TAINTED BY EXPERIENCE

*by the same author*

SPEAKING OF DIAGHILEV

# Tainted by Experience
## *A Life in the Arts*

### JOHN DRUMMOND

ff

*faber and faber*

First published in 2000
by Faber and Faber Limited
3 Queen Square London WC1N 3AU

Photoset by Faber and Faber Ltd
Printed in England by Clays Ltd, St Ives plc

A CIP record for this book is available from the British Library
ISBN 0–571–20054–0

2 4 6 8 10 9 7 5 3 1

# Contents

# List of illustrations

Title page caricature of John Drummond by Marc Boxer

1 JD's father with Uncle George
2 JD's mother
3 JD aged 6 with Great Aunt Laura and Great Uncle William
4 Great Aunt Margaret
5 JD aged 4, with his cousin, Drummond
6 Felix aged 7, 1938
7 JD's father
8 JD with his mother
9 JD at school, 1950
10 JD aged 22 (*photo A. C. Barrington Brown*)
11 Coder Drummond, 1953 (*photo G. Bailey*)
12 JD with his teacher, H. E. Piggott, 1953
13 JD with his mother and father, Graduation at Cambridge, 1958
14 JD as Iago in *Othello*, Bodmin, 1954
15 JD as Baldock in *King Edward II*, Cambridge, 1958
   (*photo Edward Leach?*)
16 JD, bit part in Ken Russell's *Don't Shoot the Pianist*, 1964
17 JD with Josette Amiel at the Paris Opéra, 1962
   (*photo Charles Edridge*)
18 Richard Dimbleby in Moscow, 1961
19 Julius Katchen, Prades, 1966
20 Cocteau decorating the BBC's Paris Studio, 1963
   (*photo Christian Taillandier*)
21 Sir Peter Maxwell Davies, Hans Werner Henze, Sir Harrison
   Birtwistle and JD, JD's 60th birthday party, 1994
22 Robert Ponsonby, Pierre Boulez, JD and Sir William Glock, Proms
   tribute to Sir William Glock, 1994
23 JD with Oscar Peterson, Edinburgh Festival, 1980
   (*photo D. I. Jervis-Read*)
24 Richard Jarman, Edinburgh, 1982

25 Brian McMaster, Peter Diamand, The Earl of Harewood, JD and
   Ian Hunter, 50th anniversary of the Edinburgh Festival, 1997
   (*photo Sean Hudson*)
26 'JP' with Sir Andrew Davis, 1989
27 John Tusa with JD, Minneapolis, 1991
28 JD with John Tydeman, 1985
29 Bob Lockyer with Sheila Colvin, 1996
30 Lady Elizabeth Cavendish with JD, 1997

The photographs are from John Drummond's private collection,
unless otherwise stated.

# Acknowledgements

My reluctance to write this book was effectively countered by my agent, Pat Kavanagh, who suggested it might be best to do it 'while you can still remember the names!' It has in effect been written from memory and inevitably others' recollection of events may differ from mine. I take full responsibility for the version I set out here.

But there would have been much less to recount without the invaluable contribution of those who made up the very effective teams with whom I worked. Many are mentioned in the text, but I must express particular gratitude to those who ran my various offices over the years: Helen Morton and Enid Praesoody in BBC Television, Annie Mackenzie Young, Victoria Boles and Julia Carruthers at the Edinburgh Festival, and Shirley Noel and Yvette Pusey at Radio 3. My special thanks are due to Anna Hutt, formerly of the Radio 3 team, who transcribed and typed the manuscript, and showed an enthusiasm for the book which went a long way to buoying up my often shaky confidence. *Tainted by Experience* is dedicated to all of them with my thanks.

My old colleague, Christopher Cook, read the first draft and gave me good advice. My editor, Belinda Matthews, was as always encouraging and my friend Bob Lockyer put up uncomplainingly with the birthpangs. I am fortunate and grateful to have had such support.

At one of the many meetings about structures and costs that came close to replacing programme-making in John Birt's BBC, one of his hench-persons lost patience with my refusal to accept his pathetic analysis of what was wrong with the organization and said, 'Why should we believe anything you say? You don't seem to me to have achieved much. In my view, you are tainted by experience.'

# Introduction – *Panic*

From the very first note, there was a low murmuring in the audience, a sense that something very different from what they expected, and probably very unwelcome, was about to take place. I looked out from my box at the packed Royal Albert Hall – the promenade crammed with cheerful young people, the boxes more than ever full of middle-aged men with faces painted like Union Jacks – and felt a certain apprehension. Lew Grade in the box next door retired to the corridor for a cigar. I caught nervous glances from faces I knew. I sat at the back of my box, trying to concentrate on the music. It was the beginning of the second half of the Last Night of the Proms, 16 September 1995, and we were hearing a new piece by Sir Harrison Birtwistle called *Panic* and dedicated to me 'in friendship and for services to music above and beyond the call of duty'.

As *Panic* (a subtle and suitable title) proceeded, I recalled the moment five years earlier when I had asked Harry to write something for the Proms' centenary. I had known him for thirty years, and had never doubted the importance of his talent or the challenge his music represented, even for people like myself well disposed to new music. He was one of a dozen major figures I sought to commission that year. He lived at that time in France, and I used to stay not far away in the house of an English singer who, generously, would put his place at my disposal to rest and recoup in after the Edinburgh Festival or the Proms, or just as somewhere to plan and think. In September 1993 I went over to spend an evening with Harry and his wife in their beautiful house at Lunegarde, high on the Causse, beyond the river Dordogne. He had lived for years in almost total isolation, first on the Island of Raasay and now here in the Lot, where, despite a steady stream of children and friends, he could retreat to a splendid summer house in the garden and pin down his visions. His music may seem daunting, but in person he is one of the most companionable of composers. I remember that evening eating huge quantities of mushrooms and ending up nervously sipping a ninety-year-old Armagnac, a present from an admirer. I asked if he had made any progress with the Proms piece. He was rather evasive, and then, surprisingly, asked me whether I had read *The Wind in the Willows*. I certainly had, but some fifty years earlier. Although I recalled Ratty and Toad and their adventures, I had forgotten that curious chapter 'The Piper at the Gates of Dawn', about the sudden appearance on the river bank of the great god Pan. Harry was especially taken with this, and wondered if it might form the basis of an orchestral piece. I was intrigued. Based on something so popular and well loved, I wondered whether the piece might not even be suitable for inclusion in the programme of the Last Night, where the presence of something new by a major British composer would make a particularly strong impression. 'Why not?' said Harry, who seemed amused. 'But I will have to think about it.'

Over the next two years his ideas shifted and *The Wind in the Willows* receded, to be overtaken by his desire to create a virtuoso piece for the brilliant saxophonist John Harle. But the Pan idea remained, concealed in the title – '*Pan-ic*' as much as '*Panic*'. Harle is a brilliant performer, very exciting to watch, and someone suitable for the Last Night, so we agreed on a piece of about ten minutes' duration for Harle and the BBC Symphony Orchestra, to be conducted by the indefatigable Andrew Davis in the final concert of the Centenary Proms. I was delighted. Another piece of the jigsaw had fallen into place.

The programme for the Last Night is by far the most difficult to put together. There are so many preconditions. There is the traditional progression of the second half from the *Pomp and Circumstance Marches* and the *Sea Songs*, to 'Rule, Britannia' (for which you need a starry singer), 'Jerusalem' and the National Anthem. The BBC Symphony Chorus and the BBC Singers must take part, and, because of their numbers, the platform is hopelessly crowded. If you want to spend as little time as possible rearranging it, piano concertos should be avoided – they mean delays. There are also rehearsal problems. For a tired orchestra at the end of a very heavy schedule, to include a tricky new piece on the Last Night was a real challenge. There was also the larger problem of what a Last Night represented. I had never attended one until I took over from Robert Ponsonby, who was in charge of the Proms for thirteen years. He obviously felt a certain distaste for the second half, and it seemed to me planned what was almost a self-contained concert before the high jinks began, at which point he would go home. During the ten seasons for which I was responsible, I moved from tolerant enjoyment to almost physical revulsion as the behaviour of the audience inexorably took over from the music. It was no longer Britannia who ruled, but exhibitionism. There was never a question of dropping the traditional format – that would have wasted everyone's time in an unwinnable battle, since the pros and antis could never be reconciled – but to make an enjoyable evening which also has some musical value is much harder than it may seem.

It was not until shortly before the 1995 programme went to press that I could find out much detail about the piece that Birtwistle was writing. I had intended it to be part of the first half of the programme, televised on BBC2 and well away from the traditional junketings of the second half. But eventually Harry produced a score that demanded a very complicated set-up, with the soloist surrounded by a group of brass instruments, all individually miked and with individually lit music stands. It would take a quarter of an hour to arrange the platform. What was the audience in the hall or on radio and television to do during this time? I was baffled as to how to make it work. On a visit to London, Harry came to see me. He was, frankly, not really concerned – it was my problem – and with his usual bluntness said, 'Well, it's the only idea I've got, and the only one you're going to get.' It was clear that, to achieve the necessary time to set up the mikes and stands, the only way the piece could be programmed was at the start of the second half, after the twenty-five minute interval.

I was not alone in foreseeing problems. There was a hysterical reaction from my Television colleagues, who were appalled by the idea of new music in the second half and begged me to drop the piece entirely. When I refused, they threatened not to televise it but to come over to the Albert Hall on BBC1 only *after* it had been performed. This made me so angry that I started positively enjoying a problem which had become a challenge. My previous hesitation seemed less than honest. I had asked for the piece fully knowing what sort of thing Harry would deliver; a mere scheduling problem should not be enough to change the plan. So to the top of the second half it went, slightly buffered by some brass fanfares to precede it. At eighteen minutes, it was considerably longer than I had asked for; but that too was perhaps justified in the circumstances. Harry had written a big, ambitious piece – tough on the players and on the audience – with no sense of 'writing down' to be popular. It was Birtwistle at his most abrasive and rock-like. During the performance the hall fell silent as the sounds John Harle produced became more extreme.

The reception at the end, led by the promenaders, who admired John Harle's shiny silver jacket as much as his brilliant musicianship, was really not bad. There were a few boos and groans from the more expensive seats, but the general feeling was one of stunned mystification. The audience simply did not know what to make of the piece. Perhaps for most people in the hall it was their first experience of the really hard edge of contemporary music. The television audience had reached for their 'off' switches, and then their telephones. The BBC switchboard was swamped with several thousand protesting calls, but it was too late, for by then it was over and a rather shaken audience moved on with visible relief to muck up one of Elgar's great march tunes with weak, anachronistic words. Few things sounded so hollow as 'Make thee mightier yet' in the last years of John Major's government.

Of course the Birtwistle piece made the headlines, with a great deal of shock horror from journalists who had not been there. But the serious critics all applauded both the piece and the decision to programme it, especially in the second half. Their tributes to my 'courage' have always embarrassed me, since I have never previously owned up to the fact that I had initially thought it could work only in the first half. But in retrospect I am glad at what happened. If the mummified corpse of the Last Night ever experiences any sort of reanimation, Birtwistle's *Panic* may have played its part. Certainly it has had a lot of further performances, and my successor running the Proms has programmed several new pieces on the final night – though none, I may say, as powerful.

At the end I went on stage to respond to a generous tribute from Andrew Davis and the unexpected gift of a marvellous work by the ceramic artist Ewen Henderson. I cannot remember what I said in reply, and I was too tired and edgy to notice whether there were boos among the applause. I had programmed nine previous seasons of the Proms and had brought off my plans for the centenary with increased audiences and many outstanding performances. It wasn't a bad way to end what I already suspected was not just the Proms job, but my public career.

When I was eighteen, a friend of my parents asked me what, in an ideal world, I hoped to do with my life. Already realizing that I was not primarily a creative person, I thought I might be able to work for organizations that promoted creativity. With the callow confidence of youth, I said that my three ideal jobs were to run the Edinburgh Festival, the Third Programme and the Proms. However outrageous it may seem, the ambition was at least honest – that really was what I wanted. Eventually, after many years of learning and of trial and error, I achieved it. By my fifties I had run all three. Through them I had unrivalled access to many of the most interesting figures of my time. Despite all the familiar problems of running arts organizations in this country, the work gave me huge enjoyment. I could feed my restless curiosity to know more about things and seek to clarify what was obscure. This continuing determination to understand has made me impatient with the reluctance of so many others to bother. But if I have been critical of the world in which I live, it is only because it is so easy to see that, with a little more application, a little more money and a little more aspiration, it could so easily be better. Utopianism? Perhaps, but the world-weary intellectual laziness that I find so widespread in contemporary society makes me irritable, as does the belief that instant gratification is the only yardstick with which to judge the merit of anything.

David Attenborough, a good friend, once said that I have 'an unlimited capacity for indignation'. It is true. But I am sick of having to justify my concern for the new, and tired of having to fight to retain support for the old. Perhaps I have expended too much energy on unwinnable causes. But how does one know they are unwinnable, without trying to win them? Now in my mid-sixties, no longer running anything, but by no means out of touch, I am all too aware of how much less I achieved than I had hoped for, and of how impermanent even is success. But, despite changing attitudes, I see no reason to question the profound belief I have always had that the arts can transform the world.

# I

# Not Being English

I was born in the early hours of the morning of Sunday 25 November 1934, in a tall Victorian house backing on to Holland Park Avenue in west London. My Scottish father was with his ship in Mozambique. My Australian mother was very much alone in London, where she had lived for only a little over a year. She had a difficult labour, and this, combined with a long-standing heart condition, meant that I was to be an only child. My father, a chief officer with the British India Steam Navigation Company – the 'BI' – came and went throughout my early life. Judging by her diary for 1934, my mother and father were together for less than four weeks that year, but at least he was back at work after nearly two years in hospital or convalescent homes recovering from tuberculosis.

My parents had met on a passenger liner, my mother returning to Australia after a stint in Europe and my father on his way to join a ship in Melbourne. It was a whirlwind shipboard romance; both of them were attractive, neither was particularly young – my father thirty-one, my mother twenty-seven. Both were doing well in their respective professions – my mother as a singer and my father destined for promotion to Captain very soon. My father pursued my mother from Melbourne to Perth, where she had grown up, and back to Melbourne, where they were married in the register office on Collins Street in July 1928. There was a ten-day honeymoon before my father left for China, but it was long enough for my mother to make a crucial discovery: my father was totally indifferent to music and tone-deaf. It seems incredible that she could have gone into a marriage without having discovered this. My parents, it would seem, knew next to nothing of each other, and this sense of difference was reinforced by a letter from my father's aunt in Scotland saying that they had always hoped he would marry a 'nice Scottish girl'. They would do their best, but my mother would, in Great-Aunt Margaret's memorable phrase, 'always be an incomer for us'. A truly Scottish welcome.

In 1929 my parents moved to Calcutta. They were there for little more than a year, but it was enough to give my mother a lifelong interest in, and affection for, India. With her typically Australian lack of formality and snobbishness, she shunned the Officers' Club, went for long walks alone, and did dreadful subversive things like not wearing gloves at all times – 'You never know what germs you may pick up' was the memsahibs' cry. For my mother, India was poetry, music, landscape and architecture. A holiday trip into the Himalayas, to Darjeeling, was recorded in a series of Box-Brownie photographs of dancers and musicians. My father, whose view of India was largely confined to the Bowls Club and the loading wharfs of the Howgli river, thought that all Indians were natives – however rich or exotic, even maharajas were little more than coolies. Yet he learnt Hindi and it seemed to me, hearing him later ordering people about on his ships, spoke it rather well. In 1930 they moved on to Singapore and set about learning Malay. Although they regretted leaving India, my mother loved Malaya, despite monsoons, humidity and insects. She adapted quickly, since she was quite without racial prejudice – except for disliking being patronized by the English.

I suppose it was too much in the 1920s to expect my father, who saw the locals largely as labourers, to have a more enlightened view of other societies. He was far from unintelligent, but had hardly any formal education. He was born in 1897 in Glasgow, the younger child of a middle-aged bank official with a previous marriage. His father died of pneumonia after catching a chill at a funeral when my father was three; my grandmother, a much younger copper-haired beauty, then dumped my father and his older sister on her family in Aberdeen and left for London. My father hardly saw her again, except occasionally in the 1920s when, having re-established contact, he was obliged to collect her from various police stations where she had been taken and charged with being drunk and disorderly. She died in 1931, when my parents were in Singapore, and my father always found it impossible to speak of her. Nor did he speak of his father, for he knew nothing about him. My grandfather's grave in Sighthill Cemetery in Glasgow tells the facts, but all my father knew was that he had worked for the Bank of Scotland and was apparently the fourth generation of Drummonds to do so, all of whom were Edinburgh-born and called, as was my father, Archibald – a family tradition happily broken in my case.

My father's attitude to his childhood surprised me. He would tell me without complaint of incidents that recalled the worst of nineteenth-century child exploitation. He and his sister were boarded out with a minister at the manse of Nigg, a village a few miles outside Aberdeen. My father suffered frequent beatings, iron discipline and manual labour. At the age of four or five he was sent out into the fields before breakfast to pick up potatoes or swedes. Yet he was not without connections: his memory of Glasgow in early childhood was of massive furniture and a great deal of silver. But if the Drummonds had money, none of it went to the children.

The Grays, my grandmother's family, were of farming stock from Donside. In addition to my grandmother and her sister, Margaret, there were two boys. My father was christened Archibald Richard George after the two uncles, both of whom in their way typified the adventurous lives of those Scots who went overseas to create and run the Empire. Though the superior state of Scottish education must have played a large part, the success of Scots everywhere in the world, including England, has always seemed to me to be closely related to the inability of the English to place a Scottish accent in class terms. A boy from an ordinary background in Aberdeen who happened to be a good engineer would prosper, while his equivalent from Birmingham or Newcastle would endure a lifetime of snobbery and discrimination. Uncle Richard had become a structural engineer and had gone to Canada to help expand the railway system across that vast country, while Uncle George had gone to India and made a fortune in textiles. George's wife, Minnie, was the sister of another Aberdeenshire boy, Logie Watson, who also made his fortune in India and was eventually knighted.

Uncle George and Aunt Minnie and Sir Logie and Lady Watson were in the background of my father's early life, but, living as they were in luxury in Cawnpore, they can hardly have been aware of what was happening to the deserted child out in the kailyard at six in the morning before hours on the school bench and frequent applications of the strap. He was most often beaten for not speaking properly. It was only when he was six that a chance inspection revealed that he was literally tongue-tied: there was a membrane below his tongue which impeded speech. Once operated on he made immediate progress and was put to school in Aberdeen, preparatory to going to Robert Watson's College, the local public school, where his fees were paid by Uncle George.

But at fourteen my father ran away and joined the fishing fleet. All his life he recalled the violence and intensity of Arctic winters and the

3

smell of fish. Incredibly, the family left him there for two years. Then Uncle George, on a home visit, rescued him and put him in a crammer to sit for entry for the Royal Navy, since my father had no other ambition but the sea. Before this could happen the First World War broke out and my father – only seventeen – enlisted in the merchant marine. The following year he was torpedoed off the coast of Norfolk and spent several hours in the water, but not even that deflected him, and the whole of the rest of his life was spent in the merchant navy. After the war Uncle George placed him in the BI – a huge company with not only passenger liners, like its great rival P&O, but literally hundreds of cargo vessels which plied between Britain and India and beyond, to Burma, Malaya, China and Australia. The principal cargo was coal, and my father believed that this was the origin of his TB.

By the time my father collapsed in Singapore in 1931, Uncle George had died, leaving a very large amount of money to charity. My father's marriage had upset the family even more than this, since they had intended him to marry the only child of the even richer Sir Logie – a plain girl called Nancy, most certainly not my father's type. After a beastly childhood and a difficult youth, my father had emerged strong, confident and outgoing. Indeed in public he always was, as everyone said of him, 'the life and soul of the party'. But a darker side was reserved for the family.

My mother's background was very different. Her father's family, the Pickerings, had moved to London from Yorkshire in the 1820s to become involved in the building boom that followed the Napoleonic wars. They were builders' merchants and surveyors in Bloomsbury, with a house in Marchmont Street, where in 1867 my maternal grandfather was born. They were a big family – five boys and three girls – unpretentious, hardworking stock, whose life revolved around the Baptist chapel and the Strict and Particular sect to which they belonged. Sunday was a day of rest, which meant chapel twice and Sunday school. If it was fine there was a walk in the park; if not, they were allowed to visit the British Museum. My Great-Aunt Laura told me that was something they longed for. She also remembered each year walking to the end of the road to see Queen Victoria passing on the way north to Kings Cross and Balmoral.

I remember the oldest of the brothers, Uncle Arthur, born in 1858, with a huge white beard, a watch-chain and clothes that smelt of sawdust. Of the other boys, Uncle Henry joined the travel firm Henry Lunn and spent most of his life as a representative in Paris and Switzerland, while my grandfather, a lithographer and printer by trade, disgusted by being fined for speeding on a bicycle in the Tottenham Court Road in 1893 at the age of twenty-six, went to New Zealand. His letters to his sister Laura are all the evidence I have of his personality. He was lively, fascinated by the fauna and flora of the Antipodes, and a good musician, playing the organ and training choirs in various small settlements in New Zealand and then, from 1896, in Australia. It is not clear what took him to Ballarat in Victoria, for the gold rush that had created that still very grand town was long over. The electoral roll describes him as an 'agent', but what for I do not know. Wool? Or perhaps timber. Certainly he seems not to have had anything to do with his original work in lithography. He married my grandmother, Mary Dingle, a schoolteacher, in 1897. They had three children: my mother's elder sister, Elva; my mother, christened Esther; and a son, Herbert, born six months after my grandfather had been killed in a street accident in 1904, when my mother was almost three.

My maternal grandmother came from a huge family. Her mother was a Graham from Tayside, and her grandmother a Dutchwoman called Vermeer. Family tradition always maintained that she was descended from one of the painter's brothers. They were early settlers, and spread widely across Australia. My grandmother's favourite sister had married a fruit farmer with 40,000 acres in Western Australia. It was there that my grandmother moved after my grandfather's death. For the next ten years she led a rather nomadic life teaching in small towns on the coast, before settling in Perth. My mother had over thirty first cousins, and during the fruit harvest they would gather and work hard and have fun. Despite considerable poverty and the problems of a handicapped sibling – her brother was what was called in those days 'simple' – her childhood seems to have had all the happiness and conviviality which my father's had lacked. Added to which she was academically very bright (winning all the prizes), good at sports (a swimming, diving and life-saving champion) and possessed of a precociously developed voice which had her singing at concerts while still in her teens.

When her mother died in the virulent Spanish-influenza epidemic of 1918, my seventeen-year-old mother was taken in by her singing teacher and given bed, board and tuition in return for looking after his and his wife's three children. Her teacher, Alexander Leckie, was a fine

5

musician. Born in Scotland, he had emigrated when young and made a career in Perth which entitled him to a long entry and a photograph in the recent *Oxford Companion to Australian Music*. It was through 'Lex', as he was known, that my mother was awarded a scholarship, raised by public subscription, to allow her to study in England. In 1921 she came 'home', as it was still called, to lodge with my Great-Aunt Laura and her husband in London.

Aunt Laura, who survived into the 1960s and died at the age of ninety-two, was a professional hypochondriac. Although only fifty when my mother went to live with her, she spent her days on a chaise longue and was pushed everywhere in a wheelchair by her long-suffering husband, the distinguished accountant William Littleton. Uncle Willie was my favourite figure from my childhood. Barely five foot tall, he was known as 'Littleun', had a tremendous bushy moustache, and smoked innumerable huge Havana coronas. He was the subject of my first recorded joke. Having travelled unusually on a single-decker trolley-bus, I told him it was like him, a 'littleun'. Not very good, but I was only four.

Uncle Willie's father was a Baptist minister at Crowborough in Sussex. Willie grew up in the country, and when he and Aunt Laura married they moved into a new house outside London in green fields near Bruce Castle. Uncle Willie walked daily down a country lane to Tottenham Hale to catch the steam train to the City. There were annual outings to Eastbourne in a hired Daimler, chapel life and many cousins. There were no children – Laura, it was said, was too delicate. I have grave doubts that the marriage was ever consummated, but Uncle Willie accepted his role of wheelchair attendant and they lived an uneventful life watching their semi-rural retreat being encroached upon by the expansion of London. The house, though damaged in the Second World War, still stands, hemmed in by the endless streets of Tottenham. But to me, as a child, it seemed deep in the country, its garden full of apple trees and roses, although only a trolley ride from Wood Green on the Piccadilly Line.

At the Royal Academy of Music, my mother fell under the spell of Harry Plunket Greene, whose *Interpretation in Song* still seems to me the best manual for singers ever written. She had a splendid true contralto voice, but with none of the boomy sound associated with Clara Butt. She was a lieder singer, and was later to attend classes with the great recitalist Elena Gerhardt. She loved Schubert, Schumann, Brahms and Wolf, but also modern composers like Armstrong Gibbs, George Butterworth and Peter Warlock. She sang convincingly in French, Italian and German. She knew a great deal of music and a lot about it. Much of this must have been due to Professor Leckie, but also there were the opportunities offered by London in the 1920s even to an impecunious student. She heard most of the great singers, always preferring the Germans to the Italians, Lotte Lehmann in particular. But she also went to the Queen's Hall and heard Rachmaninov, Casals and Cortot. It seems extraordinary today that this talented young woman was good enough to be invited to Government House in Perth to sing for the Prince of Wales, and then sent to England to study, having appeared on all the available platforms of Western Australia, yet at twenty years of age she had never heard a professional orchestra nor seen a professional opera production.

She obviously had some social connections in London, but I do not know how it was that she was invited to Petworth to stay with the Leconfields. She also went to the Sassoons' huge house on Park Lane. She was never without admirers, but had a strict moral code. Like so many Australians, she loved parties, outings, picnics, trips to the coast, and this remained true of her to the end. She never hung back for others to organize things; she got on and made things happen herself.

But her whole life was shadowed by illness. As a result of rheumatic fever and diphtheria in her teens, she was left with an arrhythmic heart – a mitral stenosis – and was advised against the strain of an operatic life. This caused her little hardship, since she was much more interested in recitals and concert music. But even in these she was constantly warned against working too hard, doing too much, travelling too far. Although she took little notice, she was frequently obliged to stop, rest and recover. All my young life I was aware of having two parents who were neither ever completely well, and both of whom had had to sacrifice much through illness.

I know very little of my mother's life in the years between her return to Australia in 1924 and her marriage. It seemed she earned her keep in Perth by teaching. Among the places at which she taught was a convent school where one of the pupils was a redheaded, rebellious Irish girl called Eileen Joyce, eventually to become one of the best-known pianists on the British scene, especially during the war. My mother later looked after her when she came through London on her way to study in Leipzig. I do know that the first major crisis in my mother's life came when she discovered that Professor Leckie's regard for her was not merely professional. By now organist of the cathedral and a professor at the university, he was married to a rather grand and starchy English woman called Hilda, and a pillar of the community; yet he and my mother realized they were in love. There was never any question of it being consummated or of his leaving his wife – quite the reverse. It was my mother who had to leave, and she returned to Europe. Who paid, what she lived on and what she did on this second visit I never discovered, except that she spent some time in Paris.

It was after this second visit to the United Kingdom and on her return home to Australia in 1928 that she met my father. Once they decided to marry and to settle in Melbourne, my mother had all her belongings in Perth – books, music and a piano she had won in a competition – shipped across to Victoria. In thick fog approaching Melbourne, in Port Phillip Bay, the ship was involved in a collision and sank immediately. My mother lost everything. So, in a literal sense, my parents entered their marriage with no baggage. But the legacy of their childhood would remain and would always colour their lives – as, eventually, it did mine also.

At the time of my father's tuberculosis breakdown in Singapore my parents had decided to move to Adelaide and start a family. My father had taken a shore job as a Marine Superintendant, but his disease was of a particularly virulent kind. He was given no more than even chances of survival, since one lung was already almost completely destroyed. There was a disagreement about treatment. My mother favoured Australia, with its excellent climate; the doctors – no doubt British – were adamant that he would do better in England. So they embarked on a small cargo vessel which took over three weeks to reach London. My mother nursed him for twenty-four hours a day, and always said she was surprised he survived. Six foot two inches tall and muscular before, he now dropped to less than seven stone. Surviving photographs show him to be little more than a skeleton. He was taken immediately to a hospital in Hampshire specializing in the treatment of TB, where he spent the next eighteen months slowly recovering. My mother lodged in a room above the village pub at Liphook and visited him every day. Her one valuable possession, a sapphire necklace (a gift from Lex?), was stolen, and she had to ask Aunt Laura for financial help. Very small amounts were grudgingly produced, together with an equally small amount via the Gray family lawyer in Aberdeen.

As soon as he was well enough my father went back to Scotland, taking his new wife with him. She got a chilly reception both from my Great-Aunt Margaret and from my father's sister, Valerie, who, after spending the First World War in volunteer ambulance sections in France, had worked for the Post Office until she married an ambitious railway manager. They had one son, my first cousin, two and a half years older than me and, though his first name was Arthur, always called Drummond.

Great-Aunt Margaret and Aunt Valerie were to dominate my childhood. Aunt Margaret, with her braided hair, ubiquitous hairnet and noisy dentures, was the moral arbiter. Nothing could be decided or done without her approval, and she approved of very little. Her only entertainment was a weekly visit to inspect the family graves. Art, music and literature counted for nothing; they were the work of the Devil. Appearing in public as my mother did – wearing make-up, smoking the occasional cigarette – was beyond acceptance. My father's sister was the only person I have known whose whole life was permeated by jealousy. She was not unattractive, having inherited her mother's copper hair, and had even been approached to model for a brand of hair dyes, to claim they were responsible for the colour. But she was far from intelligent. She married a nice man, but destroyed her marriage by her constant suspicions about his life away from her – which, since he travelled extensively on business, was considerable. She lived in thrall to the cinema, and every meeting would entail a detailed account of whatever Hollywood weepie she had seen that week. She spoiled her child, to the extent that by the age of eight he would eat only cakes, chocolates and biscuits. Above all, Aunt Valerie was mortally jealous of my mother, and let it show. Even when quite young I was conscious of the hypocrisy of these relations. Great-Aunt Margaret, the self-elected judge of everything, turned out to have an illegitimate son the same age as my father. Aunt Valerie was not only boring but devious. Is it any wonder that I preferred friends to family, for it was through my mother and her friends that enlightenment and entertainment came.

My mother had two great friends in London, both nurses: one, like a nanny, called always by her surname, Wilkie, and the other a to me exotic Belgian called Laure van Reeth. Wilkie was bossy, businesslike but good-hearted, and kept her eye on my mother and her health both during and after her pregnancy, babysitting me when required. Laure took my mother to the cinema and to tea at Lyons' Corner House, and insisted from the very start that I should be taught French.

I cannot remember actually learning to speak French, or having to make an effort to remember words or phrases. It has just always been there, part of my life for as long as I can recall. Few things have given me such rewards as the relatively painless acquisition of foreign languages. They intrigue me like a puzzle I want to solve. Far from being an end in themselves, they are like coathangers on which to hang the experiences of life. The fact that both my parents used several languages in their work was obviously an advantage. My own reliable memory and a good imitative ear seem to have provided the rest of what was needed. I am quite sure it had nothing to do with intelligence. Some of the brightest people I know are resolutely monoglot, and I never forget one of Peter Ustinov's *obiter dicta*: 'Beware of those who speak many languages – they usually have nothing to say in any of them' (which sounds fine, but of course is untrue of him – and I hope of me too). It is striking in retrospect how few of the people in my early life were English. With the exception of Aunt Laura and Wilkie, they were almost all Australian, Scottish or from various parts of Europe. I never grew up feeling English, and my vocabulary has always been scattered with Australian and Scottish words and phrases.

My mother had one other friend in London who was very much part of my life for the next sixty years, an Australian artist called Eileen Pearcey. She had heard my mother sing in Melbourne, introduced herself afterwards, and asked if she could paint her portrait. Eileen – or Eilean, as she suddenly decided to spell her name in the 1950s – was in one way a typical Melburnian of her generation, but also the nearest thing we knew to a red revolutionary. One day she would wear a hat and a veil to shop at the Army & Navy Stores – 'Since I am not the Duchess of Westminster, it seems advisable'; another day she would join a nudist colony in Buckinghamshire to tear off the shackles of bourgeois respectability. She was a Blackett, she would inform people frequently – something that possibly counted for more in Victoria than it did in Hampstead, where she lived with her brilliant husband, Ramsay Moon, and their only child, Felix.

Ramsay was one of the great pioneers of metal-frame building, and went on virtually to create the Institute of Welding, which still awards an annual medal in his honour. He was big, genial and generous. Eileen was small, self-possessed and ruthlessly selfish. She would lock herself in her studio for days at time. He would return from high-level conferences to find a cold flat with nothing in the larder and no sign of his wife or child. Felix grew up almost as an *enfant sauvage*. He was frequently returned by neighbours or even the police, having been found stark naked several streets away following the milk cart or the rag-and-bone man. He was a big-boned, redheaded child with one lazy eyelid and an infectious laugh. He was, like my cousin Drummond, two years older than me, though I was never conscious of the difference. Being with Felix was the principal pleasure of my childhood.

Ramsay and Eileen had moved to London at almost the same time as my parents came home from Singapore. Once established in London, my mother saw a lot of them and their friends – mostly Australians, like the gifted book illustrator Sheila Hawkins and the psychoanalyst Harold Link. They were a typical young professional crowd of the 1930s, into new poetry, abstract art, left-wing politics, Clark's sandals, Aertex underwear, Heal's furniture and Freud. My mother was never a fully paid-up member of the group, since she found many of their attitudes modish and shallow, but they admired her musicianship and vivacity. We were influenced by the look of the places in which they lived. I have spent my life surrounded by limed-oak furniture from Heal's, three-legged stools designed by Alvar Aalto, plain fabrics and muted colours, and have a profound dislike of prettiness. I have never got away from the ambience of my youth, nor have I really wanted to. I am sure if I had inherited an old house with good furniture and pictures I might have cherished those too. Aunt Laura's house was absolutely of its time: chiming clocks, chenille tablecloths with bobbles, antimacassars on the arms of chairs, a piano with candelabra, and a huge steel engraving of *The Monarch of the Glen*. There was nothing there I particularly liked, but I respected it as a rather sombre time capsule. My father's colleagues, home from India, filled their houses with Benares brass, teak tables, standard lamps, and family photographs in heavy frames. Great-Aunt Margaret in Aberdeen had plain white china and a heavy silver tea service which I still occasionally use today. All these settings seemed appropriate for their owners, while for ourselves my mother went for really modern design, amazingly then at prices that even we could afford. I still have a splendid chair with a reclining back, a folding table on one side and a bookshelf on the other. It cost four pounds from Heal's, and there is an example in the Victoria & Albert Museum. Just before the war, Eileen and Ramsay moved from

Hampstead to Dolphin Square, where everything in the apartment was eau-de-Nil or a pale reseda green, with bare copper-beech branches in a yellow Chinese pot. I found it elegant and restful. The 1930s may have been a low, dishonest decade, but strong elements of its design values have stuck with me.

I am unsure of how much I can really remember of London before the war and how much I only think I remember because I have been told about it. What is certain is that my eyesight must have been better when young than subsequently, because what I *can* recall is the fine details of buildings. From 1935 to 1939 we lived off Ladbroke Grove and I went most days to play in Kensington Gardens; I have the clearest memory of the Orangery and how much I liked its proportions. Apparently from earliest childhood I would comment on rooflines, windows and details of doors. My fascination with architecture was there right from the beginning.

What else can I recall with certainty? A prickly tweed coat with matching peaked cap, a fierce hairbrush purchased in Middlesborough when seeing my father off on a trip, a lime jelly quivering on the kitchen table, a picnic on the drawing-room carpet when bad weather stopped us going to the zoo, the Belgian patisserie in Notting Hill Gate where I was allowed to ask for 'Un pain d'épice, s'il vous plaît', the geometric pattern of the linen curtains in my room, and the dry rustle of poplar trees outside. I remember Casals playing the Berceuse from *Jocelyn* and Fred Astaire singing 'Night and Day', both on our wind-up gramophone. I remember going to Scotland by boat, losing a quoit overboard, and expecting to be punished. In fact everyone laughed. Great-Aunt Margaret fed me daily on pink meringues: I have loathed meringues ever since. I think I can remember the bars of my cot, and especially how I felt in the morning when light seeped through the curtains – no one could have told me that. I wanted to wander about, but knew the rule was to stay in my room until fetched. I remember the sound of music coming through the walls after I had been put to bed at night. I can remember being able to read most things by the time I was four, and I think I remember hiding under my seat at the Academy Cinema, alarmed at the wicked witch in *Snow White*. I certainly remember going to Miss Vanstone's, a sort of playgroup, though here there is a photo to remind me. I was allowed to play (if that is the right word) the tambourine. It was pure joy. I also remember the Russian family in the adjoining flat and their laughter and their parties. I recall train journeys and regular visits to Aunt Laura and Uncle Willie in Tottenham, and the clean, starchy smell of my aunt's maid, Mary, who had been sent up from Crowborough as a teenager in the 1880s and was still there fifty years later. All these things happened before my fifth birthday, because by then we had left London.

In Bournemouth for our summer holidays in late August 1939, I have the clearest memory of being driven about by a fellow guest in a big Wolseley car and being allowed to stand on the front seat with my head through the sunroof, a morning ritual when going to collect the daily newspaper. Sunday 3 September was bright and sunny, but for once we did not go to the beach. I was sent to play in the garden, and my mother came out, sat me down, and told me very simply that I would not be seeing my father for some time since we were now at war. In fact my father had already been away for over six months in Egypt. His passenger liner, the *Dumana*, of which he had been Captain for two years, was converted into a base vessel for a squadron of flying boats – Sunderlands and later Catalinas – and he was put in charge of a large contingent of both naval and RAF officers and technicians. He had been very aware of the developing political situation and had insisted that, in the event of hostilities, my mother should leave London. Now my mother received a telegram from him saying, 'Leave London at once.' But first she returned to find a totally vandalized flat, from which the burglars had taken everything of value before urinating or defecating over the rest. It was quite a way to declare war.

So we had to find somewhere else to live. My mother had few friends outside London, but Bournemouth, with no industrial or military associations, seemed an unlikely target for bombing and no one at this stage was contemplating invasion. So after a few weeks in a boarding house we rented a house in Iford, on the edge of Bournemouth. It was at the end of a road with an old semi-ruined farm, on the edge of the country, with a few remaining fields and a waterlogged golf course across the nearby river Stour. It was an area entirely built in the late 1930s – street after street of identical houses with small gardens, and on the main road a crescent of shops in the 'moderne' style. It was quite definitely the wrong end of town. The rent for our house was one guinea a week. It was meant to be a temporary solution until we got round to buying one of the slightly bigger new houses going up nearby, on the market for £1,000, or £750 if you didn't need a garage – which we didn't, because we did not own a car. We also had no money, and so the temporary solution became permanent. We lived in the same rented house for twenty years, until my parents scraped together enough to partly design and build a new house a couple of miles away on high ground, backing on to open country between Christchurch and Hurn. That area too is now so built up that the open vistas of only thirty years ago have quite disappeared.

We never meant to live in Bournemouth, and the wish to move elsewhere was a constantly recurring topic in my childhood and youth. My father, for some reason, wanted to live in the Chilterns. He bought books with titles like *Beautiful Buckinghamshire*, and spoke lyrically of Burnham Beeches. He seemed, for reasons I never understood, captivated by the area that came to be known as Metroland. My mother, after her youth in isolated Western Australia, really wanted to get back to London. It was quite a few years before I too came to feel with incipient snobbishness that the house in Iford was in every way not quite good enough.

In the final years of the war, the marriages both of my Aunt Valerie and of Eileen Pearcey broke up. Aunt Valerie and my cousin Drummond moved to Bournemouth, not far from us. Eileen got rid of Ramsay, put Felix in a boarding school, and took a full-time job in the Admiralty. Felix spent his school holidays with us. Both divorces were unnecessary and pointless, but both women were hell-bent on separation. My mother now had to cope with two 'wronged' wives, both prone to talk endlessly of their problems and both with boisterous children who were, for different reasons, increasingly out of control.

My cousin Drummond was about as different from me as imaginable. His passion was for yachts and guns – model or real. He had a brash, noisy personality, and, as with his food fads, had been allowed to develop his own approach to life. He did exactly as he liked. I was always slightly afraid, not of him, but of what he would do next. He would ride a bicycle straight at a tree to see which came off worst, not imagining it might be himself. During the war we were not allowed on the beaches, so we went inland to the hilly outcrops behind Christchurch, where we created a fantasy world among the rhododendron groves and the sandy paths. Drummond always wanted to burrow under things, but I suffer from mild claustrophobia and there was no way I was going to follow him into unsafe tunnels of soft sand. He spent a lot of time with us, since his mother had also taken a job, but he was always a problem. At times I liked him very much, but I already felt the obligations of kinship: I had to know him not through choice, but because he was my cousin.

Things were very different with Felix. Life in his company was a constant joy. In some ways he was amazingly backward – he could not write properly until he was nearly ten – but in others his imaginative gifts outran anything I have known in a child before or since. He had an infectious sense of humour, and generated jollity wherever he was. His passion was for the theatre, and by the age of six he had built one out of an old box, started designing scenery and costumes, and then presented what he called 'my stories'. He was a storyteller at all times. Since we shared a bedroom, I was used to his fantastic tales – which never frightened me, but usually made me laugh uncontrollably. I can recall my mother so often coming into our room long after we should have been asleep, attracted by the peals of laughter coming from either or both of us.

Felix went to King Alfred's School, normally in Hampstead but then evacuated to rural Hertfordshire. Eileen saw him rarely, except at the beginning and end of terms as he passed through London, to stay usually with us but sometimes with other friends and occasionally with his father, who was now deep into important secret war work. Luckily the establishment with which he was most associated, where the technology of what became to be known as Bailey bridges was worked out, was only mile or two away, and so we saw quite a lot of Ramsay. Sometimes he would take both Felix and me away for a few days at a hotel.

Occasionally Eileen came down from London for the weekend. Her eccentricity was increasing. Over a period of more than twenty years I do not recall her ever arriving on the train she said she would take. If she asked to be met at Bournemouth Central, she would get out at Christchurch. She once got off the very fast Bournemouth Belle and transferred to a slow train, as she was convinced it would arrive sooner. She contributed nothing to her keep. Invited for Christmas, she would leave two or three unwrapped paperbacks on the piano and say, 'Do help yourself.' She never got up for breakfast, never entered the kitchen, and never offered to do anything useful. She sat on the floor and talked and talked and talked. Some of her talk was quite entertaining, since she had a colourful family background – full of strong-willed women who ran things into their eighties or nineties. I was particularly fond of a story concerning her mother, who one morning caught the tram from South Yarra into Melbourne to collect an umbrella which was being repaired. It was raining, so she had another umbrella with her. As she made to leave the tram she inadvertently picked up the umbrella of the woman sitting next to her, who snatched it back impatiently. On the return journey, having collected the repaired umbrella and also bought a new parasol, she chanced to sit opposite the same woman, who looked fiercely at her and said, 'I see you have had a good morning.' This sort of thing was the best of Eileen, but when she got going on the vagaries of her department in the Admiralty, where naturally only she understood anything, it was less fun. But at least we could be confident that we were winning the war with Eileen at the helm.

My father and his cluster of flying boats had been closely involved in the evacuation of Crete in May 1941. He kept a photograph of his ship with puffs of smoke surrounding it on his desk for the rest of his life. But he was also living a very jolly social life in Alexandria. He rather played it down, for it did not much impress my mother, but later he told me that it was an amazing period – full of boozy parties, available girls and rumours of spying. Later in 1941 he moved on to Bathurst in the Gambia, a place of which he spoke with real hatred. There was no life at all apart from the occasional rather stuffy cocktail party at Government House. Things were very different when he moved again, this time to Durban. I have never visited South Africa, but my father, who had been pretty well everywhere, thought it the most beautiful of countries. For a brief period after the war there was talk of our going to live there. Happily it did not transpire. A couple my parents had known in Ceylon had moved to the Cape and came to visit us. They spoke of the good life and how cheap it was with eight servants on a small property outside Cape Town. Where did these servants live, my mother asked. It emerged that they all lived in a hut beside the chicken run, without water or sanitation. 'But what do you expect? That's what they are used to, said Mrs Gordon. They were not reinvited, and there was no further question of our moving to South Africa.

As soon as we had settled into the house in Iford, my mother found a local kindergarten for me to attend in the mornings and took a job checking and issuing gas masks in the rather unattractive former home of the son of the poet Shelley. For the duration of the war my mother was always working, fitting it around my school times and holidays. She ran canteens, and did hospital trolley service for the WVS and a dozen other jobs. We had little food and less money, but I have only the sunniest recollections of the early war years, except for the prep school to which I went in 1941 and which was already attended by my cousin.

Schoolmasters during the war tended to be those who had been rejected by the services on grounds of age or disability, and the Headmaster at this school was a martinet of nineteenth-century dimensions. I was regularly beaten with a thin cane most painfully on the back of the hands, and often dragged about by one ear. The reason for this was that I was not very good at copying what was written on the blackboard – hardly surprising, since I could not in fact *see* what was written on the blackboard. My eyesight had obviously deteriorated rapidly, but no one seemed to notice until on a brief holiday in Devon in the early summer of 1942 my mother called me to the window of her room in a hotel in Lynton and asked me to describe what was in the bay below. I could see only a black blob, and cheerfully suggested it was a whale. It was in fact a small fishing boat. Immediately on our return I was taken to the optician, and from that day on I have worn glasses, or now contact lenses. But how can the school not have suspected? I can remember asking to be allowed to get up and inspect the board closely, and then writing down from memory what I saw, but my request to do this was not often granted – administering the beatings must have been preferable. The legacy has been a lifelong hatred of physical violence. Not before time I was removed. My memory has blanked this period out to the extent that I cannot now recall the name of either the school or the Headmaster.

At this point my mother took a decision which certainly affected the rest of my life. She scraped together the money to send me to a much more expensive prep school in Boscombe, one of the best in Hampshire. It meant we had less to live on, and paying the fees was a problem, but I had no sense of going short. Once in later years I said this to my mother, and she replied with a shrug, 'Well, *you* didn't.' One only has to look at photographs of her taken towards the end of the war to see how thin, run-down and exhausted she had become. She remained, however, the centre of a group of new friends, always cheerful, helpful, bicycling about organizing things. She was the confidante of every woman we knew and the object of a certain amount of old-fashioned chivalry from the few men around – most of them rather elderly.

Her career had been completely sacrificed to marriage, to looking after me and now to work, but early in 1942 she had decided to try to pick up the threads again and wrote to the BBC. She was summoned to an audition by a music producer in Bristol, but when the day came she went down with mumps and was forced to cancel. She never rearranged the audition, and from then on sang only privately and took the occasional pupil. She never seemed bitter about abandoning what I believe was a considerable gift. Her health had initially got in the way, and then the peripatetic life after her marriage. My father's hostility to music, his illness, then my arrival and the war – all combined to prevent her making a real go of her career. Yet the house was always full of music, much of it coming from the excellent old German upright piano she had taken from Melbourne to India, Malaya and then England, and on which I still play today. She insisted that Felix and I should make our own entertainment. One by-product of the war was an almost complete absence of toys, though I had a couple of Dinky toy cars and a clockwork train. I also had a Hornby catalogue with pictures of all the wonders that were unobtainable. By the time they became available after the war, I was too old to want them. I have occasionally wondered whether the relentless energy of my life has been in compensation for not having had an electric train.

My mother loved the arts – all of them – and wanted them to be part of our lives. There were few concerts at the time, since the Bournemouth Municipal Orchestra had been 'disbanded for the duration', as we used to say. There was a scratch orchestra known as the Wessex Players, made up mostly of retired musicians or teachers, and they gave occasional concerts at St Peter's Hall in Bournemouth. I was taken on one occasion when Eileen Joyce played the Grieg Concerto. This must have been because we knew Eileen, but I remember it because I was from first exposure absolutely fascinated by the idea of a piano concerto – the pitting of one against many, and the brilliant effects that could be achieved. It was not until many years later that I realized that the conductor of the Wessex Players, on weekend leave from the RAF, was Reginald Goodall, later to become one of the great operatic coaches and a fine Wagner conductor.

For her singing, my mother had teamed up with a neighbour, Nancy Osborne, who had studied the piano and was an enthusiastic if splashy pianist. Banging her way through Grieg's *Wedding Day at Troldhaugen* was a regular turn at parties. She had been examined when young by the composer and conductor Sir Landon Ronald, whose only reaction to her playing was 'How nice to hear Schumann again!' It became a family saying. Nancy took on the job of teaching me the piano, and I made slow progress. I had some natural ability but a shaky sense of rhythm and far too little patience. With time I became a facile but untidy player, far too interested in sight-reading to spend enough time practising. But once it was clear that music was unlikely to be my profession I worried less about how well I played than about how much I knew.

By my teens I had discovered the excellent music library in Bournemouth, left to the town by a local doctor who had been part of the committee that created the Bournemouth Orchestra under Sir Dan Godfrey in the 1890s and who regularly went to London and bought the scores of everything he heard. It was an extraordinary collection. Although it had been regularly updated, the core of it was a kind of time capsule of music in England from the 1880s to the 1920s. The young woman librarian was indulgent, and from the age of twelve I was allowed to invent a wife and two children for myself and have eight tickets that were in constant use. I had no idea how unusual the library was or whether what it contained was rare or simply standard fare. There was a complete set of Mozart piano concertos in the Breitkopf & Härtel edition, with Edwin Fischer's and Artur Schnabel's timings written in. I took this as entirely normal, became fascinated with Mozart, and with the help of Otto Jahn's three-volume biography wrote out a complete list of Köchel numbers; they seemed more intriguing than the locomotive numbers that I had previously collected.

With my eight tickets I worked my way through the complete piano repertory from Albéniz to York Bowen. Much of what I was looking at and playing through was either totally forgotten or had never been very well known – all the concertos of Raff and Rubinstein, for instance. There was a copy of Rachmaninov's First Piano Concerto in the unrevised edition, very different from what we know today. By sixteen I had a right hand that could play anything and a left hand that largely filled in harmonies and vamped. In the strict sense I was never a pianist, but there are few corners of the piano repertory that I have not explored. Later I was to discover to my great surprise that I knew more of it than many professional pianists. At the same time, my mother's philosophy meant not just playing the piano and going to concerts, but trying to write music as well. By the age of ten I was writing little dance tunes – mostly waltzes, rather Schubertian in style and almost always, for some reason, in A flat. With adolescence, these became melancholy poems in A minor or rhapsodies in E flat minor.

This policy of being not just a spectator but a participant went through all our activities. Nancy Osborne's daughter had a talent for painting, so we went off on our bicycles with our sketchbooks and drew houses, churches and the surrounding landscape. I was particularly taken with Christchurch Priory and the famous Norman turret on the north transept, with its criss-cross pattern of decoration. This I drew often, for its simplicity and its attractiveness fascinated me. It was in the churchyard of Christchurch Priory that my lifelong interest in epitaphs began, leading in time to editing a collection of them. I was especially intrigued by a monument to some sailors, drowned and washed up on a local beach and buried there only to be later transferred to hallowed ground:

> We were not slain but raised,
> raised not to life
> but to be buried twice
> by men of strife.
> What rest could living have
> when dead have none?
> Agree amongst you
> here we ten are one.

I used to go around chanting 'We were not slain but raised', to the consternation of whoever heard me. The inscription, plainly legible in my childhood, has now disappeared, as have so many through pollution and neglect in this dirtiest of all centuries.

Painting trips by bicycle or by local trains took in other nearby buildings of interest: Corfe Castle, Wimborne Minster, Beaulieu Abbey. We also went to any museum or exhibition we could. The principal gallery in Bournemouth, the Russell-Cotes, was at that time a hilarious junk shop beloved only of John Betjeman. Most of the collection was the loot of a round-the-world trip undertaken by the town's first Mayor in the 1880s. It had a bit of everything money could buy – most of it awful, but some of it intriguing. There were negatives of photographs of English cathedrals set between two layers of glass in the morning-room windows; there were samurai costumes picked up in Japan. But my favourite was a full-size statue, on the stairs, of a young woman carrying a child. The woman's entire body was encased in a knitted one-piece garment, every stitch of which was lovingly chiselled out of the marble. The statue rejoiced in the title *The Bathers*.

The visual arts were also part of our everyday lives, and ours was the only house I knew with original etchings or paintings on the walls. Most of them were by Eileen Pearcey or other friends of my mother, but occasionally we would splash out a guinea or so on a print and with passepartout we would frame it ourselves. I pinned up postcard reproductions all over my room. Looking at pictures, trying to make pictures and talking about them was a daily experience.

It was the same with books. My mother read ferociously: Browning, George Eliot, Thomas Mann, Virginia Woolf. Her library tickets were always in use. She thought *Adam Bede* and *Mrs Dalloway* the two most truthful novels in the English language. She loved biography, and found Mrs Gaskell's *Life of Charlotte Brontë* extraordinary for the time when it was written. Having been able to read quite confidently at four and anything at all by six, I was then, as now, rarely without a book in my hand. I moved very quickly from children's books like *Winnie the Pooh* and *Mumfie* (Beatrix Potter was forbidden for being too wetly sentimental) to more grown-up material like Robert Louis Stevenson. I completely bypassed the boys' school of adventure writing – G. F. Henty, Percy F. Westerman, Biggles and Captain Johns. By the age of twelve I was reading Hardy, and on completing *Tess of the D'Urbervilles* I amused my mother by asking what 'seduce' meant.

I began to collect books on architecture. Every Christmas our doctor would give me a book token for one guinea, and I would agonize for weeks about how to spend it – usually settling on one of the Batsford books, with their brilliant yellow, mauve and green covers: *The Cathedrals of England, The Old Towns of England, The Abbeys of England*. I still have a shelf of them. They cost ten shillings and sixpence each, and for my guinea I could have two. My visual memory was good, and I could memorize buildings, paintings and sculpture from photographs. Ramsay offered me a book when I was eleven, and I chose Arthur Gardiner's *An Introduction to French Church Architecture*, with its over 250 pages of plates of great French cathedrals and abbeys. Fifty years later I ticked off the last major cathedral, with some sadness that I had now visited them all. But so much that I was not to see for years and years was already in my head by my early teens. On the way to and from my prep school was a big, rambling second-hand bookshop. At least twice a week I would spend an hour or two there, not necessarily buying things, since I rarely had any money, but simply luxuriating in the idea that the world was full of books and in due course

I would devour them all. But I realize now how very selective I was. I knew nothing of the natural world or of science, let alone football or motorbikes. What I sought out was history, biography, architecture and painting.

Naturally I loved poetry. I memorized it easily and, just as with painting, was encouraged to try my hand. It was pale-imitation stuff no doubt, but it poured out. Rhyme schemes and complex rhythms were like puzzles to be solved. Games and puzzles were also part of our lives, mostly memory-based like the card game Pelmanism, or 'How many writers begin with the letter C?' or 'How many composers begin with the letter B?' Every day of my life I seemed to be learning new things and caught up in the excitement of it all. It all came out of my mother's insistence that we were not just to enjoy things passively, but to participate and, if possible, to create. It was not until years later that it struck me how unusual this was and how incredibly lucky I had been to have this all-embracing but natural-seeming introduction to the world of the mind.

Apart from my mother, my most creative influence was Felix, my constant companion. He had a genius – and I use the word carefully and I think correctly – for theatre, whether it was creating a play on his toy stage or dressing up as some fantastic character he had invented. At one stage he and I put on a revue in the garden for parents and friends. It was full of sketches and songs. I must have been eight and Felix ten, but I well remember one of the numbers. Felix appeared wearing a cardboard box tied on his head with a scarf and sang, 'I am a fashionable woman of New York, and of course I never eat pork.' I am certain we had absolutely no idea that it was more than just an easy rhyme, but I remember the adults shrieking. Once, in London, Felix laid on a whole evening of entertainment in his toy theatre, and I assisted him while about eight adults sat in silence, obviously not bored. His fertile visual and linguistic imagination was not in any way academic. He hated writing and read only under protest, but he loved being read to, and constantly asked adults about their lives and especially about their travels. He had been back to Australia just before the war, and, although he recalled little of the country, he remembered very well the sea, the ship, the sun and the sense of crossing the world. That journey was part of the lives of many people I knew in my childhood, but none evoked it so colourfully as Felix, who had experienced it when he was only seven.

From the age of ten, both Felix and my cousin Drummond started to grow away from me. That two-year difference in age counted for more than when we were younger. Drummond was now totally absorbed in sailing and yachts, while Felix, at a new boarding school, was suddenly making academic progress and for the first time showing a real interest in music. How Drummond would have developed and whether Felix and I would have remained close in later years I shall never know, since in April 1945 Drummond was drowned in the local river and six months later Felix died of cerebral meningitis.

That whole period feels to me as if I am viewing it through thick glass – I can make out the outlines of things but not the details. We were in London staying with Eileen when Drummond was drowned. It was a silly, unnecessary death, typical of his dare-devil ways. Under strict instructions not to swim immediately after lunch, he plunged into a very cold river and was caught up in reeds and rushes. The two boys with him could not swim well and panicked. By the time they had fetched help it was too late. My aunt never really recovered. She became more and more suspicious and jealous of everyone, and I felt that she somehow blamed me for having survived. She got into the hands of spiritualists to try to re-establish contact with her dead son, and then became a recluse, barricading herself in her house for nine years with no running water, gas or electricity. She would creep out early in the morning to buy paraffin and fill water bottles in the public lavatory, but refused to see anyone – not my father nor a doctor. Eventually the door was broken down and my father had to authorize her being carted off to a huge nineteenth-century asylum, where she was locked in a ward with sixty other people and received no treatment at all. She was certainly highly disturbed but in no way dangerous, really needing company rather than confinement. One morning she walked out of the asylum and established herself in a bedsitter in Boscombe, mercifully in the house of an understanding woman, living there peaceably for years until one day she dropped dead in the foyer of the local cinema. It had been a poor life.

Felix I saw only once in his last year, when he came to stay for a weekend. He seemed quite grown up at thirteen, and was full of new stories. He was unforthcoming about music, but it emerged later that several times he had been found in the local parish church playing immensely complicated Bach preludes and fugues only a few months after beginning his studies. So his genius it would appear was for music too. One morning he complained of a strong headache; he was put to bed in the school sanatorium, and slipped into a coma that evening. He died four days later.

It is over fifty years since I have thought about those days, and even now I find it painful to write about them. I have quite deliberately put these two deaths to the side of my life, yet in many ways their effect has been with me always. I am not sufficiently Freudian to seek an explanation of my own development in the light of such events, but I know I had a feeling not just of having lost my two closest friends but also of a responsibility somehow to try to be a son to three women, two of whom had lost their only child and the third of whom, my mother, had a marriage which was by now obviously a failure although her strong moral sense forbade her to walk out on it. When I look back on my early years it seems that I had very few friends apart from Drummond and Felix. I can clearly recall thinking after their death that I needed not to replace them, because that was impossible, but to find some new people in my life. And in due course I did, largely through my schoolfellows and through the excellent teaching we had which made my schoolfellows more interesting. But I have never found a replacement for the sheer sense of brilliance that shone out of Felix.

I was not alone in this; all the adults who knew Felix felt the same. His mother, Eileen, took ten or more years even to start to recover, and then found a substitute love in her passion for India and all things Indian. She became a much respected yoga teacher, still working for the Greater London Council when over eighty, and made a small reputation as an artist through her action drawings of dancers – the more exotic the better. She lived on into her late nineties, fiercely independent, ruthlessly self-centred, but at times still great fun. She never swept a floor or threw away a newspaper in half a century. Clearing out her studio when she could no longer live there alone was one of the most unpleasant tasks that I have ever been forced to confront. I was more than once temped to set fire to the lot. I do not know how posterity will view her work. Her quick sketches of dancers in movement often had brilliant life; her finished paintings were quite dead. She did some marvellous sketches of Martha Graham and Marcel Marceau, who bought many, and of Indian dancers like Rita Devi and the Kathakali company. She was totally unpractical, and time and again missed chances to hold exhibitions or publicize her work. Nothing was ever possible at a time when anyone else wanted it. She went through a longish phase of being tremendously pro-Chinese, would write occasionally for the *Daily Worker*, and was a sucker for any Indian bore who came through town. My mother bore the brunt of trying to console her for the death of Felix, but hardly got a word of thanks. My father, who once tried to tell her she really should show a bit more concern for others, was shown the door.

Eileen quarrelled with almost everyone in her life at some time, and was torture for shopkeepers. At one stage she had two pairs of shoes, a coat, a handbag and a typewriter all back with the suppliers for defects that only she could see. She carried on a twenty-year feud with her neighbours over a shared drain, and kept the Noise Abatement Society busy for years almost single-handed, since she could not work, she said, for the noise of a generator in the Express Dairy's garage at the back of her studio. No one else could hear a thing. She would tele-phone at all hours of the day, especially very early in the morning, wanting long conversations about matters that interested her, without any thought as to whether they interested anyone else. 'I am very con-cerned', she said once, 'about the Burundi stool. I simply don't think the British Museum [or the BM, as she always called it] knows what it is doing.' She would complain endlessly about what she called the 'Vic & Alb' – the only person I have ever known describe the Victoria & Albert Museum in that way. Yet there was something undeniably sparky about her at her best. But deep inside I knew as few others did that her grief at Felix's death must have been partly fuelled by a real-ization of the extent to which she had neglected him. His vision and imagination had as much influence on me as anything in my life, and I still feel that, had he lived, he would have given Peter Brook and Peter Stein a run for their money.

## 2

# Willingly to School

Gorse Cliff Preparatory School in Boscombe was recommended to my mother by a friend. It had a good reputation for getting boys into public schools, though not so much Winchester or Rugby as Sherborne and Shrewsbury. I used to cycle there – about two and a half miles each way – and frozen fingers and chilblains remain a memory of my first winter. I was there for four and a half years, from 1943 to 1948, and through the outstanding ability of two of the teachers those years were the foundation of my academic ability. The Headmaster taught Latin and geography and was not exceptional, but the Second Master, Brian Mabley, who taught French and history, and Frank Pickering, English, were both remarkable.

Pickering, a chubby bachelor and model-railway enthusiast who lived in an hotel where he had a huge layout in the basement, loved the English language and its literature quite as much as trains. We were not only given a very thorough grounding in grammar and syntax but were encouraged to read widely and to have views about what we read. Every weekend we had to learn a short poem and on the Monday morning be prepared to recite it by heart. Pickering treated literary history like real history, with family trees of writers and with literature related to both politics and social change. He had a soft spot for historical novels, and we were pushed towards Meade Faulkner and Captain Marryat. He could see that *Moonfleet* or *The Children of the New Forest,* both set locally, might spark an interest, and when it came to Harrison Ainsworth's *Old St Paul's* he knew plague and fire were the kind of thing boys enjoyed. He would also read to us from a wide range of more grown-up writers: Dickens, H. G. Wells and, his great favourite, John Buchan.

A few years ago I found a notebook from my English lessons when I was twelve. The term was concentrated on the romantic poets – there is a long list of Byron's major poems, and also the date of the *Lyrical Ballads.* Pickering thought Wordsworth both too simple and too complex for young boys, but he encouraged a love of Coleridge and Keats that I have never lost. When we were ten he gave us Lamb's *Tales from Shakespeare*, but by twelve we moved on to the real thing, reading plays every week in class. If a major theatre company came to Bournemouth he encouraged our parents to take us to see it. I remember the Old Vic company with *The Alchemist*, starring Alec Guinness and directed by Tyrone Guthrie, and *The Taming of the Shrew* with Trevor Howard as Petruchio – a role I was myself to play the following year. Just as at home, things were put in a context which meant that they seemed not merely school texts, but something that could affect our lives.

Brian Mabley was even more imaginative. Propped up on the window sill was always a book of reproductions of great paintings. Each day a page was turned, and at some point in the day a few minutes were spent discussing the new picture and telling us something about both the painter and his subject. Images ranged from Bellini to Goya, from Canaletto to Monet, always with some small fact or anecdote to make them live. When it came to history he would seek out pictures of the places and people concerned; Christchurch Priory had been begun by Ranulf Flambard, the first Norman bishop of Durham, so with 1066 went pictures of Christchurch Priory, the Bayeux Tapestry and Durham Cathedral, as well as reproductions of Domesday Book. We were encouraged to take sides in the Hundred Years War and the Wars of the Roses. When it came to the Civil War, he read us excerpts from the trial of Charles I. History lived for us through him, and went straight to the heart of my own leanings.

As much as history, I still loved architecture, and the family thought I might have a future as an architect. I think it was as early as thirteen years of age that I knew that I was interested more in existing buildings of all kinds than in designing new ones. But I won a book on the new architecture of the 1930s as a school prize, and I was aware that, like all the arts, architecture was a continuum, not something that had stopped some time before I was born.

If you were as fascinated by buildings as I was, Bournemouth wasn't much of a place, especially at a time when Victorian taste was more ridiculed than admired. Yet there were several outstanding Gothic Revival churches, notably Pearson's St Stephen's, and we went to look at them. We drew Norman, Early English, Decorated and Perpendicular windows and doors in class as part of our history lessons. My belief in the interrelationship of the elements that make up social history had its beginnings in Mabley's exhilarating classes.

He taught French with the same enthusiasm, talking about his own visits to France, his time there as a student teacher and the differences in everyday life. Because of the war and the restrictions on travel afterwards, France was then a place that none of us had ever had a chance to visit. Nevertheless my accent was already acceptable, and Mabley gave me huge encouragement to master a wider vocabulary and to read both poetry and prose, from Ronsard to Anatole France. Verlaine he introduced when I was twelve, and I found I already knew some of the poems from the settings by Fauré and Debussy that my mother sang.

Mabley had rather a soft spot for my mother, and always chatted to her at parents' meetings or Speech Days. I was somewhat embarrassed by this, since he obviously found her not just interesting but attractive. But they rarely got a chance to speak for long before the arrival of his wife, Nora, the sister of the Headmaster. She taught us painting. Her own style was predictably English – genteel landscapes and floral watercolours: effective but timid – but she let us loose on wilder themes, asking for paintings of pirates, forest fires and, surprisingly, refugees. The request for refugees came on the day I lost another good friend, my immensely entertaining black cat, Tony, whom I had acquired soon after we moved to Bournemouth. On the last night of his life, in great pain with undiagnosed gallstones, he crept from his basket in the kitchen to my room at the other end of the house to be with me, leaving a trail of blood on the stairs. *Refugees*, which I still possess, has quite a lot of feeling in it for a twelve-year-old. But, as with poetry and musical composition, I was too impatient to be a really good artist, though I loved doing it and still occasionally get out the sketchbook and the brushes.

I had strong creative impulses – if not enough to make a real impression, certainly enough to fill hours of my life with enjoyable attempts. I suppose it must seem arrogant, but it never occurred to me that there was anything that I could *not* do if I put my mind to it – except those mechanical things that boys are supposed to enjoy, like taking machines to bits, mending punctures, or even putting dubbin on football boots. I was never really interested in sports and consequently never any good at them, but I enjoyed the indoor games like Monopoly, bagatelle, spillikins and darts. I loved my clockwork trains, but hated Meccano: I was simply no good at it. Instead, I had Bayco – a set of miniature Bakelite wall panels with doors, windows and roofs – and with this I used to design houses. It was a busy childhood.

The Bournemouth Municipal Orchestra was re-formed in 1947 under the German conductor Rudolf Schwarz. In the early years it gave four concerts a week with three different programmes – an unthinkable workload today. I usually went at the weekend, when there was a matinee. Schwarz was a tall, silver-haired figure, perilously thin and willowy. He had been in a concentration camp, and had only just survived. He was the first conductor I was able to see regularly enough to get used to his idiosyncratic style. He had hardly any visible stick technique, seeming to conduct more with his right wrist. It was hard to follow him until you were used to it, players said. It was certainly very different from the bouncy flamboyance of the only other conductor I had seen much of: John Barbirolli. After he had returned from New York to take over the Hallé in 1943, he came every year to Bournemouth and gave concerts for a week, each night a different programme. I was allowed to go quite often, standing at the back of the circle of the awful Pavilion Theatre; tickets were a shilling.

Sometimes there was a school outing to a concert, and on those occasions we were carefully prepared. A man called Carnegie used to come and talk about what we were going to hear, playing the main themes on the piano and occasionally using a gramophone record. Mozart, Beethoven, Schubert and Brahms symphonies were discussed, and when we got to the concert everything somehow fell into place. I remember being knocked out by Sibelius's Seventh Symphony and intoxicated by Walton's Viola Concerto, played by William Primrose. When people speak dismissively today of 'musical appreciation' I remember those preparatory sessions and how useful I found them, even though I was only eleven or twelve years old. Over the years I myself have been involved in dozens of pre-concert talks with composers, conductors and soloists, and I know they can help an already well-disposed audience to get more out of an event. Today we are told that for young people that sort of thing is too passive, and that making music matters more than talking about it, even if you have no talent. I believe there is a real place for exposition in education and on radio and television. Programme notes in those days tended to be of the rustling trees, lapping water variety; today they are often too musicological. Finding the right balance, like finding the right voice in which to talk to people, is difficult but important. I could not then know how much it was to become part of my life. But, for me, knowing more has always meant understanding more and therefore enjoying more.

It was a wonderful thing to have a symphony orchestra available at a modest price. In winter I enjoyed the thrill of the live concerts. I remember feeling positively squeamish with excitement when I first heard some of the great concertos. In summer I would come back from the beach knowing that the Proms on the radio might well include something I knew and loved, but almost certainly something to be experienced for the first time. New music was already part of my life. I recall the first broadcast performances of Vaughan Williams's Fifth Symphony and of Bartók's Third Piano Concerto, while a friend at school bought the Heifetz recording of Walton's Violin Concerto, which we thought more exciting than anything we had ever heard. Schwarz had a policy of programming a British work in every concert. This meant a few horrors and some bores, but we could follow the emergence of a new post-war generation – Malcolm Arnold, Peter Racine Fricker, Humphrey Searle and Elizabeth Lutyens – as well as the more established Bax, Vaughan Williams and Walton and the increasingly newsworthy Britten and Tippett. I was often mystified, sometimes delighted, but always intrigued enough to come back for more. If the BBC or the Bournemouth Orchestra put something on, that was good enough for me; they knew more than I did, so it was worth taking seriously. I still have a strong element of that attitude in my nature – a respect for other people's knowledge, especially in the frequent cases when it outruns my own.

There was also a new generation of soloists who came to Bournemouth. Violinists like Ginette Neveu, Giaconda DeVito and Tibor Varga. Pianists like Cor de Groot, Gina Bachauer and Mewton Wood. Cellists like Pierre Fournier and Paul Tortelier. Singers like the very young Victoria de los Angeles and, unforgettably, Kirsten Flagstad – statuesque and imperious, giving me my first taste of Wagner. Then there was Kathleen Ferrier. Still only eleven, I was considered too young to go to the English Opera Group production of *The Rape of Lucretia*, and so missed seeing her on stage, but listening to her singing Brahms, Schubert and Britten folk-song arrangements in recital I felt there was something unusually true and direct in her powers of communication, although my mother was critical of her interpretative range. Broadcasts from the first Edinburgh Festival, in 1947, brought Bruno Walter and my first experience of Mahler, while Charles Groves took over the Bournemouth Chorus and threw himself into the oratorio repertory; I heard my first *Dream of Gerontius* in Salisbury Cathedral with Ferrier's teacher, Roy Henderson, and the Australian William Herbert, whom my mother knew.

Despite school work and all the other distractions of life, music in one form or another was part of every day – even if it was only my own attempts to play through things that were frankly much too difficult for me – yet I knew even then that life without music was unthinkable. But a visit from my mother's old teacher Professor Leckie and his wife discouraged me from hoping it could be a profession for me. He gave me a good going over and pronounced me 'talented – but not enough'. Far from being discouraging, this liberated me into a conscience-free love of music rather than a bad-tempered preoccupation with fingering and phrasing. I can understand how coming to love music and wanting to be present when it was performed might seem unusual, but for me, with all the advantages I had, it was the most natural thing in the world and much more rewarding than kicking a ball about.

Ballet also found ready acceptance. In fact I was grown up before I even thought about its relevance. It, too, seemed quite natural. The first company I saw was the Anglo-Polish Ballet in *Les Sylphides*, when I was five or six. I have never forgotten the Poet, a dancer called Rovi Pavinoff, or his carrot-coloured wig, which I thought very funny. But there were moonlight, Chopin and women suspended in mid-air, and I was immediately taken with the magic of it all. Slightly later, I remember *Les Patineurs* with Harold Turner as the Blue Boy, and *Façade* with Margot Fonteyn and Robert Helpmann; it was permitted to laugh.

The war years were fertile ground for the growth of ballet, which provided glamour and enchantment against the background of a very austere world. The big break-through for me came with the International Ballet, run by the English dancer Mona Inglesby. Backed by family money, she had the foresight to recruit as producer the émigré regisseur of the Imperial Ballet in St Petersburg, Nicolai Sergeyev, who had a number of notation books containing the exact steps of the famous Petipa and Ivanov productions that had been so admired since the turn of the century. The *Swan Lake* that International Ballet presented was more accurate in a historical sense than any other production I have seen, and I loved it from the first glimpse. *Coppélia* and *Giselle* were also performed in good versions, and the company danced *Les Sylphides*, *Carnaval* and the last act of *Sleeping Beauty* in the version called *Aurora's Wedding*.

The main spur to my interest in ballet was an English dancer called

Harcourt Essex, whose stage name was Algeranoff, and whom my mother had got to know in Australia when he was a member of the company run by the great Russian dancer Anna Pavlova. When International Ballet came to Bournemouth, usually twice a year, Algy and his young French wife, Claudie, came to stay with us, and for a few days our whole life revolved around the company and their performances. Unusually for that time, Algy had also studied dance in India and Japan before joining the Ballets Russes de Monte Carlo in the 1930s. He taught me to dance the Russian *trepak*, squatting down, kicking my legs out and swinging them round like The Three Ivans. He would explain stage make-up and how important it was to emphasize the eyes of a character dancer. He himself was a touching and tragic Dr Coppélius, quite different from the camp caricature of Robert Helpmann. I begged to be allowed to go to as many performances as possible and to stay up late to hear Algy reminiscing and Claudie with her French chic cattily enumerating the shortcomings of everyone else in the company.

I found the physical discipline of classical ballet fascinating, and never once questioned dancing *en pointe* or whether ballet was really able to convey stories or situations. It seemed entirely successful in suggesting emotion and the intensity of human and superhuman relationships. Willis, swans, peasants, sylphs – all seemed to me a great deal less silly than most fairy stories in books, which I have never liked. Andersen was for me too sentimental, Grimm too Gothic, but *Giselle* or *Swan Lake* had at their heart a kind of truth about love, loss, grandeur and parade. Fifty years on, something exceptional is needed to reawaken those feelings now, but it can still happen. When I first saw Sylvie Guillem as Giselle and Baryshnikov as Albrecht (not in the same production!) I re-experienced the elation that great dancing can communicate. I was given Arnold Haskell's King Penguin *Ballet* for my twelfth birthday and learnt a bit of history – about Camargo, Taglioni and the Danes like Bournonville. I was aware of a few raised eyebrows at my enthusiasm, especially when I chose to give a short talk on ballet at my prep school – not quite what was expected!

I also saw Roland Petit's Ballets des Champs-Élysées in *Les Forains*, with its lovely score by Henri Sauguet, and Jean Babilée and Nathalie Philippart in *Le Jeune Homme et la mort*, which proved to me that dance need not be only about a fairy-tale past. My greatest disappointment was not to have seen the Ballets Jooss, since both Algy and my mother considered *The Green Table* a contemporary masterpiece. We had tickets, but on the day we were to go I went into hospital for a minor operation. It was not until several years later that I finally saw it and got to know Kurt Jooss himself.

Bournemouth was a terrifically snobbish town, though it seemed to me it had little reason to be so. Most of the parents of my school friends were hoteliers or shopkeepers, with the occasional solicitor or doctor. Once I became conscious of social distinction I realized that we were not considered to be really worth knowing, since we lived at the wrong end of town. Nevertheless, in that wrong end we made many good and long-lasting friends. Although we had to be careful, I never felt the lack of money or status. My mother made sure that everyday life was full of activity, and after the deaths of Drummond and Felix she took a lot of trouble to make sure I had friends of my own age – not only boys, but girls too. I am thankful that it was a time when girls could be friends without precociously becoming girlfriends.

The one point at which our life touched the snobby world of Branksome and Canford Cliffs was through our membership of the Bournemouth Film Society. My mother was soon invited on to the committee, and we went regularly on Saturday evenings to sit on hideously uncomfortable stacking chairs in the art college. During the years of my childhood and adolescence I saw all the great films of the early cinema, from D. W. Griffith's *Intolerance* to *The Cabinet of Doctor Caligari*, *M* and *The Blue Angel*. My mother believed the French cinema could help my studies, so I also saw all the films of René Clair, Jean Renoir and Jacques Feyder. Actors like Jean Gabin, Louis Jouvet, Françoise Rosay and Marie Bell were familiar figures – and usually rather better than their starchily stiff English equivalents. I came to love small-town France through Marcel Pagnol, and eventually fell under the spell of *Les Enfants du paradis*, probably the greatest film of the century. All cinema presents an illusory view of the world, but there seemed more likelihood that life resembled the nation's cinema in France than in England. I cannot say that I love France because of *Le Jour se lève*, *Quai des brumes* or *La Fille du puisatier*, but I cannot disassociate them from the France I eventually got to know and still occasionally glimpse.

At the same time, but in quite a different way, I was fascinated by the Russian cinema of Eisenstein and Pudovkin with their huge subjects, revolution and tyranny, and by the emerging neo-realist cinema of

Italy, in which Rossellini, Visconti and De Sica seemed to provide clues to the life of ordinary people. My mental picture of America was totally influenced by the near documentary *film noir* of the late 1940s – *Call Northside 777, Sorry Wrong Number*, 711 *Ocean Drive* – and by the looming presence of Orson Welles, especially in *Citizen Kane*. We also saw many new films at the local cinemas, from Gainsborough costume dramas with Margaret Lockwood and James Mason to the new Ealing comedies with their rolling repertory of English eccentrics: Margaret Rutherford, Joyce Grenfell, Miles Malleson and Cecil Parker. I had a soft spot for comedy, especially the Marx Brothers, and loved the stylishness of Frank Capra and Billy Wilder. Noël Coward's *In Which We Serve* seemed to me to be about my parents, especially Celia Johnson's famous speech about sailors having two wives – their real wife and their ship. I loved *Brief Encounter*, though more for the trains and for Eileen Joyce's playing of the Rachmaninov Second Piano Concerto on the soundtrack than for the love story, while David Lean's adaptations of *Great Expectations* and *Oliver Twist* still seem marvellous. Cinema was a key part of my learning about the world, and in the stuffy atmosphere of Bournemouth society I often enjoyed the films we saw more than the people we met.

Concerts, exhibitions, plays, ballet, film and (to a much lesser extent) opera were all part of my youth, and combined to reinforce the feeling I have never lost of how lucky I was in my upbringing. This also inevitably made me talkative and tiresome, too much wanting to be the centre of attention. I was tall for my age, but awkward, gangly, bespectacled and, in ways that persist, frequently shy. Without being wimpish, I hated violence and avoided fights if at all possible. I kept my head down during the obligatory boxing bouts thought so important at school to create a manly personality. I disliked rows – the more so as they were becoming a frequent part of my domestic life.

My father, who had been away since the spring of 1939, suddenly returned in late 1943. I hardly recognized him, nor he me. I remember being more intrigued by the colourful basket containing grapefruit, pineapples and bananas that he had picked up in Lisbon on the journey home by flying boat. He and my mother found themselves increasingly estranged. Apart from the evacuation of Crete, he had had a rather cushy war, eventually living in comfort in South Africa with a gang of rich friends who entertained him lavishly, while in Bournemouth my mother struggled on a proportion of his salary (eroded by my school fees) and suffering from shortages of every kind. Our social life, such as it was, he found a comedown, and showed it. It is not that I resented him, I was intrigued by him, but found it hard to make contact. I would rattle on about people and things he did not know or care for, and very soon came to feel his disappointment that I was not the sort of son he had wanted.

A few weeks after his return my father suffered the worst blow of his war. He had left his ship in West Africa and a relief captain had taken over for the return journey, while he flew home on leave. Off the coast of Sierra Leone the ship was torpedoed; it sank in a minute, and over a hundred of my father's closest colleagues were drowned. I can still recall the silence that fell on our household after the telegram arrived: it seemed to last for weeks. Inevitably he was soon recalled to sea, commanding a new ship, and he spent the rest of the war on convoys between Liverpool and North Africa, dodging U-boats in the Atlantic. We saw him every two months, and if he was in the UK during school holidays I would spend time on his ship in dock. In this way I got to know Liverpool, Newcastle-upon-Tyne and Hull – and the surrounding countryside, where I would go and look for castles and churches. The state of the cities was an eye-opener. We had had only one air raid in Bournemouth – it destroyed a hotel where my mother ran a canteen for Canadian troops – but even the crater that that made, deep as it was, had not prepared me for the appearance of Liverpool or London. But there was a grim determination to carry on as best as people could. I cannot recall there ever being a sense of defeatism, perhaps because by then the tide was turning.

Quite by chance, early one evening in June 1944 I went for a ride on my bike along the cliffs overlooking the sea and found the whole bay from the Isle of Wight to Swanage full of ships – hundreds of them. By the following day they had gone and the Normandy landings had begun. Every day I examined the maps on the front page of the *Daily Telegraph* showing the relative position of German and Allied troops. I remember wondering what newspapers put on the front page in peacetime.

That summer the flying bombs brought a new sense of danger, and one of the first of the V2s seriously damaged Great-Aunt Laura's house in Tottenham, so, Willie having died in 1942, she came to live with us, imposing her regime of piety and hypochondria on our daily life. Fragile she may have claimed to be, but, propped up by hours a day of embrocations, eye baths and indigestion tablets, at seventy-five she was stronger and fitter than my mother, who was thirty years younger. On Sundays she folded her hands on the Bible and turned her head to the wall. I was sent to my room for asking how she would cope without servants. But in due course she started talking to me about her childhood and about London in the 1880s and '90s. I had never had the benefit of grandparents – they were all dead before I was born – and only now started to feel a sense of history coming alive through eyewitness accounts. Radio and television today often feature the elderly reminiscing, but up to then I had never experienced it. Listening to my great-aunt's reminiscences was the beginning of a lifelong fascination with oral history, which later I was able to contribute to through the many interviews I conducted with my seniors, perhaps subconsciously seeking out surrogate grandparents.

When the war ended my father took command of a BI passenger liner and travelled again between London and East Africa as he had been doing when I was born. Once more life for him became parties, dances, flirtations and a world of cosseted luxury surrounded by Goanese Indian servants. He always had a willing audience for his stories and jokes; they were good stories, and the jokes were funny the first time round. Each new batch of passengers would respond. We, unfortunately, had heard them too often.

At home the immediate post-war years were in many ways worse than the war itself, with bread and potato rationing and the feeling that, though we had won, we had gained nothing. We were freer to travel – there were holidays now in Scotland, and a month in Cornwall while my father's ship was being refitted in Falmouth – and the local beaches were open again. I had made several close friends at school, and as I passed into my teens we were all starting to look to the future. My family's financial situation meant that I would have to win a scholarship for my parents to be able to afford a public school. My Latin and my maths were no more than adequate, and sometimes rather less than that, so it was decided that schools like Rugby or Winchester were unattainable. Gorse Cliff recommended Canford, a school with which it had good relations, only a few miles away, near Wimborne. It was even possible to be a day-boy. In the summer of 1948 I sat the scholarship exam and won the maximum amount without much difficulty. It was decided that I should be a boarder. I suspect that, despite his unhappy experiences, my father thought that a good thing. With considerable trepidation, I embarked on the next stage of my life.

Canford did not at that time have the reputation it has today, nor was it as expensive. Very much, as the saying went, 'a school for the fathers of gentlemen rather than their sons', it sat quite far down the league of minor public schools – respectable, but without academic fame or social glamour. It was founded on the same day in 1923 as Stowe, by the same dotty clergyman, but never became fashionable as Stowe did under Roxburgh before the war, an acceptable place for the kind of boy who failed to make Eton. Nor was it forward-looking and arty like Bryanston, its nearest neighbour up the river at Blandford, where the boys wore shorts and mixed freely with girls. Canford had few famous old boys or grand connections, but it was in a splendid setting. The park was enormous, running almost to the outskirts of Poole. Like many schools of its kind, it responded well if you chose to work.

Never having been away from home except to stay with relatives or in holiday hotels, I had no idea what to expect, and the retreating view of my mother disappearing down the drive in a hired Daimler left me feeling more alone than ever before. My first term was a hateful experience. The regime was spartan: dormitory windows open at all times – even when it snowed – dreadful food and absolute lack of privacy. I was an only child and used to my own room and my own space. Now I was never alone and subject to the usual catalogue of petty regulations and even pettier authority. Learning lists of names or mastering the school slang was easy; the constant presence of people I did not know was far more difficult. It was like starting a life sentence. After a few weeks I asked a day-boy in my form, who lived near me, if things had changed much outside in the time I had been away. I think he thought I was mad. But it was only a matter of weeks before my first exeat, and then the Christmas holidays, and by the second term suddenly things started falling into place. There were even a couple of new boys for me to be offensive to. All too quickly I came to accept unquestioningly a very unusual way of life: several hundred boys, aged from thirteen to eighteen, incarcerated in a kind of open prison with all its competitiveness and false values.

I was immediately labelled a swot in a house that prided itself on sporting achievements. The House Master, although young, was a remote figure with no skills at all in relating to young people. Life at home was constantly entertaining; here you were not even encouraged to develop your own interests or personality – you had to be one of the gang. But as winter moved into spring the attractions of the place increased, and athletics – the only sport I was any good at – allowed me to gain some small credibility with my fellows. But I questioned then, and still do, the artificiality of it all and the abnormality of such an unbalanced society. In time I came to exercise and even enjoy the kind of petty authority I had so resented in others and to view school as a microcosm of the world outside with its jealousies, friendships and rivalries. But its dangerous sense of self-sufficiency seems to me a poor preparation for a normal life.

However, once again I was incredibly lucky in my teachers. In both my weak subjects, Latin and maths, they were quite exceptional. My Latin teacher, William Strain – known, of course, as Willie Drain – had a strong theatrical streak and turned Latin into a charade. For the Ides of March the room was draped in purple, and most weeks he expostulated on the shortcomings of emperors while praising the output of poets. I came to love Latin, and – as I never had the opportunity to learn Greek, which I still regret – Latin literature became a key to an intellectual world which suggested that during two thousand years man had changed very little. Michael Hancock, a portly figure who took us for maths, had a kind of genius for making algebra intelligible. Arithmetic was obvious: it added up. Even geometry could be related to architecture or to reversing a car. But algebra had foxed me totally. What were $x$ and $y$, and why did it matter? I am not sure I can answer that today, but I knew enough about it then to get a distinction in my maths exams and even to look forward to lessons. When you could make it work there was a real sense of satisfaction.

History, English and French continued and reinforced what I had learnt and felt at Gorse Cliff, but there were choices to be made between biology and German, physics and music, and so the English system of specializing at a relatively early age has left me with no scientific knowledge or understanding. I was not really conscious of the loss at the time. Later I attended lectures on the history of science, so at least I would know who Boyle and Newton were, but science remains a great lacuna. I am typical of those whom C. P. Snow attacked in his famous 'Two Cultures' lecture. I expect and usually find that my scientist friends understand and even love music, but I have no reciprocal sense of needing to love physics and chemistry. Snow has been much sneered at, but I think he was right.

German I took to at once, partly because it was the language of my mother's lieder repertory that I knew so well, but also because my teacher was the most eccentric of them all. Yvone Kirkpatrick was a big man with a loud voice who drove an ancient Buick and commanded the school cadet corps, striding about in battledress accentuating his enormous rump. Perhaps because of this, his nickname was 'Wump'. He loved poetry, his wife was a painter, and they had talented and pretty daughters. In time, when he learnt of my love for buildings, he would organize outings to country houses in the district where he was known and made welcome. Hence I remember Velázquez's wonderful portrait of his mulatto assistant, Juan de Pareja, now in the Metropolitan Museum in New York, when it hung in the drawing room of Longford Castle, Lord Radnor's house near Salisbury. Yvone encouraged me to plan outings and eventually write to the owners myself. Most of the applications were accepted, and we saw Kingston Lacy, with its great possible Giorgione before the restoration; Charborough, the home of the wonderfully named Admiral the Honourable Sir Reginald Aylmer Ranfurly Plunket-Ernle-Erle-Drax, who had started life as Reggie Plunket before inheriting both the house and the names; and, loveliest of all, Binghams Melcombe, whose postal address was Binghams Melcombe, Melcombe Bingham, Dorset – which seemed to me perfection. Only one request was refused. I wrote a polite letter to Lord Ilchester at Melbury. Unfortunately he was away, and so it took a while to reach him. I have never forgotten his reply: 'Sir, I received your request to visit Melbury on 25 June on the 23rd. This, sir, is an impertinence. Ilchester.' But even that did not stop my growing wish to look at houses and their contents as we raced around the empty roads of north Dorset, where nothing much had changed in fifty years and characters out of Hardy's novels might well have watched us pass.

At Canford, music above all was a way of escaping from the crowd, and the purportedly haunted, almost ruined music school in former servants quarters was a frequent place of refuge. Although my piano playing was as splashy and erratic as ever, I was ambitiously trying to write more than little waltzes, and since I had a friend who was a competent violinist I embarked on a sonata for violin and piano. Over the months it grew and grew – endless pages of melancholy tunes with ambitious accompaniment. Eventually it was nearly twenty pages long, and all resolutely in the key of A minor. My inadequate understanding of music had not yet revealed to me the secrets of modulation; when I sensed the risk of moving into another key, I rapidly regained the tonic.

At this point, quite by chance, I was taken up by someone who was to become one of the great influences on my life.

H. E. Piggott was a retired maths teacher who had been recalled during the war because of the shortage of younger men. He had been a senior wrangler at Clare, taught at Westminster in the early years of the century, when Adrian Boult was among his pupils, and went on to become Second Master at Dartmouth. There he had taught not only royal dukes, but the future conductor Boyd Neel. Although a mathematician by profession, he could as easily have been a musician; Oxford University Press published several of his songs, and his chamber music was performed. At Canford he played the organ in chapel, and I loved his imaginative improvisations. He also trained the choir. He only taught the sixth form mathematics, and was reputed never to consult logarithm tables since he knew them all by heart. The Senior Music Master, an old waffler, discovered my attempts at composition and asked Piggott to hear the violin sonata. He was very restrained in his reaction, but asked me to his cottage in Canford village for tea. I met his tiny but highly impressive wife, a Cornish woman of strong personality and outspoken views. Her father had been a Member of Parliament, and the young schoolmaster had not been thought a suitable catch. Piggott proposed to her on the beach at Zennor in 1901, but felt he had to ask her to hang on until he was more established. It was not fair, he suggested, but would she be prepared to wait? 'Why not?' she replied, and five years later they married. There was one daughter, Audrey, a professional cellist, who after the war had moved to Vancouver and become principal in the orchestra there. Their little house was full of books, music and photographs and memories of their many friends, from Admirals of the Fleet to Sybil Thorndike and Lewis Casson, whose son he had taught at Dartmouth.

H. E., as I came to call him, realized how little I knew and offered to teach me. For the next two and a half years I went to tea every Monday and, after home-made cakes and conversation, had a lesson. Each week I had to prepare something – canons, part-songs, hymn tunes. Life centred around parallel fifths and false cadences. But I was reluctant to really study counterpoint, and arrogant enough to believe that I did not need it for the kind of things I wanted to write. I had by now discovered Debussy preludes and small pieces by Ravel and Gabriel Grovlez, falling in love with squishy harmonies and dominant thirteenths. I wrote a number of impressionistic piano pieces based on

Cézanne paintings – 'Cézannesques' I called them pretentiously. H. E. tolerated my refusal to work at traditional harmony and counterpoint, but he warned me I could only go so far without them. Of course he was right, and all that remains of my compositional efforts are a few songs, some short piano pieces and a mass of sketches for larger things, all of which ground to a standstill because I really had no idea how to develop the basic ideas. To that extent I was a poor pupil and he an over-indulgent teacher, but, like Professor Leckie, he recognized that I was not intended to be a professional but had, nevertheless, a deep love for music. 'You never know', he used to say, 'when things come in handy.' He certainly gave me a better understanding of music, an idea of form and an inspiring friendship.

During all this time H. E. never suggested payment, and after meeting my mother he came to be almost part of the family. Mrs Piggott taught my mother smocking and how to make saffron cakes. After her death, he lived on in a boarding house in Bournemouth with a clavichord, since there was no room for a piano. On one of the last times I saw him he was poring over the score of Stockhausen's percussion piece *Zyklus* with a slide rule and analysing its palindromic stucture. 'Dammit,' he said, 'it works!' He was eighty-six. What above all I learnt from him was that learning never stops, and that the way to keep alive is to be interested in and open to new ideas. His own music was probably closer to Holst than to Stockhausen, very much of the English pastoral school. He had collected folk songs in his youth, and was the first to transcribe 'Shallow Brown'. Cecil Sharp and Vaughan Williams were friends, but he was also fascinated by late Liszt, and wished that Bartók's collection of piano studies *Mikrokosmos* was used as a teaching instrument in Britain. He wrote an effective pastiche piano concerto for the Bournemouth Orchestra to perform with a local pianist, and a cello sonata which was broadcast but never published. Years later, in Canada, I asked his daughter what had happened to his manuscripts. She had destroyed them all. Perhaps he had been more difficult as a father than he was as a teacher, but few things in my life have made me so angry. H. E. had made settings of passages from the Apocrypha, including the words 'Where can wisdom be found and where is the seat of understanding?' He embodied wisdom for me, and his influence certainly brought me closer to understanding.

In due course I got a study to myself at Canford, and other wise voices became accessible through my having a radio. I was actively encouraged to listen to things like the Reith Lectures and the first series of talks by Isaiah Berlin on political theory. I understood little, I am sure, but was immediately taken by the sense of engagement with ideas – something rather lacking in my fact-based education. On Sundays, John Summerson chaired *The Critics*. John Betjeman shared his enthusiasms regularly, and J. B. Priestley still broadcast occasionally. I had no idea that in time I would know and work with them all. BBC Radio's Third Programme, which began in 1947, was a permanent source of enjoyment through much marvellous music: Solomon playing the thirty-two Beethoven piano sonatas (I followed them from my copies), and lots of what was still for me an almost closed book, chamber music. Haydn, Schubert and Beethoven quartets became familiar, and there were wonderful live relays from the Edinburgh Festival, such as the concerts given by Artur Schnabel, Joseph Szigeti, William Primrose and Pierre Fournier in 1947 to mark the anniversaries of Schubert, Mendelssohn and Brahms. I had always loved radio, from childhood memories of *Toytown* and *Children's Hour* to L. du Gard Peach's *The Castles of England*. Later there were adaptations of novels and great poetry readings – Marius Goring reading Tennyson's *Maud*, Paul Scofield romping through Browning's monologues, and Ralph Richardson exulting in *The Rubáiyát of Omar Khayyám*. Not having a radio in my first years at public school added to my sense of deprivation, and even at the height of my television career I still remained a regular listener. And what I missed could often be read in the *Listener*, a publication whose casual abandonment by the BBC still shocks and disappoints me. At home my mother took the *New Statesman* and, on Sundays, the *Observer*. I read them chiefly for the critics, and came to feel I really knew many of them when week by week I read Ivor Brown on theatre, C. A. Lejeune on film and William Glock on music in the *Observer*, T. C. Worsley on theatre, V. S. Pritchett on books and Edward Sackville-West on music in the *Statesman*. They covered a wide range of expertise and political and social positions. I was much less interested in politics then, but was aware that under the post-war Labour government things were changing.

The National Health Service became a reality for us when in 1951 my father's health collapsed, with another recurrence of tuberculosis demanding long and expensive treatment with new drugs. He was off work for over a year, and for the first few months very weak and helpless. With gradual recovery came a different mood, born of frustration and rage. He had been named as Captain of a brand new liner – the biggest the BI had ever built for the East African run, the summit of his career – but before he could take up the appointment he collapsed again and was forced into early retirement at the age of only fifty-three. It is not hard to imagine how difficult this was for him and how much he wanted to express his disappointment. But it is harder to justify the extent to which he took out his frustration on my mother, who once again had nursed him selflessly and given up everything else to do so.

Retirement, of course, meant that he was permanently at home with nothing to do. His sense of isolation was aggravated by increasing deafness, which, despite the best in hearing aids, made it very difficult for him to follow conversations in a crowded room or to go to the theatre with any pleasure. His life fell into a stultifying routine of slow emergence in the morning, a little time in the garden, lunch, a rest, a short drive with my mother at the wheel, and the evening slumped in a chair with the papers. In due course television took over his evenings and he became glued exclusively to the BBC, with a separate sound feed into his earpiece which made it impossible to talk to him. Like many deaf people, he believed he was being prevented from knowing what was going on, and was being talked about constantly behind his back. Since my mother and I talked often of things like music, which did not interest him, he may have had some justification. Perhaps we made insufficient effort to ensure that he felt a part of things. But for my part I found his increasingly reactionary views less than stimulating. Slightly improbably, he had campaigned for the Labour Party in 1945, but in later years he always denied it, and he made such a fuss about Kingsley Martin's pro-Indian-independence attitudes in the *New Statesman* that my mother eventually cancelled her subscription to prevent regular rows. He had been used to ordering dozens of people about and being waited on hand and foot without the need to say 'Thank you.' Now his empire was reduced to two, and we felt the full force of his personality – which, despite his physical weakness, was still considerable. We never sat down to a meal confident that it would end without a row. I am certain he genuinely loved my mother, but in a Scottish way that found expression only in childish sentimentality between bursts of unpredictable rage.

Once a week he went out on his own to a get-together with other retired naval officers in the district. It was the only time my mother was alone in the house. She, like me, had been used to her own space, and found the constant presence of this rumbling volcano exhausting. She had her weekly concerts and the film society, but apart from that was rarely out of his presence. I watched her move from being a confident, outgoing focus for fun and enthusiasm into a bitter and resentful late middle age. She became increasingly dependent on me to provide stimulus and escape, while I found it hard to get out of the house to meet my own friends. For the rest of my parents' lives, if I came home for the weekend that was where I stayed – the merest suggestion that I might go off on my own irritated my father and disappointed my mother. If only I had had a sister or a brother, I used to think. Above all, I wondered why they stayed together, and resented the implication that it was for my sake. But my mother would have never considered leaving him, since she was convinced he was incapable of looking after himself and would immediately become ill again. She was also imbued with very deep Christian beliefs that she had married him 'for better for worse, for richer for poorer'.

Our diminished financial situation, with him in receipt of only a small pension, meant that, financially, life was no less difficult now than it had been in earlier years. My mother too was frequently ill, and by my teens I was used to running the house when necessary, cooking and shopping as required. It was to prove a useful training. Nevertheless, life was not all that bad: we ran a small car, entertained friends, and had the occasional outing, but there was no fat on the budget. My father, who had always smoked heavily and probably drank too much as well, was forbidden both tobacco and alcohol. To make it easier, my mother gave up as well; it was only in later years that she crept back to an occasional cigarette – always the source of rows. My father took to a nightly whisky or two – the refusal of more led to further rows. Little of this was visible to outsiders. My father was capable of being totally charming, not only to friends, but to waitresses, shop assistants and the garage man, while in the middle of an embittered denunciation of my mother or, increasingly, of me. Everything about me was offensive to him, whether it was my love of music and books or my critical attitude to authority which was beginning to show itself.

I initially trusted that people in authority had got there for good reason. But as I got older I felt more and more that their power depended on other things, from Buggins's turn to outright dishonesty. I was never anarchic or disruptive; I just let it show too often that I was not convinced that things had to be the way they were. I frequently found myself making judgments on subjective or emotional grounds, even though I could see that they were not necessarily logical or correct. Tension between head and heart is something I have never escaped. And many of these conflicts were brought into focus by my increasing devotion to history.

My two history teachers at Canford made a sharp and healthy contrast. Gwylm Hughes, an abrasive Welshman, brought a Celtic mistrust to the behaviour of the English, whether at the time of the Reformation or in keeping Wales subservient in the twentieth century. He never ceased to celebrate the former owner and builder of much of Canford, Lady Charlotte Guest, who had been devoted to Welsh history and had edited the collection of medieval Welsh stories the *Mabinogion*. He worked out his aggression on the rugby field, where he was a tireless coach. My other history teacher, Michael Rathbone – known inevitably as Basil, because of the then famous actor who played Sherlock Holmes – was quite a different character. Tall, sandy-haired and Audenesque in appearance and manner, he specialized in the Civil War and the religious and political debates of the seventeenth century. He wrote an excellent short, privately published summary of the issues that dominated seventeenth-century politics, and challenged people like me who, devoted to Van Dyck and Inigo Jones, thought kingship sacred and inevitable. I could see how hopeless Charles I had been, but preferred a strong royalist minister like Strafford to the glum parliamentarians with their joyless attitude to life. Later I often likened myself to Strafford when faced with John Birt and the New Model Army at the BBC.

My special subject was the reign of Charles II, and I became so caught up in the interrelationships of a small ruling class that I drew up a genealogical table which, though limited to four or five families, got on to a relatively brief tree virtually every important figure of the time. I discovered *Burke's Peerage*, and more especially the Extinct and Dormant edition, and spent evenings cross-referencing the men – very few women – who had been just names to me beforehand, like the members of the Cabal. For me, biography became more interesting than fiction. And all this could be followed up in the very well stocked school library. Rathbone was responsible for acquisitions, which were remarkably wide-ranging.

I cannot imagine now how I found time to read as much as I did. And not only read, but remember. In addition to biography, I devoured everything to do with the theatre, surprising my English teacher by asking about Strindberg and relishing the prefaces to Shaw's plays, all recently published in Penguins. I read fewer novels, but loved *Wuthering Heights* and all of Jane Austen. My own small library grew, regularly fleshed out with an almost embarrassing number of school prizes. I could memorize great chunks of prose, and scattered my essays and exam papers with over-liberal use of quotations. I had a nearly photographic memory, and could always remember whether the reference I was seeking was on the right or left page and towards the top or the bottom. Today this means I have difficulty in finding things in unfamiliar editions. I have to admit that I welcomed exams, just as I loved quizzes and memory games. There is an element of arrogance in this, since one only likes that sort of thing if one is good at it. Education at that time took too much account of memory and too little of understanding.

I sat the last year of the old School Certificate in nine subjects and got a distinction in all of them except, ironically, music, where a poor response to the aural tests pulled me down to a mere credit. I went on to take a now forgotten intermediate A/O-level exam in German and Latin, and then, at seventeen, S-levels in English, French and history. I did sufficiently well for Oxford or Cambridge scholarships to be discussed. None of my family had ever been to university, and the choice of where I might go was rather random. For some reason I preferred Cambridge, and it was all quite casually agreed that I should sit the exam for the college group that contained Trinity, about which I knew little beyond its size and reputation. I gave it my first preference.

In December 1952 I went up to sit the examination, crossing London from Waterloo to Liverpool Street with difficulty in what was to be the last of the great 'pea-soupers'. It was just as I had read – virtually impossible to see one's hand in front of one's face. I took a taxi, and we crawled at a snail's pace through an invisible city. Once in Cambridge I was put in a grand set of rooms in Great Court, heated only by a recalcitrant coal fire. Term was over, and the place was almost empty but for our scholarship group. I was extremely lucky with the papers – question after question was just in those areas that I had studied, and I thoroughly enjoyed them. I was given a viva by Geoffrey Kitson-Clark, some of whose writings on the seventeenth century I had read. Perhaps impressed with my quotes, he gave me, I learnt later, an easy passage. But I had no means of knowing the standard of other would-be entrants. I had had little competition in my last year at school, but now I was up against the best of Winchester and Eton.

Two friends of mine from prep school were also there, sitting for other colleges, and, back in Bournemouth, on the day the results were to be announced we whiled away the afternoon by going to a matinee of, of all things, *Giselle*, danced by Ballet Rambert. We agreed we would not contact each other until the following day, in case one or all of us had failed. Despite that, at six o'clock one of them rang to say he had won an exhibition to Trinity Hall. A few minutes later the other, to say he had a minor scholarship at Caius. It was well after seven before Canford rang to say that I had won a major open scholarship in history at Trinity. For once there were no family rows and the good sherry was produced.

Despite my reservations about single-sex education and the socially divisive atmosphere, I had thoroughly enjoyed public school – apart from my first term. I had slowly climbed the hierarchy and ended up in my last term as head boy, rather through the departure of others than through my own qualities. I had been for the most part well taught, with imagination and humour. I had edited the school magazine, acted in a lot of plays, written yards of imitative poetry, won a medal or two for athletics, commanded a platoon in the corps, taken part in interschool debates, and made friends. I was interested in more things than there was time for, and just starting to believe that one day I might be an individual in my own right. However, the creative streak that had produced poetry, paintings and music was already beginning to wane. Sharpening my critical faculties on the work of others, it was surely right that I became tough on myself, and the more I learnt, the less original my own output seemed. But I had no clear idea where I was going or what in time I might eventually do – unlike my best friend, Brian Kenny, who was destined for the Army and ended up a full general with an impeccable record, and in retirement became Governor of Chelsea Hospital.

Another school friend had a father who was on the board of Unilever. I often stayed with them in the holidays, and knowing my family's financial situation he suggested that I see a colleague of his, Victor Bonham-Carter, who offered me Unilever backing for my university studies if I agreed to work for the company subsequently. He suggested that this would give me more money to indulge what were obviously my expensive tastes in travel and the arts. 'If you are just a schoolteacher, you will never be able to afford Glyndebourne or Salzburg,' he said. I was only seventeen but I knew he was wrong and, to the despair of my father, I declined. I may have been unfocused, but I was sure that just being an affluent spectator was not going to be enough. I wanted in some imprecise way to be a part of it all.

# 3

# Other Tongues

A few days after Christmas 1952, the Headmaster of Canford asked me to call on him. I had to choose between going straight to Cambridge or doing my two years' National Service first. I opted for National Service, and the Headmaster pointed out that, since I would be eligible for call-up in April, there was probably not much point in my returning to school for one more term. He suggested it was time I moved on. It all happened very suddenly. Within a fortnight I was a junior master in a preparatory school near Ipswich, courtesy of Messrs Gabbitas & Thring, the Dickensian-sounding educational agency which still exists. They put me on their books, and I ended up at St Edmund's Hall School, Kesgrave, Suffolk.

I had not then read Evelyn Waugh's *Decline and Fall*, but when I did a year or two later I was profoundly disappointed to find that most of my best stories had been pre-empted. Kesgrave was a perfect example of the bizarre institutions to which the middle class so enthusiastically entrusted their offspring and which Waugh caught so brilliantly. Most of the teachers were highly eccentric and probably not very competent, for the school's academic record was hardly impressive. What struck me at once was that almost every member of the staff had the kind of name that lent itself to nickname and caricature. The Headmaster, Mr McClintock, was known as 'Tick Tock'; the matron, Miss Bloomfield, was 'Bloomers'; Major Panton, Latin and rugby, 'Pants'; and Mr Curjel, maths, 'Curious'. I, inevitably, was 'Bulldog'. The most surprising person was the junior mistress, Miss Lawrence – Kay, without nickname. She was a Rubens girl – big of breast and thigh – with a deep, gurgly voice that suggested a sexy Hermione Gingold. She was a law unto herself. Within a few days she asked me whether I would keep an eye on her junior class for the first period in the morning, as she was likely to be late. Since she lived in a bungalow about fifty yards from the main building, I was perplexed. 'Got to go to London, darling. Can't miss out!' she whispered.

In no time we were closer chums than the others really liked. I was politely advised to be wary of Miss Lawrence. I, for my part, was enchanted. I had read *Goodbye to Berlin*, and she seemed to me potentially my own Sally Bowles. I have no idea what she was doing in rural Suffolk teaching six-year-olds to spell. We became conspirators, raiding the kitchen at midnight, hacking chunks off tomorrow's lunch, and exploring the surroundings on bicycles. Bit by bit she told me how, having lost her parents in the war, she had made her own way in the world, working with horses, children and company directors. One day she opened her wallet and showed me the visiting cards of some of her admirers. There were dozens of them. Every so often she would pop off to London – not always on her free days – to catch up with them and do a bit of shopping. She was enormous fun, quite without guilt or complexes and determined to get a better deal out of life. Eventually a distinguished surgeon installed her in a pretty flat in Holland Park, visiting her at the appropriate hours, between which she filled her day playing tennis and sunbathing on her roof terrace. I had never before met a woman who talked easily and informally about sex, with no hint of prurience. Sexual matters had never been discussed at home, while schoolboy smut was more fantasy than fact. 'Sex', Kay would say, 'is there for the taking, and fine. So why not? That is something my gentlemen understand!'

Teaching the kids I really enjoyed. I was responsible for French throughout the school, and for geography with the lower forms. The scholarship class, so called – the twelve- to thirteen-year-olds going on to sit for public-school entrance – were the most bewildering. They had already done at least three years of French with absolutely no idea why. It was, for them, as dead a language as Latin. They knew nothing of the country – was it a monarchy or a republic? large or small? – and seemed unable to believe that a couple of hundred miles away over 40 million people were living their lives in French. But, as so often with young people, once we got started they responded quickly. By the end of the term I was taking the lessons entirely in French and they were just about keeping up. It was the first revelation to me of the extent of British isolationism, but also of the pleasures of communicating, sharing knowledge and enthusiasm.

The principal excitement of that winter came with the devastating floods along the east coast. They were so extreme that school was abandoned in the afternoons to allow the able-bodied, like myself, to do flood-relief work, and I will never forget my first sight of Felixstowe with prefabs floating about in the town centre. It was a dramatic introduction to a county I had never visited before.

In those pre-Pevsner days, the most common source of information about England was a series of volumes by Arthur Mee, author of the *Children's Encyclopedia*. The school library had a copy of Mee on Suffolk, and I learnt that the reputed head of Oliver Cromwell was in the possession of a clergyman at Woodbridge, only a few miles away. I wrote to the owner, Canon Wilkinson, and asked if I could bring two or three of the boys to see it. He agreed, and, given the typical ghoulish enthusiasm of schoolboys, I had no trouble finding volunteers. Wilkinson produced a square wooden object about the size of an eighteenth-century knife box. It was lined with purple silk, and contained what looked like an large piece of old leather. There was a wooden spike jammed into the lower part of what on closer inspection seemed to be a human skull, or at least the front part of it. The chin, mouth, cheeks, arcades and part of the brow were there; the eyes were closed, and the back of the head had disappeared. To one side of the nose was a hollow the size of a little fingernail. Could this have been the site of the famous wart? Cromwell's body had been exhumed at the Restoration and the head exposed on London Bridge. Canon Wilkinson told us the family tradition that it had fallen off in a storm and been picked up by a soldier, who gave it to his girlfriend; it had then been handed down in the Wilkinson family for a hundred and fifty years. In the 1920s it had been examined by the National Portrait Gallery, measured, and compared with known portraits. While its authenticity could never be proved, it was thought 'permissible to believe' that it was indeed Cromwell's head. I held it in my hand for a long time – an odd experience, and one denied to later generations, since it has now been decently interred at Cromwell's old college, Sidney Sussex in Cambridge.

Ten years later, tipped off by Richard Dimbleby, I drove a hundred miles across Denmark to see in a village church the well-preserved body of Mary Queen of Scots' last husband, the Earl of Bothwell. When Mary fled into England after the Battle of Carberry Hill, Bothwell made his way to Norway, then under Danish rule, and was arrested in Bergen disguised as a woman. Christian IV, Denmark's great Renaissance ruler, clapped him in the castle of Dragsholm, a sort of Danish Bastille, and used him as a pawn in the European game. But as Elizabeth prospered in England and the Spanish threat receded, so

Bothwell's importance declined. After years of solitary confinement, in 1578 he died, still only in his thirties, and was buried nearby. In the 1950s the brother of the then King of Denmark had the tomb opened and there was Bothwell, surprisingly well preserved: reddish beard, sharp incisors, high boots, rather short (Mary had been six foot tall). After a few years it was decided to remove him from public display and a large monument was built in an adjoining chapel. But I am glad to have seen him – a much less important figure than Cromwell, but curiously attractive.

It was during my period teaching in East Anglia that I had my first experience of the perils of writing to newspapers. There had been a long-running correspondence in the *Daily Telegraph* about ancient trees, to which I contributed the following letter:

Few can claim so long a life as that of the Mount Joy Oak in the grounds of Canford School near Wimborne. It has an honourable mention in Domesday Book as a tree of considerable age, but takes its present name from Lord Mountjoy who was an associate of Elizabeth's Essex in the Irish expedition of 1600 to 1601. Canford, for so long a royal manor, passed eventually to the Guest family, and in the lifetime of Lady Charlotte Guest attempts were made to repair its decaying trunk by filling the large apertures with cement, stippled to give the effect of bark, and held in place with the aid of large chains. More recently it has survived an inexperienced attempt to rid it of a wasps' nest which caused a fire lasting several days. Despite these and other vicissitudes it is still strong, if a little lopsided, and enjoys a position of suitable eminence in the school's Coat of Arms.

I do not know where I had got all this from or what prompted me to write, but two days later there was a reply from one of my least favourite teachers at school:

Sir,

In the interest of historical accuracy, may I be allowed to correct certain statements about the Mount Joy Oak which appear in an interesting letter to you from my friend, Mr J. Drummond? This tree is indeed a noteworthy veteran, but it was not mentioned in Domesday Book, nor indeed in any document earlier than the last quarter of the eighteenth century, although it was then described as apparently very ancient. Its present name is not derived from Lord Mount Joy, but from a mythical Lady Mount Joy with whom it is associated in an apocryphal story crediting her with a feat suspiciously resembling that commemorated in the Tichborne Crawls. Finally, the stippled cement filling was not applied until after the death of Lady Charlotte Guest. Its ordeal by fire was occasioned by an attempt to smoke out wild bees – not wasps – and it does *not* occupy a position of eminence in the school shield of arms because the charge in chief is an open book.

E. Chancellor

My first reaction was to hide the newspaper and hope that no one would see it, but of course it was much too late. However, it taught me a lesson: do your best *not* to write to newspapers. Even if you get the facts right, it is hard to win the argument.

But there were happier moments at Kesgrave. With my first pay cheque I bought a pair of brown suede shoes, which seemed very grown-up at that time. In a second-hand bookshop in Ipswich I paid half a crown for an early-seventeenth-century edition of Sir Thomas Smith's *De Republica Anglorum*, which I still treasure. But, best of all, I had time to discover something of East Anglia. Today so much of Suffolk has become a refuge for weekenders, but in 1953 it still felt remote and entirely the property of the people who lived and worked there. In fifty years the landscape has also changed entirely; now there are great yellow expanses of oil-seed rape and tarted-up cottages in pink and blue, while the churches, all of which were then open and welcoming, are now firmly locked against vandals.

Even my limited travels at this time had shown me how unusual England was. While other parts of the world went on unchanged for hundreds of miles, in England fifty miles in any direction brought different accents, different building materials and different landscape. My continuing fascination with architecture was being steadily fuelled from the early 1950s by the appearance of the new volumes of Niko-laus Pevsner's *Buildings of England*. In sharp contrast to Arthur Mee, they had no purple prose or lush description; they just told you what you needed to know: when and how a building was built, and for what reason. I cherish the dryness of Pevsner. Today his achievement with his assistants in covering the whole of England in less than thirty years is downgraded by people who want charming chat, not hard fact. There is room for both, but at the root of appreciation there must be reality, not the fantasy I so naively presented in my stupid letter about the Mount Joy Oak.

In late February I was summoned to a medical examination before being allocated to one of the three services. I wanted to join the Navy, but was doubtful about what would be offered to someone as myopic as me. In a draughty drill hall in Southampton about a hundred of us stood around in awkward nudity, coughing, bending and breathing as required. My glasses were taken away from me and the man said, 'Read the letters on the wall.' I answered, 'Which wall?' It was a genuine question, but I fear the doctor sensed a desperate attempt to be rejected. I was given back my glasses. 'Which service?' I was asked. I replied, 'The Navy.' 'Well, with your eyesight you can be a cook or a clerk.' I was uncertain how to proceed. I really didn't want square-bashing in khaki, and I assumed that the RAF was even more demanding about good eyesight. Then the man asked me a very unexpected question: 'Do you have any languages?' I explained that I spoke pretty good French and had done some German at school. 'How about being an interpreter?' he suggested. 'Which languages?' I asked. 'Russian or Chinese' was the reply. 'I don't speak either.' Patiently he explained that they would teach me. I asked what the conditions were. 'Russian, two years. Chinese, three.' 'I'll take Russian,' I said. So, casually, the course of my life for the next two years was decided. I found the prospect very appealing: both of acquiring a language with a great literature, and of not wasting two years on a gun-site in Germany. My mother agreed, but of course to my father it was confirmation of his deeply held belief that I was a budding Communist, and led to a great deal of shouting and door-banging.

In April I reported to Victoria Barracks, Southsea, in the new guise of Coder Special Drummond J. CM 925253. 'CM' meant that Chatham was my home base. To begin with there was basic training and the acquisition of a skill in case I proved hopeless at Russian. There was a certain amount of marching up and down, and an obsession with shiny boots. Nearly fifty years later I still have a corn on my left foot as a legacy of the approximate fit of naval footwear. We were a jolly crowd and, as all my intake were destined for work in the communications or education branch, hardly a social cross-section, since most of us were public-school or grammar-school boys with A-levels. After the first few weeks we were allowed into the town in the evening, and I remember going to see a dramatization of Dodie Smith's I Capture the Castle, starring the young Virginia McKenna. Her role as a Wren in the film The Cruel Sea had made her the current naval pin-up, and she patiently welcomed us to her dressing room and signed autographs. We really fancied ourselves that night; it was confirmation that we were now out on our own and Navy boys. How innocent it all seems in retrospect!

Moving on to the Signal School at HMS Mercury, a converted country house on the Sussex–Hampshire border, we were taught codes and ciphers, using the then revolutionary equipment that had been spawned by the brilliant brains of the government decoding centre at Bletchley and what had been learnt from captured German systems.

Coding was pretty boring; decoding a positive pleasure, even if the messages were hardly earth-shattering. It was like completing crosswords or a difficult game of patience – highly satisfying when it worked. The principles by which it operated were as unclear to me then as now, but you do not need to understand internal combustion to drive a car.

A day or two before the coronation, at the beginning of June 1953, I went up to London to see the decorations – a moment commemorated by a more than usually gloomy photograph of me in my coder's uniform: peaked cap and folded raincoat. No glamorous bell-bottoms for coders! My expression is apprehensive and extremely un-warlike. On the day of the coronation itself I was the fourth fire picket of the port watch and confined to base, which meant that, as there were no fires to fight, I followed the proceedings on television – almost the first time I had ever seen one. The ceremony seemed a bizarre conjunction of ancient ritual and new technology, providing close-up intimacy for everyone except those who were in the abbey. My main memory is of the music and its exquisite timing – the voices of the choir bursting out in Parry's *I Was Glad* at exactly the moment the Queen appeared through the choir screen into the sanctuary, and the thrilling modulation on the words 'Let me never be confounded' in Walton's specially composed *Te Deum*.

A few days later I was sent with another coder to join the fleet. Our ship was the cruiser HMS *Superb*, flagship of the America and West Indies Squadron. We sailed from Chatham to Portland. My decoding duties were extremely light, and I spent most of the time on deck getting in someone's way and resisting seasickness. The mess we inhabited was very small but was home to over twenty of us living in very close proximity. I enjoyed sleeping in a hammock, even if my feet hung out of the end, groaned with hunger at the poor and scanty food, and tried to keep my mouth shut. Here for the first time I was among real sailors – and very jolly, profane and good-humoured they were too. But how they hated temporary National Servicemen, especially with voices like ours! My fellow coder had a particularly grand and sardonic manner, which was not appreciated. I felt a kind of snobbery in reverse, but we were gradually accepted. The star turn was provided daily by a pair of East End twins who used to stride about stark naked singing rude songs; they were abetted by a gloomy long-serviceman who had been under the command of the Duke of Edinburgh in Malta and told endless stories about his temper and his physical endowments – stories that always ended '. . . and you wonder why the Queen looks so miserable!'

The high point of my brief time afloat was the Fleet Review, when ships of the Royal Navy, together with Commonwealth and foreign fleets, gathered in Spithead off the Isle of Wight to be inspected by the Queen. It was the last appearance of the traditional Navy with battleships, cruisers, aircraft carriers, destroyers and minesweepers – a huge parade of largely out-of-date but still impressive maritime power. We sailed from Portland at nightfall, and in the pale light of early morning in mid-Channel made rendezvous with the other cruisers that were to form one of the lines at Spithead. We were at first quite alone, then at exactly five in the morning one of a dozen British and Commonwealth cruisers in line ahead, steering towards Portsmouth – an unforgettable moment. While we waited at anchor in Spithead for the big day, we watched the other arrivals. One morning a cluster of aircraft carriers, and then our only battleship, *Vanguard*. Later came the foreign vessels, headed by the ancient French battleship *Richelieu*, its towering superstructure and massive armoury evoking images from the war. Best of all were the liners that came through to show off to their passengers – the *Queen Mary*, the *Queen Elizabeth*, the *United States* – all enormous compared to even the largest battleship.

On the day itself the Queen sailed through the lines and we doffed our caps and cheered to order. I spent most of the day on the flag deck with a telescope. At one moment a voice asked if I could make out the nationality of a ship some way away. 'How the hell do you expect . . .' I started, and removing my eye from the lens saw beside me the largest amount of gold braid on a sleeve that I had ever encountered. I sprang to attention, scarlet in the face. Our admiral laughed. I wondered if he would have been quite so jolly had I had a different accent – the Navy was nothing if not snobbish. That night we waited patiently for the fireworks due to be set off at the same moment throughout the fleet. Five minutes early, rockets spewed up from HMS *Sheffield* – 'the Shiny Sheff' as she was known, the flagship of Admiral Lord Louis Mountbatten, who was the subject of a great deal of affectionate contempt throughout the Navy. 'How typical,' we all said – 'showing off as usual!'

A couple of days later *Superb* prepared to sail back to her station in the West Indies, and to our extreme disappointment my fellow coder and I were not to be of the company. Since she would not return to the UK until after the start of our projected Russian course, we could not go. We were faced with weeks of wasted time waiting around the barracks in Chatham, relieved only by trips to London, to the theatre or exhibitions, as often as I could afford on one pound, two shillings and sixpence a week. My principal memory of the barracks was of run-down shabbiness. There seemed to be very few people around, and those that were there were involved in mostly meaningless tasks. We were marched daily to a block up the hill to exercise our mechanical skills on coding machines, and then marched back to lie on our bunks. What *do* the services do in peacetime?

It had become apparent even before the end of the war that there might well be a need for Russian-speakers. I am not sure who persuaded the government that there should be a training scheme, but I have always believed that it was Isaiah Berlin, one of the very few people on our side who spoke Russian and was involved in intelligence work. I always meant to ask him, but never did. It is hardly news that there was a post-war scheme to provide the services with interpreters, but there is a problem in saying more. Over the years a number of limited accounts of the scheme have appeared and a much greater number have been prevented from being published or broadcast. In 1986 I took part in a radio documentary which was mysteriously withdrawn and never aired. The reason for all this seems to be a too literal interpretation of the Official Secrets Act, which we all had to sign. So in what I write about the next two years of my life I will make no mention of the Navy, but merely recall learning a foreign language with an intensity and total involvement which took over my whole person. So pervasive was the experience that I find it difficult even today not to feel deep inside that in some way I am partly Russian. I certainly was exposed more vividly to the Russian language and to Russian ideas than to the culture of Scotland or Australia, to which I had a blood relationship. As baptisms go, it was total immersion.

After a few weeks of basics like learning the Cyrillic alphabet – which soon ceases to be a problem if you are looking at it for about seven hours a day – we sat a test to determine our futures. Those who obtained more than 80 per cent went to a special section attached to the University of London's School of Slavonic Studies and were trained to become interpreters. Those with only 60 per cent went to Cambridge and became translators. The rest were sent back to their units. I only just qualified for London, but it meant promotion. I was raised to the glorious rank of midshipman – the lowest form of officer life, but still with a commission. It meant a new uniform of rather better material, and a degree of extremely reluctant deference from old hands.

My course group consisted of about twenty-five men, and we were sent to live in a naval hostel in Bayswater. I shared a room with two others on the fifth floor – 112 steps and no lift. You certainly checked your pockets before going out. We wore civilian clothes, were given Underground season tickets, and commuted twice a day from Lancaster Gate to Russell Square for our classes, returning to Bayswater for lunch. We spent five hours a day in the classroom and then did homework in the evening. The pressure was relentless, with long lists of words to be memorized and grammatical exercises to be written. I was slower than most and had very few evenings off in the pub with the brighter ones. In addition, we had to read ten pages a day of Dostoevsky's *Crime and Punishment*, learning all the words that were new to us. It was a tall order even for someone like me with a quick memory. Every second Friday there was an examination, and if you achieved less than 60 per cent you were kicked off the course, which in the case of Navy personnel meant you were deprived of your commission. The Army and RAF members – a minority – were only officer cadets, so the fall did not seem as extreme. I hovered around the 60 per cent mark for most of the first six months, even on one occasion resorting to a bit of mild cheating – instantly discovered, and punished by my being gated for a month. My nineteenth birthday was spent alone with the grammar tests.

It was an experimental course and, I gather, was somewhat modified for later entrants, but it worked – despite the casualties. I recall one extrovert Irishman taking to the bottle in a serious way, and others just faded. But those of us who kept up had the sense of something extraordinary happening. We were becoming different people, almost gaining an extra personality. What made survival possible was camaraderie. Several members of my own course are still friends more than forty years on, and a pretty distinguished bunch they proved to be: Lord Gillmore of the Foreign Office; Sir Derek Thomas, a former ambassador to Italy; Anthony Graham-Dixon QC, the great copyright specialist; Anthony Bosworth, Head of Classics at Bedford School; Anthony Beerbohm, a very successful producer of television commercials. The most unusual member of the course, who always came top, was an

Army officer cadet called Charles Drage, who spent the travel time each day learning Sanskrit, as Russian was so easy. He ended up running the institution where we were studying.

There was more than one course group living in the hostel, but we did not mix much, so it was not until later, at Cambridge, that I got to know Mark Frankland, who was to become one of our great Russian specialists and an outstanding journalist. I never really wanted to know the eccentric Jeremy Wolfenden, one of the subjects of Sebastian Faulks's book *The Fatal Englishman*. There was something strongly unlikeable about him, reinforced by his wearing dark glasses in winter and socks of different colours – 'to irritate people on the tube' he claimed. There were one or two dull people in my group, but the majority of them were bright and good company. That helped make the pressure tolerable, and as time went by there were opportunities to enjoy being young, independent and in London. I opened a bank account in Park Lane, and took to smoking Markovich Black & White cigarettes and lunching at the Tate Gallery. If in retrospect it seems pathetic, it felt then like the start of the high life.

Our teachers were both British and Russian. The course director was Ronald Hingley, later an Oxford don and author of a well-regarded life of Chekhov. Our grammar tutor, Brian Toms, was only a year or two older than us. In fact Anthony Graham-Dixon, who had already completed an Oxford degree, had known him slightly at Christ Church. He was obsessed with grammar and the evolution of language. Nothing thrilled him so much as the idea that in fifty years a form of usage or even the syllable which was stressed in a word (such a key element in the Russian language) might change. He was the focus of a minor palace revolution. After several months the pressure caught up with us and Graham-Dixon led a protest at the amount we were having to do each day and the interminable lists of what often seemed to be unnecessary words we had to learn. Toms, who had an unfortunate voice and a poorly judged Hitler-like moustache, challenged us to name one unnecessary word. Triumphantly, Graham-Dixon pointed to the Russian word '*khryen*', meaning 'horseradish'. 'An important word, I think you will find, in Russian daily life,' said Toms. The revolution collapsed in helpless laughter. But Toms had the last laugh. Seven years later, on my first evening in Moscow, in the restaurant of the National Hotel, Richard Dimbleby pointed to a word on the menu and asked me what it meant. 'Horseradish,' I replied brightly.

My favourite teacher was a huge-bosomed refugee from Odessa called Madame Alhazova. She had a marvellous sense of humour and a highly idiosyncratic way with the English language. Her favourite cry was a splendid Anglo-French expostulation to suggest change or sudden movement – 'There, allez-oops!' Commenting on the Crimean War, 'Your British soldiers they could not cope: they just died'; on the Revolution, 'Such nonsense was said' – all leading to a cry of 'allez-oops!' It was captivating.

The differences between the Russian teachers became more pronounced once we had completed our year in London and went on to six months' intensive interpretership training in Cornwall. A pecking order became apparent, related to the moment at which people had become émigrés, whether at the Revolution in 1917 or in the early 1920s, at the time of collectivization in the late 1920s, in the years of Stalinist terror in the 1930s, or simply as part of the diaspora that followed the Second World War. For those who had left in 1917, like the three former members of the Imperial Corps of Pages who taught us, the post-1945 lot were hardly to be spoken to – certainly politically unreliable and probably tainted by association. There were conspiratorial partnerships between, for instance, Mr Wassiljew and Mr Olkhovnikov. Olkhovnikov was the son of the hetman of the Ukraine, and barely five foot tall. Mr Wassiljew was six foot five, with a noble moustache. They would wander about together looking like Don Quixote and Sancho Panza. But what about Mr Wassiljew's name? He hated it, and simply could not understand why it was pronounced 'Wassil Jew' in England when quite clearly it was 'Vassiliev'. But, like many white Russians, he had spent the inter-war years in Germany, where transliteration into German had produced this unfortunate result for which he suffered dearly now. Grandest of all and much my favourite was Prince Volkonsky, a member of that great family on which Tolstoy had based the Bolkonskys of *War and Peace*. He looked like an eighteenth-century grandee, and could have stepped out of a painting by Tropinin or Raeburn, with a hook nose, scraped-back hair and exquisite manners. A gold half-hunter watch and a gold-headed cane were all that remained of the Volkonsky inheritance. He had a most elegant St Petersburg accent, which I strove to imitate – not difficult, since I have never been able to pronounce *r* as a rolling consonant but only as something much more French and throaty. This occluded *r* was a mark of Petersburg, since it suggested that French was a more familiar language than Russian, which in aristocratic circles it most certainly was.

With most of our teachers there was, on our side, a reluctance to ask too many questions. I never really discovered how these disparate figures had been gathered together in a remote part of England to create a sort of Russia in exile. But the language took us over completely. After a year or so it was almost easier to speak Russian than English, and it certainly drove out any other languages one might have known. I went one day in London to see the French parents of my ballerina friend Claudie Algeranova and threw them completely by answering in Russian when all the time I thought I was speaking French.

The most flamboyant of our teachers was Vladimir Kozhevnikov, known as 'Kosh'. He came from a Moscow merchant family and had spent the post-Revolution years in Berlin, where he regularly played tennis with Nabokov. He was wildly theatrical and wanted to be a dancer, even auditioning for the Ballets Russes, but was turned down. He had scraped a living in an Isherwoodish way as a tutor. Among his pupils was George Kennan, later a key figure among American Kremlinologists. I don't know when Kosh had come to Britain, but he had somehow kept his family together, since he lived with both his mother and his sister, who worked as a bilingual typist in the camp office. Kosh had extravagant moments, while constantly pleading total poverty. His flat did indeed contain practically no furniture; you sat on orange-boxes – rather hard for his elderly mother – and Kosh would say, 'You see how we poor émigrés live!' But meanwhile he would opulently entertain a small number of his pupils – myself included – to teach us the importance of understanding champagne. In the remote Cornwall of 1954 our knowledge of champagne was confined to an occasional glass of non-vintage bubbly at a wedding or a christening. Kosh thought knowing about champagne a prerequisite of social life, so at the Judges' Lodgings of the Royal Hotel in Bodmin he laid on a number of dinners where nothing but champagne was drunk. We were expected instantly to recognize the difference between Heidsieck and Mumm, between Veuve Clicquot and Roederer, Bollinger and Krug. How he afforded it I simply do not know, and when we sought to reciprocate by inviting him to a restaurant at our expense he abandoned dinner halfway through, retired to the car park, and recited Pushkin in a loud voice until the locals became alarmed.

Hardly a day passed but Kosh sought to communicate to us something of the glory of Russian poetry. The novels he felt, quite reasonably, had had good translations, but who would tell us about Fet and Tyutchev, Blok and Bal'mont, let alone Lermontov, if he did not? Lermontov's novel *A Hero of our Time* had been a set text. We all fell for its Byronic elegance, but it was Kosh declaiming his poem *The Demon* that suggested why Lermontov, like Pushkin, had been sent into exile. Nowadays, when no one seems to learn poetry by heart, it is the more remarkable that we all came out able to quote great chunks of Russian verse. I remember surprising Vladimir Ashkenazy at a lunch in Moscow a few years ago by launching into Arbenin's great speech from Lermontov's play *Maskarade*. I did not know I really remembered it, but it all came tumbling out.

Learning by heart is marvellous training for an interpreter, since one gets into one's head the proper use of language, and before long the grammatical constructions have become second nature. This was greatly reinforced by a tradition that had grown up that each course should present a play in Russian. The previous course had put on a widely praised production of *Hamlet*, with Jeffrey Wickham as the prince. The director was a youngish Australian-Russian called Dimitri Makarov. He had been born in Harbin, near the Pacific coast, into one of those families that went east rather than west at the Revolution, and had grown up in Sydney, where, as in Melbourne, there was a sizeable Russian community. His walls were hung with icons, but also with drawings by Cocteau, his great hero. He had a little Chekhovian beard and round gold glasses, and was a bundle of enthusiasms – some of them only just this side of lunacy. The play he chose for us was nothing less than *Othello*, in a marvellous translation by Boris Pasternak. I was cast as Iago. There were a lot of lines to learn, and I can remember going down to Par sands and walking endlessly up and down the beach shouting them at the winter sea. They certainly stuck, because I can still do at least two of the great speeches today. Anthony Bosworth was a brilliant Othello, strong of voice and physique, but with a real sense of poetry. Desdemona was Derek Thomas, who in later rehearsals always reclaimed masculinity by smoking a pipe while wearing a ballgown. Once, while ambassador to Italy, he astonished the company, which included a friend of mine, by announcing that he had played Desdemona to my Iago. But for his very prominent Adam's apple, it was a lovely performance. The production, however, was a total mess – in the manner of many contemporary opera productions. I have never understood why Dimitri believed that each act should be performed in a different kind of costume – an alienation effect achieved long before we had been taught about Brecht by Kenneth Tynan. The opening scenes at night in Venice were performed in masks and dominoes, early Cyprus blossomed into full Renaissance doublet and hose, the jealousy scenes had Noël Cowardish smoking jackets and evening dress, and the play climaxed in contemporary army battledress. God knows what the audience made of it.

We did two performances for our fellow students, the teachers and their families, and they were received rather well. The second performance was graced by the presence of Professor Elizabeth Hill, the legendary Cambridge Russian expert, who came especially for it. She sat in the front row and never stopped talking. It was hard enough to play Iago anyhow, let alone in Russian, and with the constant accompaniment of muttering and reactions a few feet away from me I found I could hardly concentrate. At the interval I sent for Dimitri and told him that if she did not shut up I would ask her to do so from the stage. The second half proceeded in silence, and at the end she came on stage and went down the line congratulating everybody fulsomely – until she got to me, when she just glared and moved on.

Whenever people ask me if I have ever done anything original in my life, I always claim that I am the only person who has ever played Iago in Russian in Cornwall. Dimitri moved on. He was for years Russian coach at the Royal Opera House, living in penury in a tiny garret near Charing Cross station. Improbably, he was last heard of as priest of the Russian Church in Copenhagen.

Hard as we worked at our language studies, life in Cornwall was also fun. Bodmin seemed to have more pubs than anywhere I had ever been, and we visited them all. In fact we tried to visit them all in a single pub crawl, but I fell flat on my face after about the seventh. We acquired a succession of ancient and totally unreliable cars. Mine cost twenty-five pounds and was called Byron, because of its stormy temperament. We would venture across Bodmin Moor to drink mead at Jamaica Inn, or go down to Polruan by Fowey, where three of us had rented a flat from a local doctor for days off. We would carry jugs of green cider home from the pub, since more than one pint on the premises led to incapacity. One day we drove from Polruan to Bodmin on the wrong side of the road, claiming that we were in France, and so quiet were the Cornish roads in winter that we escaped unharmed. But I also often used the trains, which covered the whole peninsula with a network of little lines running off the main Paddington–Penzance stem. You could get a train to Par, to Padstow, to Boscastle and to Newquay. Today the only branch line left is to St Ives, and the little coastal towns are blocked with lorries, buses, coaches and cars. This might well have happened anyway with greater prosperity and the growth of tourism, but it has always seemed to me that the Beeching cuts to British Rail did more to destroy Cornwall than tourism itself.

It was on the little shuttle train from Bodmin North to Padstow that I met someone quite out of the ordinary. Just as the train was about to depart, a Joyce Grenfellish figure in slacks and a pixie hat climbed aboard. Not so unusual, it may seem, and yet she was slung about with some of the most expensive camera equipment I had ever seen. I found out she was called Mary Love and was a professional photographer of shipping – the only woman in the United Kingdom to be one. Her studio, in the docks of the kaolin port of Charlestown, was full of splendid images ranging from four-masted sailing ships to the newest tankers. For my father, I bought from her some photographs of the sail training ships *Pamir* and *Passat*, taken on the only occasion they had been together in Falmouth harbour. She also made a photographic record of local traditions like the Helston Furry Dance and the Padstow Hobby Horse.

Mary was one of a number of unusual people I came across as I was finding my way into a life of my own, to the extent that I could on the pittance we were paid. A different kind of social life revolved around an institution in Bodmin known as the St Petroc Club, a private watering-hole run by a colourful character who was reputedly the boyfriend of the actor Eric Portman. We used to visit the club rather warily, expecting to be seduced, raped or otherwise interfered with, but the only experience that came my way there was with an intense middle-aged nympho who lived in a windmill – she probably, we surmised, had a man lashed to each of the sails. Much more attractive was the wife of the head of the local electricity board, who had been an actress before her marriage and was bored stiff with the round of golf- and sailing-club activities. She became part of our gang, and made the costumes for *Othello* – except for the glittering smoking jacket I wore, which was borrowed from the Portman boyfriend. Joanna became a lifelong friend, as did the fruity-voiced but wonderfully endearing Canon Harmer, vicar of Bodmin. He too only died recently, having spent his last years in a grace-and-favour apartment in the National

Trust property Lanhydrock, never missing a Christmas and writing whenever I did something that caught public attention.

Perhaps the longest-lasting influence of these Cornish months came from a chance visit to a pottery shop in Padstow, run by an ebullient man called Godfrey May. He had St Ives pottery by all the well-known names at prices which just allowed me to buy my first dish by Bernard Leach and my first jug by Michael Cardew – the dish an expensive guinea, the jug three shillings and sixpence. After I had dropped in a couple of times, Godfrey invited me to have tea with him and his wife in their flat upstairs. The teapot was by Hamada. He had several for sale; they were, I think, five pounds each. Nine years later, in Paris, I was asked to look after a broadcast for the Japanese Section of the BBC World Service during a big ceramics exhibition at the Musée des Arts Décoratifs. Into the studio came Leach and Hamada to record what was, for me, an impenetrable conversation in Japanese. But I have never forgotten the contrast between the rangy, tall, stooping Leach and the small, compact Hamada, or the warmth of their mutual affection.

I am still interested in pottery, and collect it in a quiet way. I found something sympathetic in the simplicity and practicality of stoneware pots – far from what I still find the unattractive prettiness of most porcelain and indeed much contemporary pottery. Cardew was later to become a friend, and I bought from him and also from Janet Leach and another Leach pupil, William Marshall – an uneven potter, but capable of real quality. Now the prices have risen so sharply that I am mostly a spectator at sales, often sitting with David Attenborough and trying not to bid for the same things, delighted that he at least can afford to go on refining his superb collection. In recent years I have been captivated by the work of Ewen Henderson – not a potter in any accepted sense, but a great sculptor in ceramics. He came into my life through his love for contemporary music, and the piece of his that was presented to me at my last Last Night of the Proms was exactly what I would have chosen.

We took our interpretership exams in the early spring of 1955, barely twenty months after having been total beginners. I found the written exam possible, if still difficult, and was not helped by my at times unclear handwriting. The oral test was much more fun. By now I found talking in Russian a positive pleasure, and the examiner, Professor Konstantinov from Oxford, spent most of the time flatteringly suggesting that I must have Russian antecedents or family. I passed on the written work and got the equivalent of a first class for the oral. Then we dispersed. I had made some very good friends, had a great deal of fun, played a lot of bridge, withstood the constant damp and hunger of Cornwall in winter on a small budget, and learnt both to drink and to drive. I had also acquired one of the world's greatest languages and experienced the profound enjoyment of opening the door to Russian literature and Russian attitudes to life. It has always seemed a tragedy that politics put Russia and the United Kingdom on opposing sides, since in many ways we have so much in common. I loved many of my teachers, and admired the way they had dealt with losing their homeland and their possessions. They laughed a lot, flared up when challenged, cried easily, and eventually died unappreciated and unrecognized, still circumscribed by the Official Secrets Act. But what they passed on affected me as it has affected many friends and contemporaries, not only directly through the interpreters' course, but especially through the work of the star of the translators, Michael Frayn.

I cannot say what I did next, for fear of censorship, but I spent the spring and summer in London with a lot of free time, and in fact stayed on three months beyond my official discharge date, since I had somehow to occupy myself gainfully before going up to Cambridge in the autumn. I acquired a kind of half-baked 'man about town' persona – going to deb dances, Ascot and Wimbledon, buying a brown Herbert Johnson hat, carrying a tightly rolled umbrella and wearing gloves at all times. One day my mother came to London on a shopping trip and I met her at Waterloo. She was appalled: 'You look like a middle-aged banker!' I was thrilled.

During this time I had met a delightful girl who was the best friend of the sister of one of my school friends. She was tall and very attractive, and had a splendid sense of humour. We took to meeting regularly, got to know each other's parents, and fell quite quickly into a sort of middle-aged relationship of great friendship and little passion. I found her attractive but felt no desire. I presumed that that would come. I was wrong.

# 4

# Not the Place for Me

By the time I got to Cambridge, in October 1955, I was only a month short of my twenty-first birthday. Today, many students have graduated by that age. We liked to think that the interval before going up had made us more mature and likely to get more out of university life, but I am not sure that as long a gap as we had was ideal. I had already done one course of university standard, and a very toughly disciplined one. The almost total freedom that Cambridge allowed made it very hard to force myself to study, given the numerous other distractions that I had learnt during the previous two years.

Trinity is a huge college, and the fact that there were so many people made it hard to feel part of collegiate life as friends at smaller places seemed to. As a scholar, I had a right to accommodation in college. It was a garret room in Bishop's Hostel, a detached building by the side gate in Trinity Lane. Perhaps because the ceiling was only two inches higher than myself, it seemed quite cosy. There were a small study and a smaller bedroom, a gas ring, a gas fire with three burners, and a meter. The nearest running water was a cold tap on the landing one floor down; the lavatory was two floors down on the ground floor, and the nearest bathroom a hundred and fifty yards away on the other side of New Court. By any standards it was spartan.

For almost accidental reasons, I stayed in these rooms for my full three years. In my second year, running water was installed in the bedroom – but only a cold-water tap. No one seemed to find it odd; we just accepted it, as we did the ludicrous gate rules – no entry after midnight; no visitors allowed in the rooms after 10.00 p.m. It was not even possible to cross the road to Whewell's Court on the other side of Trinity Street after ten, although you could return if you were already there. Nightly, people clambered over the gate below my bedroom window – an awkward, exposed climb – and about once a week someone impaled himself on one of the bicycles parked below it. You could not leave Cambridge in term time without written permission, and you were forbidden to visit Newmarket or keep a car. Some of my contemporaries had spent their National Service fighting Communists in the swamps of Malaya, yet, as far as Cambridge was concerned, life was much as it had been before the First World War. Gowns had to be worn to lectures and after dark. Proctors patrolled the streets. Every precaution was taken to keep the outside world at bay. Whereas my Oxford friends seemed to spend several nights a week in London, I went up for the term, a sort of prisoner on semi-parole, huddling from an east wind that came straight from the Urals and crouching close to my little gas fire.

Through reading, I had already prepared myself to find my way about Cambridge, since, in the irritating way common to London clubs, no building had any form of external identification. I anticipated hours of enjoyment looking at Cambridge architecture, but soon realized that the least desirable thing was to be taken for a tourist, so, ludicrously, there are many things in Cambridge that I have still never seen. I also discovered the total divide between town and gown, between pubs used by undergraduates and those of the townies – a race of ugly inferiors who inhabited grim Victorian brick cottages near the railway station, or so we tended to think. I learnt when not to wear a suit (to lectures) and who could be seen with college scarves (only the sporty), and decided never to explore places where games were played, nor to belong to the Union. I was a proper little snob, but it was nothing to do with class.

Trinity consisted of three blocs of undergraduates – two large and one rather smaller. The large blocs were a hereditary group of students mostly from Winchester, Eton and Harrow, many of whose fathers had been at the college before them, and a group from the great northern grammar schools: Manchester, Bradford, Sheffield and Liverpool. In between was a smaller bloc of people like myself, from minor public schools. The toffs all seemed to know each other already and had a highly casual attitude to any form of discipline. They rode their bicycles in the courtyard, came down late to breakfast, and wore a uniform of tweed jacket, cavalry-twill trousers and boots. They talked of beagles and regiments, and lunched at the Pitt Club. It was there one day that I heard a particularly rowdy Trinity Etonian say to the elderly club servant, 'Tell me, do you masturbate?' 'Probably not as often as you, sir,' was the dry response. Sometimes these oafs were a great deal brighter than the impression they gave, but they knew themselves to be the ruling class. They could be friendly in the right circumstances, but theirs was a club from which my artistic predilections and my poverty excluded me – except for very bright scholars of my year like the Hon. W. G. Runciman, who was to become a Fellow of Trinity and Chairman of the Royal Commission on Justice, and James Cornford, later Professor of Politics at Edinburgh University and Director of the Nuffield Foundation – two of the best brains of my time.

Occasional attempts were made to bridge the divide. I remember a dinner set up to get people of different backgrounds to talk to each other. It went very stickily indeed until one rather raffish member – from Bryanston, if I recall correctly – asked directly why we found it so difficult to be friendly. We broke up in embarrassed confusion and never met again. On my first Sunday I, with the other scholars, was invited to take wine and fruit at the Master's Lodge. We sat at a long table with Lord Adrian, the Nobel-winning scientist, at one end and the Vice-Master, military historian Sir James Butler, at the other. Plates of unripe fruit were passed, and we struggled to eat hard apples or unripe pears with a small silver knife and fork while Butler tried to talk about football. Lord Adrian was a remarkable and very kind man, but never seemed to notice the awkwardness of the event. I felt that class enemies were made that night.

I would eat at first in hall, but the food was both disgusting and exiguous and I soon withdrew to the gas ring or to one of the nearby restaurants. There was a Greek place, The Magnolia, in Rose Crescent, whose glutinous mushroom risotto I can still taste today – but it was only three shillings and sixpence. Quite soon I fell into a group whose principal reason for meeting seemed to be that one of them had a huge Ferrograph tape-recorder and recorded the weekly edition of *The Goon Show*, to which we listened in enchanted rapture. Otherwise the talk was mostly of football or girls.

James Cornford – Winchester and football fanatic – and I became good friends very early on, sharing the same tutors and lectures. He was totally at home in Cambridge, since his grandfather, F. M. Cornford, had been a fellow of Trinity. His grandmother, the poet Frances Cornford, lived round the corner from Newnham, and the whole university was pervaded by cousins of the Darwin–Haldane–Toynbee–Adrian connection. When Noël Annan wrote an essay called 'The Intellectual Aristocracy' in a Festschrift for the eightieth birthday of the former Master of Trinity G. M. Trevelyan, I found it riveting to see how the links worked. James thought it pointless: 'Everyone knows that,' he said. He was by nature an iconoclast. Son of the Communist poet John Cornford, killed in the Spanish Civil War before his twenty-first birthday, James had been brought up by Leonard and Dorothy Elmhirst, the founders of Dartington, and Winchester had not turned him into an Establishment figure. His great passion was the blues singer Bessie Smith, of whom I had never heard, and he believed profoundly that authority was there to be questioned. I was appallingly conformist and, despite my years in the Navy, politically naive and philosophically untutored. I had used my little free time during National Service to read novels, moving on from the great nineteenth-century masters to writers of my time, but my discovery of Evelyn Waugh, Nancy Mitford, Henry Green, Cyril Connolly and Aldous Huxley had not also included Orwell, whom James revered.

Our tutor was a demographer and former Third Programme producer, Peter Laslett, an awkward and unsociable man with whom I never felt at ease. I saw him regularly and wrote my essays, but neither they nor he struck a spark. I had dull tutorials in economic history with Sydney Checkland, later a professor in Glasgow, and attended lectures by a variety of history dons, few of whom showed anything other than world-weariness while trailing again through the feudal system or medieval kingship. The exception was Geoffrey Elton, who seemed literally possessed by the minutiae of Tudor pipe rolls and Star Chamber reports. His passionate defence of Thomas Cromwell was a healthy corrective to those of us who mourned the destruction of the monasteries and wished we were being taught by the saintly Dom David Knowles, to be seen flying by in full habit on a bicycle with strings over the back wheel to protect the hem of his cassock. The only tutor in my first year who tried hard to strike something from me was the most daunting of all. Walter Ullmann was later to become Regius Professor of Medieval History, but at this time was only a university lecturer with no college fellowship and the object of much dismissive comment by other historians. My problem with Ullmann was that he was really the only authority on his subject. Writing an essay on the impact of the Donation of Constantine or the contribution of Gregory VII, I could find practically no sources of information other than his own book *The Origins of Papal Government in the Middle Ages*. How dreary it must have been for him to have his own work amateurishly regurgitated each week by people like me! When I talk today to my contemporaries about their teachers I find that they have happier and more personal memories than I do. At no time in my three years at Cambridge did any of my tutors become friends. In part this may have been due to the sheer size of Trinity. One of my group who was reading music was taught by the young Director of Music at Trinity, Raymond Leppard. I never even met him at Cambridge, although we would later become great friends when he had left academe for the opera house.

This sense of isolation from senior members of the college conspired increasingly to make me feel both second-rate and academically irrelevant. The kind of fact-based knowledge that I had acquired, doubtless through my quick memory, counted for less than the understanding of ideas and theorizing, both of which I found particularly difficult. It was quite clear that Etonians like Garry Runciman and Wykhamists like James Cornford had been discussing and analysing ideas since the age of fifteen. I had hardly begun, and felt left out. I may have been a Major Scholar, but I came to believe myself profoundly ordinary. One evening a number of us met in the rooms of Eric James, the Assistant Chaplain, to discuss ideas. A fairly sharp divide resulted, and I found myself the only person on the same side as Garry Runciman. We walked back across Great Court together and I felt ten foot tall; yet a few days later I could not even remember the arguments I had supported. I am, as a person, pragmatic – abstraction, theoretical discussion, hypothesis and logic may have their points, but my mind is simpler. I can connect actions, attitudes and individual contributions without difficulty, but cannot separate ideas from their embodiment in human activity. I was certainly not stupid, but probably not a true scholar.

I had thought I might become a don, and the good first-class honours I won in part I of the history tripos did not suggest that this was a ridiculous ambition, but increasingly I wondered if it was right. By my third year I was spending too much time away from my studies. I had become dissatisfied with history as then taught in Cambridge: it seemed to me both fractured and partial. Now I can see that my timing was unfortunate. The tremendous popular reputation in the late 1940s of Trevelyan and his *English Social History* was not admired in 1950s Cambridge. The very phrase 'social history' was disallowed. There was constitutional history, with people like Elton and Kitson-Clark, and there was economic history, with Herbert Butterfield and G. F. Postan, but there was no sense of a whole society. Elton's widely acclaimed books on Tudor England are excellent on government, but there is only the briefest mention of music, literature or architecture, which for me matter as much as pipe rolls. Today the pendulum has swung in the opposite direction. The Parisian *Annales* school of Fernand Braudel and Emmanuel Le Roy Ladurie considers diet, clothing and language as important as government, building up a picture of society from tiny fragments of the human mosaic. In my time even biography was considered a second-rate activity.

Nevertheless, I kept on trying to write intelligent essays and occasionally found a connection that made sense. But, still doubting my command of ideas, in my third year I ducked out of the long-established Theories of the Modern State paper and opted for a subject in the first year of its inclusion in the tripos – Historiography. I found it fascinating to see how much a historian's interpretation of the past had been influenced by his own time. I read Vico, Ranke, Spengler and Toynbee with enthusiasm, but historiography proved a foolish choice. My tutor Michael Vyvyan's understanding of what kind of question would be asked was at total variance with what was actually set, and I was faced with a paper for which I was completely unprepared. My special subject, Policies and Powers at the Treaty of Paris, 1763, I had found full of interest. The use of family papers, letters and diary accounts brought it all to life. I even enjoyed the endless arguments about the Newfoundland fisheries and the rights of Saint-Pierre & Miquelon. For this paper I got a starred first. But the failure elsewhere pulled me down to a II(i).

Vyvyan talked to me about a research grant, wanting me to use my interest in Russia and Eastern Europe in some way, since Cambridge was very short of Eastern Europe specialists. But, when he proposed the second partition of Poland as a thesis subject, I knew it was wrong: Poland was not Russia, and the idea of trying to write history without access to archives, libraries and travel in those Cold War years sealed the matter. Even before that, however, something else had happened to make me look elsewhere. One morning on the way to buy my newspaper I had run into Walter Ullmann, whom I had not seen for over a year. 'What', he asked me, 'are you going to do when you go down?' 'Well,' I muttered, 'I had rather hoped to stay and do some research.' 'Oh no, get out, get out!' he replied. 'Do you mean I'm not good enough?' 'I have no means of knowing whether you are good enough, but I know you have an alternative, and only those without should stay.' I went back to my rooms uncertain what to do. In my heart I knew he was right. I didn't really have the temperament of a scholar.

No doubt my lack of real dialogue with my tutors – even with the delightfully bucolic Jack Gallagher and the elegant historian of Spanish civilization John Eliot – reflected this. They could sense that I was not going to become a real historian. Runciman and Cornford, both independently minded and confrontational, went on to have distinguished academic careers. I was strangely docile, and always knew I was not in their league.

But of course study was not everything. Looking back after forty years, I am not sure how hard I really worked, since I certainly spent a lot of time having a very lively social life with an ever widening circle of friends. It is one of the unusual things about Cambridge, and probably the result of being isolated, that you constantly met people in other faculties and with other interests. I knew all the presidents of the Union in my time without ever being a member. I always knew someone in the Blue boat, but I still don't really know where on the river they row. Oxford always seemed to be more cliquey – you were a Union man, a Bullingdon man or an actor, and paths crossed much less. At the big Cambridge May Week parties everyone who was known for any achievement – sporting, dramatic or political – met and fraternized. Everyone wanted to know the few really attractive women like Judy Innes (now Astor), Ann Dowson (now Tusa), Penelope Balchin (now Leach) and Amanda Goodfellow (now Cornford). By my second year I knew very well that I had no interest in the political societies, but I was drawn to acting and writing and generally making a fool of myself. It was for this that I tend to be remembered by contemporaries.

For nearly two years I ran the cabarets for the Footlights Society, although because I had to work for the tripos I never took part in a May Week review. My cabaret partners were Adrian Slade – brother of Julian, the composer of *Salad Days* – later Chairman of the Liberal Party, and the actor Joe Melia, at that time a passionately committed Leavisite. I wrote the lyrics, Adrian provided the tunes, Joe was a brilliant mime, and we all did silly things. My own speciality was female impersonation – not of course in drag, but quite properly dressed in a dinner jacket. It owed a lot to Joyce Grenfell, who was then at the height of her fame. I had a loud falsetto voice when required, and the piercing sound that came out of the unattractive, bespectacled six-footer made people laugh. This was one way of becoming popular: we would be asked to balls and parties, and the price for attendance was a bit of fooling around. I had one sketch that took about five minutes to write and is, worryingly, still remembered. It was called 'Party'. I was a bewildered hostess trying to get her guests to gather in clumps for party games. Today no one would know what a clump was, but then, in the age of home-made entertainment, memories of having to play games were all too real. At one point I asked all the young people to gather at one end of the room, and all the people who were 'broadly speaking not quite so young' at the other. I paused, following with my eyes a non-existent figure across the gap from one group to the other, and exclaimed, 'Harriet, how brave!' It became my Cambridge catch-phrase.

The witty and sophisticated John Villiers in King's had a splendid line in taking off critics and their jargon – 'The harpsichord does sound a trifle tubby!' Bobby Wellings' speciality was ancient dons. Collectively, smart repartee and clever-clever ripostes were known as 'clanking'. Later I suppose they would be called 'camp'. Much of our humour was based on silly voices, much of it tremendously snobbish, but it was thought funny and was not so far removed from that of the next generation of Footlights people like Peter Cook. I myself had a cabaret character not unlike E. L. Wisty. The great original humorist of my time was Jonathan Miller. There was a mad surrealism about his ideas, and something extraordinary about the way he used his body, like a tipsy giraffe. None of us had his originality, and few of us his intelligence. I had seen him in cabaret in London before I went up, re-enacting the death of Nelson, crawling about, speculating on what the 'tween-decks really were, and reacting with predictable horror to the injunction 'Kiss me, Hardy.' I met him in my first week, in the rooms of a naval friend. Our paths have crossed regularly for more than forty years, and no one except Peter Ustinov has made me feel so slow or so dull. I love his company, and have always regretted not seeing more of him.

Apart from Footlights there were college revues. Bamber Gascoigne wrote one for Magdalene called *Share my Lettuce*, which ended up in the West End starring Maggie Smith and Kenneth Williams. It was through a Trinity revue that two of my closest and most enduring friends came into my life – John Tydeman and John Tusa. Tyde was an orotund actor and a better director, while John Tusa was sporty and seemed terribly English, despite his entirely Czech background. Tyde, Johnny and I spent many years travelling, theatregoing, holidaying and laughing together. We had little idea then how interwoven our lives would become, but of all my friends they are the ones to whom I turn most frequently for advice, or just a good gossip. Johnny Tusa in particular is that rare thing in our time, a totally honest man – both in his opinions and in how he expresses them. In today's world that is not necessarily an advantage, but it did draw us closer together.

Footlights performed their cabarets frequently in Cambridge and occasionally in London. A Twickenham Ball provided a particularly unimpressed and inattentive audience, although it did allow me to say that I have played the Royal Festival Hall. But the undoubted high point was an evening in Hatfield. A Magdalene undergraduate called McCorquodale came to see me and said his mother was giving a party and would we like to do a cabaret? They would provide supper and a guaranteed welcome. I was sceptical, since we really had no time to do just any old social engagement in the Home Counties. But then one of the gang remembered that McCorquodale's mother was Barbara Cartland, and suddenly everyone wanted to go.

We turned up as requested and were fulsomely greeted by the great writer, wearing a garish floral dress with a ballerina skirt. We were given a glass of wine, then doors were flung back to reveal a long table groaning with cold dishes of all kinds and we were ordered to eat. I must have reacted, for she said to me, with dramatic intensity, 'Darling, before any public appearance you must be drunk – with food.' By now I had discovered that our entertainment was part of an evening laid on for the inhabitants of Hatfield New Town; apart from us, it included a fashion parade of Horrocks' summer dresses and a buffet by the Cheese Bureau. As we prepared to leave for the hall, our hostess emerged with every protuberance on her body glittering with diamonds – rings, brooches, bracelets, clips. Again I must have registered surprise, for in a stage whisper she assured me, 'Darling, they expect it!'

Our undergraduate humour was politely received without scoring a real success, until after the dress parade one of our number, Michael Collings – Cambridge's answer to Kenneth Williams, and quite as funny – decided to do a Cambridge Fashion Show, consisting mostly of raincoats, umbrellas and college scarves. It brought the house down.

Back at Mrs McCorquodale's for sandwiches and drinks, we were gathered in her study. All round the walls were her books, in many languages, and on top of the shelves was a huge collection of china pigs –

dangerously reminiscent of their owner. In the middle of the room was a desk, presumably where the great works were created, and on it a scarlet telephone, extremely unusual at that time. We were just about to leave when it rang. Our hostess silenced us with an imperious gesture, seized the phone, and listened in a state of growing agitation. As she put it down she turned to the room and said in a voice of doom, 'Beloved Lord Dartmouth is dead!' I am pretty sure I was the only one to recognize the significance of this, entirely due to my friend John Villiers and a quiz game we had devised based on *Burke's Peerage*, in which we had to remember the courtesy titles of peers and their family names. What Lord Dartmouth's death meant was that Barbara Cartland's daughter, the much publicized Mrs Gerald Legge, had at that moment become Lady Lewisham, since Gerald Legge's father was Dartmouth's younger brother. Barbara seized my hand. 'Do you realize what it means?' 'Yes,' I said, 'I do.' 'Lady Lewisham!' she kept repeating, 'Lewisham, Lewisham! . . . You do think Gerald's father would have had the courtesy to die first, after all the time and money we have spent making poor Raine known as Mrs Legge. Now we have to start again as Lady Lewisham – wherever that is – and in no time at all once again as Lady Dartmouth. It is so inconsiderate!' Then practicalities took over. On the following day the Queen was to open the Ideal Home Exhibition, and it had to be arranged that Lady Lewisham's car was the last to arrive before the royal vehicle, so that all the photographers could help support the family industry. It was riveting. I had never seen public relations in action before.

We drove back to Cambridge with our lives greatly enhanced, to find telegrams waiting. Mine said, 'Darling you were divine. You were superb. All Hatfield will speak of nothing else forever.' They had been sent before our performance.

A quite different encounter with a writer had taken place in my first term. A school friend, John Hale-White, in his third year at King's, asked me to tea in his rather grand rooms overlooking King's Parade. Just after I arrived he suddenly panicked, realizing he had run out of milk. He rushed out, saying, 'Be nice to anyone who turns up.' After a couple of minutes there was a timid knock at the door and a small elderly gentleman looking most uncomfortable came in and asked where John was. I reassured him that he would be back in a moment, and he sat down. He asked me if I was a King's man, and I explained that I was not but had known our host at school. He turned his head ruminatively towards the window, and as he turned I saw the back of my Penguin copies of *A Room With a View*, *A Passage to India* and *Howards End*. It was E. M. Forster. Ever since Brian Mabley at my prep school had given me *Howards End* as a leaving present, I had loved Forster's quiet but fierce characters and the vanished Edwardian world they inhabited. With nervous trepidation I told him so. At that point John returned. 'You getting on?' he said. 'Oh, very well,' said Forster, and smiled sweetly. I never really got to know him better, although I would see him from time to time in the street and he would even acknowledge me, but without stopping. In my last year, leaving a party in King's I passed an open door on the stairs and saw a little figure in a dressing gown running a bath. 'Too hot, too hot!' I heard him say.

Another chance encounter with a writer was due to my friend Julian Pettifer, who was at St John's. He said there would be a special guest in his rooms that evening, and asked me to drop in late for coffee. I climbed in and found to my delight the rumpled figure of W. H. Auden holding court. He was relatively sober and hugely entertaining, and I could see immediately why so many people found him charming. In later years he became a prize bore when drunk, which was most of the time, going on endlessly about who had sung the Third Lady in *The Magic Flute* in 1952. Happily, before that I was with him on a number of occasions when he was reading his own works, at which he excelled. Once in Edinburgh, after a BBC recording, we went to the pub to have a drink with Stevie Smith at her wonderfully eccentric best. Within twenty minutes Wystan and Stevie had started on a nostalgic journey though *Hymns Ancient and Modern* at a hideously out-of-tune piano. I rushed back to the BBC, rounded up a camera crew, and got back in time to film a few minutes of this priceless duet. It is often trotted out in commemorative programmes. Of course, in today's BBC you would have to have planned for it eighteen months in advance.

One other link to writers in Cambridge during my time was a fairly outrageous Magdalene undergraduate called William Donaldson. He inherited a shipping fortune on his twenty-first birthday, and gave us all a great deal of pleasure while he spent it. I asked him once why he never came to my rooms. 'Quite simple', he replied: 'you serve bad sherry, I serve good gin.' He was right. I was, by comparison with most of my friends, seriously poor. By the time I had paid college dues and other expenses, I had less than five pounds a week to live on. It was possible to do so, eating simply, and even smoking and drinking, but larger purchases were out. I spent my three years in Cambridge in the same clothes: one dark-grey suit and one Prince of Wales check (both paid for by my parents), one pair of grey worsted trousers, one pair of green corduroys (very arty in the 1950s), a couple of pullovers (one roll-neck – very Left Bank), one black and one suede pair of shoes, and a handed-down dinner jacket of my fathers. Books were a problem, but I won a couple of college prizes which helped.

At the end of my first year I won a bursary to study in Perugia, and spent a very happy month there with James Cornford and Mark Frankland, mastering the basics of Italian and travelling as much as I could in Umbria and Tuscany. I made my first visit to Florence on the back of a Vespa, hired by an American fellow student. We stayed in the university, and had our first taste of the glories of Florentine art and architecture. I was relatively hostile to the Roman Catholic Church, and this got in the way of understanding, let alone liking, baroque architecture, but I loved the purity of Italian Gothic and, even more, the severity and simplicity of early-Renaissance architecture like the Pazzi Chapel. Painters like Masaccio, whom I knew only from the one example in the National Gallery, were a revelation, and I began a lifelong fascination with the sculpture of Michelangelo, whose unfinished *Slaves* in the Accademia thrilled me more than the long-limbed *Dawn* and *Night* in the Medici Chapel. Everywhere I went I saw in three dimensions what I had previously known only from books and pictures, and behind it the familiar landcape still much as it appeared behind the saints and madonnas of Piero and Perugino. I also found myself immensely taken with the Italians themselves. I loved the bustle, the bravado, the formality of the *passeggiata*, the obvious love of children, the markets, and the endless variety of simple but delicious food.

At the end of my second year, through the offices of the Italian economist Pierro Sraffa, a fellow of Trinity, I was invited to Rome to work as a translator for the Bank of Italy. I was paid handsomely, but it didn't last. I was quite unprepared for the rigours of translating economic documents. Apart from my inadequate Italian, I could not find the right words in English. Patiently they put up with my slowness, until after a few weeks they paid me off. But this brief experience of working in Rome in a temperature often in the nineties and without air-conditioning did allow me to feel like not just another tourist. I fought my way on to the buses, learning that manners were pointless – charming elderly ladies drove their stiletto heels into my calf with a smiling '*Permesso!*' – so I had to use my elbows to survive. Rome is a small town full of bad-tempered people, but everywhere you look there are monuments that seize the imagination and feel familiar. I always return there with a special nostalgia. I do not really love it as I do other places in Italy, but, like the language of Christianity, it is an inescapable part of our collective memory.

Otherwise, holidays had to be spent at home. In most vacations I worked as a goods porter in a department store in Bournemouth, owned by the family of a prep-school friend. My annual naval reserve training I appreciated as much for the small amount it paid as for the chance to brush up my Russian. I never felt envious of my rich friends, but I did feel I had to earn my keep by entertaining them. I was never much overdrawn, but I was forced to ask for extra from my father in my third year, and in desperate straits at one point I sold some books which I still miss, and asked William Donaldson to lend me ten pounds. It occurs to me now that I have never repaid him.

Donaldson had an ambition to start a new literary magazine, to be jointly produced in Oxford and Cambridge. The Oxford end was to be edited by a Wykhamist friend of his, Julian Mitchell. The review was to be called *Gemini*, and at my suggestion it was printed in Ipswich by one of the best and, it turned out, most expensive printers in the country, on beautiful paper. For the first number I was persuaded to write a letter saying how necessary it was for the survival of civilization. It was, of course, a hugely expensive failure – the first of several for Donaldson, who had good instincts but no business sense. He put together the legendary revue *Beyond the Fringe*, but had to sell his share to get it into a London theatre. He eventually succumbed to his fascination with tarts, and wrote a rather amusing book about it called *Both the Ladies and the Gentlemen*. In a furniture shop in London I once glimpsed him bouncing up and down on a double bed with what he used to call a floozie. After years of lying low he resurfaced as the author of *The Henry Root Letters*, and now writes regular newspaper columns. But I haven't spoken to him or met him for over thirty years.

He invited everyone to his rooms – not only Cambridge writers and personalities, but grand figures from London. I first met Stephen Spender there. But I can no longer remember where it was that I first encountered an intense young American who had just arrived in Cambridge. Her name was Sylvia Plath. Her manic side was pretty obvious,

but I was quite unaware of the other. A number of Cambridge gradu-
ates, like Katherine Whitehorn, had made a mark in London, and
*Granta* and other university magazines were always on the lookout for
writing talent. I remember being very taken by a short story by Margaret Drabble – I think it was the first thing she ever published. But the
star of my time was Michael Frayn, already writing regular features for
*Varsity*, and one year the whole Footlights revue. Michael's mild but
hilarious view of the world has been a constant companion for most of
my adult life, whether in novels, plays or our too infrequent meetings.
His lightly disguised novel about the *Manchester Guardian*, *Towards
the End of the Morning*, is one of the funniest books I know and contains the single best parody of a television programme. Nothing can be
harder than being constantly expected to be amusing, and Michael has
felt his relatively few failures much more than his many successes. But
for me he is a supremely subtle humorist.

I too had ambitions to write, but only short poems and silly sketches were forthcoming. Then in the autumn of 1956 I was approached
under a cloak of secrecy and asked if I would write a musical. The
Musical Comedy Club had planned a show to be written by Andrew
Sinclair, a fellow scholar of mine at Trinity, who had already written a
successful novel about National Service called *The Breaking of
Bumbo*. Sinclair had delivered part of a script and some lyrics which
were pronounced unsettable by the proposed composer because they
had neither rhythm nor rhyme. Two of the committee asked me if I
would make a rival submission, to give them an alternative. I accepted
without hesitation, and in a matter of days came up with an outline
and a few lyrics for a musical set in Regency Brighton and called *The
First Resort*. The proposal was reluctantly accepted by a don at King's,
John Barton, who was responsible for undergraduate work in the Arts
Theatre. I was encouraged to get on with it, since it had to be cast by
Christmas for production the following March.

It was at this point that the Hungarian Uprising occured. It was not
just the familiar entry in *Burke's Peerage* ('by unvarying tradition the
Drummonds are of Hungarian origin') which had given me an interest
in Hungary. I loved the country's music and its dashing traditions.
From my time studying Russian I had come to loathe Communism and
the dead hand it extended over Eastern Europe. The issues of the post-
war period seemed simple. Even though we had been on the same side
in the war, Communism – or rather the state apparatus that called itself

Communism – became the next enemy. I worried a bit (not much really) about nuclear arms, generally supported alliances like NATO, found the Berlin Airlift heroic, and rejoiced in Russian withdrawal from Austria. The Hungarian Uprising seemed to have a real chance of denting the Iron Curtain and deserved total support from the West. Instead we got involved in an escapade in Egypt, where we were certainly in the wrong, and distracted the world's attention from Hungary. I joined protests not only for Hungary but against Suez, and in the middle of all this sat in my room trying to write a silly show.

Suez was for my generation a political awakening, though on nothing like the same scale as the Spanish Civil War had been for students of the 1930s like James Cornford's father. I vowed then never to vote Conservative, and I never have, though some of the finest public figures I have known – such as R. A. Butler and Edward Boyle – have been Tories. I have also often found it hard to vote Labour, and have compromised with Liberals, Social Democrats or, in local government, independents. I am a typical Butskellite of the post-war generation, and deeply resented the way in which the consensus politics of the middle years of the century fell victim to the Thatcherite need for confrontation.

*The First Resort* was written in a hurry, and with a plot that was even more ludicrous than the parody of mistaken identity I had intended. It was directed by Graeme McDonald, a future Head of Drama at the BBC, and the cast included Julian Pettifer, John Bird, David Buck, Adrian Slade, Clive Perry and John Edwards. None of the girls became as well known, but they were excellent and sang charmingly. My parents came to see the first night, and I took a bow from a box – to the derision of my friends. Then we waited for the reviews.

In those opulent days, everything of potential interest at Oxford and Cambridge was reviewed by the major London critics, and Harold Hobson and Kenneth Tynan had both been in the audience. It was the age of the overnight review, and at breakfast the following day I had the experience of reading what seemed the worst set of notices anything had ever had in the history of British theatre. 'Unfunny', 'stupid', 'irrelevant', 'ludicrous' were the key adjectives. The following Sunday, Hobson even complained of 'the worst placed harp in the history of musical comedy'. Tynan castigated the entire Cambridge arts scene for 'wasting time on trash like this, when they could be producing Brecht'. The local reviews were on the whole better and the play sold out its run at the Arts Theatre, but it was only the sight of a full house and an audience that seemed amused that kept me from running away to hide.

Were the reviews unfair? A few years ago I found the script in a pile of old papers, and I have to say it was not simply bad but crawlingly, embarrassingly awful. All that remains now is the photographs, which show the charming designs and costumes, which were probably the best parts of the production. I have never written for the stage since, although a couple of my lyrics were included in Footlights shows. On the whole it was a good lesson about the huge divide between amateur and professional standards. We were inclined to underestimate this, since the acting at Cambridge was so very accomplished. In my first year the Marlowe Society produced *Troilus and Cressida*, directed by George Rylands and with glorious fights devised by John Barton. Achilles was played by Daniel Massey, Nestor by John Bird. Robin Chapman, the dramatist, was a brilliant Thersites, and Julian Pettifer made his name as Troilus wearing nothing but a jewelled jockstrap. I could not believe how good it was; I had previously seen the famous Tyrone Guthrie production, with the action transposed to the Franco-Prussian War, but this seemed not much inferior. Meanwhile at the Amateur Dramatic Club Jonathan Miller was starring – and that is certainly the word – in *Bartholomew Fair*. On the whole the men were better than the women, since there was a greater choice in a university whose ratio of men to women was fourteen to one. But Christine Baker as Rosalind won admiring comparisons with Peggy Ashcroft from Harold Hobson, and Eleanor Bron was already a commandingly witty character actress.

People always wondered what was the secret of the verse-speaking that characterized Cambridge productions, and had done so since Michael Redgrave in the 1920s. George Rylands, known to every one as Dadie, with his sparkling blue eyes and ageless precise manner, was certainly the godfather of our ability to speak. His secret was of the simplest. 'Listen,' he would say – 'listen to what you are saying. It doesn't sound as if you understand it.' So gradually, as rehearsals went on, an understanding of the lines could be felt in the way we spoke them. John Barton, who had hated my musical and only reluctantly gave permission for it to be produced at the Arts, applied Dadie's theories to movement. The results were never less than worth looking at.

Mine was a theatrical generation. In addition to those already mentioned were excellent actors-to-be like Clive Swift, Terence Hardiman and Richard Kay, and two theatrical knights – Derek Jacobi and Ian

McKellen. McKellen came up the term after I went down, so we never worked together, but I was in two productions with Derek Jacobi – as Salisbury to his Bastard in *King John*, and as Baldock to his Edward II. No one had the slightest doubt about his potential; at eighteen he had already played Hamlet on the Edinburgh fringe.

The den mother of all this activity was Judy Messel, wardrobe mistress of the Arts Theatre. She lived in a tiny cottage next to the stage door, and kept open house for anyone involved in theatrical activities. Endless bowls of pasta and flagons of red wine were produced nightly, and she was a beacon of common sense. I can remember, after a poor performance of *King John*, sitting around there bemoaning the fact that we could well be the first generation of Cambridge undergraduates to prove totally unemployable. The company included Derek Jacobi, Clive Swift, John Bird, Eleanor Bron and myself. We may have been wrong, but we were not complacent.

*Edward II* was the last thing I did at Cambridge, in the long vacation after I had officially left. It played all through the summer, first in Cambridge, then in the open-air theatre at Stratford-upon-Avon, and finally at the Lyric, Hammersmith. My part, Baldock, was a small one, but the only one with a joke or two – as well as a touching death scene. I had been grandly boring as the dreary Salisbury in *King John*, but this suited me better and was a happy farewell to my years on the boards. From Petruchio at prep school to Tiresias in *Oedipus Rex*, by way of the King of Spain in a turgid Lope de Vega tragedy and a Noël Coward dowager at Canford, acting had been one of my greatest enthusiasms. I memorized lines easily and loved the experience of playing to an audience. In later years, lectures and even press conferences became a substitute for the theatre I miss. I am still at heart a performer, even if I lack proper training or discipline.

In addition to lacking discipline I was also a menace to my fellow actors, for I had to perform without my glasses. Sword fights, as in *King John*, meant real danger. I got unwelcome laughs as well. In Stratford one night I removed my hat in mid-scene and the whole cast collapsed in giggles. I had no idea why. It appeared that a huge moth had flown out from under the hat. I was quite innocent, but no one believed me. Parallel to all this amateur jollity we had occasional glimpses of the real theatre. The Argo company, with Rylands as editor, was recording all the Shakespeare plays on LP, and we were used for the small parts. I did practically nothing, but on the recording of *Macbeth* starring

Irene Worth and Tony Church my voice can be heard saying, 'The King comes here tonight.'

As well as acting ourselves, we went to the theatre whenever we could. The tiny Arts Theatre in Cambridge was still a major touring venue, and we had visits from Donald Wolfit in Montherlant, Margot Fonteyn with the Sadlers Wells Ballet, and several productions a year from the Oxford Playhouse, run by Frank Hauser. The most memorable was the first production of Harold Pinter's *The Birthday Party*. John Tydeman and I went to see it together, and I was so thrilled and impressed that I went again. It was rapturously received in both Oxford and Cambridge, but closed after four nights in London – hence Harold Hobson's famous *Sunday Times* notice that the public could no longer see the best new play of the year because it had folded. It was certainly strange and unsettling, but it was also marvellously observed and very funny. I can still hear the precise voices and the menace in the slow tearing up of a newspaper. I had enjoyed John Osborne's *Look Back in Anger* the previous year, which we had seen with a good touring cast, but Pinter seemed to me very special. Thirty years later, on his sixtieth birthday, I was to devote a whole evening on Radio 3 to his work and influence and recall the impact *The Birthday Party* made.

All this theatrical activity, as well as my growing disenchantment with academe, helps to explain why the results of my finals were disappointing. I wanted a double first, but not, it seems, enough to work sufficiently hard to get it. But I did have a lot of ill luck. In the Easter vacation before my finals, when I had planned a major assault on my studies, both my parents fell seriously ill at the same time and I spent the weeks shopping, cooking and ministering, since as usual there was no one else to ask.

After Walter Ullmann's injunction to get out, I had contacted the university appointments board. They gave me good advice and pointed me in several worthwhile directions. I applied unsuccessfully for a job at ITN, then to the *Manchester Guardian*, which hired Michael Frayn, and to the BBC, where I started a long process of interviews for a General Traineeship. I knew very little of the scheme, but, since radio had always been a major part of my life and television promised much in its early stage of expansion and experiment, the BBC seemed an interesting possibility. The selection process was certainly thorough. I had a detailed interview with an appointments officer who very carefully tested my claim to know about art, architecture and music. I recall being grilled about my claim to know Berg's *Wozzeck* – fortunately I did. Then there was an interview with Sir Herbert Thomson, a former member of the Indian Civil Service and then rowing correspondent for the *Sunday Times*, who tested me on politics and society, and finally I went before an appointments board of nine or ten BBC managers, at least one of whom gave me a very tough time. I knew nothing of Stuart Hood, since his remarkable memoir of life as an escaped prisoner of war in Italy, *Pebbles in My Skull*, had not then been published, but he picked up on the language course I had taken in Perugia and asked what I thought of the town. I spoke of its history, museums and galleries, of the *passeggiata* and the pasta. 'What of its politics?' he asked. I knew nothing. Did I not realize that Perugia was one of the biggest cities in Western Europe to be controlled by the Communist Party? No, I did not. Should I not have realized that? Lamely I said I had been there as a budding historian, to learn the Italian language and to understand the Etruscans. It was a damaging exchange, but the fact that I have not forgotten it probably means that it was the origin of my later interest in the Italian red belt and the striking cultural achievements of cities like Bologna, Parma and Perugia, which devoted as much time and money to culture as they did to housing.

The situation was saved by one seemingly irrelevant question, asked by a distinguished figure who ran the BBC's Outside Broadcast Department. For some reason I knew his name and one other fact about him. He asked me if I had ever found it a disadvantage to be so tall. He, I knew, was six foot seven. Cheekily I replied, 'Not really. Have you?' and everyone laughed. 'We'll let you know,' they said.

Meanwhile, much to my relief I had been turned down by the Foreign Office. I had not wanted even to apply, but had done so to please my father, who was unimpressed with the other approaches I was making. The Civil Service Commission in Savile Row took me through the routine of written exams, discussion groups and debates. I remember arguing against death duties, so as to preserve great art collections. It went down very badly. I was told that, if successful, my destination would be the Intelligence branch. My languages were tested: a smooth man in Carlton House Terrace said casually in mid-conversation, 'In a few moments the green phone will ring. You will converse with the caller in French.' I did. 'Well, we have to check,' said the smooth man. I got to the final interview, with a daunting semicircle of grandees chaired by Admiral Sir Charles Woodhouse, the hero of the Battle of the River Plate. They were very pleasant indeed, but I am sure, in addition to any reservations they might have had, they sensed my own lack of real enthusiasm. They had certainly done their homework. Why had I stood as a Communist candidate in a mock election at school? they asked. I wondered how they had discovered this. I had completely forgotten the incident, but dredging my memory I remembered that by the time I put myself forward as a candidate all the main parties had already been taken. At the end, Woodhouse said very kindly, 'We're not going to take you, because the kind of work we are recruiting for is mostly uneventful and can be boring. We are not sure it suits your temperament.' He added that if I was ever seeking a reference for a more active post he would happily provide one. Both my father and I were content with the outcome. I would have made a hopeless spy, and my father felt perhaps for the first time that I was not a total waste of space.

I had simultaneously been pursuing a hare of my own. From its beginnings, I had been fascinated by the Edinburgh Festival and had attended it in several years – either as part of family holidays in Scotland or on returning from my naval reserve training, which took place in a remote corner of Fife. I had noticed that the first Director, Rudolf Bing, had been succeeded by his assistant, Ian Hunter, who in turn had been followed by his assistant, Robert Ponsonby. Was Ponsonby perhaps looking for an assistant? I made contact with him through my old composition teacher, H. E. Piggott, who knew him slightly. Eventually I was summoned to the Edinburgh Festival offices in London's St James's Street.

Ponsonby was, as he can be, courteous and charming. He teased out my musical knowledge and my interest in theatre and exhibitions. Then, to my surprise, he asked me if I wanted the job. What did it pay? I asked. 'Six hundred pounds per annum – not rising,' he said firmly. Even then it was not much, and I visibly demurred. I got the impression that it was expected that I would have a bit of money of my own, which was very far from the case. I asked for a day or two to consider, and returned to rehearsals of *Edward II* in Cambridge. Waiting for me was a letter from the BBC offering me a General Traineeship, salary £625, with small annual increments. It was a difficult choice, and I will always be grateful to my mother, who felt strongly that the BBC offered greater opportunities. I wrote as politely as I could to Robert Ponsonby and withdrew. It was to prove a wise decision. A year later

Ponsonby, a good Director, was driven out of Edinburgh by a group of hostile local grandees, to be replaced by Lord Harewood, who immediately appointed his own assistant. The man whom Ponsonby had taken on found himself out of a job. By that time I was installed in the BBC and knew how lucky I had been to become a General Trainee, for that year they had taken only four out of several hundred applicants.

*Edward II* rambled on at the Lyric Theatre until early September. We went into Broadcasting House one Sunday and recorded it for the Third Programme. Each week members of the cast left. Derek Jacobi, who had been extraordinary, was replaced by Toby Robertson, the director. Nearly everyone was having to double – even the Gaveston, Richard Marquand, popped up in the last act heavily cowled as an abbot. But I went on as just Baldock, with my nosegay and buttoned cassock, until the end, unable to double as I kept on reappearing. Then, after the play closed, I returned to Trinity to collect my things. I went for a last nostalgic walk down the Backs, had a beer or two at the Mill, then back along King's Parade.

Despite not having had much money and feeling occasional frustration and unhappiness, I had mostly had a good time at university. My London girlfriend had faded with the competition of Cambridge social life and was not replaced. I remained emotionally unfocused and immature, but I had made many friends, whom I still cherish, and had arrived at a slightly clearer picture of who I was and what I wanted to become. I had told Victor Bonham-Carter, at Unilever all those years before, that I knew it was not going to be enough for me to enjoy the arts merely as a spectator. I wanted closer involvement, even if the price was fewer material rewards and a degree of insecurity. I don't think there has been a day in my life when I have regretted that choice, but whether I could make a significant contribution was much less certain.

# 5

# The Shadow of Reith

The BBC that I joined in September 1958 was at a crossroads. The coming of ITV three years earlier had broken its monopoly in television, and audiences had been more than halved. Radio was losing out to television in the evenings, and the early success of the Third Programme after its launch in 1947 had been overtaken by a degree of concern about its lofty tone; far from being a mark of quality, 'The Third' was now often used as a term of abuse. There were widespread rumours that the BBC's much vaunted independence had been threatened by the Eden government bringing real political pressure to bear on it at the time of Suez. There was a widespread feeling that the mood of broadcasting might be changing.

Its monopoly had enabled the BBC to win big audiences for recondite subject matter. The now almost universal popularity of archaeology began with the success of a television quiz programme called *Animal, Vegetable or Mineral?*, in which archaeologists such as Sir Mortimer Wheeler had to identify, date and explain artefacts. Natural history, with Peter Scott, was also of mass interest, and particularly suited to television. But the certainties of the Reith era and the authority that had characterized the BBC's wartime reporting were under threat in a world that was moving into a new age with attitudes that would characterize the 1960s. Nevertheless, the Reithian ethos and belief in public-service broadcasting run at arm's length from the government, rather than the American commercial model or the European closeness of broadcasting to political parties and administrations, were still at the centre of things. And even those who criticized its resolutely middle-class tone recognized that the BBC took cultural matters seriously, from its support for orchestras to its popularization of literature.

The Arts Council had begun in the late 1940s under the banner of Minister of Education Ellen Wilkinson's words 'Only the best is good enough for the working man', and the BBC confidently embodied this slogan. Some of the shibboleths of the Reith years, especially the attitude to Sunday, were now felt to be too restrictive. But no one, even in the battle to win back audiences from ITV, thought that the main role of the Corporation was just to give the public what it wanted. How could the public know what it wanted? It could certainly express its views on what it was offered, and it did so vociferously, but it was the business of the broadcaster to have ideas, to be ahead of the general taste, and adept at identifying things that people might be interested in if given the chance. Radio had done as much as anything else to invalidate the old quip about Britain being 'Das Land ohne Musik'. Spread across the Home Service, the Light Programme and the Third, music of all kinds, from specialized areas to the very popular, found a new and growing audience, while the Proms, under Malcolm Sargent's leadership, presented each summer a parade of most of the main works in the standard repertory – including all the Beethoven and Brahms symphonies, the well-known ones by Tchaikovsky and Dvořák, and the most familiar concertos. But the Proms were not concerned only with the well-known: there was a perceptible desire even then to widen the canon with new and unfamiliar things.

Television, even in its early years, had seized on music, with concerts, recitals and even operas produced in the studio, and occasionally commissioned specially. Indeed, there was much more music on television in the 1950s than in the 1990s. But, although there was a Television Music Department when I joined the BBC, the arts were still the responsibility of Current Affairs. If you seek out coverage of the famous Diaghilev exhibition of 1954 or the then shocking interview between Malcolm Muggeridge and Brendan Behan, who was far from sober, the archive reveals them to have been items in *Panorama*, the weekly current-affairs flagship programme. It was only with Huw Wheldon's *Monitor*, from January 1958, that the arts got a slot of their own.

I had always been a committed listener to radio, but after we acquired our first set, at the time of the coronation in 1953, I also began to watch a lot of television when at home. It was only broadcast in the evening then, just like the Third Programme, which ran from seven to eleven – something largely forgotten by those people today who go on about its golden age. Despite its aspirations, I found much television trivial and cosy in the same way as the British cinema, but there was a growing interest in documentary, which fascinated me, and a strong emphasis on new drama, in which ITV soon took the lead. Plays were performed live, and what they may have lost in polish they gained in immediacy. Politics were very much handled with kid gloves. Respectful interviewers gave statesmen an easy ride, and ludicrous restrictions banned the discussion of issues currently before Parliament – the so-called Ten-Day Rule. But, fuelled by the strong journalistic instincts of the Director-General-designate, Hugh Carleton Greene, things there were changing too. Under the formidable Grace Wyndham Goldie – Head of Talks, Television – Current Affairs were growing teeth and, in an altogether new departure, mixing entertainment with news and so drawing huge audiences for an early-evening programme called *Tonight*. The anchormen included heavyweights like Kenneth Alsop and Robert Kee, as well as the more emollient Cliff Michelmore and Derek Hart. What was so striking was the unrivalled access that television had both to authority and to the audience. No longer did class, education, geographical location or lack of facilities prevent people from having the opportunity to know about people and events. The cosy world of British cinema, which television had reflected in a crime series called *Dixon of Dock Green*, inexorably gave way to *Z Cars,* which was much closer to the real world of the police and the criminal.

It was also increasingly evident that, to reflect society, the BBC, although no longer monopolistic, had to represent more than one view. There was a tremendous row about the transmission of a radio series on humanism which questioned the inevitable rightness of Christianity. The first ever Reith Lectures to be delivered by a woman, Marjory Perham, challenged the British imperial record, especially in Africa. Bertrand Russell, still thought of solely as a mathematician and philosopher, began to take a more public role as a passionate opponent of nuclear arms. Although much gave the impression of being carved in stone, nothing stands still in broadcasting and I sensed from my first day an organization of enormous professionalism and authority that was beginning to be run by people of a younger generation, less convinced of the correctness of the traditional view. It was a very good time to become involved.

A couple of weeks before I joined I was telephoned by Victor Menzies, the Staff Training officer responsible for General Trainees. He told me that, after a short introductory course, I would be attached to Religious Broadcasting, Radio. I was appalled, and could not imagine why this was to be, until I remembered having given as a referee my old school chaplain, Roy McKay, now Head of Religious Broadcasting. He had asked for me. The normal pattern of the General Trainee scheme was for each successful candidate to spend up to two years with a variety of departments in both Radio and Television, usually including a spell with the World Service at Bush House. It was accepted that we each had individual areas of knowledge and interest, but it was felt that these were of only imprecise potential application. Setting us at various targets not only would find out if we were any good but would help the BBC see where best we might in time contribute. The scheme was extremely carefully administered, not only in suggesting where we might go, but in certain circumstances in turning offers of placements down. As part of our Footlights cabaret experience, Joe Melia and I had performed at the restaurant of the Royal Court Theatre, run by Clement Freud. Ned Sherrin, a producer on *Tonight*, and always on the lookout for talent, had seen us a couple of times and as a result we were given a couple of spots on that programme. After I joined the BBC, Sherrin invited me to lunch at Lime Grove to meet the Editor of *Tonight*, Alasdair Milne. Milne was friendly in his gauche way, and asked me to join the team. I was naturally very excited by the idea of being part of what was at that time the most successful show on the air, but Victor Menzies vetoed the idea at once – I was to learn first about radio, and in any case he thought I was destined for more serious things than magazine programmes, however popular. So, after four weeks of basic training in the technology of radio and a number of lectures by well-known producers, it was to Religious Broadcasting that I went.

On the introductory course I had glimpsed something of the range of skills that radio required. Val Gielgud had talked about radio drama, and his total belief in live broadcasting as opposed to the tape culture that was coming in. Barbara Bray had talked of the challenge of adapting plays and novels for the microphone, using as an example *Moderato Cantabile* by Marguerite Duras. I had learnt about outside broadcasts and lip mikes. We came to think – in my case for the first time – about the nature of sound, and experimented with sound effects played from gramophone records or manufactured on the spot in the studio. A simple edition of *Mrs Dale's Diary* involved doors opening and closing, phones ringing, teacups being rattled, and the sound of passing traffic – 'spot effects' they were called. It was better even than the electric train set I had never had. From the first, radio was presented as a creative medium, rich in potential for imagination and suggestion.

The formidable lady who ran Announcer Training found me unsuitable for microphone use: 'Soft *r*s,' she declared – 'quite useless!' Nevertheless, I wrote and narrated a mini-documentary contrasting excerpts from the Nuremberg trials with eyewitness accounts of the camps. It was ludicrously overambitious and quite unsuccessful. I did better with a magazine programme to which I contributed a feature on vegetarianism. One interview began with the unforgettable line 'In the movement we have nut cutlets.' My fellow course members came from all over the BBC, and many had already had years of experience, but behind desks or in technical areas. They were as intrigued as we few General Trainees by the pleasures and challenge of making programmes.

Eventually I joined Roy McKay in the Religious Broadcasting Department, on the mezzanine floor of the old Langham Hotel, opposite Broadcasting House. I was there for three months, and at no time did anyone make even a perfunctory enquiry about whether I shared their beliefs. They were an impressive group: Roy himself, with steel-grey hair and an intense manner, the intellectual Hubert Hoskins, Elsie Chamberlain, one of the first women ministers, and in the next office to me George Thalben-Ball, the outstanding organist, who advised the department on music.

I was set to work on a five-minute daily programme which followed *Housewives' Choice* on the Light Programme. *Five-to-Ten*, it was called, 'a story, a hymn and a prayer', and it was just that. On Mondays the stories had a Catholic bent and were read by the Irish actress Mary O'Farrell. She was already a heroine for me, notably through her performances in a series of spoof documentaries by the poet Henry Reed in which she played Hilda Tablet, a 'composeress' obviously based to some extent on Dame Ethel Smyth, although with rather more modernist tendencies. Reed's programmes were among the most memorable of those years, and still stand rehearing today. Hilda's opera *Emily Butter* had wittily atonal music by Donald Swann and starred a coloratura (Hilda's girlfriend) played by Marjorie Westbury, whose range went from small children to prima donnas. Other programmes of the series, like *Through a Hedge Backwards*, were studded with phrases that have lodged in my memory – like the description of the actress Daisy Treddle, 'whose performances delighted two generations and are now delighting a fourth', and of Stephen Shewin's experimental play, 'a sort of half-Brecht house'. Mondays on *Five-to-Ten* were always a joy with Mary. Stories on Saturdays were for children and were read by Jill Balcon, who became a lifelong friend. A roster of actors read on the other days, and I recall the first appearance of a young Oxford graduate called John Wood. After a week or two of trailing a more experienced producer I was allowed to take over, editing the stories, choosing the hymns, and even writing the prayers. 'How about a week of "Grant, O Lord . . ."?' I would say.

I had grown a beard that summer for *Edward II* and still had it, and was therefore known as the Greek Orthodox member. In those thin days I did rather resemble an El Greco. My secretary was twenty-one that month and gave a party, to which I was not invited. A few days later I asked a friend of hers if I had upset her in some way. Certainly not, came the response: it was just that it was a party for young people. How old did they think I was? (I was twenty-three.) 'About forty,' she said. I went home that night and shaved off the beard. They were most apologetic, and said that they could see I was no more than thirty-five. It was not exactly a problem, but I was often taken to be at least ten years older than I was. I took to carrying my birth certificate, but the middle-aged-banker image was winning. I don't think at any time I really wanted to be young or felt there was any particular value or virtue in youth. I wanted to be treated as a grown-up. Today I react very badly to middle-aged men in tracksuits, baseball caps and trainers.

During my first week I was asked to look after a group of archdeacons, in the studio to record a discussion. I was quite uncertain how to address them – the protocol book said 'Venerable', but it was hard to follow this when they all turned out to be about forty. Hubert Hoskins invited me along to his recordings, some of them of impenetrable doctrinal complexity and many involving a man called Reardon, one of the great theorists of Anglicanism, who in the way of these things was the vicar of a tiny parish on the edge of Dartmoor, sheltered from ecclesiastical storms by a benevolent Bishop of Exeter. I eventually made my own first real broadcast on the four-hundredth anniversary of the accession of Queen Elizabeth I, interviewing the vicar of Hatfield, where Queen Elizabeth had been in November 1558. My tape recorder – the heavy little green L2, known as a Midget, then ubiquitous among reporters – succeeded in chewing up the tape. I unwound several hundred feet of it in my bedroom and mercifully it was undamaged. The vicar went on to become a bishop; I went on to become a frequent interviewer, but I never became comfortable with the hardware.

What surprised me at the time, although I should have been prepared for it, was the total conviction of the whole department that Christianity was the only religion, and Anglicanism the major part of it. It still persists today. When I was later running Radio 3 it took me over a year to get recognition of any other religion, and then it was entirely tokenistic. I had gone through a purple patch of religious enthusiasm at school. Since my father had been born a Presbyterian and my mother a Baptist, they had decided I should not be christened until I was old enough to decide which niche I fell into. I could choose anything, I was told, except Roman Catholicism. My mother, since her Australian childhood, had considerable animosity against Roman Catholics. It was the only area where she expressed prejudice. She had none about race, class or sexual preference, but the wealth of the Catholic Church in Australia, its political involvement and its pontifications about morality offended her. My father took interdenominational services on his ship, and my mother turned to the Anglican Church really because of its music. Partly through the stimulating influence of Roy McKay, I had been both christened and confirmed an Anglican at Canford. I frequently read the lesson in chapel, and occasionally tried my hand at writing sermons – pompous and preposterous things they were too. But my religious feelings did not last. I came to realize that it was the language and the music which attracted me, not the dogma. However, I fulfilled my responsibilities in Religious Broadcasting, and, since I was given chances to be involved in many different kinds of broadcast, it proved an excellent introduction to radio. But I did have to explain to my friends that I had not had a revelation on the road to Broadcasting House.

I was expecting to be sent to Bush House in the New Year, but instead went at a few days' notice to Scotland, to cover the output of a producer who had fallen off a train, breaking both his legs. This was a frequent occurrence at Hawick, in the Borders, where the track and the platform had opposing cambers and people failed to mind the gap. It had been a dark night, the producer had been carrying a suitcase and a heavy recorder, and subsequently it was suggested that he might not have been entirely abstinent. The poor man was to be in hospital for months and his colleagues were shorthanded, so in the dead days between Christmas and New Year I packed my bags and headed north to a chilly Edinburgh.

I had begun in London by living in a room in Eileen Pearcey's flat in Dolphin Square, but moved out when she took to leaving notes on the fridge complaining that I had drunk the milk or burnt a saucepan. In those days the *Evening Standard* had page after page of advertisements for rented accommodation, and I soon found a room in a gloomy block behind Selfridges, run by a Greek widow. Six lodgers shared one bathroom and visitors were forbidden, but it was only four pounds a week and handy for work. In Edinburgh I was put up first in a reasonable hotel just down the hill from the BBC offices in Queen Street, but after a week I was told my allowance would not run to that and transferred to a private hotel at the bottom of the hill in Great King Street. The room was enormous, with three beds and a tiny gas fire. High tea was at six – a small piece of fish, a cupcake and a pot of tea.

My fellow lodgers were university students. We huddled together to avoid the Scottish winter. One of the boys tried to teach me chess. It defeated me totally – I never mastered even the simplest move. Since I had played bridge for years, I tried to interest the others in that, but cards were forbidden as the work of the Devil. One of the girls, an otherwise jolly creature, was a Wee Free from the Inner Hebrides and believed every word of the Bible to be literal truth. The boy who tried to teach me chess had a delightful girlfriend and was passionately devoted. Shyly he sought my advice; all physical contact, he had been told, was unacceptable outside marriage, and he was even unable to relieve his sexual tension in solitude, since his father had told him that masturbation was three steps on the road to hell. It is hard to know how typical they were of my Scottish contemporaries, but it all reinforced my dislike of religion.

For BBC Scotland in January 1959 there was only one topic – the impending bicentenary of the birth of Robert Burns. Every day there were programmes about him and his work, most of them a complete eye-opener to me. My father, like all Scots, could quote the occasional line of Burns. Even I knew a few of his songs. But the real richness of the writing took me by surprise. The producer and critic George Bruce was at the heart of many of the Burns projects, and soon got me involved. I have never regretted it. The high point of the anniversary was the supper to be held in the poet's birthplace, part of which was to be televised live, while the whole proceedings were to be recorded for deferred relay on the radio – deferred because of the *Nine O'Clock News*, an unmovable feast. The toast was to be proposed by Sir James Fergusson of Kilkerran, famous for his knowledge of Scotland and its history. For reasons I have never fathomed, Fergusson was extremely hostile to the BBC management and landed my poor Television colleagues in the mud by finishing his speech just as the cameras went over live to the event. Television got nothing, and it was a considerable scandal. Meanwhile in the control room in Edinburgh we recorded everything, and broadcast a rapidly edited version twenty minutes later. Unwittingly, I became a local hero for a day.

George Bruce also gave me the freedom of his crowded bookshelves, and I read widely in Scottish history and culture. For me, educated entirely in England, Scotland was largely an unknown quantity. In one sense, with my name, I felt a strong connection, but it was romantic rather than rational. Every day I became more aware of the fundamental differences between the two countries, not only in their legal and educational systems but in their attitudes to class. I went every week to Aberdeen to produce a regional news-magazine programme for the new VHF station there. Local reporters brought in tapes, I edited them, and they were presented by a young journalist who worked for the evening paper. This at least was a city and an area that I knew, but I could instantly feel how different it was from the grandeur and chilliness of Edinburgh, let alone from London. I spent a week in Dundee in a studio above the public library, recording Scottish songs and fiddle music. Craggy old men would come down from the Highlands and play for hours, and the songs showed me clearly why Beethoven was interested enough to devise accompaniments for them. There was a strength and purity about the best of them that I find unforgettable.

The music staff in Edinburgh got me involved in studio recitals, the actors introduced me to a convivial bar, and I went to the cinema and the theatre to see anything worthwhile. In the Usher Hall the Scottish Orchestra was conducted by Hans Swarowsky, an unknown quantity to me. Being used to Schwarz and Groves in Bournemouth – and to Boult and Barbirolli, let alone Beecham, in London – I thought him very small beer. Yet he was to become one of the great teachers of our time, numbering among his pupils Claudio Abbado, Zubin Mehta and Riccardo Muti. Like theatre directors who cannot act, Swarowsky obviously kept the best for his students. I went to plays at the Lyceum and pantomime at the King's, and trudged the city relishing its superb position and wonderfully varied architecture. I was often lonely, always hungry, and keen to fill my time with work to the extent of offering to take over any programme at the weekend to allow time off to my married colleagues. The most approachable was the producer and writer W. Gordon Smith, who ran a weekly satirical programme called *Scope*, which paved the way for the new attitudes that were to dominate broadcasting in the 1960s. Many of the techniques used by *That Was The Week That Was* in television and *Not The Nine O'Clock News* in radio were there in embryo. There was a mixture of comedy, comment and polemic that the authorities clearly found dangerous.

Towards the end of my time I varied the format of the magazine programme in Aberdeen. In one quiet week the only interesting report was of rat-infested public housing in Peterhead. Without asking advice, I devoted almost the whole programme to this item. A couple of days later I was sent for by my Edinburgh boss, the Assistant Head of Programmes, a very nice man called Aidan Thompson. I was asked to explain myself. I did. 'Wait here,' he said, and left the room. He returned shortly and asked me more questions, then once more retreated. This went on for quite a while, until I felt bound to ask what was going on. It appeared that he was relaying my answers to the Controller of BBC Scotland, in the next office – a godson of Reith called Andrew Stewart, who wore a bowler hat and carried a rolled umbrella. 'Could I not speak to the Controller myself?' I asked. 'Out of the question,' I was told. In the end I was reprimanded and told that I had broken a crucial rule of magazine programmes – that they were to contain a minimum of three items. I was told to go away and sin no more. I left the Assistant Head of Programmes' office. At the same moment the Controller's door opened and he emerged in his usual hat, overcoat and umbrella. We walked side by side down the corridor and got into the lift together, but he never glanced to left or right. A week later I left for Bristol, for my first Television attachment. I was having coffee in the canteen on my first morning when a familiar-looking figure wandered over to my table. 'Are you John?' he asked. 'Why not pop in and have a sherry with me before lunch?' It was Frank Gillard, the famous war reporter, now Controller of the BBC's West Region. I sensed at once that things would be very different here.

Yet my three months in Scotland were important and salutary. My ignorance of the land of my fathers was only too typical of Anglicized Scots. What I had been taught was confined to Scotland in so far as it was a problem for the English. I knew all about Edward I, about Flodden Field, the Convention and the Forty-five, but I had much to learn about the Scottish contribution to literature and philosophy. Beyond this, I found myself drawn to the toughness of character that had produced so many outstanding empire-builders, soldiers, judges, head-masters and captains of industry. My father retained his accent, despite a life spent almost entirely outside Scotland, but had not much more than a sentimental attachment to a country that had not been particu-larly kind to him in his youth. I came to feel that the least I could do to justify my name was to be better informed about and perhaps one day even get involved with what I cannot with a clear conscience call my homeland but is certainly a place which has never felt like a foreign country.

Bristol was considered the most attractive of the BBC's regional headquarters, not just because of an agreeable city within reach of splendid countryside and the coast, but because of a prevailing attitude of camaraderie and a high standard of output. Like all the regional cen-tres, it covered the whole range of output, from drama to news by way of documentaries and religious programmes in both radio and televi-sion (although the television resources were limited). Above all, it was the home of the Natural History Unit, one of television's biggest suc-cess stories. There was also a strong feeling of real cultural values. Desmond Hawkins, the Head of Programmes, was a Thomas Hardy expert; Pat Beech, his assistant, was a grandson of the famous actress Mrs Patrick Campbell. The drama producer Brandon Acton-Bond and his young ex-General Trainee assistant Patrick Dromgoole had discov-ered a local writer with a marvellous sense of comedy, Peter Nichols. Kenneth Savidge in Religious Broadcasting was passionate not just about religion but about architecture, and would make a splendid series, *The A to Z of Churches,* with John Betjeman. Douglas Vaughan, an announcer with a splendid Devon burr, was also, albeit with a slight modification to the accent, a superb poetry reader. Life revolved around the club in the basement of one of the three houses in White-ladies Road that had been joined together to make an expanding Broadcasting House. The woman who ran the bar was the only person I have ever known who always, when given the chance, used the intru-sive *l* which had turned 'Bristowe' into 'Bristol'. The bar roof had been propped up with steel girdles, she told me. Peter Scott, a famous glid-ing expert, was congratulated on being back on terral firmal. It was enchanting.

I quickly found a bedsit in Pembroke Road, a few minutes' walk away in the heart of the architectural grandeur of Clifton. Bristol, like Edinburgh, is one of those cities which has its best residential area in the centre. The university and the art gallery were just down the road; the place was full of young people. I at once felt at home, and the spring and summer of 1959 – among the hottest of the century – reinforced the feeling that I had fallen on my feet.

I was attached to a documentary producer, Ian Curtis, who made a regular series called *The Sea and Ships*, fronted by an old salt who, like my father, had begun seagoing life under sail. His name was Alan Villiers, and he lived in Falmouth. This meant regular trips to Cornwall to work on scripts, and, since we had no dubbing facilities in Bristol, to London too. I was given footage acquired from other sources to edit, and learnt about the St Lawrence Seaway, the coastal traffic of Arabia, and much else. Ian Curtis was, like so many people in television at that time, a former radio producer and depended to a great extent on his cameramen and his film editor for the visual realization of his scripts. He spent ages worrying over an evocative documentary about Dartmoor which uneasily blended amateur actors and location filming. But his major project for the year was to be a documentary about Leonard Cheshire VC.

Cheshire – the only man to be awarded the Victoria Cross for a continuous contribution rather than a single act of bravery – had been a hugely successful pathfinder pilot in the war. Under the influence of Hiroshima, he had undergone a religious conversion and now devoted his life to the care of incurables, having set up homes first in a disused RAF camp on the Lizard and later in a series of derelict country houses. It was an extraordinary story and well worth documenting, since he was now seeking to branch out overseas and found homes in Poland and India. Ian himself was busy with other projects and encouraged me to go out and assess the situation. I was asked to research where we should film and who we should interview, so I spent the spring of 1959 travelling the country by train and spending days in Cheshire Homes from Yorkshire to Cornwall, collecting stories of hardship and help. I saw more of England that year than ever before, criss-crossing the country by train after spending hours planning trips with a copy of Bradshaw's railway timetable. It was remarkable how few places were unattainable. I had had no previous experience of the kinds of problem the patients suffered – muscular dystrophy, Down's Syndrome, senile dementia and acute epilepsy – and it was a revelation to me how little concern we as a society gave to people who needed continual care, even with the National Health Service. The main problem of the Cheshire

Homes was money – there was never enough of it – and the conditions in which some of the patients lived were at best Spartan and sometimes truly appalling. The homes had all depended on private charity to start with, but local authorities were increasingly beginning to get involved and the funding mix was uncomfortable.

Curtis sought to provide a main thread to the story by interviewing Cheshire himself. Cheshire had seemed both aloof and diffident and had given away almost nothing when questioned by the then famous interviewer John Freeman, whose series *Face to Face* had wrung highly personal reflections from a series of the great and the good. The first biography was about to appear, and it too told little of the man rather than his activities. I sensed some sort of mystery and a seeming disjunction between the much decorated war hero and the self-effacing, even chilly, person we met. I became convinced that there was more to Cheshire than he wanted to let show. Ian was not interested. Nevertheless, I beavered away, finding members of his flight crew who told me of his first marriage, to a minor Hollywood actress who had then lived in a caravan on the edge of the airfield where he was stationed. The marriage was eventually annulled for non-consummation. Several people who worked in the homes knew this and delighted in it: it would make him more eligible for canonization, I was told. There was even hostility to his eventual marriage to Sue Ryder, who had sought to do for refugee children what he was doing for the incurable, through her scheme known as the Ockenden Venture. She too proved surprisingly unsympathetic – on one occasion leaving a group of kids outside in a van for hours while she was being interviewed about her work. She and her husband were of course doing admirable things, but I found it increasingly hard to admire them. The only time I saw Cheshire really animated was on a day at the Imperial War Museum when we sat together in the film library, selecting footage of bombing raids on Germany which illustrated the truly dramatic effect of carpet bombing. He sprang to life, vividly recording the exact circumstances of each loop of film.

Of course, with so emotional a story, speculation about the character and motive of the popular hero was unwelcome, and Ian eventually let me know that he thought I was going too far in my researches. The finished programme presented an entirely uncritical view of the man, the homes and the condition of the inmates. Perhaps it *was* essential to conceal one's emotions. Perhaps it *was* wrong to pry into people's motives. But what, I kept asking myself, were we doing? Making a commercial for the Cheshire Homes – an elaborate version of *The Week's Good Cause* – or trying to understand what had made all this happen? No one questioned Cheshire's achievement, but why had he taken on so much?

The tension between reputation and reality is at the heart of documentary, and the Cheshire programme confronted me for the first time with the issues that were to be a major part of my subsequent work in television. Most people turn out to have feet of clay if you look hard enough – God knows, I do myself – so is it necessary to search for them, and who are you benefiting by doing so? My instinct as an historian was seek out everything, but I was to learn as a journalist that the essential thing is to know what can be excluded without distorting the overall picture. Documentary today veers between prurience and hype. Amateur psychology seeks a sexual element in almost everything, and the quest for audiences follows the tenet that smut or scandal sells. Sometimes a totally uncritical view is presented – even, in extreme circumstances, by allowing television companies to transmit commercials disguised as documentaries and made by the subjects themselves or their recording companies. Documentary should be a question of balance and judgement, but too often the finished product is based on totally inadequate research. I may have been misguided in my attempts to deepen the portrait of Cheshire, but I learnt that research undertaken is not time wasted. I also came to question whether research is something you can delegate to an assistant, as is now common, or whether forming your own view demands that the main body of research should be done by the director. This of course takes time, which costs money, but I do not believe in short cuts.

The slowness of television was a big surprise. In radio everyone was making programmes all the time. This was largely because almost everyone had to contribute to the bread-and-butter daily or weekly programmes on which the schedule depends, but even the drama and documentary producers seemed to churn out a great deal. In television it was immediately apparent that large-scale projects like the Cheshire film could take most of a year. This impression was reinforced by my next attachment – to a subsection of Drama called Drama Documentary, back in London. Drama Documentary was very much the creation of two producers, Elwyn Jones and Bill Duncalf, with a good track record and a belief that the telling of factual stories could be helped by dramatization. This was a long way from costume drama, since it was always based on documents and contemporary accounts, though in time it would lead to a worrying blurring of distinctions in the creation of what is now known as 'faction'. At that time it was something very new, but it had been used highly successfully in a number of programmes about the history of medicine.

I was put in an empty office in a semi-derelict building in Shepherds Bush and expected to come up with ideas. I put forward several based on the state trials, especially the riveting accounts of the obviously rigged trials of people like Catherine Howard and Lord William Russell. Since the trial of Charles I had already been televised, my suggestion was thought unoriginal. I played around for a couple of boring months with themes as different as Ludwig of Bavaria, Rasputin and Byron, but got nowhere. I worked on only one programme – a pretentious failure with a strong cast produced by an intense but neurotic radio producer called Nesta Pain, who had won the Italia Prize with a radio documentary on spiders. I was really only the tea-boy, but saw already how difficult actors found it to underact to be credible as real people, rather than employing the emphatic style and elegiac tone which were so much a part of theatre and radio at that time. I loved watching actors come to terms with the limitations of television, and I was occasionally able to sit in on big drama productions in the studios at Lime Grove. I already felt a strong pull towards studio work, despite the countless problems with camera cables, microphone booms and lighting challenges. When it worked it was terrific, and, even when things went wrong, at least there was much to learn. I found myself watching television with an increasingly informed critical eye, conscious of how much the impact of an image could substitute for wordy descriptions, but also conscious of how visualization itself limited that deployment of imagination, both by the programme maker and by the interested audience, which was such a strength of radio. But I was not convinced that drama was my future – and it was an area where it took a long time to work up from assistant roles to the point where you were actually directing programmes yourself.

Victor Menzies of Staff Training was still adamant that documentary was my proper destination. There were no vacancies in the sprawling Talks Department that produced everything from *Panorama* and *Tonight* to *Face to Face* and *Monitor*, but one area that was expanding was television for schools, where a number of jobs were coming up early in 1960. I applied and was accepted, and within a few weeks was directing my first programmes.

I shared an office on the top floor of the still uncompleted Television Centre in Wood Lane, Shepherds Bush, with another ex-trainee, Colin Nears, later to be a successful producer of arts documentaries and ballet relays. It felt distinctly odd rising in the lifts through scaffolding and partly built studios to a fully occupied upper floor. Under the supervision of an experienced producer – Peter Dunkley – Colin and I were put to work on a weekly current-affairs programme for second-ary schools called *Spotlight*, which took one subject each week and explored the reasons for its topicality. The programme consisted of a film sequence – usually re-edited library film, but occasionally some-thing specially shot – interviews in the studios and often a discussion. The presenter was Dick Taverne, a successful young barrister destined to be a controversial Labour MP and one of the founders of the Social Democrats. I made programmes on Russia, British Rail, the American presidency and India.

For India we secured the participation of Lord Mountbatten, who was intrigued by the idea of being interviewed by a teenage student, and who used the occasion not only to trot out his familiar self-justifi-cation at the problems that had resulted from Partition, but also to ask me if I could guarantee the playing of a gramophone record on *House-wives' Choice* to mark his daughter's birthday. There had been much talk at that time of whether programmes of listeners' requests were rigged, so I told Mountbatten that all I could do was speak to the Head of Gramophone Programmes, the redoubtable Anna Instone. I duly rang her and tactfully explained the situation. She was outraged, so I suggested she make contact with Mountbatten herself. 'Indeed I will,' she said. Years later she told me that she had given him a good dress-ing down, and what's more it had been a pointless request since the daughter's birthday fell on a Saturday, and Mountbatten 'should have known that Saturday was *Children's Choice*'. Lady Pamela Mountbat-ten, later Hicks, was hardly still a child.

Mountbatten certainly had what we today call charisma, with his noble profile and flaring nostrils. He was quite nice to us, but I sensed an incredible arrogance. My mother had danced with him a few times in her youth, when he had accompanied the then Prince of Wales on a visit to Australia. She always said that he gave the impression that no one and nothing was quite good enough for him. My father characteristically blamed him entirely for the loss of India.

I learnt a lot from both Dunkley and Taverne and enjoyed the speed of working, since each programme was made in under a week and transmitted live. When I moved on to careers programmes the pace slackened. There was rarely any useful library film, and I had to make a fifteen-minute documentary for each programme. Since making these films took time, the total number of programmes was less. The studio element in each one was presented by the sports commentator Peter West. Unlike Taverne, he was no intellectual, but he was a total professional and more than once held things together when film cues went wrong or interviewees became tongue-tied. I made films about being a telephonist, about telegraph delivery boys, about working in a laundry, and about training to be a butcher – which involved a sequence filmed in the abattoirs of Blackpool. The head man, a jolly twenty-stone Lancastrian, dispatched hundreds of beasts a day and regaled us with gory stories in the pub at lunchtime. He had innumerable children, and I had visions of a blood-stained figure rushing home and hurling himself on his complaisant wife.

I was by now quite relaxed about the pressure of live studio broadcasts, enjoying the adrenalin, and full of admiration for the remarkable technical skills of the studio crews. There were one or two surly and tricky individuals who thought schools programmes beneath them, but most people gave as much as they would on a far more glamorous project. The readiness to solve problems and the ingenuity of operating at speed in cramped conditions was admirable. We take technical skills so much for granted in Britain: it is only when one looks at television in other countries that one realizes what an extraordinary pool of talent the BBC and its training schemes produced. Many of those I worked with went on to run the technical departments. The designers – who really had to do little more than provide a desk, two chairs and a divider unit (G plan of course) – included in their number Julia Trevelyan Oman, who was to become and remain a great friend. She brought the same seriousness of purpose to a simple talks set as she did to designing Jonathan Miller's *Alice in Wonderland* or Tony Richardson's *The Charge of the Light Brigade*, or Frederick Ashton's *Enigma Variations* and *A Month in the Country*. Surrounded by talent like that you would have to be stupid not to learn and understand the nature of teams, and how working together always achieves more than dictatorship or prima-donnaism. Well-chosen, well-balanced teams are the secret of most success.

I was much less happy in my next appointment, to be production assistant on a series of history programmes. It ought to have been right up my street, but proved frustrating and ultimately confrontational. The Schools Department contained two different kinds of producer: school teachers who happened to work in television, and aspiring television directors who hoped they were working in educational television only temporarily. In the department then were Michael Gill and Peter Montagnon, the two producers of Kenneth Clark's *Civilisation* series, Ronald Eyre, an outstanding theatre director and presenter of the religious series *The Long Search,* and Tim Slessor, who worked with Michael Gill on *Alistair Cooke's America.* At that time they were all busy making schools programmes, but with an eye on the mainstream. But did anyone really notice what we were doing?

One day the Controller of Programmes of the BBC Television, Kenneth Adam, came to our weekly programme meeting. Introducing him, the Controller of Education and the Head of Schools Broadcasting, Television, both said they realized it was quite impossible for him to see anything of our work. Speaking up from the bottom of the table, I politely asked why. It was the first of many occasions when I made myself unpopular by speaking too soon, but it seemed to me a pertinent question. Television's influence on children was a subject much in the news at that time. Hilda Himmelweit of the London School of Economics had just published a huge book of statistics and theorizing called *Television and the Child.* The newspapers were full of it, and the BBC was staunchly defending its role in providing children's programmes like *Blue Peter* and, above all, its work for schools. It seemed to me not unreasonable that occasionally the bosses should notice what we were actually doing. But my question was of course brushed aside, and I was later sent for by the Head of Department and threatened with dismissal. The following day Kenneth Adam rang me and asked me to go and see him. I was not sure what to expect, but he could not have been nicer. He showed me his overcrowded diary and said of course I was right, but . . . I could not bring myself to say that the reason we wanted to be noticed was because we were hoping for better chances elsewhere, but I am sure he knew that. Now that I had a permanent job, Staff Training's assistance was no longer available; I was on my own. I several times tried to get to meet Grace Wyndham Goldie, to see if there were openings in the Talks Department, but she was always too busy.

By November 1961 I was deep in the history series and had experienced a complete loss of belief in the way it was constituted. I could not see how dramatizing the London dockers' strike with five actors in a studio and stilted, dreadful dialogue got young people closer to the realities of working-class history. I kept my mouth shut, but I fear that, as so often, my feelings could be read on my face. In the end I was sent for by the Head of Department, who said that, since relations had broken down between me and my producer, he had a problem in knowing what to do with me next. It was news to me that things were that bad. I went back to the office to confront the producer, who spent the next hour and a half telling me in great detail what a useless and unpleasant person I was. It was not a happy occasion, and the enjoyment he showed at my discomfiture rankled for years.

But, by an extraordinary stroke of fortune, the solution was at hand. Two days later I was offered another job: working for the television service in the BBC's office in Paris. I had learnt a great deal about television in the Schools Department. I was to learn much more about the BBC and the outside world from across the Channel.

# 6

# Wider Horizons

Despite my local problems, 1961 was to prove a turning point for me, and the first year since starting work in which I spent more than an occasional week abroad. In April, while still involved in careers programmes, I had been telephoned by a senior producer in Outside Broadcasts, Noble Wilson, whom I had never met. He had learnt that I spoke Russian. He had been editing film in a cutting room at Ealing and had mentioned a forthcoming trip to Russia and the seeming lack of Russian-speakers with television experience. The editor, who had worked with me on the *Spotlight* programmes about the Soviet Union, mentioned my name. As a result, a few days later I found myself heading for Moscow in the company of Richard Dimbleby, Robin Day, David Attenborough, and BBC executives Paul Fox, Aubrey Singer and Noble Wilson. It was just after Yuri Gagarin's first manned spacecraft flight, and the Russians were keen to promote their achievements. All of a sudden, after years of non-cooperation, several television projects had been agreed. Robin Day was to present an edition of *Panorama* from Moscow, David Attenborough to record one of his series *News from the Zoos*; a performance by the Bolshoi Ballet was on the cards, but the central event was to be the live transmission of the May Day parade in Red Square.

The technical problem this presented was considerable. There were no satellite links then, and the pictures and sound had to find their way to the West by different routes. This had been tried, purely experimentally, at the time of the Gagarin flight, and had been found to work. The images went via Minsk, Warsaw, East Berlin, West Berlin and Frankfurt to Brussels and the European Broadcasting Union headquarters. The sound went via Leningrad, Tallinn, Helsinki, Stockholm, Copenhagen and Frankfurt to Brussels. In rehearsal it worked perfectly.

On the day itself we were perched on the top floor of the GUM department store, opposite Lenin's tomb in Red Square. Dimbleby had an excellent viewpoint, and I was linked to him by an earpiece so as to translate the words on the banners or identify the music played by the marching bands. We had been up half the night, with me holding up photographs so that he would recognize all the members of the government. The chief Soviet engineer was a small, fierce woman called, suitably enough, Zhelezova – Woman of Iron, which she certainly was. Twenty minutes before we went live to the West we tested the lines. The sound was perfect but there were no pictures, so the intervening stages were tested one by one. Minsk, OK; Warsaw, OK; East Berlin, silence. Noble Wilson seized the microphone and shouted, 'Would the gentleman in Berlin Ost kindly get his finger *aus*!' There was a pause, a click, and Brussels said, 'Receiving your picture.' Madame Zhelezova embraced him. It was quite clear that her job had been on the line in the event of failure.

Thereafter everything passed off without a hitch. Dimbleby – whom the public tended to think pompous but who was much more fun than his image suggested – had mastered his brief with total authority. I was constantly astonished at the easy way he inserted facts or impressions. No one since has ever done commentaries as well – his son David is never as well informed, and Tom Fleming is too lugubrious for me. It was a wonderful lesson in the art of commentary, and he treated me throughout with an affection and friendliness which I found hugely flattering. I was, after all, nobody at all in this very public world, but I could be of help since I was the one person on our side who understood Russian.

The May Day parade was only the first of our projects, and we stayed on for several weeks afterwards to record other programmes. The Soviet Union at that time did not have video-recording equipment, which was a very recent arrival in the UK. Videotape was to change the whole face of television. In the early years the equipment was cumbersome but effective. Tape could be edited only by physically cutting it as one did with sound tape or film, but with the limitation that a cut once made could not be rejoined without it showing. Editing was complicated. As there were no local recording facilities in Moscow, the BBC drove one of its huge recording vans overland and parked it in the front yard of the Moscow television headquarters, manned by very experienced engineers. We were very proud of our machines and, during the month the van sat there, innumerable technical supervisors from Soviet Television were shown around. Within a year the Russians had their own version. I suppose it would have happened sooner or later, but the BBC made sure it was sooner – without, I believe, realizing what was

happening. For the BBC the Moscow outing was a technical achievement and a jolly jaunt. Looked at another way, it gave the Soviet Union
one of its biggest propaganda coups ever, because practically every
country in Western Europe had transmitted the May Day parade live,
and in a village bar in Sicily or Spain its demonstration of Soviet military might had quite a different reverberation from the purely technical sense of achievement felt at Television Centre in London. I was
severely reprimanded for even hinting at this view, but I was conscious
of a real naivety on the part of some of my colleagues.

As the only Russian-speaker in our team, I was constantly in
demand. The Soviets naturally provided interpreters, but I was soon to
learn how selective their translations could be if there was any hint of
criticism or impatience on our side. This was the period of limited de-
Stalinization, but, as so often with such reforms, the ice thawed only
on the surface. The head of Soviet Television – an amiable man called
Kuzakov, who was reputed to be an illegitimate son of Stalin – could-
n't have been more friendly. His number two reminded me of Beria. I
was naturally subject to close attention, since the Russians were convinced I had been planted by British Intelligence. My name must have
been on their files already, since several years earlier I had met two pur-
ported students from the Soviet Union during my summer course in
Perugia, and within weeks of my return I began to receive regular visits in Cambridge from a man attached to the Soviet Embassy in London. All I had told the students in Italy was which college I was at. But
the Soviets sought me out, and others who had done the Russian
course received similar approaches. I reported back to our people and
was encouraged to go on seeing the Embassy rep – an obvious KGB
man masquerading as Assistant Cultural Attaché. I was offered books,
theatre tickets, dinners and even a trip to the Black Sea for a holiday. I
refused everything, but it made me apprehensive.

Once in Moscow, I was not surprised to be very obviously followed,
and one day I found a man in my room going through my things.
Slightly to my surprise, I hit him rather hard. It is very easy to make
jokes about hidden microphones in rooms, but much harder to live
with them – especially when you are trying to work. Spring in Moscow
was chilly, and having to go out into the street or hover in corridors to
have a private conversation was not much fun. We had with us an
excellent assistant from the Outside Broadcast Department, a feisty girl
who would stand no nonsense from the 'Commies'. She would enter a

room and say in a loud voice, 'Good morning, good morning, BBC, testing, testing . . .' On one occasion, fatuously challenged by a young soldier as we went for the fifth time that morning into the Soviet Television headquarters, she threw her handbag at him and said, 'Oh do stop wasting our time!' He dropped his gun in terror. She eventually married the chief engineer in charge of the recording machines, so she got something out of the visit.

It was very hard work in Moscow and there was practically nothing to eat except caviar and chicken Kiev. The simplest meal in any restaurant, even the best, took up to three hours for two courses. I wanted to visit the theatre, the opera, the ballet whenever I could, so I went without dinner for night after night, surviving on snacks and on oranges given me by the wife of an American correspondent. The most chilling thing was the lack of any contact with the outside world. We had to go to the head post office to telephone London, and were all too aware of how public our conversations were. The *Daily Worker* was available, but it really irritated us when the leading Soviet commentator working with Dimbleby and Robin Day would come in every morning and tell us what the weather was like in London and any vital news from the West. He had access to the World Service, whose transmissions were jammed to the general population. Nevertheless, it was a fascinating experience.

The sclerotic nature of Soviet society was everywhere apparent. The simplest request had to go through a dozen channels and endless meetings to get even a negative response. Particularly obstructive was the young woman attached to Noble Wilson and myself as interpreter. She constantly extolled the superiority of Soviet society, yet, since her husband worked for a newspaper and could travel abroad, wore French and Italian clothes and looked much smarter than any of us. Soviet society was perfect, but somehow foreign clothes were smarter. This kind of double standard was entirely typical. She had written a thesis on British education, and showed it to me. It contained much that could be found in any left-wing British publication on the subject, but also some quite dotty claims like 'The results of the eleven-plus are entirely decided by the class situation of the parents.' When I pointed out that this was far from true, she replied ominously, 'You have your truth.' For every occasion she had an appropriate quote from Lenin. We drove past the Lenin Library every morning, and every day she would say, 'The Lenin Library' and I would reply brightly, 'Where they write Lenin.' 'That is not amusing,' she would say, and I would agree with her. But she was quite impervious to irony. It was really hard to tell whether anyone believed the kind of things they said all the time or whether they just parroted what they had been told was appropriate – especially when dealing with dangerous foreigners. And we were most certainly considered dangerous.

We got a very warm welcome from Western journalists based in Moscow, and they entertained us as well as they could in those times of scarcity even for privileged foreigners. In every flat we visited there were two or three radios blaring loudly, to make bugging harder to decipher, and even in the British Embassy we were cautioned against indiscretion and moved away from the chandeliers. I went with Dimbleby to the Embassy to sign the visitors' book a day or two after our arrival. The Ambassador, Sir Frank Roberts, was an acquaintance of Dimbleby's. His secretary, a willowy youth whom I had known slightly at Cambridge, explained that the Ambassador would be unable to receive us since 'this is a working Embassy'. 'And what, pray, are the others?' was Dimbleby's tight-lipped reply.

One of the interpreters working with David Attenborough provided my first encounter with the *jeunesse dorée* of the Communist Establishment. His father was a minister, and they lived in a ten-roomed flat. He was good company and a total capitalist. During the quieter sessions, we taught each other the whole vocabulary of sex and swear words. He set his heart on a gold Dupont cigarette-lighter that David had been given by his wife. In the end, against everyone's better judgement, David gave it to him. It was not helpful in the long run. First the gas ran out, and gas for lighters was unobtainable in Russia; then, a year later, I heard that he had been sacked for receiving gifts from foreigners.

I was nervous going about the city on my own, but, since taxis were hard to find, often walked home after the theatre. People would try to get into conversation with me – it was obvious from my clothes that I was a foreigner. I longed to make contact, to find out what ordinary people said and thought, but it was impossible to trust anyone. I was reduced to eavesdropping and rejecting any friendly approach. On this first trip I never even entered the Kremlin or visited some of the more interesting areas of Moscow. But I must have had some free time, for it was in my gloomy room in the Peking Hotel – with its worn carpets, heavy curtains and chenille tablecloths – that I read Thomas Mann's novel *Buddenbrooks*. The suffocating atmosphere of north Germany in the late nineteenth century seemed not so different from Russia in the 1960s.

In the next room to me was a violinist, who began practising early in the morning and often continued late into the night. One morning we met in the corridor, and I recognized at once the roly-poly figure of Ruggiero Ricci. No wonder the Paganini Caprices sounded so good! On a Sunday afternoon when we had some time off I went to the Pushkin Museum and was admiring the Picassos when a group of young people asked me to explain cubism. We were immediately descended on by the janitors and asked to leave. We went outside and sat on the steps. Their problem, the young people explained, was that they had been told that non-representational art was rubbish, but also that Picasso was a great man. How could this be squared? Picasso's *Dove of Peace* and his public adherence to the Communist Party allowed his work to be displayed, but there was no sign of any of the work of the great Russian artists of the earlier years of the century.

We found time for one or two excursions: to the Sheremetev house at Ostankino, with its marvellous surviving serf theatre, and to the Yusupov country palace at Arkhangel'skoye, where we slithered round the rooms in felt overshoes, both preserving and polishing the floors. There were splendid panels by Hubert Robert. My comment that I had rather a good one in my bedroom at home went down very badly.

Everything about Russia – from the line of birch trees outside the airport to the skyline of the Kremlin – was fascinating and attractive. Everything about the Soviet system outraged me with its ugliness, its conformism and its denial of those human qualities which Russians have in some abundance. One night I shared a table in the hotel restaurant with a Polish engineer. He was in charge of the Warsaw sewers, and had been visiting his Moscow counterparts. He suggested slyly that a few small explosions could flood the city with excrement. I told him that Stalin and his colleagues had already done it.

Was it possible to make a real distinction between Russia and the Soviet Union? Certainly, when we went to record *Romeo and Juliet* at the Bolshoi, we saw where both worlds met and the privileged position of the artist who stayed within the bounds of what was permitted. We had a great deal of difficulty in getting agreement to record this ballet, but eventually it was granted and the company fielded their youngest ballerina, Kondratyeva, as Juliet. Everything went well until our video-recording equipment broke down in mid-session. Having taken it all the way to Moscow it was a terrible irony. I was due to take the tapes back to London the following day, in huge metal cans, for almost immediate showing. Once it became clear there was trouble with the recording, all hell broke loose. It was claimed at once that we had deliberately sabotaged the recording so as to reflect badly on their technical facilities. For hours the argument went back and forth. In the end the tapes were released and I then had to get them through customs at Moscow Airport. British Airways held the flight for me for over an hour. Eventually I fell on to the plane with my cargo. A bright hostess asked me if I would like a cup of tea, and I surprised both her and myself by bursting into tears. Later that evening, in London, I went into the West End just to walk about, look at the lights, listen to people in pubs, and sense how immensely lucky we were in our system, for all its shortcomings. But I also knew that, come what may, I would at some time go back to Russia and try to penetrate the carapace of officialdom and make friends, for the continuing survival of great artists in that society mattered more than the restrictions of Party dogma.

Even though I was an established member of staff with a secure job, I still had very little money, since BBC salaries were less than generous, but it was enough to live reasonably. After returning from Bristol in November 1959 I had spent a short time in digs with Marie Rambert's secretary, Erica Bowen, a capricious creature who some days would insist you joined her for dinner, on others make it only too clear that you were not wanted. On New Year's Eve she decided to reupholster a chair and abandon any attempt at celebration. I went out and gloomily saw in the 1960s alone on London Bridge, wondering why I seemed unable to be comfortable with myself or others – a needlessly self-indulgent piece of immature romanticism. The following spring Tony Beerbohm married and I acquired his illegally sublet mews house behind Chester Terrace in Regent's Park. It was an ideal bachelor pad, with one huge sitting room, a tiny bedroom, a bathroom and a kitchen. It felt cosy, and for the first time I had a base of my own and was able to cook, to entertain and to build a life. The only snag was that the telephone number was just one digit different from that of the Classic Cinema, Baker Street. Most days someone rang to ask for the time of the last complete performance, and as a public service I used to keep the programme times beside the telephone.

For most of these years there were restrictions on how much money you could take out of the country – not that I had a lot – and these certainly determined the length of time you could stay abroad. In the summer of 1961 I planned a long break and was away for nearly a month. I went first to the South of France with John Tydeman. For at least the last hundred years, successive generations have thought the Côte d'Azur ruined, but each new generation still finds it captivating. We had a flat on the Italian side of Menton, and met up with friends along the coast. We swam before breakfast and late at night, and I bought a very brief bathing costume and, baking in the sun, got blisters on my hips which made sleep rather difficult – not that I cared. We went up to Eze and down to Villefranche in a tiny car – three men and a couple of jolly girls. We found a little nightclub on the harbour in Monte Carlo where we danced and watched the fireworks. I loved it all – the heat, the light, the sense of relaxation, and what for Stendhal was the essence of the south, 'le parfum des citronniers le long du golfe'. Though I only really knew Paris, from visits while still in my teens, I felt strangely at home in France, even at the height of the tourist season. I remember wanting to spend more time there so as to really get to know this intriguing country whose every value seemed so different from our own.

After Menton I headed towards Venice. Not unusually, the railways were on strike and, since the journey took twice as long as planned, I arrived at four in morning with no hotel booked and a heavy suitcase. At five the left-luggage office opened, and then the station café. I dumped my case and plunged into the city, making my way through deserted markets to the Rialto and then on to St Mark's. It was a Sunday – very quiet, with just the smell of baking bread and the occasional passing boat laden with vegetables. On the Piazza were three million pigeons and one *carabiniere*. Sunlight glittered on the lagoon and the Palladio churches across the water. It was an instant love affair, and since then it has never mattered to me how crowded and noisy Venice can become by day, for the bones of the city are still there, waiting to be rediscovered at night or in the early morning. A hundred yards from the few main arteries, the city belongs only to the Venetians and triumphs in grandeur over its seedy decline. Whenever I hear people complain about the smell or the crowds I try to be sympathetic, but really I question their priorities. Venice is one of the handful of supreme achievements of the human spirit.

On that first visit I was offered the full range of meteorological drama. Violent thunderstorms blacked out the city as I sat under the arches of the Doge's Palace, seeing the skyline fitfully illuminated by flashes of lightning. The water would rise several feet in an hour or two, flooding the streets and squares. Then the sun would blaze down, dissolving marble towers into shimmering mirages, and burn one's eyelids. It was continual theatre. Venice was to become a kind of obsession; I went back again and again during the next twenty-five years, making over forty visits in all – often very brief – just to experience again the thrill of emerging from the station, or coming across the water from the airport and finding the city still miraculously there.

Through my friend John Julius Norwich, I made the acquaintance of the lively but ancient Prince and Princess Clary zu Aldringen, who, dispossessed of their great lands in Bohemia and Galicia, had ended up after the war in a house on the Zattere which the Prince's grandfather had bought but never seen. They would give genteel tea parties with tiny cucumber sandwiches. I asked the Prince about Prague in the early years of the century, when he had attended the Charles University and known Kafka. His summary of a provincial capital is unsurpassable: 'The liveries were so musty,' he said. Another friend, Countess Giustiniani, spoke excellent English. Had she spent much time in England? I asked. 'We moored our yacht off Eastbourne in the summer of 1912,' she replied, and I had an image of language wafting out on the offshore breeze. It was all captivating, but I didn't really go to Venice to meet people. I longed to be alone with the city and its magical ghosts.

Yet, despite my love for it, for some reason after a few days there a sort of depression always settles on me, a feeling of despair and lassitude, and I think it's time to get back to dry land. But when I find myself on the other side of the world, as so often these days, it is to Venice above all that my nostalgic thoughts return.

I went on from Venice to Austria – a first visit to Innsbruck, in the Tyrol – and then to Germany, where I spent my first night in a cosy *gasthof* in Garmisch. Vladimir Kozhevnikov, in one of his rhapsodic evocations of life in the 1920s, had often spoken of a holiday he had spent in a grand hotel called Sonnenbichl there, with an older woman who had admired him. He recalled sitting on the terrace in the pure air and drinking *apfelsaft*. It became for him the ultimate image of luxury, and for me of pre-Hitler Germany. I had anxieties about going to Germany, partly because my spoken German was very poor and I was unsure whether I would be able to communicate with people. But also

I was concerned about the past. We had studied very little modern history at school and university, but I had read a great deal about the Second World War, from the origins of Nazism to the Final Solution. In my early teens I had seen the film about the liberation of Belsen, and hardly a day since has gone by without those images coming to mind. Even now I find it difficult to watch television programmes about the camps, and, despite opportunities, I have never visited one. But they are inescapable without being visited. I was uncertain how I would react to ordinary Germans, the ones in the street, without constant nagging questions – 'Where were you?' and 'What part did you play?' Even forty years later I still feel discomfort when elderly Germans, whose past I do not know, speak enthusiastically about their youth. I have got used to France's myth that the entire French population worked for the Resistance, but opposition in Germany was very slight and so many otherwise admirable-seeming people had found it necessary or possible to compromise with the regime.

In 1961 the world as seen from Garmisch was one of sentimental *gemütlichkeit*. There were flowered windowboxes, smiling pipe-smoking lederhosen-clad farmers, and buxom wives in local costume. It was *White Horse Inn* rather than the SS, and my German contemporaries seemed a great deal friendlier than their French counterparts. But the evidence of fantastic and grandiose ambition was just up the road. I toured the Ludwig castles – ludicrous Disney-like follies of spectacular bogusness but undeniable charm. I went to the Wieskirche, and tried hard to understand the attraction of rococo. It eluded me totally, only reminding me of Great-Aunt Margaret's meringues. I ended up in Munich, and was captivated to find it a real southern city with its terracotta tints and golden glow, but disconcerted to notice in the main square a signpost to Dachau. How could they not have known?

Over the years, I have come to admire so much the way in which Germany has re-established culture at the centre of society, projecting its orchestras, opera companies and theatres as a demonstration of true values. Of course I regret the destruction of cities and the architectural dreariness which in most places has replaced what had been there, but I cannot avoid a feeling that the Germans got their just deserts. The bombing of Dresden or Nuremburg may not have been necessary to win the war, but it was a small price to pay considering how many died to promote the German imperial dream. Years later my friend Colin Nears made a film about Leni Riefenstahl, and I met her several times.

Her constant protestations of political naivety and innocence rang totally false. For someone of my age, *The Triumph of the Will* can never be just a piece of brilliant film-making. It was for the furtherance of something deeply criminal, and its sense of glamour only makes it more dangerous. Few things depress me more than the re-emergence of right-wing nationalism among young Germans today. As Dietrich sang in 'Where Have All the Flowers Gone?', 'When will they ever learn?'

The idea of living abroad for a while was much in my mind at this time: I was enjoying discovering the variety of Europe and experiencing places I had previously only read about. In the autumn of 1961 I was asked if I wanted to consider a job in Paris. This was a week or two before the row with my history producer. Colin Nears and I both went for an interview with the head of the BBC's operations in France, Robin Scott. Robin was tremendously friendly and amusing, and it was only later that I discovered he already knew quite a bit about me from his soon-to-be wife, Patricia Smith, who worked in the Eurovision section of BBC Television and with whom I had had a great deal of contact over the Russian outing. Colin, who had spent more time in France than I had – starting with exchange visits with the family of Madame de Gaulle's brother, the Mayor of Calais – really wanted the job. I was rather cool about it, and can remember saying that New York rather than Paris was what intrigued me most. A week later – a week which had seen the falling out in the Schools Department – I was offered the Paris job and, given the circumstances, seized it with both hands.

The rapid expansion of Television and its international involvement put new pressures on the Paris office, where Robin himself and a French secretary were the only people with television experience. The others were news correspondents or from Radio. Scott had convinced the BBC that he needed an assistant to help meet a range of new demands by the television service, from political interviews to *Maigret* sequences. It was a new job, and up to me to make something of it.

Before I left London I made the rounds of various departments and the many different programmes which were served by the Paris office, culminating in a meeting with the number two at Bush House, since, officially, the Paris office came under the External Services directorate. Tangye Lean was a curiously academic figure, and floored me completely with his first remark: 'Odd about Hoche, isn't it?' I was lost. He explained patiently that to him it was an odd coincidence that the BBC's office in Paris should be in Avenue Hoche, a street named after the admiral who had masterminded Napoleon's abortive bid to invade England. I also had a first encounter with Charles Curran, later to be Director-General, who was in charge of Bush House administration and personnel. Everyone was very kind, and it was obvious that the job would bring me into contact with a much wider cross-section of the BBC than I would ever have encountered through Schools Television.

I packed a few things, not knowing what I would eventually need in Paris, and took the Golden Arrow. Robin met me at the station and put me up in his spare room. Two days later I moved into a mezzanine flat in the same building. The flat was gloomy, and in a dreary part of the seventeenth arrondissement, near Place Wagram, but it was not far to the office and a place of my own. Its principal benefit was the largest double bed I had ever slept in. I needed to acquire very little, since it was fully furnished, but I found my French had real gaps when I went to buy bedlinen. Not only could I not calculate the dimensions in the metric system, I had no idea of the French for a pillowcase. Like the Russian for horseradish, *taie* is now something I have never forgotten.

Robin Scott was a man of enormous charm and enthusiasm. His spoken French was as near perfect as I have ever heard in an Englishman, and he radiated confident sociability, immediately involving me in dinners and outings with friends and colleagues. The office was spread over three floors of a big house on Avenue Hoche. On the ground floor was a charity that disbursed small sums to elderly Britons – nannies, cooks, housekeepers, even coachmen who had stayed on in France – and a charming concierge from Mali called Monsieur Ba. On the first floor was a fully equipped radio studio with editing facilities, manned by a splendid engineer seconded from RTF, the French radio and television service, Jean-Paul Dupuy. He was unflappable even in moments of extreme stress, and taught me all the technical vocabulary I needed. On the next floor was the Paris Representative's office, where Robin was boss. His principal secretary, Paulette, was a passionate Gaullist from Lorraine, who barely concealed her permanent contempt for all men – especially *les Britanniques* – while carrying out her duties with total dedication. Her blonded hair and pinched lips gave the lie to any idea of France being an emotionally generous country. The junior secretary, Denise, who kept the books, was the kind of French girl people write songs about – pretty, chic, slightly vulgar and very funny. She and I became fast friends. There was also a much more difficult assistant, Maud Vidal, who later was to run the office but up to this time had been responsible for the TV side. We would have many battles before we became friends, since my appointment obviously undercut her position. At the back of the building was the radio section, run by Cecilia Gillie, wife of the *Guardian* correspondent Darsie Gillie. Apart from the war years, Cecilia had been in Paris since the 1930s, and knew everyone. Unversed in television and pretty hostile to it in a very Bush House way, she had been replaced as Paris Representative with the appointment of Robin, and their relations were at best edgy. I was instantly conscious of being watched to see which party of the *fronde* I would join. It seemed to me to be essential to get on with everyone. I liked Robin immensely and admired Cecilia's knowledge of France and the Paris intellectual world. But they were chalk and cheese.

Everyone, however, loved our messenger boy, Fernand Hivert, a sixty-five-year-old former vaudeville artist and amateur painter, whose wife worked in the luggage section of the Samaritaine department store and who wrote gentle poems, privately printed. Monsieur Hivert taught me more about Paris than anyone I have known. At the end of the day, after he had run around the city for hours on his Mobilette, he would sit in my office and teach me Parisian argot and regale me with memories of Mistinguett and Maurice Chevalier, telling me about Montmartre in his youth and about the Occupation. His pale landscapes were painted on his annual holiday in Brittany and exhibited at the Salon Violet, where they sold quite well. Monsieur Hivert existed outside politics but had an evident affection for *les Anglos*. Everyone else was constantly scoring points in a permanent Anglo-French tug-of-war about how things should be done.

The differences from French radio and television were enormous. RTF was part of the Ministry of Information, government propagandists. De Gaulle, who often had a bad press, told the journalists at one press conference, 'You may have the press, but I have radio and television.' And it was true. For me, the editorial weakness of RTF threw what we were doing into a new light. I had taken for granted the BBC's distance from government. I now began to realize how much of the Corporation's standing in the world depended on it, and, because of the way it was funded, how vulnerable the BBC might be to the hostility of politicians. No one really respected RTF – not even its senior functionaries, who knew the extent to which they were placemen. Yet outside politics it did good work in documentary and drama, science and the arts.

This period in Paris coincided with the height of the Algerian War, the apogee of Gaullism and a tricky time for our correspondents, who lived on the third floor. Tom Cadett, a legendary figure in Paris journalistic circles, had been *The Times*'s correspondent there before the war, was back for the Liberation, and had survived a scandal when he had run off with the Swedish wife of the Information Councillor of the British Embassy. Tom was of the old school, highly prejudiced and highly respected. His love for France was total, and his contempt for de Gaulle as intense. He lived in a superb apartment at Saint-Cloud with a view of the skyline of Paris over the Bois de Boulogne. The head of the German Air Force had requisitioned it during the war, and Tom kept a lifesize photograph of him in the lavatory. His wife, Hellis, was scatty and elegant, their rows spectacular and their affection profound. Parties at Saint-Cloud were memorable both for the quality of the food and drink and for the emotional fallout, which was often painful. In summer the Cadetts retired to the Ile de Ré, off La Rochelle, where they had a cottage. I am sure Tom had bought it because of the name of the village – Ars!

The junior correspondent was the suave and excellent Peter Raleigh. He was away for most of the time in Algiers, but had a highly authoritative overview of France and its problems and I learnt a great deal from him. I took it for granted that to represent the BBC abroad one should have knowledge, experience and understanding of the country, and that, the longer one stayed somewhere, the more likely it was that one reported its actions and opinions with insight. How oddly that sits in today's world, where largely ignorant young men and women are sent to the world's hot spots with hardly an inkling of where they are or why! Of all the aspects of the BBC's decline in recent years, the most damaging for me has been the virtual disappearance of really authoritative news reporting. Gender balance and regional accents seem to count for more than knowledge, while no one bothers any more about correct pronunciation of foreign names or places.

My particular friend on the third floor, the den mother of the news operation in Paris, was a remarkable Berlin-born woman called Eva Dreyfuss. Daughter of a famous singer, she had grown up in the privileged atmosphere of the Jewish intellectual community of Grunewald in the 1920s. She left Berlin in 1933 and settled in France. Tom discovered her a day or two after arriving in the city at the Liberation, and she had helped to run the BBC operations ever since. Short and stout, with frizzy ginger hair and a superb sense of irony, she was trilingual, although I rarely heard her speak German. She had spent the war in the unoccupied zone, selling handbags in Montpellier, but never knowing when the next Jewish round-up would happen. She had, as was so often the case, become more French than the French, and retained an amused detatchment in her dealings with the English. She once said, 'I know your language and your country. It is your reaction to things I find hard to guess. You are so unpredictable.' She lived in a tiny apartment high above Les Halles, and from the first day adopted me as more than just a colleague. On that first day Robin had an office lunch and deputed Eva to take me out. We went to an oyster bar around the corner, and for the first time in my life I realized there was more than one kind of oyster. I could not count how many dozens we dispatched during the next twenty-five years, but the memory of them is the more poignant now that a permanent allergy prevents me from indulging in what had become my favourite food.

If I stress first of all the social side of the Paris office, it is because my colleagues did so much to make me feel welcome – and I needed it, for I found the city unfriendly and most of its inhabitants hostile. Part of this, ironically, was because my French was too good. People seemed irritated by this, as if I was trying to pass myself off as French. 'Why do you have no accent?' they would ask me indignantly. How does one reply? At times, especially when I could not find a word, I would put on an English accent to show that I was just a stupid foreigner. Often I encountered bad-tempered impatience. Cecilia, despite her long residence in France, had retained strong vestiges of an English accent. Everyone adored it. 'Que c'est charmant, ce petit accent,' people would exclaim, while I tried to keep pace with her constant references to Albert, Simone, Jean-Paul and Nancy. She was the world's greatest name-dropper, but she really did know Camus, de Beauvoir, Sartre and Mitford, and they admired her. One day, going home for lunch in her Deux Chevaux, she ran out of petrol in the Place de la Concorde. She got out and stood by the car, hoping for help. It came quickly in the shape of a gesticulating figure who made his way to her side. It was Camus.

I was the only unmarried Brit on the staff, and everyone imagined that I was having a whale of a time as a free agent in Paris. In fact I had never been more alone than in those first few months. It did not take long to discover that Maud was filleting the post every day, keeping anything of interest for herself and passing on the boring routine things to me. At first I found it difficult to understand voices on the telephone – the sound quality was so inferior to that of British equipment – and we did a great deal of our work on the phone. Oddly, both problems completely disappeared after my first trip away from Paris, when I went to Berlin for a few days. Maud realized that I was ultimately going to win and resigned, and the voices on the phone no longer confused me. Things fell into place.

My long weekend in Berlin was part of a new freedom that came because for the first time I was reasonably well-off. As an international public servant, I was not subject to income tax on my London salary and the rent of my flat in Paris was paid by the BBC. I had a small cost-of-living allowance too. I could hire cars when I needed them, and during the two years I was there I discovered much more of France than I had seen before. I could also afford a weekend abroad at least once a month – Switzerland, the Netherlands, Germany and occasionally, of course, visiting my parents in England. They rather regretted my departure, but regular phone calls kept us in touch. There was no direct dialling in those days, and I became adept at spelling out English names for the French telephonists. I can still manage 'Christchurch' at speed: 'Célestin, Henri, Raoul, Irène, Suzanne, Thérèse, Célestin, Henri, Ursule, Raoul, Célestin, Henri'. I went to concerts, the opera and the theatre, and saw every interesting new film. But it was nearly a year before I made any real friends outside the office, so I threw myself into the work, which was varied rather than demanding.

Sadly, Robin resigned from the BBC only a couple of months after my arrival, but he and his wife stayed on in Paris, where he set up an independent television recording company with a chancy American partner. He was replaced by the producer with whom I had worked in Moscow, Noble Wilson – a nice man and a patient boss, but much more formal and without Robin's mass of contacts in France. Robin had been invalided out of the RAF and had spent part of the war in Bush House, running and presenting one of the key programmes of the French Service, called *Les Français parlent aux Français*. It was often used to transmit coded messages to the Resistance. Everyone knew Robin's voice, and the combination of Robin and Tom Cadett gave the BBC a very special entrée into French politics and life. Cecilia provided the cultural background. Robin knew the world of show business inside-out and he made me realize the remarkable power of access that the BBC had. Even the fact that we were called 'Bi Bi See', not 'Bay Bay Say', was part of the special relationship. But it was under threat. De Gaulle – surrounded by a curious mixture of supporters, from gurus like Malraux to near-criminals like the Interior Minister Roger Frey – was no friend of Britain.

It was during my first months there that the campaign of plastic bombs started in Paris, and I learnt never to leave the house without my papers. We all had press passes countersigned by the Matignon, the French Foreign Office. These got us through barricades and helped distance us from the police and the CRS riot squads, with their truncheons. My friend Patrick Garland was trying to become a writer on the Left Bank. Coming face to face with a *manifestation* one day, he produced his passport and was smartly whacked on the head by a CRS with the words 'Take that for Joan of Arc!' Fifteen years after the war, there were many areas where Britain was no longer popular or admired. We had spurned the European initiatives of Jean Monnet and Robert Schuman, de Gaulle was detaching France from NATO, and the difficulties of French disengagement from Africa were putting old friends on opposing sides.

Much of my work was in support of BBC News and Current Affairs. It could be simply going to the airport to assist through Customs a can of film coming from Peter Raleigh or Robert Kee in Algiers, or it could be providing interview subjects for *Panorama* and other political slots. All the leading reporters came through Paris, and I looked after Robin Day and James Mossman on many occasions. Quite often the weekend would be spent with the *Panorama* team, and through them I met many of the leading figures in the French political world – Jules Moch, Guy Mollet, François Mitterrand, Maurice Schumann, Alain Peyrefitte. I spent a Sunday with Robin Day at Jean Monnet's house in the country, and heard the great man himself explaining patiently and persuasively why Europe needed Britain, and why Europe without Britain would achieve less than its true potential. He spoke with such clarity and modesty that I felt moved and enthused, and I have never lost that feeling, despite the ups and downs of the intervening years. Regularly into the studios came the commentators, among them Jean-Jacques Servan-Schreiber and his cousin Jean-Claude, representing two quite different tendencies in French politics. We kept an index of those relatively few who would consent to be interviewed in English. How different from today, when it seems that almost everyone in French public life speaks

English well enough to be interviewed! We also had an index of those few British politicians who could be spoken to in French. Neither list was long, but the British list remains today as small as it was forty years ago. Part of Tony Blair's popularity in France is because he doesn't sound like Edward Heath or Margaret Thatcher when speaking French.

It was easy to see why de Gaulle was so admired by people like Paulette in the office. He had given back to France a sense of greatness and international standing after the ludicrous parade of temporary coalitions under the Fourth Republic, with a change of government every few months. But there was a price to pay – a sense that France was becoming more authoritarian, more chauvinistic, a less comfortable place to live and work, especially for a foreigner. One eyed the police with suspicion, and wondered how many in public office were lining their pockets. Yet, as always, for much of the time life went on as usual. I remember an evening when I went to a piano recital at the Théâtre des Champs-Élysées and had supper with some friends afterwards. On arriving home after midnight, I learnt from the radio that more than twenty people had been killed in a confrontation between the police and Algerians in the Métro on the other side of the city. The memory of this makes me sceptical of the historical hindsight that insists that people in the past must always have known what was going on. Even in our age of rapid communications, with radio and television, one only had a limited view.

It was always curious to turn from the world of *Panorama* to the other demands London made on us. Noble Wilson went to Le Mans for the Twenty-four Hours, since he enjoyed it. I preferred rugby with Peter West, on a gantry high above the stands at Colombes, or, more elegantly, tennis with Max Robertson at Roland-Garros, crouching over a telephone, hoping I heard the cue when the time came for our insert. The Paris collections brought an influx of fashion editors and frou-frou. Ginette Spanier, the *directrice* of Balmain, was a jolly woman from Golders Green who had made a successful career in Paris. Always surrounded by famous clients, she often invited me for drinks. It was in her house that I met Claudette Colbert, who offered me her house in Tahiti for a holiday. The airfare would have cost four months' salary! Ingrid Bergman was living in Paris. I organized a viewing of the recording she made in London of *Anna Karenina*, and was depressed to find her both cold and charmless; I had idolized her when young. I was asked to invite Olivia de Havilland, married to the Editor of *Paris-Match*, to London for an interview about her autobiography. A surreal conversation ensued in which she refused to believe I was who I said I was. Eventually she was reluctantly convinced, but told me that Dirk Bogarde regularly played practical jokes on her and that she was sure that I was him, since our voices were so similar. Bogarde himself came to film an appeal for Hertford Hospital, and was as charming as I expected.

It was at Ginette's that I met Marlene Dietrich. She was, in that setting, straightforward, extremely intelligent about politics and quite without grand manners. She came to dinner at Noble Wilson's and taught us all to pour orange juice on strawberries. I asked her to do an interview about a documentary on the Third Reich for which she had spoken the commentary. She accepted at once, and said, 'No fee.' She gave me her number. The following day I rang. She exploded with indignation: how had I got hold of this number? Of course she would not cooperate. It was bewildering. On one occasion she was doing her show at the Olympia and, instead of staying with Ginette, booked into the Lancaster Hotel. I saw her letter to Ginette, asking her to provide an iron, a hairdryer and a typewriter. This was a star's life – holed up in an hotel, ironing, washing her hair and typing letters. But Dietrich was a professional telephone-user: Ginette said she ran up a weekly bill of hundreds and hundreds of dollars.

The Lancaster Hotel also entered my life during the famous elopement of Elizabeth Taylor and Richard Burton. Burton had agreed to take part in a special radio programme for Wales on St David's Day. When I finally reached him on the phone, he said there was no problem: he would walk round to the office on Saturday afternoon. Like the Ritz in London, the Lancaster has no back door, the staff exit being next to the public entrance. The world's press was camped out in front of the hotel, but Burton turned up dressed as a chef, with cheesecloth trousers and a beret. He sat down in the studio, immediately established a total rapport with Jean-Paul Dupuy, and recited great chunks of Dylan Thomas and Shakespeare from memory in that extraordinary voice. No one could have been easier or nicer.

Then there were tip-offs. One morning Peter Raleigh dragged me out of the office into a taxi. We rushed to an address in the fashionable sixteenth arrondissement and, having passed through a couple of security searches, found ourselves face to face with Patrice Lumumba, the

Marxist leader of the rebellion in the Congo. In the middle of the crisis he had come to Paris to seek support. He was indignant, volatile but eventually unable to explain where, other than the Soviet Union, his funding was coming from. On another day I was summoned to a bar in the Rue de l'Étoile, where, in the corner, Orson Welles was holding court. He had just finished shooting *The Trial* in the then deserted Gare d'Orsay. We got in to see Roger Frey, the Interior Minister, on the day tanks were circling the boulevards of Paris against a suspected invasion by the paratroops in defence of the French presence in Algeria.

One morning in the studio, while I was quietly recording a piece for *Today*, to which I regularly contributed lightweight stories from Paris, the door opened and an expressive gesture from a pair of exquisite long-fingered hands broke my concentration. It was Jean Cocteau. Out of affection for the BBC, he wanted to paint a mural on the wall of the studio and had come to measure it. A few days later he dropped by in the evening and an Orpheus face was rapidly sketched across the whole wall. I was deputed to buy him a thank-you present when next in London, and I bought a beautiful George II candle-snuffer and scissors. My colleagues thought it a very odd choice. Happily Cocteau was delighted. He later told me he took it everywhere – perhaps an exaggeration, but a charming thing to say.

Every week someone famous came into my life, and most of them were fun and lived up to their reputation. But not so Maurice Chevalier. He had been asked to take part in an edition of *This is Your Life* about Margaret Lockwood, whose first appearance on the screen had been in a 1930s musical starring Chevalier. We went to his beautiful house in the Chevreuse valley outside Paris, admired his Monets and Pissarros, and he appeared immaculate in a Prince of Wales check suit and with a gleaming silver toupee. He went into the routine with the famous accent and persuasive charm – 'Oh Maggie, how well I remember you' etc. When we finished, he said to us, 'Stupid bitch! She had no talent then or ever. Why should I remember her?' We were not even offered a coffee, let alone a drink. No one got anything for nothing out of Chevalier. I told Monsieur Hivert, but he was phlegmatic. 'Life wasn't easy for him,' he said. 'Easier than it has been for you,' I thought.

The BBC system entailed your boss writing an annual report on you, which you were then given to read and to discuss with someone higher up the tree. Being in an outpost, Noble Wilson not only had to write the report but give the interview as well. He was obviously slightly embarrassed, saying that, although the report was good, he had had to make one unfavourable comment. I reread the report and couldn't find anything at all hostile or critical in it. He pointed to the sentence 'He does not suffer fools gladly.' 'But', I protested, 'that's a compliment.' 'Not in the BBC it's not.' When I asked why the fools were in the organization, he sighed wearily and said I had much to learn. Oddly, learning about the BBC was what I did most in Paris, since we received copies of all the top management papers – records of board meetings and programme discussions. As a junior assistant, I was very privileged to be reading policy documents that even heads of department in London might not see. It gave me an overview of the organization that was unequalled at my level anywhere.

The office also brought me into contact with literally hundreds of my colleagues. In an average year over six hundred visitors turned up, ranging from the Director-General to research assistants. I got to know Howard Newby, the then Controller of Radio 3, Martin Esslin, Head of Drama, Paul Fox, Editor of *Panorama*, Huw Wheldon, Editor of *Monitor*, and dozens of others. I looked after all the TV people, and Cecilia always invited me to the lunches she gave for the Radio bosses in their elegant appartment in Rue Casimir-Périer, opposite the spires of Sainte-Clothilde. Much as I enjoyed meeting the well-known names of BBC Radio, it was the Television contacts that promised most for the future.

I made regular duty visits to London, and was invited to watch programmes being recorded or transmitted. In this way I finally got to meet Grace Wyndham Goldie, the powerful and opinionated Head of Talks. It was she who had managed to abolish the absurd Ten-Day Rule, which forbade the discussion on television of any political issue within ten days of its coming before the House. She had encouraged Donald Baverstock to establish *Tonight*, and trained his successor, Alasdair Milne. She was an alarming figure – short and aggressive – and meeting her was always risky, especially on evenings when the gin bottle had been circulating freely in the hospitality suite.

I went to Lime Grove to a *Panorama* transmission, invited by the Editor, Paul Fox. Fox had been the Editor of sports programmes before, but was a total television professional, always clear about what he wanted and scrupulous about ringing me up in Paris to thank me when I had spent the weekend working with the *Panorama* team. Robin Day had been with us often; I almost became accustomed to the clouds of cigar smoke he blew all over me at ten in the morning. James Mossman seemed to me quite different from the average journalist or reporter – much more interested in culture, with a febrile intensity which overrode any attempt at neutrality. He cared passionately about issues, eventually burning his boats in Current Affairs because of his confrontational attitude to politicians, all of whom were still treated with an almost obsequious politeness by most other interviewers. Dimbleby was the cynosure of those who, like my father, thought that anyone in a position of authority deserved respect. Mossman, and to a considerable extent Robert Kee, thought that politicians were there to answer to the public. It is a tension that still continues today with the contrasting approaches of David Dimbleby and Jeremy Paxman in television, or James Naughtie and John Humphreys in radio. At that time no one would have dreamt of interrupting all the time, but then it was more likely that the politician would at least make an attempt to answer the question rather than seek refuge in evasiveness and irrelevance or the soundbites offered today. I felt myself drawn closer than ever before to the area of news and current affairs and the cut and thrust of political discussion. Yet, just as the teaching of history had seemed one-sided at Cambridge, so political broadcasting omitted so much that was a part of life. I have never lost my interest in what is happening in the world of politics – I still feel starved without a daily injection of news and comment – but I was not certain that that was where I wanted to end up, despite the friendliness of colleagues.

Grace Wyndham Goldie, who had never responded to my previous approaches, now asked me to go and see her to discuss my future. Later that day I saw her throw a bottle at a rather dim secretary. One had to question if not her judgement, then certainly her behaviour. (Later, watching the way she promoted people like Michael Peacock, I came to question her judgement too.) Meanwhile, Huw Wheldon had also asked me to go to Ealing Studios to talk to him. He had been through the Paris office on two or three occasions, and I had got to know him slightly. He had never seemed much interested in other people or their views, but he took me out to lunch in a pub across the road from the Ealing Studios and gave me a ruthlessly thorough catechism about the whole field of the arts. He was extremely friendly, and I opened up easily to him about my hopes and ambitions for the future. He gave me to understand that he might well be interested in involving me with *Monitor* if a job came up. Nothing was promised, but I went away very hopeful.

Meanwhile my friend Patrick Garland had been offered a short-term research-assistant post with *Monitor*. He had been a very successful actor and director at Oxford, where I had met him through Anthony Bosworth, the Bodmin Othello. Patrick had played a number of roles in Peter Dews's brilliant television adaptation of Shakespeare's history plays, under the title *The Age of Kings* – a milestone in bringing Shakespeare to a wider audience. When the series was subsequently sold to the USA, he received a totally unexpected royalty and decided to spend time in Paris furthering his deep wish to be a writer. But by now his money was running out, and one evening he told me he had had two job offers: the *Monitor* research-assistant post and the post of secretary to Baron Philippe de Rothschild, the translator of Christopher Fry's plays into French and owner of the legendary Mouton vineyard. The Baron and his wife, Pauline, knew everyone and went everywhere. But I remember saying that Patrick should remember that being secretary to a Rothschild was not quite the same thing as being a Rothschild himself. In the end, Patrick chose London.

A couple of months later a production-assistant job on *Monitor* was advertised. My appointment in Paris had been for two years, but with an understanding that if after one year I found another job within the BBC I could return to London, otherwise I was obliged to stay for the second year. Interesting though the Paris job was, I thought I had got the best out of it after nearly a year, so I applied for the *Monitor* post and went to London for an interview. I was given a very hard time, and I saw quite a different side to Wheldon. Patrick had also applied, and he too had a difficult board. We waited for the result, only to be told a week later that no one had been found suitable and no appointment had been made. It was a much worse slap in the face than if somebody else had got it. The idea that none of us – neither Patrick, myself nor the other six applicants – was good enough was not only damaging but wrong, as time would prove. I later understood that Wheldon had always wanted Patrick, but, since he was much less experienced than many of the other candidates, felt unable to take him at this stage. As for me, it meant I was now obliged to spend a second year in France.

Unexpectedly it all turned out for the best, since I enjoyed my second year very much more than the first, and a year later changes to BBC Television were to create a lot of new opportunities for people with my interests. Happily the Monitor affair had no effect on my friendship with Patrick, who went on to make some splendid television programmes and to run the Chichester Festival. He remains one of the most amusing and intelligent of all my friends – quite unfazed by international glamour, as his slyly affectionate book about Rex Harrison proves.

One of the reasons why Paris got better was through a chance invitation from the television music producer Charles Rogers to the Danish dancer Flemming Flindt to take part in an edition of the monthly programme *Gala Performance* in London. Like its predecessor, *Music for You*, *Gala Performance* contained music, opera and dance with a string of big names. Patricia Foy had created *Music for You* with the oleaginous Eric Robinson as presenter/conductor, but with regular appearances by people like Margot Fonteyn, Yehudi Menuhin and Tito Gobbi; it achieved an enormous audience – over ten million on occasions. *Gala Performance* never did quite so well, but it was an integral part of BBC music scheduling. I never understood why later Controllers abandoned it – it was a perfectly respectable way of introducing a wide audience to great music, and the performers were always of the highest standard. Flindt had been a leading dancer with London Festival Ballet, where I had seen him often and met him occasionally. He was now a star of the Paris Opéra Ballet, and in a close relationship with his French partner, Josette Amiel. I arranged for them both to go to London, where they danced an excerpt from the Russian version of *La Fille mal gardée*.

Josette spoke no English and Flemming's French was at that time only fair, so I found myself in a kind of non-sexual *ménage à trois*, travelling at weekends with one or both of them on guest appearances in other cities – Zurich, Marseilles, Basle, and Munich. Josette was enchanting in a totally Parisian way – pretty, amusing, with a distinctly dirty laugh, and wonderful company. Flemming was intelligent, ambitious and a real *danseur noble* – and a good actor too. We saw a great deal of each other, and through them I got to know most of the dancers on the Paris scene, both at the Opéra and in the itinerant community, which included stars like Erik Bruhn. Bruhn was quite simply the best male dancer I had ever seen, with his aristocratic bearing and perfect technique. Very much a loner, he eventually became involved with the newly defected Nureyev, and his dancing was undermined by alcohol and unhappiness. But at that time he was supreme.

On my trips around Europe with Flemming and Josette, I got to know most of the leading figures in dance at that time – people like Roland Petit and Zizi Jeanmaire, whom I had first seen in Paris after the war and who came regularly to London in the 1950s. I loved both of them, with their very French allure – Roland's witty originality and Zizi's magical charm. Flemming introduced me to Georges Balanchine. We spent a long evening asking him endless questions about his works and his prejudices about narrative in dance. 'I will not do narrative ballets until it is possible in purely choreographic terms to say, "This is my brother-in-law,"' he told us. It was a familiar remark, but fascinating to have it from him directly, drinking Roederer Cristal in Fouquet's on the Champs-Élysées – his favourite place, he said, since Tchaikovsky used to go there.

Flemming had choreographic ambitions himself, and one day he rather shyly asked if I knew a play of Ionesco's called *La Leçon*. Indeed I did. I had a particular liking for Ionesco's surreal humour, and had enjoyed early productions of his work that I had seen in England and in France. Flemming approached him and asked for permission to adapt the play, changing the lesson from one in mathematics to one in dance. Ionesco was intrigued and agreed, and Flemming worked out a new scenario, which he showed me. Ionesco was small, round and jolly, with a fierce wife and a plain daughter. I remember Madame Ionesco watching him like a hawk, worrying about how much he was drinking and constantly saying, 'Eugène, arrête! Eugène, je t'en prie!' as he helped himself to another whisky. We went in search of a composer. Hindemith was passing through Paris, and we contacted him. He was, to my great surprise, absolutely delightful – very far from the crusty German professor I had expected. But he turned us down. 'I am an old man,' he said, 'and I want to do cheerful things. This story is much too depressing.' We eventually settled on the French film-music composer Georges Delerue.

In August 1963 *The Lesson* was about to be recorded by Danish Television, and Flemming insisted that I went to Copenhagen. I was immediately captivated by the friendliness, hospitality and wonderful food, but also by the marvellous dance tradition stemming from August Bournonville, the great nineteenth-century French choreographer who had made his career in Copenhagen. Denmark has always produced better male dancers than female, and the Bournonville style is at the heart of it. His ballets were also full of roles for older dancers, and it was a pleasure to see dancers of the right age, with real experience, in senior roles. The downside of this, of course, was that, since dancers were there for life, the talented young often found it necessary to move elsewhere, as Flemming and Bruhn had done, and as the brilliant eighteen-year-old Peter Martins, whom I also saw that year, was to do later on his way to run New York City Ballet.

The happiness of my first visit to Copenhagen was in strong contrast to the trip's continuation, with my friend John Tydeman, to Stockholm, where we singularly failed to enjoy ourselves. Having walked out of one much vaunted restaurant because it smelt strongly of cat piss, we ended up in the famous Ratskeller, in the cellars of the Town Hall. A man at the next table fell senseless into his soup, overcome by schnapps. After a day or two I hot-footed it back to Denmark, where Ionesco had by now arrived and the parties were continuing. I now know Stockholm much better and find it as lively and as interesting as anywhere else, but that first impression is hard to forget. Yet it occurs to me that coldness and rudeness are the impression that many foreigners have about Britain.

The departure of Maud had meant that I now had the pick of the television work, which included arranging all the film sequences for the *Maigret* series, then at the height of its popularity. I would be asked to provide ten gendarmes, a stretcher party, an ambulance and a quantity of old Citroën cars at some location fifty kilometres from Paris. On one occasion the producers wanted a barge on the Seine, and my researches led me to another new friendship, with a stylish Dutchwoman, Maudie Schilling, who lived with her two small daughters on a converted Dutch canal boat moored opposite the Eiffel Tower. I had moved from my gloomy mezzanine in the seventeenth to a light and airy studio and terrace on the ninth floor of a house in the Rue Copernic, off the Avenue Kléber, nearer the office and a few minutes' walk from Maudie's boat, where I spent many relaxed hours. The boat was big enough to have a baby grand and a dining table that seated twelve. On summer evenings we would sit in the wheelhouse drinking and watching the *bateaux mouches* go by, their glittering lights reflected in the water against the background of the Trocadéro. I could see the Eiffel Tower from my own kitchen window. Making meals, I would watch the lift creeping up and down the Tower and promise myself that one day I would conquer my vertigo and go to the top. I never did, and never have.

So much of Paris life fell into place in that second year. I had a string of little restaurants where I could eat splendidly and quite cheaply. I felt really settled in when I knew where to get shoes repaired, hair cut, suits made and even the one shop in Paris that sold shoes big enough for me. Another new friend was the American writer Mary McCarthy, whose husband was the American Ambassador to the Organization for Economic Cooperation and Development. Mary came to Paris looking like a typical American academic, with rather dowdy clothes and hair scraped back into a bun. Within months she was wearing haute couture and having her hair done by Carita. She was always handsome, with those great eyes and cheekbones, but now she became beautiful and fun to be with – quite different from the other writers I knew, from Ionesco to Nancy Mitford. Nancy was a good friend of Cecilia's, but I found her chilly. All these writers were having huge successes: Mary McCarthy with *The Group*, Nancy Mitford with her biographies of Voltaire and Frederick the Great, and Ionesco, of course, with a steady stream of plays, one of which, *La Cantatrice chauve*, would become for Paris what *The Mousetrap* had become for London, the longest-running play in the history of the theatre.

The other person who became a great friend and a real influence in that second year was Cecilia's husband, Darsie Gillie. Everyone had thought it an improbable match: Darsie was a confirmed bachelor, and Cecilia had had a rather erratic past, including a long relationship with the Cambridge historian Denis Brogan. But it seemed to work perfectly. However, no two men could be less alike than Darsie and Tom Cadett, and they had little time for each other. Darsie was a scholar-journalist. He had spent his early years in Berlin and Warsaw for the old *Morning Post* before joining the *Guardian*. He spoke Polish well, and became a sort of foster father to a group of young Poles who had managed to get out and move to France. He would read Polish poetry to me, especially Adam Mickiewicz, and I would reply by reading him Pushkin. We enjoyed ourselves, but it irritated Cecilia tremendously. I learnt from Darsie how the understanding that came from long residence gave real depth to reporting, even of the simply factual kind. While Tom refused to accept Gaullism, Darsie sought to analyse it and to put it in the context of a proud country which had not won a war for a hundred and thirty years.

Darsie spoke up constantly for minorities. The only dispute we ever had was about the importance of the Welsh language. Darsie's brother was a senior civil servant in Cardiff and in the middle of the language debate. Darsie could not see why I wasn't as passionate as he was about the need to protect Welsh. I sent him a list of over fifty good causes for which my support had been canvassed – from Brighter Cricket to Save the Whales. 'Too many good causes,' I said. Characteristically he replied, 'Never – not if they are really good.'

Darsie was full of recondite and amazing information about French life and attitudes, and became one of those mentors to whom I owe so much. He retired following a stroke shortly after I left Paris, and he and Cecilia went to live in Provence. Cecilia, who in Paris had never prepared a meal – a task left to her faithful maid, Marie – became, to everyone's astonishment, a first-rate cook and wrote a delightful cookery book which unfortunately failed to find a publisher. I suggested it should have been called *Bouches du Rhône*. As *Cecilia's Cookbook* it was eventually privately printed through the assistance of Katherine Whitehorn, another of Cecilia's long-time friends. In the end the Gillies' life was taken over by one of the Polish protégés, a charming man called Stas, who provided nurses to look after Darsie and eventually for Cecilia, who, after Darsie's death, was also incapacitated by a stroke. After the Berlin Wall came down, Stas returned to Poland and improbably took Cecilia with him, and she died there. I can never forget my last encounter with her, in 1995, when, barely able to speak, she showed me a copy of T. S. Eliot's poem *Sweeney Agonistes* and pointed to the lines:

> I gotta use words when I talk to you
> But if you understand or if you don't
> That's nothing to me and nothing to you

I was due to leave Paris and return to London in late November 1963, and had timed my last day in the office with self-indulgent care. I spent the morning at the film studios at Boulogne-Billancourt, where they were making *Topkapi*, and had lunch with Peter Ustinov, interviewing him about the shortly to be opened Nottingham Playhouse, of which he was a director. His accounts of recording wide-screen close-ups with Melina Mercouri were hilarious: she had a slight squint, and he could never quite decide which eye he should look at. It was the first of many happy meetings with the wittiest man I know. Later that afternoon I called on Juliette Greco at her beautiful Left Bank house, and recorded her reading 'The Owl and the Pussycat' in both French and

English for a special Christmas programme. She proved that a mature Frenchwoman can exude sexiness even in a nonsense poem. We drank tea and talked of Sartre, existentialism, Boris Vian and the little black dress. In the early evening I went back to the office with my tape recorder and, in a sentimental mood, decided to have a last drink in the bistro on the corner.

After a few minutes the balding waiter, René, who was part of our lives, came over to me and asked if I had heard the news. It appeared that President Kennedy had been involved in a shooting. I went back to the office. It was a Friday evening and no one was around. Tom Cadett had retired that summer, Peter Raleigh was at a conference in Nice, Noble Wilson was practising Scottish dancing for the Caledonian Ball, and the secretaries had gone back to the suburbs. The telex was spewing paper on to the floor and all the phones were ringing. I sat there wondering what to do. Within an hour the entire office staff had returned to their posts, the retired Tom Cadett was back in the building, and we started to animate a response from France.

I spent most of the night at the RTF headquarters, wheeling in grandees like Maurice Schumann to pay their tributes. The following morning my not very friendly concierge climbed the nine floors to my flat – traditionally she did not use the lift – and asked if I was an American. 'Why?' I asked. 'I wanted to show my sympathy,' she replied. For the next three days we hardly stopped. My farewell party, planned for the day of Kennedy's funeral, had to be postponed, and we lived in a constant atmosphere of activity and deep sadness. I had made a programme about Kennedy for schools at the time of his inauguration. In the world of de Gaulle, Adenauer and Macmillan, he seemed a symbol of a new generation – the first post-war leader with new ideas and a sense of a hopeful future. In France we had little idea of his shortcomings, and even the Cuban Missile Crisis had largely passed us by, since we had been in the depths of the first Gaullist referendum about regional devolution and had eyes only on France. But on his famous visit to Paris with his wife he had won the admiration of the Parisians just as he had later enthused the people of Berlin, and there was now a general feeling of grief and anxiety for the future. Before I left I had a small party on Maud's boat on the river, but my return to England was far from the jolly conclusion that I had hoped for.

I had learnt a great deal in France: about politics and society, but also about what we now call the quality of life. At its most obvious level, they lived very much better in France than we did in London. Attitudes to food and clothes were quite different. Much less importance was given to the idea of home: one was practically never invited into the house of a French colleague or friend – one met them in a bar or a restaurant. I learnt to accept the strange duality of professional colleagues who always used the second-person singular but never the Christian name. I experienced French directness about sexual relations but reticence about friendship. I acquired some of the French impatience and intolerance, and I learnt to respect clarity of expression even when I could not share the ideas or feelings that were being expressed. As all foreigners do, I found the use of phrases like 'le rayonnement de la France' – a favourite of both de Gaulle and Malraux – arrogant and sometimes grotesque, but saw behind it a belief not only in institutions but in ideas and their influence. I liked the seriousness of *Le Monde* and the idiotic flippancy of *France Dimanche*. I fell victim to a still continuing affection for the *chansons* of the *chansonniers*. I was depressed by the decline of painting and sculpture, exhilarated by the cinema, perplexed by the inadequacy of much music-making, but entranced by great artists like Poulenc, Pierre Bernac and Gérard Souzay, all of whom I heard or met. I hated the stilted fossilization of the Comédie-Française, but was thrilled by Jean Vilar at the Théâtre National Populaire.

Above all, I fell in love with the fabric of the city, crumbling and unloved though much of it seemed. I remember an exhibition at the Carnavalet museum called 'Le Renouveau du Marais', about the restoration of that marvellous district of seventeenth- and eighteenth-century palaces which had become a slum in multi-family occupation, full of motorbike repair shops. Eva Dreyfuss's best friends lived in the Place des Vosges, and rats would come out of the wainscot during dinner. Forty years on it is the world capital of high-camp boutiquery, but at least the architecture has been saved.

I learnt to love the changing light in the city, from the grey-brown mornings of winter to the long, pink summer evenings. I miss the dusty smell of the Métro. Today much of Paris feels like anywhere else, with fast-food outlets, traffic and tacky tourist traps. In the 1960s it was closer to the Paris of Picasso and Proust – the Paris of literature and musical comedies and that heady mixture of seediness and elegance, like old hotels, which for me is so typically French. Few countries take so long to get to know as France, but with persistence the rewards are still there, despite the changes. France, and Paris in particular, became part of my life, and, despite some unhappiness, much misunderstanding, many administrative difficulties and frequent irritation, few other places have given me such pleasure or such rewards. I knew I would never really feel abroad again when in France. But not even in my wildest dreams could I have imagined that one day I would wear the ribbon of the Légion d'Honneur.

# 7

# Breaking New Ground

The television service to which I returned in November 1963 was gearing itself up for the launch of BBC2 in the spring of the following year. A considerable expansion of staff would provide programmes for the new network, and there were also new programme areas – an extension in Further Education, and a new unit to make programmes about music. For reasons I have never quite understood, I was asked to contribute to both. It made for a rather disorganized return, with two offices in different buildings and two departments to serve.

Humphrey Burton had been asked to set up a documentary unit for BBC2 parallel to the existing Music Department, which produced only performance programmes. It grew out of the kind of small features that Humphrey had produced for *Monitor*. The most highly regarded director for *Monitor* was Ken Russell, whose film on Elgar had been shown during my time in France, but Humphrey himself had made many short documentaries about musicians, including one on the cellist Paul Tortelier and an important film contrasting the work of Peter Maxwell Davies, at that time a schoolmaster in Cirencester, and Dudley Moore, at the height of his *Beyond the Fringe* fame. Humphrey was heavily backed by Huw Wheldon and authorized to recruit. But Wheldon also knew of my Schools background, and I had told him of my interest in psychiatric medicine. I much admired the work of Hugh Burnett, producer of *Lifelife*, a pioneering programme about mental health.

Rather than working with Burnett, I was offered a series of my own for Further Education, with the doctor then known as 'the Television Psychiatrist', David Stafford Clark. Clark was a consummate television professional, able to interview or summarize exactly to the required length in live programmes and with a sure touch in using his patients to illustrate problems without endangering them or distressing the audience. He taught me a great deal, and encouraged me to visit his clinic at Guy's Hospital and the children's section, with Gerard Vaughan, its Director, later to become a Tory Minister of Health. It was my last experience of educational programming on television, and the resulting programmes were transmitted in the opening weeks of BBC2 as part of what was called *Tuesday Term*.

It is largely forgotten now that BBC2 launched itself with a strait-jacket of bizarre scheduling that would have totally destroyed the network had anyone much watched it. It could be received only in London, and further transmitters were added very slowly. It used 625-line standard, which gave a much improved picture quality but meant buying new equipment to receive it. It broadcast only in the evening, but each day was characterized by a different kind of programme. Monday was entertainment, Tuesday education, Wednesday repeats, and so on. The originator of this ludicrous scheme was Michael Peacock, one of Mrs Goldie's protégés and BBC2's first Controller. Not only was it a bad idea, but no one had given any thought to the need for common junctions with BBC1. In the days before video recording, there was not much point in alternative programming if programmes did not at least start or finish at the same time on the two networks.

The launch was frustrated by a massive power cut that blacked out most of London. BBC2 had chosen to open with a studio recording of *Kiss Me Kate*, starring Howard Keel. I missed it, since I was in the Royal Festival Hall watching a film of Furtwängler conducting *Don Giovanni* at a Salzburg Festival in the late 1940s. As with the Paris riots, I had no idea what had happened until I got home.

I was studying *Don Giovanni* because of one of Humphrey's projects for BBC2 with the Music Group involved transmitting a recording that would be made of the opera at that year's Aix-en-Provence Festival. My task was to provide a documentary element to cover the intervals. Oddly, many of the projects in my first years back with the BBC involved France, and I spent so much time there that friends claimed I had never left.

My first series for BBC2 was a set of six masterclasses with Paul Tortelier. Humphrey Burton's *Monitor* film about Tortelier had contained a short sequence of him teaching, and it was so original and entertaining that Humphrey sought to expand it. I knew Tortelier well as a soloist, but had never met him. We spent some days auditioning possible participants. One famous London teacher said, 'I am not having that bloody Frenchman coming over here filching my pupils', but most were only too happy to cooperate, even if Tortelier's methods were rather different from what prevailed in London. Jacqueline du Pré had been notably unhappy with Tortelier during a brief period of study in Paris – largely because she refused to adapt to the French system of public classes and the use of solfège. My great ally in the whole project was the pianist Geoffrey Parsons, with whom this first encounter led to an enduring and close friendship. Parsons was one of the finest musicians and most generous men I have ever met, and he gave invaluable support to me, to Tortelier and to the students. In one weekend in the small studio at Riverside in Hammersmith we made six masterclass programmes on six different composers – Boccherini, Debussy, Elgar, Dvořák, Bach and Brahms. It was a tour de force for Tortelier, and tested my directing ability to the full, since it was over three years since I had been in the studio.

Tortelier not only looked marvellous, with his striking profile and wild hair, but played superbly and also had a way with words. In his much imitated French accent, he would intervene with remarks that often seemed to have little to do with music, but were likely to stimulate both students and the television audience. In the Debussy Sonata, a masterpiece that the pupils were making very little of, he suddenly said, 'Excuse me to stop you. For once in your life you must swim in the sea naked [pronounced as one syllable] and then *perhaps* you understand Debussy.' Even this simple format – a teacher, two pupils and a pianist – generated all the different choices involved in televising music. What is the best image to make you listen? Watching Tortelier demonstrate, what mattered most: his bowing arm, his fingering hand or his face? It was impossible to include all three without pulling back so far that detail of the hands was barely visible. How often should one show the accompanying pianist? Television direction is about choices, and there is always a tension between what the layman wants – usually a personality – and what specialists might expect, which is to see the technique. I did my best, missing some things and capturing others.

The programmes were widely reviewed and Tortelier was much admired. I was reasonably pleased with the results, but I reckoned without Wheldon, who accused me of being without feeling, sympathy or understanding. What he, a non-musician, wanted was a big close-up of Tortelier's face – a marvellous image, but pointless if that was all you saw. The post-mortem on the Tortelier classes was the start of many years of having everything I did torn to shreds by Wheldon, now my head of department. Nothing I did, it seemed, was any good at all. He would often come into the office I shared with the director Barrie Gavin – a former film editor, passionate about both new and traditional music – and sit on the radiator and harangue us. I respected him and admired his editorial instinct; he was full of good ideas and stimulating initiatives. I wanted to be liked in return. But it was not to be. I came to resent his hostility, because where music was concerned he was a complete ignoramus, yet daily we had his views rammed down our throats. His particular bête noire was architecture, and through all his time on *Monitor* and as Head of Documentaries next to nothing was ever done on this subject. 'Buildings are bores, people are fun,' he would thunder. Once I got a chance I was determined to prove him wrong. But for the moment I tried to keep out of his way.

Luckily there was Humphrey Burton, who had a real gift for encouraging people. He taught me how to write film commentary, relating words to pictures in a way which would illuminate both, never saying what viewers can already see for themselves except to identify people or places. It's quite a skill, and one never mastered by some producers, who simply write a script and find some pictures to accompany it. The key thing about television is that you look first and listen second – a real problem when it comes to music. In concert relays, chasing tunes round the orchestra can be well or badly done, but even at its best there is a tension between the image of the player and the sound – especially with wind and brass instruments, which demand a physical effort which is often unattractive to watch. But we were not there to do concerts. Humphrey brought into our group only one member of the existing department, the charmingly suave and civilized Walter Todds, who had wanted to be a singer, had taught at Dartington, and became an effective radio producer before moving to television. He directed quite a few studio recitals and concerts, and I watched his work closely, for it grew out of a real perception of the demands of the score, rather than just the attraction of the performer. The best-known concert director was an Outside Broadcast producer, Anthony Craxton, from a family of musicians. On the opening Sunday of BBC2 he directed the Verdi *Requiem*, live from the Festival Hall, with Carlo Maria Giulini conducting. I produced the interval feature, which included the veteran broadcaster Alec Robertson and the critic Philip Hope-Wallace in conversation with David Attenborough.

What was exciting with the new Music Group for BBC2 was the feeling of a small team of people all pooling their ideas. Humphrey invented a monthly series called *Workshop*, which could be about anything. We began with a programme about Paganini's Twenty-Fourth

Caprice, with its dozens of versions and variants by later composers. Subsequently, no one could remember whose idea it was – it had come out of an argumentative lunch at which Barrie Gavin, Walter Todds, Herbert Chapell (recently recruited from Schools Radio) and I brainstormed with Humphrey for a couple of hours. This was all virgin territory. No one before had treated music in this semi-documentary way. Russell was making his composer portraits, with Oliver Reed as Debussy but looking exactly like Ken Russell, and the opera and ballet producers continued their relays and studio productions. But we aimed to fill in the context, ranging from Denis Matthews on Beethoven's notebooks to H. C. Robbins Landon on Haydn – standing in front of the orchestra and race-reading like Peter O'Sullevan at Ascot.

Walter Todds devised a programme showing a composer working with a director to produce the camera script the composer wanted. For this, Michael Tippett came into the studio to watch Walter direct cameras on a performance of his Double Concerto with the strings of the London Symphony Orchestra conducted by Colin Davis. In the adjoining studio I directed a second unit watching Walter choosing his shots and Tippett intervening. The victim was always poor Colin – time and again Tippett removed the shots of the conductor, insisting that the music was telling the story, not the gestures. It was a real battle, and eventually the first half of the programme, showing the rehearsals, was riveting, while the subsequent performance – with invisible conductor – was quite dull. Television, it would seem, needed a 'personality' to hold a performance together and make it come alive. Highly visual conductors like Leonard Bernstein, André Previn and Georg Solti worked better on screen than calmer maestros like Adrian Boult, Colin Davis and Pierre Monteux, since they provided more involving images, but I could always hear the voice of Adrian Boult saying, 'If you need to do so much in performance, you can't have achieved much in rehearsal.'

I made two programmes with the conductor and critic Bernard Keeffe. The first was about the evolution of the symphony, ending with an analysis and performance of Brahms's Third, one of the most unjustly neglected works in the repertory. I though it went quite well, and I hoped Keeffe would be pleased. 'They always give me the beginners' was his charmless response. The second programme was to lead to one of my happiest friendships. Entitled *The Life and Death of a Hero*, it traced the development of the piano concerto from Mozart to

Bartók, by way of Beethoven, Schumann, Brahms, Tchaikovsky and Rachmaninov. The pianist was Julius Katchen.

I had first heard Katchen fifteen years earlier, when he was very young and newly arrived in Europe. He had played the Grieg Concerto with the Bournemouth Orchestra under Charles Groves. It was quite simply the worst performance I had ever heard, and I could not believe the reputation the pianist had. We met eventually in Manchester, where Walter Todds was recording a performance of the Liszt A major Concerto under Barbirolli. I took to Katchen at once; he was amusing, intelligent, widely travelled, and packed with enthusiasm and good sense. When we knew each other better I asked him about the performance in Bournemouth. He was appalled that I remembered it. It turned out that until shortly before he had thought he was playing the Schumann Concerto, and had then learnt the Grieg in two days. In addition, he had had an acute stomach upset and really should not have been playing at all. He told this modestly, with no sense of self-justification. 'It was quite awful,' he said, and I knew I had made a friend. During the next few years I was to make many programmes with him and spend time in Paris or on tour both with him and with his highly attractive French wife, Arlette.

Julius had been a prodigy, playing his first concerto with the New York Philharmonic under Barbirolli when he was nine, and infuriating Barbirolli by pointing out an error in the orchestral accompaniment that the conductor had noticed but couldn't pinpoint. 'It's the second clarinet,' piped the child. Julius was still nervous of Barbirolli in Manchester all those years later. Through Julius I met the teacher and pianist Ilona Kabos, former wife of the pianist Louis Kentner, and den mother of the large band of émigré Hungarian musicians in London. Before they met, Julius had asked Ilona to come to an afternoon recital he was giving at the Festival Hall. She refused, but asked him to call on her later that afternoon. 'How did it go?' she asked. 'Marvellously,' said Julius. (It came out as 'mawvellously', just as he also said 'Brawms'.) 'Really?' she said. 'Marvellous, was it? All of it?' He was adamant it had been a big success. 'Well,' she said, 'you have been playing the piano in public for the best part of two hours. Are you really telling me that nothing went wrong?' 'Well,' said Julius, 'there were one or two things . . .' 'Good,' she said – 'now we can be friends.' From then on he regularly played for her and asked her advice. Through Ilona I met the conductor Eugene Ormandy, the pianist Peter Frankl and the violinist György Pauk. The Hungarian community was ubiquitous in those years, especially with Solti at the Royal Opera House.

I often asked myself what right had I, without musical qualifications or critical standing, to be mixing in this company. I gave thanks to the Bournemouth Music Library, to my mother's collection of lieder and songs, and to years of listening to concerts, reading programme notes and biographies, and trying to compose programmes myself. I may not have had professional training, but I had more than just a casual interest. When it came to repertory, I found that much that I knew was unknown to some of my professional colleagues. Even a pianist with a huge repertoire like Katchen did not know the Balakirev Sonata I had heard Kentner play, or the Barcarolles of Fauré that I had learnt from the French pianist Marguerite Long. Not only did I know a lot of music, I remembered it, where I had heard it and who had performed it. What was especially thrilling now was to have at my disposal the BBC's Music and Gramophone libraries. I had never been able to afford to collect gramophone records, and in truth was not terribly fond of recordings, except as a way of getting to know music. Now every weekend I would take home piles of LPs, listening to works I did not yet know and most particularly to the performances of musicians who were no longer around but who had huge reputations. I had seen Bruno Walter, Pierre Monteux, Charles Munch and Thomas Beecham, but not Toscanini, Furtwängler, Mengelberg or Weingartner. I had heard Schnabel, Cortot, Michelangeli and Lipatti, but never Backhaus, Rachmaninov or Gieseking. I had heard Flagstad, Hotter, Gobbi and Christoff, but not Lehmann, Leider, Melchior or Ponselle. I was learning to set the present against the background of previous performing practice and to put music in context. Listening to Klemperer in his increasingly glacial old age made much more sense when you had heard Furtwängler. Callas's originality and intelligence were enhanced by knowledge of a previous generation of uninvolving bel-canto singers.

The 1960s were a good time for orchestras and singers and for interest in the music of my own time. As was the case for everyone brought up in England during the war, for me new music was Walton and Britten, and to a much lesser extent Tippett. I must have been nearly thirty before I heard much Schoenberg, Berg or Webern. I knew something of the British serialists Humphrey Searle and Elizabeth Lutyens, but was not really convinced by their music. My eventual conviction of the importance of the Second Viennese School was a result of the arrival in Britain of Pierre Boulez, at just about the time of my return from Paris. I had heard Boulez conduct small forces in the theatre, notably for Jean-Louis Barrault, but the revelation of his status as a symphonic conductor came in May 1963, during my second year in Paris. It was the fiftieth anniversary of the first performance of *The Rite of Spring*. London had Monteux and Stravinsky (just, for he did not attend the performance, only arriving late to take the applause at the end), while in Paris we had the very building in the Théâtre des Champs-Élysées where the première had taken place as part of the Ballets Russes' first season in that new theatre. Boulez's programme was immense: the *Études for Orchestra*, *A Sermon, a Narrative and a Prayer*, *Symphonies of Wind Instruments*, *The King of the Stars* and, naturally, as conclusion, *The Rite of Spring*. It was overwhelming, as if I had never heard the piece before – which in a sense I had not, since Boulez's performance had an accuracy and precision far removed from the enthusiastic but approximate versions that I now realize were all that I had known previously. I was carried away, and the following day, taking my courage in my hands, I rang the BBC's Controller of Music, William Glock, whom I did not know. I expressed my excited enthusiasm. 'Yes,' he said patiently, 'I know all about it and we're in touch.' Boulez made his debut with the BBC Symphony Orchestra later that year. By 1964, when I was making my first contributions to the Music Group of BBC2, he was keen to cooperate.

Unlike many musicians, Boulez could see the importance of television. The main problem was that his English was at that time very limited. He had spent many years in Germany, and his German was fluent. But he had come to English through German and so was often hard to follow, using German constructions and even translating words wrongly – saying 'when' for 'if' (in German, *wenn*), for instance. Humphrey was not really interested in Boulez. Despite his film on Peter Maxwell Davies, new music for him was still largely Britten and Copland. But Barrie Gavin and I were convinced that something should be done to make use of Boulez's presence in London. Barrie's enthusiasm was the more remarkable since he had had no musical training at all and could not even read a score, but he plunged into early Boulez with total conviction. We listened to the piano sonatas, the Flute Sonatina and especially *Le Marteau sans maître*. It would be ludicrous to say that I understood everything about this last piece, but I was prepared to work at it. It is the lack of a willingness to be led in new directions that so depresses me in what are called music-lovers. I knew that Boulez was an outstanding, probably great, conductor; it seemed improbable that his own music should be without interest. Well, people would say, what of conductors like Furtwängler and Klemperer, who also wrote symphonies – and not very good ones? I was prepared to believe that Boulez might be more like Mahler – a great conductor who was also a great composer. Barrie made a programme with Boulez about the *Second Improvisation on Mallarmé· Une dentelle s'abolit*, which became part of *Pli selon pli*, performed at the Edinburgh Festival the following year. Barrie played the tape in the office three or four times a day for weeks. While not claiming I could recognize a wrong entry today, I still feel I know it in my bones. Nothing, I believed, was impenetrable given repeated hearings. That unfamiliarity was the obstacle, not complexity, became a basic tenet of my musical belief. No one would ever claim to get the best out of a great novel or poem in one quick reading, so why should it be different with music?

At the same time, Glock was demonstrating both on Radio 3 and at the Proms that there was so much more to music than the standard repertory, and that the new, like the very old, needed to be performed regularly and carefully presented rather than simply thrown at the public. Invitation concerts, analysis programmes, documentaries, all the innovations of broadcasting were moving the United Kingdom forward and reconnecting it with the rest of Europe. It was a question not of rejecting British music but of showing how much Britten, for instance, owed to Mahler, as did Shostakovich. We could still applaud British music of the Vaughan Williams kind, but saw now how that too connected with France and Scandinavia. We were inexorably moving to end the jingoistic isolationism of the BBC's music during Malcolm Sargent's years, when 'foreign musicians' and 'foreign music' were still terms of abuse. Henry Wood and Adrian Boult had been much more forward-looking in the 1930s. Now Boulez could lead the charge into a different world.

With a sense of ambition unthinkable today, we planned six one-hour programmes with Boulez. Barrie would look at the Second Viennese School, with programmes on Berg, Schoenberg and Webern, and I would cover the French contribution, with Debussy, Varèse and Messiaen. Each programme was to contain a complete performance of a major work, but with extracts from other works as illustrations. I was only too happy to start with Debussy, since I loved his music and knew it well, except for the work Boulez chose for complete performance – *Jeux*. There were dozens of performances of *La Mer* or the *Nocturnes*, and hundreds of *L'Après-midi d'un faune*, sections of all of which were included, but *Jeux* was practically never played. It felt insubstantial and was of awkward length – seventeen minutes – and had never caught on as a ballet when written for Diaghilev and choreographed by Nijinsky. But Boulez thought it the key to understanding modern developments in French music.

Boulez was about to begin rehearsing a new production of Alban Berg's *Wozzeck* in Frankfurt, to be directed by Wieland Wagner. He asked me to join him there. For a few days I stayed in a preposterous former grand-ducal hunting lodge in the Taunus hills outside Frankfurt, and drove back and forth with Boulez to the daily rehearsals. I cannot claim that Wieland Wagner made a great impression. He was certainly a great director, but not demonstrative. Most of his conversations with the Wozzeck, Walter Berry, were tête-à-tête and inaudible. I spent more time watching the Marie, Anja Silja – at that time Wagner's mistress – who wore thigh-length suede boots, had a mane of tawny hair, and exuded the Germanic sexuality typified by Dietrich or Hildegard Neff. What was unforgettable was the clarity and precision of Boulez's conducting, and his total control over the orchestra and singers. *Wozzeck* was the one work of the Second Viennese School that I knew well, and I already rated it above all other twentieth-century operas. But here I felt confronted by the reality of the piece.

Boulez was a delightful companion – easy to be with and full of catty quips, especially about the state of music in France and those who ran it – though I had initially been daunted by merely being with him. As I saw more of him, I was puzzled by the contradictions of his personality. He was totally accessible and charming, but gave a strong sense of intangibility. I knew nothing of his private life, and rather doubted that he had one. He seemed totally dedicated to music, and totally sure of what he wanted to do. Over the years he has mellowed considerably, becoming much warmer and more relaxed, but his sense of focus is still there, and no one I have ever met wastes less time. Every moment has to be grist to the musical mill. I was tremendously taken with him, but feared he thought me callow and ignorant – which by comparison, of course, I was. Nevertheless, the script for the Debussy programme emerged painlessly and I booked the Philharmonia Orchestra, since in those days ludicrous contractual conditions made it impossible for the BBC Symphony Orchestra to work for television except on its infrequent free days, which had to be paid for.

All seemed well until about a week before the recording, when Boulez started complaining of headaches and was diagnosed as having shingles in the head – a most painful and potentially dangerous condition. He nevertheless went ahead with the rehearsals and the recording. He was forced to wear dark glasses, and, so as to capitalize on this, I asked him to remove his jacket and conduct in shirtsleeves. The effect was like something out of a film by Jean-Luc Godard. Everything went particularly well with the music recording, but I had to ask someone else to direct the interview to link the music together, as it was to be conducted by me. The choice regrettably fell on a young General Trainee, Tony Palmer, who had already demonstrated a compulsive iconoclasm. Palmer shot the interview as a series of continuous panning shots – meaningless, pretentious and, because of the constant movement, extremely hard to edit. We had a big row, and it is impossible to claim that the final programme did not suffer. I was mortified.

I went ahead with the planning of the Messiaen programme – following Boulez's injunction that there should be no birds, no *Turangalîla* and no Madame Loriod (Messiaen's pianist wife). What he wanted was *Et Exspecto Resurrectionem Mortuorum*, one of the few Messiaen pieces he really admired. I was, and still am, resistant to the Technicolor lushness and overperfumed mysticism of much of Messiaen, some of which strikes me as closer to Hollywood than to heaven. But in the end the programme was never made. The shingles demanded complete rest, and Boulez spent the next two months in a darkened room memorizing *Parsifal*, which he was to conduct at Bayreuth for the first time that summer. So no time was wasted there either.

Over the years I have sometimes not seen Boulez for considerable periods of time. We meet again always with excitement on my side and with increasing warmth on his, but I would never dare claim myself a friend. We have been 'Pierre' and 'John' since the first meeting. I once said that I could never imagine using the second-person singular to him, as fellow professionals do. 'Yes,' he replied, 'I know what you mean.'

A very different composer was the subject of another programme I made at this time: Arthur Bliss, Master of the Queen's Music. The programme was to mark his seventieth birthday, looking back on his life and including not only his own music but works he admired, like Elgar's First Symphony and Stravinsky's *Firebird*. I was hesitant about approaching Bliss, as he had radiated a rather gruff, aloof manner on the several occasions I had heard him conduct or speak. I asked Wheldon, who knew him slightly, to give me a letter of introduction. Wheldon wrote very generously, saying I was one of the best of the young directors – this was news to me! – and Bliss asked me to call. He lived in a biggish house off Abbey Road with his American wife, Trudi, who, as a writer and broadcaster, was very much a person in her own right. As always, I first did a great deal of homework, listening to everything I could get hold of and memorizing his work list and the dates of composition. I find this sort of thing is necessary, even if excessive. The choice of what would be included would be made by him, but I could not function happily without the background information.

Bliss was absolutely charming, and I warmed to him immediately when he said, 'Do you know, in the course of my life I have been three things: I have been ahead of the times, of the times and now behind the times. But I don't in myself feel any different.' This described so well the position of many composers who find their voice when quite young and then use it with very little alteration over the years except for greater dexterity in handling the material. Bliss is no longer really thought an important composer, but he was an excellent conductor, Director of Music at the BBC during the war, and later on every committee of the profession – an ambassador for British music, working constantly for the British Council or the Performing Rights Society. In my youth I had been instantly attracted to his music, especially the huge piano concerto he wrote for Solomon, premièred at the World's Fair in New York in 1939. And I loved his ballet scores, like *Checkmate*. His fanfares and marches were heard on most state occasions. He was in one sense grand and famous, but in other ways vulnerable and modest, beginning to doubt whether his music would last. I hope I did something to reassure him. He certainly wrote about me with generosity in his autobiography.

However, I cannot forget the hurtful experience when we came to rehearse the music for the TV recording. Here was a programme celebrating the life and music of the President of the London Symphony Orchestra, yet hardly a single section principal turned up for the sessions. Bliss looked around and said quietly, 'Good morning, gentlemen. Quite a few new faces, aren't there?' It seemed to me a really insulting situation, and I told the orchestra's Manager, Ernest Fleischmann, what I thought. He disclaimed all responsibility, saying the orchestra was self-governing and the players chose what they wanted to do.

In the long interview we filmed subsequently, Bliss had many good stories, notably of his friendship with Elgar, whom he had known when he himself was still at school. He had turned the pages for the first play-through of the Violin Sonata with Billy Reed. It was Elgar who had commissioned Bliss's *Colour Symphony* for the Three Choirs Festival. The première was a disaster, since not all the musicians could fit on the platform in Gloucester Cathedral and several brass players never made it. Bliss and Elgar met in the gentlemen's lavatory afterwards. Elgar moved away with a shrug. Bliss was at pains to point out the difference between the image of Elgar and the reality. In photos, one saw the imperial grandee – moustache, dogs, a traditional view of England which is also there in the music. But, according to Bliss, this was only one side of Elgar, a working-class Catholic with a strong Worcestershire accent in the early years and with a deeply melancholic temperament, easily moved to both rage and tears.

It was through my friendship with Bliss that I came to love the two symphonies of Elgar. I had always loved the concertos and the *Introduction and Allegro* – one of the first gramophone records I had bought, when I was about thirteen – but the symphonies had not registered in the same way. Bliss took me through the First Symphony, commenting on the strength and ingenuity of its structure, its profoundly intelligent development, and the power of its motto in its various forms. It was a revelation. I remember driving home from one of our long sessions thinking how immensely fortunate I was to have a job where I could learn all the time while being paid for it.

There was no sense at this period that any project was too ambitious, although we came near to exhausting both ourselves and our resources with the project Humphrey devised with John Culshaw of the Decca Record Company to make a documentary about Solti's recording of Wagner's *Götterdämmerung*. After months of seemingly intractable negotiations, everything happened very suddenly, and I found myself at a day's notice on a plane to Vienna to direct the interviews and film sequences while Humphrey recorded the music sessions on videotape. I stepped off the plane at Vienna Airport, was introduced to a film crew, and was told to shoot the next plane that landed and its descending passengers, who included Solti. I had of course heard him often at Covent Garden and in concert with the London Philharmonic Orchestra, but I had never met him. He was a dynamo of relentless energy, and one was swept up in the backwash.

The *Ring* recording – the first ever to be made in the studio – was a huge enterprise and had already been grinding on for several years, dogged by money problems and a total lack of belief in the project from Decca's Financial Director, who provided the money. Culshaw told the whole story in his book *Ring Resounding*, which makes rather cool reference to our television project. At one point he says of the TV crew that it was hard to make them understand that they were, so to speak, guests at a party, so nothing could ever stop for the sake of the TV. It was of course true, but it seems to me ungenerous, as part of the commercial success of the recording was due to the huge publicity generated by the television programme in many countries.

Humphrey directed the cameras in the Sofiensaal, the dance hall that Decca used as a recording studio, taking over after the first session, in which an Austrian director had seemed quite simply lost. At this time Humphrey's German was very limited, but he soon learnt enough to get the shots he wanted. I had a complementary role, trying not to get in the way, but trying to catch the singers and Solti between the sessions, to get their views, and also filming the Decca team as they planned and carried out the most ambitious use of stereo that had yet been attempted.

The singers were a remarkable group. Birgit Nilsson, a great dramatic soprano with all the power and stamina needed for a big role like Brünnhilde, was off-stage a farmer's daughter from southern Sweden with a particularly unattractive nasal speaking voice. But you knew you were in the presence of a star. Wolfgang Windgassen, a stolid Siegfried, was near the end of his career, but brought years of experience to the recording. Gottlob Frick was the greatest Hagen imaginable – black of voice and, with beetling eyebrows, to me as sinister off stage as on. Dietrich Fischer-Dieskau as Gunther seemed to come from a different world, more sophisticated and elegant. I knew him much less well as an opera singer than in the lieder repertory, of which at that time he was regarded as the supreme interpreter. He had taken part with great ease of manner in a studio programme I had made about Schumann, complaining only about wearing white tie for a morning recording and begging me not to shoot him from below the waist – 'I look like a pear,' he said. He was unnecessarily shy about his English, and in the interview about the *Ring* came up with the perceptive description of the *Ring* as a family tragedy and of Gunther as a pocket-size Macbeth.

The mix of these great singers in *Götterdämmerung* was electrifying. The *Blutbrüderschaft* scene made my hair stand on end, and fifty feet away, on the other side of the studio, Solti was working himself and the Vienna Philharmonic Orchestra into a paroxysm of romantic passion. When they recorded the Funeral March the whole building shook with the intensity of the sound – I put my hand against the wall and felt the vibrations like an earthquake tremor. Yet the atmosphere was relaxed and full of surprises. In the Immolation scene, for example, when Brünnhilde calls for her horse, Grane, the Decca staff had organized a real horse which lumbered on to the stage. Nilsson collapsed in help-less giggles. It was a masterstroke, and her obvious tension and nerv-ousness about the big moment were dissipated – she threw back her shoulders and recorded the whole scene in two long takes.

The technical process was an eye-opener for me, and I was full of admiration for all the participants. There was a real feeling of cama-raderie and shared aspiration. Yet the orchestra was riddled with anti-Semitism, and Solti's relations with it were frequently troubled. When he later received the Gold Medal of the Gesellschaft der Musikfreunde for the *Ring* and other opera recordings, practically no one from the professors of the orchestra committee turned up. They all had their excuses – teaching, travel or prior engagements. On the morning of the presentation day, Solti was telephoned in his room at the Imperial Hotel and a woman's voice said, 'They are not coming because you are a dirty, Hungarian Jew.' After receiving the award, as Solti walked along the corridor, the door of the office of Ernst Vobisch, the orches-tra's Chairman, was open, and all the missing committee members were sitting there having coffee. Vienna doesn't change.

After our return to London we took stock of the situation. We had about eleven hours of videotape and thousands of feet of film. Where did we start? In a BBC mini-revolution, Wheldon was promoted to Controller of Programmes for both channels and Humphrey Burton became Head of a combined Music and Arts Department. He was up to his eyes in administration and dozens of other projects. I had a series of studio programmes of my own, but was given the entire task of edit-ing the *Ring*, and for several months I spent four or five evenings each week tinkering with the video, trying to see how we could use the best sequences and marry them with the filmed interviews and the location shooting. I came to feel the overwhelming power of Wagner. I had loved his music ever since hearing Flagstad and Hotter perform it, but now I came to understand why for some it can become an obsession while others find its ethos totally antipathetic. I became a 'worshipper', going home late at night after hours of Wagner in the video-editing channels and then putting more on the gramophone until two or three in the morning. I lost weight and ended up with what could, I suppose, be called a nervous breakdown – except I did not break. I went on and on and on until the job was finished, and achieved some startling music edits which even the Decca engineers had trouble recognizing. The final programme, *The Golden Ring*, ninety minutes long, is still worth watching. The overall credit must go to Humphrey, for it was his idea, but I think that not even he realized the burden he placed on me. Eventually I went on holiday to Greece with John Tydeman, and somewhere there is a photograph of me taken on a beach in Mykonos with every rib standing out. One of the great dangers for the unmarried is to elevate work into the central position in life, rather than striking a proper balance between the public and private sides of things.

I had at this time very little private life, worked relentlessly, and made a number of studio programmes on a variety of subjects from Couperin to Mendelssohn and a series of lecture recitals with Katchen (the tapes were wiped, but I still have the soundtrack). Most successfully, I directed an hour-long programme on Chopin, which was shown on BBC1 in the slot after the *Nine O'Clock News*, known then as *The Tuesday Documentary*. Presented by the teacher and pianist Kenneth van Barthold, with Tamás Vásáry at the piano, it used manuscripts, documents and dozens of still photographs. It was cheap programme-making and a good discipline compared with the cost of filming or outside broadcasts. We would knock off an hour-long documentary in one day in the studio in this way, and each one found big audiences. The Chopin programme was watched by over seven million people, which seems incredible today. It was thirty years before there was another Chopin programme on BBC1. That was transmitted at eleven at night, and the pianist, Andras Schiff, never stopped talking, even over the shortest of piano pieces, so little confidence did the director show in the power of the music.

Meanwhile, in 1966 the small Music Group of BBC2 became part of

Music and Arts, Television, which also absorbed all the old music staff and producers from Talks and from Schools and Women's Programmes. The new department totalled over a hundred people with a vast output, and every year won a string of awards. Ken Russell was making *Isadora Duncan*, Jonathan Miller *Alice in Wonderland* and Patrick Garland the *Famous Gossips* series, out of which came the unforgettable *Brief Lives* about the diarist John Aubrey. Lorna Pegram produced a long-running series called *Canvas* in which art experts discussed a single painting for fifteen minutes. Melvyn Bragg started *Writer's World* to explore literature, and old stagers like John Read continued his regular re-examination of the work of Henry Moore. Stephen Hearst, from Talks, was Humphrey Burton's deputy and looked after the arts side.

We moved from a handful of offices in the east tower of Television Centre to a dreadful building called Kensington House in a disused railway cutting on the other side of Shepherds Bush. New people were taken on every few months, and anyone with any talent was given a chance. Since the number of TV licences sold was constantly increasing, and given the higher cost of the colour licence, there was little feeling of budgetary restriction, except in the backwash of whatever Ken Russell was doing. Every time his films went over budget by thousands it necessitated a few more cheap studio programmes produced by people like me.

I was asked to assist Russell on one film he was to make in France about the film composer Georges Delerue. I knew Delerue quite well, since he had written the score for Flemming Flindt's ballet *The Lesson*. I thought I was merely to be a French-speaking production assistant, sorting out location problems and interpreting for Delerue, whose English was virtually non-existent, so I was surprised to find that I had an acting role in the film – as a sort of *film noir* mad interviewer, in a belted raincoat and trilby hat. I really had no idea what was going on, and Russell seemed totally incapable of explaining. 'Just do it!' he would shout. 'Do what?' one asked, without getting any response. So one did something, and after six takes discovered one was meant to be running rather than walking. Russell had a totally visual approach. He knew what he wanted to see, but could not explain how to get it. When he saw what he wanted he made one do it again and again. It was expensive, time-wasting and infuriating, but it was his way. His early films had not just his visualizing brilliance but also the anchor of Wheldon or Burton insisting on scripts and commentary, and in films like those on Elgar and Prokofiev the approach worked perfectly. Without the double control, things seemed to drift into aimless self-indulgence. Russell patently despised me, and relations were not helped by a serious motor accident during the filming. Russell and his wife just walked away and left the rest of us to clear up the mess while his long-suffering assistant, who had been driving, sat in the police station as the Russells went to find a restaurant for dinner. You have to admire Russell's eye, even in the dreadful films of his later years, but for me the eye never seemed connected to a brain, and his childishly selfish behaviour made it impossible to take him seriously as a human being.

For the wonderful film he made about Delius he found a new assistant in Geoffrey Haydon, whom he liked and trusted. Haydon was able to dissuade him from some of the more pretentious sequences – Delius being drawn on a barge down the canals of Bradford to the music of *Summer Night on the River*, for instance. Russell wanted Haydon to leave the BBC and continue to work for him when he moved into films. Haydon asked my advice. I suggested he was too old and too able to be merely Russell's assistant, so he stayed in the BBC, where he sadly achieved less than his promise suggested, while Russell had no one to put a brake on his disorganized fantasies. I have always regretted the advice I gave Haydon.

In the summer of 1966 I went on holiday with Arlette and Julius Katchen to Prades in the Pyrenees for what was to prove the last of the legendary Casals Festivals. We stayed in a spa hotel over a sulphur spring in Molitg, just up the valley, and went daily to the rehearsals in Casals's house, where Julius was performing trios with Casals and the great Russian violinist David Oistrakh. Even in his late eighties, Casals still produced an awesome sound, with a warmth and steadiness I have never heard equalled – not even by Rostropovich. He would peer over the music stand and twinkle when things went right or snort dismissively if he thought he was less than at his best. I turned the pages for Katchen, thrilled to be so close to such profound musicality. Both the Schubert trios were rehearsed, and for me these rehearsals were more moving than the concerts. But all around were great names. Serkin, Horzowski and Kempff were the other pianists. Serkin was an enchanter, bubbling with enthusiasm and endless stories about colleagues. I mentioned that I had much admired his performance of a huge and interminable concerto by Max Reger. He never let me forget it, always bringing it up when we met. He never quite grasped that it was *him* that I admired rather than the concerto. David Oistrakh was a fund of hilarious Jewish stories, and his placid wife, Tamara, told me a lot about the state of life and literature in the Soviet Union. They had all lived through the decline of Prokofiev and were still living with the constant oppression of Shostakovich, whose wonderful First Violin Concerto had been written for Oistrakh. Once again I was very conscious of how the human spirit can flower even in the most vile circumstances. It was after my conversations with Oistrakh that I sought out the then infrequently played string quartets of Shostakovich, which now seem to me among the great monuments of twentieth-century music.

I never completed my holiday that summer, for in early August my mother had a stroke and I had to hurry back to England to do what I could. My father was completely devastated when it became clear that she would not make a full recovery and was unlikely to walk well or ever drive again. A new doctor had given her a new drug for her life-long heart condition and it had overstimulated the heart, resulting in the stroke. She regained speech quite quickly, but was in a wheelchair. It was very painful. Even in these late years she had been so constantly active, so much the centre of things, that life as a handicapped person seemed unthinkable. She survived for two months, after which a second stroke put her into a coma from which she never surfaced. She died slowly and painfully a few days later. My father sat by her bedside for hours and hours. I sat in the car park outside the hospital, unable to watch and all too conscious of the years of animosity that my father had showed both to my mother and to me. From the time I realized she would not make a full recovery I had not wished her to live longer. Although most people thought her much younger, she was sixty-five and had a long history of illness and physical pain through rheumatism. I preferred to remember the immensely happy years of my childhood, when she had done so much to enhance not only my life but the lives of so many others. Her funeral was an occasion for much openly expressed mourning, but I felt too deep a grief to let it show.

My main anxiety was what to do with my father. He had always believed that he was not able to look after himself or cope on his own – the main reason my mother gave for never having left him. Eventually he did quite well, even to the point of driving again after a thirty-year gap, but I had to keep a constant watchful eye on him, telephoning every night between six-thirty and seven, and spending every weekend with him except when I was away filming. I would prepare enough food to last him from Monday to Friday and, if I could not be there, organize someone to do the shopping. He learnt to cook in a simple way and tried to make the best of things, but it was very hard. I never discovered if he was conscious of the extent to which his changeable moods and sheer possessiveness had undermined my mother's health. By his account it was thirty-eight years of total devotion on his side, and he talked constantly of her with sentimental adoration. It was at times hard to take, but out of it came a much better understanding between us. I was genuinely interested in his early life and travels, and encouraged him to talk about people he had known and places he had been. He was also much more interested in me, no longer convinced that I was a Communist agent. I would never be the kind of gung-ho, womanizing, macho type he had been and would have liked me to have been, but in his rather shy way he started asking for the first time about my work and was particularly nice to friends of mine he met, like the Scotts, the Tusas and John Tydeman. In the event he survived my mother by just over three years, dying unexpectedly from respiratory failure after a bout of bronchitis to which his tuberculosis had left him especially prone.

I was thirty-five when he died, and I would be dishonest if I did not say that it represented a kind of liberation. I was now on my own, without family, able to have a freer choice of what I wanted to do. In my youth, people had always said I resembled my mother – not in appearance, since she was so attractive and I was physically so ordinary – but in manner. Her outgoing, positive, Australian personality had certainly found an echo in my temperament. As I get older I find myself more and more like my father, especially since the extreme thinness of my young years has disappeared into a pear-shaped middle age. I find myself sitting as he did with one leg tucked behind the other; I flare up with impatient irritation as he did so often; I repeat the same old stories. There could never be any doubt about my parentage – I carry the genes of both of them – but I have had a more successful life, without the health problems that dogged them so persistently.

I have not kept in touch with the vast number of cousins on my mother's side, although they occasionally surface, for we found little in common and now there are few left who remember earlier times. I do have friends who come from happy families, but I have myself found happiness in friendship rather than family. My life is full of surrogate relations – grandparents, siblings and a younger generation whom I have known all their lives. I have been immensely fortunate in my friends, whose individual differences are so great that I once said, in my only aphorism that gets quoted, 'I would rather give a party for my enemies than for my friends, since at least my enemies have something in common.' But, however disparate, my friends share my curiosity about the world and my somewhat puritanical belief in the need to work for the rewards one seeks. Almost all my friends are what is known as high-achievers. This is certainly not the reason for our friendship, but it is a source of continuing stimulus and enjoyment. The only thing I fear about ageing, other than physical inadequacy, is losing friends – and that is of course inevitable since so many of my friends are older than myself.

Mine was a long apprenticeship and it was only in my thirties that I felt a real sense of independence. At last I seemed to be getting somewhere and making more sense of my life.

# 8

# Small Successes

My mother never lived to see my most successful television programme, although it was shot during the last weeks of her life. The first Leeds International Piano Competition had taken place in 1963. Devised by a local teacher, Fanny Waterman, with the help of Marion, Countess of Harewood, who had herself been a very capable pianist in her youth, it had been won by one of Fanny's pupils, Michael Roll. Without ever suggesting he was not the best of the entrants, it was not really ideal publicity for the event. Fanny and Marion were keen to seek a wider audience for the second competition, to be held in Leeds in September 1966, and after a meeting in the spring I was asked to make a programme about the event. I was interested, but also uncertain how to reflect in one hour something that lasted for two weeks and involved nearly 100 young pianists. We decided not only to record the semi-final and final rounds, but also to film the competitors at other stages and as they prepared.

The jury was outstanding. Under the chairmanship of William Glock, it included a very distinguished list of pianists – Annie Fischer, Gina Bachauer, Charles Rosen, Bela Siki, Lev Oborin, Rudolf Firkušný and Nikita Magaloff – together with Hans Keller of the BBC and the doyenne of European teachers, Nadia Boulanger. It was assumed that I would stay with the jury in the Queen's Hotel; I chose instead to live in a university hall of residence with the competitors. This was in many ways the key to the success of the venture. Making use of my languages, I was able to befriend the participants and became a kind of honorary member of the group. We had a huge amount of fun, with endless jokes around the piano and much international bonding, and I was astonished at the thoroughness of the organization and the devoted contribution of Fanny's band of voluntary helpers. Dozens of them had made available cars, houses, pianos and support for the vulnerable kids. The only crisis came when the Day of Atonement fell during the second week and virtually none of the helpers turned up.

I interviewed all the jury and many of the competitors, and, just as with the *Ring* programme, ended up with mountains of tape from the performing sessions and miles of film on the daily life of the event. Another major editing problem. I had a month to produce the finished programme. Towards the end of that month, interest in the competition was happily stimulated by Hans Keller leaking in the *New Statesman* that the jury had been hopelessly split in their final decision, having already broken the rules by nominating five finalists rather than three (four of whom elected to play the same concerto – the Tchaikovsky B flat minor). The only woman finalist, Viktoria Postnikova, had totally captivated both Glock and Keller, but the winner was a Spaniard, Rafael Orozco, who played the Brahms D minor concerto. Several newspapers took up the story, so that when the programme was finally shown the subject was in the news and there was something of the atmosphere of a real competition. Even though the outcome was already known, many people watching had not read about it.

In a sense, the film could have been about the Olympic Games, since the competitive instinct and the idea of brilliant young people doing what they did best were paramount. But it also said a lot about music. No one really likes the idea of competition in the arts, for, as Hans Keller said in his interview, 'Above a certain standard you are not better but different, and it's the difference that makes you interesting.' In 1966 this was all new to the television audience, and they certainly responded. The programme got a big audience and a huge appreciation rating, was soon repeated, and the following year won the Best Director award at the Prague International Television Festival – at that time one of the best television showcases in the world. My phone at home did not stop ringing until nearly two in the morning after the transmission, and for the first time I had the pleasing feeling of public success. I seemed to be finding my stride.

But in truth I was not totally convinced that I wanted to specialize in music, and I had already been nagging Humphrey to let me try other things, especially dance. There was, however, an obstacle to my getting really involved in this: virtually all BBC dance programmes were produced by a former Royal Ballet soloist who had moved to television, Margaret Dale. She was very skilled at transferring existing stage productions to the studio and worked regularly with the Royal Ballet and its leading dancers; but she did not believe in relaying from the theatre, and so others were asked to do that – Anthony Craxton and John Vernon from Outside Broadcasts, and occasionally one of us. I directed a live relay of the second act of *Swan Lake* from the Royal Opera House virtually without rehearsal, and made only one bad mistake, cutting too soon to an important entrance. But it was clear that Dale did not want others on her patch, since she doubted the ability of untrained people to get things right when photographing dance, which is indeed fraught with problems. If you go in close with the camera you cut off the feet and hands; if you stay out wide you might as well be looking at performing mice. If you pan the camera from side to side you negate the dancers' movement; if you remain static the shot rapidly becomes boring. It is no wonder that in recent years dance has succeeded more by creating new work for the camera than by transferring the stage to the studio.

Flemming Flindt, after the success of *The Lesson*, had won the Italia Prize for a second time with a bizarre piece based on Ionesco's story *Le Jeune Homme à marier*, with a brilliant score by the young Danish composer Per Nørgård. In 1965 Flindt became Director of the Royal Danish Ballet, with the intention of making a new work for television each year as well as ballets for the theatre. He seemed on the verge of becoming a really influential figure, and I proposed making a film about him while he prepared a new version of Bartók's *The Miraculous Mandarin* for both stage and screen.

In November 1966 I went straight from the plaudits for the Leeds film and the trauma of my mother's death to work on the Flindt project in Copenhagen. It was a disaster. Flindt proved impossible to interview – I knew him too well, and he ducked any difficult questions. The Danish film crew were slow and unimaginative, and we seemed to miss every important moment in the choreographic sessions. I tried to make a programme out of what we shot, but in the end it was reduced to a lengthy introduction to a performance of *Mandarin* after that had been completed and recorded. Perhaps Maggie Dale was right and I was not equipped to make dance programmes. However, I was successful with another, more purely documentary, project: to do something about the legacy of Diaghilev.

I had heard a great deal about Diaghilev and the Ballets Russes, since many people I knew had seen the company and its successor, the De Basil Ballet. Richard Buckle's Diaghilev exhibition in Edinburgh in 1954 and in London the following year had whetted my appetite. I was struck not only by how many of Diaghilev's collaborators were still alive (though many were by now very old) but most especially by the new and significantly different approach to artistic possibilities that had made their achievement possible. Since I have written a whole book, *Speaking of Diaghilev*, about the nearly eighteen months' work I spent making my two *Omnibus* programmes on Diaghilev, I will not devote much space to the subject here, but it was something I cared about passionately. I spent some time in 1966 exploring the possibilities, contacting leading figures and seeking their participation. They were all happy to talk, but much less keen to be filmed, especially the elderly ballerinas like Tamara Karsavina and Lydia Sokolova. I spent over a year persuading them and attempting to persuade elusive people like Balanchine and Stravinsky, who in the event never did agree to take part.

In the course of the research I became convinced that Diaghilev's insistence on total commitment by composer, designer, choreographer and dancers was the only way to achieve great results. He could persuade as experienced a composer as Prokofiev to rewrite a score. He would insist on better ideas from even great designers, and would impress on choreographers a new vision of what dance could become once it was liberated from the stuffy atmosphere of Russia's imperial theatres. It was an epic story, made all the harder to tell by there being no footage of the company performing, since Diaghilev's contracts had banned dancers from appearing on film, although he did encourage some of the best photographers of his time to make a record of what was danced. Most people, including Humphrey Burton and the proposed American co-producers, were sceptical that the programmes would work without sequences of dancing, but I was adamant that you could not explain Karsavina and Nijinsky by showing even Fonteyn and Nureyev (who in fact represented something totally different). I was convinced that the still photographs could be made to tell the story, backed by the music, so much of it well known – by Stravinsky, Prokofiev or Poulenc. There was to be no American involvement.

Shortly after the Flindt debacle, when I was gearing up to start in earnest on the Diaghilev programmes, Humphrey resigned to join the new company London Weekend Television. It was a shock to all of us, but it was the salvation of my project, since his successor let me get on with it. In 1997 – thirty years after they were made – the two Diaghilev programmes were got out of the archive, cleaned up and reshown, first at the Barbican, then at the National Film Theatre and subsequently in Sweden and the Netherlands. I was initially very nervous about this, since I was sure they would show their age in an unhelpful way, and especially because they are in black and white. But I was quite wrong. Although they are not great examples of film-making, they are remarkable documents. Nowhere else can one hear Karsavina talking about working on the *Firebird* with Stravinsky, Marie Rambert recalling the first night of *The Rite of Spring*, Massine talking about researching Spanish dance before choreographing *The Three-Cornered Hat* or Sokolova remembering how hard the company worked – and all of them talking of Diaghilev and his impact. I was gratified when the best dance critic in America commenting on the interviews in my book said that 'nothing brought one closer to an understanding of Diaghilev'. That is exactly what I sought – not just to celebrate the achievement, remarkable as it was, but to examine the philosophy on which it was based and which is so strikingly missing from most classical dance today and indeed from most theatre and opera.

One long-term result of the Diaghilev films was my increased involvement in the world of dance, from membership of the Arts Council's Dance Panel to my founding of the National Dance Co-ordinating Committee, which I chaired for nine years, and my continuing activity in association with both classical and modern companies and in defence of dance's status among the other theatre arts. For too many people – especially musicians – dance is considered an inferior art form, less valuable than spoken theatre and less important than opera. However, to my mind it was one of the key areas of artistic innovation and audience growth in the twentieth century, and without Diaghilev much of that innovation and growth would not have happened. The memory of the impact he made through getting all the arts to work together has never left me; it was to become a central part of my ideas and beliefs, and has influenced all my subsequent work.

Humphrey Burton's successor in charge of the Television Music Department was someone I already knew well. Humphrey was given only a few hours to clear his desk, but I understood that later Huw Wheldon asked him what to do about Music and Arts and he suggested splitting the department, making Stephen Hearst Head of Arts and bringing in John Culshaw from Decca as Head of Music. I had not only worked with Culshaw on the Solti *Ring* programme but had subsequently produced a long documentary study of Rachmaninov which he wrote and presented.

Culshaw's first foray into music, not long after leaving the RAF in the late 1940s, had been to write a short book on Rachmaninov – at that time a deeply unfashionable figure, very little of whose music was played. The book was a triumph over the unavailability of material, and when the typescript was completed Culshaw went to see the composer's widow in Switzerland. Ferried across Lake Lausanne in a private launch by a liveried servant, he was graciously received and asked to come back a week later, when Madame Rachmaninov would have read the typescript. Limited to twenty-five pounds in foreign currency, Culshaw had to explain that he could not wait that long. Grudgingly, Madame Rachmaninov agreed to a shorter time. When he returned, he was told to wait in the hall. Shortly afterwards she appeared holding the typescript in an outstretched hand before dropping it on to the floor. 'I have spoken to my lawyers in New York, Paris and London,' was her only comment. Yet the book is entirely favourable. It is one of the many examples of the disastrous influence of some composers' widows – *Die Unlustigen Witwen*, as Boulez calls them – 'The Unmerry Widows'. He has had to cope with Frau Schoenberg, Frau Mahler and, worst of all, Frau Berg, who for forty years spoke daily with Alban's spirit and blocked the completion of *Lulu*. In Britain we have been much more fortunate. Lady Bliss, Lady Berkeley and Mrs Vaughan Williams have been helpful and supportive, while Lady Walton has made a colourful career out of widowhood, popping up everywhere and even performing *Façade* rather well.

Our Rachmaninov programme was greatly enhanced by having as soloist the amazing Shura Cherkassky, who played excerpts from all the four piano concertos, learning the opening of the fourth as well as part of the *Corelli Variations* specially. It was very hard to reconcile the two sides of Cherkassky: the brilliant virtuoso, who presented the most interesting recital programmes of anyone, and the childlike, whining off-stage personality, racked with doubt, phobias and fetishes. I learnt later how many rolls of toilet paper had to be delivered to the dressing room before a performance. No one ever knew why they were needed. He was flirtatious and infuriating, but a magical performer, even if notoriously hard to accompany – he simply never looked at the conductor. I remember Charles Groves conducting Rachmaninov's Third Piano Concerto entirely facing the pianist, so as to have some chance of their staying together. Yet the results were always thrilling.

I persuaded the conductor Eugene Ormandy to take part in the programme, and he told how Rachmaninov had hated recording sessions and the cuts necessitated by the side lengths of 78-RPM records. The very fast tempo of Rachmaninov's own recording with Ormandy of the first movement of the Third Concerto was all to do with side lengths and quite unrelated to the composer's true intentions. Facts such as these quickly get lost.

Rachmaninov had made his name as a composer and conductor; he had become a full-time pianist only reluctantly, to make a living after the Revolution, since, like Stravinsky, he suffered from the Soviet Union's non-participation in the Berne Convention on copyright and received very few royalties. As a young man he had sold the famous C sharp minor Prelude for twenty-five dollars. He and Stravinsky both lived in Beverley Hills during the war and used to meet to play bridge, exchange gifts of honey or vodka, and complain about money. Music was never discussed. One day Stravinsky called to see Rachmaninov in his dressing room before a recital. 'Why so sad?' he asked. 'Sshh,' replied Rachmaninov – 'I am rehearsing my sadness!'

It was while working with Culshaw on the script at his mews house behind Gower Street that I had another memorable encounter. The phone rang and Culshaw seemed distracted. He explained that there were some people coming round and we had to stop. Before I could even pack up my things the doorbell rang and into the room came Benjamin Britten, Peter Pears, Mstislav Rostropovich and Galina Vishnevskaya. I decided to sit it out for at least a few minutes. At this time Rostropovich had virtually no English and the close friendship which had grown up between the four of them was conducted in what became known as Aldeburgh Deutsch – pidgin German without much grammar. Trying to be helpful, I said quietly to Rostropovich that I spoke Russian and would be happy to interpret. He was delighted. Not so his wife, Vishnevskaya, who immediately thought I must be some sort of intelligence agent. Rostropovich launched into a torrent of indiscretions about Madame Furtseva, the Soviet Minister of Culture, and also about Victor Hochhauser, his London impresario. Where did all the money go? he wondered. Vishnevskaya tried in vain to shut him up. I explained to her that I worked for the BBC and was quite discreet. But my involvement with the BBC had an immediate negative effect on Britten, who hated the organization and was deeply suspicious of all its employees. Pears was delighted to be able to chat more easily with the Rostropoviches, but Britten sulked in a corner. Eventually I made my excuses and left, hoping I would have other chances to meet them. But I recognized immediately that Culshaw was one of those people who keep their life in separate compartments and don't much like it when they overlap.

One of the other things I already knew about him was that he watched a great deal of television and – like Michael Tippett – was genuinely interested in what it could do for music. He was convinced that TV had the potential to be a great educator and popularizer without compromising its subject matter. For the majority of radio music producers, television was anathema – and our Rachmaninov project, linked to performances of all the concertos, was just the sort of thing they hated most. I happened to meet one of the Radio 3 people at a friend's house in the country. 'What are you up to?' he asked. I told him of the Rachmaninov project. 'How awful for you!' was his only comment. And what was he doing? I asked. 'Twelve programmes on the chamber music of Arnold Bax,' he replied.

Culshaw came to television with two main ambitions: to create a popular music strand for BBC1 and to persuade Britten to get involved in TV. The first was fulfilled with André Previn's *Music Night*. Previn was just becoming well known in Britain. He had a knack of introducing music to audiences with humour and a very transatlantic air of informality. I don't know why it is that American conductors like Bernstein, Previn and now Leonard Slatkin all have this gift that few of their British contemporaries share. Previn's *Music Night*, which Culshaw produced and eventually directed, was pretty unambitious stuff, but it found an audience.

The Britten project was quite a different matter. Not only did Britten dislike the BBC, he even more strongly disliked other people's performances of his work. Basil Coleman had directed a brilliantly successful production of *Billy Budd* – the first real revival of an opera that had almost sunk without trace. With a strong cast and a brilliant set by Tony Abbott, he brought the drama into close-up. But the results, although highly praised, did not satisfy Britten. The core of the problem was that at that time no studio was big enough to accommodate both the orchestra and the singers, so the orchestra and the main conductor were physically separated from but linked by monitors to the singers and a sub-conductor. It was far from ideal, but *Billy Budd* had shown that with a sensitive director and a top-flight designer and sound supervisor it could be made to work. Britten's price for getting involved with further TV projects was to transfer the whole enterprise to Snape Maltings, with its wonderful acoustic. There was then certainly enough space, but with the limitation of the capabilities of an outside-broadcast unit rather than a studio set-up.

Vast sums were spent on a production of *Peter Grimes* which Britten conducted and which was directed by a newish recruit to television, Brian Large. Large was a good musician – the youngest Doctor of Music since Malcolm Sargent – and an accomplished concert director, but he had much less talent when it came to directing stage works, and none of the expensive and complicated enterprises he produced – ranging from Britten to Prokofiev's *The Love of Three Oranges* and Verdi's *Macbeth* – made a dramatic impact in the way that Coleman had done so memorably with *Billy Budd*. Also, when it came to *Peter Grimes*, although Britten conducted it, he refused to allow himself to be shown – even in the sea interludes, which were embarrassingly visualized in a series of constantly moving graphic sequences.

This was not the only instance of Britten's non-appearance. When he and Pears recorded Schubert's *Winterreise* (with Pears in costume and distressingly made up), only Britten's hands were occasionally seen at the keyboard. And so it went on. What started as a laudable attempt to create a Britten archive became instead a Pears archive at a time when the tenor's voice was fading and he was too old for roles like Grimes. Yet nothing could change Britten's mind, and Culshaw, who had been his recording manager at Decca and a close colleague for many years, never solved the problems.

For me the biggest failure was the commissioned opera *Owen Wingrave*, which had a weak libretto and was neither creative television nor effective when transferred to the theatre. It seemed to me the least successful of the late Britten works, especially compared to his *Death in Venice*. Sadly, there is practically nothing of Britten on film or video, despite a documentary, *Britten at Fifty*, made by Humphrey and transmitted on the day that Kennedy was killed – the only programme to survive in the schedules on that famous night – and a snide documentary which Tony Palmer made about the Aldeburgh Festival, which includes a magical sequence of Britten and Sviatoslav Richter playing the Mozart Sonata for Two Pianos. In fact Britten appeared on TV *in propria persona* only twice in those years: in an edition of *The Money*

*Programme* linked to the appeal to rebuild the Maltings after it had burned down in 1967, and in a documentary I made about Kathleen Ferrier.

The Ferrier film was entirely John Culshaw's idea. He asked me to do it in 1967, not knowing how well I knew the musical material, since much of Ferrier's repertoire had been performed by my mother. As she had been dead for only a little over a year, I was not sure I wanted to get involved. Nevertheless, I was taken to lunch with Ferrier's sister, Winifred, a retired schoolteacher, who offered me her entire archive – letters, scores, photographs. At one point she opened a wardrobe, and hanging there was a splendid green and silver brocade dress that I remembered Ferrier wearing in the Proms in 1949. I had been in the front of the promenade, and remembered the intimacy with which she had sung Malcolm Sargent's orchestration of Brahms's *Four Serious Songs*.

The real problem was the lack of any film of Ferrier performing. She had died in 1953, only fourteen years earlier, but the age of video had not yet then come, and nothing survived of her television appearances. There was a snippet of news film of her getting off a plane in Amsterdam with Benjamin Britten and Peter Pears to be greeted by Peter Diamand, the Director of the Holland Festival and one of her great supporters in Europe, and there was a privately made film of her fooling around at a party, but without a soundtrack. It seemed that I was back with the Diaghilev problem – except that the use of still photographs might have been understandable for events fifty years earlier but was harder to accept when Ferrier's career was so recent. Yet there was something about Ferrier's life and the power of her personality that overcame my reservations.

Despite the intrinsic sadness of the story – a marvellous artist cut down by cancer in her prime at forty-one after a career of only ten years – the time we spent making the film was one of the happiest of my life. A devoted researcher, Rhona Shaw, sought out dozens of people from Ferrier's earlier life, from school in Blackburn and the telephone exchange where she had worked to the little town in Cumbria where she was simply the golf-playing wife of the local bank manager. Her musical associates like John Barbirolli and Gerald Moore all jumped at the chance to talk about her.

Naturally I wanted Britten involved. He had heard her first important London performance – *Messiah* in Westminster Abbey, with Pears as the tenor soloist – and had worked often with her, writing both *The Rape of Lucretia* and his *Canticle II, Abraham and Isaac,* for her. It was the disappearance of the radio recording of the canticle that was at the heart of Britten's hatred of the BBC. Pears accepted my invitation to participate at once, but Britten was not so sure. Culshaw acted as intermediary, and eventually Britten agreed to be interviewed on condition that neither Nancy Evans, Ferrier's closest friend, nor Evans's husband, the librettist Eric Crozier, appeared in the programme. In a way typical of how things were at Aldeburgh, Crozier, who had once been a very close colleague of Britten's, had fallen out of favour and been dismissed from court and written out of history. The proposal to exclude him and his wife was preposterous, and one I found it very hard to accept, since Nancy Evans was one of the most lovable and attractive singers of her time and a fund of good stories. But in the end I reluctantly agreed, and I spent a day filming at the Red House, Britten and Pears's home in Aldeburgh. Both of them were full of interest and clearly deeply attached to Ferrier's memory.

I never had any difficulty with Pears, right up to the end of his life, but with Britten I always felt I was walking on eggshells. It made for uncomfortable meetings. I was never part of the Aldeburgh set, and was treated with lofty disdain by Britten's associates while he was alive. Since his death the mood has changed totally. My frequent presence during the years when my close friend Sheila Colvin was General Manager of the Aldeburgh Festival has of course made a difference, but they are still a touchy crowd, only too ready to pounce on anything which falls short of total worship.

Britten's participation in the Ferrier film gave it authority, as did the presence of so many other colleagues who had worked with her and loved her – notably her first teacher, Dr Hutchinson of Newcastle, who, although ninety, spoke touchingly of their work together and who, to my chagrin, was subsequently deeply offended by Roy Henderson's claim that when she moved to London to study with him 'she hadn't really started'. Selecting the music for the film was tricky, as there was so much on record, but I resolved to try to recount her life through the songs she sang. Music sequences were very carefully planned and scripted to find appropriate images, while friends and the actual locations carried the story forward.

It was the only film I ever made that I still feel comfortable with as a piece of film-making, and it still packs quite an emotional punch.

Inevitably its tragic ending is painful, but the film is also full of laughter and happy memories – especially from people who knew Ferrier before she became a public figure. I gave a lunch in a hotel in Blackburn for a dozen women who had been her friends when young, and have rarely laughed so much. Juxtaposing them with recordings of Bruno Walter speaking of her understanding of Mahler, or of Pears talking of her instinctive and unforgettable approach to folk song, resulted in a musical and personal narration that I thought justified the film's success. I had rarely been pleased with my work, but this I thought made its points. As with the Diaghilev film, there is something memorable about the eyewitness accounts by people who are now dead, and the absence of film of Ferrier herself did not seem to matter – the unmistakable sound of her voice carried the message. For a whole generation she was the ideal of the singer – generous, gracious and very human. I have always felt keen sympathy for Janet Baker, who was in many ways a much more sophisticated musician, but who, in popular estimation, had to live her life in Ferrier's shadow.

We were all affected by the Ferrier story. Rhona Shaw resigned from the BBC and has since spent her life raising money for cancer research. I was constantly approached by film companies who wanted to dramatize Ferrier's life for the cinema. I also received a great many prurient enquiries about her private life. Her marriage was annulled for non-consummation, and she was permanently the object of passionate affection from men like Barbirolli and Walter, but also had very close attachments to women. My own feeling is that there was no private life. She found the role of Lucretia in Britten's opera so difficult not just because she was not a natural stage actor but because it was too close to the whole question of sex. Once she started singing professionally, at nearly thirty years of age, her work was her life. It was as if she then had to run fast to make up for lost time.

Making the film also helped me to come to terms with my mother's failed career, and I kept to myself my mother's reservations about Ferrier – mostly to do with her excursions into German lieder, where the instinct may have been right but the interpretations were not really fleshed out. Following two successful showings on television, the film was entered for the Monte Carlo Prize, which the BBC had most notably won with Christopher Nupen's exciting film about Daniel Barenboim and Vladimir Ashkenazy, *Double Concerto*. I was quite hopeful of its chances, until I met Wheldon in a corridor at Television

Centre. He said in passing, 'It seemed worth entering, I suppose, but of course it won't win.' He was right – it didn't win, but I had a couple of enjoyable days staying at the Hôtel de Paris, with all its memories of Diaghilev, and made the acquaintance for the first time of Jeremy Isaacs, who was at the festival as Editor of *Panorama*.

Culshaw found the BBC hard to understand. He was not the first nor the last person brought in from outside who was mystified by its ways, but beyond this he was by nature a shy man and found it difficult to get involved with people. The Decca team were very close to each other and he obviously missed them, while making little attempt to befriend colleagues in Television. We – the old gang – were much given to lunching in the BBC Club, talking over coffee in the canteen, or dropping in and out of offices, sharing ideas and sparking off each other. I tried endlessly but unsuccessfully to bring him into the group. Everyone knew that I knew him best, but, despite my assurances that he really loved television, he gave a very detached impression. He left the building for lunch every day, and the door of his office, unlike Humphrey's, was resolutely closed. Beyond the Ferrier programme, he made no suggestion of projects for me apart from an idea that I might go back to Russia to make a film about the Bolshoi Ballet. Envisaging nothing but endless negotiations with the apparatchiks, I was dubious. After two years largely spent filming, I was keen to get back to the studio.

I was also increasingly concerned about our total lack of involvement in contemporary music. The only living composers ever featured in our programmes were Britten, Tippett, Copland and Menotti, and even then not frequently. By the end of the 1960s a new generation of composers – Alexander Goehr, Peter Maxwell Davies, Thea Musgrave, Harrison Birtwistle, Richard Rodney Bennett and Nicholas Maw – were writing operas and big symphonic works and demanding attention. It was for this reason that I dreamt up *Music Now*, a monthly magazine programme that concentrated on new music and young performers. Michel Béroff, Pinchas Zukerman, Gillian Weir and Jill Gomez all made their British television debuts in one of the nine programmes we made between the autumn of 1968 and the summer of 1969. Geoffrey Haydon joined my team and made a series of documentaries about living composers, each of which was followed up with a studio performance or, in the case of both Goehr and Henze, an extract from a foreign opera recording.

Our first featured composer was the very young John Tavener, whose piece *In Alium* had won the audience ballot for a repeat performance of a new piece in the 1968 Proms. He had written some songs with words by Edward Lucie-Smith, based on surrealist paintings, which we performed in the studio. The first item in the series was Béroff playing Messiaen; I received messages from the Controller of BBC2, David Attenborough, asking what I thought I was doing frightening the public in this way. Yet we were allowed to continue. We invited the Pierrot Players into the studio to perform a long extract from Birtwistle's *Down by the Greenwood Side*, which brought about my first meetings not only with Harry Birtwistle but with Nicholas Snowman and Michael Vyner, who went on to run the London Sinfonietta. Richard Rodney Bennett wrote some songs for the soprano Jane Manning, and later interviewed Hans Werner Henze – at the height of his political period – who was in London to perform a rebarbative piece called *Versuch über Schweine* – 'Research into Pigs'. We showed a scene from Henze's opera *Der Junge Lord* in a Berlin production starring Loren Driscoll and the English singer Patricia Johnson. The conductor was Christoph von Dohnányi, and it was the first time I had any contact with him.

Geoffrey Haydon's films were brilliantly effective in conveying the essence of a composer through his life and surroundings – Tavener driving a white Bentley but playing the organ in a Presbyterian church, Harry Birtwistle working in a shed at the bottom of his garden in Barnes, Maxwell Davies in his country cottage with rooms hung with lurid woodcuts and engravings, most of which seemed to involve crucifixion or physical pain. Overall, the programmes were not entirely effective, since, despite an extensive search, the presenters we chose were less than adequate, but the presence of contemporary music on BBC Television was immediately recognized by publishers and promoters, and led to my long and mostly very happy relationships with Boosey & Hawkes, Schott, Chester Music, Oxford University Press, Peters Edition and the others, all of whom have devoted staff who cheerfully proselytize for new work to a largely uninterested musical establishment. As with my work with Boulez I did not always understand what the composers were trying to do, but my sense of history told me that at least some of them would mature into major figures. Also, the BBC's contribution in radio was so significant that it seemed quite wrong for Television to make so little effort in this field.

Attempts to bridge the gap between Radio and Television were fraught with problems. Wheldon once bravely invited Glock and five of his senior colleagues from Yalding House, the Radio Music headquarters, to have dinner at Television Centre with the same number of TV producers. The atmosphere was far from cordial, and probably not helped by Wheldon asking brusquely, 'Any of you chaps ever get poison pen letters?' and my replying, 'Only from Yalding House.' But the meeting did some good. Hans Keller made some thoughtful television appearances. I remember his observing after the première of Shostakovich's First Cello Concerto that Shostakovich was the only incontestably great composer who had never written a flawless work. Discuss! Barrie Gavin struck up a close friendship with Robert Simpson, leading to programmes on both Bruckner and Nielsen, and I was very happy to see Glock again. We had got to know each other on a gruelling tour with the BBC Symphony Orchestra in the depths of the winter of 1967, with Boulez and Barbirolli conducting and Heather Harper, Jacqueline du Pré and John Ogdon as soloists, giving concerts in Prague, Warsaw, Moscow and Leningrad. I produced a film about the tour, but spent most of the time locked in endless negotiations with Soviet Television about the need to hire lights or to obtain camera positions in sold-out concert halls. Barbirolli was sustained by regular supplies of whisky provided by our embassies. Ogdon spent most of his time manically practising on a dummy keyboard; we shared a couchette from Warsaw to Moscow, and he kept me up most of the night with his rattling away. Jacqueline du Pré terrified me one evening in Moscow by asking me to check in her cello and literally throwing the Stradivarius at me across a hotel foyer. Happily I caught it!

Boulez's first concert in Moscow was unforgettable. Nothing of the Second Viennese School had been heard there since the early 1920s, and he conducted Webern's *Five Pieces for Orchestra*, Berg's *Wozzeck* fragments and *Altenberg Lieder* and his own *Éclat*. All the young Soviet composers were sent to a mythical conference in Kiev to keep them out of the way, but Oistrakh sought me out and took me to a box at the back of the Conservatoire Hall, where behind a curtain sat the ashen-faced Shostakovich. I asked if he would give me an interview. Blue around the mouth and with shaking hands he firmly refused, but he was not at all unfriendly. I did not ask what he thought of Boulez's music, but he told me how much he admired his conducting of Berg.

Our party moved on to Leningrad, where the temperature was minus twenty-eight and most of the orchestra's double basses developed cracks. With typical professional camaraderie the bass players of the Leningrad Philharmonic were immensely helpful.

I discovered quite by chance that both in Moscow and Leningrad our concerts were being taped, and several of them were later issued on pirate recordings. Glock didn't seem very concerned, but I stormed out of a meeting in Moscow and took the train to Leningrad. The Soviet officials told my colleagues they simply could not understand me – I was behaving like an American. I learnt on this trip that one way of dealing with Communist functionaries was at times to be as intransigent as they were and then suddenly to be as nice as possible, moving from jolly jokes to stormy disagreements and back again without warning. That was how they behaved, but they clearly did not expect it from a foreigner. But the whole tour was absolutely exhausting and at times a bit scary. Eventually I signed a contract with Soviet Television to pay a large sum for the hire of lights that I had no intention of honouring. My bosses in London were not impressed, and when I appeared on *Late Night Line-up* to talk about the tour and mentioned some of these problems I was told off for reasons that seemed to me entirely hypocritical. It was the beginning of the longish period in which I came to be thought of as 'difficult'. Ken Russell and Jonathan Miller could be as awkward as they wished and get away with it because they had real talent as directors. I was just a house functionary and expected to toe the line. I found it increasingly hard to do so. David Attenborough was not in the least interested in modern music, although he was passionate about the music of earlier centuries. And, in addition, Attenborough hated ballet. Maggie Dale, strongly supported by Wheldon, was was determined to keep her monopoly of dance. Culshaw never really commented on *Music Now* except to express his dislike of the new-music sections. Increasingly I felt out on a limb and without any strong sense of direction.

One evening in the spring of 1969 I was at home after the transmission of one of the best editions of *Music Now* when Stephen Hearst rang me and asked me if I would like to move to the Arts Department as Executive Producer for BBC2 Arts Features, responsible for short series and one-off documentaries. We lunched the next day and discussed what he had in mind, and I accepted. It seemed just the kind of new fillip I needed to get going again. I had already come to the conclusion that, despite Leeds and Ferrier, I was not going to be an outstanding director, nor did I really want to go on directing full time. I also felt, as I often still do, that only music – however marvellous – is not enough. I liked the idea of the wider canvas the Arts Department would provide.

Culshaw made no attempt to retain me, and I wound up my five years in the Music Department with a curious programme in which five of the young composers featured in *Music Now* came to the studio to discuss their work with Michael Tippett. It says much for the affection in which Tippett was held that they had all accepted. He was quite tough on them, particularly on Maxwell Davies, who had been represented by his honky-tonk-piano version of the fantasy on *L'Homme armé*, moving from the Middle Ages into the world of the tango. 'How old are you, Max?' Tippett asked. 'Thirty-five' was the answer. Tippett looked reproachful. I do not remember Birtwistle saying a word, but I came away convinced that for me his was the voice of the future. Michael Tippett was somebody we all loved. It was impossible not to, since he was so genuinely enthusiastic and affectionate with everybody. I have no idea whether posterity will think him a great composer – to me, his works often seem an uncomfortable mixture of blinding vision and awkward amateurishness – but there was an integrity about him which was profoundly affecting. I took to calling on him from time to time and asking his advice or his opinion. He was always generous with both.

Although I left the Music Department, for the next few years I never actually left music. I went on interviewing, writing commentaries and occasionally adapting foreign films for my colleagues, and I kept up many of the new friendships that my involvement in new music had provided. In retrospect, the work of Television Music under Humphrey Burton seems a golden age, reflected in a whole wall of awards along the corridor of Kensington House's fourth floor. It had been a real adventure, but the sense of exploring virgin territory was already over. So much had been done. It would, of course, be done again – and perhaps better – but the initial excitement had faded. The wider field of the arts was to provide new challenges.

I had started the 1960s as an unattached General Trainee alone on London Bridge. I ended the decade as a newly appointed Executive Producer. Along the way I had learnt a great deal about communicating with audiences and how to shape material. I owe much of that to Humphrey Burton. Despite being twice passed over promotion to full producer and being overtaken by younger men like Melvyn Bragg, I had eventually made a mark, with some worthwhile films and studio programmes. I had travelled widely – to Russia and Eastern Europe with Boulez, to Sweden with Humphrey to remake the *Ring* programme for Nordvision, to Denmark for Flemming Flindt, to America, where we tried to set up co-productions for the Diaghilev project, and on holidays to France, Italy, Spain, Greece and Austria. As important as any of this, I had with my assistant on the Diaghilev films, Bob Lockyer, established a friendship which has been central to my life for over thirty years. Other friends, like John Tusa and John Tydeman, were moving into interesting jobs both in broadcasting and other areas of life.

I had been influenced by the changes associated with the 1960s, from flared trousers and long hair to the Beatles, and felt a new spirit in society – less trammelled by convention and precedent. I had been quite unaffected by the events of 1968. While Paris was in an uproar and Tariq Ali was invading the Television Centre, I was in the Lake District filming the Ferrier story. I despised the fellow-travelling of some of my colleagues and, despite my growing friendship with Henze, was quite unimpressed by Castro's Cuba or the cult of Guevara. I admired what the Wilson government had done in creating a Department of the Arts, and found its first Minister, Jennie Lee, inspirational in her continuing belief that the arts were for everybody.

For all its limitations, television could bring great artists into people's homes and allow them to demonstrate what art meant to them and why it mattered, and the audience responded in numbers that far outran attendance at concerts or opera. My colleagues and I had at our disposal an unrivalled tool for popular education and enjoyment, and were part of an organization that still believed in raising standards rather than counting heads. There may never have been a real golden age, but, compared to the flabby unadventurousness of television in the 1990s, the 1960s certainly felt like one, and many of the most effective vehicles, like masterclasses, cost practically nothing. We cared about the audience, but did not think this meant giving them only what they wanted or knew about already. Anything, Wheldon thought, could connect if presented in the right tone of voice, and in that belief there was no dispute between us.

# 9

# Words about Pictures, Pictures about Words

I probably owe as much to Stephen Hearst as to any of my professional colleagues – which is not to say we always agreed or thought along
the same lines. What was and still is attractive about him is his sense of
aspiration. Coming to this country as a teenage Jewish refugee from
Vienna, he is one of that extraordinary generation of immigrants who
have given Britain so much. As a result of the anti-Jewish policies in
central Europe, we in this country gained some of our most outstanding public figures, and their contribution seems to me insufficiently recognized. In almost every field, they worked not just for British society
but for international values.

Hearst felt quite clearly that, though the world was our oyster, we
were inadequately informed about vast areas of it. He enthused about
everything – from programmes on Mexican archaeology to Indian
writing, from Japanese cinema to American architecture. He was a true
internationalist, while also recognizing that there was both a historical
and a contemporary contribution that was distinctively British. He
wrote and spoke the English language rather better than most of us. He
worried away at prejudice and ignorance. It was refreshing, but at
times bewildering when confronted with the several directions in which
he wanted to move at the same time.

I also had to become more closely involved with the politics of the
BBC's staff structure. All departments had a Head, and some also had
an Assistant Head. The jobs of assistant heads varied. When Stephen
Hearst was Assistant Head of Music and Arts under Humphrey Burton, he was effectively Head of Arts – which he later became when the
departments were separated.

Below this there were editors, usually of continuing strands like
*Omnibus* or *Chronicle*, while executive producers were responsible for
groups of single programmes or small series. I had been Editor of
*Music Now* in the Music Department, and was now Executive Producer for BBC2 Arts Features.

The programmes were made by producers, who in documentary

departments like Arts Features were almost always directors as well. (This was not the case in Drama where, as in the cinema, the functions of producer and director were separated.) But many of the producers making programmes in Music and Arts were not full producers, but on the lower grade of either Assistant Producer or Production Assistant. 'Director' was not a grade: it was simply a description. People often took a double credit – 'Produced and directed by . . .' – and for a time a triple credit – 'Written, produced and directed by . . .' – was possible, though this was later disallowed. People were very touchy about how they were described.

The departmental structure changed all the time, according to the remit of successive Controllers or departmental heads, who appropriated territory and empire-built whenever possible. The confusion was considerable. At one time there was a Documentary Department, a General Features Department and a Documentary unit in the Presentation Department, and any one of them could have produced the same programme. It was hard to fathom even for those of us inside the system, while journalists and the general public could never make head nor tail of it. It was like the remains of the statue of Ozymandias in Shelley's poem, with bits of departed empires randomly sticking up out of the sand, without much rational explanation. No attempt to tidy it up ever entirely succeeded.

Arts Features, when I joined it, consisted of a number of very established producers older than myself who had been part of Talks Department, a number from educational television, and a growing number of bright young men. There were also more women producers than in any other department, but in the way of things they had had to wait longer for opportunities than the Oxbridge men. Some of the senior figures – like John Read, son of the critic and writer Herbert Read – lived very much in their own world, with their own projects, keeping to themselves. By the time I joined Arts Features, Michael Gill and Peter Montagnon were embarked on Kenneth Clark's thirteen-programme series on Western civilization; they had been colleagues in Schools Television, but now worked very much as a separate unit within Arts Features. Lorna Pegram, from Women's Programmes, concentrated on the visual arts and was for a long time Editor of the weekly BBC2 arts magazine programme *Release*, the successor to *Monitor*, which had ground to a standstill under Jonathan Miller's editorship. But Jonathan Miller was still around from time to time, working like Ken Russell, Patrick

Garland and Jack Gold on short-term contracts. The flagship programme which replaced *Monitor* on BBC1 was initially called, not
very imaginatively, *Sunday Night*. It became *Omnibus*, with the very
experienced documentary producer Norman Swallow as Editor. Paul
Johnston ran an archaeology unit – much involved with the new world
of underwater exploration and the retelling of historical events, with
presenters including John Julius Norwich. My responsibility was for
one-off documentaries and smaller series – of fifteen- or twenty-minute
programmes – on anything we could sell to the Controller, largely
produced by a group of young directors most of whom had been General Trainees.

Stephen Hearst was attracted to General Trainees because of their
obvious intelligence. I was less convinced, since most of them had had
virtually no experience of the BBC before joining the Arts Department.
Huw Wheldon thought that no one should be a producer at the BBC
unless he or she had spent some years doing other things; although I
myself had not, I had at least had six years experience elsewhere in the
BBC – in London, the regions and abroad – before starting to specialize. I felt that the young should learn their craft as I had done in areas
like Schools Television before being allowed near the arts. The danger
was that there was rarely enough work for them to become comfortable with the mechanics of programme-making. Making live studio
programmes, re-editing library footage and my other tasks in Schools
had given me a grounding which they lacked. Once we moved from
Television Centre to Kensington House, people never saw studios and
began to concentrate their ideas entirely on film. The pace of production with film is naturally slower, so it takes longer to get a body of
work under one's belt. Also, many of the young came to believe that
they need only do what they wanted to do. I knew from my experience
that often the best programmes were those commissioned by enlightened editors. It had not been my idea to make either the Leeds Piano
Competition film or the Kathleen Ferrier biography. Left to one's own
devices, one always tends to limit one's aspirations to what one already
knows, walking round the ramparts of what is safe and comfortable
rather than branching out into new areas so as to extend one's knowledge and eventually become more valuable to the organization. There
were young producers in the department, like Lesley Megahey, who
understood this at once and embraced opportunities enthusiastically.
Others were not convinced. How could they bring something to sub-

jects they were not really conversant with? they would ask. Trust your editor to match subject and producer and do some homework was my view.

Shortly after I began in the Arts Department. I became aware of a large exhibition, 'The Age of Neo-Classicism', which was to take place at the Royal Academy in London, planned by the Council of Europe. I had always been interested in this period, chilly and severe as it might seem, and I suggested a series of short films on some of the leading figures – David, Schinkel, Canova, Thorvaldsen, Soane and Ledoux. I gathered the young directors and laid out my proposal. They seemed tremendously uninterested. I suggested that they think about it. They came back a week later and told me that, except for David, there was no one on the list that they could 'relate to' – a new phrase just coming into vogue. I tried further exhortation. We made no progress, and I was forced to abandon the proposal. The programmes were eventually made for the Further Education Department by a former *Monitor* producer, Nancy Thomas, who just got on with them and did them rather well. My backing down gave me a temporary reputation for democracy, but it made me uncertain about the extent of executive authority. Was it right to accept life only on the producers' terms, or should I have insisted?

I tried again with a series on writers' houses. Since a number of the producers had read English or history at university, this was safer ground and they accepted with a degree of enthusiasm, as also happened with a series that John Read proposed on craftsmen. But I had long, heart-searching conversations with Stephen Hearst about how I could convince people that my own ideas were worth taking seriously. No one had ever questioned Wheldon's authority on *Monitor* or Jonathan Miller's quite different but highly influential approach. I found myself treated by the young directors like a superior tradesman – they came to me to be measured for their new programmes. I did not want to run an authoritarian regime, nor was I convinced that I was always right, but I did feel that at least some of the time I had a responsibility to insist that the output we produced was balanced, that it covered a wide range and that it also contributed to their training. Their view was that beyond the arts-magazine strand – a kind of bread-and-butter thing they had to do – their work should be entirely at their own discretion.

Wildest of the wild cards was Tony Palmer, who from the start went his own way, eventually producing a weekly topical arts show which broke every rule and won few plaudits. It had energy but precious little else, but it was a child of its time – a period when 'doing your own thing' was the ideal and rock music was claimed the equal of the classics. William Mann, the music critic of *The Times*, maintained that the Beatles were the best songwriters since Schubert. I greatly enjoyed the Beatles, but it seemed a very stupid remark then and seems even sillier now. There is absolutely no need to compare rock music with the classics: they both have a place.

My real complaint about some of the younger producers was that they quite simply did not work hard enough. They arrived late, had long lunches, wrote for magazines or other outside bodies, and spent their evenings at the cinema. There was no commitment to television and its audience. They treated each other's work with hushed reverence, but never watched anything else. I remember one of them being outraged when I suggested he might watch *Z-Cars* or *Coronation Street* to learn more about how good popular television was made. He dismissed me as ridiculous and irrelevant. I think Stephen Hearst has to accept some responsibility for having brought these bright young men into the department and allowing them to do what they wanted. None of them was to make an impact comparable to that of the people that Wheldon had so strictly schooled on *Monitor*. I still find it hard to believe that the most disorganized of them all, Alan Yentob, ended up running BBC Television.

To achieve good programmes, much depended on the chemistry between director and writer/presenter, and during this period several long-term relationships were built up – such as that between Dennis Marks and the writer Michael Frayn, who for more than twenty-five years have made programmes together. One of the most effective couplings was between the director Mike Dibb and the critic John Berger, whose series *Ways of Seeing* still stands up well as a radical way of looking at art. It made a fascinating contrast to Kenneth Clark's *Civilisation*. I was fairly critical of *Civilisation* at the time, finding Clark's manner unengaging, until while the series was first being shown on television I sat next to a clever young woman from *The Economist* at a dinner. I was droning on about whether Clark was as reliable on political history as he was on art history when she interrupted me and said coolly, 'My father is seventy-four years of age and lives in Stoke-on-Trent. He has never been interested in art. Last week he came to London to see me, and his first question was "Where is the National Gallery?"' That is what *Civilisation* achieved, and I felt properly reproved.

What great communicators like Clark and Berger had in common was an ability to involve the public in their own enthusiasms. This was something that the bosses of Television and Radio then understood completely, but it has since been almost entirely replaced by a superficial clever-cleverness that touches no one. Today I cannot but feel that people are chosen because they look odd. Would anyone have bothered with Sister Wendy had she been an ordinary-looking creature? There is an excellent technical and scientific historian, Adam Hart-Davis, who is filmed riding around on a bicycle, wearing Lycra pants and a crash helmet in brilliant colours. There is absolutely no need for him to be dressed in this ludicrous way, but I can't help feeling that that is what television wants nowadays. It is all a way of down-grading seriousness and of undermining scholarship. Anything else invokes the deadly word 'elitist'.

Later I got to know Clark well and came to understand his sense of irony and admire his judgement. Looking back, I now find *Civilisation* a most impressive achievement, but the young all hated it. They disliked its confident convictions and its sense that there was only one way of looking at history and culture. I could see a place for Clark, but was more drawn to Berger, whose uncertainties and anxieties felt closer to my world than did Clark's sense of an ordered society, which seemed at that time very much under threat. Today, offered a choice between Brian Sewell and Sister Wendy, both Clark and Berger look like Old Testament prophets, so low have we sunk.

What was particularly enjoyable about this period in my life was the realization that I had now learnt enough to see how editing works and how small adjustments can lead to big improvements, whether at script stage or most particularly in the cutting room. I very much enjoyed looking at rough cuts with directors and film editors and seeking ways to make them more effective. Sometimes we would look at a sequence which made no sense at all to me, though the director would say, 'Well, I understand it' – which meant that he could not step back and see whether it was in fact saying what he wanted it to. I had myself made many mistakes of this kind, and was sometimes able to help achieve clarification to the satisfaction of all concerned. At times, however, discussions became highly confrontational, and the day was saved only by the imaginative grasp of some of the excellent film editors with whom we worked.

Although I lacked really committed interest in the techniques of filming – Geoffrey Haydon always said I simply did not care enough about lenses – I loved the process of editing, watching things come together and, through collaboration, often improving on one's initial vision. I know that my Diaghilev programmes, in particular, were saved only by the dedicated contribution of an assistant film editor who saw what I was trying to achieve with the still photographs while the editor did not. All of us learnt as much from editors and cameramen as we did from executive producers and heads of department, and we were immensely fortunate in the depth of talent available to the BBC in both areas at that time. Cameramen like Tubby Englander, John McGlashen and Ken McMillan, editors like Alan Tyrer, Peter Heelas and Mike Bradsell were outstanding, often with a surer instinct than the producers as well as the necessary knowledge of the technical processes to make a primary contribution. Some directors planned every shot and every sequence like a military operation, and proved absolutely incapable of flexibility when one did not work. These were the hardest to help – followed closely by those who wrote yards and yards of script and sprayed celluloid at it almost regardless of whether the image and the narration ever married, let alone fed off each other. Producers with a background in education were often the most literal, those with current affairs experience the most disconnected. Neither group was easy to help, and some of the worst programmes of this time fell into one or other of these categories.

Sometimes, however, the imaginative elements really took off. Lesley Megahey made a number of truly original films, notably one about Georges Rouault – set in a circus – which I thought a work of art in its own right. We had trouble getting permission from the Rouault family to make the film, and I recall a viewing of some of Megahey's previous work with the daughters of the painter, who had to be convinced. The unmarried daughter, Isabelle – a real French *vierge professionelle* – said we could go ahead, but that none of Rouault's drawings or paintings of prostitutes was to be included. 'But your father did paint them,' I pointed out tentatively. 'Cela c'est entièrement autre chose.'

I suppose at times I may have been heavy-handed in my dealings with some producers, but I could never believe I was there just to rubber-stamp their ideas. I always sought to help them to realize the programme that *they* wanted to make, not to impose on it my own approach. Both Wheldon and Burton had a tendency to want you to do things their way. With gifted producers, I found it more appealing to have a diversity of approach. But the programme had to work, and, not surprisingly, it often didn't. The greatest area of dispute was the use of dramatization. We were not, in my opinion, geared up as a department to handle this. Not only did it involve considerable expense, it also required experience of directing actors which was often missing. It was one thing for Jonathan Miller with *Alice in Wonderland*, or Patrick Garland with *Brief Lives*, to produce a kind of drama that the Drama Department would never attempt. It was quite different when almost entirely inexperienced directors sought to outdo Alain Resnais or Antonioni or any of the other film icons of that time. Historical situations using actors were always dangerous: the dialogue rarely worked and the whole thing creaked. Even a gifted producer like Colin Nears, whose documentary film on Colette was quite outstanding, came a cropper with a dramatization of the early life of Lenin – an unsuitable subject in my view. Most obdurate of the dramatizers was Gavin Millar, who spent most of his time as the *Listener*'s film critic and very occasionally made a short film for the department. He was an undoubted hero to the other young producers, but I simply could not see why. Even his subsequent work for the cinema has not justified the claims made for him. Tristram Powell was rather better, making sensitive explorations of the world of writers like Jean Rhys, as the excellent Jack Gold had done with A. E. Coppard.

There was always a huge amount going on, with demand for programmes increasing as the number of hours of transmission expanded and the coming of colour gave a new dimension to art films. We were always looking for new and effective presenters. Robert Hughes swept in like a breath of fresh air with his very Australian intolerance of art-speak, and James Mossman – exiled from Current Affairs for questioning authority too fiercely – brought his sensitive mind to bear on writers from Muriel Spark to Gore Vidal. Roy Strong, despite his bizarre sartorial predilections, proved a compelling talker about portraiture. Patrick Nuttgens, in his quirky way, was good on the environment. Basil Taylor made an excellent series on watercolours, and Edwin Mullins one on the art trade and the auction houses. In an unsubtle attempt to neutralize Mullins's reservations about the ethics of the art world, Peter Wilson, the Chairman of Sotheby's, invited

Mullins and me to spend a weekend in a chateau in the South of France with him. For all his upper-class smoothness, there was something deeply sinister about Wilson, but he was far too clever for us to pin anything on him. I am sure it was Bruce Chatwin's realization of Wilson's trickiness that led him to leave Sotheby's.

It was through Mullins that I undertook one of my most enjoyable journeys – tracing the Camino de Santiago. I hardly knew Spain at that time, but my interest had been caught by the enthusiasm of Sacheverell Sitwell, who had become a friend since taking part in the Diaghilev films. I hesitated, partly because I did not speak the language, but also because of a lingering hostility to the Franco regime, fuelled by friends like James Cornford. Eventually Mullins, who was planning a book on the pilgrimage route to Santiago, suggested an accompanying film, and I used my holiday to test whether there was enough material. I travelled with Bob Lockyer from Paris, darting about between the different routes across France, taking in Conques and Moissac, crossing the Pyrenees at Roncevalles, and continuing across northern Spain by way of Burgos and Léon, arriving at Santiago on the eve of St James's Day, in time for the celebrations – Mass and fireworks. It was a revelation of the scale of medieval enterprise. Roads, bridges, hospitals, hospices – still surviving after eight hundred years – had been erected in honour of a piece of ludicrous fakery. St James was no more buried in Santiago than St Andrew was in Amalfi or than the Virgin's birthplace had been miraculously transported to Loreto, which I had visited the previous year. I still had difficulty in squaring the aesthetic achievements of Christianity with its preposterous tradition and damaging dogma.

The fact that Spain had never known religious reform was particularly fascinating, with the cluttered dark church interiors and, in places like San Domingo de Silos, the superb choirs. The trip was to be the start of a longer association with Spain which in time led to my being invited to meetings of the Tertulias Hispano-Britannicos, the informal Anglo-Spanish talking shop. New friendships grew out of meeting other members, notably writers and historians like Raymond Carr, Hugh Thomas and, less obviously, Iris Murdoch. Her annual speech on the need to protect our language from the corruption of Anglo-American laziness was always a high point of the meetings. There was something both impressive and ludicrous about Murdoch's manner and appearance. She was obviously profoundly intelligent and well-meaning, but unbelievably grubby and disorganized. I had enjoyed her early work, but found many of the later novels too fantastic for my taste. I have never been comfortable with her picaresqueness, any more than with the science fiction of Doris Lessing. All science fiction seems to me a cop-out from the real business of the human condition. Who needs invented worlds when our own is so extraordinary? And I had by now embarked on a happy and continuing preoccupation with the French novel – most especially Balzac, but without losing a long-established love for Stendhal and Flaubert.

Our coverage of literature on television was decidedly patchy, with too many minor figures and not nearly enough about poetry. Here again individual choice prevailed over network needs. When the BBC spent a large sum on the serialization of Trollope's *Palliser* novels, it seemed to me important to provide some sort of introduction or biographical study, to provide a fuller picture of Trollope as a novelist who also had an interesting life. But there were no takers: nobody was in the least bit interested in him. And when it came to the centenary of Dickens's death the job was done by Ned Sherrin as a guest producer, his truly awful dramatization of the writer's life using characters from the novels as if they were real people. It was saved by the casting. Half the British theatre took part in it, from ancient figures like Sybil Thorndike and Gladys Cooper, both of whose last appearance this was, to people better known for their film careers, like Michael Wilding and Margaret Leighton, through to young people like Jenny Agutter and most particularly, in the role of Dickens himself, Anthony Hopkins, right at the start of his remarkable career. The acting honours were almost entirely stolen by Arthur Lowe as Dickens's father (with dialogue lifted from Mr Micawber) and by Joan Greenwood as one of Dickens's wimpish women. Anything to do with Sherrin was always fun and always involved a fleet of stars – never more so than in the obituary he made of the actor-manager Donald Wolfit, probably the funniest programme I ever saw on television, with people like Ronald Harwood and Harold Pinter capping each other's stories about being young actors in Wolfit's company.

One had to have something of a bird brain to cope as Executive Producer for so varied an output, sometimes in one day dealing with five or six different films in the course of preparation or scripts being written on quite different subjects. It was exhausting and at times confusing, while sometimes I also had the feeling that, just as with the Paris job, I was running a service station but was not able to drive the cars.

Yet I was convinced that in the long run I had made a right decision. I was not a born director in the way that many of my friends were. As a generalist in an age of increasing specialization, I was sure I could contribute more as a producer.

Meanwhile by 1969 the BBC was going through one of its periodic departmental and administrative upheavals. Paul Fox, an immensely effective Controller of BBC1, even if not much interested in music or the arts, left for the new Yorkshire Television. His place was taken by Brian Cowgill, who was even less interested in what we were doing. At BBC2 David Attenborough, who had been a reluctant executive in any case, although much liked by production staff, decided to return to his gorillas and was replaced by Robin Scott, my former Paris boss, who in the intervening years had been the first Controller of Radio 1. I had wanted my appointment as Executive Producer ratified by Attenborough, who was not a total supporter because of his reservations about *Music Now*, rather than by Scott, who was a friend – a scruple that, Stephen Hearst observed, no one in Vienna could have understood. It was a time of much mobility, as new independent companies started up. Producers as well as executives were leaving, and unfortunately the ones who left were usually the best, so people like me were obliged to make a schedule with the unambitious, the ineffectual or the unready. But for the time being I had guest-producer posts that could bring in talent from outside on short-term contracts.

Another rejigging of the departments in 1970 was said to have been made to prevent Aubrey Singer from leaving for the commercial sector. Singer, who had been the driving force behind most of the BBC's international expeditions – from Moscow in 1961 to satellite links like Telstar and the moon landing – was a Bunterish figure, almost circular in shape, much given to whistling and jingling the coins in his pocket. He loved to travel, and was always setting off to far corners of the world to see what the BBC could quarry. He took with him quantities of gifts, like an old colonial explorer, and on at least one occasion – in Ulan Bator – was forced to bring them all back since no one really wanted to talk to him. He was extremely energetic, but to my mind he confused activity with action. In Moscow, after I had spent six or seven hours interpreting, he needed to find something else to do and called on my services relentlessly. But I always liked him, however infuriating he might be. A new group – the Features Group – with Singer at its head was pulled together out of the departments based at Kensington

House. It included Arts Features, Science Programmes and a loose collection of producers called General Features, as well as the then popular weekly programme *Man Alive*, run by the hugely self-regarding Desmond Wilcox. It made very little programme sense and generated a new layer of bureaucracy and more meetings, all of which lasted twice as long as necessary if Wilcox was present. As with the Duke of Edinburgh, there was no subject on which Wilcox did not have views.

Singer would roam the corridors whistling and jingling, and one learnt to sweep anything important off the desk at his approach, since he would invariably volunteer to get involved with a hundred needless initiatives. He was tremendously well-meaning, but a dangerous bundle of undirected energy. His greatest achievement was to have boosted the BBC's commitment to science programmes, but his longest legacy was the move into co-production. The impetus for this was the tapering off of the income from the licence fee and rising costs, yet co-production failed to recognize a central fact: that the requirements of different networks in different countries were very different. Singer struck a deal – a lucrative one, it must be said – with the Time–Life Corporation. From then on, all our ideas had to be run across Time–Life's executives. The head man reminded me of an exchange between Danny Kaye and Curt Jurgens in a long-forgotten film: 'You have one of the best minds of the century – the fifth century.' All Time–Life seemed to care about was what it called 'marquee names' – usually Hollywood stars – so anything to do with the arts had to have Charlton Heston or James Mason introducing it. Jackie Kennedy was thought right for the Hermitage, in Leningrad, since she had redecorated the White House, and when John Wells wanted to adapt and dramatize *Gulliver's Travels* Time–Life insisted on Burt Lancaster as Gulliver. It may have been easier for the science producers, since there was more common ground in science, but the kind of programme we made had nothing in common with mainstream American television, where documentary hardly existed outside social issues.

We already had good links with public broadcasting companies in other countries, although financially they were too poor to contribute much. Stephen Hearst did a deal with Bavarian TV, Munich, under which an Anglophile Head of Documentaries, Kurt Hoffman, bought into a very large number of BBC programmes and in return we were lumbered with trying to make broadcastable versions of some of theirs. I was the BBC representative on a European committee looking at art, architecture and history projects. We met in Paris, Amsterdam, Rome, Munich, Brussels and London in turn, and after four years we produced one unsuccessful series. The German element was an academic lecture on the Ottonian empire, illustrated by still photographs. Italy made an attractive film about the Palio in Sienna, but it was hardly ground-breaking. France made an immensely stylish but virtually untranslatable study of the role of popular song and music in the French Revolution – I was faced with having to translate 'Ça Ira' and 'La Marseillaise' in ways that might explain their significance for a British audience. My main memory of the whole venture is of the arrogance of the French, who, if they were present, insisted that the entire proceedings be conducted in their language. I spent days translating from French into Italian and from German into French. It was as useless as Unesco, whose art-film committee I also attended for a while, where the bleatings of disaffected French documentary-makers about not getting royalties for resold programmes brought the whole committee to its knees. The only decision it ever made was where the next meeting would be held, coupled with a thorough discussion of whether there were any good restaurants.

Stephen Hearst and I were both believers in European cooperation, but it rapidly became clear how little could be done to bridge national differences. In co-productions there was always a winner and a loser, and I was determined we would not be the loser. But there were other effects of co-production too, like the downgrading of on-screen experts in favour of off-screen voices, so that programmes could be more easily dubbed into other languages. Perhaps this matters less with natural-history programmes, but we were told that powerful critics with things to say, like David Sylvester, were unacceptable for the 'international version'. I worried about the future of what television does best – putting up the right specialist to buttonhole the public with his enthusiasm and expertise. Attenborough was able to continue doing it in natural history, but in our area we lost out.

Even more serious in the long run, co-productions removed a crucial element of editorial control. We no longer made what we thought important: we made what we could finance. I am quite aware that this is the system that prevails in most other areas of life, from manufacturing industry to the cinema, but the uniqueness of the BBC until then had been that it had been free to select what it did. It was in the best sense editorially independent. Today it still insists on its political independence, but it caved in pretty unresistingly to commercial interdependence and we found some very strange bedfellows. An American public-relations company was quite prepared to put money into a film about Alexander Calder and his mobiles, except that it thought the project was 'too inexpensive'. It could not really be serious if it was so cheap – could we not up the budget a bit with a few days' helicopter filming? Norman Swallow, the Editor of *Omnibus*, built a cosy relationship with the Soviet Novosti agency, leading to a programme about Leningrad with a sequence celebrating the jolly life of young poets. This was in the wake of the scandal about Boris Pasternak being pressured to refuse the Nobel Prize for Literature and the difficulties he had in getting his work published. Hearst and I were outraged, but Swallow insisted on keeping avenues of communication open. I found his political position puzzling, and it became more troubling when Stephen Hearst was appointed Controller of Radio 3 and Swallow took over the Arts Features. He brought in a group of ageing documentary producers who kept the bar going flat out and produced a large number of dull programmes, few of which seemed to have much to say about the arts.

Naturally, when Hearst left in the summer of 1971 I felt I had to apply for the job, although I knew I had no chance of getting it as I was nothing like experienced enough after less than two years as an executive. I flew back from Rome in the middle of an Italian holiday to be interviewed. Because I knew I would not be taken seriously as a candidate, I found myself under much less pressure than usual and did probably the best interview of my life. Certainly with David Attenborough, who had never really been a friend, I felt a quite different relationship from that day on. I was neither surprised nor depressed not to get the job, although it added to the growing number of times I had not been appointed to posts in the BBC. What I did regret was the departure of Stephen Hearst, who, despite occasional differences of opinion, had been an inspiring colleague and a most supportive friend. Others found his intense and almost neurotic concern about things irritating, and he could be very dismissive, but he cared passionately about the kind of society we lived in – and most particularly about the place of the arts in that society. I had taken many aspects of this attitude for granted, but I was now learning how much they had to be fought for even in the BBC.

Norman Swallow had none of Hearst's fire and energy; he was

friendly, but quite without obvious passion – for the arts at least. But inevitably he was much better liked than Hearst since he was so easy-going. His technical knowledge of documentary was impeccable and he was terrific in the cutting room, but I could not work out what he really wanted the department to be and was concerned that he gave the impression that it did not really matter. 'It's only television,' he would say with a shrug of the shoulders when I got steamed up about something we had done or, more often, things we were not doing. Whereas Hearst had spent the lunch hour swimming in the Lime Grove baths, Norman presided every day over long, boozy lunches in the BBC Club, giving the impression that he found almost everything faintly ridiculous – especially me. I realized that, as with Culshaw, I would have to carve my own furrow. I am usually depicted as knowing exactly what I want, and eventually that may be so – but only after a long process of brooding and discussion. I need a dialogue with superiors or colleagues; I want to tease out reactions and to test ideas. I like teams, and, as a result of what I learnt from Humphrey Burton, Stephen Hearst and others, have spent a good deal of time putting teams together, being extremely lucky in finding the right people in the past twenty years. Life was to be decreasingly satisfying after Hearst left.

Nevertheless, I had a lot of programmes to carry forward – probably never fewer than fifty or sixty going across my desk at any one time. I didn't seem to have much trouble keeping the details in my head and in constantly shuffling the programme offers and ideas to try to achieve a balanced output which matched the staffing, the service requirements, the money and the aspiration. I was also making new friends through a wider range of contacts. A visit to Turkey to set up a series of films on the history and archaeology of Asia Minor led to a lifelong friendship with the presenter of the series, John Julius Norwich, who shares my love of history, of *faits divers*, of unusual personalities and of France. John Julius took me to meet his mother, the legendary Lady Diana Cooper. I found her quite as captivating as did the rest of the world, with her piercing blue eyes and pale skin. She seemed quite ageless. After our first meeting I sent her flowers. She wrote back on the first of many postcards, 'Glad you enjoyed the lunch. I adored you.' Heady stuff! She was a hostess of considerable charm and grace, with a capacity to bring out the best in everybody. At one jolly lunch around her circular dining table, one of the guests, Gladwyn Jebb, a former ambassador to France, had really been left out of the conversation and had contributed practically nothing, Diana turned to him and said, 'Gladwyn, you speak such beautiful French, why don't you read us some French poetry?' And he did, and had his moment of glory.

It was at Diana's table that I met the Queen Mother, who usually came to lunch once a year. The conversation turned to attractive men whom she and Diana had known in their youth. The most fascinating, it appeared, was Lord Sefton. Lord Sefton was for me a bluff, aged racehorse owner whose charms were hard to see. Why had he been so attractive then? 'Well, you see,' explained Queen Elizabeth, 'he used to ask one to dance and then sneer. It was captivating.' I remember her once pausing in the doorway as she left to go to a garden party and saying, 'Oh, how I wish I could stay here with you and laugh for ever.' I was being increasingly drawn into a world of rather grand and well-known people. My reasons for enjoying this had little to do with snobbery – they were just such good company, told such good stories, and were such generous hosts.

Much of my time was now spent in pursuit of writers – especially ones who had previously been unwilling to be interviewed or filmed. The list of these was long and contained some of the most popular names, like Agatha Christie. We never succeeded in getting her, but we did eventually gain access to Daphne du Maurier, who had become very reclusive in her later years. The price of access was an interviewer of her choice and the BBC showing a film made by her son, based on her book *Vanishing Cornwall*. The film was well shot and attractive, but sank under the weight of a relentless commentary by Michael Redgrave, who, by reading extracts from the book, simply told you unnecessarily what you could already see. I tried in vain to persuade her and her son that the film would benefit greatly if the commentary was thinned out. I think it was found outrageous that I should attempt to interfere with her writing. In the interview, however, she was surprisingly frank and straightforward – rather mannish in her gruff way, but full of interest.

Norman Swallow sent me to see J. B. Priestley in his large and chilly house in Warwickshire, a very 1930s construction with a marble floor in the hall and pale colours in all the rooms. It sat oddly with the phrase with which Priestley started most sentences, 'Speaking as a life-long socialist . . .' We had at that time a regular programme in which people chose favourite extracts from books or poems and read them with an actor or actress. Priestley chose oddly dull chunks of mostly his own work, including an enormously long and boring description of a visit to New Zealand. I suggested, as politely as I possibly could, that it was simply too long. 'I'll have you know, young man, I know what I am doing,' he said. He was altogether very unimpressed with me, since for temporary medical reasons I was not drinking and he had opened a rather good bottle of wine for lunch. The programme which resulted was a near disaster.

I was sent off one day to Paris to make contact with Terence Rattigan, to discuss a bizarre proposal which had been suggested to Norman Swallow. It was that we should make a large documentary about Alexander the Great, but interleave it with a new production of Rattigan's play *Adventure Story* about Alexander, for which Rattigan would write new scenes and linking material. He was living in a small flat in Passy, and I was asked to call at four in the afternoon. He was the only person I have ever seen who actually wore a silk dressing gown and used a long gold cigarette holder. It was plain that he was not impressed with the project, despite my valiant attempt to sell it. He cut across me and said, 'You don't believe a word of this, do you?' I could not help laughing and readily admitted it. 'Well, then, now let's have a drink and get to know each other.' He produced a bottle of Bollinger and we talked for ages. He was obviously lonely, hated his tax exile and felt out of things, and was depressed by the constant critical attacks he received from people like Kenneth Tynan. As I left, I asked if there was anything he *would* like to do for the BBC? 'Yes,' he said, 'I'd like to write a programme about Borley Rectory.' This, I happened to know, was an Essex vicarage famous in the 1930s for a series of dramatic hauntings, all of which it emerged were a hoax, perpetrated by the man who ran the Society for Psychical Research. I tried to interest my superiors in the idea, but without success.

Peter Ustinov came into my life again, and I produced one of the still remembered programmes of *After Dinner Conversations*, in which he told stories and answered questions. The surprising thing was that these conversations were very carefully planned, and all the stories were cued in in an agreed sequence; the sense of improvisation was an entire illusion. I always enjoyed seeing Peter, who had done the commentaries for my Diaghilev films. His wit was so wonderfully ready, and we always laughed a lot. I remember him pausing in the middle of recording the Diaghilev commentaries and saying, 'Do you think Diaghilev was the kind of person about whom you could say, "Hail,

Fellatio, well met?"' But behind all the jokes there was an element of sadness, for it was quite clear that he really wanted to be taken extremely seriously as a playwright, a theatre and film director, a novelist, a short-story writer and a cartoonist, but all the world seemed to want was chat. It was brilliant chat, but just chat, and his sense of frustration was very evident.

One of the real high points of these years came with the involvement of Samuel Beckett in our output. Tristram Powell had persuaded him to allow the BBC to record some of his short plays which had been presented at the Royal Court Theatre. In 1973 Powell very kindly invited me to meet Beckett and to look after him when he came to a viewing. I was immediately entranced; not only did he look so wonderful – like a great eagle – but his manner was so warm and approachable. I remember that he was wearing the most wonderful expensive grey suede coat, which was rather a surprise. Years later I spent a long evening in Paris with him and his enthusiastic champion John Calder. We started in the very expensive, long-established restaurant the Closerie des Lilas, but Beckett was obviously deeply unhappy in such luxurious surroundings and we left without ordering, ending up in a small Chinese restaurant where he was well known. He told stories about Ireland, about France, about James Joyce and taking Joyce's daughter dancing. It was hard not to pinch oneself, and to believe that one was really in the presence of someone so extraordinary.

Meanwhile, back in Kensington House, in the early 1970s I made a number of small programmes myself, just to keep my hand in. The most notable was a series of conversations about the theatre with John Gielgud, whose memoirs were just about to be published. Strictly speaking they seldom were conversations: one question was usually enough to set Gielgud off for the ten-minute duration of the programme. This was certainly the case when I asked him about his cousin the designer Gordon Craig. The question released an unstoppable torrent which was transmitted as it stood without any editing. Gielgud was marvellous company, though frequently given to mildly depressing comments on the state of classical theatre. He and his great friend Ralph Richardson had got a new wind with writers like David Storey and Harold Pinter, and he was furious when people kept asking him why he was still not playing romantic leads. 'They want me to go on being Richard of Bordeaux!' he would groan. He became quite violent when asked whether he thought contemporary dramatists' use of four-letter words was acceptable. After a performance at the Royal Court of *Veterans*, Charles Woods's play about the making of Tony Richardson's film *The Charge of the Light Brigade*, he told me that during the pre-London run in Brighton 'You couldn't hear the dialogue for the noise of seats tipping up as the audience trooped out.' At dinner we were joined by Alec Guinness. It was wonderful to watch them playing off each other – so different, yet so equal in authority.

Gielgud's faux pas were legendary; I am sure they were not intentional. In one of our conversations he mentioned Peggy Ashcroft and said, 'She is one of the great actresses I have had the misfortune (*pause*) – I mean the good fortune – to work with.' It was about Ashcroft that he made one of his most unexpected observations. We were sitting side by side on a banquette in the Poissonnerie de l'Avenue in Chelsea at the end of a splendid lunch for which he had insisted on paying when he said, 'Funny about passion, isn't it? It just doesn't show.' I asked him to explain. 'Well, look at Celia Johnson – totally happy, lots of money, nice husband, lovely children, beautiful house, big success, yet she looks like the back of a London bus. Whereas Peggy's been in and out of every bed in London and not a line on her face. Passion, you see, just doesn't show.'

We went together to Cecil Day-Lewis and Jill Balcon's house in Greenwich, to record some poetry – a charming idea of Norman Swallow's to cheer up the obviously dying Poet Laureate. Gielgud invited me back to Cowley Street in Westminster, where he lived, sat me down in the drawing room, and said, 'I'll be back in a minute.' He was gone for ages – no doubt trying to persuade his reclusive companion to join us. He eventually returned, calling from the stairs in that wonderful, much imitated voice, 'Don't worry, I'm not wearing a frilly nightie!'

One of the things I was most pleased about in these years was being instrumental in persuading the Australian Broadcasting Corporation to put up some money to help us make a series of programmes about Australian architecture with John Betjeman. I had always been delighted by Betjeman's contributions to television, whatever the subject. He was marvellous company, and his infectious laugh was irresistible, but behind the teddy-bear exterior there were sound scholarship and deep passions. He loved out-of-the-way places, neglected artists and undervalued writers, and had the knack of sharing his enthusiasm with no hint of patronage. He gave the audience confidence. I recall him appearing once on the David Frost show. When Frost, with his usual sneering philistinism, suggested that there was something odd about writing poetry, Betjeman got up, walked across to the studio audience, and asked how many of them wrote poems. Hands went up all over the place, and at his suggestion several people quoted things they had written to their wives or lovers. They felt safe in his hands; they knew whatever happened he would not laugh at them. Frost looked on in baffled amazement.

Betjeman had fallen in love with Australia on a previous visit, and longed to go back. It is almost impossible today to realize how little the British knew about Australia thirty years ago, and everywhere attitudes were full of contempt. John just loved it – from the wrought-iron balconies of Ballarat, my mother's birthplace, to the elegant Georgian houses of Tasmania; from tarantulas in the loo in Brisbane to the horrors of the penal colony at Port Arthur. Just as in his poems the smiles fade and a serious point is made, his account of the solitary-confinement cell at Port Arthur made one's blood run cold.

From now on I saw him regularly, and grew also to know and to love his companion, Lady Elizabeth Cavendish, a woman of remarkable strength of character and beliefs whom he characterized by the nickname Phoeble. (His extraordinary wife, from whom he was not quite separated, though she spent much of her time in India, where she had grown up, he called Philth.) Every meeting was both entertaining and instructive. We went to see an exhibition called 'The Destruction of the Country House', which Roy Strong had organized at the V&A. There was a big gallery full of photographs of demolished houses. John went round and, in highly audible tones, to the consternation of the other visitors, commented on the hideousness and architectural shortcomings of almost all those that had gone. The only good ones, he said, had caught fire or collapsed of their own accord. 'Why the mourning?' John asked. 'The best have all been saved.' But there would have been less mileage in 'The Saving of the Country House'.

John had a line of quiet asides that was memorable too. About a fierce woman producer with whom he had made a short film on the Isle of Man, he said, 'I would like her to chastise me – and I don't mean pretend.' Of a good-looking young male director, 'Brings out the Scoutmaster in us all.' Perhaps our most extraordinary occasion together was a dinner following a viewing of the Australian films organized for the Prince of Wales, who loved Australia, and for Princess Margaret, who was about to go there for the first time. Elizabeth Cavendish was a lady-in-waiting to Princess Margaret, and she made the connections. The other guests were Lord Snowdon, Elizabeth's mother, the Dowager Duchess of Devonshire, the writer and diarist James Lees-Milne and his formidable wife, Alvilde, Patrick Garland, who like me had Australian connections, and his then girlfriend, Jenny Agutter. We dined in a top-floor room at Rules in Maiden Lane, chosen by John – perhaps not entirely tactfully, because Edward VII used to entertain his girlfriends there. At one moment four of us trooped in procession through the crowded restaurant to the gents. I could sense people saying to each other, 'The Prince of Wales, Lord Snowdon, John Betjeman, and who's that with them?' 'He must be the private detective,' I heard a woman say. The evening culminated in a spectacular row between Princess Margaret and Lord Snowdon, after which he refused to leave and she had to be driven back to Kensington Palace in Patrick Garland's Mini. In fact we all trooped back and were there until two in the morning, since the Princess never seemed to tire. James Lees-Milne wrote of the occasion in his diary, but better than that was the letter he wrote to John Betjeman, in which he said he found Princess Margaret 'very very very frightening but beautiful and succulent like Belgian buns'.

Though my social life was expanding, I never stopped seeing my Cambridge friends – especially those who had gone into the theatre, like Derek Jacobi and Ian McKellen. John Tydeman was happily installed in Radio Drama, where he produced many of the most outstanding radio plays of the time and was responsible in the 1960s for developing Tom Stoppard and discovering Joe Orton. My longest-running theatre friendship was with Judi Dench, whom I had met when I was eighteen and she was the girlfriend of Julian Belfrage, who had been one of my school friends and became her agent. I feel lucky to have been around to watch Judi's career from its beginnings, and even more to know her. These days we meet rarely, but always with joy on my side and a degree of hysterical laughter. For someone who is so funny, she has unrivalled power to move me. On the night of the moon landing, Colin Nears and I produced a bizarre programme of music and words about the moon. Judi read Matthew Arnold's 'Dover Beach', the only time I can remember being in floods of tears in a television studio.

The most significant new friendships of these years came out of my continuing ambition to get architecture on to television. The BBC film for our European series had been a brilliant survey of the effects of the Industrial Revolution on the landscape and look of England, written by Patrick Nuttgens and directed by Christopher Martin. Martin shared my interest in architecture, and we had collaborated on several projects – including a big studio discussion which involved Hugh Casson, whom I had known since school days and who brought into the studio legendary figures like Maxwell Fry and Jane Drew. I was convinced that, following the success of Kenneth Clark's *Civilisation* and Jacob Bronowski's *The Ascent of Man*, we should do something about architecture. In 1973 I asked Casson and Nuttgens to join a working party with several producers in the department to see if we could devise something interesting. I was certain we did not want to produce a chronological study starting with the Saxons and ending up on the South Bank.

It was difficult to make progress. Casson was still teaching at the Royal College of Art and was in demand everywhere from Windsor Castle, which he was redecorating, to the Anti-Apartheid Movement meetings which he chaired. Nuttgens was running Leeds Polytechnic. My BBC colleagues also had plenty of other work, and we were slow in formulating a proposal. What eventually emerged was a suggestion that we should look at architecture not through the passage of time but in response to changing requirements. It was really a history of building types, although Nikolaus Pevsner had not yet published his book with that title. I wanted to look at the architecture of power, of entertainment, of education and so on, and provisionally called the series *The Measure of Man* – from the Alberti tag that architecture should be 'to the measure of man'. We presented it to Norman Swallow and one or two other colleagues. They were completely unimpressed, and nothing we said could shift them.

One morning I woke up and thought, 'Why are we causing all these problems? Let's just do the obvious.' Christopher Martin and I walked around Holland Park for an hour and by then had roughed out a series of eight programmes on British architecture from the Saxons to the South Bank. We even had a title – *The Spirit of the Age*. But who was to write and present it? All the obvious names were examined but were found problematic. John Betjeman was deeply involved in programmes for the General Features Department produced by Edward Mirzoeff, and in any case, much as I loved both him and his approach, I felt he was not right for something on this scale. John Summerson had made a film the previous year about Inigo Jones, but he had been thought stiff and too remote as a presenter. Pevsner, a seemingly obvious choice, had made one film with us about his Penguin *Buildings of England* series. He had hated the filming process, and complained bitterly that the fee he received for two weeks' work was equivalent to that for one lecture in America. Casson was too busy. Nuttgens, although tremendously ambitious, also could not spare the time: *Civilisation* had taken over two years of Kenneth Clark's life.

I wondered how it would be if, like so many books on architectural history, the series had more than one author, each selected to cover the period he knew best. In this way we could use most of the big names, but make fewer demands on their time. Swallow was initially sceptical, but eventually accepted it and I started fitting names to periods. Some were easy – Roy Strong was a natural for the Tudors, Summerson for neoclassicism, Nuttgens for the Arts and Crafts movement and Casson for the moderns. After a lot of toing and froing I sounded them out. Summerson would like to have done them all, but accepted the period I suggested, as did the others. Several gaps remained – the age of Wren, the Palladians, the Victorians and, most important of all, since it would inevitably be the first programme in the series, the Middle Ages.

I went to see Pevsner in his little office in Bloomsbury Square. He was as friendly as he always was with me, but adamant that he could not do even one programme – he was racing to complete the *Buildings of England* series. He had recently lost his wife, and was already suffering mildly from Parkinson's Disease. 'Who could do the Middle Ages?' I asked him. He ran through several names, none of which struck sparks from either of us, and promised to think about it further. I went back to the office and by chance met Eddie Mirzoeff in the corridor. He was carrying the galley proofs of a book – *The English Parish Church as Work of Art*, by Alec Clifton-Taylor. He asked if I knew him. I did not, but I had a copy of his invaluable book on building materials, *The Pattern of English Building*. Mirzoeff enthused about the galleys, and offered to lend me them. I read them for less than an hour, seized the London phone book, found a number, and rang. Clifton-Taylor replied at once. 'Could we meet?' I asked. 'Is it urgent,' he replied. 'Well, fairly,' I said. 'Nine-thirty tomorrow morning.'

I was greeted next day by a tall, white-haired, tweed-suited rubicund figure with an almost boyish manner. We went through to his garden, where he worked in a heated summer house, and sat down and began to talk, in very general terms. I was immediately captivated, and within half an hour had offered him the opening programme of the series. He had never appeared before a camera, but he was a very widely admired lecturer. Also, as he was rich and self-employed, he could certainly find the time and not worry too much about the small amount the BBC paid. I went back to the office both thrilled and extremely apprehensive about what Christopher Martin and my other colleagues would say. On my desk was a postcard from Bloomsbury Square. It read, 'The name that eluded us was Alec Clifton-Taylor. I think he's your man. Good luck. Nikolaus Pevsner.' The meeting with Clifton-Taylor was the beginning of one of the happiest friendships of my life and the start of what was to be for him a ten-year career in which he became almost as well known as his old friend John Betjeman. There are times when one is tempted to think the gods are on your side.

The eight programmes of *The Spirit of the Age* were filmed during an eighteen-month period in 1974–5 and became the BBC's contribution to European Architectural Heritage Year. In addition to Clifton-Taylor, Strong, Summerson, Nuttgens and Casson, the three remaining slots were given to Robert Furneaux Jordan for the age of Wren, John Julius Norwich for the Palladians and Mark Girouard for the Victorians. It was a strong line-up, balancing recognized scholarship with television experience. I decided to direct Alec Clifton-Taylor myself, as I felt he was my discovery, and also John Summerson, since I longed for an opportunity to work with him and was convinced he could be more confident than he had been in the Inigo Jones programme. Christopher Martin took on Furneaux Jordan and Girouard – two absolute newcomers to television presentation – and worked again with Patrick Nuttgens. David Cheshire had previously got on well with Roy Strong and Hugh Casson, so they were teamed up, while David Heycock had also worked happily before with John Julius Norwich. Some presenters knew exactly what they wanted to include, others had a long list of alternatives, but the key thing was that there would be a lot of time for research, since the selection of places was obviously of the greatest importance. Research is much less expensive than wasted filming, and I was keen to keep the costs down where we could, since the travel element, as well as the lighting, was going to consume much of the budget. It was clear that I was going to find it difficult to carry on as Executive Producer for all the BBC2 output with this series as well, and Norman Swallow agreed to release me for a year to make the programmes.

I began in the middle, as it were, with Summerson. I was so respectful of his knowledge and his Olympian manner that our early collaboration was uncomfortable. We used to meet on the top floor of the
extraordinary Sir John Soane's Museum in Lincoln's Inn Fields, where
he had been Curator for over twenty years. His deputy, officially
known as the Inspectress, was Dorothy Stroud, an architectural historian in her own right and a jealous guardian of access to Summerson.
We made very slow progress. I felt we needed to look at things together, to gauge how he would react on film. I knew he was giving a lecture
at Attingham Park, outside Shrewsbury, and I suggested that after the
lecture we spend a couple of days travelling together. We saw
Cronkhill, a pretty Nash villa, and were charmingly received by Lord
Cawley at Berrington, a very good house by Henry Holland. We visited Downton Castle, the creation of the aesthete Richard Payne Knight,
with a castellated neo-medieval exterior and a totally classical interior.
We scrambled over Chepstow racecourse looking for the ruins of a
Soane house – it was quite a sight to see Sir John shinning over a six-
foot barbed-wire fence. We ended up in Bristol, seeing how neoclassicism tailed off with the early Victorians and looking at the recently finished Catholic Cathedral in Clifton, which to Summerson's amusement
had won the annual award of the Concrete Society. He proved wonderful company, and I quite got over my fear of him.

On the last day, he asked if I would care to dine with him and his
wife at their home in Primrose Hill on our return. I was thrilled, for I
already knew that practically no one was ever invited to the house and
I was keen to meet his wife, the sister of the sculptor Barbara Hep-
worth. (The two sisters certainly proved a justification of genetics,
since they both produced triplets.) As we arrived at the house, Lady
Summerson said, 'Did you have a good time?' 'Simply wonderful,' said
her husband, and, indicating me, 'He knows everything.' I locked
myself in a bathroom and heaved a sigh of relief. Of course it wasn't
true: I didn't know everything, but I had done very careful research and
was usually able to pick up his references. Research, like editing, was
always for me the really enjoyable part of the programme-making
process.

Over the several months we worked together I came to have a deep
affection for Summerson as one of the great teachers. He was much
more amusing than first impressions suggested, incredibly well read,
and interested in much more than architecture – he had, after all,

chaired the radio programme *The Critics* on the Home Service for many years, and he loved the theatre and literature as much as landscape and buildings. His speaking manner, like his writing, was measured and notable for a huge vocabulary, with very careful use of adjectives and adverbs. I asked him once about his style. He was genuinely puzzled – he didn't think he had one. In the 1930s he and Betjeman had worked together on *Architectural Review* and Betjeman had coined the name by which Summerson was still known to friends: Coolmore. It fitted perfectly. Reading him today, and most especially hearing his voice in recordings, seems to evoke a vanished age. Summerson may not have been a natural performer, but he commanded attention and radiated authority – which is more than can be said for Janet Street-Porter as a presenter of architectural programmes. Why has the BBC come to believe that knowledge is inessential, that any old TV personality will do? It is stupid, lazy and damaging – a typical by-product of the claustrophobically metropolitan Groucho Club attitude to culture that characterizes so many television executives.

The film Summerson made was far from being the most admired in the series, but I always had a soft spot for it. It was a vindication of my earlier belief that neoclassicism could be made to live, and whether in the Soane Museum itself or walking around Edinburgh's New Town, or in the Wye Valley talking of Wordsworth's 'Tintern Abbey', Summerson exuded a combination of scholarship and understated passion that won my total loyalty. We had a private viewing of the finished film, to which he invited Dorothy Stroud. At the end they were both in tears. So much for the chilliness of neoclassicism!

I went on seeing Summerson from time to time for the rest of his life. He was thirty years to the day older than me, and on his eightieth birthday, my fiftieth, I presented a tribute to him on Radio 4. He eventually succumbed to Parkinson's Disease, and the last time I saw him – at Hugh Casson's eightieth birthday party, in the Royal Academy – he could hardly control either his arms or his legs. His voice, however, remained unaltered. It was very moving.

Meanwhile, Christopher Martin and the others got on with their planning, trying to get a workable script out of the tetchy Furneaux Jordan and to bolster the confidence of the very shy Mark Girouard. In the end both their programmes were successful and I wished that Girouard could be persuaded to do more, but, like Pevsner, he did not really enjoy the mechanics of film-making with all its delays and interruptions. Roy Strong cantered through the Tudors changing his clothes about seven times in the fifty minutes – a stupid distraction for which the director, David Cheshire, must take the blame. Cheshire was too pleased with himself to think it mattered – so many people had told him he was promising that he came to believe he need not make an effort. Eventually, when his marriage broke up, he took to the bottle and destroyed himself. It was a sad story. David Heycock, who had made a good job of the John Julius Norwich script, also had a problematic life, since soon after *The Spirit of the Age* he developed MS. He bravely struggled on on sticks, hardly able to walk but determined not to give up. I much admired his courage.

All the time when I was not working with Summerson or involving myself with other directors I devoted to Alec Clifton-Taylor. He sent me haring all over the place to look at churches, bridges, houses and castles I did not know, and often we travelled together. He always took with him his notebooks. After every visit to a building he would write an account of its condition. We stopped one day at Gedney, a wonderful church by the Wash, and he brought out three different accounts of it written over the previous forty years. He was obsessed with architecture – and not only in Great Britain. He travelled widely in Europe and elsewhere, and once lent me his copious notes on Turin, a city he thought seriously undervalued.

A lifelong friend of his once said that Clifton-Taylor had only ever had one idea in his life, but thank goodness it was a good one. His great idea was the importance of building materials. He knew which quarry provided the stone for every cathedral or great house in England; he could gauge for how long bricks had been fired by their colour. He saw every roof slate as part of a larger design, and was frequently choleric about the state of windows when glazing bars had been removed or unleaded glass had been inserted. Most of all he hated churchyards with green granite chips and plastic flowers. He could have been tiresome and pedantic, but I found him fascinating, and he fundamentally altered the way I looked at architecture from then on. I knew lots about style and could date things pretty accurately, but I had simply not realized how much of the pleasure of buildings lay in the raw materials, the satisfaction of stone, brick and slate well used.

On our first meeting I told him that, although exteriors were freely available, we could probably afford to light the interior of only one cathedral, and I knew how difficult the choice would be. 'Not at all,' he said. 'There are several wonderful cathedrals in this country, but only one supreme example on a par with the great churches of France.' He then made me guess. Of course I got it wrong – oscillating between Durham, Salisbury, Gloucester, Canterbury and Wells. 'No, no,' he said. 'They are all interesting, but Lincoln is by far the best.' So off we went to Lincoln, where the Dean – the splendidly named Oliver Twistleton-Wickham-Fiennes – lent us his keys and let us climb all over the building. I suffer from vertigo and so have problems with heights. Clifton-Taylor knew no fear and would lean out from the choir gallery over a 100-foot drop, pointing out details of the roof while I cringed against the wall. We climbed into the space between the nave vault and the external roof; it was like a huge tithe barn. Clifton-Taylor would fling open doors and gaze into the void, jumping about with enthusiasm.

All over the country, he took me to places that may not have been the best known but always had the most atmosphere – something he recognized as being useful for filming. Great Chalfield Manor in Wiltshire, Lower Brockhampton's Gate House in Herefordshire, Cullompton Church in Devon – we filmed them all. He was highly companionable, full of stories and a great gossip, always keen to know more about the famous and the infamous. He had inherited a sizeable fortune and devoted his life to his interests. He was that rare thing in our time, but so familiar to our forebears, a confirmed bachelor. He asked me once if I thought sex mattered. I said I did, and he replied, 'I am so lucky – it has never been of the slightest interest to me, and that has given me so much time for other, more fulfilling, pursuits.'

So as to familiarize him with filming, I took him with a camera crew to Harefield church in Middlesex, stood him in front of a wall, and asked him to talk about the stone. He started telling me all kinds of interesting things, and I stopped him quietly and said, 'Don't tell me, Alec – tell the camera. That's where your audience is.' Punching his right fist into his left palm – a very characteristic gesture – he said, 'Right', and turned to the camera as if it were the most natural thing in the world. He never needed to be told again.

It was an absolute joy being with him, and we only fell out about shirts. Remembering the irritation of the Roy Strong programme, I insisted on him wearing the same clothes throughout the film. He had a very expensive blue-grey check suit made, which was fine, but what was he to do about shirts? He could not wear the same shirt on successive days. 'Well, why not buy three or four of the same colour?' I suggested. That he was unwilling to do, so eventually I offered to take his shirts home and wash and iron them. He had never ironed a thing in his life.

I made only this one film with him, but I was the godfather to his first series about English towns, having suggested Dennis Moriarty as the director. They became fast friends, and Moriarty was eventually his executor. At the time of his death, in 1984, his final series on English towns had the largest audience of the week on BBC2 and he had become a national institution. He left me his copy of the *Survey of London* for Kensington, with all his annotations in the margin. I use it often. And it was as a result of my speaking at his memorial service that I was asked to succeed him as President of the Kensington Society – a largely figurehead job, but a happy link with his memory. He was a much loved figure whose life was literally transformed by my accidental meeting with a colleague bearing galley proofs.

It was while I was filming with Alec Clifton-Taylor that I heard that Norman Swallow had resigned and was returning to Granada Television, where he had worked for years before taking over *Omnibus*. The Head of Department job was vacant again, and I threw my hat into the ring for a second time with what I thought was a strong chance. But once again I was unsuccessful, for the opportunity was taken to bring Humphrey Burton back from London Weekend Television. I could understand why Wheldon, who was now Managing Director of BBC Television, wanted him back – they had always been close – but disturbed to learn from Stephen Hearst that some kind of lobby had been organized against me. I have never got to the bottom of this, nor really tried to, but it hardly made me feel confident about my future. I was now forty, and seemed to be marking time. At Humphrey's insistence, I was made Assistant Head of Music and Arts. But there was a well-known BBC saying: 'Assistant Heads will roll.' Humphrey asked me to take responsibility for all the music and arts programmes on BBC2, which was a lot of work – covering not only the arts programmes I was already looking after, but opera, dance and concerts as well.

Meanwhile *The Spirit of the Age* was shown. Although quite well received, it failed to make the impact of earlier series. Was it the subject matter, or the fact that eight different presenters meant eight different kinds of programme and a much less homogenous result? I had done everything to promote the series, including commissioning an opening fanfare from Arthur Bliss – the last piece he wrote. He came to the studio to record it with the brass from the London Symphony Orchestra, and looked very frail. He died shortly afterwards. I felt his death keenly. He was the first really public figure to befriend me, and he had been immensely generous and kind over the years. *The Spirit of the Age* was shown twice on BBC2 but, unlike other series, was never repeated on BBC1 and the beautiful book produced in association with the series was allowed to go out of print in a matter of months.

Christopher Martin went on to become a sort of resident film-maker to the Prince of Wales – responsible for the, to me, shocking film in which Prince Charles rubbished the work of Denys Lasdun and a number of other major architects. I have always found the Prince's lack of interest in anything to do with the arts in our time depressing, since all his opinions get so widely reported. It seems to me that he has had unrivalled opportunities to get to understand the twentieth century, but he has rejected it without hesitation. Both Lasdun and Colin St John Wilson, of the British Library, found work hard to get in this country in the aftermath of the Prince's criticisms. I cannot believe it is a proper use of royal patronage to increase unemployment among architects. And it is the same with music. Having listened together at a Bath Festival concert to a superb performance of Alban Berg's String Quartet, written in 1910, the Prince turned to me and said, 'Well you can't call that music, but I suppose you would, John.' 'And so should you, sir,' I replied defiantly. We had quite an argument, and later that evening he told our host that he liked me but unfortunately I was wrong about everything.

I took up the threads of Music and Arts for BBC2 in the autumn of 1975, with the opportunities offered by having a major performance slot every Saturday evening and an hour-long documentary slot every Sunday. It is the memory of these hundred programmes a year that justifies recent criticism even from BBC governors about Television's inadequate coverage of the performing arts. Not everything we made or showed in the 1970s was first class – a great deal had to be bought in from abroad – but much was popular, successful and worth doing. Regular placings for arts or music programmes on BBC2 disappeared in the 1990s. We were told such programmes had become too expensive. This, of course, is complete rubbish. It is simply that the people running the network had no concern for the arts. Where controllers have interest – or, now, where the focus groups have told them there is an audience – there is always money. For a brief period in the late

1990s the Controller of BBC2, Paul Jackson, suddenly seemed interested in arts programmes. In no time at all he was whisked off to some
non-job to do with the regions. Dance has been the subject of some
interesting programmes, as it certainly was in my time. Coverage of
opera has become intermittent and based much more on what other
people will fund than on what our own audience might require, with
Glyndebourne lost to Channel 4 – quite unnecessarily. Concerts, other
than the Proms, hardly exist on TV, and recitals not at all. Music documentaries, except for one series in 1999, have become promotional
films for stars. It is a vicious circle: we are told the audience is not
interested, but audience interest is not stimulated. I do not believe that
the experience of thirty years ago is irrelevant. At that time we found
sizeable audiences for serious programmes on music and the arts. It is
about time such programming was tried again, rather than Alan Yentob claiming there has been no dumbing down. The few *Omnibus* programmes shown today are mostly about rock stars or comedians. A
proposal to make a film about Simon Rattle's appointment to the
Berlin Philharmonic was turned down as being of insufficient general
interest.

Humphrey Burton's return to the BBC was on highly individual
terms. He negotiated himself a contract that allowed him to work for
part of the year for other companies, usually making recordings of concerts or studio performances with Solti or Bernstein. In addition, he
presented *Omnibus* each week on BBC1, doing interviews and commentaries, so there was not much time left for him to run the department and he passed most of the day-to-day business to me. I came
increasingly to feel that I was doing a job without receiving the com-
mensurate grade or salary. I had nothing personal against Humphrey,
although his editorial sense seemed to have been somewhat blunted by
his years in commercial television: it was just that the situation was not
a happy one for me. Money for programmes was tighter than before,
the guest-producer posts were closed, and we were depending increasingly on co-productions for almost everything we wanted to make.

But there were a few compensations. For the first time we achieved a
proper reflection of the Proms on BBC Television, going from two or
three a year to twelve. Why this took so long to achieve I have never
understood. The increase was welcomed by everyone except the Controller of Music, Robert Ponsonby, who had taken over from William
Glock. He deeply resented the presence of cameras – especially in the

arena of the Royal Albert Hall, as of course was essential for covering a concert with soloists. You simply cannot record something like the *Missa Solemnis* with cameras only at the side of the hall. Ponsonby felt that cameras in the arena got in the way of the promenaders and changed the nature of the event. In later years I too was to have strong feelings about what television could do to a public concert, but I always recognized that the Proms belonged to the BBC *in toto*, both Television and Radio, as well as to the audience in the hall, and some compromises had to be found.

Bringing the cameras to the Proms and increasing the number of concerts broadcast meant reductions elsewhere, and one of the victims of this was the Edinburgh Festival which throughout the 1960s and the early 1970s had been very substantially reflected by BBC Television. Ironically, having lured the cameras back to London for the Proms, I was to suffer in later years from their disappearance from Edinburgh.

The principal limitation with music on television was the totally inadequate sound quality. This was a huge disadvantage, especially with opera, where the audience had become accustomed to much more refined sound quality from their own hi-fi systems. The problem was not the BBC's responsibility. The sound left the transmitter in good shape, but even the most expensive TV sets had cheap and inadequate loudspeakers. When Humphrey and I challenged the manufacturers about this, in a typically British way they said there was no demand for anything better. However, as time went by it became possible to play the sound through a hi-fi system and, in the case of simultaneous broadcasts, to have the radio sound aligned with the television.

One of the other pleasures was a major project with Martha Graham and her dance company, who were coming to the Royal Opera House in London in the summer of 1976, not having appeared in London for ten years. Graham had now stopped dancing herself, and the Royal Opera House was apprehensive as to whether the season would sell. I managed to acquire from New York a first-rate programme about Graham and her work, made as part of WNET's series *Dance in America*. Much of the repertory in the programme was being presented in London, but the New York tape contained no appearance by Graham herself, which was what I wanted most of all. The company's Manager, Ron Protas – a controversial figure, who had certainly saved Graham from her drinking, but had also alienated all her friends – was adamant that she never gave interviews. I went to New York to see her attorney, the most famous show-business lawyer in New York, who looked after everyone in dance from Martha Graham to Rudolf Nureyev. Arnold Weissberger was the prince of wheeler-dealing, and I thought it worth trying to persuade him. I pointed out that, since I had the rights to the WNET programme, I could undermine the London season by showing it all. On the other hand, if Miss Graham were to agree to an interview we would show only sections of it, and it could well be helpful publicity for the season at the Royal Opera House, for which the bookings were very poor. After several deeply unpleasant meetings with Protas, I was allowed to meet Graham herself. She was extremely professional, as I expected, and immediately saw the point. So two days later, with Weissberger's backing, after a long session in make-up and attired in an extraordinary gown by her sponsor, the designer Halston, she turned up at the BBC office in New York.

Bob Lockyer had organized a film crew, and we set to work. She was, as I had been sure she would be, quite marvellous. I knew from my own experience that she was a great dancer and a wonderful choreographer, and from her pupils it was obvious that she was a great teacher. Now I could feel the force of her personality face to face. She had an eloquence and a passion that defied the years. She may have been more than eighty already, but looked ageless – like some oriental goddess. She had a way of peppering her speech with aphorisms – 'Music is what we dancers lean on', 'You are never alone with a myth' and so on. Perhaps she said them often, but most of them were new to me. We interleaved the interview with archive film and parts of the WNET recording, and it was shown on BBC2 the week before the London season began. At that time Covent Garden had sold 25 per cent of the seats; within two days this had risen to 60 per cent, and eventually the season sold out. It was one of the only clear demonstrations I have ever had that television promotion can work.

I went to see Graham at the Savoy, to thank her again. I found her gracious but troubled. My friends Robin Howard and Robert Cohan had spent ten years creating an outpost of Graham technique in London with the highly successful London Contemporary Dance Theatre. What they most wanted was for Graham to visit the company and see something of their work. Protas rejected the idea entirely, describing them as parasites who owed their positions entirely to Graham and did not deserve the acclaim they had received. This seemed to me wicked, and I begged Graham to go to the LCDT's studios at The Place. At once she became a troubled old lady and said sadly, 'I don't know who to believe. I don't know what to do.' It was quite tragic. She never did make the visit, but when the LCDT company came to a closing party at the Opera House she at least spoke to some of the dancers, which in some way compensated.

I used to visit Graham regularly when I went to New York during the next few years, and was always generously received. My saddest memory is that in the early months of my friendship with Bob Locky-er I had taken him to see her dance Klytemnestra. She was extremely drunk and deeply embarrassing, and I insisted that we left – I did not want him to see the ruins of a great artist. But I was wrong, for even in decline there was a spark of genius, and Bob – who has devoted much of his life to the legacy of Martha Graham – has never quite forgiven me.

One evening in 1976 I heard Aubrey Singer whistling and jingling his way down the corridor outside my office. He asked if I would like to go to the Round House with him to see Peter Brook's production of *The Ik*. I was delighted – I loved Brook's work, and also had a real fondness for the Round House itself, that converted engine shed run so brilliantly by the charismatic Thelma Holt, already an acquaintance and soon to become a close friend. After *The Ik*, which I enjoyed without thinking it as good as Brook's *A Midsummer Night's Dream* or *Marat/Sade*, Singer took me to dinner in, as usual, a very good restaurant, and we fell to discussing gaps in our output. I was very concerned about the lack of attention we paid to our archives. No one seemed really to know what we held or on what principle things were retained or destroyed. All of us had had to sign destruction orders for programmes, as was inevitable since there were limits to the number that could be kept in the library. We also had no experience of the long-term problems of storing videotape. It was claimed that tape had to be regularly rewound, otherwise there was a risk of images printing through like text on poor-quality newsprint. Film negative had to be stored at temperatures slightly below zero, and the requirement for shelving was growing at the rate of hundreds of yards a year, even though less than 30 per cent of what was shot was retained. I myself had lost most of my early programmes and had authorized the destruction of hundreds of other studio programmes we had made in black and white – especially programmes on the visual arts. Much was also destroyed for contractual reasons: after two years the rights on anything involving actors or musicians lapsed and had to be completely renegotiated if the programme was to be shown again. For this reason, most of the drama, light-entertainment and music output of BBC Television in the 1950s, 1960s and early 1970s was lost. A committee had deliberated the question in the late 1960s and had decided that the BBC was primarily a production house, not an archive, and that financial priority must be given to making new programmes rather than storing old. It was an understandable decision, but in retrospect disastrously short-sighted, since no attempt was made to find outside bodies that could reliably store what we could not. Some of the best of the BBC's output was taken by the British Film Institute, but the great majority has totally disappeared.

I suggested to Singer that evening that I should investigate what remained, with a view to making a regular archive strand, or perhaps even a month-long festival in summer – a time when repeat programmes tended to dominate the schedules. I spent weeks in the film library and with the tape archive, and even longer with the Contracts Department to try to persuade them of the value of reshowing some of the most memorable programmes, however complex the contractual difficulties. Eventually in both 1976 and 1977 I put together four weeks celebrating our earlier output with programmes every evening on BBC2. We rebroadcast forgotten things from the early years like *Asian Club*, as well as samples of famous series like *Quatermass* (of which one episode remained) and the Saturday revue *Not so Much a Programme, More a Way of Life*, the only example of which was the uncharacteristic programme broadcast the day after Kennedy's death. I was particularly gratified to show again Basil Coleman's production of *Billy Budd*, which stood up to the passing of time even better than I expected and produced a terrific response. I believe that the quite different attitude the BBC now has to its archive had its origins in these festivals. Its methods are still slightly random, but today there is more likelihood of valuable material being retained. What still tends to slip through the net is the ordinary – often the most valuable evidence for future historians. The backing Singer gave me for this initiative showed the best side of him – energy helpfully applied and support enthusiastically given.

Yet I was increasingly uncertain of where my future might lie. I had worked for the BBC for nearly nineteen years and had not really found a totally satisfactory niche. At regular intervals Wheldon urged me to get out, since, in his view, I 'lacked the common touch'. I knew that I antagonized colleagues by sometimes reacting too sharply to lazy ideas and sloppy programmes. If the bosses did not believe in me and the staff did not support me, it was surely time to start looking for something else. I had only ever worked for the Corporation and to that extent was somewhat institutionalized, but occasionally I would learn of other possibilities.

I was never tempted to get involved in running a dance company, although once or twice I was asked if I might be interested. I was, on the other hand, often attracted to those areas that we now call heritage, and would look at organizations with which I worked from time to time, like the National Trust, and wonder whether I might be happier there. After we had finished *The Spirit of the Age*, John Summerson one evening asked me to the Sir John Soane's Museum for a drink, and introduced me to his Chairman, Lord Holford, architect of the University of Kent among other things. I thought it was a purely social get-together, but slowly realized that I was being sounded out as a possible successor to Summerson, who had come to recognize that I not only admired but also, I hope, understood Soane, the oddest and quirkiest of all English architects. I cannot deny that the job was tempting, because it was quite well paid and did not involve very heavy responsibilities, but I was certain that others had better qualifications. When the same job came up again twenty years later I once again looked at the advertisement and wondered. But there is a line between professional skills and amateurism which one crosses at one's peril. For the same reason, despite being so drawn to the world of architectural scholarship, I doubted that I had the necessary knowledge to accept one of the most flattering invitations I ever received: being asked to write one of the volumes of the Penguin *Buildings of Scotland* series. Colin McWilliam, the Editor, was a friend, and he knew how much I loved architecture. Once again I ducked out, believing – correctly – that other people, such as the admirable John Gifford, would do better.

Aubrey Singer, who was fascinated by China, took me one Sunday to lunch in Kew with the great sinologist Joseph Needham. I found him immensely impressive. After lunch we walked around Kew Gardens and he asked me about my position and my ambitions. I told him I seemed to be in something of a rut. 'Why not come and join me?' he said. 'I'm looking for intelligent historians with wider experience to join my team.' 'But I don't speak Chinese,' I answered. 'You can – it's no more difficult than the languages you do speak,' he said. 'I could get you a grant. Why not?' For a few days it was very tempting, but in the end I thought it too extreme a reaction to my current situation. After all, I did have some experience, and none of it would really have been relevant in China. But the fact that a great scholar like Needham found me interesting was more than reassuring. Perhaps there were possibilities nearer home. When the Theatre Museum was established at the Victoria & Albert Museum I applied to become its Director. I had been a trustee of its predecessor at Leighton House. Fortunately, I did not get the job, as the Theatre Museum only came into existence with its own premises eleven years later, during which time the man who was appointed sat in a cupboard in South Kensington cataloguing and purchasing without a real museum to run. It would not have suited me at all.

I went on a financial management course at Ashridge, in Buckinghamshire, and experienced for the first time the hideous jargon of management-speak, but was pleased to find that concepts like cash flow were a pleasure to deal with once you understood them. There was also some pleasure in living for a month in a Wyattville castle – something for which I had a rather particular affection. I had even for a time contemplated buying a Wyattville ruin in Wiltshire, for the sheer delight of looking after something so outrageous.

My travels, both through work and on holiday, were beginning to convince me that other countries were coping rather better than we were with culture, even if their broadcasting organizations were not a patch on the BBC. I visited several European festivals, and relished the cross-fertilization that they provide between the different arts. I very much liked what I heard about the festival in Adelaide, then run by Anthony Steel, who had previously worked at the Royal Festival Hall. Joan Bakewell, who had been in Adelaide, told me they were looking for a new Director, and I let people know I could be interested. But my mind kept coming back to Edinburgh. I had visited the Festival regularly over the years, and it had never lost its attraction for me. On several occasions I had been involved in the BBC's reflection of its offerings.

One morning in the spring of 1977 I was sitting in Humphrey's office, trying to get his attention for departmental matters, when there was a phone call from Ian Hunter – the boss of Harold Holt, the concert agents – who had been the second Director of the Edinburgh Festival. He told Humphrey the Festival was looking for a new Director and asked if he was interested. Humphrey said, 'No, but John might be.' I hoped Hunter would take it up with me, but he did not. It all went to the back of my mind until late that summer, when, in a small shop on the Greek island of Paros, I bought a copy of the *International Herald Tribune* and saw the job advertised. I returned just in time to meet the deadline for applications, and produced a very full CV. My secretary, who typed it in strict secrecy, said that reading it she thought I might be in with a chance, and when I looked back over the different areas in which I had worked I certainly seemed better equipped than I had been nineteen years earlier when Robert Ponsonby had offered me the job as his assistant. I sought references from both Huw Wheldon and Hugh Casson, and sat back to wait for Edinburgh's reaction. Wheldon sent me a copy of his reference. He pointed out that many found me difficult and said I was not always good with people, but he wrote something which after all the years of our misunderstandings seemed to me quite extraordinarily generous: 'I have never met an artist who did not respect and admire him.' I never saw Casson's reference, but I understand it was particularly warm.

I told no one else at the BBC about my application to Edinburgh. In November I was invited to go north for an interview. A few days before the chosen date Anthony Steel, over from Adelaide, had lunched with me in London. He told me he was on his way to Edinburgh and the job was almost completely sewn up. I said nothing, but thought that, if it were true, Adelaide might be a good place to begin a new trade – in a country which I had always loved from a distance, but which at that time I had never visited. On the day appointed I turned up at the City Chambers in Edinburgh and was grilled very thoroughly for three-quarters of an hour by a very large board chaired by the Lord Provost. I knew no one on the board, but felt I had acquitted myself reasonably. On the stairs as I left, I passed Steel going in for his interview. He looked totally pole-axed, no doubt remembering what he had told me. I later learnt that he had been interviewed earlier in the year but that they had been divided about him, and on this occasion he did not make a strong impression. I went back to my hotel – one I had chosen deliberately because I felt sure I would see no one I knew there – and after a rather melancholy solitary dinner went out for some air. On the steps of the hotel two boys were fighting with knives, the pavement was covered with vomit, and an old man was urinating against the railings. 'Why in God's name', I thought, 'do I want to come and work here?'

I slept badly, and taking my seat on the next morning's train I was put out to be joined by Magnus Magnusson, whom I knew very well since he presented the archaeology programmes made by our department. What was I doing in Edinburgh? he wanted to know. I was evasive – I wanted to avoid the reason being known, because I was fairly certain that I would not get the job and I didn't want yet another failure to be widely broadcast – but eventually he teased it out of me.

As I walked into my flat in London that evening the phone was ringing. I answered it, and a voice said, 'This is the Lord Provost of Edinburgh speaking. I require to know whether you would accept the job if offered it.' 'Well,' I said, 'I did apply for it, but there has been no discussion at all of salary, of conditions, terms of contract or anything else.' 'I need an answer now,' he said. 'One of our board is returning to Canada tonight, and we wish to make a decision before then.' This, I knew, was the Vice-Chairman of the Festival, Ronald Mavor, son of the dramatist James Bridie and a former Director of the Scottish Arts Council. He had been the least friendly of all the board members. I thought for a second, then said, 'Well, in the circumstances, if you wish for an immediate answer then I accept.' 'Very good,' said the Lord Provost – 'we will be in touch tomorrow.' I went round to Bob Lockyer's studio, where John and Ann Tusa asked me how the interview had gone. 'Who cares about the interview?' I said. 'I've just been offered the job – and, what's more, I've said yes.'

The announcement a few days later was widely publicized, and both the English and the Scottish press were largely friendly. Only the *Guardian* managed to be snide, referring to me as 'forty-four, unmarried and fond of ballet'. At a press conference in Edinburgh I was asked if I was the youngest person to be appointed. 'No,' said the Festival's press officer, Ian Crawford – 'he's in fact one of the oldest.' I was the same age that Rudolf Bing had been, but much older than Hunter or Ponsonby, and slightly older than Lord Harewood. The BBC were pleased for me, but mildly irritated. Alasdair Milne, now running BBC Television and Director-General designate, said he had wanted me to become Controller of Radio 3. Humphrey Burton's first reaction was to say, 'But you know nothing about opera!' Two years later he said, 'If I'd known it was such an interesting job, I would have taken it' – almost worthy of Gielgud for unintentional offence. Among my friends, only John Betjeman lamented. 'We will never see you again,' he said, and, although we kept in touch, he was almost correct. Just before Christmas the department gave me a big send-off, with several colleagues in kilts singing new versions of McGonagall adapted to my name. Eleanor Warren, formerly of the Radio 3 Music Department, who had left the BBC for the Royal Northern College of Music, wrote and said, 'You may feel apprehensive after all these years in the BBC, but the water outside, if cool, is clean and fresh.'

I had been a passionate believer in the power of television to promote so-called minority interests and to spread knowledge and enthusiasm. But, except for the time spent making *The Spirit of the Age*, the 1970s had not been a fulfilling or happy period of my life. My restlessness and the way in which I was looking around at other possible goals give evidence of it. I had a sense of having taken a wrong turning. Now, with hindsight, I can see that the waiting time gave me more experience – especially with things like money – and perhaps greater maturity.

A couple of weeks later two chaps in brown coats turned up at my flat to collect my television set – which seemed quite reasonable, since it belonged to the BBC. After all my insistence on knowing what television was up to, and the relentless way in which I had watched everything, I found life without one quite possible and it was nearly two years before I replaced it. I had other things to do than watch TV.

# 10

# Getting in the Way

As I prepared to get to grips with the Edinburgh job, I was very aware of the long shadow of history on present-day Edinburgh and Scottish culture, and most especially the history of the Festival itself. Founded in 1947, it was one of many remarkable artistic developments in the post-war years: the creation of the Arts Council, the growth of ballet and opera at Covent Garden, the founding of the Aldeburgh Festival and the English Opera Group, the renewal of Glyndebourne, the Old Vic and the Stratford Shakespeare Memorial Theatre, and the development of London and regional orchestras. In all this artistic advance, Scotland played a smaller role. It had neither opera nor ballet companies and only one orchestra – by no means among the best – and its theatres depended as much on touring operations out of England as on indigenous productions. There was in many ways a deep-rooted suspicion of the performing arts – in contrast to the long tradition of academic excellence. Scotland was still full of architects, poets and painters, but musicians and actors had mostly sought their luck in the south.

The impetus to create the Festival had come partly from a visionary Lord Provost, Sir John Falconer, who had an idea that Edinburgh could be a focus in reconciling the formerly warring nations. He was helped by the desire of Glyndebourne Festival Opera to find a way of expanding beyond its short season in its small Sussex opera house. Rudolf Bing, the Vienna-born General Manager of Glyndebourne, who since arriving in England had hardly ever travelled beyond Sussex and London, went in search of another stage. His first choice was Cambridge, but, like Oxford, it turned out to have no concert hall or suitable theatre. Eventually, at the suggestion of the British Council, he visited Edinburgh and a committee of local interests was formed. The newly created Scottish Arts Council gave £25,000, and Bing used all his contacts to persuade major figures to join the scheme.

From the first Festival in 1947, when Glyndebourne brought operas by Mozart and Verdi, the standards were of the highest. From England came the Old Vic company with two Shakespeare productions, Sadler's Wells Ballet with *Sleeping Beauty*, the Hallé and Liverpool orchestras, and the chamber orchestra of Reginald Jacques, while from Europe came the Vienna Philharmonic Orchestra – reunited with the conductor Bruno Walter for the first time since the mid-1930s. There were also the Colonne Orchestra from Paris and Louis Jouvet's theatre company with productions of Molière and Giraucoux. The tradition of morning concerts was established and, most memorably, Bing created a Festival Quartet with four of the most outstanding musicians of the day: Artur Schnabel, Joseph Szigeti, William Primrose and Pierre Fournier. They gave three recitals of music by Schubert, Mendelssohn and Brahms – all of whom had significant anniversaries that year – and set new standards. The Scottish Orchestra had Michelangeli as soloist, and there were concerts of Scottish songs and choral music. It was a truly international programme, and made an impact I can still remember. The BBC broadcast many of the concerts, and Edinburgh's reputation for excellence was established from the beginning. To cap it all, the Festival made a small profit – something no Director was subsequently allowed to forget.

Yet right from the start there were tensions. Who was the Festival for: visitors or the local population? Was a festival really what Edinburgh needed most? Despite the close involvement of prominent citizens and local grandees like the Countess of Rosebery, the idea took hold that somehow the Festival was imposed on an unwilling city and that the smart thing to do was to leave town so as not to be disturbed by all that activity and all those flighty performers with their demands for food and drink late in the evening and taxis at all hours. Apart from the big hotels, Edinburgh had only one licensed restaurant, and – like the pubs – that closed at nine o'clock. Social life in the Festival therefore focused on a temporary club installed in the Assembly Rooms, which, as it was the only choice, brought performers and audiences together. Over the years, changes in licensing laws and in restaurant provision destroyed the need for the Festival Club, and many people felt it a considerable loss.

The city's halls and theatres had all been made to work for the Festival. The excellent Usher Hall had no bars but a splendid acoustic, the gloomy Freemasons' Hall was home to the morning concerts, while the King's, the Royal Lyceum and the Empire theatres all played a role appropriate to the limitations of their relatively small stages. It took forty years to get an orchestra pit in the King's, and fifty for the Empire to be rebuilt as the Festival Theatre, with a stage big enough for ballet or large-scale opera. But in the early years the limited resources were seen as a challenge rather than an obstacle, and visiting international opera, drama and dance companies made do with what was available, even if half their scenery never made it on to the stage.

In 1948 the brilliant Irish director Tyrone Guthrie succeeded against all expectation in turning the Assembly Hall of the Church of Scotland into a daring thrust-stage theatre and produced a long-forgotten Scottish classic, *Ane Pleasant Satyre of the Thrie Estaitis*, Sir David Lindsay's sixteenth-century pageant of good and evil – real festival material, and Scottish too. And once again the best of Europe took part alongside British companies and orchestras.

Bing masterminded only two Festivals, but his imprint on the whole enterprise can still be felt today. He was the only one of my predecessors whom I never really knew. I used to telephone him when I was in New York and we would talk, but I never achieved a meeting. When he returned to Britain in the 1980s he was already a victim of Alzheimer's Disease and beyond reach. His successor was his assistant, Ian Hunter, who maintained the standards and added a new and, to my mind, vital element: art exhibitions. Hunter had a real talent for finding the right people to help him. David Talbot Rice, Professor of Fine Art at Edinburgh University, was his link to the world of exhibitions. Hunter was succeeded in 1956 by Robert Ponsonby, whose years have been insufficiently recognized. He was extremely young when appointed, and was poorly treated by the local grandees, but his record was excellent. The legendary revue *Beyond the Fringe* – which was not part of the Fringe at all but a main Festival offering – appeared during his time. The Fringe itself was also growing in importance. Starting with a few disaffected Scottish groups who had not been asked to the party, it became an important adjunct to the Festival, using the city in quite new ways and bringing a feeling of innovation, notably in drama. The fact that drama all over the world was evolving in informal ways and preferring black boxes to proscenium theatres was a great advantage. Over the years the Fringe has grown into a huge and, to my mind, less attractive operation – taken over now by rapacious commercial considerations and with far too great an emphasis on stand-up comedians who vie with each other in obscenity and outrageousness. There was always an element of outrageousness on the Fringe, and it was a great help – the annual protest of some of the more reactionary public figures added a great deal to the sense of occasion. I cherished the Fringe then, but regret its current domination of the media. In those days not only Radio but also Television presented numerous programmes from the main Festival; now television coverage is almost entirely reduced to Fringe vulgarities with ignorant presenters.

I mentioned earlier Ponsonby's offer of employment to me in 1958 and how fortunate it was that I did not take it up, since he and his team departed the following year, to be replaced by Lord Harewood. Harewood opened up the Festival to all kinds of new ideas, from contemporary music to the arts of India. The full revelation of the genius of Janáček and the range of Czech opera is also due to him, while his use of thematic concert programming with pairs of featured composers was at that time something very new. Harewood's time in Edinburgh was cut short by the revelation that he was no longer with Marion Harewood but had a second family and a previously unknown child. Sent for by the Lord Provost to be asked if the stories in the papers were true, Harewood admitted the situation and asked what he should do. Resignation was suggested, and Harewood obliged. A year or two later, I was told, the Lord Provost in question was found hanging near the body of his mistress in a North Berwick hotel room. Such are the ways of the world.

Despite my admiration, I hardly knew George Harewood, and shortly after I was appointed a mutual friend suggested a dinner at which I could get to know him better. I was delighted. He was accompanied by his now second wife, Patricia, an Australian violinist and sister of the horn player Barry Tuckwell. 'Well,' said George, 'I was sacked for adultery. That, I presume, will not be your problem.' It was the beginning of what to me has been one of the most influential and helpful friendships of my life. George came to every one of my Festivals and gave me wise advice whenever I asked for it. He is a truly creative and imaginative colleague, and his fifty-year contribution to the arts in this country – at the Royal Opera House, the Edinburgh Festival, the Philharmonia Orchestra, English National Opera and Opera North – is unrivalled. Given his royal background, making his own way in the world of the arts could not have been easy. But he has touched our lives in many ways, including founding *Opera* magazine and revising *Kobbé's Complete Opera Book* twice. I love the company of George and Patricia and their continuing enthusiasm for musicians – both the great and established and the young on their way up, so many of whom he has helped. The Harewood legacy was constantly in my mind when I was Director, and I am still convinced that he was the best of us all.

None of this, however, is to disparage the contribution of the Director who followed George in 1966 and whom I succeeded, the longest serving of all, Peter Diamand. Born in Berlin and working first as secretary to Artur Schnabel, Peter moved to Holland before the war and had a difficult time during the Nazi occupation. After the war he worked for the Concertgebouw orchestra and became the first Director of the Holland Festival, a position he occupied for seventeen years. So for thirty years he ran two of Europe's most important festivals. He did so in a way that was highly idiosyncratic. It was all done on a personal basis. He avoided managers and agents and worked directly with the artists, winning from them a loyalty which was truly impressive. In public he was taciturn and withdrawn, hating the promotional demands of the job. In private he was witty, passionate and wonderful company. Considering how much he had done for Edinburgh over thirteen years he was little appreciated there, but he never seemed to care much what people said, provided he could maintain the artistic standards.

He had a group of colleagues, known as the Diamand Mafia, whom he invited back year after year. They consisted of most of the greatest musical names of the time – Carlo Maria Giulini, Dietrich Fischer-Dieskau, Isaac Stern, the Amadeus Quartet, Teresa Berganza and so on. But he also did a great deal to bring on the careers of young performers, notably the conductors Daniel Barenboim and Claudio Abbado and singers such as Jessye Norman. His policy was one of two possibilities open to a Festival Director. Do you try, as Harewood and I did, to vary the roster of performers as much as possible from year to year, seeking out new talent and unrecognized areas of artistic activity? Or do you reinvite the tried and trusted, hoping that audiences will follow no matter what they do? The advantage of the latter method is that as the public knows the performers it is perhaps more ready to book seats. The disadvantage is that over the years each Festival, however grandly cast, tends to feel like the same mixture as before. The current Director, Brian McMaster, has chosen the Diamand route and regularly achieves big audiences for innovative work once artists and companies have become known. In this way the Mark Morris Dance Company, which went five times to Edinburgh before coming to London, drew audiences north especially to see them. Directors like Luc

Bondy and Peter Stein, regular Festival visitors now, never show their work in London.

Harewood and I tended to start again each year, and the results were often disappointing at the box office. The historic achievements of the Festival or the reputation of the Director were not enough to persuade people to book for companies or performers they had not heard of. Often the result was thin houses for opening nights and then, after the notices appeared, queues for returns by the end of the week. It was extremely frustrating. Naturally some performers in whom I believed came back each year, but not as many as Peter had invited, and my first decision on taking over was to drop some of the people who were not always making quite the impact they had done in earlier years, as seemed to me the case with both Isaac Stern and the Amadeus Quartet. There was a need for new energy, particularly in the drama area. However talented their leading actors, there was surely another drama company beyond Prospect Players, who seemed to come so often. I was also determined to take the editorial control of drama back into the Director's hands. Much of the feeling that drama was a second-class citizen within the Festival stemmed, I thought, from the fact that all the previous Directors had been primarily music men. It was here that the generalist nature of my Television years bore fruit. But getting a foothold was not easy. The handover in all organizations is difficult, and mine was to last for nine months, since I was in waiting throughout 1978 and I took over officially only after that year's Festival.

I had met Peter Diamand quite often over the years, but no doubt came into the category of people from the press and the media whom he preferred to keep at arm's length. He had always been perfectly charming, but nothing more. I expected some sort of regular meeting or discussion after my appointment. None took place. In March 1978 I went to work in the Edinburgh Festival office in St James's Street, London, where I received a distinctly chilly welcome and was given a table in the corridor next to the lavatory. In truth there was little alternative – the office was a former bachelor apartment with three decent-sized rooms, a kitchen and a bathroom. The secretaries occupied the biggest room, Peter and his assistant, Bill Thomley, the other two. Peter rarely appeared before mid-afternoon and spent all his time on the telephone, emerging only to dictate letters just as everyone wanted to go home. Thomley was responsible for the theatre side of the Festival and did his best to avoid me. But 1979 had to be planned, and I needed some assistance. I largely managed without.

Peter passed me the file on the 1979 Festival. It contained only one letter – from the Boston Symphony Orchestra, about possible dates. My attempts to see him were frustrated by his constant travels in pursuit of Placido Domingo. The 1977 Festival had seen a remarkable production of *Carmen* by Piero Faggioni, conducted by Abbado and starring Berganza, Domingo, Mirella Freni and Tom Krause. It was the high point of Peter's time, and by any measure an outstanding achievement. Nevertheless, it cost over a third of the Festival's budget – largely through the huge expense of keeping the London Symphony Orchestra in Edinburgh for over three weeks. *Carmen* was to be revived in 1978, but Domingo had agreed to appear only in the first season. Peter simply refused to accept this, and doggedly turned up at every performance Domingo gave across Europe and America in the vain hope of persuading him to reconsider.

But there was also a subtext to Peter's attitude to me that took a long time to discover. The Edinburgh job, as a local-authority post, had never been at all well paid, and a pay freeze meant that Peter had had no increase in his salary for four years. After thirteen years, he was receiving a ludicrous £9,500 a year, but, to his understandable offence, the job was to be advertised at £12,000. The salary was not mentioned in the *International Herald Tribune* and I had never been sent the conditions, but when I came to negotiate with the administrator I asked for more. My BBC salary had been just over £12,000, and I felt Edinburgh was worth an increase. We settled on £15,000. Peter of course learnt this from the Festival Council papers and quite understandably resented somebody with no previous experience of running a festival starting off with a salary nearly 60 per cent higher then he was getting after thirteen years in Scotland and seventeen in the Netherlands. But it was hardly my fault.

In the end, he brought the stand-off to a conclusion. We both happened to be in New York at the same time that spring, and he telephoned and asked me to lunch at the Russian Tea Room. His reserve disappeared totally, and he gave me much good advice – although I never did discover whether there had been a more extensive plan for 1979 in addition to the Boston Symphony Orchestra.

Peter's resentment against Edinburgh was real, and overshadowed the tributes paid to him at his last Festival. I will never forget the cynicism on his face as he listened to lavish praise from the Festival

Council that had opposed him on so many occasions. The concert and party after given by the artists in his honour were quite a different matter. Even Giulini, who never attended social functions, turned up and hovered just inside the door for a few minutes. I had been to see Giulini at the George Hotel and begged him to return in 1979, but he refused. It was nothing personal, he said, but his relations with Peter were very special and he had promised always to support him. Perhaps he might reconsider in a year or two. I met him at Amsterdam Airport shortly after my first Festival and he told me he had heard that things had gone well. One morning he called at the London office just to say hello. He was a dear man, but did not come back to Edinburgh. The future was to lie with a younger generation.

It was at that lunch in New York that I experienced for the first time a typical example of Peter's ironic observation of colleagues. I had only recently met Abbado, and found him hard to read. 'Is he difficult?' I asked. 'No,' said Peter – 'not difficult, but obstinate. For instance, one day you will certainly want to do an opera with him in which in the fourth act a servant appears with a letter saying "Ecco una lettera" and exits, never to reappear. And Abbado will say, "For that I think we need Ghiaurov."' And indeed, a few years later, when we were casting Act 2 of *Lohengrin*, in which the Herald has all of twelve bars of music to sing, Abbado said that he couldn't conduct it without Wolfgang Brendel. It was always like this, and if you demurred he would say, 'So you want it to be less good?' – an unanswerable question.

It was impossible for me to receive visitors in the corridor of the London office, so I decided to go out and call on people. I made the rounds of the London orchestras and concert agencies, and got a very warm reception. Quite a few artists, I discovered, had kept time free, hoping or expecting to be invited to Edinburgh. I have never understood the hostility of some of my colleagues to concert agents. Some agents can certainly be difficult, but without their support it is increasingly hard to make plans, and at that time I did not have the direct access to many artists that I have now, or that Peter so strikingly had. My visits to agents made me a lot of friends. Among the most helpful was Emmie Tillett of Ibbs & Tillett. She was a straightforward person, originally a secretary who had married the boss, and I already knew and liked her. She had been helpful on several occasions, notably in lending me the entire office files on Rachmaninov, whom they had represented in Europe from 1920 until 1939. Emmie asked how she could help. I knew that she represented two artists I much admired but had never met – Janet Baker and Clifford Curzon. She said, 'Leave it to me', and in due course asked me to lunch at her home with Curzon and gave a dinner party for Janet Baker and her husband.

Curzon was of a mind to withdraw from Edinburgh, where he had been a regular visitor since the early years. Although I was dropping a number of much loved artists, I wanted to be sure of retaining him, whom I hugely respected despite knowing how difficult and neurotic he could be. Peter had told me that driving one night to the Usher Hall, where Curzon was to perform, he saw him walking back towards his hotel. Peter stopped to ask him where he was going, and only with difficulty got him back to the hall. Listening to Curzon's recordings, it is hard to feel the technical insecurity which troubled him so much. We sat on in Emmie's garden for most of the afternoon, talking music, and happily I persuaded him to come back in 1979 but suggested new partners. He was intrigued, and eventually agreed to a concerto appearance with Simon Rattle (making his Edinburgh debut) and a quintet with the young Medici Quartet.

The first meeting with the Medici was a near-disaster – they were all too nervous to play. Then suddenly Curzon started laughing, the mood changed, and the relationship became a love affair. Although Clifford felt guilty about deserting his long-term Amadeus partners, he came to love the Medici and appeared several times with them in his remaining years. The situation with Rattle was rather different. Curzon had proposed Mozart's 'Coronation' Concerto, K537, an infrequently played work generally thought inferior to the other late concertos. Rattle questioned this, and foolishly I let Curzon know of Rattle's reservations. From then on it was 'young Master Rattle', and a great deal of pursed lips and reluctance.

I had also persuaded Curzon to play Franck's *Symphonic Variations* for the first time in years, and it was not a success. Nevertheless, he accepted my invitation for a recital the following year. Some months later he asked me to his beautiful house on the edge of Hampstead Heath – full of impressionist paintings and excellent furniture – and offered me a superb lunch, just for the two of us. Having subtly softened me up, he then told me he was not coming back next year, or ever again. It was too much effort. It saddened me, but at least he had shared that first year with me.

The dinner for Janet Baker was fascinating. She knew quite well that

I had made the Ferrier film, and it hung like a cloud over the earlier part of the proceedings. I learnt quite quickly that, although her nickname in the profession, Dame Granite, sometimes seemed deserved, once you paid proper and deserved tribute to her a much warmer and less formal personality was allowed to appear. As the evening wore on, traces of a Yorkshire accent re-emerged, and we parted affectionately and have remained good friends. She also had some excellent ideas for extending her repertory – just the sort of thing I was seeking.

The most challenging of the agents was the Director of Ingpen & Williams, Howard Hartog. Though I knew him only slightly, I realized he was someone to listen to. He represented Boulez, Solti, Alfred Brendel, Jessye Norman and Joan Sutherland – all people I wanted to invite. Before the war Hartog had been in the tea trade, but finding himself in Hamburg in 1948, while still in the British army, he had set about trying to revive music in that city. He became a publisher, running the London branch of Schott of Mainz, then, with his friend Joan Ingpen, moved into artists' representation. He was quite certainly the rudest and most aggressive person I had ever met, given to one-line letters – 'Dear John, What about making up your mind? Howard' – and impetuous telephone calls in which the phone was replaced in the middle of my answer if it did not seem what he wanted. He also often tried to pre-empt me by offering jobs for his artists – 'I know Boulez will want her.' It was infuriating. Yet he loved music, was a superb champion of the things and people in which he believed, and became over the years one of my most admired friends.

We would lunch together quite often, usually in very good restaurants. Much of the lunch would end up on his cuffs or his shirt front, but he seemed not to notice as he rushed to light the huge cigar that came with coffee. He taught me about so many aspects of the music business, and his value to me far outran access to his artists – many of whom, like Boulez, I never did succeed in luring to Edinburgh. He demanded the highest ethical standards. When for no good reason Jessye Norman, at the height of her career, cancelled some recording dates he had spent two years organizing, he had no compunction at all in refusing to continue to represent her. Howard had two assistants who now run the firm, David Sigall and Jonathan Groves. They had a first-class training – as in a sense did I.

The separation of programmes from contracts in the BBC meant that I had never had to deal directly with negotiating fees, which is not the most congenial of tasks. Some agents are cowboys, some deliberate time-wasters, and some fly kites to see how high they will rise. But even the trickiest of London agents was as nothing compared to the vultures of New York, who have seriously damaged the music scene in Britain by refusing to maintain the old understanding that, since subsidies are lower here, fees should also be lower than in France, Germany or Italy. Ronald Wilford of Columbia Artists in New York, for example, saw no virtue in helping the impoverished British orchestras or festivals, and hyped fees up to a level that now seems scandalous. It was like the coming of co-production in television – control passed out of one's hands, and one was caught in a spiral of rising costs that bore no relation to need or often achievement.

Strenuous attempts were made to limit remuneration, but they never worked. Shortly after I started in Edinburgh, there was a meeting of opera intendants in Munich, chaired by August Everding, boss of the Bavarian State Opera. Over thirty opera houses agreed never to pay more than $15,000 a performance to anyone, yet within a month Munich itself had broken the agreement. Great artists have always commanded enormous sums – Caruso, Tetrazzini and Chaliapin were all paid vast amounts, but they really delivered, staying in one place for months at a time and building audiences, while at the same time prolonging their careers. Today the fact that you can sing in Vienna, Paris and New York in the same week – and some do – has changed the whole musical environment. In addition, while there are still lots of singers (except for Wagner tenors), there are very few conductors who can be compared to the best of the past or who deserve the kind of fees they demand. Happily, I was to discover that some of the ones I valued most were far from being the most expensive or the most difficult.

Humphrey Burton's claim that I knew nothing about opera was not wholly true. I had not worked in an opera house, and still never have, but I had sat in many auditoriums and knew the repertory fairly well, especially Russian and French opera and Rossini, which particularly appealed. But I did need help and advice in evaluating what might be available for Edinburgh. The days when major companies were happy to crowd on to Edinburgh's inadequate stage were over. Companies would look at plans of the King's Theatre and ask where our real theatre was. I started by making a list of opera houses of good standing whose theatres were not much bigger than ours. It seemed practical. I was also struck by the fact that, although we had had orchestras, theatre companies and dance from both France and the USA, we had never heard a French or an American opera company. I turned to the doyenne of artists' representatives, who for many years had been closely associated with opera in Europe – Lies Askonas. Lies was Austrian, a tall, handsome, former champion skier, who for thirty years had represented not only singers and conductors (the young Abbado and Mehta were first championed by her) but also companies of both opera and ballet. She had been much involved with Edinburgh, especially in the Harewood years, when she had gone to Prague with George and helped him plan the hugely successful visits of the Czech National Opera. She could be autocratic, especially with junior staff, and her very Viennese *gemütlichkeit* could seem artificial, but once you gained her confidence and got down to serious work she was unrivalled. Like Hartog, she became a close friend and somebody whom I miss very much.

Through Lies Askonas I met Hugues Gall and Gérard Mortier, who were then running the opera houses in Geneva and Brussels and now run the Paris Opéra and the Salzburg Festival. Lies and I travelled together to Stockholm to see whether the Drottningholm Court Theatre company would work outside its exquisite eighteenth-century home. We went to Nancy and to Strasbourg to look at French regional companies, and to Zurich, whose productions of Monteverdi with Nikolaus Harnoncourt had been an important element of Diamand's last year. Lies introduced me to Peter Hemmings, the former Director of Scottish Opera, who was now in Sydney and hoping to bring Joan Sutherland to Europe with the Australian Opera. And she made sure I was on good terms with Peter Ebert, who now had Hemmings's old job in Glasgow. Scottish Opera's record in the Festival had been splendid, with daring productions of *The Trojans* in 1972, *Macbeth* (with Vishnevskaya) in 1976 and the world première of Thea Musgrave's underrated *Mary, Queen of Scots* in 1977, and continued close collaboration – helping them achieve more strong international casting and playing to the strengths of their Music Director, Alexander Gibson – was a plank of my policy from the start. But how much of the Festival's budget did I wish to devote to opera? That was the question.

It was impossible at short notice for me to achieve anything very spectacular, let alone the kind of world-beating production that Diamand had presented with *Carmen*. I was concerned to even up the representation of the arts, so I decided to make my first year a statement of intent, putting more money into theatre, dance and exhibitions than Peter ever had. It was a risk, but I just got away with it.

I had much admired the work of Roger Norrington and Jonathan Miller at Kent Opera, and believed they were now ready to compete in an international context. Not everyone agreed, but I was sure they were worth a try, so in 1979 Miller directed a new production of *La Traviata*, and they revived their founder Norman Platt's perfectly decent production of *Iphigénie en Tauride*. Although *Traviata* had many good things in it, it never quite achieved the level of such previous Miller productions as his excellent *Eugene Onegin*. And it was not helped by the indisposition of the Violetta, Jill Gomez, who after a tentative first night went back to London without telling anyone. She did return, but her absence meant an understudy for the second and third performances. Above all, *Traviata* was sung in English, and to some that was unacceptable. Riccardo Muti, in Edinburgh to conduct the Philharmonia Orchestra, heard of the English *Traviata* and with characteristic directness said, 'At one stroke you make the Festival provincial.' Having heard Wagner in Italian on distinguished Italian stages, I thought that a bit rich. But it was a worry. Scottish Opera offered a revival of their brilliant production of *The Golden Cockerel* and a new production of *Onegin*, which David Pountney set almost entirely behind a gauze, greatly reducing its impact. When the gauze was finally lifted in the last act, the audience broke into unwelcome applause. This relative weakness in my first year meant that an international season of opera in my second year was essential.

Other elements of 1979 worked rather well. For the first time I attempted a thematic link running right through the Festival. In 1954 Edinburgh had been the setting for an important exhibition devised by Richard Buckle to mark the twenty-fifth anniversary of the death of Diaghilev. I was naturally well aware that 1979 would mark the fiftieth anniversary. Sitting quietly in my kitchen in London in the spring of 1978, looking at a calendar, I suddenly realized that the 1979 Festival would open on 19 August, the actual day of the Diaghilev anniversary. Given how well I knew that Diaghilev's influence could be traced in opera, concert music, drama and lectures as well as dance, I started to explore the possibility of making it a main feature, and it proved valuable in discussions of programmes with artists and companies. The great advantage of Edinburgh as opposed to Salzburg or Bayreuth is that there is no obligation to feature any one composer. This gives wonderful freedom of choice, but it can also make it difficult to know where to begin when a conductor asks you what you might want him to do. Having a theme helped me focus the planning. In the end the Diaghilev motif was reflected in two of the four operas, six of the Usher Hall concerts, two of the plays, three of the ballet programmes, six lectures and an exhibition. Themes are poor masters but good servants, and we have probably seen too much of them in recent years. But most people reckon that the two most effective Festivals I planned for Edinburgh were my first and my last – both themed: Diaghilev in 1979 and 'Vienna 1900' in 1983.

In the summer of 1978 Peter Diamand's assistant, who had given me no help at all, announced that he was leaving to run the Lyric Theatre, Hammersmith. It was a considerable relief, but it meant that I urgently needed to find someone to help me, since I was now whizzing about all over Europe and the USA, contacting people and companies and trying to get a long-term plan in place. Through my involvement with the Arts Council I had met a young administrator, Richard Jarman. After Oxford, he had worked in concert management, in publicity and for both the Arts Council and the British Council. He was now freelance, and the Festival Council allowed me to offer him a short-term contract while we advertised for a permanent replacement. We hit it off immediately, and I persuaded him to apply for the job full time. We saw several other candidates, some of whom went on to do interesting and important things elsewhere, but Jarman was head and shoulders above them all – especially since he had experience and an interest in contracts and administration as well as knowledge of music and dance. He was particularly strong on opera, which was also an advantage. My five years working with him were of the happiest, and I greatly respect his talents. I once described him as 'the best gun dog in the world', as whatever I shot he retrieved. I was told that this sounded patronizing, but it was very much meant as a compliment and was certainly true – he never failed to bring back a deal, however difficult or complicated the situation.

Diamand's secretaries also left one by one, and by the time I took over, in the autumn of 1978, I was in a position to put my own team together. But what I needed most was an experienced senior figure to run the London office and coordinate all the different elements, and this was not going to be found at the salary that Edinburgh paid Peter Diamand's principal secretary, who had a much less influential role. It

1 JD's father with Uncle George *left*

2 JD's mother

3 JD aged 6 with Great Aunt Laura and
Great Uncle William

4 Great Aunt Margaret

5 JD aged 4, with his cousin, Drummond

6 Felix aged 7, 1938

7 JD's father

8 JD with his mother

9 JD at school, 1950

10 JD aged 22

11 Coder Drummond, 1953
12 JD with his teacher, H. E. Piggott, 1953
13 JD with his mother and father, Graduation at Cambridge, 1958

14 JD as Iago in *Othello*, Bodmin, 1955
15 JD as Baldock in *King Edward II*,
Cambridge, 1958

16 JD, bit part in Ken Russell's
*Don't Shoot the Pianist*, 1964

17 JD with Josette Amiel at the Paris Opera, 1962

18 Richard Dimbleby in Moscow, 1961
19 Julius Katchen, Prades, 1966
20 Cocteau decorating the BBC's Paris Studio, 1963

21 *Left to right*: Sir Peter Maxwell Davies, Hans Werner Henze, Sir Harrison Birtwistle and JD, JD's 60th birthday party, 1994
22 *Left to right*: Robert Ponsonby, Pierre Boulez, JD and Sir William Glock, Proms tribute to Sir William Glock, 1994

23 JD with Oscar Peterson, Edinburgh Festival, 1980
24 Richard Jarman, Edinburgh, 1982
25 *Left to right*: Brian McMaster, Peter Diamand, The Earl of Harewood, JD and Ian Hunter, 50th anniversary of the Edinburgh Festival, 1997

26 'JP' with Sir Andrew Davis, 1989

27 John Tusa with JD, Minneapolis, 1991

28 JD with John Tydeman, 1985
29 Bob Lockyer with Sheila Colvin, 1996
30 Lady Elizabeth Cavendish with JD, 1997

took several months to get the Festival Council to discuss the question, let alone find the money for an enhanced post. But I was determined that they should – not only because such an appointment was so obviously necessary, but because by then I believed I had found the right person.

Sheila Colvin came into my life through mutual friends in Edinburgh and the gallery owner Richard de Marco, with whom she had worked in his earlier years. Lancashire-born but Edinburgh-educated, Sheila had worked in radio and television, having been assistant to Rudolf Cartier, the doyen of drama producers at the BBC, and later to Humphrey Burton at London Weekend Television. She had also been part of the team that founded the Traverse Theatre in Edinburgh, and was an excellent musician. She had worked in publishing in Brazil, and knew as much about opera as Richard Jarman. She was now twiddling her thumbs in London as PA to the head of an American oil company who visited London only once a month. Despite being well paid, she was bored and was extremely keen to work for the Festival, but I simply couldn't offer her an acceptable salary and had to turn her down. She was obviously upset and, unfortunately for her, we met by chance at the opera later that evening, when I was certainly the last person she wanted to see. But I did not forget her, because I was sure she was right for the job. It took me several months to persuade the council to agree to a more substantial increase, and, even though it was still 25 per cent less than she was being paid by the oil company, she then accepted.

Sheila Colvin's arrival was the best thing that happened to me in the Edinburgh years. From the start she proved invaluable. She was to spend ten years at the Festival – five with me and five with my successor – before moving on to run the Aldeburgh Foundation. She is one of the most capable and gifted women I have ever met, and certainly the most hard-working, with a loyalty to colleagues that is unmatched. So by my first winter as Director I had the makings of a real team around me in the London office. We were all new to festivals, but we all had enthusiasm and commitment and we all knew the Festival well. Inexperienced as my colleagues were, I felt total confidence in them – which was more than I could say about the set-up in Edinburgh.

The Festival's administrator was a local-authority man called George Bain, very much of the old school. After thirteen years, he and Peter Diamand still called each other Mr Diamand and Mr Bain. I called him George from day one, and he slowly accustomed himself to calling me John. He was a good man, as straight as a die, and did what he thought necessary. But he was completely out of his depth in dealing with the pressures and complexity of the Festival. In the strictest sense, he really ran only the Edinburgh office and handled local hirings, the Festival Club and relations with the District Council and the Festival Council. But even with local hirings there were problems. I decided to increase the number of performances on Sundays. George negotiated a key contract which excluded access on Sundays. When I protested, he said, 'But we have never done that' – which of course was precisely why I wanted the change. I am not for a moment suggesting he did not do his best; it was simply that I was accustomed to working with an intensity and speed that he could not respond to but which the Festival demanded. On one desperate day when a major company had withdrawn, I went into his office to discuss the crisis. He waved me away with the long-cherished and much quoted reply 'I am on the phone to Linlithgow.'

He had a deputy whose role I never fathomed. Apart from administering the Festival Chorus – hardly a full-time job – he kept out of the way and was famous for putting his coat on and going home at five o'clock precisely, whatever the situation. Everything we did had to pass through the local authority, whose Deputy Finance Director was responsible for authorizing payments and supervising the budget. It was an uncomfortable situation which frequently became intolerable. While I initially had sympathy for the Edinburgh staff's difficulty in understanding the full import of what was going on, they seemed unwilling to learn and treated us as if we were certainly irresponsible and probably dangerous.

Edinburgh was suffering under the two-tier system of local government introduced by the Tories. The old City Council had been abolished and reduced to the District Council, now surrounded by the newly created and much larger Lothian Regional Council. The District Council was small, relatively poor and Conservative, while the Regional Council was large, rich and Labour-controlled. Both bodies had been represented on the Festival Council, but the year before I took over the Regional Council withdrew, leaving the District Council to put up all the subsidy. This was administratively simpler, but made us more vulnerable. The level of Council support had long been a political issue, largely opposed by the Labour group and reluctantly supported by the Tories. The smaller parties – the Liberals and the Scottish National

Party – wanted greater Scottish presence in the Festival as the price of their support. For Richard, Sheila and myself it was daily evident that what was seen in London as one of the great glories of the Scottish year was for many in Edinburgh a tiresome, expensive irrelevance.

I set out to try to raise the level of understanding in Edinburgh, and spent much of my first year accepting every invitation I was offered to speak and write about the Festival, to demonstrate not merely its cultural significance but also its economic contribution to the city and the country. It was tough going. The division between the two local authorities meant that many of the benefits from the massive attendance went to the wrong council. Relations between the two were so bad that in the event of snow the Regional Council ostentatiously refused to carry out its responsibility for gritting the roads outside the City Chambers, home of the District Council. I never felt any real sense of appreciation of what the Festival was about and, when once a year I was given the chance to address the District Council, I always felt that there was resentment at more than the cost of the Festival. One year I carefully examined the District Council's budget to find an equivalent cost to that of the Festival. It was the graveyards. I mentioned this, and an elderly councillor said thunderously to me, 'What you ignore is that we have a statutory duty to bury the dead. There is no such duty regarding the Festival.' In his column in *The Times*, Bernard Levin christened the annual debate about financial support 'the Grudging of the Money'.

Yet the District Council was by no means the only source of funds, or even the largest. Most income came from the box office, and by my time all the audience surveys revealed that the majority of the audience lived in the city or its surroundings. Fewer than 10 per cent came from abroad, especially after the high inflation of the early 1980s, when hotels increased their prices dramatically without any improvement in their quality. The rich American and Continental tourists of early years then went away, to be replaced by the back-packing young who made themselves at home on the Fringe.

Support from other local organizations was mixed. The Scottish Arts Council had funded the Festival from the start. Indeed, its grant to the Edinburgh Festival was greater than the sum of all other grants to British festivals, for in England the Arts Council supported festivals in a very small way indeed. In the early days the Festival had been seen as a part of a much needed seeding operation to extend arts awareness in

Scotland, and there is no doubt that such organizations as Scottish Opera, Scottish Ballet, the Scottish Chamber Orchestra, the Traverse Theatre and the Scottish Arts Council's own exhibition space had all come into existence on a wave of enthusiasm for the arts that the Festival had helped to generate. But by the 1980s the seeding operation was over and pressure on Scottish Arts Council funds grew every year, with new clients from Orkney to the Borders. I had genuine concern that Arts Council finance might not be permanent. The then Director, Sandy Dunbar, seemed more concerned with Scotland than with Edinburgh, and I found him tricky. Luckily I had an ally in the Chairman, Lord Balfour of Burleigh, who went out of his way to support us and could not have been more helpful.

The Festival also benefited from a large number of private enterprises – brewers, banks, insurance companies and shipping firms – who made donations. But we were only at the beginning of the age of sponsorship, and turning donors into sponsors was to take up a large amount of my time. BP had come in on the *Carmen* production with £35,000. By the time I left, total sponsorship had risen to £240,000. Today it is well over £1 million a year – a truly astonishing figure, since many companies prefer to support round-the-year activities rather than one-off events. As sponsorship increased, so donations declined, but keeping everyone on board was a major part of our task. No one on the Festival Council was prepared to help. They had in Peter Diamand's time established a Fund-Raising and Sponsorship Committee, but its only achievement was to decide it was unnecessary and vote itself out of existence.

Attitudes in the community were also complex. Since the Festival took place during the summer vacation, Edinburgh University said it did not see how it could contribute apart from leasing accommodation in its halls of residence. The Music Faculty was notably absent. Peter Williams, a baroque specialist, wrote brilliant programme notes for us, but left the city during the Festival unless he was asked to perform. My first official function as Director was to attend a lunch given by the Scottish Tourist Board in its expensive new headquarters. The Chairman, in the presence of several senior bank executives and business leaders, chose the occasion to emphasize that the Tourist Board had no intention of helping the Festival in any way, since there was already 'a healthy level of tourism in Scotland at that time of year'. He could see no connection between the presence of the tourists and the attractions of the Festival. He might consider some assistance, he said, if we were to move the Festival to April. Every time I went out, people would pin me against the wall and tell me what was wrong and what they thought needed to be done. At one party, given for me by the designer of the new logo which I had insisted on, a group of grandees grilled me for an hour while I stood there with an empty glass. Eventually one of them said, 'Well, come on, tell us what you think.' I replied, 'I think I should be allowed to go out in the evening without having to do a fucking board for the job.' They retired in confusion, and word got around that the Director used quite unacceptable language. No one expected the local press to be in the Festival's pocket, but I found it odd that the editor of our programmes was the *Scotsman*'s principal music critic, Conrad Wilson, whose response to my annual press conference was always to produce a long list of works that we were *not* performing.

Meanwhile my Scottish base was a small room at the back of the George Hotel, which had lost its former standing and was increasingly given over to coach parties. I was spending a great deal of time in Edinburgh, in an effort to make friends and get to know people, but also to try to change the mood. Diamand had avoided Edinburgh except when it was essential. He would come up for a meeting with the Festival Council and return to London immediately it was over. This was much resented, which I could understand, but it was soon clear to me that, although the funding of the Festival might be controlled from Edinburgh, the artistic side demanded my presence elsewhere – anywhere else, in fact.

The London office had been the subject of heated controversy since the beginning. No Director had ever lived in Edinburgh, and the physical circumstances of the Festival offices – in a well-sited but wretchedly unsuitable building overlooking Waverley Station – made doing so an unappealing prospect. The building had formerly been the offices of the *Edinburgh Evening News*, and the offices clung to the outer walls round a huge central well which might have been useful to the paper but was no good for us except when operating as a box office, and even then it was fraught with problems. Access for queuing customers was through the same entrance that the staff had to use, and the booking methods paid little heed to contemporary requirements. It was not even accepted that credit cards could be used. That soon changed, and within three years the system was computerized, but with painfully slow equipment that took ages to print out the tickets. Despite a hard-working staff, this gave an impression of amateurishness and lack of purpose. We were even forbidden to put up a sign outside to say that that was where the box office was. The offices themselves were adequate but awkwardly interconnected, and one aged lift served the whole building. Above all, there was no accommodation for visiting staff. We were paying a sizeable rent for the place – money from the District Council going straight back to the Council. I wanted a better building, and went in search of one. But when I found a possible place it was rejected out of hand, and only in 1999 did the Festival administration finally move to a specially converted building on a prime site.

I suggested that accommodation be found for the Festival Director if I was to spend more time in the city and be able to receive people or entertain during the Festival. Eventually, a disused children's crèche at the lower end of the Royal Mile was suggested at a very low rent. It was far too big, but it had some splendid features. The Labour group found out about the low-rent proposal and created a major political row. Accommodation for the Director or staff was never mentioned again, and we went on paying hotel bills for four of my six years at the Festival. I stayed first in the George then in the North British, where a bloody-minded receptionist would again ask me my name as I checked in for the fortieth time that year. I spent one year in the spare bedroom of two councillors, but this had to be kept secret as they were not only Regional but Labour councillors, and my last year was spent in the spare room of our Vice-Chairman, the architect James Dunbar-Nasmith. It was very generous of him, but not really very satisfactory. Every year for the Festival itself I tried to rent a house, as previous Directors had done, and sometimes these houses were splendidly situated and really comfortable, though twice the best we could find on the market was a top-floor flat without a lift.

Despite the kindness and hospitality of a number of people in different walks of life, I never really felt welcome in the city and came to dread evenings alone when there were no performances to attend and no social events. I am quite used to eating alone in restaurants, since I have travelled so much on my own, but I never got used to the intrusiveness of other diners in Edinburgh, who would come over and tell me what was wrong with me and the Festival at every turn. Over the years I came to realize that my campaign of befriending and being around in Scotland bore little or no fruit. One night, at the annual dinner of the Scottish Licensed Victuallers Association, the then Secretary of State for Scotland, George Younger, asked me what on earth I was doing there. I wondered myself.

What was essential was my presence at meetings with the Festival Council and its advisory committees. The Festival Council was made up partly of elected local councillors and partly of lay men and women. In the early years the numbers of local-authority members were proportional to the strength of the parties on the District Council, which meant that the governing body of the Festival had on it a number of people from the Labour group who were opposed to its very existence. Such is democracy. Just before my time, the Tory group used their majority to take almost all the places. We had one Labour man, one Liberal and one SNP, with the nine others all being Tories. Some of them were helpful enthusiasts; others were quite bewilderingly uninterested. I met one of the Tory councillors on the Festival Council at a party during the Festival and asked if she was enjoying things. She replied, 'My sister is over from Spain, so I have not been able to go to anything.' The lay members were much more supportive – both in attendance and in understanding – but whenever there was a potential difficulty or a financial problem they tended to remain silent and they could always be outvoted. Much depended on the attitude of the Lord Provost, who was ex-officio Chairman. For Kenneth Borthwick, who had overseen my appointment, what mattered was the Commonwealth Games. He did his best, but the Festival was quite alien to his real interests and he always sided with George Bain and the City Treasurer if there was any dispute about money or administration. His successor, Tom Morgan, was a great deal more interested, and became a good friend, but I never lost the feeling that they thought me a wild card who had to be watched closely. Even the Vice-Chairman, Dunbar-Nasmith, was pretty timorous.

All innovations were considered risky. Depressed by the dreadful conditions of the halls and theatres that the city owned and charged us a high rent for, I tried other solutions, like inviting the Royal Ballet to bring its travelling tent, the Big Top, to the Meadows. I had the impression that every department of the local authority, especially Building Control, was doing its absolute best to obstruct the plan; Richard Jarman went through the tortures of the damned to get it agreed. The licence to use it was insultingly delivered to us only a few minutes before the royal car swept up to the entrance on the opening night. 'We'll keep these whippersnappers in their place,' I overheard one official say. Of course every previous Director had had the same problems and had triumphed over them, so we were not going to allow ourselves to be defeated, but I resented to my last day the expenditure of time and energy it took to cause anything new to happen.

The Director of the National Gallery of Scotland, Colin Thompson, was an old friend with whom I had made several television programmes, and he shared my wish for exhibitions to feature again as they had done in Ian Hunter's time. There was a new temporary exhibition area, carved out of the Mound beneath the National Gallery itself – not an ideal space, but it offered opportunities. As part of my policy of redressing the balance of expenditure between the art forms, I went ahead with Thompson and Ronald Pickvance of Glasgow University in planning a major Degas exhibition for my first year. I was sick of being told it took seven years to plan a major exhibition and that you could no longer borrow the great impressionists. Pickvance focused the exhibition on 1879 – an important year in Degas's life, and well represented by pictures already in Scotland. Without too much difficulty, we achieved loans from the Louvre, the National Gallery in London and leading American collections. The show was a huge and deserved success, and I was delighted with all the work that went into it. It cost the Festival the equivalent of four concerts or less than an opera company. At the end of its run, the National Gallery's Keeper of Paintings, Hugh McAndrew, told us, 'Never again! We can't have the janitors so overworked in a holiday period.' Colin Thompson had no authority to overrule him, it would seem, and it was the only time in my years in Edinburgh that the National Gallery cooperated with the Festival. Every year London art critics would complain, but I could hardly admit the real situation.

Even more controversial was the role of the Royal Scottish Academy, whose dilapidated building sits next to the National Gallery. It had neither temperature nor humidity control, nor funding to assist with exhibitions. What is more, the Academicians really wanted to display their own efforts at Festival time. Although there were some excellent painters and sculptors among them, the general impression, as with the Royal Academy in London, was of very mixed quality. The President of the Academy, Sir Robin Philipson, was Chairman of the Festival's advisory committee on exhibitions, which also included a former Director of the National Gallery of Scotland, David Baxendall. They opposed almost everything I suggested. In my second year, which featured the arts in the major Commonwealth countries, I was offered a splendid exhibition of Australian impressionists, already curated and ready to be shipped. The Advisory Committee turned it down flat – Streeton, Roberts, Conder and the other leading Australian artists were not good enough for Edinburgh. When, as politely as I could, I asked why they had rejected it, Philipson said wearily, 'It's all so provincial.'

I did what I could for exhibitions over the years, but always against a background of non-cooperation. Douglas Hall, at the National Gallery of Modern Art at Inverleith House, went his own way. Given two years' notice of an Italian emphasis in the Festival, he opted for a German sculptor. The university's Talbot Rice Centre was pointedly uncooperative, and the Director of the Royal Scottish Museum threatened to have me thrown out of the building when I suggested he might open an exhibition a few days earlier to coincide with the Festival. Nevertheless, we achieved several good shows, but always in the face of coolness from the advisers and carping from the critics, who wanted things like the Degas exhibition every year. In the end we got rid of the advisory committee and set up a new body under the aegis of the Art Department of the Scottish Arts Council, but it was really no more effective. In recent years there has been a total stand-off between the Festival and the National Galleries of Scotland, with public disagreements, very much on a personal level, between Brian McMaster and the gallery's Director, Tim Clifford. While I understand McMaster's financial concerns and share his resentment at Clifford's high-handed manner, I regret this situation, since exhibitions are very much a crossroads and meeting place for all the different audiences, both for what people will call the 'official' Festival and for the Fringe. It is the cross-fertilization between those audiences that makes for a good Festival.

Mention of the Fringe was a real red rag to the Festival Council. I could understand this attitude but thought it foolish, since the two operations, however different in approach and attitude, were complementary. The Fringe did little for music, but was making a very strong contribution in the area of theatre. The focus of drama in the city was much more at the little Traverse Theatre than it was at the Royal Lyceum. I admired what the Traverse were doing and in my first year I invited them into the Festival with two new plays: the very remarkable *Animal* by John McGrath, and a rather silly piece by Billy Connolly called *The Red Runner*. No one among the critics or the audience thought it inappropriate that they should be part of the main programme, but the Festival Council was deeply shocked when I gave a joint press conference with the Fringe administrator and toured the city on the top of an open bus with Billy Connolly. The truth was we needed the Traverse's audience to counteract the increasingly ageing profile of our own. I wanted a new cooperative spirit, and despaired of previous attempts to get local support.

There was an organization called the Edinburgh Festival Guild – several hundred loyal supporters, all of them, it appeared, over sixty. They were known to the staff as 'the woolly hats'. Eventually the Guild was wound up, and I tried to establish a new organization, the Friends of the Edinburgh Festival. I asked eight effective people I knew from the city and surroundings to help. We never even achieved a meeting which all eight attended. More could have been done if our press and publicity officer, Ian Crawford, had been a bit more energetic. He was notably welcoming to me when I first arrived, and I enjoyed his bucolic company, but he simply did not work hard enough and he spent too much time rubbishing the Fringe – an organization of which he had no direct experience, since throughout the Festival he sat in the Press Office dispensing good champagne to all and sundry. A fund of splendid stories and with a wide range of friends and contacts, he frittered away my support through overlong lunches and missed deadlines. His relations with George Bain were poor to the point of non-existence: he and George could not bear each other. Eventually I had to get rid of him – the first time I had ever had to do this to a member of staff. It is a measure of his personal qualities that he behaved impeccably and we are still friends, but of course it was not a popular move with the press, who had enjoyed his generous hospitality. His replacement as the locally based publicity officer, although younger and more ambitious, never became one of the team.

All these anxieties about the level of local support for the Festival drained me of energy, and greatly diminished the enjoyment I got out of what was, and still can be, one of the best jobs in the arts anywhere in the world. In the winter of my third year George Bain went down with a very bad attack of flu, and to everyone's regret he died unexpectedly a few months away from his retirement. I was genuinely saddened, since he had tried hard to adapt to the new team and been very supportive of both Richard and Sheila. He was a very nice man in quite the wrong job. In the vacuum following his death, I asked Richard to move to Edinburgh temporarily to hold the fort. When I saw the difference made by having someone there who embodied our policy, I asked him to make the move permanent. Despite his reservations he agreed, and in time I think he came to enjoy living in the city, but without ever loving the local authority. I well remember the meeting of the Finance Committee at which agreement could not be found for paying the expenses resulting from his move.

The arguments about the London office continued. I worked it out that in my third year I spent four months in Edinburgh, four in London, and four on the road exploring or negotiating with potential visitors. Of course none of these four-month totals formed a single block. A typical week saw me in Edinburgh for two days, in London for three, and abroad for the two remaining ones. I worked seven days a week throughout my time as Director, and with so small a staff it was barely enough – especially as, unlike Diamand, I was constantly seeking new things each year rather than rebooking the already known. The cost of the London office was relatively small. The rent was about £12,000 a year, and the staff would have cost little less had they been based in Scotland. Its closure would have meant that for two-thirds of the year the Director would be without a base or secretarial support, or the contacts that came from being in a city like London which saw almost every musical organization or artist at some time during the year. I wrote a report on the London office in my first year, and it was grudgingly agreed that we should keep it on. But it was a constant irritant to many in Edinburgh, and especially to the Nationalists.

I wanted to deliver the best Festival I could, and did not believe it could be done by spending more of my time in Edinburgh. I worked out that the extra we would spend on travel and expenses if we closed the London office would be almost as much as what was saved in rent. My successors have felt differently. Frank Dunlop downgraded it; Brian McMaster closed it and has moved to Edinburgh. I wonder how much time he spends there – though the fact that he invites the same people year after year means that he probably needs to travel less than I did.

It was the fact of my being in London that led me to the most outstanding company which appeared in my first year. I was telephoned by the Soviet Cultural Attaché and asked to lunch with the Minister of Culture and the Director of the Hermitage, who were visiting London. We had a lively lunch, just the four of us. I took at once to the Minister, Popov, who, though a Communist apparatchik, was well versed in cultural matters. He had a well-known association with the mezzo-soprano Elena Obraztsova, and had travelled widely outside Russia – quite unlike Madame Furtseva. I had been chasing up a play by Robert David MacDonald about Diaghilev, called *Chinchilla*, presented a couple of years earlier by the Citizens' Theatre in Glasgow, and I had remembered that the text had been printed in the monthly magazine *Plays and Players*. Leafing through back numbers of the magazine, I chanced on a review by Michael Coveney of a theatre festival in Mexico where the star attraction had been a company from Tbilisi, in Georgia, called the Rustaveli. I had never heard of them. On the morning of my lunch with Popov, I received out of the blue a letter from our Cultural Attaché in Moscow saying that the Rustaveli company had just completed a season there and he thought we ought to be interested since they were remarkable. I asked Popov if he had seen them, and he went into an ecstasy of praise and excitement. Did *I* want to see them? 'Certainly,' I said. 'When?' 'Well, soon.' Five days later Richard Jarman and I were in Moscow, where we did the rounds of some dull companies, and a few days later we arrived in Tbilisi.

I really had no idea what to expect. As a language, Georgian is about as remote from Russian as is Chinese, and the prospect of seeing unfamiliar plays in a language I did not know was daunting. The first evening we saw something called *Machika*. I never worked out if it meant mother-in-law or step-mother, but I have rarely laughed so much in my life. Here was a brilliant company of character actors from the old school, with every theatrical device at their command. The following night we saw the exceptional and highly visual production of Brecht's *The Caucasian Chalk Circle* which Coveney had raved about, and I was immediately determined we should bring it to Edinburgh. The company's showpiece, and the secret of their Moscow success, was a satirical political drama about a Georgian tyrant and his subversion of a society. For any Russian or Georgian, it was full of coded messages about Stalin. Even Popov thought it brilliant. But I was not sure it would work for a non-Russian audience. It was too talky. Foreign-language drama must be visually exciting and, like opera, carry the audience with it through the language barrier.

People often ask me why they should be expected to derive pleasure from something they cannot literally understand line by line. My response is always to say, 'Look, and you will get a comparable pleasure.' Great acting also tends to override language barriers. I have seen productions in Swedish, Polish, Greek, Japanese and other languages I do not speak, and have been as moved and involved as by anything in the languages I do understand. It is a matter of careful selection. The World Theatre Seasons in London, run for years most imaginatively by Peter Daubeny, were full of revelations, and after his death I felt a lack of contact with international drama. One of the great advantages of Edinburgh was that it gave me a chance to redress the typically British feeling that we did not need to know what those foreigners were doing. But the Stalin play was not what I wanted, and to bring just the Brecht seemed too much of a box-office risk – brilliant though it was. What else did Rustaveli have to offer?

Extremely reluctantly, they told me that their current enterprise was Shakespeare's *Richard III*, but that they were not yet satisfied with it. It had been in rehearsal for several months, had been given a couple of performances, but had then been withdrawn for further work. Like the other plays, it was directed by Robert Sturua, who ran the company, and starred the amazing Ramaz Chkhikvadze, whose Asdak in *The Caucasian Chalk Circle* had seemed to me Olivier-like in its theatrical bravura and intensity. In between partying a great deal and eating the most enormous quantity of extremely good food – something that differentiated Tbilisi quite clearly from Moscow – we argued endlessly about the rest of their repertory and what might happen.

Sturua, Chkhikvadze and a couple of other actors took us to lunch in a restaurant in the country outside Tbilisi. They wanted to talk about anything but *Richard III*. Halfway through lunch, two cases of wine arrived at the table, an unsolicited gift from a neighbouring table, for our hosts were all stars and local heroes. With great reluctance, on our last morning they finally agreed to run the first act of *Richard III* for us in the theatre. Richard Jarman and I sat there in stupefied amazement. It was unforgettable, and from the first moment when Chkhikvadze, in a long leather coat, leaning on a stick, limped towards the audience with the words 'Now is the winter of our discontent', I felt he had joined the ranks of the great Shakespearian actors.

But the production was not yet ready. I offered to come back when they themselves were satisfied with it, and two months later I returned to Tbilisi and saw the whole play, which maintained throughout the extraordinary impact of Act 1. I had to have it. But now the company got a really bad attack of cold feet. It was one thing to bring Brecht to Britain, quite another to bring Shakespeare. They were immovable.

Eventually Sturua agreed that I could speak to the whole company. Summoning up my increasingly rusty Russian, I harangued them for twenty minutes, digging up from the depths of my memory every word of praise I could think of. But what finally got to them was my saying simply that I had seen Shakespeare directed by Guthrie, Brook, Vilar, Bergman, Gielgud, Hall, Welles and so on. They must trust me: what they were doing was in its way as remarkable and original as Brook's *A Midsummer Night's Dream*. I knew that Sturua worshipped Brook and had seen quite a lot of his work. In the end they agreed, and so became my first foreign theatre company.

They played Brecht for three performances, then four of *Richard III*. Bookings were very slow, and the Royal Lyceum Theatre was less than half full for the first two days. Then the notices appeared, and the bush telegraph got to work. The latter is a key element in evaluating the Fringe, but on this occasion it was very helpful to me too. Directors and critics from all over Europe descended on the Lyceum, and we turned away hundreds of people for the last performance of *Richard III*. It was a triumph by any standards, and most valuable for me in that it represented my calling card to the British and international theatre community. My reputation, such as it was, was largely for music and dance; this was a first chance to see what I supported in theatre. Peter Hall, with whom I had had friendly conversations about the non-involvement of the National Theatre, promised to come and see what I was doing. He saw both Rustaveli productions and McGrath's *Animal*, and agreed to the National Theatre taking part in subsequent years. This was to prove more problematic than I had hoped, but at least we were on the same wavelength.

The Glasgow Citizens' Theatre revived *Chinchilla*, the play about Diaghilev, the following week, and paired it with the Goldoni play on which the ballet *The Good-Humoured Ladies* had been based for Diaghilev. Traditionally, Edinburgh has a dislike for Glasgow's most experimental company, but in the Festival context their productions worked, both supporting the Diaghilev theme and lending the presence of a major Scottish company. I have always enjoyed the Cits, but often felt they looked better than they sounded, which may be why they have been so successful abroad – their high-camp, visually brilliant style has always seemed more European than British. Sadler's Wells Royal Ballet presented three programmes in their Big Top, one linked to Diaghilev, including the world première of Kenneth Macmillan's *Playground*, a powerful and disturbing piece with a new score by Gordon Crosse. Alicia Alonso, already in her sixties, brought the National Ballet of Cuba for its British debut, and danced Giselle herself – three times the age of her partner, but with glimpses of her former greatness. In the last week the Merce Cunningham Company made their first appearance in Britain for eleven years and began a love affair which has led to their regular returns ever since. Cunningham himself – one of the great performers of our time – and his lifelong friend and colleague the composer John Cage became friends of mine, and we gave a birthday party for Cage, who sat on the floor with his picnic basket of macrobiotic food and an ill-concealed bottle of vodka. Sitting around him were young Scottish composers like Edward McGuire and Martin Dalby, and the great figure of Witold Lutosławski, who had conducted his cello concerto that night. This, I felt, is what Festivals should be about.

At the College of Art we had an adventurous, if not totally successful, exhibition of ballet costumes, called 'Parade', which overcame the lighting restrictions placed on showing old fabrics by creating a *son et lumière*, with moments of disorientating darkness being followed by brilliant illumination for no more than thirty seconds. We were deluged with complaints about the risk of pickpockets or more intimate contact, but theatre costumes make no impact without theatrical lighting, and the Edinburgh designer John Patterson was full of ideas – most of them extremely expensive. Edinburgh's twin city, Munich, gave us a free display of small works by Kandinsky, and I was able to feel at the end of the first year that theatre, dance and the visual arts had done much to compensate for the lower level of expenditure on opera. I just wished that Kent Opera had been at its best. A distinguished colleague said, 'They had a chance to step up. But in the event they just came.'

The concert programme followed the traditional pattern, with visiting orchestras in the Usher Hall and chamber concerts in the morning. But here, too, a new element came into play. From 1947, morning concerts had been given in the Freemasons' Hall in George Street, with its bathroom acoustic and hideously creaking chairs, or in Leith Town Hall, gloomy and difficult of access. A disused church in Newington, not far from the old Empire Theatre, had been earmarked for conversion, and work was in progress when I took over. I went to see it with the Chairman of the rebuilding appeal and the architect. It was a most attractive 1820 building, oval in plan, with a central area and raised seating around it. The gallery sightlines were poor, but it had real atmosphere. Despite its having no ceiling and no stage at the time I saw it, I felt confident of its eventual attractions and decided to take a risk. I booked it for six morning concerts, retaining the Freemasons' Hall for the majority. I was naturally apprehensive as to whether the conversion would be ready in time, but I think the Festival's support was a fillip to the hall's fund-raising. They managed to get the job done, and in July the Queen officially opened the hall and christened it the Queen's Hall. The opening concert was made embarrassingly memorable by the appearance in a kilt of the Master of the Queen's Music, Malcolm Williamson, who seemed to think that the sporran should be worn at knee level. Afterwards, I broke protocol and asked the Queen what she thought of the Hall. She said with a smile, 'Being who I am, I probably shouldn't say this, but it seems a good thing that the congregation went away.' The Queen's Hall has been a real asset both to the city and to the Festival, and is now accepted by everyone as a first-rate chamber venue. It is hard on pianists, in particular, to achieve a proper balance with singers, but it has real presence and has also proved excellent for broadcasting.

The Usher Hall saw the familiar parade of orchestras – nine in number: something totally taken for granted by Edinburgh audiences, but unthinkable in most other European festivals. Abbado returned with the London Symphony Orchestra for two concerts, and in the third week Riccardo Chailly made his British debut. The two leading Scottish conductors, Alexander Gibson and James Loughran, brought the Scottish National Orchestra and the Hallé. The Scottish Chamber Orchestra sold out their first Festival appearance in the Usher Hall. The brilliant Polish Chamber Orchestra made a fine impression. It was Jerzy Maksymiuk's Scottish debut, but he was to become a frequent visitor for many years at the helm of the BBC Scottish Symphony Orchestra. The Festival opened with a Diaghilev programme of Prokofiev's *Chout*, with the Fringe Chairman, actor Andrew Cruikshank, as the narrator, and *The Rite of Spring*, both conducted by Gennadi Rozhdestvensky with the BBC Symphony Orchestra – a deliberate nod of recognition and gratitude to the musical contributions of my former employer. Boston came as planned, with Seiji Ozawa.

The orchestral high point for me was a series of four concerts given by the Philharmonia. Two were conducted by Riccardo Muti. He had not been one of the Diamand Mafia, and his only previous Edinburgh appearance had been to conduct Beethoven's disappointing and rarely heard cantata *Christ on the Mount of Olives*. I had sought an early meeting with him, and we had had lunch in an Italian restaurant in London. I knew that others had found him difficult, but we got on right from the start. I very much admired him in the right repertory, which to my mind is not the Brahms and Bruckner that he now specializes in with the Vienna Philharmonic, but music of great colour and theatricality. In Edinburgh that year he conducted Mussorgsky, Tchaikovsky (with Salvatore Accardo) and Ravel, and at my suggestion learnt especially Falla's *The Three-Cornered Hat*, a score he had never even looked at before but which subsequently became a favourite. With Janet Baker he conducted a set of Liszt songs – her idea, and a very interesting one – and he also performed Mozart and Penderecki. We were to have a very fruitful collaboration over the next few years. After our first lunch, we walked back to St James's Street on a sunny afternoon, and as we parted he said, 'I wished very much to see the face of the new Director. I like what I see. We will work together.' In fact the only row we ever had was when he discovered that Abbado's photograph was slightly larger than his in the Festival programme book. He flung it at me across the Artists' Room.

The Philharmonia also gave a concert with the underestimated Jésus López-Cobos, now another stranger to our shores. But their fourth concert was the start of a long collaboration and warm friendship with Simon Rattle. This involved the concerto with Curzon. Although they had had their problems, I had none with Rattle, whose energy, enthusiasm and charm were matched by an improbably mature musicality. He was, after all, still only twenty-four.

At the end of the first Festival I could feel that, with Rattle, Muti, Chailly, López-Cobos and Maksymiuk, I was starting to build my own 'family'. To our relief, we had had only one cancellation – and that well in advance of the Festival. There was a procession of great singers – Christa Ludwig, Elisabeth Söderström and Jessye Norman for the first time in the Usher Hall – and the presence of pianists such as Maurizio Pollini, Krystian Zimerman and Jean-Philippe Collard did not suggest any falling off in the overall standards set so admirably by my predecessors. When the final accounts were completed, the out-turn was four pounds off forecast on the budget of £1.3 million. Not even our severest critics could find much to complain about in that.

The relentless treadmill of planning never lets one sit back and be complacent. I found the three weeks of the Festival exhausting, but also exhilarating. On parade for at least sixteen hours a day, I never felt tired and was only astonished when people would say, as they often did, 'You'll be so glad when it's over': for me the end of the Festival meant back into the darkness for another forty-nine weeks of preparation and planning. What I did find difficult was adjusting from the steady flow of television work, with something broadcast every few days, to the concentration of a year's work being realized in just three weeks. Pacing life was a challenge. I always went on holiday immediately after the Festival, but I took my plans and notes with me. After a few days' complete rest, the future surfaced again. Indeed it never left me, since there are deadlines to meet at many moments of the year.

The most difficult problem was that we never knew how much money we would have until very late in the day. Both the Edinburgh District Council and the Scottish Arts Council would confirm their annual grant only in the spring of the year, when the main elements had all been booked. We hoped for an increase each year, and usually got something, but how much was unclear. We planned in relative darkness, and even the best prepared budgets could be undermined by inflation or changing exchange rates. But after the first Festival I knew the score and could see more clearly what was possible and what we might have to abandon – not just because of cost, but through changing circumstances and conditions. The arrival of a new building like the Queen's Hall was an advantage, but the continuing inadequacy of the King's (with no pit), the Royal Lyceum (with ancient stage machinery) and the Usher Hall (with its total absence of air-conditioning and its limited space backstage) meant a constant search for new solutions. There wasn't a building in the city I did not look at to assess its possible value. Increasingly the Fringe was expanding, and used any hall or church that we did not. From its days of unlicensed cafés and early closing, we were moving to a situation where Edinburgh had more entries in *The Good Food Guide* than any other city outside London. The pubs were now open all day and, on application, for most of the night. The role of the Festival Club became more questionable. It was expensive to run, the caterers seemed unable to produce interesting food, and the social needs had changed.

I wondered whether we couldn't find some better use for the Assembly Rooms. I very much wanted to involve writers in some way, and in 1980 we launched a four-day conference of poets, novelists, lexicographers, biographers and critics. Not much attention had been paid to literature since John Calder's conference in the 1960s – remembered by everyone for the moment when a naked girl was wheeled across the gallery of the McEwan Hall during one of the sessions. Nothing so dramatic happened in 1980, but a roster of distinguished figures – including Robert Burchfield, Margaret Drabble, Michael Frayn, John Mortimer and Gore Vidal – turned up and found enthusiastic and receptive audiences. This event was the precursor of the now annual Edinburgh Book Festival, and I am happy to have been its godparent. It took a great deal of organizing – a task undertaken by Sheila Colvin, working with the broadcaster Frank Delaney. There were many cancellations and much last-minute toing and froing, but most of it was good-humoured, even though I recall Anthony Burgess's Italian wife threatening me with her walking stick for reasons I cannot now remember.

In 1979 we had presented a series of lectures about the world of Diaghilev, in the tiny but charming St Cecilia's Hall. In 1980 we looked at 'The State and the Arts' with Arts Minister Paul Channon, Roy Hattersley, Peter Ustinov, Lord Goodman, David Steel and distinguished foreign guests. The following year we had a conference on 'Television and the Arts' with Jonathan Miller, John Mortimer, Melvyn Bragg, Humphrey Burton, Jeremy Isaacs, Robert Hughes, John Julius Norwich and others, under the chairmanship of Huw Wheldon. I felt the Festival was improved by having so many well-known faces around.

In my first two years I used the Festival Club to entertain, but found the formality of seating plans infuriating, especially as people would either not turn up or bring their family and their agents, their cousins from Dallas and so on. We eventually abandoned the Assembly Rooms to the Fringe and moved the Club to the university's Senior Staff Club. This was also not successful, but I don't think anything much was lost. I took to entertaining in whatever house I had rented for the Festival. Sheila found a wonderful young farmer's wife from East Lothian, Tina Bain, who coped no matter how large the numbers. I insisted on hot food: the endless round of cold salmon and salad or, at the City Chambers, spam and WWW, as one of my assistants christened the warm white wine, was deeply depressing for artists who had spent the evening acting, dancing, playing or singing. At home we had one good hot dish, lots of salads, fruit and cheese, and unlimited quantities of inexpensive sparkling wine, cooled in ice-filled dustbins and dispensed by the invaluable Bob Lockyer, who took his holiday every year to help me by running the house and the parties.

We had three or four evening supper parties each week, with anything from forty to ninety people present. Everyone whom I invited came – especially the artists, but also local notables and visiting celebrities and friends. The total cost was a fraction of what we paid at the Club, and the goodwill generated was enormous. I remember an opening night when Paul Scofield and his wife were deep in discussion with Riccardo Muti, the Beaux Arts Trio with a clutch of local musicians, and visiting grandees included Lords Goodman, Bernstein and Harewood. Someone brought the splendid Dru Heinz, who as a result helped fund the writers' event, and on two occasions Princess Margaret came – once to celebrate her birthday. I was always the last to go to bed. In addition we usually had people to stay: Judi Dench, Michael Williams, Ian McKellen, John Tydeman, Robin and Pat Scott, and, after his retirement from the *Sunday Times*, J. W. Lambert and his wife, Catherine. The only people we did not invite were working critics and local journalists, but David Palmer, the most experienced and able press officer in Britain, whom I brought up especially from London, looked after them in the Press Club, backed up, as we all were, by a posse of university students from Edinburgh, Durham or St Andrews, who came and worked with us for fifty pounds a week and acquired a taste for the arts. Many of them went on to play major roles. Stephen Carpenter, now Manager of the City of London Sinfonia, started by driving a van. Andrew Nairne, later to be Art Director of the Scottish Arts Council, ran errands. One night in my house, the wife of a London orchestral manager asked a young woman what she did. In her normal life she taught music at Fettes, and came from a very distinguished Edinburgh family, but for me she looked after the transport plan, booking taxis and arranging buses. Discovering this, the orchestral manager's wife said, 'Should you be at a party like this?' It passed into our collection of memorable remarks, along with the famous phone call to Linlithgow.

Today, twenty years later, people still talk to me about the parties. For me they typified what I was trying to do: to get the arts and the city to talk to each other and to generate a really festive atmosphere. The Fringe found the latter so easy; middle-class prejudices were much harder to dissolve. Inevitably the local press got on to the subject and hinted at profligacy and elitism, but then they had not been invited. Some of the locals who were invited found it hard to mix, but I will never forget the sight of the American dancer Tom Jobe, in leather and safety pins, deep in discussion with the Duke of Hamilton. Edinburgh has little of the warmth of Glasgow, but at least at Festival time I was determined to break through its snobbery and exclusivity and show its citizens a warmer and more companionable world. And, however much they still disapproved, I believe there was a palpable difference in feelings about the Festival over the years I was there. I do not think it too immodest to suggest that we might have made a small contribution.

Despite the short preparation time, I was reasonably happy with my first Festival. It came quite close to representing my idea of what a festival might be, demonstrating how something that was not just a random collection of events, however distinguished, gained an excitement that differentiated it from the year-round arts life of big cities. No important festival of the arts takes place in a really big city. Attempts to create one in Chicago, Houston, Sydney and Paris have all failed to do more than reinforce existing patterns. The truly influential festivals all take place in middle-sized towns, where you can walk, absorb the atmosphere, and meet people by chance at events or in the street. A festival can effectively disrupt the ordinary life of the place, and that should be the aim. Challenged on the pavement outside the Freemasons' Hall by an elderly Edinburgh citizen who claimed that I was getting in her way, I assured her that it was quite deliberate – that was my primary intention. I have been in some large cities during their festivals and been quite unaware that anything was happening. This is not the case in Edinburgh – or indeed in Cheltenham, Brighton or Bath, while Salzburg, Aix-en-Provence, Spoleto and Adelaide become totally different places during the festival period. It is not just a question of tourists, or the visible presence of art events; it reaches deeper into the community. Sensible places recognize the huge benefit that festivals bring at many levels.

I think the last twenty years have seen a difference in Edinburgh, with a less stuffy attitude from the main Festival – especially under my successor, Frank Dunlop – and an ever increasing investment in the Festival from the local community, both public and private. The eventual improvement of the theatres has made them much more attractive and more practically effective. The city now has almost too many stages for its budget and its audience, and in the winter months this overprovision shows. I was completely unsuccessful in getting improvements during my period as Director, but the many meetings I attended and the large sums I spent on converting buildings may have sown the seeds of the eventual recognition of the need for change. Before my time, improvements – if any – had been to the front of house. It was wonderfully ironic to see substantial sums being spent on the Royal Lyceum's decor and foyers while students of nineteenth-century theatre came to see its antiquated stage machinery – the scenery being changed by pulling on ropes, without even a system of counterweights. But it was in the basement of the Lyceum that I found another crucial member of my team: the Technical Director, Nicholas Beeby. Up until 1980 the Festival had always had to depend on outside firms to oversee the installation of its productions or the conversion and adaptation of venues. Beeby was tireless, inventive and wholly supportive. It meant that we never again had problems of the kind we experienced with the Big Top.

There was a continuing problem in providing a stage good enough for ballet. It is often claimed that I did a lot for dance in Edinburgh, but the facts are quite otherwise. In my first year, the combination of the tent and the conversion of Moray House Gymnasium gave the Festival three weeks of dance at a high level. But this never happened again. Some of my more painful failures were with dance companies. Even with new commissions, Scottish Ballet, London Contemporary Dance Theatre and Ballet Rambert all failed to deliver outstanding work, and the use of the vast but underequipped Playhouse cinema as a theatre for the first visit of the San Francisco Ballet was only a partial success. Ironically, it is Brian McMaster, with an opera background, who has made the biggest impact on dance, year after year bringing major companies and drawing large audiences, even for experimental work. At the same time, my record in opera is a great deal better than some doubters expected. But I had a lot of help with this, and also a degree of luck.

My second Festival demanded the return of a major foreign opera company, but it happened only as the result of the worst crisis I faced in my first years. In pursuit of a French company, I had, with Lies Askonas's support, settled on L'Opéra du Rhin, based in Strasbourg. Although I did not especially admire their Principal Conductor, Alain Lombard, their administrator, Jean-Pierre Brossmann – later in Lyons, now at the Châtelet in Paris – was a helpful colleague and became a good friend. Nineteen seventy-nine was Offenbach year. Everywhere people were putting on *The Tales of Hoffmann*, a surprisingly popular but extraordinarily difficult piece. I heard Domingo in new productions of it in Salzburg, Cologne and London. Strasbourg also was to have a new production, by one of the European new-wave directors, Virgilio Puecher. Shortly after my first Festival, I met up with Lies in Strasbourg and saw what they had done. It was only a partial success, which they recognized, and needed more work before it was to be revived in 1980. I was not totally convinced, but decided to pursue it for Edinburgh, for I seemed to have little alternative. Opera planning taking so long to achieve, I was already in discussion with Cologne for 1981 when suddenly in the late autumn of 1979, while sitting in on a meeting of the Edinburgh Festival Guild – six elderly ladies with cups of tea, in a flat in Moray Place – I was summoned back to the office to be told that Strasbourg had withdrawn. This was the moment of George Bain's phone call to Linlithgow.

I was due to be in Stockholm with Lies the following day. It was a good chance to pick her brains as to what I should do next. In the event I flew on to Cologne and asked the Intendant, Michael Hampe, if there was any chance of Cologne coming a year earlier. I was not hopeful. Hampe examined his schedules and saw a possibility, depending on the availability of the singers, but it would all depend on the support of his Music Director, John Pritchard. We talked, and with his usual courtesy and professionalism Pritchard volunteered to contact personally the leading singers in two operas – *Così fan tutte* and *Il matrimonio segreto* – to see what they could offer. I had always both liked and admired JP, as he was known. A consummate musician, he had at Glyndebourne in particular shown an instinctive understanding of Mozart rare in our time, while during his years with the Royal Liverpool Philharmonic being willing to tackle the most difficult areas of the contemporary repertory. I knew him, but we had never really worked together. He knew Edinburgh very well, and understood at once how important this moment was, not just for me but for the Festival. He rang every soloist during the next three days, and with one exception they all agreed to come to Edinburgh a year early. Hampe, not unreasonably, insisted that the invitation for 1981 should be maintained, especially as they were planning a new production of *The Barber of Seville* to open at the Festival.

The first Cologne visit, in 1980, was to my mind entirely successful, with wonderful performances by Julia Varady and Ann Murray in *Così* and simple but stylish productions. After the visit, JP went on holiday to a local hotel and wrote me an extraordinary letter, guaranteeing his support for me and my ideas and offering to provide any help he could muster. It was a splendid gesture of confidence which led to a close and important friendship until his death in 1989. His great qualities were known to all the musicians with whom he worked, but he was completely ignored by the recording companies and taken for granted by audiences. In a way, JP was almost too talented. He could sight-read the most complex new score, and his easy-going, relaxed manner belied a fierce determination to achieve high standards. Large, bulky men are often thought to be lazy, but no one took on more work than JP. We achieved a kind of pupil–teacher relationship which was one of the most valuable of my professional life. He was a good man, a great musician and an awful warning of the increasing shallowness of the commercial music world, where hype and public relations were taking over from sound musical judgement. No one could suggest that JP was not tremendously successful. In his last decade he was Music Director of the opera companies of Cologne, Brussels and San Francisco, and Chief Conductor of the BBC Symphony Orchestra. But, as he told Robert Ponsonby when he joined the BBC, 'I won't sell many seats for you.'

The second Cologne visit was ruined for me by the unacceptably arrogant attitude of Michael Hampe. Hampe, who had been quite easy to deal with in the previous year, now showed a different side with a new production to mount. While always being nice to me, he railed at the rest of my staff the moment my back was turned. Without Nicholas Beeby, *The Barber* would never have got on stage, since the Cologne workshops had misread all the stage plans for the King's Theatre and half the scenery had to be altered or remade. Cologne Opera Studio's production of Thea Musgrave's *The Voice of Ariadne*, very effectively directed by Willy Decker, came close to being cancelled through Hampe's hostility – or was it jealousy?

The major operatic success in my second year was provided by Scottish Opera, who, on two consecutive nights, presented new productions of Janáček's *The Cunning Little Vixen* and Berg's *Wozzeck*, the latter with a shaven-headed Benjamin Luxon in the title role and Alexander Gibson at his very considerable best in the pit. This was the kind of contribution I wanted from the Glasgow company. Both casts were strong in characterization and perfectly adequate vocally. Both productions were modern, but without cliché or pretentious distractions. The company's presence was a real piece of joint planning and budgeting, and exactly what was needed. But, sadly, it was to be the last time that Scottish Opera made such a contribution in my years. Their General Director, Peter Ebert, left and the company went into a period of interregnum which gave me only one effective production in my three remaining years and a couple of real duds – a truly dreadful *Beggar's Opera* and a *Death in Venice* co-produced with Geneva, whose stage is twice the size of the King's. *Death in Venice* was destroyed by our inadequacies. But why had Scottish Opera proposed this production? By the time I saw it in Geneva it had been advertised and it was too late to cancel. There were terrible arguments about who should bear the extra cost of adapting the scenery, and even then it still looked hopelessly cramped and inadequate.

My most unexpected success in 1980 was with a newly commissioned work by Peter Maxwell Davies, *The Lighthouse*, premièred at Moray House Gymnasium. It went on to become the most successful small-scale opera of its time, chalking up close to two thousand performances all over the world in the intervening years. I had never lost touch with Max after our early encounters in Television, and, although we weren't always on the same wavelength, I hugely admired his practical approach to music, his involvement in education, and his willingness to try to create a new kind of popular music theatre with his group The Fires of London. *Eight Songs for a Mad King, Miss Donnithorne's Maggot* and other works convinced me that he had a flair for fusing music and dramatic ideas lacking in so many composers of our time. He approached me about his ideas for *The Lighthouse*, based on a true story of the unexplained disappearance of three keepers from a northern lighthouse in the early years of the century, and we negotiated a new form of sponsorship from the brewers Tennant Caledonian, who were to provide £25,000 a year to create new work. The gestation of the sponsorship was a much longer and slower process than the creation of the opera. Tennant Caledonian initially wanted a sort of retrospective award, like the Fringe Firsts; it took me over a year to convince them to take the risk of backing something new. In this I was greatly assisted by the then Chief Executive, Hamish Swan, an excellent man who, without being musical or even really knowing much about Max, trusted us. At the launch he said, 'Business is about taking risks. Why should arts sponsorship not do the same?' It was the only time in my life I have ever heard a sponsor express belief in creativity or trust in an arts organization. It was heady stuff, and Swan remains the only corporate sponsor I have known with such vision.

Max had a long list of commissions already in place but was burning to write *The Lighthouse*, so we jumped the queue. He wrote the libretto himself in a few weeks, and came to the office in London to read it to Sheila, Richard and me. We were enthralled. He then returned to his home in Orkney, on the island of Hoy, and wrote the piece in a couple of months. It poured out at white heat, and sounded like it. With a cast of three and a small ensemble, it was to prove an ideal work for small companies, universities and festivals, and thoroughly deserved its immediate success. The singers Neil Mackie, Michael Rippon and David Wilson-Johnson and conductor Richard Dufallo, with simple scenery and a highly effective production by David Williams, brought it to life with the impact of a Grand Guignol ghost story.

Never again were my opera plans to work as well as in 1980, with a major foreign element, two exciting new productions from the local company, and the world première of a brilliant piece by a living composer. Just as with dance in the first year, I felt I had got it right with opera in the second. Although there were good things in later years, the balance was never as effective and there were serious failures – notably with the visit of the Dresden State Opera in 1982. I had long admired their wonderful orchestra, and they had a great tradition. Encouraged by Brian McMaster's enthusiastic reports about the work of Harry Kupfer and Joachim Herz, I went to Dresden to see several productions. It was difficult to find productions that would fit the Edinburgh stage, and negotiating with the East German authorities was not easy. In the end we took a Herz production of *Ariadne auf Naxos*, which, despite good features, was dully conducted and visually cramped in Edinburgh. And with it came a totally inadequate Kupfer production of *Die Entführung aus dem Serail*, which I had been unable to see. I will never forget the chill of the Edinburgh reaction as the long-faced grandees trooped out of the dress circle on the first night. Hugh Trevor-Roper, now Lord Dacre, said glacially, 'So you think *that*'s Festival standard, do you?' I did not, and I could hardly blame anyone but myself.

The other main operatic event planned for 1982 – a visit from Florence's Maggio Musicale company with an unknown baroque opera and the première of a new version of *Macbeth* by the contemporary

composer Salvatore Sciarrino – collapsed when Sciarrino failed to complete his score and the ever helpful Director of the Maggio, Massimo
Bogianckino, left Florence to run the Paris Opéra. Instead, at very
short notice, we secured the Piccola Scala from Milan, with two excellent small-scale operas, very well cast. But somehow the shadow of
Dresden's failure even overshadowed the fascinating Milan production
by Pier Luigi Pizzi of Handel's *Ariodante*. Welsh National Opera were
bringing a production of *Tamerlano*, and it was far from ideal to have
two Handel operas within a week of each other, since many, even twenty years ago, still considered Handel to be second-rate and dull. Philip
Prowse's dramatic vision of *Tamerlano*, which the critics hated, seemed
to work against the grain of the opera, whereas Pizzi's stylization of
*Ariodante* was a revelation – all the action growing out of the foot of a
huge Doric column which revolved and split open to bring on the
singers. I very much admire Prowse as a designer, but I have reservations about his directing. Pizzi seemed able to do both.

I travelled relentlessly during this time, looking for companies all
over the world – which became increasingly necessary given that major
European opera houses who had come in the past now steadily refused
to compromise their directors' intentions on our inadequate stages. In
Tokyo I saw a Japanese production of Britten's *Curlew River*, hoping
to present both the opera and the Noh play on which it was based side
by side. But the Japanese singers were not good enough. Peter Hemmings invited me to Australia to formalize his plan to bring Australian
Opera to Europe for the first time, with an exciting double bill including Joan Sutherland in a role she had not previously sung. The intention was to visit Moscow first, for which the Australian government
would bear the main costs, and then Paris, which had offered to pay
generously, and then poor old Edinburgh, which could not pay much
but which would do its best.

I stepped off the plane in Sydney to find myself in the middle of a
full-scale row. Hemmings, it appeared, had planned all this activity
without any reference to the Music Director, Richard Bonynge, or to
Bonynge's wife, Joan Sutherland. Bonynge was apoplectic – especially
as Sutherland had not even agreed to study the opera that Hemmings
had chosen – Verdi's *I Masnadieri* – let alone tour it. I was entirely sympathetic to Bonynge's point of view, and to this day I have never understood how Hemmings, an experienced intendant, could have been so
crass. Admittedly Bonynge could be a difficult colleague, but surely the

one thing the General Director of Australian Opera had to ensure was that his Music Director was involved in his planning. Sutherland was her normal delightful, straightforward, unflappable self and shrugged her shoulders and said she understood how I felt. Bonynge set his face against even examining whether the project was worthwhile, and the whole scheme had to be abandoned. However, it took me to Australia for the first time, and it was the beginning of a long involvement with the Australian arts scene which is still continuing. I was also lucky to find there a brilliant young company, Australian Dance Theatre, run by an ex-Rambert dancer, Jonathan Taylor, which came to Edinburgh in 1980 and had a huge success with an original, splendidly staged piece of total theatre called *Wild Stars*. We could have run it for a month.

My continuing wish to present a French opera company also came to nothing, but I was more fortunate in the United States. I had been very impressed with the work of a number of American regional opera companies I had visited. Much the most interesting was the Opera Theatre of St Louis, run by two British expatriates, Richard Gaddes and the former Director of the English Opera Group, Colin Graham. Gaddes, who had previously worked in Santa Fe, had an amazing capacity to find and develop new talent. Many of the most promising American singers of recent years were first heard at St Louis. There was, however, a problem: there was not a permanent company, just a three-week festival in the month of June. In addition, the theatre had a thrust stage, for which all the productions were designed. Prompted by the British conductor Raymond Leppard, who now lived in the USA, I turned reluctantly to Santa Fe, whose opera festival, close to the Edinburgh dates, was run by its long-time conductor-director John Crosby. The Santa Fe stage was huge, but Leppard believed we could work together and arranged a meeting in New York. For over an hour Crosby totally ignored me, moving his chair in the restaurant closer to Leppard and talking only to him in a way that made it impossible for me to hear or follow what was being said. Leppard tried bravely to involve me, but without success. Then suddenly Crosby turned to me and, with a liberal use of four-letter words, questioned any possibility of collaboration between Santa Fe and Edinburgh. I later discovered that Peter Diamand had got very close to a deal with Crosby ten years earlier but had withdrawn, and Crosby bore a continuing grudge against the Festival. No one had bothered to fill me in on this bit of history.

I was flying back to London the following day, and at breakfast I thought I really ought to talk to Gaddes in St Louis to see if anything could be salvaged there. Because of the time difference from New York, I resolved to ring him later that morning, after I had been to an exhibition at the Metropolitan Museum. It was in the pre-Christmas period, and I decided to buy some presents in the museum's shop. I was queuing up to pay when I looked up and saw Gaddes standing six feet away. We went to the bar – open already, although it was still early in the day – and sank a couple of stiff vodkas, and as a result the St Louis company came to Edinburgh the following year. We were very limited in what could be brought, since nothing involving a chorus was affordable, but we presented a new American opera by the young Minneapolis composer Stephen Paulus, based on the famous novel and film *The Postman Always Rings Twice*, and an almost unknown Delius opera, *Fennimore and Gerda*, brilliantly directed by Frank Corsaro and just about adapted to a proscenium stage, although it lost some of its magic on the way. Also, I asked Gaddes to line up all the young singers he could and invited Alistair Cooke to host a concert presenting them in the Usher Hall. That, anyhow, was a huge success. And the whole visit was characterized by total enthusiasm and support from the opera-minded community of St Louis, many of whom came to Scotland to cheer on their company. This, too, led to a long association, and for several years I returned to St Louis to give lectures or, on two occasions, to MC the annual fund-raising gala – a rare chance for me to be back on stage again.

I had known Alistair Cooke since 1970, when he began to work on his television series *America*, though I had listened to his 'Letter from America' from my teens and read him in the *Guardian*. I met him for private rather than professional reasons. His producer, Michael Gill, was a neighbour and often invited me round for drinks, and it was there that I got to know the Cookes. In a sense it was a curious friendship, since I was pretty ignorant of his greatest enthusiasm, jazz, totally uninterested in his passion, golf, and almost entirely without experience of the United States. Yet from the start we got on marvellously, and I was also very taken with his attractive and stylish wife, the portrait painter Jane White. Over the years, I have stayed with the Cookes in New York and in their house on Long Island, travelled with Alistair in the United States, and been his host in Scotland. I have never for an instant been bored – even by his golfing stories. He is one of the greatest raconteurs – much funnier in real life than on the radio and television – and endlessly generous and hospitable. He is the quintessential townie. The only landscape he knows is the golf course. Their remarkable house on the north shore of Long Island – a kind of Gropius beach house, twice the size of its seemingly modest exterior – sits on a deserted stretch of Peconic Bay, with a white sand beach and warmish water. In the more than fifty years that Alistair has lived there, he has never set foot on the beach, while in her late seventies Jane, a daily swimmer, took up single sculls and could be seen before breakfast streaking across the bay. In New York, dinner at the Carlyle – with the obsequious reverence of the *maître d'*, the acknowledgement by the pianist, the slow examination of a menu that Alistair must have memorized long ago – takes on the characteristics of a ritual. Alistair attributes his and Jane's long marriage – a second for both of them – to their differing timetables: she up early to paint, and he up late to talk. Only the middle part of the day seems to be shared. In summer Jane never leaves Long Island, not even for the White House. Once when I was with them she refused dinner with the Reagans, preferring the summer light in the studio on the beach.

I added Alistair to the list of father figures I had often sought out to compensate for my unsatisfactory relations with my real father. Alistair teases me relentlessly about knowing famous conductors or members of the royal family, but becomes aggrieved if I don't telephone. On his regular visits to London he nearly always makes time for an evening together. For me, his genius is having the essential ability of the great journalist to find the right particular from which to generalize. In a week that had seen a major international disaster, his 'Letter from America' would begin with a casual conversation with a taxi driver or a headline in a local paper. Today, at over ninety, his grasp of the present is still sharply honed, although he dwells much more on incidents from his long past. Yet he remains a fixture in my life both on the radio and in reality. I find his friendship not only marvellous and companionable, but very flattering.

The high point of my visit with Alistair to the 1983 St Louis Festival, before the Edinburgh visit, was when he was fêted by his old friend Joseph Pulitzer and then followed by crowds of admirers wherever we went. The Pulitzers' three houses were all crammed with superb pictures, and the one in the suburbs of St Louis had Monet water-lily and wisteria paintings reflected in a pool surrounded by sculptures by Matisse and Maillol. In addition, the Miss Universe competition was being held in the hotel in which we were staying, and the foyers were thronged with girls in bathing costumes and sashes. Alistair and I entered the lift to be confronted by Miss Guam and her minders. It has been a running joke ever since. I also recall first hearing the beautiful Sylvia McNair in St Louis, singing Héro in Colin Graham's brilliant production of Berlioz's *Béatrice et Bénédict*. I wished I could have brought that to Edinburgh.

Opera continues to be a presence in the Edinburgh Festival, but never these days on the scale of the early years. Times have changed too much, and the costs involved have gone through the roof. Small-scale productions and concert performances have been tried, sometimes successfully, but I find it ironic that Brian McMaster, one of the most gifted opera intendants of our time, has at Edinburgh made so much less impact with his opera plans than with dance and theatre.

Theatre was always thought to be the poor relation in the Festival. It wasn't always true. I had been lucky in my first year with the Rustaveli, but had not overcome the continuing challenge of the Assembly Hall of the Church of Scotland, where Guthrie had recreated the thrust stage to such effect in his 1948 production of *The Thrie Estaitis*. Over the years many different companies tested themselves against its awkward shape and tricky acoustics, and playing there was never easy. Since it had to run for at least two weeks and sometimes three, whatever was presented represented a big element of the Festival's finances and a real albatross if it was poorly reviewed. Using my friendships in the British theatre, for the first year I invited the Bristol Old Vic, then run by Richard Cottrell, whom I had known well since we were at Cambridge. The visit was notable not so much for a *Troilus and Cressida* that he himself directed, but for the second play, Farquhar's *The Recruiting Officer*, the first major revelation of the talent of his young assistant, Adrian Noble, who now runs the Royal Shakespeare Company.

Part of the problem with Edinburgh theatre was that our programme book went to press months before the Festival took place. Casting in the theatre is decided at very much the last moment. Prospect Players had a permanent pool of actors like Ian McKellen and Timothy West, but a company like the Bristol Old Vic did not, and, although there were good performances, they were not quite what I wanted. What I really wanted was the National Theatre at its best, and as a result of Peter Hall's visit to the Festival we achieved in 1980 the most memorable use of the Assembly Hall since Guthrie, with Bill Bryden and

Tony Harrison's major reworking of the York and Wakefield mystery plays under the title *The Passion*. The designer, William Dudley, turned the space into a magic box in which the audience promenaded around the actors and everyone ended up dancing at the end. The transformation of the space was so unexpected that my first reaction on seeing it was to burst into tears. A very strong company of wonderful actors – including Brian Glover, Jack Shepherd, Bryan Pringle, Barry Rutter, J. G. Devlin and the very young Brenda Blethyn – embodied the biblical characters, and in addition to the evening performances took various scenes into the city, performing in the streets on carts, as had been done in medieval times. Noah's releasing the dove on the space in front of St Giles' Cathedral drew crowds of hundreds. The whole venture, expensive as it was, was a real vindication of the Assembly Hall, the role of theatre in the Festival and the potential of the National Theatre.

To show a different aspect of the National Theatre's work, Peggy Ashcroft led a company in the Royal Lyceum with a new production of Lillian Hellman's *Watch on the Rhine*. Once again, as with Scottish Opera, I felt this was the kind of collaboration I had sought and hoped that it could be maintained in the future. Sadly, it was not to be. A plan to play *King Lear*, with Gielgud in the title role, back to back with Howard Brenton's *The Romans in Britain* collapsed in 1981 when Gielgud discovered that the Assembly Hall in Edinburgh was being considered. He had thought the intention was to play only in the small Cottesloe Theatre in London. I was disappointed, of course, but, given the subsequent row about Brenton's play and the court case that resulted from Mary Whitehouse's campaigning against it, I was ultimately relieved. In its place I was offered the première of Tom Stoppard's adaptation of a play by the Viennese writer Johann Nepomuk Nestroy which he entitled *On the Razzle*.

From the beginning it was fraught with problems. The fee demanded by the National Theatre seemed to me to be outrageously high. To make matters worse, their workshops failed to take on board the fact that the stage of the Royal Lyceum Theatre was raked. All the scenery was on boat trucks. To prevent it sliding into the audience, the stage had to be levelled. This meant that the front rows of the stalls had to be removed and all those who had bought seats there had to be reseated elsewhere in a theatre that was largely sold out. And, to cap it all, we were told that the play could not be reviewed since it was, in director Michael Rudman's immortal words, 'an out-of-town try-out'. The published text of the play, by no means Stoppard's best, claims that the first performance was given at the National Theatre in London – and for this I paid not only for the cast but for the remade stage and for a stage crew of nineteen to work within an already fully crewed theatre. My hopes of a long-term association with the National Theatre were not to be fulfilled. Peter Hall was sympathetic about the financial problems but did not feel he could intervene, and I have rarely in my life met such lofty arrogance as there was in the attitude of the National Theatre's administration.

For the Assembly Hall that year I had invited the Birmingham Rep, now run by another ex-Cambridge friend, Clive Perry. They presented a rather indifferent *As You Like It*, and a lively *Candide* with a strong cast which almost succeeded in papering over the cracks in Bernstein's flawed but fascinating piece. The following year I was unable to find a company prepared to play there, and it remained dark – a rare black hole in the Festival's programme. On several occasions over the years the Festival had mounted its own productions in the Assembly Hall, sometimes successfully, but it was always an administrative headache as well as a big risk. We were just not staffed or equipped as producers. I wished we had been.

Ironically, because of the different attitude in other countries to running the same show over long periods, it was much easier to find foreign productions. Companies from France, Romania, Greece, Canada, Spain and Italy all featured in our programmes, and in the majority of cases with success. In 1981 Gilles Bourdet's Théâtre de la Salamandre brought one of the most brilliant productions of Racine I have ever seen, converting the Moray House Gymnasium into a wing of Versailles for a *Brittanicus* which still reverberates in my mind after twenty years. The scenery weighed several tons, and the illusion of a day passing from early dawn to a spectacular sunset was recreated on a tiny stage very different from that of the Odéon in Paris where I had first seen it. It made the Birmingham Rep's *As You Like It* seem very ordinary. The French government official who brokered the deal told me she would not have agreed to bring *Brittanicus* if she had known how poor the standard of other productions might be. Even if she was right about the Birmingham Rep, she was wrong about the second company in Moray House that year: the National Theatre of Romania. Romania has a great theatre tradition, and even in the worst years of the Ceauşescu regime it continued to reveal such outstanding directors as

Andrei Serban, Lucian Pintilie and Liviu Ciulei. I went to Bucharest on
a recce armed with Olivia Manning's *The Balkan Trilogy*, about the
coming of the Second World War, and ate in the restaurant she had
described. Even if the city had not been recently damaged by an earthquake it would have been hard to tell if we were in 1940, when Manning had been there, or in 1980. The National Theatre in Bucharest is
bigger than its equivalent in London, and its main auditorium was the
first I had seen which had movable walls – a '*salle modulable*' of the
kind planned for the Bastille Opéra in Paris, but still not complete or
functioning there. I saw several good or worthy productions, but nothing that really caught my imagination until the last evening, when I
went to the small studio theatre. There a young cast much influenced
by Brook's *A Midsummer Night's Dream* were breathing riotous life
into a Roman comedy – *The Girl from Andros*, by Terence. It was
enchanting, and offered no real obstacles of language since most of it
was acted out in highly inventive mime and with brilliant use of music.
I loved the company and its director, Grigori Gonta, and his very beautiful wife. Their visit to Edinburgh was a total success, with big audiences and a tremendous sense of friendship beween the company and
our people. Unlike the Rustaveli, whom I have met up with in various
parts of the world since Edinburgh, I have never managed to keep in
touch with the Romanians and have no idea how – or even if – they
survived the horrors of Ceauşescu's last years. They were, incidentally,
the cheapest foreign company ever to come to the Festival. I made them
a preposterously low offer which, to my astonishment, was instantly
accepted, such was the need for hard currency.

Though *The Girl from Andros* triumphantly leapt the language barrier, two other productions that I brought, from Greece and from Italy,
did not. They were both oddities and I knew I was taking a risk. Sadly,
it did not pay off. The Greek theatre company, Amfiteatro, from
Athens, brought an eighteenth-century reworking of the classical story
of Iphigenia as performed by an amateur group at Luxouri on one of
the remoter islands. The audience in Athens fell about with laughter,
easily able to differentiate the amateur script from the professional
actors pretending to be amateurs. I should have realized that this was
something that would not be apparent to the audience in Edinburgh,
where it played in total silence. The other failure I would defend more
strenuously. Sandro Sequi, the opera director, devised a staging, without music, of a famous opera libretto by Metastasio set by dozens of

composers, *L'Olimpiade*. It was choreographed like a ballet, with a chorus of actors speaking in unison and the movements stylized into a kind of ritual. Again, it was something that had worked in front of an indigenous audience when I saw it in Rome, but its magic disappeared before foreigners. I must take full responsibility, though I still believe Sequi's ideas were fascinating and worth exploring.

All this brought into question whether my view of world theatre could be sustained. Few of the great directors like Peter Stein or Giorgio Strehler would even discuss coming to Edinburgh unless they were assured of an extended period of rehearsals in the theatre, which was simply not possible in the context of a twenty-one-day festival. For his famous production of *Peer Gynt* in Paris, Patrice Chéreau had obtained three weeks of lighting rehearsals alone. It was impossible to persuade local people of the difficulties. If major opera houses and major drama companies had come in the past, why was it not possible to present them now? The answer was that the world had moved on and rebuilt its theatres, creating demands from both directors and audiences that Edinburgh could not respond to. We were increasingly forced back on to smaller-scale productions. Some of them were very successful. The traditional puppets of Italy were represented by the Collo company of Milan with its fully staged ballets on rod puppets. A tiny company from Sardinia retold *The Little Match Girl* by Hans Christian Andersen, and a black company from South Africa brought a different ethos with *Poppie Nongena*. The hugely entertaining *Billy Bishop Goes to War* – a two-hander about a famous Canadian pilot in the First World War that I had found in Vancouver – later played very successfully both in London and on Broadway. The amazing Japanese Sankai Juku with their ritual Butoh theatre – half dance and half mime – astonished people when they performed outdoors suspended on ropes from buildings in the Royal Mile, bringing a Lothian Regional Council meeting to a standstill as they drifted past the windows, seemingly naked and covered in white rice flour.

In 1980, for the first time in the main Festival, we presented the work of the Polish director Tadeusz Kantor, who on several previous occasions had been one of the biggest hits of the Fringe. Kantor, a painter by training, had evolved an experimental drama company which by then had moved from Poland to Florence, where they were given a theatre space and accommodation by the city. It is hard to imagine any city in Great Britain offering such opportunities. But, as so often happens when the experimental becomes the established, this had led to decline and delusions of grandeur. Kantor, who had always been difficult but was previously happy to appear for Richard de Marco for almost nothing and to sleep on the floor, now insisted on two suites at the George Hotel – one for himself and his wife, and a second one so that he would have somewhere to go if he couldn't sleep. Nothing we could do would satisfy him or his equally difficult wife. When she found an electric kettle did not work, she telephoned me and said, 'We are not used to being treated like this' – which was certainly true, but not in the way she meant it. Their visit, successful in artistic and audience terms, concluded with a reception at the City Chambers where the company – wonderful actors but brain-washed human beings – were ordered to stand outside in the courtyard in the rain, as a protest at the way Kantor had been treated. I find it hard to believe how such a remarkable creative figure could in his personal behaviour be such a total shit.

By no means all my journeys produced the results for which I had hoped, although I always learnt something about different societies and their attitudes to culture. Edinburgh was twinned with Vancouver, and I was instrumental in bringing, from the museum at Victoria on Vancouver Island, an important exhibition of North-West Indian art. There is such a patronizing attitude in Britain towards ethnography. Even where we have fine collections, as in Edinburgh at the Royal Scottish Museum, they are rarely appreciated. Berlin, Brussels and Paris have much more successful museums, although their collections are of no greater importance. With the Canadian-Indian material, I sought to add an element of performance, and we obtained the presence of a pole carver, who worked away quietly in the City Arts Centre throughout the Festival. The pole was subsequently donated to the city by Vancouver. For years tucked away in a corner, it has now disappeared.

But what I had really wanted was a performing group – preferably of dancers. In the far north, right on the Alaska border, there was just such a company, which had appeared in folk festivals in the United States. I arranged with colleagues in Vancouver to visit them. I have never been anywhere else as remote – there was nothing but mountains, rushing rivers full of salmon, and a small settlement reminiscent of an old western, with one street and a hotel. We were unlucky in that one of the tribal elders had died just before our visit, so no full performances by the dancers were permitted, but there was a potlach at which I was prevailed upon – pretty reluctantly – to join the salmon dance. Then we went back to the hotel, where the proprietor, a white woman, was the agent for the local group's activities and tours. My two Canadian colleagues had rooms at the front of the hotel but – by mistake, I assume – I was given one at the back, overlooking a small off-licence where the Indians were being sold alcohol in unlimited quantities. Drunken figures lay sprawled across the grass; noisy teenagers raced motorbikes up and down until they collided with trees. It was a scene of gross and appalling debauch. Here were two kinds of response to the Indian question. At the front of the building they organized tours and dances, showing off the splendours of native culture; at the back they rotted their brains in the interest of commerce. I was so outraged that the following day I found it hard to speak to the hotel proprietor, who anyhow had made it clear there would be no government funding to take a company to Europe. We did attempt to bring another group from Victoria Island, but they proved extortionately expensive. In a sense you cannot blame them.

Sheila Colvin and I had a fruitless visit to Poland in 1982. Much as we wanted to help our colleagues there, we found nothing that was transportable or available that suited our requirements, but it did bring me one of the most moving moments of my life. Andrzej Wajda, the great film director, also ran the Stary Theatre in Cracow, that marvellously preserved city. In the old Franzuski Hotel, eating sour rye soup and stuffed cabbage, nothing seemed to have changed for centuries. Wajda had, for reasons quite as much political as literary, mounted a production of T. S. Eliot's *Murder in the Cathedral*. In Warsaw the authorities had closed it down. The debate about where power lay – with the Church or the State, God or General Jaruzelski – was too close to the bone. But in Cracow they were still able to perform it – and, what's more, in the cathedral in the Wawel Castle, the Westminster Abbey of Poland. The audience walked up the hill in driving snow and bitter cold and sat in the nave of the great church for the first part of the play. Then, when the moment came for the famous Christmas Day sermon, we trooped through and sat in the choir stalls. The actor playing Thomas à Becket, Jerzy Radziwilowicz, already well known even in the West from his leading role in Wajda's films *Man of Iron* and *Man of Marble*, was robed in the vestments of the former Cardinal Archbishop of Cracow, now Pope John Paul II. It was unforgettable. We sat surrounded by the tombs of the kings of Poland to watch the murder and the knights' justification of it. The acting was superb, but the impact came as much from the setting as from Eliot or the production. I toyed with the idea of trying to perform it in St Giles' Cathedral, whose minister was a good friend and a keen Festival supporter. But it would still have lost the profound irony of the Polish setting, just as the Rustaveli play about Stalin meant more in Moscow than it could ever have done in Scotland.

An even more remote trip which yielded nothing but happy memories was my first and so far only visit to China. I had been tipped off that the People's Art Theatre of Peking had a spectacular production called *The Teahouse*, which told the story of China in the twentieth century through the comings and goings in a typical teahouse of the many characters who frequented it. We had an extremely helpful Cultural Attaché in Peking, Keith Hunter, who went on to become Arts Controller of the British Council, which partly funded my trip. I had been a member of the Council's Dance and Drama Panel for some years, and in return for their help I offered to lecture or do anything I could to improve Anglo-Chinese relations at a time when China was slowly starting to recover from the ravages of the Cultural Revolution. My Chinese contact was an actor called Yin Ruo Cheng – known as Stephen. He was very well known and later, in the liberalizing period that led up to Tiananmen Square, became Deputy Minister of Culture, but subsequently endured a period of house arrest. He was to play the role of the tutor in Bertolucci's film *The Last Emperor*. His English was perfect, and he translated for me both in whispered asides at the theatre and in meetings.

*The Teahouse* was a revelation of an old school of naturalistic acting that has disappeared in the West. The first scene, set in 1900, had a cast of over sixty people of all kinds – birdsellers, fortune-tellers, mah-jong players and waiters – all rushing about and providing a picture of brilliantly choreographed chaos. Later acts were set at the time of the Long March and at the Communist takeover in 1943. These were less spectacular, but even so the play was breathtaking as a piece of political theatre and as a picture of society in evolution. I wanted it badly, but how were we going to pay for something involving over a hundred people? I needed help from the Chinese government, and, since they had already paid for it to go to North America, I thought there was some chance of receiving it. But there was already a vague agreement that the European première would be in Germany, and as Germany couldn't take it until October the dates did not work. This was one of the many times when the three-week window of the Festival severely limited what was available. There was also the political question of whether the Chinese would help financially. The British Ambassador, Sir Percy Cradock, was sure the Ministry of Culture would not budge on Germany or find extra funds for Scotland, and he proved correct. I was taken to see the Minister – an elderly woman no more than five foot tall, wearing a grey trouser suit and with a grey fringe that made her look exactly like Stevie Smith. I think she spoke only three words, and each of these was 'No'. It was not to be. Part of me regretted that ten days in a busy season had been given up to this wild-goose chase. But, on the other hand, I was so fascinated by everything I saw and heard that I could hardly think of it as time wasted.

The People's Art Theatre were in a dilemma. They had been told that they had the right to choose what they presented, but with the proviso that there should be no politics, no religion and no sex. They asked my advice. It was hard to know what to suggest, but unbelievably they opted for Tom Stoppard. They put on *Rosencrantz and Guildenstern are Dead* and *The Real Thing*. All Stoppard's recondite wordplay could apparently be translated effectively into Chinese. Ironically, the following year Toby Robertson went to Peking and directed *Measure for Measure* – a play entirely about politics, religion and sex, but which was also a huge success.

Every morning I would be taken to visit a group of artists – one day actors who wanted to know about our training methods, another day dancers. I sat in on class at the New China Ballet and, at their request, intervened in a pas de deux class for soloists. It was quite apparent that the notation from which they had learnt the steps gave no clue as to what was really going on. They danced the famous final pas de deux from *Don Quixote* about as un-Spanishly as it is possible to imagine. The girls wiggled their fingers over their heads without any understanding of what it might mean, and when I asked what they were doing they looked blank. The castanet was unknown in China. They were so willing and so enthusiastic, although their physical shape – long body and short legs – still sits uncomfortably for me with classical technique.

A group of theatre directors grilled me for two hours on European theatre. An old man clutching a big leather-bound volume asked me what I thought about the plays of J. M. Barrie. A young man in full military combat gear, with a gun in a holster at his waist, quizzed me with passion about Gordon Craig. Did we revere him as he did? I had to admit that for most people in Britain he was a totally forgotten figure. They knew about designers such as Gordon Craig and Adolphe Appia and directors such as Peter Brook. They wanted to know about the Royal Shakespeare Company and what I thought about Olivier and Gielgud. It was quite extraordinary. During the hideous years of the Cultural Revolution, when most of these people had been put to forced labour in remote provinces, they had somehow held on to the idea of an international culture. The young girl who looked after us was the daughter of one of the great actors of the Peking Opera. He had escaped to Hong Kong. She had spent nine years up to her knees in the rice paddies of the Yangtze Delta without pen, paper or books. There was something so all-embracing about the petty thoroughness of oppression, but the great message was that it had failed. These people had survived both in mind and in body.

Stephen Ruo Cheng took us to tiny restaurants in back streets in the city and in upper rooms we had wonderful food about as far removed from the average Chinese restaurant in Great Britain as is imaginable. We walked on the Great Wall in a temperature of minus ten degrees, we saw little farms like Han funerary models, and we descended into the Ming tombs. In the bus on the way back an elderly woman, who radiated benevolence but rarely spoke, suddenly started singing 'All Things Bright and Beautiful' – a memory of her mission-school education long ago: something it was still daring to admit.

In the intervening years I have been often to Japan and enjoyed it, but the impenetrable nature of Japanese social life and behaviour is a real barrier. China, on the other hand, although so very different from Europe, seemed to share the same fundamental human feelings. More than anywhere else in the world, I have longed to go back. One of my many reasons to be grateful to the Edinburgh International Festival was that the adjective 'International' in the name encouraged and allowed me to see more of the world than I had before, and it changed my perspective on life and art.

# 11

# Towards a Real Festival

Looking back on the five Festivals for which I was responsible, there were outstanding moments in opera, dance, theatre and exhibitions, as well as a fair number of less successful ventures. But for many people they were of less importance than the extensive music plan, which, involving different concerts every day, represented the bulk of our work and, in the case of the Usher Hall concerts, the largest element of financial risk. Even after negotiating group-travel deals for orchestras, there remained the problem of hotels. While Eastern Europeans would accept student hostels, American orchestras demanded single rooms for all the players – and a hundred single rooms in first-class hotels were not there to be reserved even a year in advance. Above all, there were limits to what the audience was prepared to pay for even the starriest of concerts.

People who pontificate about the arts often fail to distinguish between the economic situations of the different audiences. The opera audience and the audience for concert music are by no means the same, and the concert-going audience – who are generally much less well off – often want to attend more events. The Usher Hall audience was very sensitive to seat prices, and also conservative in its musical tastes. I didn't want merely to provide established popular repertory, but the presence of an unknown piece in a programme, let alone a major piece of contemporary music, had an immediate negative effect on bookings. My natural inclination was to make really adventurous programmes, but my commercial sense realized how risky this could prove. Every year I would reluctantly persuade myself to modify imaginative plans in the interest of the box office, but at times I thought the overall balance was reliable enough to let us afford an all-Henze programme (in 1981) or an all-Berio one (in 1982), since they were in the smaller Queen's Hall. When I invited Berio to conduct a programme in the Usher Hall and he insisted it should consist entirely of his own music, I withdrew. I felt a certain shame in doing so, but it was a necessary decision.

The box office was not the only problem, however. While not having the need, however pleasurable, like Salzburg to include a great deal of Mozart, I did have essential elements that had to be programmed, like the Royal Scottish National Orchestra and the Scottish Chamber Orchestra, and, since they were so readily available to local concert-goers outside the Festival, it was not always easy to get a big audience for them without very grand soloists. But to leave them out would create political problems.

One group that had to be found a place – or rather several places – was the Edinburgh Festival Chorus, an admirable body and a truly national organization, with sections drawn from Glasgow and Aberdeen as well as locally. The chorus rehearsed every week all round the year for just the few concerts in the Festival – an outstanding example of the enthusiasm of amateurs and how much they can still contribute to musical life. But they were demanding about whom they worked with, and in what repertory. On my arrival they presented me with a wish list of conductors and a hate list of works – headed by Brahms's *German Requiem*, which they said they had performed too often. In my first year they sang in Mahler's Third Symphony with Abbado, *Belshazzar's Feast* with Loughran, and *Daphnis and Chloë* with the Boston Symphony Orchestra under Ozawa. They opened my second year with Beethoven's *Choral Fantasia*. Later, they also sang Tippett's *A Child of Our Time*, Handel's *Creation* and the Berlioz *Te Deum*.

The Berlioz gave rise to one of our more daring plans. Due to the hopeless state of the Usher Hall organ, we decided to link the hall to St Mary's Cathedral and relay Gillian Weir's contribution from there. The concert was being televised live by the BBC (those were the days!), who set up the sound and vision links. At the rehearsal there was some difficulty about pitch, but nothing major. As Abbado and I walked to the stage entrance on the night, he turned to me and said, 'What if it goes wrong?' I shrugged my shoulders and said I had no idea, and we both started to laugh. The videotape shows him coming on to the platform wreathed in smiles. In fact everything worked perfectly, and the Lothian police – entering into the spirit of the party – whisked Gillian in a police car to the Usher Hall within a minute of the end, so she could take her bow. It was a real Festival moment.

My first crisis with the chorus came in 1981, when I unwisely agreed to open the Festival with Abbado conducting Bach's *St Matthew Passion*. There seemed good musical reasons for this, since he always attracted an amazing line-up of soloists – in this case Margaret Price, Jessye Norman, Peter Schreier, Hermann Prey, Philip Langridge and Gwynne Howell. But, although he reduced the orchestra, he never really made up his mind about what size chorus he required. All 160 of them rehearsed before the Festival, but at the first get-together Abbado reduced them to 140, then the following day to 100, and finally to 80 – 40 on each side. The chorus were outraged and wrote me a letter saying, among other things, that they would never work with Abbado again. I should have foreseen the problem. In fact the whole event went off at half-cock: Abbado's Bach was very un-German, the alto part was by then too low for Jessye Norman, and the length of the piece caused problems for the Edinburgh grandees. At the end, the wife of the Chief Constable said, 'Don't you ever do that to me again!'

The chorus were back at full strength for the Berlioz *Romeo and Juliet* with Muti, Mahler's Second Symphony with Rattle, and the Bruckner *Te Deum* with Gibson, and when Abbado opened the 1982 Festival with the Verdi *Requiem* they were all there en masse and in splendid voice, as the still available video shows. So much for 'never again'! They were a huge asset, and, although scheduling rehearsals during the Festival was difficult for people in full-time employment, the Festival would have been much the poorer without them.

While I did have some control over what the chorus did, it was not always so with orchestral repertory. I think most people believe you just ask conductors to perform what you want and, given appropriate rehearsal opportunities, it happens. Not so. All kinds of obstacles can be put in your way. For instance, American orchestras on long European tours are subject to union-imposed limits on the number of programmes they can take, and everything has to be rehearsed before they set out. Even with a couple of years' notice, you get what you want only if others want it too. One year, Riccardo Muti was bringing to the Festival his American orchestra, the Philadelphia. They had recently recorded Elgar's concert overture *In the South* and, as I had suggested an Italian focus in the Festival that year, it seemed an ideal work for them to include. But no one else in Europe wanted to hear it, so they played Schumann, Prokofiev, Ravel and Mahler. Incidentally, this was the only time a visiting orchestra came to Edinburgh *after* appearing at the Proms in London, and it certainly affected the box office. In those days, it was quite normal for orchestras to visit Edinburgh first and then travel south with broadly the same programmes. The financial advantages were considerable, and it always seemed to me a good thing. When Solti conducted the *Missa Solemnis* in Edinburgh, the performance was repeated in London two days later with the Edinburgh Festival Chorus travelling south to take part, and I was grateful to Robert Ponsonby for finding some of the necessary funding for travel and accommodation, and to the chorus for raising the rest themselves. If the Edinburgh concert was not broadcast live, it gave the Proms no problem, and I cannot understand why my successors have set their faces resolutely against this arrangement. Today you do one or the other.

Very early on I had invited Solti to conduct *The Dream of Gerontius*, a work he admired but had never performed. The plan fell apart because of the choral element. Since a recording was needed to justify the time and expenditure, and that had to be made in London, Solti felt obliged to use the London Philharmonic Chorus; but for both political and financial reasons I was not willing to bring them to Edinburgh. Solti never came in my time with the Chicago Symphony Orchestra. After their last concert in Diamand's final Festival, there was a huge row about the potential for damage to the orchestra's double basses, since the orchestra left the platform by the same stairs and at the same time as those members of the public who had been seated there. The Players' Committee vetoed a return unless the public was banned from the platform. I was already concerned about the revenue lost when we had a chorus on the platform, and to lose that income when there was no chorus seemed to me too high a demand.

There were other conductors I approached who were just not interested in coming back, even though they had been to Edinburgh before. Karajan said it could not be fitted in because, at the end of the Salzburg Festival, the Berlin Philharmonic Orchestra went on an annual visit to Lucerne and then reopened the Berlin season. I doubt in any case whether I could have afforded him. Bernstein was never available. Carlos Kleiber agreed to come and then, as so often, withdrew. One long-held hope was to bring about the return of Rafael Kubelik, but this was thwarted by the tactlessness of Peter Hemmings. who had by now left Australia to run the London Symphony Orchestra. Kubelik – a personal hero of mine, and one of the greatest musicians of the age – was conducting much less often, but on one of his rare visits to London, for the LSO, I spent a couple of hours with him and we worked out two possible programmes, one of which was to consist of Bruckner's Eighth

Symphony, a work in which no one equalled, let alone surpassed, him. For financial reasons, the concert would have to be repeated in London, at the Barbican. Hemmings joined our discussion, but when Kubelik told him enthusiastically that I wanted the Bruckner he said brusquely, 'How do you expect me to sell that in the Barbican in August with the Proms going on?' Kubelik quietly left the room and I never saw him again.

Even those conductors who were always happily available for Edinburgh in my time – Abbado, Muti, Chailly, Rattle, Tennstedt – imposed limitations on what they were prepared to offer. Abbado had never conducted Mahler's Seventh Symphony and said he could not possibly do so for the first time in as bright a light as shone on Edinburgh. When, at my suggestion, he agreed to Berlioz's *Symphonie fantastique*, a work he had not conducted since his student days, Conrad Wilson of the *Scotsman* complained about him doing something so unadventurous. I have never been afraid of standard repertory, just of routine performances, and Abbado's Berlioz was very far from routine. Rattle always had a central idea; he knew what he wanted the main work to be, but it could take an age to fill in the rest of the programme, and the necessary conversations, and others like them, became one of the great attractions of the job.

No two people will ever entirely agree on what makes a satisfactory programme, but the careful game of suggestion and compromise is of endless interest – provided it does not go on for too long. It is sometimes hard to dislodge an *idée fixe*. One year no less than five conductors made it clear that it was *essential* for them to conduct Mahler's First Symphony. To allow any of them to do so would have upset the others, so no one did it, and reaching agreement on that took weeks of meetings and phone conversations. But I was gradually becoming more confident. I had started inventing concert programmes when I was in my teens, spurred on by the annual publication of the Proms programmes. Even though by the 1980s programmes were much shorter than they had been, averaging ninety minutes of music, there was still room for imagination and new approaches, and as I got to know the conductors better I came to know what sort of thing they would suggest and how they would react to my ideas. There is no point at all in trying to force a conductor to programme works in which he has no real interest, even though generous conductors like Pritchard and Gibson could be open to almost any suggestion. The great thing was to find works or conjunctions of works which intrigued them, producing a programme which felt new or different and caught both their imagination and that of the public.

Today, in my advisory work for orchestras, I still get more satisfaction from making programmes with an interested conductor than from any other aspect of planning. Conductors are extremely selective, and are more likely to be led into new paths by recording contracts than by festival engagements. And it is a mistake to think that they know everything in the orchestral repertory – even all the standard works. The only conductor I know who seems to have looked at everything that exists, however recondite, is Gennadi Rozhdestvensky, whose suggestion it was that we perform Prokofiev's quite unknown ballet score *Chout* on the opening night of my first Festival. He had almost too many ideas, but could pull extraordinary rabbits out of his capacious hat. He had inherited a considerable music library from his father in Moscow, and added to it compulsively. I once asked him if he knew any interesting pieces about Italy by non-Italian composers, other than Elgar's *In the South*, Mendelssohn's *Italian Symphony* and Wolf's *Italian Serenade*. He replied, 'There is a piece by Charpentier – not Marc-Antoine – called *De l'Italie*.' When I asked if it was any good, he said, 'Well, it's salon music – but a very high-class salon.' It never got into the programmes, and I have still never heard it. But I have also never met anyone else who has heard it.

It was Rozhdestvensky who enthusiastically took up the most large-scale commission in my Edinburgh time: the *Akhmatova Requiem* of John Tavener, one of his best works. Teamed up with a Schreker overture and a Haydn concerto, it achieved the lowest attendance of any concert I put on in the Usher Hall, with only about two hundred people in the audience. At the Proms later in the week it was heard by several thousand.

One area I was very keen to expand was the participation of youth orchestras. I have a total enthusiasm for the excitement and energy that a good youth orchestra can generate with a fine conductor. Both the National Youth Orchestra and the new Scottish National Youth Orchestra came to the Festival, but the outstanding memory I have is of the European Community Youth Orchestra with Abbado. Among other works, they performed Abbado's regular showpiece, the suite from *The Miraculous Mandarin*, by Bartók. The New York Philharmonic were to play the following day, and their conductor, Zubin

Mehta, a close friend of Abbado's since student days, was already in Edinburgh. He came to the concert and sat with me. At the end of the Bartók he said, 'The thing about youth orchestras is they just don't know how dangerous it is. They give everything all the time.' More mature musicians find it hard to be so giving; there is always a sense that they are holding something back – worried about their lips or their fingers, their mortgage or their wives. With the young, playing is an affair of the heart and everything is on offer.

Abbado has a kind of genius with young people. He is never more relaxed or more obviously enjoying himself than with the various groups he has created or supported: the European Community Youth Orchestra, the Chamber Orchestra of Europe and now the Gustav Mahler Jugendorchester. The ECYO – now the EUYO – was the remarkable creation of an American dynamo, Joy Bryer, who with her South African husband has kept this marvellous idea going for over a quarter of a century with the help of the best conductors of our time. But money is always a problem. Each year she treks around the European capitals begging for support, and achieving it. It is one of the true glories of the European idea, and shamefully the only one in the arts – but always at risk.

Early on she involved the then Prime Minister, Edward Heath, with the orchestra, since he at least loved music. But the price of his support was a tricky one: he wanted to conduct. From my point of view his support was splendid, but there was a difference between his seizing the baton for a consciousness-raising concert in Bonn or Brussels and his appearing with the orchestra in a major music festival. I indicated that I would not expect him to conduct in Scotland, since Abbado was what Edinburgh wanted. Mrs Bryer said it was up to me to tell him. I wrote him as polite a letter as I could – he was no longer Prime Minister, but I knew him slightly since he had been a regular visitor to Edinburgh in Diamand's days and I had entertained him once or twice. In reply I received a phone call and then a visit from a friend of his, Lady Elles. She told me my attitude was a disgrace, and ordered me to back down. I refused, and the next development was to me truly shocking. Pressure was brought on the sponsors of the concert to withdraw their funding unless Heath was allowed to conduct. Since I ultimately cared much more about the orchestra and Abbado, I agreed that Heath could conduct the overture to *The Marriage of Figaro* – just about the shortest in the book. When the day came, he conducted the much longer overture to *The Magic Flute*, and then addressed the audience for fifteen minutes. I have no idea how it went, for Abbado and I decided to go for a walk while it was happening.

I later asked Mrs Bryer if Heath had insisted on conducting the orchestra the previous week in Salzburg. The issue had been raised, but Karajan, a great friend of Heath's, had absolutely refused to allow him to conduct a Mozart overture. 'You must', he said, 'conduct the Jupiter Symphony. And, what's more, I will come and listen.' Heath did not conduct in Salzburg.

I owe to Edinburgh important friendships with two great German conductors: Klaus Tennstedt and Kurt Masur. Tennstedt was hardly known in the West until the last two decades of his life, but he rapidly built a relationship with the London Philharmonic Orchestra that generated music-making of a rare intensity. He was a shy man, not given to long talks. Programmes were settled quickly, and in the Conductor's Room both before and after the concert he seemed in a kind of trance in which human contact was neither needed nor welcome – in marked contrast with Abbado, who filled the room with a cordon sanitaire of chattering Italians. I learnt to be very discreet with Tennstedt, but on non-concert days we and his splendid organizing wife would share a bottle of champagne and roar with laughter at the follies of the world and the foibles of the profession. Sadly, by the time I got to know him well his health was already failing and we had almost as many cancellations as performances. But when the performances did take place I was truly aware of what a great conductor can do with music that one may think one knows everything about.

Tennstedt was booked to come to Edinburgh one year with his German orchestra, the North German Radio Orchestra, but in the previous season he suddenly left the orchestra and after a month or so of reflection the management named a successor, the to me totally unknown Günter Wand. They begged me to keep the Edinburgh date in the book, but reluctantly I declined. I was unsure how we could sell an unknown conductor with an orchestra that, although good, was not absolutely in the top league. Robert Ponsonby at the BBC took the trouble to go to Hamburg and hear Wand, and this led to Wand's appointment as Principal Guest Conductor of the BBC Symphony Orchestra and his regular presence in London in subsequent years, and later in Edinburgh as well.

Long before the fall of Communism in East Germany with which he was so closely involved, Kurt Masur was already a kind of hero. He had maintained a career both in the West and with the Leipzig Gewandhaus Orchestra in the East, seeming to keep his integrity untarnished while serving one of the most corrupt of all regimes. He has often been pictured as a kind of earnest kapellmeister – Professor Masur – without charm or humour. Nothing could be further from the truth. My relations with him both in Scotland and subsequently have been among the most cordial of any, and I admire and respect him not only as a musician but as a remarkable man. The soloists he brought for his two Gewandhaus concerts in 1980 were the great pianist Claudio Arrau, making his final visit to Edinburgh, and a quite unknown cellist, Natalia Gutman. Masur had proposed Gutman. I knew from her teacher, Rostropovich, how good she was. But Masur's reasons went beyond music. Gutman was Jewish and had never been able to get a visa to travel abroad, since in addition her first husband had been sent to detention camps for his political views. She had had a very hard time making a career. It was a typically generous gesture of Masur to insist on her coming, and through his authority she obtained a permit from an initially hostile Soviet concert agency.

Some conductors can be casual in their relations with soloists, but the best realize the advantage of close collaboration. I saw one of the most outstanding examples of a conductor behaving nobly when Emil Gilels came to Edinburgh to perform with Muti in 1980. In the second movement of Brahms's Second Piano Concerto, Gilels got lost. For what seemed an age, piano and orchestra were several bars adrift. It was a truly frightening experience, like an out-of-control tank coming down a hill at you. It probably lasted for no more than fifteen seconds, but everyone was shaken. Immediately after the concert, Muti asked me if there were any Russian journalists in the audience. There was one from the Novosti agency, and also the Cultural Attaché of the Soviet Embassy. Muti asked to see them. Then, with a very disconsolate Gilels sitting beside him, he told them, 'I do not like pianists.' I was horrified, but he continued. 'I only like musicians. Emil Gilels is one of the greatest musicians I have ever had the joy of working with, and I want him, and you, to know that he will be my chosen partner with any of the three orchestras in Milan, London or Philadelphia that I conduct.' There was much embracing and not a few tears. Two days later Gilels gave one of the most profoundly satisfying piano recitals I can remember, to a packed house and a standing ovation. Things so rarely go wrong these days that audiences tend to forget how difficult and dangerous making great music can be. You don't just turn on the tap. Gilels had had nearly fifty years on the world stage, as had Arrau, but the challenge remained as great in their older years as it had been before. Greatness has to be worked for tirelessly.

As a failed pianist, I have always had a special affection for those who succeed, and Edinburgh gave me the chance not only to bring back my heroes, like Gilels and Arrau, but to explore the work of the younger generation. Like almost everyone else, I had a huge enthusiasm for Martha Argerich. We had worked together a couple of times in Television, notably when we made a documentary about preparing a performance of the Tchaikovsky First Piano Concerto with Charles Groves and the Royal Liverpool Philhamonic. Argerich has a kind of genius, but with a worrying flaw: her temperament seems not to match her talent. She is frankly bored by the routine of concert life, and in her younger years she preferred to go dancing. The night before I first made a television recording with her, of the Chopin C sharp minor Scherzo, I think she had not been to bed at all. She still brought it off in one take, without a single note out of place and with the fiendish octave passages impeccable.

She hated to practise. Murray Perahia told me of an occasion when Argerich was living with Stephen Bishop. She was prowling about like a caged animal, and Bishop suggested she might go and do some practice, as she had an important recital that week and hadn't touched a piano for days. When she said how little she enjoyed practising, Perahia suggested she just play something. So she sat down and played the Chopin B Minor Sonata and, as Perahia told the story, 'What do you say? It was just about the greatest performance of it I had ever heard. Hard to tell her to practise!'

I did not have any problems with her seeming laziness, but I came to hate her too frequent cancellations – which included the opening concert of my second Festival. But in this case there was a compensation. Needing to find not only a soloist for the opening concert but a recitalist for a date later in the week, I was encouraged by a Scottish friend to consider a then little-known French pianist who had given a concert in Scotland for his music club. He insisted she was brilliant. So I booked my old friend Peter Frankl for the opening concert, since he was a pianist that Muti knew and liked, and for the recital I chanced my arm on Cécile Ousset. For the next ten or more years Ousset had a big career in Britain, which she has always traced to that Edinburgh Festival recital. Like Maria João Pires today, she had an interrupted career, retiring after a brilliant start and returning to the concert platform only when she was considerably older. There were several outstanding French pianists around at that time – Michel Béroff, Pascal Rogé and Jean-Philippe Collard among them – but Cécile had something special, and I was present on many happy occasions when her strongly dramatic playing and her very French elegance of style combined to make truly fine music.

Apart from those I have mentioned, two of my favourite pianists are both Polish: Krystian Zimerman and Emanuel Ax. Zimerman, whom I had already worked with shortly after he won the Chopin Prize in 1976, has always seemed to me the most aristocratic pianist of our time, with rare sensitivity allied to keen intelligence. Off stage he has a great sense of humour, and always a new Polish joke. 'What's half a mile long and eats rice?' Answer: the potato queue. Ax, a consummate musician whether on his own or with his trio, may look like a benevolent bear, but he has real subtlety in his playing and the biggest fund of Jewish stories of anyone I have known since David Oistrakh. At one stage we planned to found a chamber-music festival together somewhere in Europe, but other opportunities intervened for him, and my work took me in a different direction. Whenever we meet, I feel a continuing desire to work with him more closely. His musicianship seems to grow with every year.

Ax came to Edinburgh in 1980 having just won the first Rubinstein Prize. Radu Lupu and Murray Perahia had already won at Leeds, so perhaps competitions do get it right some of the time. But I cannot see a competition today bringing forth the idiosyncratic talents of Shura Cherkassky or the even more individualistic Jorge Bolet. Bolet had been very successful when young, but then retreated almost entirely to a teaching career at the Curtis Institute in Philadelphia. He re-emerged in his late years as a phenomenon of the keyboard – a sort of *Wunderalte* – and, although he looked like a melancholy gorilla, conjured from the piano performances of extraordinary virtuosity and delicacy. As if the Chopin *Études* were not hard enough already, he chose to play Godowsky's elaboration of them, daring one to believe that only two hands were involved. Like many virtuosi, he was not at his best in concertos. He never looked at the conductor, and could be wayward in tempo with a capricious individuality unknown among the more careful younger generation. But in recital he was unexcelled, throwing off cascades of notes as if they posed no problem. He was marvellous company off stage, full of stories and dry comments and with a relaxed manner quite unlike his brooding concert presence. I caught only the last years of his career, but they were a delight.

Much more demanding on both me and the audience were the intellectual pianists Alfred Brendel and Maurizio Pollini – both enormously choosy about whom they worked with and what they played. While I understood their reasons, this made for what could be thought unnecessary expenditure. Anything that Abbado or Rattle conducted would be well attended, so it was not really necessary to have a soloist at all. To include a very expensive one looked confident and demonstrated Edinburgh's continual drawing power for musicians, but from my point of view it would have been much better to pair great conductors with younger or less well known soloists, and great soloists with conductors who outside the Festival might not have a chance to work with them. Nevertheless, Abbado often insisted on Pollini, while Rattle's enthusiasm was for Brendel. One of the hardest things for someone in my position is to gain the trust of a major conductor when suggesting a soloist he does not know. I regularly proposed Philip Langridge to Abbado when we first started working together, but Abbado did not know him and would not accept my endorsement. Then one day he rang me from Milan to say he had heard a very good tenor singing with the London Sinfonietta and would like to work with him. It was, of course, Langridge. But there was never a ghost of an acknowledgement that I had suggested him rather earlier.

Confidence can come through regular contacts and growing friendship – but not always. I became very friendly with Alfred Brendel, one of the most intelligent people I know, and have enjoyed his hospitality in a household where musicians, apart from Boulez or Brendel's pianist pupil Imogen Cooper, are less frequent visitors than writers, philosophers and men of ideas. I tend to share Brendel's feeling that many musicians, however eminent, are often quite uninterested in life outside music. It is one of the reasons I always wanted to work in a multidisciplinary context, like broadcasting or festivals. But, despite our social contacts, I have rarely worked with Brendel. The dates were seldom right, the conductor was wrong, the orchestra not one he admired, and so on. As Brendel's reputation grew, I saw him less and became troubled by his attitude to repertory. Whole years would be devoted to one composer or one group of works. I remember Artur Rubinstein saying that, even in advanced age, it was a good thing to play a great variety of music. He had played three concertos in one concert at his debut in Vienna, and always wondered why pianists had to rest for two days after only one. Brendel is certainly remarkable, but not the easiest of colleagues.

Pollini came several times to Edinburgh without ever becoming a friend. In fact, even sharing meals with him, I have hardly ever heard his speaking voice – except on one occasion when he turned up in Edinburgh unexpectedly, demanded six seats for a sold-out concert, and bawled me out when I was able to find only four, and those by sacrificing my own. There is nothing so imperious as a rich card-carrying member of the Italian Communist Party. Yet what a musician! And what imaginative recital programmes – culminating for me in one in which, after two late-Beethoven sonatas, he played the Schoenberg piano pieces and a marvellous Nono impression of Venice with electronic tape called *Onde Sofferte Serene*. The hall was, of course, less than a third full, but as often with small audiences they cheered for ten minutes.

But with the years one pianist emerged who combined the intelligence of Brendel with the exuberant zest for life of the older generation like Rubinstein. This was the remarkable Mitsuko Uchida. Though her repertory is quite limited and her performances are relatively infrequent, she radiates understanding and musicality. She also talks brilliantly about music, on one occasion giving a pre-concert talk about the Schoenberg Piano Concerto which would have melted the stoniest heart. She is, most unusually among major pianists, fascinated by new music and can be seen at all the more challenging concerts. Above all, she has an enthusiasm not only for music but also for literature and especially for wine. After hearing her play or meeting her, I always come away feeling better and more positive about the world.

Though my years in Edinburgh gave me a wide choice of pianists, the situation with violinists was more restricted. The older generation of Arthur Grumiaux, Nathan Milstein, Isaac Stern and Yehudi Menuhin were all past their best, and there were few, if any, younger players who could arouse public enthusiasm. I greatly admired Salvatore Accardo, who became a regular visitor, and the eternally ageless Ida Haendel. But Gidon Kremer, Shlomo Mintz and Pinchas Zukerman each came only once, and I could never lure Itzhak Perlman to the Festival since he spent his summers in Aspen. Kyung-Wha Chung was brilliant at her best, but her career was already very uneven. I did invite Henryk Szeryng one year and he played well, although the travelling circus that accompanied him was less than entertaining. I don't think I have ever met a vainer man, with his stacked heels and lacquered hair. He was ranked as an Ambassador to the United Nations by his adopted country, Mexico, but I always found it odd to hear a Pole talking about 'our great national composer Manuel Ponce'. He handed out LPs like confetti, though many of the sleeves were found to contain nothing at all.

After long discussions, my old friend Ian Hunter persuaded me to invite Menuhin, and we planned a three-day visit in 1981 to show a range of things he was still able to do, focusing particularly on his work with young people and his talent as a communicator. He talked about Bartók before playing the sonata written for him. Unfortunately a string broke and this completely disconcerted him. He played a Bach concerto with the Camerata Lysy, the orchestra of his Swiss summer school, and the Brahms Double Concerto with a young pupil from his school in England. But it was all very depressing. Here was an undoubtedly great musician who simply could no longer get round the notes. Beyond this, Menuhin was a pretty hopeless conductor, and it seemed to me wrong to use his huge and deserved fame to pretend otherwise. He was intelligent, generous and likeable, but I found his public performances embarrassing. The record companies seemed to me to be cashing in on past reputation rather than marking current achievements. He must have known himself how great was the falling off, but outwardly he seemed quite unconcerned.

His dragon wife, Diana, who would usually answer for him if you asked him a question, daunted most people. I rather liked her, and was unfazed even when after the Festival she wrote to me a postcard, which I cherish, saying, 'Darling John, what a pity that, unlike your predecessors, you did not find time to sit down and tell the old man how wonderful he is.' The last time I saw Menuhin was at a dinner at Lord Weidenfeld's. He arrived with his wife. She was unwell, and dropped to the floor like a stone. He put her in a taxi, sent her home, and returned to the dinner. We sat next to each other and had an enthralling conversation about the nature of memory and our seeming inability even in this scientific age to work out exactly how it operated. He was never less than fascinating to meet, and his generosity to the young was admirable.

Every year other instrumentalists and chamber groups came in considerable numbers, and it was not always possible to get to know them well. I rarely, if ever, missed a morning concert – 'the best possible way to wake up', as J. W. Lambert said in the *Sunday Times*. The Beaux Arts Trio were always a joy, especially the ebullient Menahem Pressler, a great and undervalued pianist. I also had a soft spot for all accompanists – so essential and so often overlooked. Geoffrey Parsons was already a close friend, from whom I use to ask and receive priceless advice on singers and repertoire. I also admired the work of Dalton Baldwin, Irwin Gage, Thomas Schuback, Philip Moll, Bruno Canino and Martin Isepp, while the young generation of Roger Vignoles and Graham Johnson were beginning to make their mark. The best of them were not in any way mere accompanists but duo partners, contributing as much as the singer or instrumentalists with whom they worked, yet uncomplaining about the casual way in which critics and audience considered them little more than superior servants.

Edinburgh always had a special attraction for singers, and over the five Festivals for which I was responsible I became almost complacent about our continuing ability to attract the best. When Abbado said that for the Verdi *Requiem* he required Margaret Price, Jessye Norman, José Carreras and Ruggiero Raimondi, I was doubtful only of their availability, not about the attraction of the invitation. In fact they all accepted at once. When Abbado wanted Herman Prey, Wolfgang Wagner moved the date of a Bayreuth performance to allow him to come to Edinburgh. Casting for Edinburgh was in many ways a much easier job than for many places elsewhere, since the already thirty-five-year-old tradition worked very much in our favour. I have my predecessors to thank for that.

Most of the great singers were without pretentiousness or grand manner and a pleasure to have around. Some, like Elisabeth Söderström, became real friends. And when Elly Ameling refused to go on stage at the Usher Hall until the lighting had been adjusted I felt she was not being difficult but absolutely right – it was pointless for the spotlight to light a patch of floor rather than her. Many of the singers ended up in my flat, and I got used to Phyllis Bryn-Julson playing blues on the piano, and Jessye Norman climbing eighty stairs and helping in the kitchen. My only tense moment was when Norman refused the flat her agent had rented for her and told us to sort it out. She ended up staying in the palatial grandeur of Hopetoun House, by courtesy of the

Marquess of Linlithgow, whose daughter was one of our helpers. It was perhaps unfortunate that the Mini that transported her to Hopetoun broke down in the drive, a quarter of a mile from the house, but she just laughed. It was all very different from the present day, when she requires the tea bar at the Barbican to be closed to the orchestra in case the noise disturbs her, and insists that no one speak to her. I fear she has spent too much time being worshipped by Parisian hairdressers. We never had nonsense of that kind, and thought of her as almost one of the team.

I had a similar affection for the lovely Lucia Popp, whose early death was such a loss to music. In a recital programme of folk songs arranged by great composers she could get away with wearing a sort of gypsy costume with gold coins sewn into the tassels. Her charm outrode the kitsch. It was also a real pleasure to be able to invite so many British singers, including Felicity Lott, Ann Murray, Thomas Allen and Anthony Rolfe Johnson, who were taking their place on the world stage during these years.

One innovation in 1982 was the organization of masterclasses, first with Elisabeth Schwarzkopf and then with Hans Hotter. What a contrast! Schwarzkopf and I spent two chilly days auditioning in a hall in London, and she listened a bit then. Once we had chosen the singers it was practically the last we heard of them, so relentless were her interruptions. She was obsessed with words, and felt that no one who was not a native-born German should sing anything in that language. Half a phrase was the average before she leapt to her feet and intervened. The audience certainly got their money's worth of Schwarzkopf, but I felt for the young singers.

Getting her to Edinburgh was not a problem. She had done some classes in Germany, and wanted to do more. During the years of her marriage to Walter Legge she seemed in public entirely in his shadow, but after his death she never drew breath. Her visit gave me one of my most revealing experiences of how much rich admirers really care. I happened to spend a weekend in a great house in Scotland the winter before she came. One of the other guests, a multimillionaire who had been associated with Glyndebourne, spent most of the weekend professing his undying love for Schwarzkopf. When we planned the masterclasses, I thought he might help with some of the associated costs, perhaps by paying her hotel bill. I sought a meeting with him, only to be shown the door. 'How dare you', he shrieked, 'presume on a chance acquaintance!'

Hotter's visit the following year was quite a different matter. One of the greatest musicians I have ever known – certainly the greatest Wotan – he presided over classes with generosity and benevolence, and actually seemed to like the young people. I could not get over the joy of having him around, and felt privileged to be in the audience watching him at work. Elderly as he was, I could not have imagined that twelve years later, in my last year running the Proms, he would still be performing the role of the Narrator in Schoenberg's *Gurrelieder*.

Changes and developments in musical taste were pushing at both ends of the repertory: both unfamiliar early music and new music were now available, with specialist performers. I had never been a fully paid-up enthusiast for the so called 'authentic' movement, since the quality of performances was so chancy in the early years. But things were improving – though Bob Lockyer said he resented that more time was spent tuning than playing, just as with new music more time was spent moving the music stands, since no two pieces ever seemed to be written for the same combination of instruments. One longed for the simplicity of a string quartet. Roger Norrington, John Eliot Gardiner, Christopher Hogwood, Gustav Leonhardt, Reinhard Goebel, Frans Brüggen and Anthony Rooley all came with their ensembles, and it was evident that a quite different audience was emerging that wanted baroque music rather than the nineteenth century. The girls bought their dresses at Laura Ashley and the boys wore brown tweed suits and gold-rimmed glasses, and my goodness they were serious. But they were right to be interested, since so much music had been forgotten. There was, however, a tendency to think that any Italian concerto grosso was a masterpiece, and demanded the same reverence they accorded to Bach. While it was enjoyable, I felt much eighteenth-century music was written to be a background to life rather than a new religion.

What was less enjoyable was to discover what a set of prima donnas the early-music conductors were, and how inadequate their administrators. Goebel and Musica Antiqua Cologne managed to lose all their music at Heathrow Airport, and my team spent the whole night copying new parts from scores borrowed from the university library. John Eliot Gardiner, whom I had first met at his parents' house when he was still a schoolboy, always gave the impression he was doing you a favour in agreeing to perform. I was surprised that these conductors often achieved impressive performances, since practically none of them had even a shadow of conducting technique. The new-music groups were infinitely better equipped, with organizers like Amelia Freedman of the Nash Ensemble and Reinbert de Lieeuw of the Amsterdam-based Schoenberg Ensemble. My only regret was that, for box-office reasons, we couldn't work much more with them.

My quest for diversity in the music plan led to the first involvement of jazz in the Edinburgh Festival. I invited that much underrated British musician Mike Westbrook to transfer from the Fringe, and his huge piece *Cortège* was a real hit. I was also delighted to be able to present Oscar Peterson on two occasions, since I found him almost as exciting as Martha Argerich and a great deal more reliable. Crossing frontiers and expanding taste was central to what I wanted to do, whether it was having the Netherlands Wind Ensemble playing in the streets or putting on late-night shows with James Galway, Richard Rodney Bennett or Benjamin Luxon. We were always being told that we didn't reach the local population, but to the extent that this was true it was not for lack of trying. With five hundred shows on the Fringe, we were not without rivals in the field, and in planning alternative events we had to be careful not to seem to be patronizing people. I lost count of the times I was told that Yehudi Menuhin had played in a tough, working-class district back in the 1950s, as if that were the only thing to do.

That now regular feature the Fireworks Concert began in my time. The idea originated with the Scottish Chamber Orchestra, but the first contact with their potential sponsor was inauspicious. I was asked to lunch by the boss of Glenlivet, Ivan Straker. He lined up his directors on opposite sides of the table and put himself at one end and me at the other. The conversation began as follows: 'I don't suppose a long-haired weirdo like you has ever seen a balance sheet.' I replied coolly that I had been looking at his, and could see why he wanted more publicity. The fireworks concert went ahead as a totally independent event but listed in the Festival programme – I had wanted a contribution to the Festival as well in return for the Glenlivet name on everything.

Straker's tone of voice and attitude were something I was now familiar with in Edinburgh: it was as if those of us who worked in the arts were the lower orders, and really did not deserve to sit at the top table. But all those who patronized us nevertheless wanted to be asked to the parties and to meet the stars, and were not above asking Jessye Norman if she would 'Give us a song' after dinner.

There were two kinds of patron: the Edinburgh professional class, mostly lawyers, who inhabited the New Town and believed they represented a kind of permanent autocracy – a *noblesse de robe* – and the new and expanding business community, mostly first-generation bosses who really had no experience of the world of culture but thought it could be bought when it suited them. Government policy – increasingly insisting on multi-source funding – and the rise of sponsorship meant that we had to spend a great deal of time courting potential sponsors. There were some absolutely admirable people, but many who, while recognizing the possible benefit to their company, were not sure what or why they should be helping. BP, the first Festival sponsor with Peter Diamand's *Carmen*, put up £25,000 for the 1979 Degas exhibition. The following year I suggested they help with the cost of the Australian Dance Theatre. They were very doubtful, and I spent a surreal afternoon at BP House in London with a group of refinery and chemical managers, trying to explain why modern dance was worthwhile. In the end they agreed to contribute, were delighted with the result, and went on to become one of the company's principal sponsors through BP Australia.

Other sponsors would come and go. One of the big insurance companies supported us generously one year, to mark their centenary, but did not come back. Sheila Colvin and I spent many lunches and evenings in pursuit of financial help. Sheila noticed that the Banque de Paris had opened a branch in Edinburgh and befriended the manager. Eventually, after several meetings, they sent a cheque for twenty-five pounds. I was tempted to tear it in two and put it back in the envelope, but, as Sheila wisely pointed out, twenty-five pounds was still better than nothing. It was significant, however, that the most generous support was international or London-based rather than local.

The three Scottish banks – the Bank of Scotland, the Royal Bank of Scotland and the Clydesdale – had always clubbed together to give the Festival a joint donation. It stood at £12,000 in my first years, though the banks' collective profits were several hundreds of millions. Through Lord Balfour, who was not only Chairman of the Scottish Arts Council but also on the board of the Bank of Scotland, I sought a meeting and we came together in the office of Sir Michael Herries, the Chairman of the Royal Bank. Lord Polwarth represented the Clydesdale. I explained the risks of grants falling in value through inflation, the danger of raising seat prices too much, and the widening gap between what we needed to maintain the artistic standards of the past and what we were now receiving, and as politely as I could I suggested that they could do more. They gave me a very patient hearing and told me they would consider my suggestion. A few weeks later they increased the donation to £15,000, each putting in £1,000 more. I was grateful, but found it hard not to be disappointed. The following year by chance I sat next to the new Chairman of the Bank of Scotland, Tom Risk, in the Shuttle up from London one morning. We talked in very general terms. I made no new appeal, but a few days later he called me to say that he had decided to break the cartel and come in as a sponsor to the tune of £20,000. It was a marvellous moment, and Sir Tom remains one of my heroes.

The constant pursuit of funds sapped not only my energy but my enthusiasm for the job. I was travelling relentlessly. One day a girl thrust a questionnaire at me at Heathrow Airport. Was I a frequent traveller? 'Yes indeed.' How many times had I used the airport in the past year? Since I had been working on my tax papers and calculating the days I had worked abroad, I knew the answer. Counting the regular London–Edinburgh trips and the foreign travel, I had been through the airport 146 times in the preceding year. 'You have ruined my statistics!' said the girl. I came more and more to feel that some part of the financial responsibility for the Festival should be shared. I turned to the Festival Council and asked whether they did not feel that the members of the Festival Society and its Council should assist. They most certainly did not. In the first week of the 1982 Festival, the Council were complimenting themselves on how well things were going. From our point of view we had had a very troubled opening, with failures and inadequacy in almost all the halls and theatres, none of which was our fault. I pointed out the sort of things that had gone wrong, and one young councillor started giggling. I said, too testily, 'I'm glad you find it funny, but neither I nor my colleagues do.' A chill fell on the room, and I never again felt the Council was on my side.

My five-year contract was to run out in 1983, but, despite our cool relations, I was offered an extension for another five years. I thought that too long, and said I could probably do two more years – until 1985. Yet in the following weeks I became more and more anxious about whether I really could keep up the pace and whether my energy and commitment were still at their former level. I spent a gloomy weekend alone in London, and on the Monday morning I told my colleagues there that I had changed my mind and had decided to leave after the 1983 Festival. I felt guilty in so far as they were affected. Everyone, including my two secretaries, Annie Mackenzie Young, later to run orchestras and tours, and Julia Carruthers, later Deputy Dance Director of the Arts Council, was outstanding. They had given me superb support and had become a real team. They were upset, but I knew they understood my feelings.

I returned to Edinburgh and went to see the Lord Provost. All hell broke loose. It was put about that I had resigned. Since no new contract had been issued, I had in no way resigned. I had simply decided not to extend my old contract. I am not by nature a resigner – although I have quite often felt the desire to do so – but deep in my heart I felt it was time to move on. Where to, I had no idea, but I knew that I might endanger both the Festival and myself if I started to doubt my ability to continue doing the Edinburgh job as I had tried to do it for almost five years. It is not easy to relinquish one of the best jobs in the world, but I knew myself well enough to know that the fires of my enthusiasm were dying down. So much energy was expended in Edinburgh with such puny results. All the problems I had inherited – inadequate buildings and finance, widespread prejudice and philistinism – seemed quite undented by a hard-fought campaign to improve things. Perhaps it was arrogant and Utopian to believe I could change deeply engrained attitudes, but, whereas my predecessors had largely just got on with the job, I had spent endless time explaining the Festival and its needs, and in doing so had given up more time than I had wished – time away from the real work of running the Festival, and time out of my own life. I was increasingly feeling that I did not have any life at all apart from the job.

My withdrawal was accepted with ill grace, and I was left in no doubt that it was I who had behaved badly, and that the Council's conduct and attitude had been unimpeachable. I was very surprised at the number of affectionate and understanding letters I received from Edinburgh people, many of them long-time Festival supporters. But they all seemed to accept that things would not, and could not, improve. Even some of my close friends could not understand my deep belief that, *unless* things improved, the Festival would have a much diminished future. But two friends who understood that very well were George Harewood and Peter Diamand. Yet I still had one more Festival to run, and I had a quiet suspicion that it might just prove to be my best.

Like many key events in my life, the origins of 1983's 'Vienna 1900' Festival were almost accidental. I had long known the *Lyric Symphony* of Zemlinsky – a fine work, but understandably overshadowed by Mahler's *Das Lied von der Erde*, also a symphonic song cycle on Chinese texts, but a greater masterpiece. Zemlinsky was for me little more than a name in the history books: Schoenberg's teacher and eventual brother-in-law, Mahler's assistant, a one-time lover of Alma Schindler, and by all accounts a very fine conductor. But I knew practically nothing of him as a composer. In 1980 a friend gave me a recording of his settings of five Maeterlinck poems for mezzo and orchestra. I was intrigued, and on several occasions used the recordings as a test with friends, asking them to name the composer. Some said Mahler, others early Berg, a few Schoenberg, but no one guessed correctly. In 1982, the Hamburg State Opera put on two one-act operas by Zemlinsky based on Oscar Wilde's *A Florentine Tragedy* and *The Birthday of the Infanta*, known in German as *Der Zwerg, The Dwarf*. Accompanied by Lies Askonas's assistant, Robert Rattray, I went to Hamburg to hear them. *A Florentine Tragedy* is a piece of late-romantic Grand Guignol, second cousin to Puccini's *Il Tabarro*, but *The Dwarf* seemed to me to be that very rare thing, an incontestably major work that has somehow been overlooked. Little more than an hour long, it was given a spare but effective production by Adolph Dresen. Inge Nielsen was brilliant as the Infanta, and as the Dwarf the American tenor Kenneth Riegel gave a performance of extraordinary dramatic power and vocal intensity. It is difficult enough to sing a high tenor role like the Dwarf, but even harder when, like José Ferrer as Toulouse-Lautrec, you are performing on your knees with your legs strapped up behind you. I immediately wanted to bring the opera to Edinburgh, and started negotiating with Hamburg's Music Director, Christoph von Dohnányi, and his excellent administrator, Christoph Albrecht.

Back in London, Sheila Colvin asked a sensible and pertinent question: who *was* Zemlinsky and why, if this piece was so good, did we not know him? In a sense the whole 1983 Festival was an answer to that question. The idea that Vienna at the turn of the century was the furnace out of which came many of the ideas that affected our lives had long been in my mind. I had not previously found the peg on which to hang an exploration of a period which found strong expression in music and theatre, but also in architecture, painting, literature, philosophy and the birth of psychoanalysis. Once I started thinking hard, it was almost too rich a mixture. I needed help.

During my Television years I had had a number of contacts with the

English art historian Peter Vergo, a recognized expert on Jugendstil – the Viennese art nouveau – and much else in the culture of Austria. I invited him to lunch and tentatively explored whether the Vienna 1900 idea would work and whether there might be an exhibition which would show how interrelated the arts were – how, for instance, Schoenberg the painter stood in relation to Schoenberg the composer. Vergo was voluble and intrigued. He always reminded me of Van Gogh's Doctor Gachet, with his red beard and intense blue eyes. He obtained his doctorate in Vienna, speaks Viennese rather than German, and knows everyone in that tricky city. I wondered if he could help me. He was, and still is, a full-time university teacher with a very busy diary. But again luck was on my side. He had a sabbatical coming up and, although he had intended to use it for writing, he agreed to find time to work with us.

I began discussions with conductors and orchestras about Vienna-based repertory (there was also a Webern centenary in 1983), and Vergo and I went to Vienna to see the museums and gallery people. Before this I spent a few winter days in the city, enjoying not only *Die Fledermaus* on New Year's Eve, but also the traditional New Year's Day concert, conducted that year by Lorin Maazel. I looked at the Schoenberg paintings in the Historical Museum, including his full-length portrait of Alban Berg. Bob Lockyer, who was with me, commented that if he were Director of the museum he would be reluctant to part with such an important work at the height of the tourist season. I felt he was probably right, but we reckoned without Vergo's persuasiveness. The museum agreed to lend everything we asked for, with the single exception of Schoenberg's painting of the Gerstl family, which was too fragile to travel. The Theatre Museum section of the National Library was similarly hospitable, and agreed to find stage and costume designs from its collections. In a very un-Viennese way, doors kept opening to our requests. It seemed too good to be true.

I had no idea, however, how big the exhibition might be, who would pay for it, or – crucially – where we could display it, but I took Vergo on as curator and set about filling in the gaps. The Austrian government is not allowed to lend any of the paintings by Gustav Klimt in the Belvedere: they are regarded as too fragile and too valuable. The only important Klimt in the United Kingdom is in the National Gallery in London. Michael Levey, the Director, so often helpful and supportive, agreed to lend it. Ironically, only one institution refused to help, and that was only one likely to make money out of the plan – the publisher Universal Edition. Although they would receive royalties on anything we played by Schoenberg, Berg, Webern or Zemlinsky, they would not lend even a scrap of manuscript or answer letters.

There was one request which had totally unforeseen consequences. When the Theatre Museum came to look for the famous Alfred Roller designs for the Wagner productions that Mahler had conducted in Vienna, they found some of them missing. They were eventually traced to the walls of Lorin Maazel's apartment. It was absolutely not his fault, although in a very Viennese way he got the blame. As Music Director of the Vienna State Opera, he had been provided with a flat and it was suggested it might be nice to have some suitable pictures on the walls. The Roller designs were borrowed without authorization, and Viennese intrigue used the fact to undermine Maazel's position at the opera house. There were headlines praising Edinburgh for having uncovered the scandal, which I found tremendously embarrassing. I had always got on very well with Maazel and had no axes to grind with him – except for the size of his fee.

Other elements started to fall into place as if by magic. Scottish Opera was to put on a new production of *Death in Venice*. Visconti's film had anchored the character of Aschenbach, the writer, inaccurately but memorably in the music of Mahler. The Municipal Theatre of Haifa had a new play by the excellent Yoshua Sobol, *The Soul of a Jew*, about the Viennese philosopher Otto Weininger. Although himself Jewish, Weininger had written passionate anti-Semitic diatribes and eventually, while still in his twenties, killed himself in 1903 in the very room in which Beethoven had died. His writings had a strong influence on Hitler. The Director of the Haifa theatre had been at the previous Edinburgh Festival and knew our stages. I went to Israel to see the production and found that, in addition to being of great quality, it would fit on to the stage of the Music Hall in the Assembly Rooms, which I was now intending to use in partnership with the producer William Burdett-Coutts as a sort of halfway house between the main Festival and the Fringe. So keen were the Haifa company to come that they even had the programmes printed in Israel, and I brought them back with me.

I asked the three directors of the Glasgow Citizens' Theatre to come and talk to me about my Viennese theme, since I knew that Robert David MacDonald had long had an ambition to dramatize some of the writings of Karl Kraus, the best-known satirical journalist in Vienna in the years before the First World War. The Cits improved the idea by also suggesting a production of Hugo von Hofmannsthal's libretto for *Der Rosenkavalier* as a play. Only with a wordy writer like Hofmannsthal could such an idea work. Both productions demanded a big cast and excellent design, something I knew Philip Prowse could provide. Giles Havergal directed with ingenuity. It looked a very expensive plan, so I decided to put a sum of money on the table and say, 'If you can do it for this, fine. But beyond that you are on your own.' They thought about it and agreed. Recently Havergal told me that he found it a very satisfactory way of working, for right from the start he knew where he was. *The Last Days of Mankind*, as MacDonald called the Kraus piece, was an epic, lasting over four hours, with moments of genius and similar in its range to Robert Musil's *A Man Without Qualities* – a work I have always preferred to Proust. It was entirely worthwhile. Hofmannsthal, it turned out, needed the talents of Richard Strauss to make his text really enjoyable. But the production was lovely to look at, and made audiences aware of what a libretto was rather more successfully than poor old Metastasio's *L'Olimpiade* the previous year.

Ballet Rambert, offered that year's Tennant Caledonian-sponsored award for new work, approached Glen Tetley, who chose to base a piece on the painter Kokoschka's expressionist drama *Murder, Hope of Women*. Graham Johnson of The Songmakers' Almanac compiled a programme about Alma Mahler, using her letters and her own compositions as well as those of her husband; Janet Suzman brilliantly impersonated Alma Mahler herself. The excellent Schoenberg Ensemble from the Netherlands put together three programmes based on the concerts of the Society for Private Performances, including Schoenberg arrangements of Busoni and Johann Strauss as well as music by Webern, Zemlinsky, Hans Eisler and Debussy. *Das Lied von der Erde* with Brigitte Fassbaender and Herman Winkler was to be conducted by Tennstedt, *Verklärte Nacht*, by Haitink, *Erwartung*, by Abbado, Webern and Mahler by Rattle. Cherkassky offered the Berg Sonata, Charles Rosen the Webern Variations, and both Lucia Popp and Ileana Cotrubas included songs by Schoenberg and Berg. A very young student at the Royal Northern College of Music, Mark Tinkler, devised a whole programme of Zemlinsky songs to perform on the Fringe.

One of the greatest elements was provided by the Scottish National

Orchestra and its Music Director, Alexander Gibson. Gibson had memorably conducted Mahler's Eighth Symphony in an earlier Festival, and with characteristic modesty asked very tentatively if he could do it again. 'No,' I replied firmly. He looked crestfallen. 'No,' I said, 'because I want you to conduct *Gurrelieder*. Lord Harewood had opened his first Festival with this great, sprawling, early-Schoenberg epic. It was, and remains, an absolutely favourite work of mine. Gibson, as always when offered a challenge, rose to it splendidly, with an excellent group of soloists including Marilyn Zschau, Ann Murray and Philip Langridge, and gave one of his greatest performances with Hans Hotter as the Narrator. Making another link, the text of *Gurrelieder* is by the same Danish writer, Jens Peter Jacobsen, who provided the story for Delius's *Fennimore and Gerda*, which the St Louis Opera were to perform. Parts of an enormous mosaic were falling into place – as much by luck as by deliberate action.

But how to open the Vienna Festival? My long-term plan had been to start with Beethoven's Ninth Symphony, conducted by Reginald Goodall. Brian McMaster, then directing Welsh National Opera, with which Goodall was working, regularly tried to persuade him to come, but after several meetings he declined, and I was fortunate to find that Andrew Davis was free, and this allowed me – daringly for Edinburgh – to precede the Ninth Symphony with Berg's thrilling *Three Orchestral Pieces*. Just as with the *St Matthew Passion*, this caused long faces among the local bigwigs, but it set the course for the following three weeks, in which every day somewhere in the programme something happened relating to the Vienna 1900 theme.

After months of arguing and negotiating, we finally managed to house Peter Vergo's exhibition in the Museum of Antiquities. Although not vast in size, the show was a revelation and the perfect link to the rest of the Festival, showing clearly how the work of Mahler, Freud, Kokoschka, Berg, Kraus, Zemlinsky and the architects and designers Kolo Moser and Josef Hoffman interrelated. At the last minute a generous sponsor, Bruce Dawson of Autobar, came up with the funds to design and install it. A series of lectures on Vienna and its influence brought, in addition to Peter Vergo, the philosopher Sir Alfred Ayer, the theatre historian Martin Esslin, the composer Alexander Goehr, the painter George Eisler (son of the composer Hanns) and Leonard Stein, Director of the Schoenberg Institute, to talk about the period. The Fine Arts Society reconstructed the famous room that Charles Rennie

Mackintosh had designed for the Vienna Secession exhibition in 1902, and Piers Plowright of Radio 3 devised a literary programme about life and letters in Vienna. One of Schoenberg's sons came to Edinburgh with his American wife and a charming child known as Arnie Schoenberg, Jnr.

Collectively the impact was at least impressive and for some revelatory. This at last seemed to me what a major festival should be doing, though the costs were high and the receipts were inevitably lower than if we had performed Shakespeare and Tchaikovsky. But it wasn't all Vienna. The Spanish actress Núria Espert produced a tender and beautiful production of Lorca's play *The Spinster*, and Joan Plowright led a distinguished cast in Lindsay Anderson's production of *The Cherry Orchard*. At the Royal Scottish Museum there was an excellent exhibition curated by the ethnomusicologist Jean Jenkins, called 'Man and Music', which brought together a marvellous collection of musical instruments from all over the world, while groups of musicians from India, Bali, West Africa, Mexico and Morocco, plus bagpipe players from Scotland, Ireland, Yugoslavia and Galicia, invaded the city and performed in all kinds of places, many of them quite unexpected.

I spent the three weeks in a kind of permanent high. Not even the relatively few disasters could alter the atmosphere, though Glen Tetley's inexplicable decision not to perform the twenty-five minutes of new choreography that he had created for Ballet Rambert, but instead to use the dancers as actors in a largely unintelligible version of the Kokoschka play, came close to causing a scandal and contributed to the sad demise of the Tennant Caledonian award. The award had been a fine initiative, but only one of the new commissions, *The Lighthouse*, had really succeeded and my successor abandoned the scheme, which had never had the support of Tennant Caledonian's parent board, Bass Charrington in London.

Musically there were highlights beyond the Viennese theme. Abbado's conducting of Act 2 of *Lohengrin* was powerful and impressive. The Chamber Orchestra of Europe under Alexander Schneider, with the Beaux Arts Trio, made one believe that Beethoven's Triple Concerto was better than its reputation, while Neville Marriner with the Academy of St Martin-in-the-Fields and Frans Brüggen with the Orchestra of the Eighteenth Century showed equally valid approaches to Mozart and Schubert. The Labeque sisters thundered their way through the Brahms Waltzes and Hungarian Dances, while Pinchas

Zukerman played the three Brahms violin sonatas and two viola sonatas. Yo-Yo Ma, Emanuel Ax and Young Uck Kim gave quite simply the best performance I have ever heard of the Brahms First Piano Trio. The Festival ended with a traditional Viennese night conducted by Neeme Järvi, who has a real feeling for both Strauss R. and Strauss J., while Elisabeth Söderström lent lustre to my final concert not only with the closing scene of *Capriccio*, but by singing 'Meine Lippe sie kussen so heiss', and 'Vilja' by Lehár.

We had much to be pleased about – not least the critical response. Most of the London writers, both on music and on drama, agreed that collectively the Viennese theme had made sense and added to the understanding of the period. Only Conrad Wilson of the *Scotsman* slagged off the plans, with his usual long article listing all the things we were not playing. According to him, even the Zemlinsky quartet that the Melos Quartet were to play was the wrong one, and why had we not produced Schreker's *Der ferne Klang*? At my last press conference, I found myself suggesting that Edinburgh's greatest need was not an opera house but a music critic on the *Scotsman*. The previous year I had had enough and decided to get rid of him as editor of the concert programmes. He denied me the pleasure by resigning. Critics are entitled to their views, but whether you agree with them or not is less important than your general belief in their ability. I often had poor notices from Peter Heyworth, who wanted much more contemporary music. I agreed with him, but he didn't have to pay the bills. I had, every year, support from David Cairns, who seemed to have a real understanding of the problems we faced both in funding and in facilities. Retrospectively, I know that what we achieved that year sowed seeds. Hugh Canning has often said it was the Vienna 1900 Festival that made him want to be a critic. I totally support the independence of critics and their right to find fault and denigrate. What I cannot accept is the too frequent tendency of arts journalists to get the facts wrong. I am amazed at their seeming unwillingness to undertake thorough research. Time and again, where I have inside knowledge, I see them writing rubbish. Standards in Britain in writing about the arts are much lower than we would tolerate about economics or the law.

I was very grateful for the support I had had from broadcasters, notably the BBC, although their departure from Edinburgh at the end of the second week of the Festival was always irritating. Radio 2, Radio 3 and Radio 4 all came to Edinburgh, but without ever speaking to each other. BBC Television naturally never noticed BBC Radio, and local radio, though supportive, really wanted gossip and scandal rather than art. I spent hours a day being interviewed, trying to encourage audiences to take risks and to build an awareness of the importance of the Festival to the city and to Scotland. Occasionally my patience was overstretched. Brian Matthew invited me on Radio 2's *Around Midnight* for a few minutes every night – a wonderful opportunity to update and trail the next day's events. It was on this programme that I finally burnt my boats as far as the local authority was concerned. After a particularly ill-tempered Festival Council meeting, revolving mostly around the problems caused by Scottish Opera's *Death in Venice*, I told Brian Matthew and his audience that there were six months until the next District Council elections. Would it not be a good thing if Edinburgh got itself some better candidates? I may have been foolish to say it, but it was not a stupid suggestion.

I had been at meetings not only of the full District Council but also of the Labour group, currently in opposition, and had been appalled by the latter's 'little Scotland' attitude. I had a strong suspicion – which proved justified the following year – that Labour might be in a position to take over the Council, and was extremely worried about their attitude to the Festival. It was easy to agree with them that too much of the year's provision for recreation and leisure was spent in the three weeks of the Festival, making for a pretty thin spread for the rest of the year. But I could not believe that the answer was to sacrifice the Festival, with all the publicity and the huge income it brought into the city, for the sake of small-scale activity in the suburbs. This was also the time of rate-capping and Thatcherite hostility to local authorities. I was sure the situation would not get easier. Perhaps a new Director with a new approach might achieve more.

The search for my successor was a matter of urgency but in many ways half-hearted. The Lord Provost kept asking me if Humphrey Burton, Melvyn Bragg or Jonathan Miller would be interested. I pointed out that my salary, by now a little over £20,000 a year, was probably a fraction of what they earned. Although it had increased over the years, it was still tiny by international standards. Since I had neither family nor outside claims, it was possible to live reasonably well on it, but others would not see it in that way. In addition, the constantly reported problems of the Festival made it hard to attract the best candidates. I had got the job without previous festival experience but in competition with what was, frankly, not a strong field of candidates. The list of applicants to succeed me was no better, with no one of real stature either as a festival director or particularly in their knowledge of music.

Frank Dunlop's application, he has often said, was a sort of joke – not really taking the idea seriously. He was well known in Edinburgh and had produced some very successful shows for the Festival. I knew him and liked him a lot. But when I was told he was to be appointed I was frankly astonished. I could see the case for having a theatre person at the helm, but surely some knowledge of music was essential as well. By any standards, music was not well served during Dunlop's eight years as Director. He did, however, help to solve one of the key problems – the state of the theatres – and it was in his time that the King's Theatre finally got an orchestra pit, the Royal Lyceum a new stage, and the plan to turn the disused Empire into what is now the Festival Theatre took shape.

Dunlop had a terrible time from the new Labour-controlled council in his first years. The air was full of populist contempt for higher forms of culture. Frank argued with the councillors, turned many round, and achieved a great deal in terms of increased sponsorship and local support. Generously, some people have said that I sowed the seeds for this, but I had not been able to make the seeds grow. I have a reputation for impatience, and after I have explained something more than twenty times it is hard for me to do it again – and again and again – with equanimity. It was just as well I never joined the Foreign Office, and I was certainly right to have left Edinburgh when I did.

However, I had no job to go to and no clear idea of what I wanted to do next – other than taking a real break to restore my energy, which after six relentless years was at a low ebb. I had been approached earlier that year by the BBC through my old boss, Aubrey Singer, to see if I wanted to return to television. I had no desire to become an executive or a producer again, but late in the day I had come to enjoy appearing on television. During the Edinburgh years I had done a lot of this, from fronting two series of *Dance Month* for BBC2 to presenting a monthly arts magazine for Scottish Television – a cynical operation on their part to improve their chances of getting their licence renewed. I had no illusions about my looks or the fact that many felt my voice to be too posh, but in areas where I have knowledge and commitment I felt the obstacles could be overcome, and there was hardly an arts programme on radio to which I had not contributed – especially *Kaleidoscope* on

Radio 4, where I had been the almost resident dance reviewer for nearly ten years. I enjoyed these broadcasts just as I enjoyed public speaking, and liked the idea that something of my own enthusiasm could be communicated to others. I am not a specialist but a generalist, but with more than superficial knowledge of several different areas.

After talking to Aubrey Singer, I proposed to the BBC a series on Franco-British relations, notably in the cultural field but also in education and social attitudes. I called it *The Unknown Neighbour*, and suggested that we could make the series in French as well, under the title *Mésentente Cordiale*, as the BBC was at that time actively pursuing co-productions with the new television channels in France. I was led to believe that the proposal might be accepted, so I roughed out a synopsis and started approaching leading figures in Britain and France about their possible participation. Meanwhile the BBC seemed to go cold on the idea, and one day in the summer of 1983 I had a curt note from Singer saying it was not wanted. I wrote to Singer suggesting that the decision might at least have been taken with some reference to me. His reply began, unforgettably, 'You of all people should know better than to write to me like that.' When I was in the BBC, I always resisted claims that it was high-handed and impervious to criticism. After I left, I found myself singing a different song. Time and again the BBC's attitude to contributors or to events like the Festival seemed offensively casual and patronizing. So, whatever I was to do after Edinburgh, I did not think it would involve a return to the BBC in any way that I could imagine. In this, as in many other things, I was to be proved wrong.

# 12

# A Mid-Career Break

When I left Edinburgh at the end of the 1983 Festival I was in a state of profound nervous exhaustion. We had had a marvellous Festival, but for the first time there was a considerable deficit, and I had no job to go to. I talked glibly of a mid-career break, but I had really lost my sense of direction. I knew I could not stay, but had no idea where to go. I had worked out that I had enough put by to survive for about eighteen months without a full-time job.

As so often in the past, I went to Venice, which I always associated with the words inscribed on Diaghilev's grave 'Inspiratrice éternelle de nos apaisements'. Usually a short stay in Venice did the trick and I was ready to start up again, but not this time. After two melancholy days in the rain I knew it was not the answer, hired a car, and drove down the coast to Pesaro – unrecognizable from my student days in Perugia, when we used to go there to swim: now like part of an Italian Costa Brava. I turned inland to Urbino, and was rewarded with the largest parking fine I have ever had in my life. I ended up in that most remote and mysterious of Umbrian towns, Gubbio. Gubbio is on no main tourist route and retains an inward-looking independence that I have often found attractive. I looked at a flat which was for sale – the upper floors of a sixteenth-century palazzo, with a superb view over the plain. Why not? I thought. It was inexpensive and extremely attractive. Luckily, before I did anything foolish I realized how stupid I was to think that I could make a home in a town which was in international terms almost the most inaccessible in Italy – four hours' drive from Pisa and six from Rome, the nearest airports. It was one thing to hide away for a few weeks, quite another to go into voluntary unpaid exile.

I rejected Gubbio and drove down through southern Umbria to Orvieto. This was better. I read and sketched, ate well, and drank good local wine. But I could not shake off the depression. After a week, I ended up staying with my friend the composer Hans Werner Henze, who lives in glorious isolation in the Alban Hills, only forty-five minutes from the centre of Rome but in an island of tranquillity surrounded by vineyards.

From our first meeting when I was Editor of *Music Now* in the 1960s, Henze – a frequent visitor to Britain, with a home in London – had become a regular part of my life. We had met often, and I had on several occasions programmed his music in Edinburgh and come to value his friendship. The highly political stance he took in the 1960s, with visits to Cuba and outspoken attacks on capitalist society, endeared him to few, while the avant-garde of music as represented by Boulez and Stockhausen spoke of him with real contempt. I had succeeded in ignoring his politics while admiring his music. It is immensely gratifying to see how his true worth is now appreciated. He is a brilliant composer of both opera and ballet, an inventive symphonist, a versatile creator of sounds for every instrument from the double bass to the guitar, and a real force in musical education for both amateurs and professionals. But, beyond all that, he is also wonderfully well read, highly intelligent and fun to be with. His slightly pedantic manner in English (less so in Italian) and his often justifiable hypochondria can usually be pushed aside with a joke or a good piece of gossip. He lived in high style, but with a punishing schedule – teaching, conducting, composing, organizing. I attribute my rapid recovery from the post-Edinburgh failure of nerve to the loving and supportive atmosphere of his marvellous house at Marino.

The house rules at Marino are geared to both work and play. Morning is for work, and no one speaks. There is a simple late lunch, an afternoon at leisure and, in the evening, drinks in the library and a grand dinner with friends who come out from Rome or further away to enjoy the arguments, the ribaldry and the superb cooking of Henze's long-time partner, Fausto Moroni, a fascinating man in his own right with a genius for designing and gardening. I have been fortunate to return to Marino on several occasions, and the magic always works. The house, built in the 1960s using old materials, looks as if it has been there for ever and feels remote from the pressures of the everyday world, though in the evening from the terrace you can see the floodlit dome of St Peter's.

It is a symptom of our time that Henze's sheer productivity has been used as ammunition against him, as if agonizing over one short piece is a greater guarantee of quality than writing ten. In an address I gave some years later in Munich, when Henze received the Siemens Prize, I said that while with many composers it feels like autumn, for Hans it is always spring. New buds are always bursting forth. He was not entirely pleased with my speech, which somehow failed to be a total eulogy, but his autobiography, *Bohemian Fifths*, deals frankly with the conflicting elements within his personality which have given friends concern and which go a long way to justify and explain what to me was the aberration of the Cuban years. I have always disliked trendy lefties, such as the members of the French Parti Socialiste Unifié, who, it was said, would arrive at the barricades in their Jaguars. I recall the BBC producer Peter Adam returning from Havana, festooned in Dior luggage, exclaiming, 'The revolution is wonderful!' I simply could not understand how a regime that imprisoned artists and legislated against homosexuality could be thought so admirable by homosexual artists. But the serious political face of Henze, as it appears in his musical manifesto *The Raft of the Medusa*, was both truthful and timely. One can never know how taste will evolve or how the art of today will appear in the future, but Henze is to me a major voice in the music of our time.

Much restored, I returned to London to face a totally new situation. For the first time in my life I had no obligations, no timetable and no demands on me. I could wake up in the morning and ask myself what I would like to do that day. Anything was possible, from staying in bed to going to Paris or to simply reading a book. But this state of affairs could not last, and my puritan side said it should not. Within a few weeks I had agreed to undertake an inquiry for the Arts Council on the need for a dance theatre in London, and within days I was locked into as heavy a schedule as ever. But it was a different kind of work, and one that I particularly enjoyed. During all the years of my membership of the Arts Council Dance Panel, the problem of where dance was to be performed had ranked high in our discussions. Sadler's Wells, the only receiving house in London which could be rented by national or visiting companies, had a tiny stage and a front of house hardly geared to the demands of the new world of sponsorship and corporate entertaining. There were a number of smaller spaces, like Riverside Studios, the Institute of Contemporary Arts and Battersea Arts Centre, but they were short of money, had limited facilities, and, because of their size, had little box-office potential. Even the Royal Opera House, like all horseshoe-shaped theatres, had a majority of seats with a restricted view of the stage, when ideally a straight-on view is needed to read the patterns of choreography.

Throughout the 1960s and '70s we had lived through what the Canadian critic Jan Murray christened the Dance Explosion. There had been a proliferation of small companies in Britain and a mass of new and exciting activity around the world, very little of which we saw here. The fact that the Merce Cunningham company's visit to Edinburgh in 1979 was their first British appearance in eleven years says something about the problem, while companies like Paul Taylor's or the Nederlands Dans Teater rejected Sadler's Wells as too small and were not offered the Coliseum or the Royal Opera House. The problem of access to adequate theatres was obvious, but no one had tried to quantify the need for better conditions. What made a good theatre for dance? How big should the stage be, and, for that matter, how big the auditorium? How much dance activity was available, and how big was the potential audience? It seemed obvious to me that the Royal Ballet would be able to perform much more often than they did if they had a theatre of their own. In the jargon of the times, they would then be better value for money.

Largely through my friendship with Peter Williams, Editor of *Dance and Dancers* and Chairman of the Arts Council's Dance Panel, I had got to know almost everyone on the British dance scene. Some, like Peter Wright, I had known since my televison years; others, such as Kenneth MacMillan, were more recent friends, but they all shared with me their anxiety about the future of dance without proper facilities. The modern-dance people were especially concerned, since they were having to perform in the more inadequate places.

I devised a questionnaire and went through it with over seventy people on the British dance scene, as well as asking a number of foreign companies to complete it. I was assisted in assessing the development potential of existing theatres by an enthusiastic architect, Nicholas Thompson, of the partnership RHWL, who, with an excellent assistant, provided the technical details of every building that was suggested or had been used, and of some that were our own idea. Everyone's preference was for a purpose-built theatre, but of what size? The larger companies all wanted not only a big stage – ideal for dance – but a big auditorium as well, to maximize their income. The smaller companies wanted just as big a stage, but – a combination never thought of in theatre design – a small auditorium linked to it. The model for many was the Théâtre de la Ville in Paris, which had only 1,200 seats but a huge stage. Everyone was convinced that the auditorium must be not curved but straight on – like the Theatre Royal Drury Lane, where the back of the circle is nearer the stage than the front of the Grand Tier at the Royal Opera House. The then Director of the Royal Ballet, Norman Morrice, pointed out that a dancer's face was unreadable beyond eighty feet, and ideally should be no more than sixty feet from the audience. At the Royal Opera House it was frequently well over a hundred.

We examined old cinemas occasionally used for stage performances, such as the Dominion and the Astoria, admired the marvellous sight-lines of the Coliseum, despite its daunting size and hopeless backstage conditions, and despaired of ever improving Sadler's Wells to make it really effective for dance, since it was built on such a narrow site. We were not even allowed to look at the Lyceum Theatre, since the GLC had granted Mecca a new lease to use it as a dance hall, but I had never been convinced of its long-term value except for musicals. After two months of inquiry the answer appeared to all of us to be Drury Lane, where, in addition to the splendid Grade I-listed foyers, the auditorium had a close and involving feel, the stage was the deepest in London, and behind it was a vast paint-frame workshop several hundred feet long, hardly ever used, inside which Nicholas Thompson proved you could build an 800-seat theatre for the smaller companies. The weeks of interview and discussion with everyone of importance on the dance scene reinforced my sense of their practicality and modest good sense. They live their lives in frequently dreadful conditions, but often manage to create great theatre. How much better could they do with up-to-date facilities? But two problems interposed themselves: first, the weakness of the Arts Council in embracing a positive policy which could convince the government of the need to spend on capital requirements as well as on annual grants, and, second, the depressing feeling that there was not enough money around nor enough high-quality dance to justify a theatre that presented nothing else. Audiences were slightly in decline. The bubble of the Dance Explosion had burst and I could not put my name to a report which failed to recognize this.

Lack of unanimity in the dance world was also a weakness. I presented the report to a packed meeting of dance representatives from all over the country at the Arts Council's headquarters in London. I met a mood of almost total hostility, culminating in a dance animateur from Humberside declaring that he had no interest at all in better provision in London, since life was so difficult in Hull. This seemed to me a classic example of myopia. The Arts Council had already embarked on its Chairman Sir William Rees-Mogg's *Glory of the Garden* report and a massive policy of devolution to the regions and the Regional Arts Associations. It was quite clear that the Greater London Arts Association was only going to get involved in small projects, with an understandable emphasis on ethnic minorities and experimental dance. As so often in Britain, the bigger picture was invisible, and the lack of leadership from the Arts Council or the government was palpable. I presented my report to the Council, most of whom seemed devoid of any professional understanding. Only Roy Strong of the Victoria & Albert Museum showed any real interest. I asked Rees-Mogg if they intended to cause something to happen or just sideline the debate. He shrugged his shoulders. I had listed a number of recommendations, of which the final one was 'On no account do nothing.' But nothing is precisely what they did.

Sixteen years later the National Lottery has seen the rebuilding of both the Royal Opera House and Sadler's Wells, while the Barbican Theatre and the Queen Elizabeth Hall have started to present dance. But the basic problems remain. It is still both difficult and expensive to bring a company into London, and, compared to most other European cities, the British public sees little of the international dance scene. The Paris Opéra Ballet has not been to London for more than twenty years, though most critics rate it the best in Europe. It took more than ten years of effort to get the outstanding Frankfurt Ballet of William Forsythe to London, or the brilliant but expensive Mark Morris company that had been seen so regularly in Edinburgh. I would worry less about the absence of the international component if British companies were better, but, except for Birmingham Royal Ballet, under both Peter Wright and his successor David Bintley, there is a dreary sense of repetitive programming, with constant revivals of full-length nineteenth-century classics by the Royal Ballet and English National Ballet and diminishing returns in their desperate attempts to find popular success with new works.

Surprisingly, despite some of the same problems, opera has thrived in this period, for it has had heavy backing from sponsors and a growing public to support it. Television, which now practically never looks at the big classical dance companies, has continued to televise opera, albeit often for reasons that have to do more with filling a hole in the catalogue of the video companies than with the quality of the work.

Yet ballet on television always used to attract larger audiences than opera, and the cost of opera far outruns that of dance. One area of dance that *has* flourished on television is the creation of small special-ly commissioned pieces. The several series of *Dance for the Camera* have revealed real ideas and new talents. The same kind of commit-ment by independent producers and Bob Lockyer at the BBC has ensured that the remarkable work of Lloyd Newson and his company DV8 has been recorded for television, winning a string of internation-al prizes into the bargain. But ballet as it used to be, regularly on tele-vision at Christmas or Easter, has as good as disappeared.

Unusually, I was paid to write the dance-house report – the first time the Arts Council had ever put money into the authorship of a report. The voluntary, unpaid, aspect of support for the arts in this country is often thought to be a healthy expression of citizenship and community involvement. In fact it produces weakness all along the line. It restricts membership of committees to those who can afford to take time off to attend, and it also limits authority since no one has ultimately to answer for policy as they would have to if they were part of a real Min-istry of Culture on the French or German model. I have never been able to understand why everyone expects to pay for legal or financial advice but thinks it is a good thing not to pay for comparable advice in the arts. The age of the well-off and knowledgeable enthusiast who can afford to donate his time is now largely over. When I joined the Arts Council, the chairmen of the music, opera and dance committees were, respectively, Lord Harewood, Simon Townley and Peter Williams – all men of independent means. If governments and local authorities want a true range of opinion and advice about the arts, they have to come to terms with the need to pay for it. Over the past twenty years I have given up months of my life to sit, totally unpaid, on boards, commit-tees, trusts and interview panels. But I fitted this around a salaried job in which I could schedule my work accordingly. Most full-time employees cannot do this, and it weakens the whole advisory system – particularly since the rich men who knew a lot have been replaced by people who may be rich but who know very little. You have only to look at the recent history of the Royal Opera House to see what hap-pens when you appoint people who know nothing but nevertheless think they own the place and can dictate policy.

My departure from Edinburgh led to a string of invitations to join boards and committees. Where I felt there was real work to be done, I agreed – though sometimes saying, 'Use my name, but please don't ask for time or money'. But committee work is for me ultimately frustrating, especially since I have actually run things and want action rather than endless talking around the alternatives. One organization which did prove useful, however, was the National Dance Co-ordinating Committee, which I founded and chaired for nine years, initially as an informal group of artistic directors, but later as a useful element in dance coordination, administered by the Touring Department of the Arts Council. It tried to bring dance companies closer together and give them a stronger collective voice. But many committees were absolutely useless, and first among that number I would count that for the Theatre Museum.

With our great theatrical tradition, a museum of theatre would seem an obvious national requirement. But, when eventually the various disparate collections were brought together under the aegis of the V&A, the Museum was established in quite the wrong building, with no funds to run a programme of exhibitions. Without sponsorship, nothing could be done, and the mandarins of the V&A had not only no interest in the place, but a dismissive attitude to what they considered ephemera. The Theatre Museum contains several million objects, from costumes to stage designs, from play texts to personal effects, but it needs the eye of a brilliant exhibition designer – with a budget – to animate it. I sat for years on the board, while successive directors of the V&A – Sir Roy Strong, Dame Elizabeth Esteve-Coll and Alan Borg – found good reason not to fund it. It was at one stage suggested that the main floor should be rented out to Andrew Lloyd Webber's Really Useful Group, so as to raise money for exhibitions. It was grotesque. At least three members of the Theatre Museum Committee on which I sat were millionaires, but their purses remained closed. Why join if you do not intend to help? An attempt to break away from the V&A and establish the Museum independently failed for lack of funds and will. And what incentive is there to work for an institution like this when Westminster City Council says you cannot even put a sign up saying 'The Theatre Museum' outside? I have often had reservations about Ministries of Culture, but I have even more now about the flabby bureaucratic weakness of the British system, divided between institutions like the Arts Council and local authorities with different priorities. The problem is that running arts organizations has very little to do with democracy. You need a very healthy dose of executive authority.

Diaghilev would never have achieved anything in today's world.

The 1980s were a troubled time for both the Arts Council and the British Council, working against the background of Margaret Thatcher's dislike of subsidy and all politicians' suspicion of the role of the arts. In the case of the British Council, the Arts Division had never had more than about 12 per cent of the total budget, and was increasingly unable to fund our great national companies to travel abroad. Small companies like Cheek by Jowl did splendid work, but was that all we were able to show the world? With enormous difficulty, funds were found to take the Royal Shakespeare Company to Poland and the Royal National Theatre to Russia in the 1980s, but these tours were very much exceptions. Alongside successive director-generals of the Council, I tried to persuade the politicians that the British Council was not about teaching Morris dancing to the natives, but a valuable contribution to our influence in the world. They were mostly unimpressed. Even the huge educational influence of the Council, through its language courses and its libraries, was downgraded by smug Treasury officials and frequent cuts, paralleled by the inexplicable parsimony of government to the World Service of the BBC. Government went on about Britain's importance in the eyes of the world, while other countries – notably France and Germany – put money where their mouths were and spent on culture as well as on trade shows, stealing the ground from under our feet.

I remember an acidulous lunch at the British Council during the directorship of the admirable Sir John Burgh – another of those refugees from Nazism who has contributed so much to his adopted country. The guests were members of the Conservative backbench 1922 Committee, and they droned on about satellite broadcasting as a substitute for language courses and about the irrelevance of art. Michael Kustow, then at Channel 4, and I sat in gloomy silence until I could restrain myself no longer. 'While pointless conversations like this are going on in London,' I said, 'France is taking over as the main influence on culture in Africa, South America and South-East Asia.' They looked offended, but John Burgh observed quietly that throughout Uraguay's recent history English had been the country's official second language, but the previous month the government had opted for French instead. Burgh's trenchant criticism of government policy had already resulted in his being denied the chairmanship of the Trustees of the Tate Gallery – a typically shabby piece of petty revenge.

So many good people in the arts and education were manifestly, in Mrs Thatcher's phrase, 'not one of us'. I remember Lord Hesketh, a junior minister, telling me that we had better get used to Thatcherite culture, for that was where the future lay. But when I asked him what it was, I got no intelligible answer. Speaking out as John Burgh or Peter Hall did was widely reported, but in the long run probably achieved less than they hoped. But at least those of us who expressed our dislike of the situation had a clear conscience. We were not placemen or courtiers. The people for whom I felt a lack of affection were those who climbed on the bandwagon, as Melvyn Bragg and David Puttnam have done more recently with the Blair government. Over the years, in different parts of the world, I have worked with politicians of every persuasion from the extreme Right to the extreme Left without, I think, losing my independence. In H. L. Mencken's immortal phrase, 'Never accept a free lunch or a free ride and you will find shaving in the morning a positive pleasure.'

Meanwhile I was spending more time with friends and rediscovering England. Bob Lockyer made a splendid film about Elisabeth Frink – someone I had known for years but rather lost touch with. As a result of Bob's film, Lis and her third husband, Alex Csaky, took to inviting us to Dorset for the weekend. In the almost secret valley below Bulbarrow Down where they lived, I discovered another place like Henze's Marino which refreshed the spirit – but in a quite different way. While Marino meant silence and contemplation, Woolland was full of dogs, bustle and the pop of champagne corks. The whole valley was peopled with Lis's sculpture – horses, dogs, wild boars and running men glimpsed through trees against the Dorset skyline. It was quite magical.

I loved Lis, with her Roman profile, frizzy hair, gravelly voice and huge, capable hands. I last saw her a few weeks before her death in 1993, when she was still working on the great figure of Christ for Liverpool's Anglican Cathedral. Alex was already in hospital, not to return. Lis and I crunched across the garden, stiff with the hardest frost of the winter, and drank a last bottle of champagne. I gave the address at her memorial service in Salisbury Cathedral – an honour and a challenge which I only just got through. As I get older, the tears come more readily, though, like John Gielgud, I have always been prone.

There was also time to see the Wise Men. Denys Lasdun taught me so much about the presence of architecture and its superhuman power, and through David Sylvester, archpriest of critics and master of exhibition design, I learnt that, if one is to have a chance of really seeing and understanding art, the spaces between pictures matter as much as the pictures themselves. Denis Forman invited me to work for Granada and produce his longed-for series on the history of music. Though I did not accept, I found it easy to admire a commercial-television tycoon who had also written a book on Mozart piano concertos. Then there were Arnold Goodman, Pat Gibson and Kenneth Robinson, all three former chairmen of the Arts Council who, unlike Rees-Mogg, had a clear understanding of what the Council was for. In their time the organization was geared to saying yes to ideas and innovation, unlike the negativism forced on it today by a mixture of political correctness and the sheer inadequacy of the people who run it.

All these people seemed to see some quality in me that they thought worth encouraging, which did much to alleviate my own uncertainties and to sharpen my attitudes. I found these older men more thoughtful and more generous than most of my contemporaries. In public life you learn to accept the fact that, rightly or wrongly, many people dislike you, and there is little point in worrying about it. But all of us would like to earn the respect of people we admire. In this, as in many other things, I was extremely fortunate.

Regular invitations to lecture, address organizations, preside over graduation ceremonies and so on forced me to be much clearer in my mind about those things in which I believed. I had decided from early on to speak impromptu, even though it meant that I risked losing the thread or, as sometimes at press conferences, omitting important things. But I felt people responded better to enthusiastic talk than to less risky prepared readings. My growing sense of confidence in what I felt was matched by my increasing reluctance to go along with that very English feeling that it is bad form to show emotion, impatience or dislike for the terms of the discussion. In this, as in many other things, I sensed my Australian half coming to the fore.

More time also gave me more opportunities to write, especially for that much lamented weekly the *Listener*. Its Literary Editor, Derwent May, became a friend and sent me a wonderfully eclectic list of books to review. Unburdened by a full-time job, I found not only that writing became a pleasure but that I now did it better than when I had *had* to write dozens of short things to promote broadcasting or the Edinburgh Festival. It was at this time that, renewing my passport, I rather cheekily changed my occupation from Television Executive to Writer.

I needed a new passport because I was determined to travel, even though I was hardly in a position to afford it. Despite all my journeys on behalf of Edinburgh, I had never visited India, South America or most of Africa, and I thought this might be the time. But I was getting old for travelling rough, and also getting less pleasure from travelling alone. But I did want to spend more time in Australia, and I decided to go to Adelaide in February for the 1984 Festival. Both *The Times* and the BBC asked me to review various events in what looked like an excellent programme. Looking back, I think there was a real question in my mind as to whether my future lay in the United Kingdom. I was sick of the problems that surrounded arts organizations here, and felt that new stimuli from elsewhere might have a rejuvenating effect. Above all, I wanted to find out more about my other country, Australia.

I realized immediately how very like Edinburgh the Adelaide Festival was, with a mixed programme covering all the arts and also a very healthy Fringe – and many of the same disputes and rivalries. The sheer quality of the companies and individuals that Adelaide attracts puts it on the short list of the world's major festivals; indeed, it is the only one of any real consequence in the southern hemisphere. Australians regard Adelaide itself rather as we do Cheltenham or Bath: as an attractive, civilized place, but without much energy. But at festival time it becomes a hub of frenetic activity and real enjoyment.

Among the exhibitions in 1984 was one devoted to the wardrobe and memorabilia of Dame Edna Everage. I went to the official opening, performed by the Dame herself in full fig. I knew Barry Humphries only slightly, but we shared a deep affection for John Betjeman. Noticing me in the crowd, he asked a gallery attendant to bring me round to see him. Sitting back with his stockinged legs on the table, drinking a cup of tea between engagements, he asked me if I had news of John, who was in hospital and likely to die at any moment. He said he had talked to Kingsley Amis, who had been going to the hospital to read to John, and wondered if I had been in touch with Elizabeth Cavendish. All this was a normal part of our shared concern for a much loved friend. But, though he can apparently do the voice when wearing male clothes, he cannot stop using the voice when got up as Edna, and I found it quite intolerable to be talking about the imminent death of one of my most cherished friends with this shrieking virago. I have always had more than a soft spot for Dame Edna, since she bears a dangerous resemblance to my mother's sister, but in these circumstances she was too much and I excused myself apologetically. John Betjeman died the next day.

Despite this disconcerting moment, Adelaide was hugely enjoyable. It was a novel experience to have no responsibilities other than to attend performances and do a fair amount of partying. I came under real pressure to accept the directorship of the Festival in one of the coming years, and I actually was interviewed for the 1988 Festival – in the Australian Bicentenary year – but negotiations broke down over salary and conditions.

The 1988 Festival was eventually directed by Lord Harewood, who shares my love for Australia and, through his wife, identifies closely with the country, but I came to feel that the Festival should really be directed by Australians, and since 1988 it has gone in that direction. For too long Australian arts institutions were run by expatriate Britons or Americans, and not always the best. It is surely the right thing for Australia to bring on its own people, using people like George Harewood or myself only as advisers if need be. One of the real attractions of Australia is that, unlike the UK, you feel it is a country which has more future than past. Though often bad-tempered in its debates, it does very much avoid the world-weary British attitude that the arts are to be admired but not really supported.

It was while I was in Adelaide that I received a phone call from Alasdair Milne, now Director-General of the BBC. He wanted to know how long I was away for, and asked me to come and see him on my return. He was not specific, but he hinted at changes that might interest me. I was flattered, but not really attracted. I was certain, above all, that I did not want to return to Television. But it turned out that it was not Television that he wanted to discuss. Back at Broadcasting House, he told me that the Controller of Music, Robert Ponsonby, was due to retire the following year and that he, Milne, was looking for a successor.

The job of Controller of Music seemed to me in most ways an inappropriate one. It had always gone to qualified musicians rather than to people who were professionally involved in broadcasting. But events a few years earlier had radically altered the Controller's role. As a result of some well-meaning but half-baked plans put forward by Aubrey Singer, brought from Television to run Radio, there had been a Musicians' Union-led official strike which caused the beginning of the 1980 Proms season to be abandoned. Broadcasting House was picketed by famous musicians, and Ponsonby courageously joined the ranks of the protestors. The plans had involved getting rid of the BBC's light-music orchestras, the training orchestra in Bristol and, more controversially, the BBC Scottish Symphony Orchestra. The situation was sorted out by Arnold Goodman, representing the Union, and the BBC backed down on some of its proposals. The long-term casualty was Robert Ponsonby's relationship with the Corporation. Almost as a punishment, a new element – the Radio 3 Music Department – was created, working directly to the Controller of Radio 3 and taking all programme responsibility away from the Controller of Music. It had always been a messy situation, with two controllers serving the same network, one providing music programmes but with no control over their scheduling, while the other had to put together a schedule consisting for over 80 per cent of the time of music, about which he knew nothing. Only a herbivorous organization like the BBC would have tolerated such a confusing and illogical situation. Ponsonby post-strike was left with responsibility for the BBC's orchestras and the Proms. Otherwise, music programmes were agreed directly between the Radio 3 Music Department and the Radio 3 Controller. There was a total separation of operation, and even of the buildings the two groups occupied.

When I had left the BBC for Edinburgh, Milne had discussed with me the possibility of my eventually becoming Controller of Radio 3 – a job for which I think I had real qualifications and in which I was keenly interested. Neither Stephen Hearst, when Controller of Radio 3, nor his successor, Ian MacIntyre, who had been shunted over from Radio 4, had achieved a good working relationship with Ponsonby, and the results were in my opinion damaging. How would it be, I asked Milne, if the two Controller jobs were merged?

In common with most television executives, Milne had little real interest in or feeling for radio and was, I thought, unaware of the tensions within Radio 3. He agreed to think about changes, and we planned to meet again a few weeks later. Meanwhile I checked Ponsonby's age in *Who's Who* and found that he would not reach retiring age until late 1986 – over two years away. I relayed this to Milne, but he had meanwhile already seen Ponsonby and told him he was to go in 1985. The BBC has always denied this part of the story, but I am sure it is true.

Milne and I had a further meeting, which also involved my old friend Dick Francis, a General Trainee of the same year as myself, who was now Managing Director of BBC Radio. He was sceptical about whether the two Controller jobs could be done by one person, and had a regard for MacIntyre which I did not feel Milne shared. As a result, I was formally offered the Controller of Music post from November 1985, but with no extension of responsibilities to get back the broadcasting elements that had been shifted away. After a few days of reflection, I declined. Of course I longed to direct the Proms, but I was certain that the situation with Radio 3 would become a permanent problem. I went away to America, and then to Italy and France.

In the late summer Milne again asked me to see him. He made no promises – I am categorical about that – but he said he would keep the Radio 3 situation under review. Would I trust him to do that? By now my money was running out, there were no other real jobs in the offing, and, even with the new limitations, it was quite something to be asked to take on a post once filled by William Glock, whom I had so much admired as Controller of Music. I was sure that, since I did not have a music degree, my appointment would be strongly disapproved of by the Radio 3 music producers, but I suspected that the orchestras and the profession might feel differently. So, very much following the advice of friends like Robin Scott and Denis Forman, I agreed to take a chance on it. But I told Milne that there might be rocks ahead and that I hoped he would continue to keep the Radio 3 situation in mind.

I ran into Huw Wheldon at a party a few days later and told him that I was going back to the BBC. 'Completely misguided, absolutely wrong!' he cried. I observed that, during the more than twenty years we had known each other, he had never missed a chance to reprove me. 'Indeed yes,' he answered. 'You are one of nature's reprovees!' He rang me up a few days later and asked me to lunch, but I was not free. I never saw him again, for he died a month or so later.

As I expected, the announcement of my appointment, in November 1984, received a mixed response. Nicholas Kenyon, then writing for *The Times* but having written the history of the BBC Symphony Orchestra with considerable BBC experience behind him, speculated on how I would fit into the broadcasting hierarchy, having been so much my own man in Edinburgh. It was a good question, and one I asked myself. I hardly knew MacIntyre, and did not believe Milne to be a strong Director-General. Nevertheless, I had agreed to return to the BBC in February 1985 and to wait in the wings until Ponsonby's retirement in November.

I undertook to write a confidential review of the whole position of music in the BBC, especially as Milne wanted my responsibilities to include music on television as well as radio. I was allocated an attic room in the old Langham Hotel, then almost entirely emptied of BBC staff, and I sat there for eight months, with Asa Briggs writing the history of the BBC in the next office as my only neighbour. I had the services of one of those amazing women who had for so many years been the backbone of the Corporation. Monica Atkinson had been in the organization all her life, latterly as assistant to senior controllers, including Stephen Hearst. She knew everyone and how to get hold of things. In two days she furnished an office with everything I needed, from chairs to a CD player – not neglecting the permitted quantity of curtains and the content of the drinks cabinet, both officially graded according to the job. (Previously, as an Assistant Head of Department, I had curtains that would not draw.) Monica became a great friend, and was typical of a BBC now totally lost. Her husband worked in the Engineering Division, her son in Data. She loved the place and all its oddities, and helped me avoid a hundred elephant traps with a cheerful 'Let me call Maisie', or Harry, or whoever it was. She always had a way around any problem and an answer to any question, and, unlike anyone in Birt's BBC, she enjoyed her job.

I set about meeting people. MacIntyre generously gave two drinks parties for me to meet the Radio 3 staff, very few of whom I knew. Most of the old guard had retired, and there was a mass of young producers brought in by the Head of the Radio 3 Music Department, Christine Hardwick, who before the strike had been in charge of the Gramophone Department. There was an air of palpable hostility from many of the producers, but there were also one or two friends. I knew Hardwick quite well already, and was sure that we could find a way of working together. I asked permission to interview her department, one at a time, for half an hour or more each, and over the next two months I saw all of them.

I also visited the regions, to see the music producers there and to meet the orchestras and their staff – who, in the way of the BBC, were quite separate. The senior producer in Birmingham asked me pointedly whose Controller did I think I was – the orchestras', London's, or perhaps even the regions'? It was hard to see how I could be the BBC's Controller, since the bulk of the musical output had precious little to do with me, while the regional producers worked to their local bosses.

In the national regions of Wales and Scotland there was a permanent feeling of incipient UDI and resentment of London. I sensed that I risked being a generalized figurehead who would be appealed to when help was needed and ignored when it was not. Nevertheless, I promised to spend more time in the regions than my predecessors had done and to try to represent everyone at least as far as standards went, which was very much within my remit.

The report I wrote – *The BBC and Music* – underlined problems which ranged from poorly paid orchestral musicians to indistinct lines of communication and Television's total hostility to anyone from Radio having any say about anything. My appointment as Controller coincided with Alan Yentob, a former General Trainee under me in the 1970s, becoming Head of Music and Arts in Television. I knew him well – and knew how little he knew about music. We had several meetings, and things were fine as long as I went along with his ideas. But there were inevitable differences. Knowing so little, how could he decide, for instance, what operas should be televised? I was also concerned about the BBC's standard contract with its musicians, which was full of exclusion zones. Neither gramophone recording sessions nor television appearances could happen except on the orchestras' free days. They were not part of the basic contract. Nothing, it seemed to me, had been looked at systematically for years and years, while a series of petty restrictions and obstacles had grown up which made resources on which the BBC was spending millions of pounds a year much less useful than they ought to have been.

John Pritchard, then Chief Conductor of the BBC Symphony Orchestra, was, not surprisingly, pleased with my appointment. But he had a string of grievances to air, especially about the inadequacies of the Maida Vale studio where the orchestra was based. During the spring and summer of 1985 I built up a dossier of problems and challenges, and then embarked on an extensive European-festival tour, since I knew that from then on the Proms would prevent me from going to Bayreuth, Salzburg, Edinburgh or Pesaro. Salzburg memorably made me pay for my seats, whereas in the past they had always provided complimentaries. When I asked why the change, the Festival President's secretary replied with a smile, 'Well you're no longer in Edinburgh, and not yet *en poste* at the BBC', and handed me a bill for the equivalent of £400. At Bayreuth I saw the last year of Peter Hall's production of the *Ring*, which by then had settled down. Although nothing like as imaginative as the great Patrice Chéreau centenary cycle, it was still impressive in its more literal response to Wagner's intentions. The atmosphere at Bayreuth is very much to my liking, with its seriousness and attention to musical detail. It is a pleasure to be a part of an appreciative and knowledgeable audience – so unlike Salzburg, where the foyer fashion parade seems to count for more than the productions. Yet after both of them I longed for the informality of the Proms.

During these months I had hardly any contact with Ponsonby. Eventually I rang him and requested a meeting. He kept me waiting for a quarter of an hour in a scruffy little ante-room in Yalding House. I said I had heard that he rightly resented the conditions of his departure, but assured him that they were nothing to do with me. I said I was also sure he did not approve of my appointment. He denied this strongly, but said he could not imagine how I could possibly do the job without previous experience of orchestral management. He, after Edinburgh, had for some years been Manager of the Scottish National Orchestra. I bit my lip. What I wanted to say was that *I* could not see how the job could be done effectively without experience of broadcasting and the ways of the BBC, and I had over twenty years of that. But there would have been no point.

It was quite clear to me that MacIntyre, through his minions – notably his press officer – was working against me. I hated his supercilious manner at meetings, and could not admire his habit of sending biting personal memos to people with copies distributed all over the organization. He was capable of great charm and was by no means unintelligent, but he seemed to be in a permanent war against all but his close circle – which did not, with the possible exception of Christine Hardwick, involve music. It was not a happy time for me, for Ponsonby or, with hindsight, for MacIntyre, who had certainly got wind of the possibility of a subtext to my appointment. Long handover periods are always a big mistake and, despite the opportunity mine gave me to identify problems and meet the extensive staff, I was as much relieved as apprehensive when I finally took over in November.

But even that nearly didn't happen. In the preceding week a series of cuts was imposed on Radio 3. MacIntyre made sure that the bulk of them were in areas for which I was responsible, such as the Music Library and the BBC Symphony Orchestra management. A considerable number of posts were to be forfeited. I begged for a stay of execution, to give me time to assess what *I* felt were the needs of the situation. An uneasy compromise was achieved. The BBC management announced the number of posts that would go, but not which they were. This made certain that I took over an unhappy and extremely nervous ship. Not for the first or the last time, I wondered why I had accepted Milne's offer. Then I remembered the Proms. I was certain that, whatever happened about Radio 3, the Proms would provide one of the great challenges, opportunities and pleasures of my life.

# 13

# Controller without Control

The first impression I had on becoming Controller of Music was of how very little back-up or support there was for the job. There was a post of chief assistant, which Ponsonby had filled a few months earlier with someone whom I had indicated would not have been my choice. While the regional orchestras and the BBC Singers each had a producer attached to them, the BBC Symphony Orchestra did not, although there was a curious outfit called Concerts Division which worked with the Controller and had a link to the orchestra. The BBC Symphony Orchestra's Concerts Manager, Anthony Sargent, helped devise concert programmes, but did not produce the broadcasts. This was left to two studio managers, who were not on my payroll and behaved with considerable grandeur, one of them writing long dissertations on acoustics. They knew their job as recording engineers, but where did the radio programmes come from? Who generated them? The words spoken seemed to come from something in the back room, called the Music Information Index. This collated existing material about individual works and, on demand, provided a script which was then passed to another department, Presentation, where an announcer with no previous connection with the material would read it. The regional orchestras sold their programmes directly to the network through Christine Hardwick; the Controller of Music was involved only in contractual matters or conductor appointments – except for regional orchestras' appearances in the Proms. Is it any wonder that there was a lack of cohesion and of commitment in the broadcasting of the output of the orchestras?

It was quite hard to find any cohesion in the planning of the Proms either. Ponsonby had had a kind of committee for both the BBC Symphony Orchestra and the Proms, with a considerable number of people gathering in his office and making suggestions. Otherwise, he had worked with the door closed and, as with the BBC Symphony Orchestra, there was no coordinating producer responsible for broadcasting the Proms. I tried for over a year to make this system work, but it was always impossible to achieve any change in areas that related to broadcasting. My remit, it was pointed out, was to decide what music was played, and where. I realized that I would do much better by concentrating on the orchestras themselves – how they were run and, more especially, who was to conduct them. That at least was in my sphere of operations.

The BBC Symphony Orchestra demanded the most time and energy, but even that created problems, since the regional orchestras in Manchester, Wales and Scotland felt that the Controller was interested not in all the orchestral forces but in only one. Just like Yentob and the Television Music Department, they welcomed support but resisted any criticism or suggestion that things might be done differently. There was a further problem in the attitude of the Radio 3 Music Department to the orchestral output. As Christine Hardwick put it in one of our conversations, 'I am not interested in hearing the BBC Welsh Symphony Orchestra play Beethoven.'

Ironically, that was the one thing that BBC Television *was* interested in. The Principal Guest Conductor of the BBC Welsh Symphony Orchestra, Mariss Jansons, conducted the whole cycle of Beethoven symphonies on TV – paid for, it must be said, not by BBC2 or Alan Yentob, but by BBC Wales, who chose to make music programmes as part of their devolved output. These programmes came to the Controller of BBC2 free – a deal masterminded by me some years earlier, when I ran the performance slot on BBC2. That is why the BBC Welsh Symphony Orchestra appeared so often on television. It caused great resentment among the other orchestras, who never appeared on TV but, in the way of orchestras, believed themselves to be better. A national region can to a great extent deploy its funds where it sees an advantage. Wales chose music on TV.

The 1980 strike had left the BBC Scottish Symphony Orchestra in a weak position. It had been reduced in size, with a resulting limitation on the range of music it could perform, but it was fiercely led by the composer Martin Dalby, who persuaded the Controller of BBC Scotland to invest money in rebuilding the orchestral studio at Broadcasting House in Glasgow.

There was energy and ambition in Cardiff and Glasgow, but there was little evidence of a similar spirit in Manchester, where the BBC Philharmonic had become the seemingly independent fief of a senior music producer, himself a would-be conductor, and of its Principal

Conductor, Edward Downes, who, despite his huge repertory and considerable talents, failed to excite much interest on the British music scene.

Three orchestras and three different kinds of problem. But they were as nothing compared to those of the BBC Symphony Orchestra in London. I was extremely happy to have inherited John Pritchard as Chief Conductor, although ill health and overwork had greatly undermined his musical determination and sapped his vitality. A new Principal Guest Conductor, David Atherton, had just begun a three-year contract. While JP was a close friend, I hardly knew Atherton, but he came to see me to say he was sick of conducting new music, with which he had made his name at the London Sinfonietta, and wished to avoid new scores entirely. Since one of the main functions of the BBC Symphony Orchestra is to perform new music, this seemed to me to augur badly for an effective collaboration. His repertory of non-twentieth-century music was extremely small, but there was at least some – which was not the case with the other guest conductor, Peter Eötvös. The earliest music on his repertory list was Debussy's *L'Après-midi d'un faune*. In twentieth-century scores he was masterly, but he had no public recognition. Günter Wand, the other main guest conductor, came only twice a year and it was quite clear that he would conduct only nineteenth-century repertory – and not much of that.

When I asked Robert Ponsonby why Pritchard conducted so relatively rarely, he said it was a jolly good thing since he was so expensive. I found this surprising, because by international standards it was hardly true. In fact Pritchard, being also Music Director of the opera houses of Cologne, Brussels and San Francisco, had hardly a day without being either in an aeroplane or on the podium. The orchestra depended too much on guest conductors. Before my time both Charles Mackerras and Mark Elder had had contract posts but had not been thought successful. Foreign conductors of any stature were either very expensive or committed exclusively to other orchestras in Great Britain, especially the four major ones based in London.

What, indeed, was the role of the BBC Symphony Orchestra outside the Proms, whose backbone they had provided since their foundation in 1930? In the situation I inherited, they made occasional foreign tours, which had to be entirely financially self-supporting, and performed in a number of regional towns in England, although it seemed to me that the list of these – Bedford, Southend, Slough – was much less significant than might be expected for an orchestra that under Adrian Boult, Pierre Boulez and Colin Davis had been thought one of Europe's best. There was in the music profession a hostility to the BBC orchestras, notably from the Association of British Orchestras, an organization of which the BBC was itself a member. Some orchestral managers, such as Clive Smart of the Hallé, conducted an unremitting campaign against the BBC orchestras performing in public. Why should they not stick to studio recordings and invitation concerts? This view was shared by Ian MacIntyre, the Controller of Radio 3.

It was, of course, unthinkable if you wanted a great orchestra that it should be confined to the wretched Maida Vale studio, with a maximum audience capacity of a few hundred. But it was also evident that the kind of programmes that Glock, Ponsonby and I all thought necessary drew very small audiences in the Royal Festival Hall or the Barbican, while regional audiences were even more conservative. Though all the major European broadcasting organizations have their own orchestras, few of them are considered among the best. Kubelik and his successors at the Bavarian Radio Symphony Orchestra in Munich consistently overshadowed the Munich Philharmonic, and the North German Radio Orchestra in Hamburg with Tennstedt or Wand outplayed the Hamburg Philharmonic, but elsewhere the situation was quite different. One reason why radio orchestras have rarely achieved the eminence of, say, the Vienna, Berlin or Amsterdam orchestras is that all radio orchestras are required to programme a very wide range of music, especially that of the twentieth century, and rarely play it more than once. The luxury that Simon Rattle had in Birmingham of performing the same programmes four or five times – good for the orchestra, their conductor and their joint relationship – was largely denied to a radio orchestra except when on tour. But the need to broadcast most dates from a tour within a limited period meant that Radio 3 would then be lumbered with four or five performances of the same programme, differing only in that each was played in a different hall – not the main concern of the radio listener.

The need for a big repertory also affects the availability of conductors for radio orchestras. Most top conductors have a relatively small repertory which they have made their own. As they get older and more in demand, this repertory usually shrinks. Wand had conducted everything, notably Messiaen, when young, but now it was only to be Mozart, Schubert, Brahms and Bruckner. However outstanding he might be with these, this limited his value to a broadcasting organization. Christine Hardwick, who had previously run the Gramophone Department, would wish to broadcast the best available performance of a work, from whatever source; hence her attitude to the Welsh orchestra and Beethoven. Although the BBC's orchestras needed to reflect the whole range of orchestral music of both the past and the present, the paying public in the hall had more limited interests. There was, and still is, therefore, a permanent three-way tug of war between the public and its expectations, the BBC and its broadcasting function, and the orchestras and their conductors. I do not know how this can be resolved.

I am, nevertheless, absolutely convinced of the importance of radio orchestras in the total picture of British musical life. It is undoubtedly true that by abandoning its orchestras the BBC could save money, in the same way that hiring a taxi costs less than running a car. But it would severely limit the BBC's freedom of operations. When I looked in my first year at the collective output of the four BBC symphony orchestras and compared it to what was available elsewhere, especially in London, it was immediately clear that we could not have offered the radio listener anything like the same choice if the BBC's own orchestras had not existed. Yet this argument – Reithian and aspirational – sat increasingly uncomfortably in a changing BBC into which management consultants were being inserted by a hostile government and a willing BBC board.

The Governors of the BBC had little understanding of anything to do with music and, apart from the Proms, really took no interest. They had the same attitude to other areas of the BBC's resources, such as the remarkable and immensely valuable Music Library. 'Why is it needed?' one governor asked me. 'I thought musicians played from memory.' It was against that kind of background that I set about trying to explain to the BBC itself, then to the world outside, why the BBC's orchestras and resources mattered, and why their cost should be considered as an investment in a world where the BBC's contribution had brought about radical changes of perception. If you seek to know why Britain is no longer thought of as '*das Land ohne Musik*', then the existence of the BBC and its huge investment in the performance and dissemination of music must be seen as key elements.

In addition to any broadcasting staff, the orchestras also had management teams, similar but less numerous than those of the commercial orchestras. But, whereas other orchestras had gone in the direction of sponsorship, subscription concerts and marketing, BBC structures were basically as they had been for the previous forty years. There was a general manager, responsible for personnel and overall activity, an orchestral manager, who arranged the schedule of rehearsals and performances, and assistants to roster the players, look after instruments and facilities, and liaise with libraries and publishers.

In London there was once again a complete physical separation between the BBC Symphony Orchestra at Maida Vale, the Controller of Music at Yalding House and the producers at Broadcasting House. In the regions their equivalents inhabited the same building and often had closer understanding simply through physical proximity. In London no one ever met or saw a member of the BBC Symphony Orchestra unless they went to Maida Vale, and I cannot remember a single occasion when the Managing Director of BBC Radio, let alone the Director-General, visited Maida Vale – except once when there was a threat to close it down. Marmaduke Hussey, after nine years as Chairman of the BBC, did not know where Maida Vale was when he decided to visit it only because his friend Georg Solti was quite exceptionally rehearsing the BBC Philharmonic there. I remember being present on one occasion when Lady Solti spoke dismissively of the BBC Symphony Orchestra. This was at a time when Solti had convinced Margaret Thatcher that London needed only one orchestra – provided it was conducted by him.

Studio 1 at Maida Vale – a converted roller-skating rink – had been home to the BBC Symphony Orchestra since the 1930s, except during their wartime evacuation to Bedford. It was, and still is, quite the wrong shape, with a low ceiling which makes it virtually impossible for the conductor and the players to hear what is going on. The management offices are two hundred yards away, at the other end of the building, and the conductor's room – a subterranean burrow – would disgrace a local radio station. Through all the years I was Controller, I conducted a permanent campaign to have the place rebuilt and upgraded. At one point in 1991 agreement seemed attainable, owing to a brilliant development plan devised by Nicholas Thompson, with whom I had worked on the dance-house report, but the BBC's nerve failed at the last moment and the Director-General, Michael Checkland, struck the scheme out of the budget. Yet when I approached Simon Rattle to see whether we could involve him in any way with the BBC Symphony

Orchestra, it was the inadequacy of Maida Vale that was a major element in his refusal. It was a typical British situation: no one at the top knew enough to care, and no one seemed to trust the message from the people who did know. Eventually, all I could achieve was a redecoration which got rid of the submarine government green and brown paint and brought a bit of light and colour to the place. But the studio still had a lowering effect on morale, which certainly affected musical standards.

But I am jumping ahead. My first task was to decide which of the posts that had to be sacrificed were in the orchestral management team and which in the supporting services of the library, with its copyists, binders and clerks, or the Concerts Division or the Music Information Index, a constantly growing archive whose cost was increasingly controversial and whose value I questioned. My lack of managerial experience with orchestras, which Ponsonby had commented on, made it hard to evaluate what was needed. In the event, every area lost some of its staff in the kind of equal inflicting of misery that disaffects everyone and rarely sorts out the problems. I was very much dependent for advice on the General Manager of the BBC Symphony Orchestra, the well-respected Bill Relton. Relton – a long-time administrator, with a high reputation as an adjudicator in the brass-band movement – was at least friendly and, it seemed, helpful. I found most of the others suspicious and, understandably, fearful for their jobs. Time and again, as in Edinburgh, the answer to questions was 'We've never done that' or 'That's not the way it works.' There were so many no-go areas.

The co-principal system in the BBC Symphony Orchestra, introduced to give the orchestra access to a wider range of top players, seemed to me to work entirely to the advantage of the players rather than the orchestra. Conductors' requirements came a poor second. While the orchestral management tried to give conductors a stable group, particularly of key players, things often went wrong and I had irate conductors on the telephone asking why the principal oboe or the principal cello was not there on that day, as they had requested. As to the two leaders, Rodney Friend and Bela Dekany – both distinguished and able men – they had complete freedom to pick and choose concerts at will. Friend usually led for Pritchard and Dekany always for Wand, but in other cases one never knew who would lead and could not control it. There were many fine players in the BBC SO – some of whom had been there for ever, like Alan Civil, the principal horn, and Colin

Bradbury, the principal clarinet – but there was very little feeling of community, of their being friends and colleagues. The full-time contract attracted some players, especially those with families who were nervous about the merry-go-round of freelance life, but the low salaries kept away many experienced men and women and increased the proportion of young players, who were often very talented but lacked the years of collective experience which tend to produce a great sound. What the orchestra needed above all was a dynamic music director, and, for all his great qualities and profound musicianship, dynamic leadership was not within JP's grasp at this stage of his career. This was the more frustrating in that he had put together a totally new orchestra for the Théâtre Royale de la Monnaie in Brussels with marvellous results. But the employment conditions and established practices of the BBC impeded a similar rejuvenation at Maida Vale, and – importantly – he was not there often enough.

My first hint of the real scale of the problem came when I went with the agent Howard Hartog to Paris to see Pierre Boulez and firm up a list of planned concerts with the BBC Symphony Orchestra in the coming years. He cancelled everything, claiming that, having just passed his sixtieth birthday, he must limit his conducting activity and devote himself almost entirely to composition. I felt a real sense of betrayal from someone whose work and music I had always strongly supported. Eventually, however, when relations were partly restored, it emerged that the change of personnel had been so great that he felt he knew no one in the orchestra and could not rely on them for the quickness of response or the commitment that he had enjoyed during his years as Chief Conductor. Christoph von Dohnányi, whom I brought in two or three times in my first year, with his characteristic brutality of manner put his feet on the table and said, 'I don't know if this orchestra has a music director, but he certainly has some work to do.' Dohnányi knew perfectly well that it was Pritchard's orchestra, and that Pritchard was in failing strength and spirits. I had been seriously considering Dohnányi as Pritchard's successor, but his appointment in Cleveland intervened and I knew I would only ever get a small amount of his time, even if he liked the orchestra, which it was clear he did not.

My first executive decision, even before taking over, had been to extend JP's contract for two more years. This was done partly out of friendship and affection, but also to buy me time. I was conscious that I would make few more important decisions than the choice of the next

Chief Conductor. Remembering how short Colin Davis's term had been – a little over three years, after which he had left to run Covent Garden – I wondered how he might feel about a return to the BBC, now he was nearing the end of his Royal Opera House contract. We had a curious courtship, since Davis was convinced that I should take over as General Director of the Royal Opera House following John Tooley's retirement, scheduled for 1988. For several months the ball went to and fro, with Davis and his wife even coming to dinner at Broadcasting House with the new Director-General, Michael Checkland, who enthusiastically supported my idea. In the end Davis said no. I found out later that the key to his decision was advice from William Glock, who had said one should never return to old ground.

Meanwhile, in the midst of all the challenges, Bill Relton decided to take early retirement – or so he claimed. I was somewhat surprised when, a few weeks after leaving, he accepted a job running the Eastern Authorities Music Board, which programmed concerts for all those towns on the eastern side of England which had no resident resources. His number two at the BBC was a former Philharmonia Orchestra violinist whom I had taken to immediately, Lawrie Lea. Running orchestras – especially difficult ones like the BBC Symphony Orchestra – is a game for tough guys or thugs, and Lea was certainly no thug. In fact Robert Ponsonby warned me that Lea was not the strongest of men either in health or in temperament. Nevertheless, I promoted him, and found him a positive pleasure to work with, but it was true that he had a tendency to worry about things in a way that might not make the job as rewarding for him as his presence was reassuring for me.

Another departure was that of Anthony Sargent, the Concerts Manager, an idiosyncratic creature known for wearing Doctor Scholl sandals, even at La Scala when we went to see Berio, for sending faxes at three in the morning, and for having on one occasion booked two distinguished baritones for the same concert. His leaving to be the cultural boss of the City of Birmingham gave me an opportunity to achieve the structure I required. I persuaded my superiors that it was essential to create two new posts: a producer for the BBC Symphony Orchestra, to be responsible for all aspects of their concert and broadcasting work, and a producer to coordinate the Proms, since there was really no one with an overview except the splendid planning assistant, Jacky Kohn, and me. And I had a number of other preoccupations.

In 1985 I had taken part in a conference run by the Association of

Professional Composers, the more forward-looking of the two organizations that represent British compositional talent. The APC had among its members almost all the British composers whose work interested me and whom I wished to commission. At the conference, I was impressed by the intervention of a young man who worked for the British Music Information Centre, a useful sorting house for those with an interest in British music. His name was Roger Wright, and at his suggestion we subsequently lunched together. I was not only struck by his knowledge but taken with his personality. When we advertised the BBC Symphony Orchestra job he applied, and he seemed to me head and shoulders above the competition. He and Lawrie Lea became great friends, and for the three years we worked together he made a real contribution. It did not surprise me that, after a spell in Cleveland and then at Deutsche Grammophon, he returned to the BBC in charge of the orchestras, and now has my former job as Controller. In addition to his real ability he has a splendid sense of humour – always an advantage in any large organization.

Despite the presence of a considerable number of admirable people, the Players' Committee of the BBC Symphony Orchestra always seemed to attract the awkward squad, while the Musicians' Union representative saw his role as one of permanent opposition to any innovation or change. I had often been in contact with the Union, which was also in a state of flux. Some of the old guard, who had fought worthwhile battles for many years, had now ossified into a permanent negative stance. I believed in the need for the Union and wanted good relations with it, but I wanted constructive dialogue – which need not mean getting my own way all the time, but should at least allow for discussion of long-running issues. The BBC was, and still is, the biggest employer of musicians in the country, yet the activity of its employees was ringed around with restrictions and barriers which made it hard to make headway in the modern world. It was, for instance, ludicrous that the BBC SO was barely represented on disc. A totally inadequate internal department, BBC Records, had little or no interest in classical music, and very little money, and when I took over there was only one available CD – a recording made by Pritchard of Scriabin's Third Symphony, hardly likely to be a best-seller. Union regulations and contract clauses made it virtually impossible to issue the work of the BBC orchestras on disc – something available to all the German broadcasting orchestras. Günter Wand's work with the Frankfurt Radio Symphony Orchestra, although much less distinguished than that with the BBC Symphony Orchestra twenty years later, was being released on CD. It was extremely galling. Television, as I have indicated, was hardly possible except for live relays from the Proms. There were restrictions on the broadcasting of recorded concerts that seemed to me no business at all of anyone except the BBC. Why did all concerts from a tour have to be broadcast within thirty days? It seemed to me that, since the basic contract between the BBC and its own musicians had been devised for Adrian Boult in the 1930s, little had changed except for the addition of dozens of small side clauses, all of which were in some way intended to prevent unfair treatment, but which collectively had come to impede the maximum usefulness of an investment costing millions of pounds a year.

I set myself the task of completely reviewing the standard contract. The renegotiation with the Union and the orchestras took just over four years, and was probably the most important single contribution I made as Controller of Music. I was backed throughout by Michael Checkland, even though he realized that it would result in considerably increased expenditure by the BBC. I was helpfully assisted by the Head of Contracts, Jeremy Hill, who had many years of experience and proved a great deal more flexible than I had been led to expect. The increased remuneration that resulted from renegotiation gave the BBC access to better players, and the abolition of restrictions on recording resulted in greater visibility. The long list of CDs now available is much more representative of the range and quality of all the BBC's orchestras.

My other success was the appointment of Andrew Davis as Chief Conductor. As I have indicated, he was not my first choice, and after the withdrawal of Colin Davis I spent nearly a year pursuing Esa-Pekka Salonen, to the point of his conducting the opening concert of the 1988 Proms. But his London roots were with the Philharmonia. Like Boulez, he is also a composer, and he already had a radio orchestra in Stockholm. I admire him greatly and was not surprised that he had Boulez's backing, but I was seeking someone who actually wanted the job, rather than someone who had to be reluctantly persuaded. The BBC Symphony Orchestra post does not pay all that well, but at its best it gives a conductor considerable freedom to follow his tastes and his ambitions – a rare thing in music anywhere today.

I had known Andrew Davis since his early beginnings, and had watched him with choirs, in the opera house, with orchestras and with

contemporary-music groups like the London Sinfonietta. He had conducted most of the great American orchestras – Chicago, Cleveland,
New York – but rather fewer in Europe. He had all the talents, but,
despite the security offered by more than ten years as Principal Conductor in Toronto, he did not seem to be maturing in a way that excited people. He brought the Toronto Symphony Orchestra to the 1986
Proms, following an invitation from Robert Ponsonby. I found the
results pretty dull, yet I knew him to be capable of much better work,
especially with the Berg *Three Pieces for Orchestra*, with which he had
opened my last Edinburgh Festival. His manager told me that Davis
was intending to leave Toronto but had no fixed plans. He was in discussion with one of the less prestigious German radio orchestras, and
had some vaguely developed opera plans. I wondered how large he
wanted opera to figure in his career. He seemed to have most of the
desirable qualities, but I had a reservation about his drive. Some of his
work had seemed to me routine in a way that reminded me of other
gifted British conductors like Charles Groves and Alexander Gibson –
people who seemed to need a high hedge to jump to produce exceptional results. I wanted exceptional results as a matter of course.

We arranged for Davis to work with the BBC Symphony Orchestra
for a month, with a carefully chosen repertory which would include
two Royal Festival Hall concerts, some studio recordings and a popular Christmas special on the South Bank. The results were immediate
and electric. After the first concert, Rodney Friend asked me if I had
plans for Davis. Even the normally grouchy Players' Committee sent
word that they hoped he was on my list. We met and talked at length.
He was the right age, had the right ideas, was willing to undertake new
repertory as well as a wide range of older music, and – not necessarily
an important factor, but nevertheless useful – he was British and would
not flinch at the Last Night of the Proms. Some of his predecessors,
including Boulez and Rozhdestvensky, had always ducked out of that.
I was confident of being able to work with Davis. I have never regretted his appointment, but I have to say that his accepting the music
directorship of Glyndebourne at almost the same time was something I
could have done without. Since the Glyndebourne season and the
Proms fell during the same time of year, this created a real planning
headache if he was not to have his attention fatally divided between the
two. How was he ever to have a summer break? In the long run he
managed to cope, but not without a great deal of rejigging of rehears-

al schedules and performance dates, trying not to keep him in perpetual motion between Sussex and Maida Vale.

Davis is a fine musician and an easy colleague, yet even after several years I found it hard to get him to say what he really wanted to do. He would, like Pritchard before him, accept most suggestions – even to the point of accompanying the piano roll of Percy Grainger playing the Grieg Piano Concerto on the Last Night in Australia's bicentennial year. But it was rare for him to have ideas himself. After one of JP's least impressive performances – of a little-known and, for me, not very exciting piece by the American composer Roger Sessions – I asked him why he had programmed it, since he admitted that he had not much admired it. He replied, 'Because Ponsonby asked me.' I begged him never to accept pieces he did not believe in, because I or anyone else suggested it. Andrew Davis was similarly willing to undertake most things, even some of the most difficult and challenging new works, but I didn't always feel the sense of commitment that so characterized his work in the opera house. Yet, considering the many different and sometimes conflicting qualities that the BBC Symphony Orchestra job demands, few people could have fulfilled them as conscientiously as he did over what stretched to a ten-year tenure. But I suspect that his new position at the Lyric Opera in Chicago is something he cares about more deeply.

The other conductor appointments I made at the BBC Symphony Orchestra were all, in different ways, unsuccessful. The brilliant but capricious Oliver Knussen accepted a post as Guest Conductor, but withdrew almost before he began, struggling, as he still does, to balance the demands of composition, teaching and conducting, at all of which he has outstanding ability. He finds it hard to commit, and leaves behind a trail of cancellations and unwritten music which saddens me greatly – and he is getting too old to rely on charm and apologies. I had high hopes of the young German conductor Lothar Zagrosek, despite the reservations of some of my colleagues. I found it hard to understand why the orchestra, who claimed to like him personally, rarely delivered their best for him. Then one night on tour in Madrid I sat on the platform and watched him from the front, and at once saw the problem. He never acknowledged what the players did for him. Most conductors respond to what has just been done, with a nod, a smile or some simple gesture of recognition, while continuing to shape what is coming up. Zagrosek never relaxed, and his nervousness made the players nervous too. My other appointee, the Russian conductor Alexander Lazarev, was still more curious. A conductor of manifest brilliance, he achieved stunning performances with orchestras in Bournemouth and Glasgow, both less good than the BBC Symphony Orchestra, but never seemed to achieve the same results in London. Like all Russian conductors, with the exception of Rozhdestvensky and Valery Gergiev, Lazarev had little real interest in new music, and he also gave me a long list of great names from the past whose music he did not wish to conduct. Making programmes was therefore difficult, and he found the orchestra hard to control, since, despite his excellent English, they mistook his very Russian sense of irony for superciliousness.

The chemistry between orchestra and conductor is hard to analyse. Why did Simon Rattle have problems with the Concertgebouw? Why should the Vienna Philharmonic like Muti or Bernstein – two men so far outside the Viennese tradition? Some orchestras go their own way regardless of who is conducting. Some put their skills at the complete disposal of a conductor they trust. Some simply do not concentrate. I used to despair at the shambling way the BBC Symphony Orchestra entered on to the platform for a concert, with a visible lack of focus or determination to succeed. In rehearsal they talked or walked about, always suggesting it was the conductor's job to convince them rather than the other way round. They complained endlessly about Wand, but stood up when he entered the studio. They hated Rozhdestvensky for his laziness and refusal to rehearse, but greeted him with shouts of acclamation when he returned. With the exception of Andrew Davis, whose honeymoon lasted for years, the BBC SO approved only of conductors from their past or those not yet appointed. I had hoped to have a great deal of shared enjoyment but in many ways my relationship with them was one of the least satisfying of my career.

Despite every effort, audiences at their public concerts remained pathetically small, and personal relations were bumpy to the point of hostility. A gruelling Russian tour in midwinter with an ailing Pritchard and a tired and emotional Yuri Temirkanov culminated in a member of the orchestra telling me I was a 'fucking cunt' and one of the principal players shouting drunken abuse both at me and at John Tusa, who was travelling with us as Managing Director of the World Service. My years with the BBC Symphony Orchestra did nothing to dim my love for composers, conductors, soloists or music, but I have no desire ever again to be involved in the day-to-day life of orchestras, who seem always to look on the black side and carry complaining to the highest level of art. As a special gesture, to give them a good send-off on what was to be a long European tour, the BBC SO were once put up in a five-star hotel in Brussels. I asked a group of players how things were going. 'Dreadful,' they said. 'We had to wait three minutes for the lift.'

Because I was never so close to the other orchestras, my relations with them seemed less troubled. I was determined to find ways of augmenting the BBC Scottish Symphony Orchestra so as to give them a fairer chance of competing both in Scotland and on the radio. Reduced size had limited them to a diet of Haydn, Mozart and smaller-scale twentieth-century music. Their Chief Conductor, Jerzy Maksymiuk, was at home in this repertory. I knew him well, since I had invited his brilliant Polish Chamber Orchestra to the Edinburgh Festival. He is the only person I know who, after many years spent in Glasgow, seems to speak English less well today than when he arrived. But he has a kind of demonic energy and is a thoroughly nice man. Successive BBC controllers in Scotland saw the orchestra as a plus, and gradually both its size and its quality rose. Today, in Osmo Vänskä, it has one of the most exciting new talents in European music at the helm. It has successfully resisted a plan to be merged with the orchestra of Scottish Opera. There is certainly a problem with orchestral provision in Scotland, but that never seemed to me the way to resolve it. I opposed it when I was Controller, and as Director of the Proms I only reluctantly endorsed it when it seemed the chosen way forward, which made me very unpopular with the orchestra. The threat receded, but London's ignorance of the national importance to Scotland of the BBC SSO will always make them vulnerable.

The BBC Welsh Symphony Orchestra were in a different position from the others. They are the only orchestra in Wales, and are partly funded by the Welsh Arts Council and, to a much smaller extent, by the Welsh-language television channel S4C. Their public role grew in importance after the opening of St David's Hall in Cardiff. They were lucky to have had Mariss Jansons for a while, at just the right moment in his career, and they reinforced their position under the Japanese conductor Tadaaki Otaka. But their natural prickliness made the Welsh hard to deal with. At European Broadcasting Union meetings they would sit at a separate table from the BBC delegation, and the eventual Head of Music in Wales, Huw Tregelles Williams, was a political operator of a kind I personally found unattractive, although he may well have raised the orchestra's profile. An unsuccessful attempt was made to bypass me over a proposed change of the orchestra's name. The Welsh Controller wanted to call it the National Orchestra of Wales, with no mention of the BBC, and intended to put it to the BBC Governors without any prior discussion. The eventual choice, after my time, of BBC National Orchestra of Wales was an ungainly compromise, but the idea that the BBC's own Welsh managers should propose dropping all acknowledgement of the orchestra's main funding source and broadcasting role was an extreme example of the tendency towards UDI which always bubbled under the surface in Cardiff and was regularly fuelled by Tregelles Williams. It seemed to amuse him to be difficult.

Administratively, the real problem lay in Manchester, at the BBC Philharmonic, an extremely important element in the performing of British music, and the workhorse of the BBC's orchestras. Internal relations there were appalling. Shortly after I returned to the BBC I went to Manchester to hear Edward Downes conduct Berlioz's *Romeo and Juliet* in the Free Trade Hall. The then Head of Music in Manchester, David Ellis, gave a supper party afterwards for me to get to know Downes better. After the concert I ran into the orchestra's producer, Peter Marchbank, and asked if he was coming with us. 'I have more important things to do than have supper with David Ellis,' was his reply. Marchbank had studied conducting under Boult and had strong views about the conductor's role, hating anything that suggested showmanship. Apart from Downes, the orchestra was saddled with a string of guest conductors like Bernhard Klee and Günter Herbig – solid, reliable musicians, but hardly exhilarating. I once said to Klee after a performance of Zemlinsky's *Lyric Symphony*, 'I really do love that music.' He replied glacially, 'I love my children. I quite like Zemlinsky.' Most of the BBC Philharmonic's performances sounded as if the conductors *quite liked* music.

Downes had an amazing repertory, more than twelve foolscap pages of everything from the eighteenth to the twentieth century, but he seemed most at home with unknown figures like Reinhold Glière, whose symphonies he recorded, or with what I considered the duller end of British music, like George Lloyd. In the wider context of the BBC's national role, it could be seen as part of our job to programme composers like Lloyd, but time and again the BBC Philharmonic under Downes opted for those parts of the repertory that I personally found less than stimulating. David Ellis left, through a combination of illness and conflict, and a troubled interregnum followed during which I was aware that none of the Manchester music staff were on speaking terms with each other. It was also quite apparent that Marchbank was bad-mouthing me to Downes, and, despite regular attempts, I never really got on friendly terms with Downes. Eventually we brought Trevor Green, former Manager of the BBC Scottish Symphony Orchestra, back from Australia as Head of Music, and, after a long period of attrition, both Marchbank and Downes also left.

Green had energy and drive and real ambitions for the orchestra. As Principal Conductor we appointed Yan Pascal Tortelier, the son of the cellist, who had done very good work in Ulster and with the Royal Liverpool Philharmonic Orchestra, and the excellent Brian Pigeon moved from Liverpool to become senior producer. The BBC Philharmonic today seem to me to be the best-run and the most positive of the BBC's orchestras, and I continue to have close relations with them. Now, following Green's return to Australia, they have recruited an excellent senior producer from Wales, Mike George, to programme them, and there is a real feeling of a team, a body of men and women with shared aims benefiting from the new Bridgewater Hall in Manchester. The mood is strikingly different from the depressing story of the Hallé in recent years.

By the time I left, I was really confident about the role and quality of all the BBC's regional orchestras, and was able to reflect that confidence in the challenge and the number of programmes I could offer them in the Proms. I never succeeded in spending as much time in the regions as I had intended. It was extremely difficult to get the Heads of Music or senior producers together for meetings, whether in London or, as I had initiated, in the regional centres: Glasgow, Cardiff and Manchester. But I don't think that any of them could have claimed that I was merely Controller to the BBC Symphony Orchestra.

The extent to which the BBC broadcast the music of non-BBC orchestras was not in my remit – at least to begin with – but a quota system of the same number of broadcasts from each of the major London orchestras, which had worked quite well for years, was under considerable threat from rising costs and the emergence of a multiplicity of new groups – chamber orchestras in Scotland, Newcastle and Bournemouth, and also the orchestras of the early-music movement, which were making huge inroads into eighteenth-century repertory and drawing big audiences. Some conductors, such as Roger Norrington, worked happily with the BBC's orchestras as well as their own groups, but if musical fashion was dictating that a Mozart symphony could no longer be played by the BBC Symphony Orchestra, and only just by the BBC Scottish, there were problems ahead. And behind it all was a debate not only about style and repertory, but also about funding.

There were several reports on the orchestral situation, particularly in London, where I greatly resented the constant claim that there were only four symphony orchestras: the London Symphony Orchestra, the London Philharmonic Orchestra, the Royal Philharmonic Orchestra and the Philharmonia Orchestra. I did not see how the Arts Council could overlook the role of the BBC Symphony Orchestra. I had hoped, when Nicholas Snowman was appointed to run the South Bank Centre, that things would improve. They did not. Snowman, who constantly talked about the need for more ambitious and adventurous programmes, never came to any of the adventurous programmes given by the BBC Symphony Orchestra, except on the increasingly rare occasions when they were conducted by his former boss in Paris, Pierre Boulez. He would occasionally suggest that we needed help in marketing, which was certainly true, but at the coordinating meetings at which the BBC Symphony Orchestra was represented there was no sense of our being central to his thinking.

We had much better relations with the Barbican. Robert Ponsonby had daringly programmed a festival of Stockhausen there, just after my appointment. I attended most of it, and found the hall unexpectedly but gratifyingly full for most of the events. The idea of presenting an annual weekend of the music of a major contemporary figure at the Barbican grew from that, and the credit for the idea must lie entirely with Ponsonby. Each January we devoted a concentrated period to, in turn, Berio, Birtwistle, Boulez and Henze. None was as well attended as the Stockhausen Festival, but Henze was surprisingly more successful than the others. They all represented real challenges of programming, and especially of rehearsal, while giving audiences at the Barbican and on Radio 3 a chance to hear a wide variety of a composer's output in a short period of time. Only the BBC can risk doing that. Other orchestras have mounted successful seasons of contemporary composers, as the Philharmonia did with Ligeti and Lutosławski, but spread over a much longer period. I suppose there are not that many people who are prepared really to work at something difficult and largely unknown, but the fact that even a few hundred live or a few thousand on the radio *did* take up the challenge reinforced my belief that we needed not less but more of this kind of planning. It has been a real disappointment to me that, since my departure, the January weekends have been entirely devoted to dead composers like Hindemith or Martinů, who may interest some people but lack the daring of Ponsonby's original plan.

The most trusted of my colleagues in all this was the Editor of Contemporary Music, Stephen Plaistow. An excellent pianist and a fine all-round musician, it was he who held the reins of the commissioning policy. The sums available were small – only £50,000 a year when I started. Although the amount increased quite a bit in my time, it still represented only a tiny fraction of the millions the BBC spent on music. Yet its importance was out of all proportion to its size. Plaistow was a skilful diplomat and fielded the constant demands of the third-rate with tact and subtlety, as well as seeking out the best of the young figures emerging on the scene. There were literally hundreds of people each year seeking BBC commissions, and we were probably never able to programme more than about twenty-five. Scotland and Wales had their own lists of composers – a great advantage to a young Scottish composer, though the lack of outstanding new talent in Wales was, and remains, a problem. The really difficult cases were those composers who had received BBC commissions in the past, some as long ago as the 1950s, but whose music had not established itself and who were still writing to us. One composer in particular bombarded my office with scores, letters and demands for meetings, but seemed to have no talent whatsoever. He had, I suppose, once seemed promising. Now there were many others who not only had seemed it, but had justified the BBC's earlier investment.

We tried to keep a balance, and Plaistow and I never had a real disagreement. I depended greatly on his judgement, and later on that of his successor, the excellent Andrew Kurowski. My own response to new music is more instinctive than rational. I may find it hard to follow, let alone read, some of the most complex modern scores, but I have a keen sense of whether a composer has something to say. What we could offer someone of real promise was their first chance to write for a big orchestra. The funding situation and the lack of interest in new music mean that most new music that gets performed is written for small groups. While there is nothing wrong with the concentration of ideas that this can present, there comes a time when a composer needs to tackle a bigger canvas and a bigger challenge. This is what I tried to allow, especially with Prom commissions. The results were, of course, mixed. There is no formula for success, but it seemed to my mind more important to give a Young Turk like Simon Holt his first orchestral commission than to return yet again, as Wales did, to established figures such as William Mathias and Alun Hoddinott. I once cattily said that the Welsh scene was dominated by Mount Mathias in the north and Mount Hoddinott in the south, and they had both already been climbed.

The overall picture with composers in the 1980s was of lots of new people, new ideas and new aspirations. I doubt whether there has ever been a period with so much talent around, and we tried to reflect as much of it as we could. I was especially keen not to overlook composers of ability whose music I did not find immediately attractive. There are those like Brian Ferneyhough whose music I simply cannot understand, though I recognize the support given him by my colleagues, but there are also others like Robin Holloway whose music provides no barriers to understanding but which I simply cannot get on with. My own tastes are extremely eclectic, but I came back again and again to those whom I felt had found a real voice and whose music was showing growing confidence and achievement with each work. Commissioning is a bit of a bran tub, but I was adamant, and my view was shared by Plaistow and Kurowski, that it should not be a case of Buggins's turn coming round to old so and so who hadn't had anything for a while.

When it came to major international figures, who commanded very high commission fees, it seemed better with our limited resources to try to secure British premières. This worked well, particularly with Lutosławski, whom I came to admire both personally and musically above all other major European figures. There was a quality of mind at work which, combined with his enchanting personality, with its very Polish charm and exquisite mannners, made all encounters with him a delight, whether musical or social. I really loved him, and he responded by giving the BBC Symphony Orchestra the British premières of his Piano Concerto and Fourth Symphony and the world première of the song cycle *Chante fleurs et chante fables*.

A vital link in our dealings with composers were the music publishers and their hard-working and long-suffering promotional staff. There were a number of remarkable women and a few men who represented many of the major British and international figures and became friends – especially Sheila McCrindle at Chester Music, Janis Susskind at Boosey & Hawkes and Sally Groves at Schott.

Sheila McCrindle was one of the most entertaining people I have known, trudging about from concert to concert, from festival to festival, promoting composers with unflagging enthusiasm. Unusually, she was as supportive of composers whom she did not represent, like Richard Rodney Bennett and Hugh Wood, as she was of those whom she did, like Robert Saxton, John Tavener and Lutosławski. She was at her best with the trustees of the estate of Lord Berners, as eccentric a band as the composer himself. She mocked them in private, but with great affection. She was a repository of splendid gossip, and the origin of innumerable bad jokes. She took to writing regularly to my London home with dotty messages, often inside ludicrously addressed envelopes which must have been as surprising to my postman as they were entertaining to me. She once sent me an Albanian railway timetable with the terse comment 'Perhaps this will help you remember!' Behind the jokes, she was both serious and seriously sad, with years of poor health and a mass of unfulfilled ambitions. I will never forget the warmth and tenderness of her protective relationship with Lutosławski and his equally lovable wife, who, after the composer's death, tidied his papers, cleared up everything in their apartment in Warsaw, and silently faded away. A terrible testimony to true love. Sheila's death, only a couple of years later, was followed by a commemorative concert in the Guildhall School which was not only moving but extremely funny – just as she would have wished.

My constant link to Hans Werner Henze was through Sally Groves at Schott, who never failed to keep me abreast of developments in his work and even withstood my lack of enthusiastic endorsement for her protégé Steve Martland. It was through Janis Susskind at Boosey & Hawkes that I got to know and appreciate the marvellous mind of Elliott Carter and to renew my struggle to understand his music. Among the men, Bill Colleran at Universal Edition became a real friend and adviser, representing not only the glories of the Second Viennese School but also my own particular enthusiasm, Harrison Birtwistle, whose *Earth Dances* was certainly the most important BBC commission to be completed in my time. None of these people earned much, but they never faltered in their belief in new music.

Sometimes it was even possible for us to help them. I had learnt of the early work of James MacMillan in Scotland and found it highly intriguing. I asked him to visit me. At that time no note of his music had been heard outside Scotland and he had no publisher. He is a fascinating mixture of old-fashioned socialism and very modern commitment, a devout Catholic and a devoted family man. The directness and modesty of his ways were most attractive. I resolved to commission a piece, and was more than rewarded by *The Confession of Isobel Gowdie*, which won an ovation at the 1990 Proms. A few days after our first meeting a depressed Bill Colleran told me that one of his brightest young hopes had left him for another publisher. I suggested he take a look at MacMillan; he did, and took him on. The combination of having a publisher and a Prom commission changed MacMillan's life. He continues to interest me in all that he does, and I only wish I saw him more often.

But commissions can lose you friends as well as make them, and this was sadly the case with my contemporary Nicholas Maw, whom I had known for ages and much admired. When I returned to the BBC, I knew that he had been struggling for many years to complete a vast orchestral score and had eventually put it to one side. I asked him if he wanted to take it up again and if the BBC could perhaps commission it. He agreed, and the saga of *Odyssey* began. The complete score arrived several months late and over half as long again as we had expected. There was a problem in preparing the orchestral parts and with the conductor Mark Elder's conviction that he had insufficient time to learn it thoroughly. I offered Maw a number of alternatives: to postpone the performance for a year, to withdraw from the project entirely, or to give a partial performance. Without any hesitation, he opted for a partial performance – of four of the seven projected movements. I pressed him hard so as to be certain that this was really what he wished, but he was adamant and we went ahead. The partial performance took place, very successfully, but I was lambasted by every critic in town for my failure to support the composer's intentions. The following year we scheduled a complete performance at the Royal Festival Hall and made it the centrepiece of a whole day of Radio 3 devoted to Maw and his music, but the speculation about the earlier partial performance continued. Maw never spoke to me of it again, and never acknowledged our support. *Odyssey* has subsequently been taken up by Simon Rattle, recorded by the City of Birmingham Symphony Orchestra, and hailed as a masterpiece, having 'triumphantly survived the dreadful treatment given it by the BBC'. I fear the situation still rankles all round and, despite its success, I find the piece overlong.

But this was a unique case. The opportunity to commission was in so many other ways a real joy, and it will be posterity's task to see which of the many pieces that resulted win a place in future concert programmes. It was apparent from the first moment of its première that the BBC commission from John Tavener of *The Protecting Veil* would be a success. Despite its many performances and several recordings, I still find it one of Tavener's weaker pieces, but it certainly gives pleasure.

I will continue for as long as I can in trying to understand the compositional process and to find opportunities to promote it. When I think of the uphill struggle of people like Sheila McCrindle, even in promoting a great composer like Lutosławski, I feel I can take little credit for something that was easy to do with the funds and the patronage at my disposal. Every time I am foxed by a new work, I remind myself of the seemingly impenetrable difficulties of the Bartók quartets when I first heard them in my teenage years, and my certainty that such music would never catch on. But time passes, the mind absorbs and adjusts, and the problems of yesterday become the mainstream of the present. How depressing it is that so few musicians feel a commitment to the music of their own time! I can respect Brendel, who goes to hear new music regularly even if he does not play it, but I have less time for the many who don't even bother to explore it or, even worse, who perform it out of a sense of dreary duty. Of course not everything new is good. But how can we know what is without the chance to hear it? And how much of that chance would there be without the BBC? Yet in a world increasingly hell-bent on maximizing audiences, even at the expense of quality, presenting new music was becoming an increasingly uphill task. It is, however, one of the main justifications of the BBC and its licence fee. If the BBC just does what the others do, why should it have the advantage of its special funding?

One of the benefits I felt on my return to the BBC after eight years away was that I knew the people who ran the place. Paul Fox in Television and Dick Francis in Radio were old friends. Even some of the newer faces who had been with ITV, like Michael Grade and Brian Wenham, the Controllers of BBC1 and BBC2, had become friends through their visits to Edinburgh for the Television Conference. Wenham, in particular, spent more time with us at concerts or the opera than he did with his colleagues discussing the state of TV. It was in Edinburgh that I had also met the new Chairman of the BBC, Stuart Young, brother of the Tory cabinet minister David Young. Sadly, Young died after only eighteen months in the job and was replaced in 1986 by Marmaduke Hussey. I was on holiday in France when I heard of Hussey's appointment, and wondered if I was the only person in the BBC who knew him, since we had both sat for years on the Drama and Dance Panel of the British Council. In that setting we had usually been on the same side in our efforts to maximize the effects of the pathetically small budgets the Council had for promoting British companies abroad. Yet he seemed a curiously anachronistic figure, and I was not by any means enthusiastic about his appointment.

Chairmen impact relatively little on the life of most BBC staff, but, largely through my involvement with architecture, I had in the 1970s become very friendly with Young's predecessor, George Howard, of Castle Howard. Howard, a truly eighteenth-century figure with his bulky girth and bald head, was a wild card, useful on a board but an improbable chairman. He had taken to inviting me to his London home or to Castle Howard, and I greatly enjoyed his baroque company. He would ring and say, 'What are you doing on Sunday?' I would tentatively ask what he had in mind. 'Why not come on the river with some actresses,' he once growled. 'Which actresses?' I asked. 'Claire Bloom and Lee Remick. Good enough for you?' He kept an exquisite launch, all teak and brass, moored on the Thames at Windsor, and we would consume huge quantities of Coronation Chicken and vintage champagne with his youngest son cycling along the towpath from Eton to join us for lunch. Claire, who was to become a good friend, sat in the bows in a big hat trailing a hand in the water. It was very unlike ordinary life in the 1970s. One night I went to a party in Ennismore Mews and was confronted by the Chairman of the BBC sitting on a sofa between the Director-General, Ian Trethowan, and the Home Secretary, William Whitelaw, both of whom were wearing dark-grey three-piece suits with gold watch-chains. Howard was in a turquoise kaftan with a rope of amber beads to the knee. Also present were Jeremy Irons, Penelope Keith and other well-known faces. He was a constant surprise.

Once in Venice during the Italia Prize competition he gave a dinner at Cipriani's Locanda on Torcello for the BBC delegation. Finding I was there on holiday, he generously asked me to join them. It was during my Edinburgh years, and I had not been confronted by the massed ranks of BBC Television for some time. Aubrey Singer had thoughtfully arranged for the cathedral to be open before the dinner. The Television executives trooped in dutifully. None of them had ever been there before or knew anything of its history, and I found myself conducting a guided tour, explaining the relationship between Torcello and Venice. Bill Cotton, Controller of BBC1 and former Head of Light Entertainment, listened and then said, 'I suppose it was rather like Television Centre in relation to Kensington House.' It got a laugh, but reinforced my feeling that television people have no other world than television, and can neither appreciate nor discuss anything else.

Hussey had no experience of broadcasting or public service and showed little aptitude to grasp their at times infuriating but often admirable intentions and values. Knowing I knew him, people would ask me if he was quite as dim as he seemed. Although he claimed not to know the Prime Minister, Margaret Thatcher, and that his appointment was a surprise, we had little doubt that, having been used by Rupert Murdoch to sort out the union problems at Times Newspapers, he had not been brought into the BBC to encourage its independence. All governments, of whatever persuasion, really want a Ministry of Propaganda that they can control, and the air at that time was heavy with antagonism to the BBC: to the manner in which it was funded and to its refusal to be merely a mouthpiece for the government as the French and Italian state broadcasters were. David Young, Norman Tebbit and Thatcher herself radiated hostility, while creepy little horrors like Woodrow Wyatt in the wings did all they could to undermine us. I spent a weekend with friends in a house in Northamptonshire where Wyatt and his wife were also guests. He talked endlessly of the 'traitors' who were running the BBC. He was so grotesque that I could never understand why anyone thought him worth listening to. In the event it was probably only the presence of the much more balanced Douglas Hurd at the Home Office that prevented Thatcher from bringing the whole BBC edifice down, as she would certainly have wished. It was clear that Hussey would have a tricky time politically, even though he was certainly in Thatcher's terms 'one of us'. But he never became one of us at the BBC. When in 1967 Harold Wilson brought Charles Hill, the former Radio Doctor, over from being Chairman of the Independent Broadcasting Authority to become Chairman of the BBC, it became clear that Hill had a kind of Pauline conversion. To Wilson's irritation, he became a staunch supporter of both the licence fee and the BBC's editorial independence. Hussey resisted a similar conversion.

Alasdair Milne in his memoirs, *DG*, alludes to a failed attempt to persuade the Governors of the need for certain changes. I learnt later that this referred to the idea we had discussed of merging the jobs of Controller of Music and Controller of Radio 3. But his timing was bad, and the Governors were not interested. Shortly after, Hussey peremptorily sacked Milne – between a Governors' meeting and the subsequent lunch – and there followed a hiatus during which no one really had any idea who might succeed him. It became known that Hussey was backing David Dimbleby, a familiar figure to the audience and an experienced broadcaster but perhaps more significantly in this connection the proprietor of a newspaper which was totally non-unionized.

The interview board for the Director-General happened to be held on the day that Humphrey Burton was giving a rather splendid party at Leighton House to celebrate his wife's fiftieth birthday. Brian Wenham, a candidate for the job, turned up late at the party and rather the worse for wear, and none of us thought that he, with his detached and sardonic manner, could have been the choice, despite his wide experience of both television and radio. In the end the job went, very surprisingly, to the former Chief Accountant of BBC Television, Alasdair Milne's deputy, Michael Checkland – a man without any direct experience of making programmes. Previous director-generals had all had programme experience of one kind of another, from Ian Trethowan's political reportage to Charles Curran's work for the World Service at Bush House and Milne's editorship of *Tonight*.

I knew Checkland well from my Television days and liked him very much. On my return to the BBC he had been extremely helpful to me on a project on which I had set my heart. Michael Tippett's vast cantata *The Mask of Time* had been premièred in Boston by Colin Davis, and subsequently Andrew Davis had performed it with a splendid cast at the Royal Festival Hall in London. We had made a digital recording of the concert with an eye to issuing it on gramophone records, but the costs were very high since everyone had to be paid large supplementary fees – including, of course, the members of the BBC Symphony Orchestra. I had little success in finding the money. Tippett was unimpressed by this, and at a reception in Bristol following the award of an honorary doctorate to Pierre Boulez he had chided me for lack of will. 'Come on, John, come on,' he said. I went to see Checkland, who asked how much I needed. As Deputy Director-General, he had some funds available for special projects. I told him the missing sum was £42,000. He agreed without demur, and it was the foundation of a relationship that moved quickly into friendship and which served me well in my time as Controller.

Many people have written Checkland off as weak, and it is true that he failed to give leadership in an editorial sense, but he had a real understanding of the role of public-service broadcasting and fielded innumerable problems and challenges with more skill than he is given credit for. Unfortunately he was socially shy and did not give the impression of knowing people in the way that Hussey certainly did. Going about London a lot – to public events, embassy parties and performances, as I did at that time – I never seemed to see the bosses of the BBC, except for John Tusa, who was by now running the World Service. The Radio bosses all seemed to come in very early, before breakfast, and go home to the commuter belt in the late afternoon, and the absence of visible BBC management was something of which I was very conscious. Even before Edinburgh I had been on the invitation list of major embassies such as those of the United States, France, Germany, Italy and Spain. Not only the cultural staff but the ambassadors were people I got to know and often liked very much. At their receptions I met politicians and diplomats, generals and captains of industry. I found it fascinating. These were the people running things and, even if we did not need to know them, the BBC needed their support. It was often left to me to make the BBC's case, and I felt that was a weakness. Although I did it willingly, ideally the advocacy should have come from higher up the ladder. My own attitudes had been much affected by Edinburgh and I never felt on my return that I was entirely a BBC man – one foot remained firmly on the pavement outside. But I did support the principle the BBC stood for, if not always the practice of its management.

I was never confident that Hussey believed in the BBC or its ethos. When in 1987 he brought John Birt in from London Weekend Television as deputy to Checkland, this impression was strongly reinforced. They were a curious pair: the blustery, harrumphing old Hussey and the chilly, Armani-suited Birt. They seemed to me to have only one thing in common: a fundamental contempt for the BBC and what it stood for. Birt sought me out one day, insisting on meeting in my office, since he said offices told him a lot about people. He sat in my room, with its red walls and brilliant display of Sean Hudson's photographs of Edinburgh productions, pulled up the sleeves of the Armani jacket, and talked about only one thing – the refuge, always, of the uninterested: 'Do we', he asked, 'do enough about jazz?' I explained that whatever we did would never be enough, since no audience in the world is more divided in what it likes. He did not seem impressed. He listened impassively to my defence of the money the BBC spent on orchestras, and I felt it unlikely we would become friends. Yet he took to asking me to the dinners he gave for visiting politicians – occasions that Checkland avoided. At dinner in 1990 with the Reith lecturer, who was soon to be appointed Chief Rabbi, Jonathan Sacks, Checkland kept looking at his watch and brought the proceedings to an early close. He lived in Sussex. His driver told me that he clocked up over twenty thousand miles a year just going back and forth. Checkland said it gave him time to read and think. Meanwhile, Birt was taking over the public and editorial roles.

On one occasion – at a dinner he gave for the then Chancellor of the Exchequer, John Major – the other guests were Conrad Black of the *Daily Telegraph*, the columnist Barbara Amiel – Black's wife – and Mrs Thatcher's foreign-affairs adviser, Charles Powell, and his noisy Italian wife. I sat next to the news reporter Kate Adie, whom I had never met before. Powell laid into the BBC for its attitude to South Africa. Nelson Mandela had recently been released from prison and was much in the news. According to Powell, Mandela was of no consequence at all – 'a busted flush', he called him. South Africa was a wonderful country, where he sent his children on holiday. Barbara Amiel leant forward in grovelling agreement. Kate Adie coolly asked him if this was the kind of advice he gave the Prime Minister. There was an awkward silence. One night after one of these dinners I thanked Birt and said how much I appreciated being invited – which was true. He rather spoilt things by saying, 'Well, there is no one else around I can ask.' Presumably the fact that I had made the major part of my reputation outside the BBC saved me from the blanket dismissal he extended to my colleagues.

Checkland knew all about the discussions before my return and told me of Milne's failure to carry the merger proposal. I had by now spent eighteen months as Controller of Music, and was increasingly frustrated by my inability to have any influence whatever on the broadcasting side of things. MacIntyre seemed to feel that Radio 3's standing was preserved by endless broadcasts of academics uninspiringly reading wordy scripts. The failure to relate music and performance to anything around them, especially in the intervals of concerts or operas, was disconcerting. I shared MacIntyre's aspiration for intellectual distinction, but could not see why he disallowed any text that had been previously published. I could not see why the weekly review programme *Critics' Forum* never looked at opera, concert music, dance, architecture or design, or why musicians were never invited to talk. I knew how bad MacIntyre's relations were with the Drama Department, since my friend John Tydeman was now Assistant Head. All drama scripts, regardless of the views of the department, were vetted by a special committee of the Controller, who had the final say. No music producer was allowed to make speech programmes, with the exception of the Sunday-morning magazine *Music Weekly*. It was as if there were quite different parallel threads running through Radio 3 and only the spoken element mattered, even if it was less than 15 per cent of the output.

I asked Christine Hardwick if she felt the situation was ideal. She was reluctant to discuss it and said point-blank, 'I am not joining any conspiracies.' I was not looking for conspiracy: I wanted cooperation. I knew that the Presentation Department shared my hopes for closer integration, but, since practically no one in the BBC ever listened to Radio 3, I found few allies. David Hatch, the former Head of Radio 2 and Radio 4, who took over from Brian Wenham as Managing Director of BBC Radio, was a nice man from a very different background to me and was visibly daunted by MacIntyre. He seemed very much to admire the Head of the Talks Department, George Fischer, whose attitudes were even more dismissive than MacIntyre's. Their treatment of young producers at Radio 3 meetings was so destructive that the Drama Department refused to attend.

I did not get the sharp memos that Ponsonby had had to cope with from MacIntyre, but I had no conversation and precious little contact with him. It was profoundly unsatisfactory to someone like myself who had spent years making programmes and seeking ways to involve a wider audience in the world of music. Through the winter of 1986–7 I became increasingly impatient. Hatch reproached me for not going to Programme Review, a weekly meeting that assessed the output, but when I went I was frankly appalled at the attitude of MacIntyre and Fischer to individual producers, notably a gifted woman, Judith Bumpus, who was highly regarded in the world of the visual arts but who was subjected to a vitriolic personal campaign against her and her work. I decided that, despite the pleasure the Proms were giving me, I was largely wasting my time. Prompted partly by Colin Davis, I wondered whether I should after all apply for the General Director's job at the Royal Opera House, which was being advertised prior to the departure of John Tooley. It seemed possible that knowledge of my application might concentrate the BBC's mind on the Radio 3 question.

It was quite a dance. Jeremy Isaacs of Channel 4 – a candidate for the Director-General's job without, it seemed to me, much chance of being successful – was looking for a move and was already on the board of the Opera House. Word got about that he was the board's choice, but I felt I had little to lose in applying since I knew that I was one of only two candidates with any knowledge of the Royal Ballet. I had never worked in an opera house, and was not sure I wanted to, but I felt increasingly that making my application public knowledge was a good bargaining counter, and so it proved. Within a few weeks of my being seen by the Opera House board – a quiet and unsuccessful conversation early on a Sunday morning in Denis Forman's office at Granada Television – I was told by Checkland that the Governors had decided to merge the two BBC controllerships and that if I wanted the new job I would have to apply in the normal way. There had been some resentment that I had been appointed as Controller of Music without an interview board, and it seemed to me quite proper, especially in the circumstances, that I should have to make my case. MacIntyre was also invited to apply, but it was in a sense more difficult for him to represent music than for me to represent Radio 3.

I was grilled pretty thoroughly by Checkland and Wenham, and early the following morning, as I was packing my suitcase to join the BBC Symphony Orchestra on tour in Italy, I was telephoned by Wenham and told that they had decided to appoint me and that MacIntyre would take early retirement. By the time I returned a few days later he had cleared his desk, and we managed the transition without confrontations or rancour. I had real sympathy for his position. He had been shunted into Radio 3 because he had not proved a successful Controller of Radio 4. His knowledge of music was minimal, and the mere proposal to merge the jobs told him that the management were looking for a different way of doing things.

So, by the early summer of 1987 I had achieved what I had hoped for: I was Controller both of Radio 3 and of the BBC's music resources. Two sizeable jobs to restructure or reinvent. And of course there was also the Proms, which meant three strands to be kept in balance, and a volume of work which would challenge even my considerable energy. But there was a real chance of making sense of the network. Whether I could do so in the face of the continuing hostility of the Music and Talks producers was a key question. I attended one meeting of Fischer's department, where I mentioned a few of my concerns. They treated me with derision. There followed a confrontation in my office where I told Fischer that he could be quite sure that *I* was the Controller and that it was more likely that my policy would prevail than his. A few days later he decided to take early retirement. Christine Hardwick committed herself to be as helpful and positive as possible, provided I respected her role, which I had every intention of doing. The Drama Department got characteristically drunk, although they were perhaps more delighted by MacIntyre's departure than by my arrival, while a meeting of all the announcers produced the sulkiest group of grown men that I can ever recall. The main obstacles had gone, and it was up to me to prove that what I felt was needed was not only an improvement on what had gone before but could actually be delivered by the existing staff. That would be the challenge of the next few years.

# 14

# Reputation and Reality

When the Third Programme began, in 1947, the main anxiety expressed by the BBC's Director-General was that it might prove too popular, for if so it would be failing to meet the high intellectual standards it set itself. In these days of focus groups, head counts and audience research, the mere idea that something should deliberately exclude the great majority of the audience seems almost unbelievable, yet exclusivity was what Sir William Haley, the then Director-General, and his assistants wanted. The BBC should be seen to be leading the intellectual debate, not merely reflecting or following what went on elsewhere.

There was something heroic about such aspirations, but the results were not quite what was expected. The audience was indeed small, but the by-product of the network's tone of voice and lofty ambition was that the Third Programme became a joke. Any populist speaker, any would-be comedian, had only to say 'Third' in that particular BBC voice to get a laugh. Happily, in my home we were not put off. We tuned to the Third for concerts, recitals, some plays and occasional talks. I followed, with the score, Beethoven's piano sonatas played by the British pianist Solomon. I remember Stephen Potter and Joyce Grenfell's series *How?*, beginning with a strongly satirical view of the BBC and its output called *How to Listen*. It contained a cod dramatized biography of Wordsworth, parts of which I can still quote. I later came to value great readings of poetry: Ralph Richardson with the *Rubáiyát of Omar Khayyám*, Paul Scofield with the Browning monologues, Marius Goring reading Tennyson's *Maud* – still one of the great neglected poems.

At school I was allowed in my study to listen to Isaiah Berlin discussing political thought, a first awakening for me to ideas rather than facts. I recall Terence Tiller's extraordinary journeys in pursuit of the origins of mystifying phrases like 'Green Grow the Rushes, O!' or 'The owl was the baker's daughter' – a line that can apparently be found in many other countries apart from its appearance in Shakespeare. I remember the plays of Anouilh and Ugo Betti, my first encounter with

Beckett through *All That Fall* with the amazing Mary O'Farrell, and the first squeaks and thumps of *musique concrète*. I can clearly recall not understanding some things and feeling left out of many others, but I never ceased to feel the need to come back and try again. The fact that almost everything was repeated allowed this.

Yet, however wide the range, its actual duration was small. The Third Programme was on the air for a mere four hours a day. People who claim that the Third did *everything* so much better than today are entitled to their views, but they certainly cannot claim it did as much. Later it was supplemented by the daytime Music Network, devised by William Glock and his chief assistant John Manduell but hotly contested by colleagues like Hans Keller, who thought that the too ready availability of music would dull its impact and cheapen the currency. A Further Education buffer broadcast between the two strands was eventually got rid of, and Radio 3 emerged through the reorganization of broadcasting proposed in an internal document called *Broadcasting in the Seventies*. To a great extent this reorganization ghettoized music and hived off experiment. Certainly the BBC's role as the educator of a wide public was better served when, for instance, the Proms were broadcast on the Third Programme on Monday, Wednesday and Friday, on the Home Service on Tuesday and Thursday, and on the Light Programme on Saturday, though the new Radio 2 and Radio 4 carried some classical music and, in the case of Radio 4, an excellent series in Antony Hopkins's *Talking about Music*. As late as the 1980s Radio 4 carried one concert a week, and Radio 2, through its link to the BBC Concert Orchestra, could still provide a wide range of entertaining music, by no means all of it already popular.

Radio 3 never lost the much parodied exclusive image of the Third Programme's early years. Nevertheless, a generation of features and music producers who had given it its reputation for knowledge and intelligence retired or died, and by the time I returned to the BBC in 1986 there was practically no one of the stature of Douglas Cleverdon, Deryck Cooke or Barbara Bray. There were a few highly imaginative producers like Piers Plowright and a few internationally known experts like Robert Layton – a world authority on Scandinavian music – yet the young generation certainly considered themselves worthy successors of the founding fathers. I was not so sure.

During my Television years, it had seemed that at Radio 3 there was a European mafia, with Hans Keller in Music Programmes, Martin

Esslin as Head of Drama, George Fischer in the Talks Department and Stephen Hearst as Controller. They certainly knew about academic and intellectual standards. They also knew about vicious infighting and the unresolvable confrontations that so dog academic life. The real question was whether they were in step with a changing world whose language had moved on. The Olympian tone of Radio 3 had begun to sit oddly, even with its core audience, as society changed in the 1960s and '70s. There were new views of what information was needed and what constituted authority, and perhaps a less rigorous view of the use of language. My predecessor as Controller, Ian MacIntyre, was known to use the word 'rigorous' as a touchstone of quality. He seemed to believe, like the Scottish schoolmaster he is at heart, that importance and seriousness are somehow inseparable. This made for stodgy speech programmes, while the separation of music from the rest of the output resulted in a grinding change of gears between programmes which seemed designed to discourage listeners from staying tuned. I once described Radio 3 as a network of pauses, silences and various kinds of applause, together with apologies for the late commencement of the next programme because the concert had overrun. There was little sense of joy, very few laughs, and a dogged dullness of presentation which, however worthy the intentions, distanced even interesting programmes from any audience not already disposed to listen. Surely, I thought, standards could be maintained within a more attractive framework. There were good programmes and intelligent producers, but for most people the network was invisible.

At the time I took over Radio 3, a journalist whom I had never met wrote a very perceptive article about the difference between MacIntyre's vision of the network and mine. He said that for MacIntyre Radio 3 was a kind of senior common room, while for me it would be an artists' café. I thought it a good metaphor. While Radio 3 did carry programmes on science, religion, politics and philosophy, the bulk of the output was about the arts – music in particular, but also drama, literature, the visual arts and cinema. Yet the preoccupations of the network bosses were summed up for me by an evening at the Italia Prize in 1985, when I arranged a dinner for senior Radio 3 staff at a waterfront restaurant outside Cagliari in Sardinia. The fish was excellent, it was a beautiful summer night, the moon was high over the Mediterranean, yet for much of the dinner the conversation revolved around the correct use of the semicolon. It was like a parody by Michael Frayn.

No reference of any kind was made to our surroundings; we could have been in the basement of Broadcasting House.

Although the arts had a major role in the network I inherited, I felt little sign of creative imagination in the way the network was planned. There had been occasional seasons of linked programmes, but in the main the various programmes had no relation to each other. I remember only one evening in the year when I was waiting in the wings when the interval talk in a concert related to the concert itself: the BBC Symphony Orchestra was on tour to a contemporary-music festival in Turin, and in the interval there was a well-researched feature on arts funding in big Italian cities. The norm was demonstrated at the same year's Brighton Festival, where the Finnish Radio Symphony Orchestra were to play the cycle of seven Sibelius symphonies. The interval fare included 'Democracy Romanian-style', 'Aspects of Egypt' and 'Four Continents' – a dreary weekly round-up of press cuttings read by announcers. Yet Finland is an important country when it comes to musical education and standards, Sibelius studies were revealing new aspects of the old man, and Brighton – alone of British festivals – had had its grant greatly increased that year. None of this was thought relevant. The people producing the concerts and the people producing the interval features inhabited different departments in different buildings, and did not feel in any way related to each other. I could see no reason why Talks and Music producers could not work together.

We began in the autumn of 1987 with opera. A relay of Berg's *Lulu* from Glasgow had two interval talks. One, with George Steiner, discussed the theme of the *femme fatale* and the other, with Martin Esslin, examined the light that *Lulu* cast on the society world of *fin de siècle* Vienna. No one much noticed, but it was a start. Yet the apathy among the senior producers was palpable. I asked Leo Black, who had for many years produced many distinguished programmes, what he wanted to hear in an interval. 'I want to make a cup of tea' was his helpful response. One of his scripts had given me useful ammunition in my campaign for better presentation. It was introduced with the words 'Dr Leo Black has contributed the following elucidatory note.' What was basically wrong with the speech element of the network was its total impersonality and the fact that it was all in written rather than spoken English – full of phrases like 'elucidatory note' which you would never think of saying to anyone.

I was astonished at how few of the producers seemed to feel or understand the difference between written and spoken English. For me it is total. There is a tradition – no doubt arising from university practice – of standing up in front of an audience and reading. I hate it in lectures (despite the true meaning of the word), and it seemed particularly inappropriate to broadcasting. The rest of radio had become conversational. Sometimes this had gone too far, and I knew MacIntyre wanted to avoid that at all costs. So did I. But I wanted living people talking well, rather than what I christened 'handouts from the Ministry of Music'. We needed to find presenters who could communicate enthusiasm and knowledge, and producers who could broadcast effectively and explain the intentions behind their programmes. Some of the announcers took to this new approach with ease; others fought me all the way. The senior announcer Peter Barker, a very familiar and much admired voice, told me he could make no contribution since he knew nothing about music. He had been presenting music programmes for over twenty years. It seemed to me he had had time to learn a bit along the way. During the next year a number of announcers decided to move on and a number of producers showed unexpected ability in presenting, but bringing about change was a slow business, especially so in the regions. The entire Radio 3 output from Manchester, for example, was always presented by the same voice – and that one of the most old-fashioned and inflexible.

The Proms gave me the best chance of making related intervals work, and Anthony Cheevers, who was chosen to coordinate the intervals for me, was full of ideas. I wanted to involve composers, conductors and soloists in the presentation of concerts, and within a year this had become established practice to the extent that a non-related interval stuck out like a sore thumb. It put a great deal of strain on the music producers, and created problems in finding room in the schedules for short stories and the academic talks that the new intervals replaced. But the old radio talk – twenty minutes of closely written polemic – was in any case on its last legs. For the small sum we paid, few outstanding people would spend the necessary time preparing a script, especially when the demise of the *Listener* meant there was little chance of the talk being published. I knew that many reluctant writers would be happy to talk to an informed interviewer, so in some areas we substituted animated conversation for dead readings and, although the result may have been lighter in intellectual weight, this greatly enhanced the communication of ideas. A distinguished scientist like Lewis Wolpert was sufficiently respected by colleagues for them to agree to be interviewed by him, and his interpretative skill made many of the more advanced areas of scientific research intelligible even to a non-scientist like me. The only people who complained were the very few who understood it all already.

The death of the *Listener* in January 1991 was the final nail in the coffin of the radio talk. In my first year as Controller I asked two leading radio journalists what they thought of the Reith Lectures. 'I haven't read them yet' was the reply. Their job was to review radio, not to read magazines. The lectures that year were for the first time about music, given by the composer Alexander Goehr – chosen by my predecessor. The producer put him under such constraints that he was initially told he could not include musical examples to illustrate the points he was making. It really was like *Alice in Wonderland*.

There were only two contributors under contract to the network when I took over: Michael Charlton and Anthony Thwaite. Charlton, a formerly much admired *Panorama* presenter, had declined into crusty middle age and was extremely hard to enthuse and difficult to produce. He continued for a couple of years, making a good series on Africa, with particular reference to the Rhodesian UDI question in the 1960s and '70s, then in 1988 I asked him to revisit his homeland, Australia, and talk to some of the leading figures in different spheres. It was very hard to persuade him to go, and harder still to convince him that I had any knowledge of public or political affairs. His attitude to Australia also seemed to me out of date and extremely patronizing in a very British way. When his chosen producer moved on to run the Russian service at Bush House I decided not to renew Charlton's contract – clear evidence, I was told, of the trivialization of the network. But an annual retainer not much smaller than my salary for one series every eighteen months seemed to me excessive, even if his work had been as good as it had been in earlier years. In his place we invited Peter Hennessy, Anthony Howard and several others who seemed more lively and were a great deal less difficult to deal with.

Anthony Thwaite was the Poetry Editor on the network. He had been the last General Trainee to join the old Features Department under Lawrence Gilliam, and I had known him slightly since my earlier days in Radio. He lived in Norfolk and came to London to present the regular monthly series *Poetry Today*. I wanted much more poetry across the network, with much less formality in its presentation. Thwaite addressed me as if I were the office boy. His programmes would have had to have been a great deal better than they were to persuade me to keep him on. His departure caused a temporary fuss, but we soon found a young producer in the Talks Department – also a poet – who had a more friendly and flexible approach.

The problem with many Radio 3 people, it became clear, was that it was unheard of for them to have to respond to the requirements either of the Controller or of the audience. They thought their job was just to do what *they* wanted, to pursue only what *they* thought interesting. Luckily there were a few, like the outstandingly gifted Piers Plowright, who were interested in a multitude of things and who had a real feel for the medium, but many of the others were set in their ways and simply could not recognize that the world was changing.

The most productive of the Radio 3 producers was Philip French, who, in addition to his weekly *Critics' Forum* and many documentaries, had for years been film critic of the *Observer* and a much respected figure in the world of cinema. He could not be faulted in the quantity of output he generated, but much of it was extremely formulaic. *Critics' Forum* was, for me, set in aspic, if not concrete. At his invitation, I had taken part in it several times in my break between Edinburgh and returning to the BBC, and had even chaired it on a couple of occasions. French has likened me, on the record, to a dictator who wants only applause. What shocked him, obviously, was that I felt I had the right to commission programmes and not just wait for them to emerge.

For me, the Controller's role could never be just planning the schedules and making sure we did not overspend. I wanted not only to know what I was getting, but, even more, to open up areas that we neglected. This meant the editorial and commissioning function being exercised not only by heads of departments and producers, but also by the Controller at the top. I am quite unrepentant about this, because the most depressing aspect of my time at Radio 3 was how very few new ideas or formats the producers or departments generated. Although the names changed – *Music Magazine* became *Music Weekly* and is now *Music Matters*, for example – the basic format of programmes like *Critics' Forum* had been around for over half a century. There had to be other ways of devising programmes that even a strongly conservative audience like Radio 3's might respond to if they were seen to be an improvement. We might even acquire new listeners. During my months of conversations with the music producers before I took over from Robert Ponsonby, not one of them mentioned the audience. They talked about everything else, but whether or not an audience existed seemed not to matter to them at all.

The biggest change I made, which related both to new formats and to my belief in high-quality conversation, was the introduction of a twenty-five-minute programme called *Third Ear*, broadcast five days a week at seven in the evening, in the slot before the evening concert. Subject matter varied from day to day, but usually Monday was about theatre, Tuesday literature, Wednesday public issues, Thursday music, and Friday the visual arts, design and architecture. It was produced across departmental boundaries, with three departments participating – too difficult an idea for many people to grasp. It took time to get established. The first programme – a conversation between two potentially excellent talkers, the Director of the National Gallery, Neil MacGregor, and Julian Spalding, at that time running the Manchester Galleries – was of stupefying dullness and seemed interminable.

*Third Ear* eventually found its pace, though the theatre editions were always the weakest, the issues presented by the excellent Robert Hewison the most controversial, and those on the visual arts the most surprisingly successful. All the visual-arts programmes were produced by Judith Bumpus, whose career revived with a bit of support. I really admired her ability to find ways of talking about the visual arts in a manner that compensated for the absence of images. Twenty-five minutes is a long time on radio, and you need the right protagonists to fill it, but frequently I found the best broadcasting of the week in this series. It never achieved much of an audience, but it attracted a considerable amount of journalistic attention, especially in areas like dance and design that had been woefully underrepresented in the past. Major writers, painters, composers, choreographers and architects came to the microphone and demonstrated that there was a multiplicity of voices capable of serious talk and of generating stimulating controversy. In every way it seemed an improvement over dull dons reading.

The danger of all arts broadcasting is that everything is treated as equally important, with a permanent mood of celebration. No one on Radio 3 ever says that some composers are second rate, or that some writing is vapid and some poetry gobbledegook: everything is presented with equal reverence, as if it all had profound importance. You would never believe from listening to Radio 3 that the arts are as much about controversy as about achievement. When I began as Controller there were very few lighter moments on the network, and far too many dull hobby-horses being ridden. The Music Department was particularly susceptible to that favourite feature of the gramophone industry, 'the complete works' – all the quartets, all the sonatas, or whatever. Anniversaries were relentlessly celebrated, and my reluctance to overrule Christine Hardwick often led to totally disproportionate attention being paid to minor figures such as Cipriani Potter or Howard Ferguson.

Christine had brought into the department a large number of young producers. Young in age they may have been, but their tastes and attitudes seemed to me extremely middle-aged. They all had music degrees – a prerequisite for their job, it was felt, although neither Christine herself nor I had one. Most of them knew a lot about the past, only a handful had any interest in music today, and none had had any training in writing scripts which sounded as if they were spoken by a living person with feelings and enthusiasms. The long shadow of the Music Information Index and *Grove's Dictionary of Music and Musicians* hung over them. Their ability to recognize high standards of performance was not in doubt, but their musical tastes were often questionable and their communication skills were virtually non-existent – an occasional session with one of the senior announcers was held to be training enough. The fact that some of them thought Arnold Bax or Herbert Howells more important than Mahler or Britten was, I suppose, a matter of taste. But their lack of interest in the BBC's orchestras was bewildering. When the BBC SO Producer, Roger Wright, left to work with the Cleveland Orchestra, only two producers out of more than forty applied for his challenging and important job. The music producers preferred their gramophone records, their studio recitals and staying within their narrow grooves. There was only one of them who cared about jazz, only two who were interested in non-European music, and not many were even interested in opera.

Despite improvements in recent years, I have always found the music faculties of British universities to be bastions of conservatism and musical jingoism. I wondered why we could not recruit from a wider base. My trying to explain this was seen as seeking to justify the fact that I did not myself have a music degree. Interestingly, nor do many of our best critics. The real problem was not the extent of the producers' knowledge of music, but their ignorance of almost anything else. As a generalist myself, I wanted producers who had not only 'good ears' – the phrase Christine Hardwick used so often – but also well-stocked minds. Combative though the old generation of music producers may have been, people like Hans Keller and Julian Budden did have knowledge and understanding of much beyond the world of music. They deserved their reputation. Some of the young behaved as if they were Robert Simpson or Deryck Cooke, but without the necessary qualifications. Meetings with the Music Department were slow, sulky and ultimately quite unstimulating. If, as is often said, I talked too much, it was to bridge the silences. In my last year as Controller, I asked a group of twenty music producers what they had thought of that year's Proms season, just ended. No one had a single word to say. It is one of the great pleasures of my post-BBC life that I no longer have to go to such meetings.

What I really wanted was to establish teams of producers working together and bringing different skills to a common idea. We achieved it only twice in my time on Radio 3: first in Berlin in 1990 and a year later in the 'Twin Cities' of Minneapolis and St Paul. The peg for the Berlin weekend was the first democratic election in post-Communist East Germany. I wanted to show something of the vitality and diversity of a city that was still functionally divided, and to use all our resources in doing so. The principal agent in achieving it was my planning assistant, Brian Barfield. He had been a producer on the Radio 4 programme *Kaleidoscope* when I first knew him, and should have become its Editor, but he moved to Radio 3 to take charge of planning the schedule a couple of years before I took over. He was extremely hard-working and conscientious, and had a very constructive relationship with Christine Hardwick in the placing of the music output. He had obviously got on well enough with MacIntyre, but from the start he was eager to discuss the possibilities of change. We talked endlessly about the weekly schedules and the shape of each day, asking all the insoluble questions: When is the best time of day to broadcast contemporary music? Is there a real audience for drama on Radio 3? Should opera always be in the original language? What place does jazz have, or ethnic music? What kind of science programmes should we be making? With Barfield, I made several attempts to alter the familiar pattern – usually with no evident gain in audience size, and often producing a violent reaction from the letter-writing public.

My first clash came with the News Division. I decided to stop Mac-

Intyre's relatively recent innovation of broadcasting World Service News on Radio 3, since, for all its wide range of subject matter, it sounded as if it was being dictated to a shorthand-typing class. I asked for specially written Radio 3 news bulletins. Despite the millions being spent on News and Current Affairs by the new John Birt dispensation, they were not forthcoming. No one in the News Division, it seemed, could understand what I meant by a Radio 3 news bulletin. This was at the start of the tabloidization of BBC News which, with its triviality and lack of authority, has so damaged the BBC's reputation. Most news programmes now show as little insight as local newspapers. Juggling with the schedules, I decided to move news bulletins to the half-hour rather than the hour in the morning. This was certainly a mistake, and I withdrew it quickly, admitting at a press conference that I had been wrong. (I was told by the doyenne of radio critics, Gillian Reynolds of the *Daily Telegraph*, that she had never previously heard a Controller admit to making a mistake.) But this still left unsolved the question of why there was news on Radio 3 at all, as so many of the audience said that they turned to the network to avoid it, especially in the mornings.

There was a mild disagreement with the Religious Broadcasting Department. *Choral Evensong*, a long-standing feature of the network, had been increased from one to two transmissions a week by MacIntyre. For me it was too redolent of the Anglican domination of BBC thinking, and it was also surprisingly expensive, so I reverted to one broadcast a week – to the irritation of the Central Religious Advisory Council.

I suggested that *Composer of the Week* should be repeated in the evening, since not everyone could hear one of our most useful and informative series in the morning. Christine Hardwick was against this, for it took up more of her precious 'needle time'. The BBC was at this period subject to an agreement of sorts to broadcast no more than 40 per cent of its output from gramophone records. Sixty per cent had to be live music, specially performed for radio. While totally supporting the work of living musicians, both in public and in the studio, I was never sure why an organization that did so much for live music – much more, indeed, than anyone else – should be compelled to clog its schedules with endless rather ordinary recitals by inexpensive musicians because an outside body demanded a restriction on the use of recordings. We were not in control of our output. I thought the BBC should be able to make its own choices, but everything we did was strictly monitored by some other body – the Performing Right Society, the Musicians' Union, the Association of British Orchestras, the Composers' Guild or the Association of Professional Composers. At our regular meetings with them I would be constantly pilloried about percentages, quotas and balance. I rapidly learnt that no matter what we did we would be lucky not to be attacked by someone with a vested interest. There was hardly ever any sense of gratitude for what the BBC was doing: spending millions of pounds a year on music. Within a few weeks of the coming of classical music on commercial radio with Classic FM, 'needle time' quietly disappeared. Why had the BBC not challenged it earlier?

I retained a Utopian vision that occasionally we should throw away the schedules, do things differently, and perhaps catch the imagination of a different audience. I was completely against change for change's sake – the philosophy that Birt seemed always to talk about and that was such a feature of the Thatcherite monologue – but I did believe that at times it was necessary to shake up audiences and question whether a practice that had been around for a long while was the only way of doing things. When we talked about devoting a whole weekend to one subject, I was warned that there were real no-go areas which I touched at my peril. Principal among them was *Jazz Record Requests*, which had to start at five o'clock on Saturdays or the world would come to an end.

Our Berlin weekend broke every rule. For forty-eight hours the entire network went abroad to examine the resources, assets and challenges of a different place and a different set of circumstances. Some established points of reference, like an opera on Saturday night, remained, and we broadcast from Berlin the first production of Henze's Mishima opera, *The Sailor Who Fell from Grace with the Sea*. But we did much more that was unexpected, shuttling from East to West, from one radio studio to another, using their archives and their local artists. Around this was constructed a series of features and talks about aspects of the life of the city. Music producers, Talks producers, planners and presenters worked side by side in a kind of cultural commando. It was extremely exhilarating. Elizabeth Burke, then a young producer on attachment from Bush House, made a number of distinguished contributions in Berlin, notably with the well-known German scholar Philip Brady. On our return to London she sent me a postcard.

It said quite simply, 'Why can't London be like Berlin?' By working as a team and crossing the departmental barriers, we achieved a network that sounded fresh and alive.

The Berlin weekend was heavily trailed both on the air and in the newspapers, yet no one reviewed it and no single member of the BBC Board of Management listened to even half an hour of it. The only reaction I had from the Managing Director of BBC Radio was a query about what had happened to *Jazz Record Requests*. It was the most graphic example in my time of the way Radio 3 seemed of no consequence to the management of the BBC. At the weekly Programme Review meeting, it was usually only the Further Education or Staff Training people who had heard any of our output. David Hatch, Managing Director of BBC Radio – not a natural listener to Radio 3 – flatteringly said that he trusted me, but there was an intellectual vacuum at the top of the organization and no debate at all about serious programming.

Yet, despite the dispiriting lack of reaction to the Berlin weekend, I planned a similar outing a year later to Minneapolis and St Paul. We had very good links, especially in drama, with American Public Radio, whose headquarters are in St Paul. Richard Imison, the Assistant Head of Radio Drama, knew all the people there, and John Tusa, Managing Director at Bush House, was on the board of American Public Radio.

John and I had collaborated on the presentation of the Berlin weekend, and it had been a delight to be working side by side only for the second time in our long friendship. The previous occasion had been a not very successful television quiz in the early 1970s. Since then John had gone on to become not only a brilliant administrator at Bush House, but a very familiar face and voice on both television and radio. His knowledge of the world outside politics was extensive. In this we were like mirror images: he had worked mostly in current affairs but loved the arts; I worked with the arts but was much more concerned with the political world than most of my artistic colleagues realized. Both he and I believed that the separation of the two worlds was artificial and damaging, and our international experience had shown us how much more successfully other countries had bridged the gap. A photograph of John and myself at the microphone in St Paul, co-hosting the Twin Cities weekend, is one of my most cherished souvenirs of the Radio 3 years. This time I made sure that most people in the BBC management knew what we were doing, and in the main they thought

it was a good thing. The music producers, however, were as patronizing as usual about American music – especially about the works we
broadcast by a group of young Minnesotan composers, who may not
have been geniuses but were as much worth hearing as some of our
own young talent.

Despite the attraction of these weekends, I came to believe that any
alteration to the schedule irritated more people than it pleased, and I
saw ahead of me years of grinding away at the familiar pattern. But
there were some innovations. Despite widespread scepticism, I finally
achieved a programme on food and drink – a growing preoccupation
of our audience. *Table Talk*, presented by the excellent Leslie Forbes,
was really imaginative and won several awards. I also insisted on a
late-evening music strand which recognized that there were gaps in our
coverage, genres that for all kinds of reasons fell between Radio 1 and
Radio 3: ethnic music, minimalism and some kinds of experimental or
advanced rock. It must have worked, for, alone of my changes, *Mixing
It* lasted beyond my time. But otherwise few new ideas came forward,
few new presenters of real intelligence were found, and most scripts
still tended to lack imagination and insight. However, there was only
so much one could do, especially in a BBC which was moving into a
period where senior staff were expected to attend meetings for four or
five hours a day, leaving little time to talk to colleagues let alone listen
to what was broadcast. I relied on tape machines in my car, my bathroom and my kitchen to keep in touch. Occasionally I would take a
'day off' to listen continuously, usually with dispiriting results. I wanted to spend more time at the coalface, but it was becoming less and less
possible. There were serious administrative and political threats to deal
with, and several attempts either to impose things on the network or to
take others away. For over a year I was told that the only way that
Schools broadcasts could continue was for primary schools to take an
hour a day out of our schedule. When it finally had to be admitted by
the Controller of Education that sending out tape cassettes would serve
the purpose more effectively and at less cost, Schools backed off.

Then there was the wavelength question. Radio 3 was broadcast
simultaneously on both medium wave and FM. It was clear that in
ideal conditions the quality of the signal was better on FM, especially
for listening to music. What the BBC engineers refused to accept, however, was that great areas of the country were unable to obtain a decent
FM signal, whereas medium-wave reception, though vulnerable to

interference, was practically universal. Eventually, except for Radio 4, government policy forbade the BBC to simulcast on two wavelengths, and Radio 3 lost medium wave. It was probably inevitable, but no one at the top seemed to recognize that large areas of the country had thus been disenfranchised. It was hard to accept the constant assertions of the Engineering Department about reception once research had revealed that, unlike in France, the BBC's FM transmitters were too far apart to give reliable coverage. The whole of Greater London was served by only one transmitter in the south. Unless you lived on a hill, FM was virtually unobtainable in north London. Even on my expensive equipment at home in central London, Radio 3 on FM was accompanied by a loud hiss not unlike that of a 78-RPM gramophone record. Yet I was expected to sell FM to our hi-fi-conscious audience, while at the same time attending demonstrations of digital radio which was in every way superior and bound to be the eventual choice.

The loss of medium wave created a problem for *Test Match Special*. Not being a real fan of cricket, I found the quasi-religious cult surrounding this programme, with its 'Johnners', 'Aggers', cakes and chattiness, curiously dated and self-indulgent, but it had a real following and greatly boosted the figures of the network in the summer, when it replaced music on medium wave. What I found hard to understand was that when the BBC planned a new national network to carry sport – Radio 5 in its first version – no provision was made to include *Test Match Special* on it. I was told it would replace Radio 3 on FM, effectively silencing the only classical-music network for many hours a year. After months of argument, it ended up on the still split Radio 4 and irritated a different audience. I liked the sports people, and much of *TMS* was entertaining; what depressed me was their conviction that, however inconsequential, the chat was sacred and not one word could be missed. If Television could cope with several big sporting events on the same day, why could not Radio 5? I was told that I had missed the point: *Test Match Special* had an audience which included the then Prime Minister, John Major. Like the Health Service, it had to be safe with the Tories. David Hatch, rather unnecessarily it seemed to me, in the middle of the arguments sent John Major a cricket bat autographed by all the commentators.

Further hours of meetings were spent on discussions about rebuilding Broadcasting House on a new site at White City, the brilliant plans of Norman Foster to replace the old Langham Hotel opposite Broadcasting House with a new broadcasting headquarters having been abandoned. It was this that had led to the departure of my old friend Dick Francis, the Managing Director of BBC Radio, who moved to the British Council and killed himself with overwork. Admittedly the Langham Hotel replacement would not have covered all the needs of drama, let alone music, but it would have been a distinguished piece of architecture, unlike the appalling prefab Lubianka put up at White City as the corporate headquarters, thus giving senior managers three different offices in three different buildings: Broadcasting House, Television Centre and the Lubianka. Such a sensible economy of resources for a cash-strapped organization!

It was, for a time, the intention to move the whole of BBC Radio on to the White City site. Having spent years of my life in White City and Shepherds Bush, I could understand the reluctance of centrally based staff to move to what they saw as the sticks. But the BBC was renting a bewildering number of expensive properties in the West End, and trying to achieve cohesion was partly a geographical problem. As Controller of Music, I started out at Yalding House in Great Portland Street – an awkward building which I shared with the Music Library, the Concerts Division and the BBC Singers. On becoming Controller of Radio 3, I moved to Broadcasting House – to the red-walled office on the fourth floor which John Birt had visited. I was next door to the Controller of Radio 4 and just down the corridor from the Managing Director of BBC Radio, David Hatch, who called in frequently to tell me about things or to kick around ideas. I enjoyed the proximity, but realized eventually that I really needed to be close to my Proms planning team and the Music Department, since they were my major points of reference. I therefore moved to a building opposite Broadcasting House in Langham Street. I could now drop in on them and they on me. David Hatch resented it, and from the time I moved to Langham Street I felt increasingly marginalized from policy and how it was evolving. But, since it was evolving in a direction I was coming to despise, I preferred to be more available to programme-makers rather than to the growing crowd of corporate functionaries brought in as the first impact of Birt's changes started to be felt.

My last office, when I was running only the Proms, was in yet another building: Henry Wood House, on the site of the old Queen's Hall in Langham Place, where the Proms had begun. While Birt went on telling the world how money was being shunted from administration into programmes, I watched floor after floor of this building being taken over by apparatchiks with no involvement whatever in broadcasting, and no desire to learn about it. There was even a floor devoted to what was called Corporate Writing. I would get long papers about our 'mission', written in a language that denied everything I had been taught or learnt about communication. I would send documents back with 'Please translate' scribbled across them. Attempts were made to send me on courses to be taught how to do my job. Since the people running the courses were mostly half my age and totally ignorant of what my job was, I refused. It caused a real row, but I watched colleagues going at great expense to spend days in hotels in the country being taught about performance indicators and setting objectives, then playing war games which were videoed to show them their shortcomings. John Tydeman, by then Head of Drama, was sent on a course to teach him about body language and relations to staff, including the correct way to respond if spoken to by the Director-General. He was fifty-five years of age, with thirty years of experience behind him. It was insulting in the extreme, and of course intended to undermine the house style and ethic of the BBC, for which both Hussey and Birt had such contempt.

One day I was summoned to a business breakfast – a hateful American import – to meet the head of a new department, Corporate Management Training, who had recently joined the BBC from a period of working with large organizations in the commercial world. Conversation with all the Radio controllers was desultory. In the end, I could stand it no more. Why was he here? I asked him. What had attracted him to the BBC? Well, he explained, he was 'interested in change' and perceived that the BBC was 'an organization going through a process of change'. It would be worthwhile seeing how it happened. I pointed out that everyone else in the room was there through conviction, and that we had not made popular or financially advantageous choices. We had chosen the BBC rather than the commercial world, Radio rather than Television, administration rather than production, although we were all good producers. It was absolutely clear that, despite our different disciplines, we shared a set of values about the BBC, and particularly about public-service broadcasting. What, I asked the new man, were his values? There was a long silence. He then said he did not understand the question. The meeting broke up, and I was attacked by my colleagues about how unkind I had been. Two days later I met the Head of Corporate Management Training in a corridor. He said he was sorry to have been so silly and he now understood that what I had been talking about was value for money. When told to go on one of his courses, I said I would rather resign. He did not insist, but the Corporate Management Training Department had over thirty people in it by the time I left, and was costing as much in a year as a BBC orchestra. The BBC had become a favourite organization for management consultants, who were raking in millions of pounds of licence-payers' money. This was the promised land to which Birt was leading us.

Meanwhile, back in my office, I was still trying to answer the questions Brian Barfield and I had asked each other from the start. Who was the network for, and could it go on justifying its cost of nearly £50 million a year for a small audience? Even if one subtracted the cost of the orchestras – over £20 million a year – it was still expensive. But I felt passionately that the expenditure was justified, as long as the audiences – the many different audiences – were significant if not in size then in nature and quality. Stephen Hearst had told me of an occasion when he challenged a producer about a particularly recondite programme. 'Who listened to that?' he asked, to receive the answer 'Anyone who needed to.' It was a brave answer, but passive. Unless you believe in your bones that long-term influence counts for as much as short-term impact, you will join the ranks of the doubters about the need for serious radio. There has to be an act of faith. Radio will always get audiences for background music, for undemanding chat and occasional news updates. The craft of making closely reasoned documentaries and imaginative features, or promoting new drama, will always command less immediate support, especially in a world increasingly geared to phone-ins and the Top Twenty.

Television – short of money in most areas, it claimed, but profligate with it in all – was a permanent enemy. The Controller Alan Yentob, trying to keep BBC2 creative and not just given over to snooker or darts, claimed he needed more money. The strong suggestion was that it should come from retrenching in Radio. Why not in preference limit Television's wastefulness? Why does a simple television quiz show need the ten production staff listed on the end captions? Why does every television programme need to be headed by a title sequence which must have cost ten times as much as the programmes I used to make? Why did it cost millions to design a new set for the evening news, and why did it matter? Why, when we had meetings with our Television colleagues at the Albert Hall, were taxis kept outside with the meter running for the duration of the get-together? Compared to Television, Radio is a very tight ship.

I cared enormously about costs and was determined that we should continue to bid strongly for what we needed but cut out all unnecessary expenditure. I virtually ended the practice of extraordinarily expensive studio recordings of opera, which seemed to me to have little justification beyond filling a gap in the record catalogues. Was recording Meyerbeer's *Robert le Diable* in Manchester with a rather ordinary cast a real necessity? But cancelling it was a small gain against the background of a world in which the cost of music and musicians was rising much faster than our income. In place of studio recordings or expensive special relays, we got access to the Texaco-sponsored broadcasts from the Metropolitan Opera, New York. Technically we were unable to accept sponsored broadcasting, but, rather than reject them out of hand, I suggested to the Editor, Opera, that he process the Met programmes through the European Broadcasting Union in Geneva. In this way not only the UK but all the EBU member countries got the Met free. It did not make us popular with our own opera companies, who suffered a big reduction in the number of broadcasts they had each year. But it had to be admitted that, despite the often interesting productions in London, Cardiff, Glasgow and Leeds, the voices at the Met were often superior – and we were, after all, a radio station.

There were other things on Radio 3 that seemed to me to be there for reasons of history and whose relevance had to be questioned. Here I bumped up against the vexatious question of radio drama. I have referred to the difficulties the Drama Department had with MacIntyre. I am not sure they did much better with me. I did not insist on reading every script in advance, but I did reduce the number of plays, partly because of cost but mostly because of the very uneven quality of the work. In all my years as Controller, I never met anyone not professionally involved who listened to a play on Radio 3 unless it was by a major writer or an established classic. The majority of what we offered was new, and much of it gloomy and pretentious. I was sick of plays in which the Woman, the Dictator, the Philosopher and the General tried to sort out the world in an hour of undistinguished writing. I disliked the feeling that we were being offered rejects from both television and the theatre – and accepting things that no one else would take because no one in Drama could see their limitations. Moderately interesting writers like Howard Barker were presented to me as if they were major modern masters. Hardly anything Drama proposed showed a glimmer of wit or comedy, and we practically never won any awards.

This was all very difficult for my relations with the now Head of the Drama Department, John Tydeman, almost my oldest friend and a frequent travelling companion in younger days. John had an impeccable track record as a producer, not only having directed some of the classic radio productions, but having discovered or developed the talents of such fine new writers as Tom Stoppard and Joe Orton. He had won every international prize – some of them several times. In private he admitted the shortcomings of the output; in public he defended his producers valiantly. The problem was that the members of the Drama Department reasoned with their emotions rather than their heads, and confrontation and rows were easily triggered. Sometimes I simply could not understand the extent of their belief in quite ordinary plays that seemed to me all right but not exceptional. For every Richard Nelson – a very interesting writer largely developed by Radio 3 – there were hours of pieces by writers like Peter Barnes, who in forty years has rarely hit the jackpot. There was total resistance to producing the classics: I was told that they had all been done. A production of a Shakespeare play fifteen years earlier was held to disqualify it from further consideration. If I recall correctly, only *Pericles* and *King John* were given new productions in my time. I insisted that we repeat some of the old triumphs: Gielgud's Prospero, Scofield's Othello, and the great Henry Reed comedies of the 1960s.

One innovation I proposed was called *Critics' Choice* and brought to the radio a number of theatre works which had had only limited exposure in London or elsewhere but which had won high plaudits. Not everyone, I had to point out, went to the National Theatre or to Shaftesbury Avenue every week. Critics like Michael Billington of the *Guardian* and Michael Coveney of the *Financial Times* were part of the selection committee, and the series allowed some of the best new theatre to find a wider audience.

But, beyond artistic considerations, I was also concerned about cost. We were spending more than £1.5 million a year on drama for Radio 3, and a surprisingly large proportion of it was generated from the regions – particularly from Belfast. There happened to be a couple of good producers in Belfast, but there were few actors to speak of, so entire casts were flown in and put up in hotels, greatly increasing the overall cost. Drama from Belfast cost as much per hour as opera from

371

Covent Garden, yet any attempt to reduce it was refused on political grounds. Checkland told me that we had to provide a full range of broadcasting output from Ulster, regardless of cost. In one year it seemed to me that every second play on the network came from Ireland and, however much I supported my colleagues, it was simply too much.

We eventually reduced drama to one play a week on Radio 3, with occasional special additions to reflect seasons or anniversaries. Deep in my heart, I believe listening to a long, serious radio play is like playing the harmonium: something that people simply do not do any more. But try and argue that with the Society of Authors, which guards its members with the same inflexible tenacity as the Composers' Guild! The Drama Department clearly thought my lack of appreciation was a mark of ignorance and insensitivity.

Whatever we did on Radio 3 bored and irritated more people than it pleased. What people want is what they want, exactly when they want it. Anything else is to them irrelevant and evidence of decline. Few people – and practically no journalists – seem able to accept that they cannot impose their taste on a network as they can on a private record collection or library. There has to be an allowance for other people's requirements. Simon Jenkins, during his years as a *Sunday Times* columnist, wrote a scathing dismissal of Radio 3, using as his peg the fact that the current Composer of the Week was someone of whom he had never heard. It seemed to me a clear illustration of the worst of British traits: to invite applause for ignorance. Because Jenkins had never heard of him, the composer could not possibly matter. It was ironic that the composer in question was Zemlinsky, who had been the mainspring of what I still feel was my most successful venture – the 'Vienna 1900' Festival in Edinburgh.

I received a large correspondence as Controller, and would generally spend one of the weekend days trying to summon up the patience to answer it politely. Here were some of the most highly educated and supposedly intelligent people in the country writing to protest in ways that were often personally offensive and frequently just plain idiotic. I had previously berated the BBC for its intolerance of criticism, but dealing with it required more patience than I could sometimes muster late on a Saturday afternoon after a hard week, when I should have been taking some exercise or restocking my tired mind with a book. I received letters claiming that I was in the pay of the record companies, that I was secretly promoting the collapse of society through allowing four-letter words in plays, that I was trying to corrupt the minds of all right-thinking people with contemporary music, and so on. One woman said that salvation lay in having ninety minutes of organ music every evening at seven o'clock. Someone else – the head of a polytechnic, no less – said that all piano music should be banned. I had a letter in careful calligraphic script, from a fourteen-year-old, accusing me of outrageous neglect of the composer Havergal Brian. The letter was signed 'Thine Faithfully'. When I wrote a pretty sharp reply, criticizing both the boy's musical taste and his linguistic pretentiousness, his parents passed it to their Member of Parliament, who sent it to Hussey, who passed it to Checkland. 'Do try and be a bit more patient,' Checkland said. I remembered Noble Wilson's old criticism that I did not suffer fools gladly. Yet if at fourteen I had written such a preposterous letter to a Controller at the BBC, my parents would have been the first to tell me off.

I was, however, in every sense a public servant, so with time I learnt to say that I had 'noted the points' the correspondent made and would 'bear them in mind'. Of course, for many this was not enough and they returned to the attack. One indifferent composer whose music had not been broadcast for many years challenged my support of his more significant colleagues and demanded that I spend a day with him going through both his scores and the scores he hated, so as to reveal the latter's inadequacy and mine. I acquired a thicker skin with time. Every now and then there would be a critical letter with which I agreed. On one occasion I said so, and the correspondent sent my reply to the producer of the programme, saying, 'Told you so!' Luckily the producer in question – one of the more tiresome – was not someone whose support I counted on or had ever had.

The truth is that if you let the public decide what you do you will become both repetitive and lacking in imagination, for what the public want is always more of what they have already experienced and liked. The real challenge is to find ways in which they can be persuaded to listen to something that they do not find immediately attractive, so that eventually that experience extends their knowledge and their taste. If that is arrogant, then so be it, but I cannot think of any other reason why one should become an editor unless one is prepared to believe in the importance of the generally not yet known and loved and to seek ways to persuade others to share that belief. You must exercise your own knowledge and judgement and know when to ignore criticism.

Just as in my Television years I had had in my desk drawer a list of names of people I wanted to bring to the network, so with Radio 3 there were people who had broadcast in the past but had dropped out, or who had never been interviewed. My old friend Howard Hartog, in the last months of his life, came and talked with extraordinary fascination about getting culture going again in Europe at the end of the war, and about the whole business of representing artists and what it involved. It was both moving and revealing. Peter Diamand, also near the end of his life, talked about running festivals and orchestras, about working with conductors, and about his deep belief in standards rather than cheap popularity.

At the top of the list of people I wanted to return to Radio 3 was Isaiah Berlin. I had been strongly influenced by his broadcasts in the 1950s and '60s, and regretted that he had disappeared from our output while still being very evident socially in London and Oxford. I got to know him largely through my friendship with Asa Briggs, and I undertook a campaign to bring him back to the microphone. He had had a mild stroke, and his doctors' insistence that he should avoid strain had led him to give up lecturing, but he could still talk. One day, after a lunch with Briggs and his wife at Worcester College, Isaiah and I walked round Wadham College's garden for an hour while he told stories – mostly about Stravinsky, whom he had known well, and about the great poet Anna Akhmatova, by whom I was fascinated and whose poetry I would from time to time attempt to translate. When we parted, I said to him, 'You know, one of these days we must have a serious conversation.' He replied, 'Oh yes, Plato and Aristotle – I know. Very boring for me!' But that wasn't what I'd meant at all. What I meant was getting him to broadcast again – and eventually, using the peg of his eightieth birthday, he agreed. We devoted a whole evening to him, with his great friend Alfred Brendel playing music Isaiah loved, a Turgenev story that he had translated, a repeat of one of his early lectures, and a linking conversation with me about his life and some of the people he had known. Once again, this refreshed the schedules, brought to the network someone of immense distinction, and I hope revealed to some new listeners the fascination of one of the great minds of our time.

No one could have been more generous or more friendly to me, and no meeting passed without marvellous anecdotes and serious exchanges. On a later occasion I interviewed him about his life in Oxford, about the creation of Wolfson College (whose first President he had been) and about not only the people he had known and liked but also those he had disliked. We hit a rock when it came to talking about Kenneth Clark, who had been a close friend. He embarked on a real eulogy – what a great scholar Clark was, how knowledgeable and how illuminating. Yet he felt he had to say that Clark had had a failing: 'He was a terrible snob.' Here he checked himself and said, 'I can't possibly say that.' So we started again, and again the same thing happened; and then a third time. Brian Barfield was with me during the recording, and he and I were by now helpless with laughter – as was Isaiah too. I promised Isaiah we would not broadcast that section of the tape, but I very much hope that it still exists. He had a marvellously sly sense of humour, and I will always cherish his reaction to my asking a banal question about the differences between Oxford and Cambridge. He pointed out that Cambridge was inward-looking and full of engineers, adding that he had lectured there some weeks after the Second World War had begun and 'you know, they really hadn't noticed'. The Cambridge lecture was the only occasion on which he had met Wittgenstein.

Isaiah Berlin, for me, was not just an ideal Radio 3 participant, but also exemplified the highest representatives of the audience for whom I hoped we were working – people of real intelligence and ideas, whose interests spanned more than one subject. Whether we will or can continue to produce people like Berlin, and whether we will cherish them if we do, remains a key question. Far too few of our prominent intellectual figures have his breadth of knowledge and his power to connect. Without the latter, both study and scholarship seem unfulfilled. As I have said before, I am no true scholar, but I do have a huge respect for scholarship where it makes connections. And, as far as I was concerned, making connections was what running Radio 3 and the Edinburgh Festival was all about. I am all too conscious of how daily difficulties and structural problems left many of my aspirations unrealized. I am much more aware of what we failed to achieve than of what we did. But I don't think the rightness or wrongness of my approach has ever been closely examined – certainly not in Humphrey Carpenter's book on the Third Programme and Radio 3, *The Envy of the World*, which starts splendidly with the early years but tails off into too many unexamined quotes from me and others.

I do not believe that in my time there was a falling off in standards. Despite reducing the number of prepared scripts broadcast, we did not decline into inconsequential chat. That would come later. I think we did change the climate at Radio 3, making it a much more open and lively network, where both the staff and the audience could feel that there was not a single authoritative viewpoint but a broader imaginative challenge. Both Ann Winder's Features Department and the Radio 3 Music Department, where there was a greater output of speech programmes, revealed a growing confidence in dealing with major issues in a way that was different from that of Radio 4 and less desiccated than that of the old Radio 3 that I had inherited. But there was no overall increase in the size of the audience, no major breakthrough in removing the curse of the old jokes about the Third, and little evidence even in academic or professional circles that Radio could again command the respect it had done in my youth. Whether that means it has outlived its purpose is for others to decide.

Depressingly, on my return to the BBC the debate about broadcasting seemed concerned less with the quality of programmes than with the size of the audience. And yet minorities matter, especially since majorities are so often wrong. Minorities have a way of growing, and the balance within society shifts all the time. The BBC was created not by a focus group, but by a highly opinionated individual who identified a need and saw opportunities. Recently, the Managing Director of one of the commercial television networks told me that the days of the cultural tsar (his phrase), like Wheldon or me, are over. 'Only because you choose it to be so,' I replied. Whether broadcasting peddles junk or reaches to the stars depends on the will of the people in charge. It does not depend on the people as a whole voting for what they like. I have always been flattered when people have said I am Reithian in my attitudes and beliefs. However odd Reith may seem today as a man, there are worse things to be called and worse exemplars to follow.

One of the most attractive things about radio is that it is simple and direct. It is easier to tackle difficult subjects and to take important issues seriously when only the words matter and there is no need for images. Television constantly courts and achieves trivialization. Its hatred of talking heads and lack of faith in the power of words leads to irrelevant dramatization of even serious scripts, and news bulletins order their topics according to the available images rather than the importance of the subject. Radio – despite the spin doctor and the soundbite – will continue to be a focus for polemic and for serious debate, and, as the pendulum starts to swing away from the corporate-management ethos of the 1980s and '90s, it is in radio that the improvement will appear most tellingly. But it will always be a struggle to retain quality, since sloppiness, laziness and trivia are so much easier and cheaper to provide and so much more voraciously consumed.

# 15

# Standing up for Music

It was always a positive pleasure to turn from matters of administration, or the schedule of Radio 3, to the planning of the Proms. I found again, as I had in Edinburgh, the satisfaction there is in running something really popular. The sense of the tide flowing in my direction went a long way to mitigate the problems which inevitably occurred.

In fact, during the ten Proms seasons for which I was responsible, there were only a handful of really serious crises. For the most part, once launched, the great vessel moved forward with a relentless drive, and, however long it looked in the first week or two, the season was all too soon over. The whole of life took on a rhythm in response to the demands of the evening concerts. In my first two and last three years I was running only the Proms. I look back with astonishment on the 1988 season, when I had taken over Radio 3 a few weeks before the Proms began and was deep in the internal discussions that would contribute to the changes I made that autumn. How I found the hours in the day I hardly know, but it was as important to demonstrate that I was aware of everything on the network as to concentrate on the Albert Hall. When everything went well, it was *just* possible to combine the jobs of Controller of Music, Controller of Radio 3 and Director of the Proms, but there was a clear priority in my mind. The Proms were a hugely important public institution, and failure there would be damaging not only to me, but to the institution itself and to the BBC.

My own memories of the Proms went back to radio in the 1940s. I first went to one in 1949. Since then, as for so many people, they had been part of my life. I had benefited from their expansion under Glock in the 1960s, and welcomed the wider range of music and the additional elements like late-night concerts. What I had not realized was their international, as well as national, significance. In my journeys in pursuit of artists and orchestras, I found that I was now even better known than I had been in Edinburgh. The Proms brochure was on every desk; every artist and orchestra wanted an invitation. The only obstacles were concurrent events like other major festivals – Aix,

Bayreuth, Salzburg, Santa Fe and Edinburgh – which meant that artists were sometimes not free, and the very limited availability of foreign orchestras within tightly structured tours. If I could not give a visiting orchestra the dates they wanted I risked losing them entirely, but there was only so much that could be done in terms of flexibility.

The whole Proms operation was geared to the regular presence of the BBC Symphony Orchestra, and to a lesser extent the other BBC orchestras. The BBC Symphony had been the backbone of the Proms since Henry Wood's time, when they played almost every day. Wood was well known for rehearsing only starts and ends and occasional passages with soloists. He and his orchestras knew each other well and had performed the same works often before, so he could skimp on rehearsals and get away with it. Standards and expectations had since risen, however, and this was no longer acceptable, but it was impossible to explain that to the management consultants who now infested our lives. Since the BBC Symphony Orchestra had played over thirty times in a season in the 1930s, they reasoned, they should still be able to do so today. However much I explained that thorough rehearsal was now found to be essential, and that the orchestra could therefore play only every fourth night, or thereabouts, the management consultants continued to insist that this was merely a matter of choice – only my opposition was preventing the orchestra playing every night. I must have had at least five meetings a year on this topic, and could never get it into their heads that the old ways were no longer valid. But then the consultants not only knew nothing, they refused to learn. Were we to allow the future of a great institution like the Proms to be decided by people like this?

The planning process started with a sheet of A4 paper divided down the middle, listing the dates and days of the week for the whole period. Into this list I inserted the rota of the BBC Symphony Orchestra, who played the opening and closing concerts and in between had a schedule of two days' rehearsal, concert, day off, three days' rehearsal, concert, day off, with very occasional variants like skipping the first day off and then having two together. The rule was that the orchestra could never, either in the Proms or on tour, work for more than eight successive days without time off. Then into the BBC SO schedule I had to insert the conductors, starting with the Chief Conductor and the guest conductors and ending with anyone else I wanted to invite. In most years the BBC SO played thirteen or fourteen concerts. This is a lot, and meant a very packed schedule – almost always containing a considerable amount of new music.

The orchestra went on leave for most of June each year, then returned to three weeks of rehearsals running up to the Proms. During this period the new pieces were worked on in advance and studio recordings were made to be broadcast within a few days of the public performance so as to give a chance of hearing a piece twice. I always hoped the musicians would come back from their holiday having had a real break and feeling refreshed. It was often far from the case. When the former principal cellist Ross Pople founded an orchestra for a summer tour of British cathedrals and abbeys, paid for by British Gas, I was alarmed to see it contain so many well known faces from the BBC SO. Pople's band were running the length and breadth of the country, playing in York one day and Exeter the next – not my idea of a holiday. When challenged, the players pleaded poverty: we paid so little, they had to moonlight. It was another demonstration of the need to increase their salaries, despite my deeper feeling that, however they much are paid, orchestral musicians are reluctant ever to turn down offers of work.

Once the BBC Symphony Orchestra was in place, all the other elements could be considered. Some had already been planned, like the National Youth Orchestra and Glyndebourne, both which could be decided two years in advance, and visiting orchestras were known about anything up to three years ahead, although the actual dates remained variable while tours were being finalized. There were also other considerations to remember. The BBC Welsh Symphony Orchestra had to be available for the Eisteddfod; the London Philharmonic were at Glyndebourne until mid-August; several other British orchestras were on holiday; some conductors, like Colin Davis, insisted on a proper summer break. Within these constraints, a schedule slowly emerged showing who would be performing, and at the same time discussions were proceeding about what they might play.

I made very few changes to the basic shape of the Proms, but I did give myself the prop of a theme for the first two years of my own programmes. In 1987 it was dance, which allowed me to programme Stravinsky's masterpiece *Les Noces* and follow it with John Cage's James Joyce-based piece *Roaratorio*, for which the promenade arena filled with dancers of Merce Cunningham's company. That was something new for the Proms! Merce later told me that John Cage's last piece, *Ocean*, was written with the Albert Hall in mind, but it proved too difficult to install and rehearse in the context of daily concerts. The following year we explored, rather more conventionally, the links between music and literature, but it did allow me to programme four different treatments of the Pélleas and Mélisande story – by Debussy, Sibelius, Fauré and Schoenberg – on consecutive days. But ultimately there are few topics universal enough to animate a whole Proms season, and after a couple of years I no longer felt the need for themes.

Until shortly before my time, the Proms had only occasionally included concerts on Sundays. I wondered why, since it seemed a good day to find an audience. In fact I was wrong: Sunday was always a difficult day, and unless the concert was in some way exceptional the hall was hard to fill. So a standard programme made for thin houses, whereas something special like a Handel opera did very well indeed. The promenaders – especially the season-ticket holders – told me that they hated Sunday Proms: they wanted at least one day a week off. At the same time, I made an effort to revert to slightly more popular programming on Saturdays. It always worked very well.

Another developing area was Late Night Proms. They had started under Glock and had been carried forward by Ponsonby in a variety of locations. I liked the late-night concerts as they gave a different dimension to the season and, with the right artists, drew enthusiastic audiences. The question was, how many should there be and where should they take place? Some previous venues, like the Round House, were no longer available. St Luke's, Chelsea, much used by my predecessor, had a long, narrow nave and dreadful sightlines which made it hard for the majority of the audience to see anything of the performers. As I had done in Edinburgh, I went on a building search, looking at every space within a mile of the Albert Hall to see if there might be good ones we had not used, easily accessible by public transport. We looked at the V&A, the Royal Geographical Society, the Royal College of Art, the Natural History Museum, Brompton Oratory and many others, but either their capacity did not convince us or there was a problem with intrusive noise. What I wanted was a church for choral and early-music late nights, and a neutral space for new music. In the event we found both, but only temporarily.

The church was St Paul's, Knightsbridge, with a beautiful interior and excellent acoustics. Using the gallery, the capacity was not far short of 900. We already knew the place well, since the BBC Singers had recorded there often. Though so close to Knightsbridge traffic, it was marvellously quiet. We used it for my first four seasons, and then the fire and safety authorities declared that the gallery could no longer be used as there were insufficient fire exits. Apparently the regulations did not apply to church services but only to concerts: you could be burnt to a cinder as long as it was in pursuit of a religious experience. We found a neutral space in the small hall of Kensington Town Hall, just off the High Street and close to the Underground. This could seat 500 and, although acoustically very dry, answered well to the requirements of contemporary music. But it never caught on with the promenaders, on one occasion producing the smallest audience in the history of the Proms – less than 100. Eventually we were offered so few dates when it was available that I had to withdraw. We then looked at the excellent St John's, Smith Square, but it would have meant a long journey from the Albert Hall even if we laid on buses.

I hesitated for several months, then finally came off the fence. The Proms were synonymous with the Royal Albert Hall, so why not do everything there? It meant that some very small ensembles might be excluded, but the Albert Hall is surprisingly flexible in its acoustics and kind to the human voice, so many possibilities were still available. We ended up with a concert in the hall every Sunday and a late night once a week. This gave us over seventy slots to fill, and sharpened the focus of the event by having it all happen in one place.

Perhaps the most surprising thing about the large and prestigious institution of the Proms is the tiny number of people involved in making it happen. More than twenty thousand people are employed by the BBC, but there was in my day only one person who worked full time on the Proms: my planning assistant. Everyone else had other responsibilities. The finance assistant also looked after the BBC Symphony Orchestra and the BBC Singers; the publicity and publications people likewise; while I too had one or two other things on my mind. Yet, in time, there was a growing sense that I had a team at the Proms who worked together and knew each other well and knew everyone else's role. I had originally brought in a producer full time, as with the BBC Symphony Orchestra, but there was not enough to do all year round. It was enough to have the cooperation of a coordinating producer from the Radio 3 Music Department, and that for several years was the excellent Stephen Wilkinson. He liaised with the presentation people on how each concert was promoted and introduced on air, and, with visiting orchestras and the BBC's regional orchestras, made sure that the technical side was adequately taken care of.

Initially my planning assistant was a very able and alarmingly hard-working woman who had been part of the Concerts Division when I arrived. Jacky Kohn (later Guter) was large, ebullient and at times explosive, and everyone told me she was difficult. I found her enthusiastic, committed and full of humour, and we achieved a splendid working relationship. At times doors did bang, but she made more connections than clashes, and was tenacious in pursuing people and getting answers. (It is astonishing how slow agents are in checking the availability of artists. One would think it would be in their interest to move a bit more quickly.) After Jacky married she moved on and was replaced by Henrietta Smythe – a much quieter but equally efficient assistant – and when Henrietta went on maternity leave her place was taken temporarily by Stephen Maddock, a PA from the Radio 3 Music Department. Stephen proved dauntingly knowledgeable, and when Henrietta decided not to return he moved into the job as if it had been designed for him. I don't recall any young man having a more extensive knowledge of the repertory or a more practical approach to planning. After my time he was upgraded, and he has since become General Manager of the City of Birmingham Symphony Orchestra, who are lucky to have him.

The publicity side of BBC Music had been an area that Ian MacIntyre thought unnecessary, but it was, of course, essential in promoting both the Proms and the BBC Symphony Orchestra. I was lucky to get a former publicity assistant from English National Opera, Nicola Goold, herself a singer and an enthusiast. No one could have asked for more attentive or lively cooperation. She knew all the music critics, and was assiduous in trying to placate their constant grumbles about where they sat in the hall. She also understood me well enough to know instinctively what line I would take on issues, and what journalists I would encourage to write not just about the Proms but also, as they increasingly did, about me. As programme editor there was George Hall, a quirky, highly idiosyncratic specialist, with an excellent instinct for commissioning articles and notes. George gave an impression of almost constant uncertainty, but I soon learnt that his aims were set fast and doggedly pursued. He too was much respected by the profession, and I was shocked by the way my successor got rid of him.

The finance assistant was the least well paid but probably the most important of my helpers, and Elizabeth Russell was a remarkable mixture of determination and modesty. An excellent clarinettist, she was also passionate about horse racing. Throughout the time she worked with me she spent several nights a week on the Samaritans' switchboard, and was obviously greatly gifted as a counsellor. In my last year she finally decided to follow her vocation, went to university, and is now a minister of the Church of England with her own parish. A quite exceptional woman, she was constantly undervalued by the BBC, but nevertheless carried out her work without complaint. One of her most remarkable abilities was to predict the size of audiences. The Proms' audience had suffered a major decline at the time of the 1980 strike, and only slowly climbed back to earlier levels. It averaged 75–80 per cent, and we all wanted to increase it, yet without compromise or vulgar populism. Liz would look at a programme and say quietly 'Seventy-two per cent. If you changed this, it could be more.' She would also advise me on which concerts were sure sell-outs, since I needed on those days to bid for the whole hall to be available for sale by us.

It is hard to explain to outsiders how the Albert Hall works, and why very large numbers of its best seats are empty on Prom nights with a 'sold out' sign outside. The hall, a private venture, was built with money advanced by investors who, in return, got seats or boxes in perpetuity. These privately owned seats – which include all but three of the Grand Tier boxes and over 700 stalls seats – cannot be offered for sale to the general public. By agreement with the Council of Management of the hall, the BBC is allowed five exclusive lets during the Proms season, provided that none of the five is the Last Night. I tried without success to increase this number and to find a way to fill the privately owned seats. It seemed ludicrous that the seat-holders would neither use their seats nor return their tickets for sale. On opening nights, if the work programmed was not obviously popular, most boxes would be almost empty. For some ridiculous reason, the rules applied only to concerts. When the Bolshoi Ballet or English National Ballet went into the hall, they were able to sell every seat, yet we – the main user for more than a two-month period every year – were perpetually disadvantaged, despite providing a large slice of the hall's income through steadily increasing rental charges and the hall's percentage of the ever increasing ticket sales.

When I started running the Proms, the hall was run by an unbending Aberdonian, Cameron McNicholl. McNicholl always wore a dark suit with impeccable white shirt cuffs, his manner was that of a sergeant major, and his hostility to users of the hall was total. He would walk about with a watch, and if there was a possibility of an overrun he would hold it up to me as if I had broken some Mosaic law. He had his minions seal the doors with clanking chains within minutes of the end of a concert, with no thought for audience comfort or reaction. One day I was contacted by the Cultural Department of the City of Glasgow to talk about his application to run the new Glasgow Concert Hall. I instructed my secretary to say that I was out of the country for an indefinite period. Mercifully, he got the Glasgow job and left, to be replaced by a very different kind of person.

Patrick Deuchar came from the world of sports promotion. He had worked for Mark McCormack in the UK and South Africa, and had run professional tennis tournaments in the Albert Hall. He knew the place inside out, and all its shortcomings. He took over on the eve of a Proms season, and quietly observed the operation. Immediately the Proms were over, he sacked almost everyone. Box office, security, catering and backstage staff were all replaced, and in every case with significant improvements. We had had dreadful difficulties with the box office, which was old-fashioned and incompetent. I would ring up to see how they were handling enquiries. If they could be bothered to answer at all, they often told me that concerts were sold out when I knew that to be far from the truth. Andrew Stokes, brought in from the Philharmonic Hall in Liverpool, changed everything. The operation was successfully computerized, and we sold thousands more tickets as a result. The new stage crew were admirable and all became friends, responding cheerfully to the increasingly heavy schedule of rehearsals and quick turn-arounds with two concerts a night.

I was less happy with the catering side of things, but that was not for me the most important element. To the hall, however, catering profits mattered greatly, and the aim was ever higher consumption in the private boxes, where, for the kind of people who often occupied them, the music seemed to take second place. They crashed about, opening bottles, pouring drinks and passing sandwiches even during the quieter passages. Nothing, it seemed, could make them realize the insulting inappropriateness of their behaviour. At the back of the box next to mine, owned by Lew Grade's wife, Cathy, who was Vice-Chairman of the hall, an elderly man frequently laid out a three-course meal with china and silver cutlery and, having munched through it, started noisily clearing up during the last work on the programme. People walked about chatting and seemed quite oblivious that their behaviour was deeply offensive to the promenaders and the rest of the audience – especially to those few, like me, who were also seated in the Grand Tier. I lost count of the number of times I had to move to the very back of my box so as not to be enraged by the constant movement or conversation in adjoining boxes. People behaved as if it were the Last Night, which of course is the touchstone by which the event is perceived in the wider community, especially internationally. (One year a French woman asked one of my staff when we would sing 'Rule, Britannia'. 'In about six weeks' was the reply.) Much of the secret of the Proms' success lies in their informality and their sense of companionship and good humour. In these days, when so many people seem to need to eat, drink and talk all the time, emphasis on the atmosphere is in danger of downgrading the importance of the music. But I always found that, however frivolous or silly the promenaders might be before the music started, there was nothing but silence and close attention from them once the concert began. Would that this were so in the privately owned seats.

People often commented that the promenade itself seemed less crowded than they remembered from their youth, and they were right. The capacity was much reduced, again on safety grounds, and as a result even on sold-out nights a lot of the prommers now sit or even lie down – unthinkable in the past. Those who lie down usually manage to allow all the loose change in their pockets to clatter on to the floor in the slow movement.

I became worryingly aware of the emergence of a band of 'heavies' who were seeking to control the promenade and any newcomers. No more than about twenty in number, they had season tickets, came back year after year, and were aggressively hostile to anyone who invaded what they thought of as their territory. They were usually the source of the increasingly unamusing Prom chants, and were the main reason why I decided to abandon the tradition of an annual meeting between the Controller and the prommers. Usually they had nothing but a dreary list of complaints about things that were not my responsibility, like the state of the lavatories, but I hated a sense of hostility in any way. Fortunately, as they were so few in number, once we realized how they were operating they found it hard to exert their so-called authority. But it shows how fragile even this kind of institution can be. My private anxiety was always that the promenade might be taken over by an extremist group such as the British National Party. The complicated arrangements to get tickets for the Last Night were very much designed to prevent anyone getting tickets for a whole block.

Seat prices for the Proms are lower than for any other concert series in London. I was always being told by right-wing politicians and captains of industry that the BBC had no idea what it was about and could treble prices and still sell tickets well. While this might have been true for a few concerts, most of which already had higher prices, low prices were, for me, integral to the whole operation. Nicola and I had several audience-research surveys carried out during my years, and – apart from the audit firm being shocked by the discovery that the audience went to the Proms expecting to enjoy themselves, something no other musical inquiry had suggested – the real revelation was of the social background of the audience. Our audience research showed that most of the Proms audience belonged to the least well-paid section of the qualified classes. They were teachers, nurses, social workers, librarians, students and so on – people with tertiary education, civilized tastes and little money. In my opinion, the failure of promoters to recognize this is at the heart of the seeming decline in concert-going. For a social worker on £18,000 a year, to pay thirty-five pounds for a top-price ticket at the Royal Festival Hall or the Barbican – plus travel, parking, a programme and an interval coffee or a drink – is simply out of the question, and even in cheaper seats the marginal costs remain the same. The Proms are packed partly because they are cheap. Music-lovers can afford not only to go more than once, but to take their children as well.

This subsidizing of seat prices by the BBC is for me the hallmark of public service. For many in the 1980s it was evidence of the BBC's lack of commercial sense. I am confident that the key to understanding concert audiences in Britain is a matter less of taste than of cost. Very few rich people I know go to concerts; their playground is the opera house or the musical theatre. While many music-lovers also go to opera, and would love to go more often, more of the Proms audience can be found at English National Opera, where the tickets are cheaper, than at the Royal Opera House or on the South Bank. I could never understand why so many members of the South Bank board thought that the key to success was an expensive restaurant. Some of the proponents of this hugely wasteful idea had, to my certain knowledge, never attended a concert in their lives. All through my time at the Proms, the Royal Festival Hall was trying to go socially upmarket – insisting on black tie for corporate events, trying to make concerts smart. In the Royal Albert Hall we were selling thousands of tickets a night at lower prices but offering much more fun. It must be said that we were not offering much else, because of the appalling state of the building, but Patrick Deuchar, the new Manager, recognized this and drew up a plan for refurbishment and reconstruction which is now, with Lottery funding, at the halfway stage. Unlike many applicants, the hall was lucky in being allowed to divide its lottery bid between two sources: the Arts and Heritage funds. The Heritage fund is restoring the building, and the Arts fund is making activity within the building more effective.

For all its shortcomings, I love the Royal Albert Hall, and every evening during the Proms season I would feel again its power to project music and make it vibrate in the often clammy air. Yes, air-conditioning would be lovely for both performers and audience, better toilets would be a good thing, and proper backstage accommodation was desirable, but even without all these the hall has a presence and a resonance lacking in any other building in the capital. The rebuilding plans and the actual state of its fabric meant we were always worried that it might not be available for the Proms. One year, when the hall demanded a rent rise of over 40 per cent, I went in search of alternatives. We looked at and costed all the big spaces in London. They all proved more expensive than the Albert Hall, and most of them were far away and had dreadful acoustics. In any case, I could not imagine the Proms audience trailing out to Alexandra Palace or Wembley Conference Centre, or enjoying the atmosphere of Earls Court or Olympia. In a sense, the BBC is over a barrel with the Albert Hall, but the hall does well out of the Corporation and should have no real wish to alienate it. We eventually achieved an accommodation on the rent increase, and the rebuilding is avoiding the Proms season. But I don't believe one can ever count on the Council of the Albert Hall for altruism. They have a very expensive, totally unfunded building to run, and will always have to keep a sharp eye on their financial priorities. But with Deuchar, who became a real friend, our relations were good and we felt that everyone was on the same side. I will never forget McNicholl and his minions striding about kicking cello cases and ordering people to 'Get out, ASAP!'

Another contentious issue was the intermittent presence of television cameras. This was a long-running saga. Even beyond BBC Radio's inbuilt hostility to BBC Television, there was tension between the Controller of Music and the Television Music Department over who had priority. I recalled arguments about the placing of cameras in the arena from my Television time. The cameras in boxes were out of the way, but once you put them in the stalls or the promenade they not only were distracting, they actually blocked people's view. But television was necessary both to raise the visibility of the Proms and to reach a wider audience. Compromises had to be made. Important as it was, the audience in the hall was only part of the equation. The radio broadcast greatly increased the size of Radio 3's audience, and television had the capacity to go far beyond that. Yet two elements conspired to confuse the issue. One was the determination to show Proms on both BBC1 and BBC2; the other was the very late stage at which Television decided which Proms it would take live rather than recorded.

In my Television days, this latter question was held to depend on the availability of outside-broadcast units, which shifted between Wimbledon, Henley, test matches and other sporting events which naturally had greater priority than we did. In the 1960s we did broadcast a few Proms live, but only when OB units were available. By the 1980s and '90s, as the BBC disposed of its own resources, there was greater flexibility in that units could be hired as and when required. I was entirely in favour of live broadcasting of the Proms, but I had reservations about the deferred relay of only part of a programme. The partial relay not only disturbed the balance of the programme we had planned, but was frequently transmitted against a live Late Night Prom on Radio 3.

We eventually achieved much earlier decisions about what was to be televised, but the split between BBC1 and BBC2 still exists – and never more worryingly than on the Last Night. I could never understand why the whole of the Last Night of the Proms could not be on BBC1, and I put this to Michael Grade when he was Controller of BBC1. He agreed that if the first half was really popular, why not? So I programmed a really popular first half and he refused to take it, being unwilling to drop the fourth rerun of a dreary old western. Just as the BBC returns year after year to Edinburgh and unimaginatively televises the increasingly irrelevant Tattoo, so the pattern of the Last Night is maintained. Only the silliness can be shown on BBC1. Now the Marketing Department has dictated that further concerts elsewhere – in Hyde Park or around the country – are essential to allow *everyone* to feel that they are involved. I would feel much more involved sitting at home watching my television rather than sitting in a damp park hearing the BBC Concert Orchestra playing something completely different, or watching Michael Flatley of *Riverdance*. The thinking behind all this is the essence of mindless populism imposed on an event which is already dangerously rabble-rousing. But the Marketing Department, Radio's newest discovery, say that this is what is needed – and they, of course, cannot be denied.

Despite niggling difficulties with the hall, with our Television colleagues and sometimes even with the audience, these were never enough to undermine the pleasure and fascination of the planning process that lay behind deciding what was to be played and by whom. The Proms of my youth had had several fixed points: Bach and Handel on Tuesdays, Beethoven always on Fridays, the Ninth Symphony always on the penultimate night. By my time only the placing of the Ninth Symphony remained, and in due course I was to move that. It seemed to me that we should get the best performance we could of the work, and that might well be one by the BBC Symphony Orchestra. But that could never be given on the penultimate night, since they were needed for the following day – and to take the BBC Symphony Orchestra, Chorus and Singers out of the Last Night would have caused a real riot.

I inherited the main outline of the 1986 Proms season from Robert Ponsonby, who had completed about two-thirds of it by the time he left. I proceeded to fill in the gaps, and in one or two minor cases changed things he had suggested. I was somewhat surprised when, nearly three months after leaving, he came to see me to complain that he had heard I was interfering with his programme. If he had really thought it was his responsibility to complete the plan, I wondered where he had been for the last few months. His plan contained some splendid things – notably a visit by Colin Davis with the Bavarian Radio Symphony Orchestra – and as a whole it gave me a gentle introduction to the job, since I was only the caretaker of much of what went on. But I had already been planning my first season, and beyond, long before taking over.

Central to my first years was the role of John Pritchard. There was never any trouble in discussing with him what he might do, but his availability was tricky. During the summer he needed some sort of break from his constant travels in Europe and America, and it was not in my interest to bring him to the Proms if he was tired and lacking in real drive, though this was increasingly the case. By 1987 it was clear that he was far from well. There always seemed to be some small ailment – trouble with his legs or his liver. He was overweight, and his fondness for food and good wine was obviously a contributing factor to his condition, but since our Edinburgh days the light within him seemed to have dimmed. I tried hard to find programmes that would strike something of the old spark. In the planning I inherited, he conducted three Proms, which included Strauss's *Alpine Symphony*, Bruckner's Fourth Symphony and Berlioz's *Grande Messe des Morts* – all very big works. I had hoped to have him more than three times a year, but it seemed this was all he could manage – not much for the orchestra's Chief Conductor.

Everyone takes special care over their opening programme with a new venture. In Edinburgh it had been a Stravinsky evening for the Diaghilev anniversary. In the 1987 Proms, I wanted to open with a celebration of two major twentieth-century figures: Janáček – such a recent discovery – and Michael Tippett – to my mind Britain's greatest living composer. Pritchard and I agreed to juxtapose Janáček's *Sinfonietta* with Tippett's *A Child of Our Time*. Typically for a First Night with music of the twentieth century, it did not sell out. Also, the Janáček was given a performance that was less than thrilling. Unfortunately, when JP was at less than his best he was the first to know it, and all my affection for him could not compensate for a distinct feeling that the piece had gone less well than we had hoped. Things were better with the Tippett, but from now on it was a matter of luck whether JP was ever really on form. The orchestra, who respected him greatly, would sense his uncertainty, giving rise to a vicious circle. There were still great moments, but he could never again full realize those tremendous musical qualities that he had shown so impressively in earlier years.

It was bad luck to have caught only the end of his career, but I tried never to let my disappointment show. He had been such a good friend, and on many occasions a generous host in his beautiful house in the hills behind Nice. In 1983, a month or two before my 'Vienna 1900' Festival, I had suddenly got cold feet about the risk it represented. I went to stay with JP and showed him the plans. Sitting beside the swimming pool, he examined them carefully and then said, in that much imitated voice, 'Well I think that looks rather good.' Immediately I felt my anxieties disappear.

Over the next two years I sought out soloists he loved, like Ida Haendel and Felicity Lott, and works he especially liked. But the results were often less than we had hoped for. With the exception of a concert performance of Bellini's *I Capuleti e i Montecchi*, his best performances in later years were almost all in the opera house. The 1989 season was to be his last year as Chief Conductor, and I asked him to do two things he had never done before: conduct Beethoven's *Missa Solemnis* and preside over the Last Night. His other concerts were to consist mainly of works he had conducted on the South Bank as part of a highly successful Mozart–Strauss series we had planned for his farewell season. From the early summer, it was plain that there were going to be real problems. But what actually was the matter with him? He had phlebitis in one leg; his digestive system was out of order; he spoke of a possible blood clot. He went in and out of hospital, constantly fighting the doctors' reluctance to let him work or travel. It was typical of him that he hated cancelling anything – 'letting friends down' he called it. It was only with the greatest reluctance that he abandoned the planned performance of the *Missa Solemnis*. With characteristic understanding, Colin Davis broke into his holidays to take over. But JP was absolutely determined to appear on the Last Night.

It was a real cliff-hanger. I insisted on talking to his doctors, but they refused to discuss his case with me. I found their attitude bewildering: if he was not suffering some curable ailment, was there perhaps a darker truth that they were unwilling to admit? So as to be sure of being able to go ahead with the Last Night, I contacted Charles Groves and asked him as a personal favour if he would stand by to take over if necessary. He accepted at once – something I was particularly grateful for, since he had been very upset by my failure to offer him an engagement in the 1987 Proms. Happily he had returned in 1988 and had had a personal triumph with Delius's *A Mass of Life*. He agreed to cover for JP, and set about learning a couple of small pieces in the programme that he did not know. JP managed a limited amount of rehearsal, and on the Last Night his only compromise was to sit down to conduct. 'Klemperer always did,' I said. He smiled bleakly. Backstage, we turned the Artists' Room into a virtual hospital ward, with a nurse, a physiotherapist and oxygen supplies on hand. One of the soloists, Sarah Walker, when asked to move to the Conductor's Room, to our outrage chose to throw a quite unacceptable tantrum. Ida Haendel, who was devoted to JP, proved too worried about him to play at her best, but JP got through the concert and made a very moving and charming speech at the end. It was obvious to everyone that it would be his last appearance. We were all very emotional, and no one noticed Charles Groves sitting at the back of my box and creeping away quietly afterwards so as not to attract attention. His presence was the generous gesture of a very nice man.

JP went on holiday after the Proms and then to San Francisco, where he was caught up in an earthquake and stranded for several days on a high floor of the building where he lived. Later he managed to conduct a couple of performances at the Opera, but in early December he collapsed and, after a few days in hospital, died. The official cause of death, we learnt, was lung cancer. He was completely riddled with it. Did he know? Should we have been told? I only know that getting through that Last Night was an act of superlative courage and loyalty to his orchestra, to his colleagues and to me.

Even after his death he had a surprise in store for me. Well though I had known him, I had not known that he was a devout Catholic. At his funeral, the Catholic church in Soho Square was packed with friends and colleagues. The word on everyone's lips was 'undervalued'. More than ten years after his death, the BBC is still sitting on a collection of outstanding performances by him over a long period, none of which has ever been issued on record. He is still, I am told, not a box-office attraction. Is it surprising that I have such dislike for the recording companies and their cheap successes with wretched compilations of the best of Mahler's slow movements and the vulgar exploitation of scantily clad teenagers? Pritchard embodied for me the qualities that I seek in a conductor: not just flash and fireworks, but profound consideration for both the score and the performers. I learnt much from him, and miss him a great deal. His qualities are increasingly rare in this market-driven world.

JP was especially pleased that he was to be succeeded as Chief Conductor by Andrew Davis. From his first season, in 1990, Andrew conducted six Proms every year – a heavy load, since he was also conducting right through the Glyndebourne Festival. He also nobly stepped in to replace an indisposed Günter Wand one year, and in 1990, at a couple of days' notice, he took over in difficult circumstances for the Last Night, replacing Mark Elder.

Through the summer of that year, the crisis in the Gulf was building up and it seemed very likely that at some time there might be a war.

Mark Elder, who is a curious combination of obstinacy and indecisiveness, began to worry about the 'Rule, Britannia' element of the Last Night, given the developing political climate. I was rather too busy to share his concerns, until at the beginning of the last week of the Proms he asked me to meet him to discuss the situation. He told me that, if we were at war by the day of the concert, he would find it very hard to conduct the patriotic element in the programme, since for him it would be inappropriate. We talked at great length. I was fairly certain we would not be at war by Saturday, but I also felt that, if we were, the public would be better disposed than ever before to bellow their way through 'Land of Hope and Glory'. Mark disagreed, but said he would keep in touch. The following day his views were splashed all over the *Evening Standard*. It turned out that he had shared his uncertainties with the journalists before he had talked to me. I thought that was idiotic. In all our two hours of talk he had never hinted that he had already gone public with his views.

I spent a troubled lunch hour alone in my office with a copy of the *Standard*, then made a phone call to the Director-General, Michael Checkland, and explained the situation. Checkland agreed with me that, in the circumstances, we could not go ahead with Elder. I called Andrew Davis at Glyndebourne. Before I could even put the question to him, he volunteered to take over. I then rang Mark, and told him his services would not now be required. I have a great respect for his musical abilities and a personal affection for him, but he had put us in an impossible situation and I felt I had no alternative but to replace him. He was genuinely shocked by my action, and asked for a meeting to discuss it. I said there was no point: the decision had been taken. I took no pleasure in it, nor do I in recalling it now, but I am sure I was right. The press, for once, were on the BBC's side, and after a short hiatus my friendship with Mark was soon resumed. But it was a day I would not wish to live through again.

The following year I once again found I had the press on my side – this time over the strange affair of Nigel Kennedy. I had spoken at a conference about 'Music, Money and Marketing' and had been scathing about the vulgarization of artists in publicity material and record sleeves – typified by images of the cellist Ofra Harnoy appearing to have a too intimate a relationship with her instrument, or Peter Donohoe stripped to the waist against an upturned piano keyboard, or Nigel Kennedy's ludicrous clothes and grotesque, self-invented accent.

All the hype around his recording of the *Four Seasons* failed to conceal the fact that there were several better recordings available, despite the sales figures. I feared that Nigel was putting appearance before values. For the sixtieth-anniversary concert of the BBC Symphony Orchestra he had turned up to play the Berg Violin Concerto wearing a kind of Dracula outfit – a long cloak and green make-up. When I challenged him about this, he said, 'Well it's about death, innit?' I remembered Nigel from his first years at the Yehudi Menuhin School, when he had sounded just like his mother, speaking classless standard English, and had rather a sweet personality. BBC Television had returned every six months over a period of several years to watch his progress – an imaginative idea, and one that I fear backfired badly. I had always believed that the Aston Villa lager-lout persona that emerged in late adolescence was a reaction against the cosy world of the Menuhin School and the media attention he was already attracting. He was certainly a very talented violinist, but in my conference speech I had suggested he would do well to concentrate more on his technique and less on his appearance, since there was a new generation of very gifted violinists coming up who would give him a real run for his money.

All this was at a private meeting, and was well received. People were accustomed to my speaking frankly about things that worried me, and in this case I had had at the back of my mind the memory of the pianist Eileen Joyce, whom my mother had looked after, who had destroyed her serious standing through her obsession with changing her dresses. It was a bonus for the popular press, but did nothing for the music. I feared that Nigel, whom I was fond of, was going the same way. To my amazement, these views all leaked out several months later when the *Independent* newspaper obtained a tape of my talk. They became headlines in every paper for days. I was doorstepped by the press, the phone never stopped ringing, and my life became a misery – except that, wonder of wonders, almost everyone appeared to agree with me. Total strangers came up to me in the street and shook my hand. 'It needed saying,' they all told me. Even Yehudi Menuhin, who had been so close to Nigel, told me that, although saddened by the affair, he understood clearly what I meant. For the second time in a year I became, for a few days, the subject of praise in the popular press. Yet I would gladly have avoided both incidents.

I am often dangerously frank in my lectures and speeches, but, since I find so much double-speak around me, I refuse to apologize for that.

Sometimes my frankness makes unexpected friends, and sometimes it confirms expected enemies, but I decided a long time ago that I would rather have a clear conscience and say what I think rather than settle for the cosy comfort of pretended acquiescence. I am far from claiming that I am always right – one of my remarks about Nigel Kennedy was seriously wrong and actually defamatory. In general I find there is a kind of hypocrisy at work. Everybody knows something is wrong, yet no one dares say so, because it makes for an easier life. I don't think life was made to be easy. I know that many compromises are both necessary and undamaging, but I nevertheless have a hatred of those that are unnecessary.

There is, of course, always the risk that by speaking out you may damage the cause you seek to support, as Peter Hall is reputed to have done when Mrs Thatcher caught him on television in very vocal disagreement with the Chairman of the Arts Council. The occasion is said to have sharpened her general hostility to all of us in the arts. But no long-term damage was done to Mark Elder or Nigel Kennedy by my actions. Nigel is now playing extremely well again, although he is still caught up with a lot of loony ideas about Jimi Hendrix and jazz improvisation. Mark Elder has found a new musical base at the Hallé Orchestra and is also widely respected as one of the best opera conductors around. All of us may have learnt something from the confrontations.

There were one or two areas in which I altered the balance in the Proms. One of these involved youth orchestras. I have written earlier about my enthusiasm for the fierce commitment of youth orchestras, especially when conducted by a great musician. The National Youth Orchestra's performance of Schoenberg's *Gurrelieder* conducted by Pierre Boulez in my first season, part of Robert Ponsonby's plan, was of thrilling quality. To hear that splendid score played with total commitment by such a large body of musicians (twelve flutes!) was unforgettable. The NYO, one of Britain's undervalued glories, had appeared before in the Proms, but never regularly. I told their Director that, if we could jointly discuss who might conduct them for their summer course, I would guarantee them a Prom every year. It worked very well. With conductors like David Atherton, Tadaaki Otaka, Matthias Bamert and Mark Wigglesworth in charge, the NYO certainly deserved their place.

In 1989 Mark Elder suggested the NYO might play some Wagner, something few youth orchestras get a chance to do. 'How about the third act of *Walküre*?' I suggested. Mark was enthusiastic, but wondered who we could get to sing Brünnhilde. I volunteered to ask Gwyneth Jones, an old friend and someone I knew would enjoy the experience. She accepted immediately. We put together a very strong supporting cast, with Simon Estes as Wotan and Jane Eaglen as Sieglinde, and Mark had the brilliant idea of preceding the Wagner with some short tone poems by Sibelius. The standard of playing was remarkable. Reginald Goodall sat beside me in my box. In my first year he had conducted the English National Opera Orchestra in the last act of *Parsifal* – his final appearance on the podium – and Mark had very much wanted him to come and hear the *Walküre*. I was astonished to find that he knew the unfamiliar Sibelius pieces as well as he knew the *Ring*.

Also present was the now elderly Wagnerian soprano Dame Eva Turner, a very frequent visitor to the Proms – and, I have to say, a very time-consuming one, since she always arrived an hour early and expected constant attention. She was delighted with Gwyneth, but telephoned the following day to protest 'in the strongest possible terms' about the dreadful shock she had experienced when some of the Valkyries appeared wearing trousers. I could not share her horror. It seemed to me a good idea – better than a *Walküre* at the Proms in my youth, when each of the women had worn not only a different colour but a different neckline – everything from long sleeves to practically topless was on display. In 1989 I had asked them all to wear black, except for Brünnhilde, and the trousers, although not my idea, seemed very appropriate. But Dame Eva was not to be placated.

It was after this concert that Gwyneth asked me rather shyly if I would consider her taking part in the Last Night. I had thought her much too grand, but the following year she turned up in full Britannia costume and brought the house down – a very jolly memory. But my longest-lasting memories of National Youth Orchestra concerts in the Proms, apart from the enthusiasm of the audience and the commitment of the players, is of tearful farewells in dark corridors at the end, for the NYO's summer course is as much about affairs of the heart as about the love of music.

The indefatigable Joy Bryer was on six occasions able to fit a Proms date into the European Community Youth Orchestra's summer tour, and their standards surpassed even those of the National Youth

Orchestra. They came twice with Bernard Haitink and once each with Vladimir Ashkenazy, Kurt Sanderling, Carlo Maria Giulini and Mstislav Rostropovich – a roster of conductors even the world's greatest orchestras would find it hard to top. It was always striking how much visible pleasure conductors got from working with these young people. Giulini, who never went to parties, came to the German Embassy after his concert and sat for over an hour surrounded by intense young people plying him with questions, which he answered with his characteristic charm and gentleness. Ashkenazy seemed as young as the players, bouncing on to the platform and grinning with delight at what they did.

The Rostropovich concert was of special interest to me, since it was very hard to get him to the Proms: as his fee had become so enormous, it was only within the planning of a very clever operation like the ECYO tour that it could be made to work. But I was alarmed when Mrs Bryer suggested that Martha Argerich might be the soloist. I was assured that, given her close relationship with Rostropovich, she would certainly turn up. When the day came, I was telephoned to say she had at least played in Brussels the previous night and had arrived in London. She did not, however, attend the rehearsal in the afternoon, deciding instead to go for a walk in the park. When I arrived at the hall as usual at about 6.30, I heard the piano in the Artists' Room being put through its paces with unmistakable effect. I heaved a sigh of relief, and quietly let myself into the room.

I had not seen Martha for several years, but she greeted me as an old friend and asked what time the concert began. I told her it was 7.30. 'No,' she said, 'I am absolutely certain it is eight o'clock. I am very hungry; I need to go and eat something.' I pointed out that by eight o'clock she would have played her concerto and would be free to eat for the rest of the evening. 'I don't believe you,' she said – 'I know it doesn't start till eight.' I excused myself, found two security guards, locked the door of the Artists' Room, and said, 'In no circumstances whatsoever is she to be allowed to leave the room.' She banged on the door for a bit, but at 7.30 sharp she went out and gave one of the most brilliant performances of the Prokofiev Third Concerto I have ever heard. Such genius, and such a lack of professional discipline!

Claudio Abbado had by now moved on from the ECYO, of which he had been the first conductor, to a new youth orchestra, based in Vienna, which he called the Gustav Mahler Jugendorchester. I christened it the Hapsburg, since it drew its members from Hungary and Czecho-slovakia as well as from Austria. Eventually it recruited from all over Europe, including Poland and Russia. The orchestra came only three times, but memorably – although there was always a serious problem. While the National Youth Orchestra and the ECYO came for a rea-sonable fee, both through sponsorship and because they were ama-teurs, the Gustav Mahler Jugendorchester failed to find either sponsor-ship or state support. They came into the Proms costing a good deal more than many professional orchestras. My initial response was to say that they had to raise the money to reduce the cost. When they failed to do so, I was left with a dilemma. Abbado had given up the London Symphony Orchestra and was now a very rare visitor to Lon-don. I was confident in my belief that he was a very great conductor – and never better than with young people – so in 1991, 1993 and 1995 I swallowed my objections, knowing that the concert would sell out. In 1995, to Liz Russell's indignation, I even increased the prices – some-thing we had never done for a youth orchestra. I wanted Abbado to be there every year if we could find a way.

Such was my enthusiasm for youth orchestras that in 1993 we actu-ally had five of them: the National Youth Orchestra, the National Youth Chamber Orchestra, the National Youth Orchestra of Scotland, the Gustav Mahler Jugendorchester and the European Community Youth Orchestra. We also, on other occasions, brought in the Aus-tralian Youth Orchestra, the Junge Deutsche Philharmonie and the Chamber Orchestra of Europe (no longer really a youth orchestra, but from the same stable). There seemed so much in common between these young players and the predominantly young audience in the promenade that I was never happier than on these evenings, the play-ers' attitudes being such a contrast to the gloomy, moody manner of many adult orchestras. But there was one lamentable exception: the visit of the Schleswig-Holstein Festival Youth Orchestra under Leonard Bernstein in 1988.

It was always a matter of luck whether the task in hand commanded Bernstein's full attention. I had first met him in the 1960s, when he came to the television studios to conduct a performance of his *Chich-ester Psalms*. I was a huge fan of his theatre music – *On the Town*, *Fancy Free* and especially *West Side Story* – but I couldn't understand why his so-called serious music was taken so seriously by many critics, since for me it seemed so very ordinary. All through the rehearsal and recording of the *Chichester Psalms*, Bernstein was going on about how essential it was for him, after the recording, to visit a then-fashionable disco in the West End. It was members only. Of course none of us was a member, but I suspected that my friend Robin Scott, who was running Radio 1, might be. Indeed he was, and he agreed to ring the club and arrange for them to let Bernstein in. So, after the television recording, a group consisting of Bernstein and his wife, Felicia, Martha Gellhorn, Richard Rodney Bennett and I set off for Leicester Square. It was a Monday night and the club was almost empty. Bernstein became instantly maudlin and sat there saying, 'To think that this place is more famous in New York than Buckingham Palace!'

I met Bernstein occasionally over the years, especially after I became friendly with the management of the New York Philharmonic. I would go to their concerts in New York, and several times my visits coincided with Bernstein's appearances. One evening he conducted a whole programme of music by living American composers, all of whom were present: Roger Sessions, Ned Rorem and William Schuman. Halfway through Rorem's piece – a song cycle – Bernstein started coughing and left the platform. We sat in embarrassed silence while his hacking cough could be heard off-stage. Afterwards I went round to see him and found a huge group in the Green Room, most of whom were in tears of emotional commiseration. Bernstein wept his way slowly through the crowd, kissing, sobbing and acknowledging the cries of 'You're the greatest', led by the unlikely pairing of Billy Rose, the band leader, and Isaac Stern. It was America at its most flesh-crawling. At one stage a young man came over and said, 'Do we know who you are?' I replied, 'Well, your father does.'

Later came a famous occasion when Bernstein conducted the BBC Symphony Orchestra in a performance of the *Enigma Variations* and spent forty-five minutes tuning up, reducing the players to nervous wrecks. The performance, issued on record, is the slowest in history – and the schmaltziest. Yet he could be remarkable. I worked closely with him on a television programme about Stravinsky's *Les Noces*, and he was perceptive and amusing both about Stravinsky and about the work, which he conducted with precision and passion. Yet there was always the feeling that Bernstein the conductor was what mattered, rather than the composer he was interpreting. His better work was with the Vienna Philharmonic Orchestra, whom he respected, and the Concertgebouw, who reacted to him with characteristic Dutch reserve.

His most questionable performances, for me, were with the Israel Philharmonic and the London Symphony Orchestra. He visited Edinburgh with the Orchestre National de France the year before I took over and did not return in my time, although I invited him, as I did to the Proms.

Bernstein made his first appearance at the Proms in 1987, with the Vienna Philharmonic. It was a very successful concert, with a memorable performance of Mahler's Fifth Symphony, and he was on his best behaviour, as he usually was with the Vienna Philharmonic, who, despite their legendary anti-Semitism, liked him very much. Backstage afterwards, he was full of praise for the audience, especially for the attention and stillness of the promenaders. He explained to me, as if to a slightly backward child, that nobody knew about the Proms. He would make it his ambition to tell the world. So we looked for further possibilities of collaboration.

The following year he was scheduled to conduct the youth orchestra specially formed for the newly established Schleswig-Holstein Festival, an initiative of the German pianist Justus Frantz, who had gone out of his way to befriend Bernstein. Negotiations were carried out through Bernstein's manager, an inscrutable American called Harry Kraut, distinguished by one of those bizarre Abraham Lincoln beards that cover only the jawline. Kraut said – and Jacky Guter, who was with me, can confirm this – that Bernstein would do a concert in the Proms with the Schleswig-Holstein Orchestra either free, out of enthusiasm for them and for the Proms, or, at the very worst, for a special low fee. Kraut has always denied that this exchange took place.

The administration of the orchestra proved totally incompetent. Despite warnings from us, they failed to sort out work permits for the non-EEC players, and two days before the concert Frantz was ringing up none other than the German Foreign Minister to sort out the mess. The van with the instruments and the orchestral parts arrived in London the day before the concert, but was unable to find the Albert Hall; most of the rehearsal on the day of the concert was lost because of its late arrival. In the first half of the programme, three young conductors from the summer course were to conduct short pieces. They got no rehearsal at all, because the second half – which was to be televised – consisted of Bernstein's own song cycle *Songspiel*. The evening came, and by 7.25 there was no sign of Bernstein. He showed up at 7.28 and was obviously under the influence of some substance or other. He could not be persuaded to get ready to go on. Jacky said, 'We're live on the radio in two minutes.' 'Who gives a fuck about radio?' said Bernstein. 'Well, we do – and they are, after all, paying your fee,' said Jacky – a reference to the fact that we had in the end been forced to pay something approaching Bernstein's normal rate.

Grossly unfair to the young conductors, Bernstein took all the limelight. And when afterwards a considerable number of people were invited back to the Savoy for supper, he kept the company waiting for over an hour and a half. I was tired and wanted to go home. Humphrey Burton and his wife begged me not to. When Bernstein finally arrived and we were seated at several tables in a private room, I found myself with Bernstein at a table with a lot of women whom I did not know. Bernstein started telling a string of really disgusting stories, full of four-letter words and sexual references. After a while, I protested. Bernstein turned to me and said, 'What's the matter with you, you dreary old queen?' The project to tell the world about the Proms came to an unhappy end.

Bernstein holds a special place in the history of American music as the first American conductor to succeed with a major orchestra, and his musicals could be brilliantly entertaining, but the constant attempts to elevate him to the highest level of the compositional ladder seem to me ridiculous. Shortly after Bernstein's death, Christoph von Dohnányi, not the most generous of colleagues, said over lunch in Cleveland, 'I don't know how Lenny dared to conduct Mahler. He had neither the musical nor the intellectual qualifications.' It was a preposterous remark, which I countered by pointing out that Bernstein was at least a Jew. In fact he embodied the best and worst of Jewishness: both the ambition and the sentimentality. I think his best theatre music sums up his time, but his relentless attempts to be taken seriously, whether with symphonies or in the vapid opera *A Quiet Place*, for me fail. But of one thing I am quite certain: he understood Mahler very well, and his performance of the Fifth Symphony in London just about effaces the unhappy memory of the last time we worked together.

One of the other changes I made in the Proms was to reduce the number of appearances by the London orchestras. It seemed to me that they operated throughout the rest of the year, and I could not see why they needed so many Prom dates – a total of eleven in the season I inherited. I decided to cut them down and to offer more opportunities to the BBC's regional orchestras and to foreign visitors. I guaranteed at least one concert a year for each of the London orchestras, although involvement with Glyndebourne always gave the London Philharmonic at least two. I was aware that this move was much resented, but when the orchestras did come I wanted them to do something truly special, bringing major conductors or major works.

The Philharmonia had had a difficult time with my predecessor, who had always booked the orchestra, but never with their Principal Conductor, Giuseppe Sinopoli. I felt that created real problems for the orchestra, and I hastened to invite Sinopoli – an uneven conductor, but very interesting at his best. He is a man of great intelligence – qualified in medicine and psychology, and a gifted composer – but somehow he does not always deliver as a conductor. He had fallen foul of the London critics, as Franz Welser-Möst was to do later, and whatever he did seemed to be negatively received. Yet the performance of Mahler's Sixth Symphony which he gave in the Proms in 1987 was, for me, a high point of the season.

At the London Symphony Orchestra, Michael Tilson Thomas was extremely keen to make a strong impression, and every year he came up with at least one work that he was determined to include which often involved well over a hundred players and led to a commercial recording soon afterwards, for which I had effectively paid for the necessary rehearsals. In this way we had a complete *Klagende Lied* of Mahler, Prokofiev's *Scythian Suite*, Copland's Third Symphony and *The Rite of Spring*, as well as music by his mentor, Bernstein. Tilson Thomas has undoubted talent, but sometimes has a way of upsetting people. I had met him on one of his early visits to London, in the 1960s, and had not been entranced by the one concert he gave with the BBC Symphony Orchestra. He was certainly not much liked by them. When I took over at the BBC the orchestra begged me not to invite him, but his manager, the *éminence grise* of American music, Ronald Wilford of Columbia Artists, came to see me and offered him as a successor to Pritchard. It seemed to me that there was a risk that too many aspects of British music were being dictated from New York, so I declined. MTT found his niche with the LSO, where the chemistry worked pretty well. I became so tired of the constant enquiries as to whether his Prom would be televised that in my last year I booked the LSO on a date when I knew he was not free. I rather resented the feeling that the Proms were being used to advance his career. But he has been a big success in San Francisco – perhaps a more suitable environment for him than London.

The London Philharmonic were very important to me because of Klaus Tennstedt, their Chief Conductor, though the perilous state of his health made booking concerts with him very risky. When he did turn up, it was always a major event. I came to have the greatest possible admiration for him, so modest in his manner and such a servant of music. It seemed unfair that his late flowering and international success were constantly undermined by the cancer that, despite long periods of remission, finally killed him. I would try to reduce the strain on him by programming something non-orchestral in the first half – a piano or organ solo. But he was unlucky, and on three occasions was forced to cancel. In 1991, apparently fully recovered from cancer, he fell and broke two ribs on his way to see a physiotherapist a week before the concert, and was unable to lift his arms to conduct. He was scheduled to conduct Beethoven's Ninth Symphony. I immediately tried to contact his old friend and colleague Kurt Masur. After a day of phoning New York and Leipzig, it turned out that Masur was on holiday with his family in Devon. I tracked him down to the Belmont Hotel at Sidmouth, and during the next few hours became very friendly with the hotel's switchboard. It was a hot day, and the Masur family were on the beach. When I finally got him, in the early evening, I asked him where he intended to be on the date of the Tennstedt Prom. 'In the audience,' he said – 'we've bought our tickets.' With characteristic generosity, he interrupted the family holiday to take over, just as Libor Pešek was to do three years later. Tennstedt's last appearance was in 1992, when he conducted a Wagner evening with wonderful intensity and grandeur. Going out on to the platform to announce his non-appearance was always the most unpleasant task I had to face, so great was the anticipation of his visits.

Dealing with cancellations – usually at short notice – brought out the best in one's colleagues and in the concert agents. Word got around like wildfire, and often people would helpfully ring up to suggest substitutes. Singers were the most likely cancellers, and it was always easy to understand their problems. Who was around to take over depended largely on luck. Within an hour of Margaret Price's cancelling on the very day of her concert, Rosalind Plowright was in the hall rehearsing. Only on one occasion did I have to change a programme, in 1986, when the Russian bass Paata Burchuladze cancelled a planned performance of Shostakovich's *Suite on Verses of Michelangelo Buonarroti*. No replacement could be found who knew the work. We substituted

Shostakovich's First Violin Concerto for the song cycle, and in this way Dmitri Sitkovetsky made a very successful Proms debut. The Shostakovich song cycle took its place in a later year, and saw the improbable Proms debut of Dietrich Fischer-Dieskau at the age of sixty-two. He had, quite simply, never been invited before.

I tried to be even-handed in offering dates to the British regional orchestras, although the poor state of the Hallé for most of my time and of the Royal Scottish National Orchestra meant that they were only occasional visitors. The Bournemouth Symphony Orchestra, under both Andrew Litton and later Yakov Kreizberg, certainly earned their place. It was unthinkable that we should not plan for two Proms with the City of Birmingham Symphony Orchestra and Simon Rattle, but an unexpected and very satisfying relationship grew up between the Proms audience and the Royal Liverpool Philharmonic under their Czech Principal Conductor Libor Pešek. In my first year, Pešek came to the Albert Hall for a meeting to discuss his ideas. I did not know him and he had never been to the hall before, but with typical practical intelligence he wanted to see the place and tailor his ideas to its scale. After our meeting, he asked if he could stay on for that evening's concert. I took to him at once, and was sure we could find interesting things to programme. What he really wanted, above all, was to conduct the *Asrael Symphony* of the Czech composer Josef Suk – for British audiences, totally unknown territory. I said I would certainly consider it, for it is a fine work, but not for three or four years. I wanted time for him to build a reputation, and this he did with impressive confidence. He made his debut with Dvořák the following year, then conducted Smetana's complete *Má Vlast*, and in 1990 the *Eroica* and the Janáček *Glagolitic Mass*. By now Pešek evenings at the Proms were selling out, and when in 1991 we finally included the *Asrael Symphony*, preceded by the Elgar Cello Concerto, the attendance was 85 per cent. It is extremely satisfying to build a long-term relationship like this with a conductor. It creates real confidence on both sides. Twice Pešek stepped in at short notice and took over difficult programmes, and I have the happiest memories of working with him.

There was only one bumpy moment. At a dinner after his second appearance, he invited me to bring my main guests, great friends, the writer John Mortimer and his wife, while he brought the RLPO's Chairman, John Last, a noted supporter of Margaret Thatcher. Pešek told us all what a heroine Thatcher was in Czechoslovakia and how lucky we were to have her at the helm. Mortimer and I caught each other's eye, and I wondered what would happen next. Quietly and firmly, Mortimer said he could understand Pešek's point of view as seen from Prague, but seen from the Royal Court Theatre, whose Chairman he was, things looked rather different. Not for the first time with such moments, the wives saved the day. Penny Mortimer and Jarmila Pešek launched into a passionate rhapsody about the Proms and their audience, and the tension disappeared.

Yet Pešek was right: Thatcher *was* a hero for Eastern Europe. On the only occasion I was involved in a conversation with her, after a performance at Glyndebourne, she gave a very perceptive description of the changing situation in the East and showed real understanding of the different cultures and attitudes of Poland, the Ukraine and the Baltic States. What was fascinating was her obvious contempt for France and Germany. She constantly referred to her friend *Mr* Gorbachev, then dismissively to Mitterrand and Kohl *tout court*. 'The Germans have got to be patient,' she cried several times. In our group was the German conductor Lothar Zagrosek, the first West German to take on a major job in the former East Germany, at the Leipzig Opera. He was unable to get a word in. I realized why Thatcher was so hard to interview, for she never looked anyone in the eye – she spoke to the gaps between people and hectored. Eventually I managed to say, 'Prime Minister, if you'd spent forty years under Ulbricht and Honecker, you might not be quite so patient.' She fixed me with a gimlet look and snapped, 'No doubt', then went on about the dangers presented by Franco-German cooperation. During the half-hour we talked she sank three large tumblers of whisky, not much diluted, and then swept out to 'get back to my boxes'. The production she had seen that night was the controversial Peter Sellars version of *The Magic Flute*, with all the dialogue cut. Predictably, she hated it. But she totally approved of Glyndebourne, operating as it did without subsidy. As she made her exit, George Christie, who had borne the brunt of the evening, said quietly, 'Well, I think that's worth a knighthood', which of course he duly and deservedly received.

I never had much say in what Simon Rattle would conduct in the Proms: he had very clear ideas of his own. There was not much point in arguing, since he was always quite immovable, but it wasn't really necessary, for his ideas were always interesting. There was, however, rarely a complete programme, and the interest for me was in the tennis match that completed the plan, lobbing works, ideas or soloists to each other. I much enjoyed seeing Simon – so much so that I rather hoped we would not reach too easy a conclusion, as I used to relish my regular visits to Birmingham to settle the deal over a lunch or a late supper. Like many conductors, he knows what he is good at, although his range of special enthusiasms is much wider than most. He believes in the music of our time, as he showed in his admirable championing of Mark-Anthony Turnage as composer in residence, and he cares about great neglected composers like Carl Nielsen. He had the huge advantage in Birmingham of being able to perform a programme three or four times before it was brought to London to face the national press, and this gave his performances a degree of polish and refinement denied to London orchestras.

The question always asked was whether the City of Birmingham Symphony Orchestra were as good under other conductors. It is difficult to answer, since on most of the occasions when I have heard them they have been conducted by Simon, and yet there was an undeniable improvement in the whole sound of the orchestra during his time there. This has been excitingly maintained by his successor, Sakari Oramo.

It was eminently sensible for Simon to have stayed in Birmingham and learnt his craft thoroughly and to have rejected rushing about guesting until he finally felt ready to take on the world. I first met him in 1974, when he won the John Player Conductors' Competition, and was immediately struck by his electric personality. Yet he was modest, lacking the arrogance that so many conductors develop. He was not universally successful after that. He had unhappy experiences in early years with the Cleveland and Concertgebouw orchestras, and was reluctant to become a Blu-Tack travelling maestro. He wanted to move on from standard programmes, and was fierce in his belief for the need for change. One night at Henze's house, after conducting the London première of Henze's Seventh Symphony, he got into a discussion about Aldeburgh with the Princess of Hesse and the Rhine, who was President of the Aldeburgh Foundation. She was alarmed at the disagreements that had emerged following Peter Pears's death and wanted to know why the directors of the Festival could not recapture the mood of earlier days, when things seemed so simple and straightforward. Simon became really angry. 'You cannot ever go back, nor should you want to,' he said. 'It is a recipe for death and decline. Aldeburgh, of all places, must be about the future.' Simon's approach to music reflects his continuing belief that nothing can stand still and you must find ways of intelligently moving forward. His skill, both in chosing reper- tory and in the careful preparation of programmes with a stable body of players, was matched by that of the CBSO's long-time Chief Execu- tive, Ed Smith, who was as full of ideas as Simon and managed to raise the money to realize them.

Rattle is very tough indeed where work is concerned, and no one is ever going to persuade him to do something he feels himself not ready for. He avoided Beethoven symphonies for years. Given his very wide musical tastes, he is also unwilling to repeat successes. When I realized we were likely to have a Sunday Prom on the exact fiftieth anniversary of the outbreak of the Second World War, I asked him to conduct Brit- ten's *War Requiem*, which he had done very successfully in Birming- ham and London a couple of years earlier. He would not revisit the *War Requiem* for several years, he said. Instead we programmed Brit- ten's *Sinfonia da Requiem* and Mahler's Seventh Symphony – just as appropriate for the anniversary, and more challenging for him and his orchestra. It has been one of the keenest pleasures of my musical life to have watched his steady growth and striking individual approach to music of all periods. It is no surprise to find him as happy with the Orchestra of the Age of Enlightenment as he is with the Berlin Philhar- monic.

So much talent is today endangered by the pressure placed on con- ductors by too much travel, by too many new musical relationships and by unthinking demands by record companies. One night at Glyn- debourne I sat next to Franz Welser-Möst, a highly talented and inter- esting musician. What was he doing next? I asked. The answer was horrifying. There were plans for him to record some Dvořák sym- phonies, some Haydn symphonies, Stravinsky's *Oedipus Rex* and a major symphony by Bruckner. He was still in his twenties. I never doubted his talent, and am delighted that a period of sensible retrench- ment working under less pressure at the Zurich opera has now led to his appointment in Cleveland, but it was a close-run thing. He could have burnt out completely, as other highly praised young prizewinners have done.

There is a serious shortage of great conductors nowadays, and the failure of most of them to stay in one place to serve a long apprentice- ship is one of the main reasons. Examination of the careers of Mengel- berg, Ansermet, Ormandy and Mravinsky shows that these conductors were associated for long periods with one orchestra, as in our time Haitink in Amsterdam and Masur in Leipzig have been. Jansons in Oslo and Dutoit in Montreal also show how much can be achieved by staying in one place with an orchestra which may not yet be great, but which might become so. Yet people like me are among the guilty, constantly making demands on conductors' time and pushing them on matters of repertory. In the case of the major figures, I know how little leeway there is. With conductors like Haitink and Colin Davis I could make a programme in ten minutes on the telephone, since I know them, what they like and what they do best. It is the conductors without such a strong personality or with a huge repertory that often take more time. The size of the repertory is what makes conductors valuable for radio orchestras. They have to be willing not to repeat the same thing time and time again, even though repetition is often the key to deeper understanding and great results. It is a tricky balance. It was marvellous to have Jansons in Cardiff for his years with the BBC Welsh Symphony Orchestra, but his repertory was relatively small. Downes in Manchester conducted everything from Albéniz to Zemlinsky, but with less memorable results. I was fortunate to have a hand in the transition to Tadaaki Otaka in Wales, to Yan Pascal Tortelier in Manchester and to Osmo Vänskä in Scotland, all of whom combine wide range with strong areas of special interest.

Broadcasting makes huge demands on conductors, and in regional orchestras they rarely have the very best raw material to work with, but throughout my time the steadily improving standard of the BBC's regional orchestras was something I could take pleasure in demonstrating in the Proms. It was not a case of saving money or of being nice to colleagues. By involving the BBC regional orchestras, we managed to achieve a broad range of programmes including much new music and impressive performances of standard repertory. It was considered very risky of me to have asked Otaka and the Welsh to play Mahler's Fifth Symphony the year after Bernstein had conducted it with the Vienna Philharmonic, but I never heard the Welsh orchestra play better. They rose to the challenge, and that satisfied everyone – players, audience and organizers.

The role of chamber orchestras and early-music groups in the Proms was a relatively new one, but their rise in popular appeal made it necessary to find appropriate ways of including them with programmes that did not get lost in such a big hall. Groups like the Norwegian

Chamber Orchestra, the Chamber Orchestra of Europe, the Orpheus
Ensemble from New York and the Moscow Virtuosi were so disciplined and produced such a body of string sound that they presented
no problems of either audibility or impact, but an early experience
with the excellent Amsterdam Baroque Orchestra showed me that such
groups needed a chorus, strong vocal soloists or a major brass ensemble to really carry. When they had these, ensembles as diverse as Marc
Minkowski's Les Musiciens du Louvre and Trevor Pinnock's English
Concert presented dramatic works by Purcell and Handel in a way that
really connected with a growing audience.

John Eliot Gardiner had a strong personal following. For me, both
Roger Norrington and Nikolaus Harnoncourt were much more impressive conductors, but Gardiner's Monteverdi Choir Prom would usually
sell out and give us our annual chance to have a falling out with Gardiner himself, whose lofty attitude to colleagues and the BBC did not
endear. One year he proposed Gluck's *Orfeo*. I took it largely to obtain
the Proms debut of the American soprano Sylvia McNair, whom I had
much admired since hearing her at St Louis. She made a dramatic
entrance at the top of the side stairs, dressed in a brilliant lemon-yellow
dress. Slowly descending the staircase, she reached the stage for her
entrance aria. At this moment, Gardiner stopped the orchestra and
retuned. I was furious: it was so grotesquely offensive and unmusical.
When I went round to commiserate with Sylvia, she told me he had
done it at every one of the preceding performances. One year Gardiner
persuaded me to accept a performance of the Bach B minor Mass without soloists, using members of his own excellent Monteverdi Choir for
the solos. Much as I admired the choir, I was not entirely sure that individual members could carry such major parts in such a big building.
However, I need not have worried. Without reference to the Proms
office or any regard for the financial implications, Gardiner changed his
mind and booked a roster of five distinguished soloists which cost me
thousands. He was quite unapologetic, and I was considered imperti-
nent to have questioned his judgement. His judgement was probably
correct; his manner of achieving it was unacceptable.

Gardiner's extraordinary arrogance was admirably demonstrated at
a *Gramophone* magazine awards ceremony when, claiming he had to
get back to Paris for rehearsals, he insisted that his award should be
presented separately and before the celebratory lunch. He was nevertheless still in his place at table when the ceremony ended some three

hours later. It was always a relief to work more happily with other baroque specialists like Paul McCreesh or Robert King, with a modest approach to their role, and a particular pleasure to renew contact with Roger Norrington, who has combated illness in recent years with such remarkable fortitude.

Giving concerts every Sunday and reducing the presence of the London orchestras gave me the space for another key development: an increase in the number of foreign orchestras. In the year I inherited, there were only two. By 1990 the number had risen to seven, and in 1992 and 1995 there were ten. Among the visitors, the European radio orchestras were nothing like as expensive as some British orchestras, largely because their rehearsals were counted as part of their basic contract and I was liable only for the costs of travel and the concert fee. In this way the radio orchestras of Berlin, Paris, Stockholm, Copenhagen and Helsinki came to London, and often with adventurous programmes and outstanding conductors like Esa-Pekka Salonen, Vladimir Ashkenazy, Riccardo Chailly, Marek Janowski, Ulf Schirmer and Jukka-Pekka Saraste.

The Concertgebouw from Amsterdam came to the Proms four times with Riccardo Chailly. It has been a cause of real regret to me that so little of Chailly's career has been in the United Kingdom. From his debut in Edinburgh and concerts with the Royal Philharmonic and the London Symphony Orchestra, I came to have a very high opinion of his all-round ability and intelligence. I would dearly like to have seen him in charge at Covent Garden. Like his Italian contemporaries Abbado, Muti and Sinopoli, he is torn between the opera house and the concert platform, but for me he excels in both. He makes adventurous progammes and is fun to be with. I was totally surprised when he went to work for the Concertgebouw, the most serious-minded of European orchestras. The relationship took a number of years to settle down, but now seems both logical and comfortable and the orchestra play for him at their very considerable best.

Mariss Jansons also came four times, with the Oslo Philharmonic, the most improved and unproblematic of European orchestras, whose presence was always a delight. The Leipzig Gewandhaus Orchestra came with Kurt Masur, Gothenburg with Neeme Järvi, St Petersburg with Yuri Temirkanov and Jansons, and Dresden twice with Colin Davis. There was also Rotterdam with James Conlon, Budapest with Ivan Fischer, the Orchestre de Paris with Semyon Bychkov, and the St

Cecilia from Rome (the first Italian orchestra ever to play at the Proms) with Daniele Gatti. From further away the Sydney Symphony Orchestra came with Edo de Waart and the Israel Philharmonic with Zubin Mehta. Any festival in the world would be glad to have these orchestras, but, such was the attraction of the Proms, their presence was not hard to achieve.

It was much more difficult to achieve the visits of the Vienna Philharmonic. Their visit in 1987 with Bernstein, and with Abbado the following night, was hugely successful. A later visit led to endless rows and recriminations about costs, since they had failed to tell us that half the orchestra were coming from Barcelona and half from Vienna, and the financial implications were substantial. When the Berlin Philharmonic came for the first time, in 1991, I was extremely apprehensive about the backstage conditions of the Albert Hall and the lack of appropriate changing space. On the night, I was confronted by a row of double-bass players in their underpants changing in the corridor, using their bass cases as wardrobes. Far from being difficult, they thought it hilarious, and they were even more taken with the Proms audience. Since Abbado had insisted on programming the Brahms Second Piano Concerto with Brendel and also Mahler's Fourth Symphony with Cheryl Studer, the concert has the distinction of being by far the most expensive in the whole history of the Proms, but it was worth every penny and meant another much hoped-for element ticked off my wish list. The Berliners came back again in 1994 and, under Abbado, gave the most memorable performance of Mahler's Ninth Symphony I had ever heard. At the end, as the sounds of the symphony faded into silence, time seemed to stand still and the audience held their applause for what felt like minutes. It was one of the great occasions. This was the kind of thing I wanted, and, provided we could balance the books with less expensive ventures, justified its expense entirely.

Almost every year we had a visit from one of the major American orchestras, and those highly professional bands in their different ways showed some of the possibilities open to orchestras who are properly funded, even if privately, and maintain a stable body of players who play like a real ensemble. We had visits from the New York, Chicago, Cleveland, Boston and Philadelphia orchestras and in 1994 a remarkable juxtaposition of Cleveland, Los Angeles and Pittsburgh one after the other. What was so striking was the sense of corporate morale in these orchestras. More than half the players would be on stage ten or fifteen minutes before the concert began, psyching themselves up for the occasion – in contrast to British colleagues, who, with the exception of the harpist, tended to wander on at the last possible moment and spend the first work in the programme settling down. Having the American orchestras also guaranteed the presence of conductors like Mehta, Solti, Dohnányi, Ozawa, Salonen, Maazel and Sawallisch, and when I looked at the prospectus and saw such names alongside those of our own leading figures I really felt that the claim of the Proms to be 'the World's Greatest Music Festival' was justified.

With the visiting orchestras, I would always go on stage at the beginning of rehearsals in the hall to welcome them and explain some of the Prom traditions, such as the promenader's chants (to the Boston orchestra, 'Welcome to *our* tea party'; to the Orchestre de Paris, 'Bienvenus au Promenade des Anglais') and the cheers that would greet raising the piano lid or the leader giving the orchestra a tuning A on the soloist's piano. They were always amazed when I told them the extent of the series – approximately seventy concerts with some thirty-five orchestras in fifty-eight days, and all this at a time when most concert halls in Europe and America were shut for the summer and very few festivals featured more than, at most, three or four orchestras.

The breadth of the Proms is taken totally for granted by the British audience and by the management of the BBC. It was nevertheless a highly complex operation, like playing multi-dimensional chess, to fit all the orchestras all in, and to make sure they did not all play the same music, much as they seemed to want to. I depended very much on my good relations with conductors and my growing friendships with orchestral managers like the excellent Tom Morris in Cleveland, Trond Okkelmo in Oslo and Elmar Weingarten in Berlin.

The Proms programme was a huge collective project to which innumerable people contributed and in which disagreements were rare. On one occasion, however, the Boston Symphony tried to insist on a work that was already programmed for another orchestra. They rang the other orchestra and told them to withdraw, but it was Boston rather than Bournemouth who withdrew having nearly lost their concert as a result of their attitude. Unlike many festivals, the Proms had an artistic director and a policy, and orchestras could not do just what they wanted. The knack was to get in early on the planning of the repertory, to air my own preoccupations and see how they could be accommodated in a way that suited both ourselves and the other places an orchestra would visit. Sometimes we failed, and looking back on a few programmes I think we could collectively have done better, but usually the discussion process became the foundation of better musical understanding and a happy outcome. As I have said before, it is no good forcing someone to do something they don't want to do or don't like, but first thoughts are not always the best and blocking the intention of *everyone* to play Mahler was a public service.

A former colleague recently told me that, though my enthusiasms were very visible, it was much harder to see what I disliked. I was happy to hear that, for I was often worried that by omission I might too strongly bias the institution towards my own taste. When I first talked to John Pritchard about the Proms, he said, 'I'll do anything except the Chausson Symphony.' I immediately scheduled it for the following year with another conductor. Though there are better works, even by Chausson, the symphony was not a problem for me. Few composers are, except for some early-twentieth-century windbags with all the technique in the world but nothing much to say. Reger is for me the worst. I have a particular dislike of the nineteenth-century French organ repertory, but it did not prevent the inclusion of Franck or Widor if the organist could make an interesting programme which suited the hall. I was perhaps too tough on a number of English composers of the first half of the twentieth century. I did find room for several Bax pieces, but not for his symphonies – Nielsen and Sibelius seem to me so obviously better. But more important than my personal taste was the imperative to make good programmes. Over the ten seasons, I must have had a hand in more than six hundred: some simple, some very complex, and some that did not achieve what we hoped.

I am often asked what makes a good programme. There are so many possible alternatives that it is an unanswerable question, but I knew very quickly what made a bad one. I tried to avoid the pitfalls of, for instance, too long a first half or too much that is unfamiliar, whether it is old or new. I never felt anxious about key relationships, as did so many musicians of the older generation, but only in exceptional circumstances did I like programmes of the music of only one composer – a key feature of the Proms in early years. I tried to avoid the juxtaposition of similar kinds of music, such as Ravel and Debussy or Prokofiev and Stravinsky, since one of the composers always tends rather to cancel out the other. There is no winning formula, and we have nowadays a much less restrictive attitude to programmes than our forebears. It is still possible to perform an overture, a concerto and a symphony and make a satisfying whole, but there are lots of other approaches too, and some of them lead to a wider trawl through the music of the past and a better context in which to place the music of today.

With a festival as extensive as the Proms there is no question of one person imposing their own taste, as Robert Simpson claimed in his 1981 pamphlet *The Proms and Natural Justice*, since such a large-scale operation can never reflect just one view. But the deliberations of the kind of committee he suggested seem to me equally dangerous. I suppose that William Glock came closest to imposing a single view, but his tastes were wide-ranging and his programmes highly imaginative. I have a few musical blind spots, of which Gilbert & Sullivan are one, but when I dropped G&S from the Proms it was not because *I* didn't like them but because the public seemed to have lost interest. I was criticized for almost always including the major symphonic works of Debussy, Ravel and Stravinsky, but they were for me the touchstones of twentieth-century taste. I came late to a love of Bruckner, and found the Albert Hall an ideal building in which to undertake the long but so satisfying journeys through his works. I sought advice about baroque music, but was found wanting in my decisions by many who looked for less familiar lists of works by Bach and much more Handel. But I was very much dependent on what the performers in this area were performing elsewhere. None of the early-music groups is a permanent body: they tend to come together for a tour on which they perform the same works wherever they go. It was no good my asking for six rare Bach cantatas when the other venues all wanted something better known. I no longer found it necessary to programme all the Beethoven symphonies every year, as had been the tradition in my youth. I remember once wondering if I would be attacked for leaving out a popular concerto like the Tchaikovsky B flat minor for the second year running, but in the event no one noticed, and when we brought it back for the London debut of the very young Evgeny Kissin it seemed fresher than ever.

In standard repertory I wanted the best possible performance, not just another parade of the familiar, and because of this I also wanted the best soloists. This set up an inevitable tension between the role of British musicians and that of foreign ones. The presence of British music and British orchestras was an inevitable part of the overall plan, but when it came to soloists we had a much wider choice. I was lucky that my time coincided with a golden age of British singers, and I sought every year to include leading figures like Ann Evans, Felicity Lott, Ann Murray, Anthony Rolfe Johnson, Philip Langridge, John Tomlinson and Thomas Allen, as well as to give opportunities to rising younger artists like Michael Chance, Janice Watson, Judith Howarth, Jean Rigby, Simon Keenlyside and Catherine Wyn-Rogers. But it was good to keep in regular touch with outstanding foreign singers like Barbara Bonney, Brigitte Fassbaender, Jessye Norman, Arleen Augér, José van Dam and Dmitri Hvorostovsky, even though they cost a great deal more – sometimes, as with Jessye Norman, eventually pricing themselves out of our range.

With instrumentalists, the choice was more tricky. I wanted the best, and thought that nationalism should not play a leading role. In fact, provided the concerto was popular, who performed it seemed to have very little influence on the sale of tickets. There were of course a number of stars like Mstislav Rostropovich, Alfred Brendel and Anne-Sophie Mutter who had their own following, but they were relatively few. In my first year I offered engagements to fourteen British pianists. It had no adverse affect on the box office, and gave me a chance to see how some of them handled big occasions. Some, like John Lill and Peter Donohoe, already had a following. Others, like Kathryn Stott, became regulars. Some I did not invite back. My time coincided with the emergence of a remarkable new generation of violinists. In my Edinburgh years there had been only Kyung-Wha Chung. Now there were Frank Peter Zimmermann, Joshua Bell, Gil Shaham, Raphael Oleg, Antje Weithaas, Christian Tetzlaff, Pamela Frank, Tasmin Little, Dong-Suk Kang, and the very young and extraordinary Maxim Vengerov. Vengerov had made his debut for the same fee as Bell and Zimmermann, but within a year it had gone up by 400 per cent and I could not keep pace.

Artists' fees were negotiated annually between the BBC's Contracts Department and the concert managements. Usually we arrived at what was called an 'agreed fee' for the year and there was then no further debate. But with debutants and fast-rising stars it was more complex. British artists tended to start at the bottom of the BBC scale, and it took even someone like Felicity Lott many years to reach the level at which some foreign artists began. I thought this unjust. To bring in foreign artists, one had to justify their professional standing in order to get a work permit, and I sometimes felt that the agents upped the fees to demonstrate the international reputation of their clients. We had few fallings out with British agents, but when the Americans started taking over it became more difficult. Most of the British agents understood our problems, and managers like Joeske van Walsum, Stephen Lumsden, Martin Campbell-White and David Sigall became not only necessary professional colleagues but friends. Others were more nakedly rapacious, and I sometimes tackled them when I thought they were behaving unreasonably. There was one occasion when I invited an American soprano who lived in Europe, and her agent said he would not approach her without being offered a fee much in excess of what had been agreed earlier in the year. So I rang the artist, who was a friend, to find that her agent *had* contacted her and she had already accepted the engagement at her normal fee. The agent was forced to back down. Negotiating was a two-way street. I knew how little we paid on the international scale, but also how prized a Proms invitation was, especially for a young artist but even for an established one. Just as with Edinburgh, once you had appeared at the Proms you never left it off your CV.

A personal difficulty was that there always were more people I wanted to invite than I had room for, and every time I booked someone new this inevitably excluded someone else who had perhaps come to regard a Proms engagement as part of their regular pattern of work. There are a number of good British pianists who did not do well out of my time, but when the choice had to be made between them and a brilliant newcomer like Leif Ove Andsnes or Lars Vogt I felt I had no choice. It was so important not to let the Proms become repetitive and routine, as they had been in the years before Glock transformed them. When outstanding new groups emerged, such as the Ensemble Moderne in Germany and the Asko Ensemble in the Netherlands, I wanted to show their qualities, while still keeping a place every year for the London Sinfonietta and being very careful about what they did. In my early years they gave concerts made up of a mass of short pieces and spent more time rearranging the platform than playing. It is a problem of contemporary music that composers refuse to write for standard formations; everything has to have something bizarre included. But getting the platform ready holds up proceedings and frequently kills the atmosphere of the event. It is hard for multi-work programmes of contemporary music to make the impact of a major piece like Messiaen's *Des canyons aux étoiles* or the Henze *Requiem*. These two works not only attracted big audiences, but drew in the best possible way on the very special skills of outstanding performers of new music.

When I started in Edinburgh, and again with the Proms, I said both privately and publicly, 'Let me get on with it as best I can, and I promise I won't stay too long.' Outstaying my welcome was something of which I was very conscious, having followed thirteen years of Peter Diamand in Edinburgh and thirteen years of Robert Ponsonby at the Proms. I organized only five Edinburgh Festivals, and I was not expecting to spend more than six or seven years with the Proms, but coming up on the horizon, in 1995, was a very special anniversary – the Proms' centenary – and I was tempted to stay on to oversee that.

My contract to run both the BBC Proms and Radio 3 was due to end in the spring of 1992. Late in 1990 David Hatch, Managing Director of BBC Radio, offered me a five-year extension. It was generous, but I was beginning to find holding down three overlapping jobs too much. I was not happy at the direction the BBC was taking as John Birt was moving his troops into position. I was not sure that I wanted to continue with interminable and unconstructive interrogations about resources, and the growing emphasis on audience size as the only means of determining quality or effectiveness. Yet I loved the Proms and had ideas for the centenary. I was also determined that the overall control of Radio 3 and Music should not be separated again, so I suggested tentatively that I might not extend my existing contract but would stay until the centenary to run only the Proms. I knew this could cause difficulties in finding a successor, since the Proms were the most enjoyable part of the job. I also knew that my continuing presence might be a problem for whoever took over the network. But I felt that for once I should ask for things to be on my terms. I had spent over thirty years trying to be a good servant of the organizations that employed me. I had not put my own requirements, let alone financial rewards, at the top of the list. For once I thought I had perhaps earned the right to go on doing something I loved and to shed the less enjoyable part of things. So it was agreed that I should give up Radio 3 in 1992, but continue as Director of the Proms until after the centenary season in 1995. Typically, and stupidly, I suggested I take a cut in my salary without waiting to see what they would offer. Compared to the salaries then being offered to outside appointees I was far from overpaid. I wonder how many others would have volunteered that.

When the two jobs of Controller of Radio 3 and Controller of Music were merged in 1987, I had asked to retain both responsibilities in my job description. Why could I not be Controller of Radio 3 and Music? But Michael Checkland was adamantly opposed; it was Controller of Radio 3 or nothing. I pointed out that I was sure that the music profession would see this as a downgrading of the place of music in the BBC's corporate thinking. Even though at that time no such downgrading seemed to be intended, I thought it necessary to insist. But I lost the argument, and subsequently I came to wonder whether there was in fact a long-term strategy to diminish the BBC's public role in music, either by getting rid of orchestras or by reducing the budget of Radio 3.

By 1990, this seemed a real possibility. Libraries, archives and many other traditional craft centres of the BBC were being disposed of or greatly cut back. There had been renewed attacks on the BBC Singers, on the need for the Music Library, and on the cost of the orchestras. An internal financial inquiry, whose members somehow had not found time to consult me during their deliberations, came up with the requirement to cut orchestral costs by 10 per cent. Why 10 per cent?, I asked. Why not 9 per cent, or 12, 36 or 3? On what basis had this figure been arrived at? There was no answer. It was one of those brisk managerial diktats whose implications had simply not been thought through. I went to see Checkland and explained to him that a 10 per cent cut in the cost of the orchestras – a saving of about £2 million a year – could be achieved in only one of two ways: by sacrificing an orchestra or by obtaining commercial sponsorship of the Proms. Consternation! Surely we could sell a few more tickets, make a few more commercial recordings, put up our hire charges to outside promoters. It was cloud-cuckoo-land.

I was totally opposed to losing an orchestra, especially since since it would have had to have been the BBC Philharmonic in Manchester, as the Welsh and Scottish orchestras were protected by their national regional status. I was also totally opposed to the Henry Wood Proms becoming the BP Proms or the Royal Insurance Proms or whatever. I was in due course strongly resistant to their being renamed the BBC Proms, since this clearly contravened the agreement with Wood's heirs that his name should feature in perpetuity in the title. Yet this decision again was taken without consultation with me, as part of the 'branding' of the BBC imposed on the organization by public-relations people like Tim Bell, who was paid huge sums for the deep originality of telling us we should say not 'Radio 3' but 'BBC Radio 3'. It was true that many people thought that the Proms just happened or were run by the Albert Hall, so I was not unsympathetic to enhancing the visibility of the BBC in the operation, but I was unhappy about being bypassed. These things needed open discussion. It all augured badly for the future.

To avoid the 10 per cent cut proposed, Checkland opted for sponsorship of the Proms, and I was mandated to seek it. I took on an experienced but abrasive fund-raiser, Wendy Stevenson, who had achieved a great deal at the Edinburgh Festival after my departure. But her attitudes were not those of a public-service organization. Many, including Alan Yentob of BBC Television, felt that the BBC's ownership of the Proms was one of the prime examples of the Corporation's public-service role and should not be sacrificed for the sake of a small financial advantage. Surprisingly, John Birt was also against sponsorship. But the project never really had a chance. The quest for sponsors coincided with the worst recession in business for a generation, leaving those banks, insurance and oil companies who had been among the leaders in arts sponsorship in the 1980s retrenching fast. All the big players were contacted; most of them wanted only the Last Night. But I was adamant that the Proms could not be sold off in bits. It was the whole season or nothing. The Proms had to be worth somewhere in the region of £2 million a year to a sponsor. Royal Insurance was giving the Royal Shakespeare Company £1 million, but no one offered anything like double that. A dreary campaign went on for the next nine months, with Ms Stevenson submitting invoices for thousands, but there were no takers.

Eventually Checkland not only was forced to back down on sponsorship, he also found himself with a £2 million increase in orchestral costs through the new contract that we had been negotiating with the musicians – much more favourable to the BBC, but still very expensive. He came up with the money, but, despite the Proms' steadily rising attendance figures, I was not everybody's favourite person. But the orchestral costs were only a tiny part of the BBC's £2 billion budget. The BBC Symphony Orchestra cost no more than a TV drama series. The Proms were incredibly cheap, since the concerts performed by the BBC orchestras were already covered as part of the orchestras' annual contracts, and the overall income from concerts, programmes and associated advertising covered all the other expenditure except the cost of the Albert Hall. George Howard, when Chairman of the BBC, had made the hall rental the subject of a special financial grant. It was only the rent rise that made the Proms seem pricey.

There was a curious double standard at work. No one ever said that a drama production *lost* money: it simply *cost* money. But the cost of an orchestra was always presented as a loss. As far as I was concerned, putting on concerts cost money, just as putting on plays or making documentaries cost money. It was part of the cost of broadcasting. But the figures were not presented this way, and the fact that the orchestras and their personnel were charged to Radio 3 made it disproportionately expensive compared to the other networks. Accounting can be done in all kinds of ways, but this seemed to me totally uncreative accounting. Not even Checkland, an accountant by profession but also a keen music-lover, could sort it out.

This situation was to be reinforced in 1993 by the ludicrous invention of so-called Producer Choice, which, by creating business units covering everything from carpets to pensions, made the BBC's orchestras seem more expensive than hiring orchestras from outside. However, as I said earlier, while owning a car does cost more than taking the occasional taxi, it gives you a quite different control over your life. The BBC's extraordinary role in British music came from its having orchestras, libraries, commission funds and all the rest. The Corporation's contribution to the artistic climate of the country could not be assessed by a simple profit-and-loss account as suggested by the corner-shop mentality which lay behind the whole market-forces movement. Simple cost accounting is not the way to evaluate the significance of Oxford University, the British Museum or an organization like the BBC, which had led the world in standards of programme quality, editorial judgement and political independence. None of that seemed to register with the new men of the Birtist BBC.

Even some members of the Thatcher government had reservations about what was happening. Timothy Renton, when Minister for the Arts, was invited to a concert in Manchester given by the BBC Philharmonic, with the aim of interesting potential sponsors. He made a good speech, but rather spoiled the occasion by turning up with the Chairman of the Hallé, with whom he was staying. During the course of dinner, he asked me a pertinent question. 'Why,' he said, 'having so successfully resisted Margaret Thatcher, Norman Tebbit and David Young, is the BBC now destroying itself?' Renton had been Douglas

Hurd's number two at the Home Office during negotiations about the BBC's licence fee and was someone whom the BBC considered a friend. The only answer could be that, in their understandable obsession with the need to win renewal of the BBC's charter, Hussey and Birt had decided that demonstrating a willingness to grovel was the only way to achieve favourable results. It was not clear that they had any idea of what the BBC was really about or what had given it its stature over the years. Now value for money and corporate management training were the battle-cries, not the timeless values of education, information and entertainment which the BBC had so long stood for, long before we were all told to write mission statements and set objectives.

It was during this period that the conversation took place that gave this book its title. 'Tainted by Experience' was what a young Birtist consultant called me, and I proudly shared that description with some of my colleagues. Before long, a select group of us had T-shirts emblazoned with those words. But the Birtists had the last laugh. Within a year or two, all those of us who thought 'Tainted by Experience' outrageous had left the organization.

# 16

# Moving to a Close

It must have been early in 1991 when I had a call from Nicholas Kenyon, inviting me to lunch. We had known each other for years, and I liked him and admired his work. He had done a lot for the BBC Music Department in his earlier days and had written the official history of the BBC Symphony Orchestra, not an easy task. He had spent a year in New York deputizing for Andrew Porter on the *New Yorker*, and we had passed some time together there before he returned to become principal music critic of the *Observer*. For my predecessors, Kenyon was a controversial figure. After years of experience, he had been effectively banned from broadcasting on Radio 3, and Christine Hardwick always referred to him as 'squeaky Kenyon'. I had no problems with his voice, and thought the reaction rather silly. I had asked him to write an article on the BBC's orchestras for my first Proms brochure, in 1987, and I knew from other things he had written that he supported the general thrust of what I was trying to do, especially in bringing words and music closer together on Radio 3.

At the lunch, he asked my advice about his future. He had recently been offered a senior post at the *New York Times*, but had declined it, not because he disliked New York but because his wife had serious misgivings about bringing up their children there. Though he shared his wife's anxiety, it was obviously a great disappointment to him, and he was not sure which direction he might now take. Only half seriously, I said, 'Do you want my job?' He laughed, and said it had occurred to him. I knew I was leaving in a year's time and he seemed to me a promising candidate, so I undertook to tell my senior colleagues about him since I suspected – quite rightly – that they would never have heard of him.

There was a real shortage of suitable candidates for senior posts in the BBC, and the changing nature of the organization was making it harder and harder to attract the best people, especially in areas which seemed as if they might be under threat. Only two producers had applied for the job of senior producer to the BBC Symphony Orchestra. We had had a very poor short list to replace Christine Hardwick on her retirement, and the choice we made proved unsatisfactory. I had thought that Adrian Thomas, Professor of Music at the Queen's University in Belfast – a composer, teacher and experienced broadcaster – might have brought new ideas to the job, but even before he started I discovered that Belfast had offered to keep his chair open for him in case he did not settle at the BBC. I should have taken this more seriously, for no one ever gives their all to a task if they are at the same time seeking a safe exit. My job, created by merging Radio 3 and Music and including the Proms, was to say the least daunting, and still demanding even without the Proms. Of one thing I was convinced: the successful candidate needed to be someone with a reputation in the world of music, both to reassure the musical world of the BBC's continuing commitment and to be a figurehead in the battles which were sure to come with the arrival in 1992 of Classic FM and over the future of the orchestras. Birt showed no interest at all in the orchestras, never attended concerts, and usually paid only one visit to the Proms – except for the Last Night, when he filled his box with Conservative politicians and right-wing journalists. If he was getting rid of studios and cutting back on film crews, outside-broadcast units, libraries, archives and the rest, why should he not move against the orchestras?

I told David Hatch about Kenyon and said that in many ways he seemed to have the necessary background, even though he had never run anything more than small-scale publications like *Early Music* and the occasional festival. I also quite properly told my deputy, Brian Barfield, that, despite his excellent work and totally loyal support, I felt he was not likely to become Controller as he had no standing in the world of music. Either he refused to take this seriously or he believed he could win on his own terms, for he did in due course apply for the job, did not get it, and took the failure very badly indeed. For several years it was more than he could do to bring himself to speak to me, which I much regretted since we had worked together so enjoyably. Being a brilliant number two, as Brian was, has often proved an obstacle to promotion. Of course if you are an uncomfortable number two, as I had been, that too can prove an obstacle. But bringing people in from outside also had its problems.

Although the BBC was not necessarily bound by the past, it was often extremely difficult to find out exactly how it worked. Neither Brian Wenham nor Dick Francis seemed to me to have a real under-

standing of radio, and gave the impression of marking time while waiting for something better. David Hatch had spent his life in radio but,
though totally professional, had a less intellectual approach. The BBC
had always depended on a lead from the top, but after my return in
1985 I had little sense of strong editorial leadership anywhere. Paul
Fox, the Managing Director of BBC Television, having returned from
Yorkshire Television rich but without his earlier drive, seemed to spend
most days at the races, while Michael Grade always gave the impression that it was commercial television that had got its priorities right.
Milne was too abrasive, and Checkland too modest. We all tried, in as
polite a way as possible, to encourage Checkland to express his views
about the output, to become a more public figure. If you are the boss,
you somehow have to be seen to be the boss. Wheldon's relentless glad-
handing could be irritating, but at least he behaved as if he were in
charge, though he never made it to the top. The same was true of
Gerard Mansell and John Tusa, both of whom had run Bush House
brilliantly, and had infinitely better qualifications to become Director-
General than the men who actually got the job.

The chemistry between the Board of Management and the Governors was always interesting to watch. I would go in front of the Governors about three times a year, and was given a minute or two to talk
about the orchestras, the Proms or Radio 3. The Governors rarely had
much to say and few questions to ask. When I was allowed to stay on
for the regular programme discussion, I was staggered by how little
they had seen or watched, and it was rare for them to make any reference to Radio. I was aware that the main purpose of the Governors
was not to review the output, but they seemed to lack any interest in it.
Discussions revolved around whether we had offended anyone. Hussey
would bluster, the token ethnic-minority-representative governor
would claim under-representation, and P. D. James would occasionally
comment on a drama series or a soap opera. As I watched Checkland
wriggling with discomfort and Birt grinning like a ventriloquist's
dummy, I wondered where and how the real decisions took place.

The Governors always seemed pleased about the Proms, but not one
of them ever had anything to say about Radio 3. Birt seemed not even
aware of the existence of Radio. I asked him one day what he thought
of the BBC's orchestras. He replied that they were 'a variable resource
centre whose viability depends on the business plan of the Controller
of Radio 3'. A year later I repeated this pathetic remark to him. At first

he denied having said it, and then claimed it had been meant as a joke. I certainly could not have invented it, since, mercifully, that kind of language does not spring to my lips. It reveals the extent to which ludicrous jargon had replaced normal speech in a organization that one would have hoped would have been dedicated to intelligible communication. This was the 'croak-voiced Dalek' of which Dennis Potter complained.

I felt in an increasingly alien world, but I was nevertheless concerned that my successor should carry some clout through having a proven track record from elsewhere. I had come back to the BBC with a public reputation after Edinburgh, and I hoped my successor would be in a similar position from which to ward off attempts to cut the budget or to question the need for orchestras and resources. Nicholas Kenyon got the job on his own merits. Correctly, I was not party to who applied or who was seen. By that time I had been reluctantly swept up into another job, which resulted in my leaving Radio 3 some months before the end of my contract.

In the autumn of 1991, Jeremy Isaacs asked me in the Crush Bar at Covent Garden whether the Arts Minister, Timothy Renton, had been in touch with me. He had not, and Isaacs was unwilling to tell me why he should have been. The call came nearly two months later, and when I went to see the Minister he explained that the government had decided to mark the British presidency of the European Community in the second half of 1992 with an arts festival, and asked if I would be prepared to organize it. I was very sceptical about what, if anything, could be done at little more than six months' notice and astonished that something so ambitious had been left so late. In addition, Renton was unable to tell me exactly how much money might be available, though he hinted at sums in the region of £10 million.

It was an inconclusive meeting, for I explained that I was under contract to the BBC to run Radio 3 until the late spring of 1992. But Renton contacted Checkland and asked if I could be released early from my Radio 3 contract. I talked to Checkland, who saw no objection to my going early. My own friends and advisers were divided. Anyone with relevant expertise recognized the difficulties of the timescale and wondered how much control the government would allow me to have over what was done. Others thought it a good chance for me to use my contacts and to prove that some things were possible even at short notice, and believed that the offer of additional funds for the arts should not be lightly refused. After further meetings I said without arrogance that I could be persuaded only if I would have a degree of independence from committees and the Civil Service.

I was not told until after I had accepted the job that meetings had already taken place with the heads of various arts organizations, who had been encouraged to claim considerable chunks of the money. Several million pounds had already been asked for by the Royal Opera House, English National Opera, the Royal National Theatre and others. Since the overall government contribution had now been set at £6 million, if their bids had been accepted as they stood there would have been virtually nothing left for anyone else. I insisted that everything should be put on hold until I had formed a committee, recruited some staff, found an office, and formulated a policy. All this was done in a matter of weeks, and in January 1992, with six months to go, the European Arts Festival started work.

When it came to staff and offices, we had several very lucky breaks. The Japan Festival of 1991 was winding down, and I was fortunate to be able to recruit David Pickard. He was enthusiastic, very hard-working and a delight to be with, and is now successfully running the Orchestra of the Age of Enlightenment. My former Proms planning assistant, Jacky Guter, came to work for us and did a brilliant job of coordinating the planning and the very complicated costings. I took on two outstanding women, Sally Lewis and Kate Needham, who had also worked for the Japan Festival to run the education programmes. The property developer John Ritblat provided me with an office on part of the recently vacated Thames Television site on Euston Road. Jacky spent a few hundred pounds on second-hand office furniture and soon made it habitable. It was also within walking distance of Broadcasting House, so I could divide my days between the Proms office and the urgent planning needed for the European Arts Festival.

But what was the Festival to be? The Prime Minister, John Major, insisted that he wanted something both widespread and popular and with a European dimension. It should not be a metropolitan event, even if that had been possible at such short notice. The London and regional symphony orchestras, opera houses and ballet companies had the coming season fully planned, and their bids for additional funding looked pretty thin when I had a chance to examine them. But the large organizations continued to believe that they would get considerable sums of additional money, and became extremely hostile when it became clear that they would not. I decided to try to present or underwrite activity in every region of the United Kingdom and Northern Ireland, while spending quite large amounts on bringing to Britain a small number of major European companies which limited funding had made it impossible to bring in previous years. Despite the valuable work of Lift, the London International Festival of Theatre, many of the leading European drama companies had not come to Britain since the days of Peter Daubeny's World Theatre Seasons at the Aldwych in the 1960s and '70s.

I contacted Thelma Holt, who was running her own production company and advising the National Theatre on international links. Thelma, a remarkable actress, enthusiast and operator, had her hands full already, but since we had worked together so satisfactorily before, notably with the Rustaveli company's visit to London after their Edinburgh debut, she agreed to help. It was entirely due to her tenacious efforts that Ariane Mnouchkine's Le Théâtre du Soleil returned to Britain after a nineteen-year absence, along with Giorgio Strehler's Piccolo Teatro of Milan and Franco Zeffirelli's company from Rome. By paying the orchestral costs, we achieved the first visit for fifteen years by the outstanding modern dance company in Europe, Nederlands Dans Teater. These were the big items of expenditure, and corresponded to my long-held ambition to ensure the presence in Britain from time to time of the best of European dance and drama, and not just orchestras or small companies.

Determined to enhance the regional impact, I offered the regional Arts Boards in England and the Arts Councils of Scotland, Wales and Northern Ireland a sum of £50,000 each to develop events with a European dimension in their area, in any art form. We obtained from the Museums and Galleries Commission a list of hoped-for exhibitions which were in trouble with their funding, and were able to contribute to making over a hundred of these possible. We gave money to small publishing houses to promote outstanding European poets and novelists in new translations. For months we worked at white heat, cajoling, enthusing, encouraging people to have ideas and ask us for money.

But in many areas of the arts there was a real resentment at the way we had been funded. Most arts organizations had had their Arts Council grant frozen, some had even had cuts, yet here was the government suddenly providing £6 million extra for something that the media were convinced was unnecessary. I had lunch one day with a group of leading arts journalists and, far from finding any enthusiasm for our plans, was roundly attacked – notably by my old friend Robert Hewison of the *Sunday Times*, who said, 'You have fatally compromised your well-known editorial independence by accepting this tainted money.' Little did they know of the struggle going on behind the scenes to resist the politicians' suggestions for money to be spent on their friends or their constituencies. The Arts Minister thought it would be a good thing to fund some sort of Christmas exhibition to be put on by Christie's and Sotheby's, both of whose chairmen, Lords Carrington and Gowrie, were former Tory cabinet ministers. Neither auction house had any idea at all what it might do, but one elegant young man told me that the Minister required it and that a quarter of a million pounds should do the trick. I noted that they were offering space only over the Christmas period, when there were no auctions taking place. Renton sent the impresario Harvey Goldsmith to see me. He had very successfully put on *Aida* at Earls Court the previous summer and had made a profit. He now wanted to revive it at the National Exhibition Centre in Birmingham, and claimed he needed half a million pounds of our money to do so.

Relations with the Ministry were pretty cool. The senior civil servants had deliberated for weeks on whether we were covered by government indemnity in the event of an accident to staff working in a building which was not government property and for which no rent was being paid. But at least wrestling with this problem kept them busy. One of Renton's aides, a patronizing young man, phoned to inform me that the Minister was worried about whether we knew what we were doing, and offered me the services of Jeffrey Archer. I said we were not quite that desperate.

But I was not only reporting to the Arts Ministry. I had approaches from the Department of the Environment, the Scottish Office, the Welsh Office, the Northern Ireland Office, the Department of Education, and the Foreign Office. The Foreign Office were particularly tiresome, since they were busy compiling their own schedule of possible arts events, which they were reluctant even to discuss with me. It turned out that they were merely responding to unsolicited letters sent to them by a variety of organizations and, instead of passing them to us, were insisting on having their own list of important events, many of which were anything but. I had to appeal to my old friend David Gillmore, who was now Head of the Foreign Office, to intervene. I had trustingly always thought that the mandarins of Whitehall were talented and capable. My year with the European Arts Festival suggested that most of them were terrified of anything new or of creating a precedent.

John Major was helpful and encouraging at every stage, but it was quite clear that the initiative was not widely supported, especially by the Treasury. I spent considerable time trying to raise additional sums from the European Commission, and made two trips to Brussels to argue my case in front of its cultural boss, the attractively named Madame Flesch, a former Mayor of Luxembourg. In the event they gave me 100,000 écus for the education programme, with the immediate result that the equivalent amount was deducted from my budget by the Treasury. No one had bothered to explain to me the concept of additionality. I suppose I should have known about it, but I didn't. No one had warned me that I had been effectively wasting precious time.

The brochure eventually produced ran to twenty pages of closely printed events, grouped by region and ranging from youth theatre to opera, from folk festivals to special displays in local museums. Some of the education initiatives were brilliantly carried through, and literally hundreds of schools became involved. At the centre of the plan was an idea I had long wanted to try: that of a travelling festival which moved from place to place, bringing together all the arts in a circus tent for a weekend. We had a special tent designed and built, and recruited a permanent crew to rig it, man it and move it from place to place, led by the remarkable Julian Sleath, later Technical Director of Scottish Opera. The tent was operational in twelve weekends during the summer, beginning in Chatham and ending in Omagh by way of Lowestoft, Castle Douglas, Glenridding and seven other towns. In each place, there was music of all kinds, cabaret and drama. Local groups appeared alongside leading European entertainers in a continuous programme of different activities. Sometimes it poured with rain, sometimes attendance was thin, but in the best places – like Omagh – there was the feel of a real artistic carnival, involving artists from all over Europe together with the local community. The tent and its tour cost over £1 million, but it left more trace in the communities it visited than if I had bailed out English National Opera.

The whole Festival was conducted in an increasingly hostile political climate. I had strong expressions of support until the signing of the Maastricht Treaty. Suddenly all those ministers who had agreed to attend events or speak on our behalf lost interest, and by the summer they had disappeared entirely from view. After the general election in April 1992 Renton was replaced by David Mellor, and the Arts Ministry quintupled its remit, now also covering broadcasting, sport, the film industry and heritage matters, with the arts relegated to one section among many. At my first meeting with Mellor as Secretary of State for the Arts, after a desultory conversation about our plans, he sent the civil servants out of the room and asked, 'What are they saying about me?' I replied that, whereas before we had had a part-time Arts Minister (who had always also been the Minister responsible for the Civil Service), now we had a Secretary of State, but with a portfolio in which the arts represented a much smaller part of his responsibilities.

Mellor always made much of his commitment to music, but I never saw any evidence of interest in the performing arts. With great reluctance he came to Halifax to the opening night of Mnouchkine's production of *Les Atrides*, presented in a specially converted woollen mill. It was a hot night, and soon after the play began he whispered to me, 'How long does it last?' 'Two and a half hours,' I said. He looked appalled. 'Do I have to stay?' The whole performance was accompanied by his groans of boredom. Of course it was in French, a language he could not be expected to understand, but the glittering brilliance of the staging and the exhilaration of the music and the dance seemed not to impress him one jot.

Following the problems of his private life, Mellor soon departed and was replaced by Peter Brooke, whom I met once, briefly, at the Barbican later in the year. He obviously knew nothing at all about the Festival, and showed no desire to find out. We were even deprived of a highly visible inauguration by Haydn Phillips, the civil servant whom Mellor had brought in from the Treasury as Permanent Secretary. We had planned to launch the Festival with the opening of a very impressive Manet exhibition at the National Gallery, to which I had contributed a much needed £100,000. The plan was that, on 1 July, the European Commissioners and the government would travel from the Westminster Conference Centre to the National Gallery to see the exhibition and have a buffet lunch there, with speeches on the importance of European culture from both John Major and Jacques Delors, the President of the European Commission. About a month before the launch, I was sent for by Phillips. When I entered his office, he brandished an advance copy of the catalogue of the Manet exhibition, which showed on the front a detail of a partially destroyed painting of the execution

431

of the Emperor Maximilian of Mexico. The exhibition was devoted to bringing all the surviving fragments of the picture together for the first time since Manet's death. 'How', shouted Phillips, 'can you expect a government to associate itself with an image like that? It is unthinkable', and he promptly cancelled the National Gallery reception.

All I was left with for an opening event was some Italian flag-wavers outside the Westminster Conference Centre. There I noticed Mellor among a group of ministers waiting on the pavement for the arrival of the EC Heads of State. I joined him, and he introduced me to the then Minister of Education, John Patten. Mellor explained what I was doing. Patten looked supremely uninterested. I ventured that we had quite a few events planned for Oxford, his constituency. He turned to me and in a voice of real contempt hissed, 'There is far too much bloody culture in Oxford already.'

The high point of the Festival for me was the visit to the National Theatre of the Piccolo Teatro of Milan with Giorgio Strehler's extraordinary evocation of eighteenth-century life on the Venetian lagoon in Goldoni's *Le barruffe chiozzotte*, one of the most magical evenings I have ever spent in the theatre. It was mostly acted out in misty silhouette, with marvellously atmospheric lighting. The dialogue, in eighteenth-century Venetian dialect, was impenetrable, but it did not matter: the production was a total evocation of a society's members living their daily lives. Richard Eyre of the National Theatre had gone to considerable lengths to help Thelma Holt and myself secure it for London. Strehler was old, idiosyncratic and purportedly high on cocaine most of the time. The critical responses were pretty good, but we were unable to motivate the National Theatre staff, who totally refused to publicize the event. All reference to the European Arts Festival was left out of the programme, and they told us if we wanted posters we should put them up ourselves. For this we paid over half a million pounds.

I had relied on the cooperation of my colleagues not only to credit the Festival, but also to indicate the extent of our financial help with the major projects. In almost every case no acknowledgement was given. I gave Opera North £100,000 to fund entirely a production of a previously unseen opera based on Sheridan's play *The Duenna*, by the distinguished Spanish composer Roberto Gerhard, who had spent his later years in Britain – an ideal 'European' project. Nicholas Payne, the General Manager of Opera North, had been very supportive of the idea, and we went together to see a production in Madrid. Yet the

Opera North production carried no credit for the Festival. We had to drape the foyer of the Grand Theatre, Leeds, ourselves, and Opera North mentioned our financial contribution in their annual report only in an overall list of sponsors. I realize now that I should have insisted in the financial contracts that due recognition be given to the European Arts Festival for being instrumental in making the events happen. Sadly, this lack of acknowledgement meant that there was much less awareness of the Festival than I had hoped.

Luckily, away from the big cities, much more was made of our involvement, especially in Scotland and in Ulster, where we had supported a very wide range of events and exhibitions. A great deal was written about the tent. People still speak of the Mnouchkine and Strehler visits as worthwhile and a big success. Neither company has been back to the UK since, nor, without the help of the kind of funding we could provide, is it likely that they ever will.

Though I was on Proms duty in the Royal Albert Hall every evening during the Festival, I saw all the main productions and exhibitions and hoped that they would have made a sufficient impression to convince the government that something like the European Arts Festival should become a regular part of our cultural provision. But it was not to be. When I finally reported to Peter Brooke and suggested that something like this might happen on a regular basis, his response was to say, '*Étatisme, étatisme* – that's what the French do', as if that somehow justified our isolationism and lack of curiosity. I wrote a final report, admitting what had gone wrong but making a case for similar events in future. I told Haydn Phillips I was going to send a copy to the Prime Minister. He was appalled. 'Out of the question,' he said. 'It must be sent to the Secretary of State, Peter Brooke, and we will see if it should be passed to No. 10.' Of course it never was, and a year later I sent John Major a copy myself. I have often wondered whether I was wise to have got involved, but, despite everything, I enjoyed the challenge and still believe we need initiatives like that.

The BBC to which I returned full time after the European Arts Festival was already, after only a few months, feeling like a different place. John Birt, who had now taken over as Director-General on Checkland's departure, had succeeded both in alienating executives and in demoralizing producers. It was hard to believe that anyone could be so insensitive, but he was protected by his belief that only he understood anything. His influence was soon visible in a sharp loss of focus in programme ideas and quality. This was more obvious in Television, but Radio also suffered from new structures and the promotion to senior positions of people who had no understanding of the radio audience. When inappropriate change was foisted on that audience, they turned very publicly against it. Yet Birt somehow got away with his schemes, even claiming that halving the audience for Radio 1 was proof that his system was working. So hell-bent were the Birtists on the pursuit of a non-existent youth audience that they showed no concern whatsoever for older listeners, who were not only a large element of the radio audience, but key supporters against the incoming tide of cheap commercial radio.

The BBC was a woolly organization, and there was undoubtedly room for improvement and modernization, but the way in which these were carried out was, to chose a mild adjective, inept. At the centre of my disenchantment was the intolerable way in which the BBC's most effective executive, John Tusa, was got rid of. Hussey refused him an interview for the post of Director-General, claiming there was no point since he would not get the job, and then made sure that his contract at the World Service was not renewed. When I challenged P. D. James about this, she twittered on about how essential it was to achieve renewal of the BBC's charter. Hussey had convinced the Governors that only by appointing Birt and bringing in more outsiders could that be guaranteed. Yet Tusa was a reforming figure, and had reorganized Bush House and the External Services without losing their distinctive ethos or the support of his staff. The Governors – a wet lot – had no understanding of the damage that was being inflicted, being reduced to catatonia by Birt's droning on. I have never in my entire life observed anyone else with such an inability to provide leadership.

Meanwhile Nicholas Kenyon was making drastic changes to Radio 3, and many of the things I had introduced had already disappeared. Faced with the challenge of Classic FM, my view had always been that, as Classic FM was seeking to do a different job from Radio 3, it was not, in the strict sense, a direct competitor. It was providing something many people wanted – classical music as a background to their lives. Radio 3 should be making programmes which needed to be listened to – foreground listening, if you like. There is, for me, a real distinction between listening and just hearing something in the background. It may be unrealistic to expect people to sit at breakfast time between perfectly balanced loudspeakers, reacting purely musically, but it was the BBC's job to make programmes, not just play any old discs with a bit of chat in between. Kenyon, it seemed to me, was aping Classic FM almost before it was on the air. He would from time to time come and ask me about various specific points of detail, but we never discussed policy. I kept out of the way, and, since I was no longer asked to meetings or shown minutes or papers, I could no longer detect the thrust of the BBC's policy.

One day, after almost a year running Radio 3, Kenyon dropped into my extremely small office, previously occupied by the Proms planning assistant, and seemed to want to talk. 'I know I have been a very big disappointment to you,' he said. I said it was not worth thinking like that. He must do what he felt right, but I did wonder whether the changes he had made had been his idea or had been imposed as part of the corporate obsession with bigger audiences. I was thinking particularly of the new pattern for Sunday mornings, where, in place of *Music Magazine* (which under various names had been there for forty years) and concerts by the world's great orchestras, we now had a former King's Singer, Brian Kay, with a pleasant manner but musical tastes suited more to Radio 2 than to Radio 3. I felt it was odd that my policy that Radio 3 should not seek change, but try to do better what it had always done, had been reversed the day after I left. Why had nothing of the sort been suggested while I was in charge? Kenyon said the changes were his idea entirely, but he had found a willing response from his superiors. 'I was pushing on an open door,' he told me. When I asked again why they had not suggested such changes to me he said, 'They were scared of you.' I was astonished, for, though I certainly fought my corner as strongly as I could, I always recognized that my superiors had the absolute right to impose a policy on me if they wished. The fact that they didn't suggested to me that they were content with what we did.

It seemed best for me now to keep quiet, and publicly I did so for the next few years, while the BBC simply didn't speak to me any more. I was to all intents and purposes sent to Coventry, and became a nonperson. When Nicholas Kenyon got rid of the Manager of the BBC Symphony Orchestra, Lawrie Lea, I was not invited to sit on the selection panel to find a successor. Despite the fact that the orchestra's most prominent engagements were in the Proms, which I was still running, it was considered more appropriate to invite the Manager of the London Symphony Orchestra to help in the selection. They appointed a totally unsuitable candidate, who had little relevant experience and no feeling whatsoever for the BBC's role in contemporary music, though this was much insisted on in the job description. To my sadness, Andrew Davis went along with this, and also with the removal of Martin Cotton, the senior producer whom I had appointed to replace Roger Wright.

There seemed to me a real risk of the BBC Symphony Orchestra losing its crucial role in the vanguard of programming ideas. The first commission of the new era was to a composer, Michael Nyman, whose talents seem to me overstretched even by movie scores, to be conducted by Richard Hickox, someone whom I had never invited to conduct the orchestra. The new Manager, Louise Badger, cheerfully told me that the orchestra had had no one managing it in the previous seven years – exactly the time that I had been there – and brought in a number of foreign conductors of the second rank with no interest in new music. I was determined that in the Proms, at least, the BBC SO should maintain its traditional role, although Ms Badger let it be known that she thought it ought to be her job to choose their Proms programmes.

The 1993 Proms involved all the conductors that I had appointed – Andrew Davis, Alexander Lazarev, Mark Wigglesworth – and those I had inherited from Robert Ponsonby – Günter Wand, David Atherton and Mark Elder. Lutosławski returned to conduct his Fourth Symphony, and I invited the young Yakov Kreizberg to work for the first time with the BBC Symphony Orchestra. After his first rehearsal, he telephoned me and asked, 'What do you have to do to get this orchestra's attention?' Ms Badger also rang me to tell me that the orchestra didn't like Kreizberg. I told her that I thought his view of them was rather more significant. By the day of the concert they had graciously decided that they did like him, but he was still to be convinced. Like many Russians, Kreizberg has little interest in new music, but he has a formidable personality and I was responsible for suggesting him to the Bournemouth Symphony Orchestra, where he became Principal Conductor over the head of Richard Hickox, their Principal Guest. It is important to know what an orchestra think about a conductor, but at times you have to insist they just get on with their job. The BBC Symphony Orchestra have real feelings of grandeur – often, it must be said, justifiably – but one of the Players' Committee once told me it was unacceptable for them to be conducted by other than great conductors.

I felt like telling them how poor an impression they often made on visiting maestros. Simon Rattle always said his basic hostility to the BBC SO was because of the hard time they had given Lutosławski before they generously decided to like him.

We opened the 1993 season with a thrilling concert performance of Strauss's *Elektra*, something I had suggested as especially appropriate for Andrew Davis, a very committed Straussian. William Cochran, who was singing Aegistheus, fell off the podium during the final rehearsal and spent most of the night before the concert in the Accident and Emergency ward at Hammersmith Hospital, but bravely carried on and was part of a terrific cast led by the extraordinary Marilyn Zschau, backed up by the ageless Eva Randova as Klytemnestra and Deborah Voigt making her debut as Chrysothemis. By no means all operas make a real impact in concert form, but this *Elektra* had quite as much dramatic punch as any opera-house production I have seen. It was semi-staged, but not in the way that Glyndebourne Prom productions were, with the singers on a raised platform behind the orchestra. Here they were downstage, with the conductor and orchestra behind them, and Andrew Davis held the whole thing together with monitors in the no man's land to help the singers.

There was more Strauss when Mark Wigglesworth conducted the closing scene of *Salome* with Maria Ewing, one of the best roles of a highly idiosyncratic singer, who could make such difficulties for herself and her colleagues but who always showed me her best side. She came to the Proms on several occasions, in pieces as different as *Pulcinella*, *Les Nuits d'été* and *La Mort de Cléopâtre*. In my first year, when she appeared twice, she was the only singer who wrote to thank me for her flowers. She had a fascinating way of dressing specially for the role: shimmering rhinestones for Berlioz, a cocktail dress for *Pulcinella*, a black crinoline for *Kindertotenlieder*. Her hair too was always arranged differently, and she seemed to want to make her appearance part of her interpretation. I was really sorry that when one year she sang American songs of the Cole Porter/Jerome Kern vintage the arrangements we had made for the BBC Concert Orchestra rather overwhelmed her, but when accompanied on the piano by Richard Rodney Bennett she was the essence of classy cabaret. Yet for all her success, and despite her great musical intelligence, she seemed to me a sad person, full of insecurity and subject to that most undermining of problems – insomnia. I am sure her marriage to Peter Hall foundered partly on this, since she never slept at night and he got up at five in the morning to write his diaries. I interviewed her once about her preparation for roles, and found her much more perceptive about her work than many less troubled artists. She is also something I specially value – a singing actress, rather than a singer who is forced to act. But, just as with Gwyneth Jones, I never saw her difficult side. 'That is because you are not a director!' said Graham Vick.

Mark Wigglesworth had come to my notice in 1989 when he took part in the conductors' competition in the Netherlands in memory of the Russian conductor Kyril Kondrashin, whose early death shortly after leaving Russia to take up a post in Amsterdam was a real tragedy. During the competition, several members of the jury, including Riccardo Chailly and Kees Hillen, Artistic Manager of the Rotterdam Philharmonic, rang me to ask if I knew anything about him, so powerful was the impression he made in the early rounds. I did indeed know something about him and, characteristically, it was through John Pritchard, who had spotted him when Wigglesworth was still in his teens and had taken him to San Francisco to do some sub-conducting and watch how opera was put together.

Wigglesworth won the Kondrashin competition, and soon afterwards we started discussions about how he might get involved with the BBC. Eventually he made his debut with the BBC Symphony Orchestra in a Barbican performance of Shostakovich's Tenth Symphony; later he conducted Deryck Cooke's controversial completion of Mahler's Tenth. He showed real and unusual talent. The Mahler was notably well prepared, since he had managed to programme it on a tour with the Dutch National Youth Orchestra and by the time he came to conduct it in London he had already performed it more often than any other living conductor. This kind of intelligent planning, both in the choice of work and in its preparation, impressed us all. His technique was sketchy, but he had real ideas. I was keen to give him opportunities with the BBC's orchestras, and this led to a contract which I believe to be unique. He was given a roving brief to be at the disposal of any of the orchestras in Manchester, Glasgow, Cardiff or London. His Prom debut in 1991, a programme shared with Lutosławski, who conducted the world première of his song cycle *Chante fleurs et chante fables*, was far from happy, however, and it was my fault. I had simply not allowed for the time it took to reset the platform between the Lutosławski and the final work, Bartók's *Music for Strings, Percussion and Celeste.* There was a break of nearly fifteen minutes, and the whole concert went off the boil. But Wigglesworth came back the next year to conduct the very tricky 'Babi-Yar' Symphony of Shostakovich, and later for *Turangalîla* and Shostakovich's Fifth Symphony. He had the intelligence to realize that great sprawling masterpieces like these were less difficult than a Mozart symphony.

Wigglesworth then had a very small repertory, and was extremely reluctant to expand it under the bright lights of the Proms. Of all the BBC orchestras, the one with which he got on best was the BBC Welsh Symphony Orchestra, and in due course he became their Chief Conductor – outrageously insisting on the grand title of Music Director, though not as far as I am aware ever having accompanied a piano concerto. The BBC Symphony Orchestra took against him, and the relationship I had hoped for fizzled out. He came to dread working with them, and it was pointless to persist. Despite his considerable charm, he is not an easy person, being most inflexible in the choice of repertory and not always successful in the realization of his own choices. In the 1994 Proms he conducted a very dull performance of Ravel's *Daphnis and Chloë*, which Pierre Boulez, who was conducting the following day, sat in my box to hear. He was not impressed. Irritated by Wigglesworth's general complacency, I told him of Boulez's reaction. His response was to ring Boulez and ask to see him in Paris. They spent several hours together going through the score – generous of Boulez, and certainly intelligent of Wigglesworth. When he conducted *Daphnis* again more recently with the Welsh orchestra there was a noticeable improvement. Yet at the time of writing he has still not made his mark in the way I had hoped. Several orchestras have reacted strongly against him, though others are entirely favourable. It is mysterious. But he is still young, and I have no doubt of his basic talent.

Other high points of 1993 included the Proms debut of Maxim Vengerov, a musician of exceptional quality, and the first appearance in the Royal Albert Hall of the wonderful Wynton Marsalis band, jazz musicians of the highest ability and some of the nicest young men I have ever met. There was also the Proms reappearance of a very old man: Berthold Goldschmidt, ninety that year. Simon Rattle, who had championed Goldschmidt's music in Birmingham, was keen to conduct something of his in the Proms. Goldschmidt's life was being much written about: how he had shown brilliant promise in pre-Hitler Germany but had later been forced to leave, and how after successful years in

Britain, including conducting the first performance of Deryck Cooke's version of Mahler's Tenth in 1964, he and his music had faded from view. I found it very hard to evaluate Goldschmidt's music: it had obviously seemed remarkable in the 1920s and '30s, but struck me as less so after sixty years. The work Rattle chose, the *Ciaccona Sinfonica*, was the first piece that Goldschmidt had written in Britain, in 1936. It had a triumphant reception, as if the audience wanted to compensate for years of neglect by refusing to let the composer leave the platform, and Goldschmidt really revelled in the applause. We gave him dinner afterwards in a nearby restaurant, during which he became seriously unwell and eventually slumped forward apparently dead. It was a dreadful moment. Simon Rattle stood behind him and felt for a pulse. I rushed about phoning ambulances and looking for a doctor. By the time the ambulance arrived Goldschmidt was sitting up chatting, quite unaware of the panic he had caused. 'It's rather hot, isn't it?' he said. He went home in a taxi, accompanied by a charming young woman, as if nothing had happened. At his ninetieth birthday party his publisher, Anthony Fell of Boosey & Hawkes, said it was marvellous that Goldschmidt was not bitter at his roller coaster of a life. In reply, Goldschmidt said, 'Bitterness is a question of taste.' I am glad he lived long enough to hear his music performed again and to return to Germany and be fêted everywhere, but I am still not sure how good the music is.

If 1993 was a successful year for the Proms, it was against the background of further loss of support at Broadcasting House. David Hatch, the Managing Director of BBC Radio, had been close to Checkland and critical of Birt, but when Birt took over he was neutralized by being appointed Birt's special assistant. I simply could not understand how he could swallow his reservations. The top job in Radio went, according to the new pattern, to someone from outside the BBC and with no previous experience. Liz Forgan had been Women's Editor of the *Guardian* and then for a time at Channel 4. She arrived in a flurry of open-door goodwill, posting up a silly letter saying how super radio was and issuing an invitation to anyone to drop in when they wished. She soon realized how hollow an offer that was in the Birtist world of continous meetings about meetings. While Hatch, although not musical, had been a valiant supporter of the Proms, Forgan not only did not come but claimed subsequently that she had. When I suggested she visit the rather demoralized BBC Symphony Orchestra at Maida Vale, she told them she would be 'on your side in the battle to come', which did not improve their confidence in the future. She refused to give me any undertaking that the BBC SO was safe in her hands, since she said she could not commit herself to something she might not be able to deliver. Perhaps unwisely, I suggested that guaranteeing the survival of the orchestra should be central to anyone doing her job. She seemed quite out of her depth, and certainly could not understand someone like me who believed so passionately in the BBC's role.

That year was exceptional in that I had nothing to do but concentrate on the Proms and the upcoming centenary. We were faced with a familiar dilemma: when does a century start? The Proms had begun in 1895, and each year was advertised by the number of the season, 1993 being the ninety-ninth. It followed that 1994 must be the hundredth, but, since the institution had begun in 1895, which year was the real centenary? Inspired by the Boston Symphony Orchestra's approach to a similar problem, I devised a scheme to spread the centenary over two years. It was extremely hard to persuade anyone that it would work. Michael Checkland had been particularly sceptical, but I persisted and eventually the plan took root. We would devote 1994 to looking back over the history of the Proms' first century, and 1995 to looking as much as possible to the future. There would be few new commissions in 1994; instead, we would carry the funds over to 1995 to make a bumper year for new music, seeking to include some of the biggest names among living composers from whatever country. We placed commissions with Luciano Berio, Elliott Carter, Kaija Saariaho, Steve Reich and Tan Dun. On the British side we added Harrison Birtwistle, Peter Maxwell Davies, John Casken, Judith Weir, James Wood and Judith Bingham. This part was simple.

What was extremely difficult was discovering what had been done in the past, since there was no way of finding out except by leafing through old programmes. Every year in the Proms brochure we would put an asterisk against a piece of music being performed for the first time, regardless of when it was written. In 1991 Andrew Davis and I had decided to include Mendelssohn's *Elijah*, a work now rarely performed but a staple of our younger years and one that Andrew particularly liked. When the proofs of the programme book came back, I noticed an asterisk against it. I rang George Hall, the editor, and questioned this, since I had clear memories of having heard *Elijah* in the Albert Hall. Surely there must be a mistake. George agreed to check again, going through seventy years of programmes from the 1920s onwards, big

choral works having begun to feature in the Proms only after the First
World War. George proved correct and suggested that my memory was
probably of Royal Choral Society concerts under Malcolm Sargent or
the Goldsmith's Choral Union. The result was a growing belief on my
part that we needed a complete index to the history of the Proms, and
that this should be put on a computerized database.

It was slow and very expensive to bring this about, but by 1993 we
had the database to hand. We could now find out at the touch of a few
buttons not only what had been done, but when and by whom. The
system was complicated by works appearing under different titles – *Le
Sacre du printemps* sometimes appeared as *The Rite of Spring*, for
example, and Piano Concerto No. 2 as Second Piano Concerto – and
this took some time to sort out, but eventually the whole ninety-odd
years were there to be examined. I realized how defective one's memory can be. I had clear recollections of Eileen Joyce regularly playing the
piano concerto by John Ireland. The concerto had in fact been played
on more than thirty occasions, from its première in 1930 to the early
1990s, but only once by Eileen Joyce. It had been played often by its
dedicatee, Helen Perkin, and by Eric Parkin, the guardian of the Ireland legacy, and on two other occasions the soloists were, surprisingly,
Artur Rubinstein and Gina Bachauer – a fascinating discovery. The
other strong impression I had from exploring the archives was of how
almost entirely British the Proms were for their first sixty years. Rubinstein's presence in the 1930s was exceptional, for almost none of the
great international soloists of the earlier years had appeared: no
Casals, Cortot, Rachmaninov, Horowitz, Heifetz, Kreisler, or Szigeti.
Benno Moiseiwitsch was an exception, but he lived in London, and he
was a far less frequent performer than Myra Hess, who came every
year for over fifty years.

We started compiling lists: all the first performances, all the commissions since the BBC took over the Proms in 1927, all the conductors
besides Henry Wood who had played a major role. It was a fascinating
game, and it had practical results. I was able to compile a sequence for
1994 in which most of the concerts contained a work which had been
first performed in London or in Britain at the Proms, and also to build
special programmes around the leading figures of the Proms' history.
To mark the fiftieth anniversary of Henry Wood's death, on 19 August,
we devised a special programme in which every piece had a direct connection. Elgar's *Grania and Diarmid* funeral march had been dedicat-

ed to Wood, the Schoenberg *Five Orchestral Pieces* had incredibly been sought out by him and given their world première in 1912, Vaughan Williams's *Serenade to Music* had been premièred at Wood's jubilee concert in 1938, with sixteen of the best British singers of the time, and Beethoven's Seventh Symphony was the last thing he conducted, three weeks before his death. I invited sixteen of today's singers to take part in the *Serenade*, offering everyone only a token fee, and was delighted that everyone we asked accepted – and particularly by the return to the concert stage of Heather Harper after a period of serious illness. We also made programmes dedicated to Malcolm Sargent, Adrian Boult, John Barbirolli, Constant Lambert and Pierre Boulez. We reinstated a complete cycle of Beethoven symphonies, a Wagner night and a Viennese night, and for the second concert of the season we reproduced the exact programme given on 6 September 1900 – sixteen pieces in all, including songs, marches and concertos for violin and bassoon. In this way we rescued from oblivion such masterpieces as Florian Pascal's *Fairy Fretting* and Frances Allitsen's *When the Boys Come Home*. We printed special programmes identical in style to those of 1900, and a patient audience sat through a marathon concert lasting over three hours.

I was determined not just to make an academic and historical compilation, but to show how tastes had changed and to remind people of when pieces like the Schoenberg had first appeared – and how wide-ranging were the composers Wood supported, and how quick he was to find them. Mahler's First Symphony was first performed in the United Kingdom in the Proms of 1901, the Fourth in 1905. Sibelius's Violin Concerto came in 1907, Rachmaninov's First Piano Concerto in 1900, Debussy's *L'Après-midi d'un faune* in 1904, *The Firebird* in 1913 and Frank Bridge's *The Sea* in 1912. The list of BBC commissions was much more uneven. It contained most of the right names, but often with less than major works, though I was pleased to be able to include Nicholas Maw's *Scenes and Arias* from 1962 and Hugh Wood's Cello Concerto from 1969, while we repeated James MacMillan's *The Confession of Isobel Gowdie* – one of my own commissions, already becoming a repertory piece after only four years.

Of all the concerts, the one that took the most careful planning was the tribute to William Glock. No single programme from his seventeen years as Controller seemed to me to sum up his contribution, so we put together a three-part concert to show different aspects of his ideas. The

BBC Symphony Orchestra was conducted by Pierre Boulez and Colin Davis, the two chief conductors that Glock had appointed, and by George Benjamin, to represent the young generation of composer-conductors, while Martyn Brabbins conducted the Nash Ensemble, and Philip Pickett the New London Consort in memory of David Munrow. We included music by Elisabeth Lutyens and Roberto Gerhard, composers whom Glock had championed. Boulez conducted Stravinsky's *Symphony of Psalms* and his own *cummings ist der dichter* with the BBC Singers, while Colin Davis conducted a Mozart piano concerto played by Imogen Cooper, a pianist Glock had always admired, and Haydn's Ninety-ninth Symphony. Glock himself, at eighty-six, was paper-thin and frail, and his enchanting French wife, Anne, was even frailer, but they stood up to the test of the long evening with enthusiasm. I cherish the photographs taken of three Controllers of Music and Pierre Boulez.

Making special programmes and creating events is essential to the continuing vitality of the Proms, and the historical elements proved as enjoyable as I had hoped. Without the database we could never have had them, and this went a long way to convincing me of the practical possibilities offered by the new world of information technology.

There was always a strong social element to the Proms. Across the corridor from my box in the Grand Tier was the Henry Cole Room, which Robert Ponsonby had originally retained so as to get away from the crowds. I preferred to fill it – before concerts and during intervals – not only with the guests in my box, but with the guests of other BBC colleagues and any composers, publishers, musicians and friends whom I met in my regular journeys through the hall, from the Grand Tier to the backstage dressing rooms. I always called in on conductors and soloists before and after their performance, whether I knew them well or not, and usually went down to the control box in the interval, to see how the broadcasting side was going. It was important to have direct contact with the artists, especially if they were more than usually nervous – which was often the case, since the Albert Hall feels so enormous. Over the years, I seem to have seen most of the world's great conductors in their underpants.

Guests in the Henry Cole Room were from every background. As a matter of course I invited the heads of all the music colleges, the directors of the museums and galleries, and all those people like Arnold Goodman who had become friends through involvement in and championing of the arts. Goodman was infuriating in that he would never decide when he wanted to come until a day or two before the event, despite having had several months' notice like everyone else. On one occasion – a totally sold-out Abbado concert – he threatened to go to 'my friends in the Union' if I did not come up with what he wanted. I was very fond of him, but he was a terrible old bully. Of course he got his tickets. Far from being a burden, the jolly intervals were, like the parties in Edinburgh, my way of relaxing. The tricky nights were the ones when I had no guests.

Over the years, there were innumerable encounters which led to gossip, like the night the Editor of the *Sunday Times*, Andrew Neil (not invited by me) brought with him a young woman rather scantily dressed for a concert. We subsequently found out she was the infamous Pamella Bordes. My favourite exchange was when Rose Luce, wife of the Arts Minister, Richard, asked Neil what he did, and, on being told he worked for the *Sunday Times*, said, 'And what do you do there?' I was told to leave my own room by the Muti groupie Lord Weinstock, because I lit a cigarette. Weinstock's self-importance was so great that he thought it within his rights to demand that the BBC provide him with a recording of every broadcast that involved Muti. When he asked for tapes of a performance of *Parsifal* which we had relayed from La Scala and Weinstock had attended, I refused. Our engineers had more important things to do. Weinstock complained to Checkland, but got no sympathy. We saw a lot of actors, since Prunella Scales and Timothy West, Patricia Routledge and Peter Eyre were frequent visitors under their own steam. They just loved music. Peter Mandelson came one night as someone's guest and, talking in a corner to Germaine Greer, responded to my greeting by asking, 'And who might you be?' But on most nights there were more entertaining encounters or the pleasure of seeing old friends.

The royal family were regular attenders. The Duke and Duchess of Kent came often, and the Duchess sang when I booked the Bach Choir. I invited both the Prince and the Princess of Wales, in different years, to come to the opening concert. The Princess told me she loved the Verdi *Requiem* and wanted it played at her funeral. In due course a short extract was. Prince Edward came as patron of the City of Birmingham Symphony Orchestra and the Scottish Youth Orchestra, and the Duke and Duchess of York came, predictably, to the Last Night. But the Queen had never been to the Proms, and I was determined in

445

the hundredth season, in 1994, to invite her. She came with the Duke
of Edinburgh in the first week, to an English programme which included the *Enigma Variations*. 'This is the one about the dog,' Prince Philip
exclaimed at the appropriate moment. The Queen was friendly and
stayed longer then we expected afterwards, talking to performers and
BBC staff. She told several people how surprised she was to find that
the promenaders actually stood. The evening was made still more
enjoyable by the absence of the Director-General: John Birt thought
that attending the World Cup was more important. Hussey did not
agree, and for the first time I sensed that, although he had got the
Director-General of his choice, they were not always seeing eye to eye.

Having played all the historical cards in 1994, it was important that
the centenary season of 1995 should be really forward-looking, though
it needed to contain a substantial number of works from the established repertory, otherwise we would never have sold the tickets. I
decided to include a complete cycle of Mahler symphonies, almost all
played by British orchestras. Critics tended to think there was too
much Mahler around, but playing all ten symphonies in two months,
together with four of the vocal works and the early version of the first
movement of the Second Symphony, seemed to me something that only
the Proms could do, using such a range of conductors and orchestras.
It also seemed to me the counterpart of the old Prom tradition of playing all the Beethoven symphonies: for our time, Mahler had come to
have similar significance.

I wanted as many programmes as possible to include major twentieth-century works by composers who were no longer controversial:
Bartók, Ravel, Debussy, Shostakovich, Britten and Messiaen, who all
now draw big audiences and disprove the idea that *all* twentieth-century music, except the minimalists, is alarming to the public. There
were two anniversaries to note: Webern – difficult in the huge expanse
of the Albert Hall – and Hindemith – difficult for me, since I find so
much of his music lifeless. But what took most time was ensuring that
the range of new music was both extensive and authoritative. We had
had some losses. The death of Lutosławski deprived us of the piece he
had promised for the BBC Singers, and Oliver Knussen failed to complete his planned piece, as also did Steve Reich. Reich was enormously
apologetic but agreed that we should play what existed, so it was
another partial performance, but without the recriminations that had
followed Nicholas Maw's *Odyssey*. Some of the pieces were disap-

pointing. I found Kaija Saariaho's violin concerto *Graal Theatre* hard
to get to grips with, even with Gidon Kremer as soloist and Esa-Pekka
Salonen conducting; its shifting colours and transparent texture
slipped away into the dome of the Royal Albert Hall.

Most elusive of all was a clarinet concerto by Benedict Mason,
which the London Sinfonietta and their Principal Conductor Markus
Stenz had persuaded me to commission. Mason is, to say the least, a
quirky and highly individualistic composer, but to offer for the Proms,
with its broadcasting requirements, a work where the platform of the
Albert Hall was occupied only by a solo clarinet while the other players walked about outside the building seemed, to me, unreasonably
dotty. By compromising and having the players move along the
ground-floor corridor it was possible for the radio audience to hear
something, but it made little or no sense in the hall, and led me to wonder whether some composers are more concerned with being different
than with being intelligible. Mason had written some interesting pieces
using unusual sources like the rhythm of lighthouse signals, but this
was just silly and we had a couple of chilly meetings about it. What a
contrast with the joy of working with Elliott Carter, who at eighty-
seven was writing with a fluency and speed not typical of his earlier
career! The *Adagio Tenebroso*, which was to become the middle movement of his *Sinfonia*, was truly impressive and a great deal easier to
decipher at first hearing than some of his other works. Carter is such
an attractive figure – so intelligent, amusing and modest – that the
sheer complexity of his musical thought sometimes surprises. But I
expect future generations will take it in their stride, although they will
be denied the pleasure we had of knowing him and his equally interesting wife, Helen. Carter's visits, like Lutosławski's, were high points
of any year.

I wanted also to give opportunities to a number of younger composers whose work I admired. John Casken, one of the most intelligent
figures in British music, had long wanted to write a violin concerto.
Having moved from Durham to Manchester as Professor of Music, he
was building a fruitful relationship with the BBC Philharmonic and
they performed the work, which Casken generously dedicated to me.
Judith Bingham, a long-time member of the BBC Singers, was winning
a reputation writing for voices and contributed *Salt in the Blood*,
which included a setting of the Beaufort scale of wind speeds.

The BBC Scottish Orchestra brought the young Chinese-American composer Tan Dun to the Proms for the first time, but were the victims of a most unfortunate incident. They performed his *Orchestral Theatre 1*, which he had introduced in Scotland the previous year, and were about to give the world première of the commissioned *Orchestral Theatre 2* when all the lights failed and the Albert Hall was plunged into darkness. The reserve lighting from the hall's generator was insufficient except for finding one's way out and was not going to last for more than fifteen minutes. After I learnt that the power cut had affected not just the hall but the whole of that part of Kensington, I had no alternative but to go on stage and ask the audience to leave, which they did only after several appeals and with some understandable hostility. It was not the BBC's fault, nor that of the hall, but of course we got the blame. We were assured by London Electricity that it could not happen again – but it did, the following night, in the middle of the last movement of Schubert's 'Tragic' Symphony in a concert by the Chamber Orchestra of Europe under Nikolaus Harnoncourt. They struggled on manfully to the end of the symphony, but they were not able to play their encore, for which they had rather foolishly brought in extra players. On this occasion it was the players who turned aggressive. I must say I had more sympathy for poor Tan Dun, who lost his world première, than for the Chamber Orchestra, who simply lost their encore. The next day power was restored and extra generators were brought in as a standby, but it gave a new sense of risk to the whole enterprise. It was clear how close to the wind we sailed in an old building with ancient facilities in an age where the renewal of public utilities had become the victim of political dogma.

I was fortunate to obtain the British première of Henze's Eighth Symphony, brilliantly performed under Simon Rattle, and the first London performance of a piece by Tom Adès, the newest kid on the block. Peter Maxwell Davies provided a new work, *Beltane Fire*. I did not find it up to the level of the previous year's marvellous Fifth Symphony, the only major work premièred that year, but it was essential to include something by Max since he had such been a key figure in the wider understanding of contemporary music. He has done as much for musical education and awareness as any of my contemporaries. His best music is of the highest quality, but for every really outstanding piece like *The Lighthouse*, *St Thomas Wake* and *Vesalii Icones* there are sometimes less effective works. But of all his generation it was Max who most keenly heeded Benjamin Britten's injunction that the composer's job is 'to be useful and to the living'. Watching him work with young musicians or in the context of his own remarkable festival in Orkney is compelling. With his bright, beady eyes and intense manner, he compels people to feel involved and that music matters in their lives. Every city needs someone like Max, for he is, to use that awful Arts Council expression, an 'animateur' – and a brilliant one. He makes things happen, and that is an important aspect of creativity. He shares this gift with the excellent Judith Weir. Judith has wit and seriousness in equal measure, and her wider sympathies have made her an imaginative festival director at Spitalfields. Her new piece, *Moon and Star*, was elusive but attractive.

Another Scottish woman composer whom I have always admired is Thea Musgrave. Long residence in America, where her husband runs the Virginia Opera and she has a prominent role as a teacher, has kept her away from Britain, and her music has had a hard time keeping its place in the repertory. She has been particularly unfortunate in the past twenty years with opera commissions. After the big success of *Mary, Queen of Scots* in the Edinburgh Festival of 1977, just before I took over, she was commissioned by the Royal Opera House, but they eventually refused to produce the work that resulted, the oddly named *Harriet, the Woman Called Moses*. The fact that it required a largely black cast was apparently one of the reasons, but that did not stop Glyndebourne from putting on its brilliant production of *Porgy and Bess*. Later the tenor Placido Domingo commissioned her to write an opera in Spanish to be produced jointly by the Los Angeles Opera and Scottish Opera. It was based on the life of Simón Bolívar. When Domingo was unable to find time to learn it, however, Los Angeles cancelled the production and Scottish Opera could not afford to go it alone. The piece was eventually premièred in Norfolk, Virginia, and I went to hear it, determined to do something for Thea in my last year. With her husband, the conductor Peter Mark, Thea and I worked out a twenty-five-minute concert suite, and luckily three singers from the Norfolk production were free to come to London. It was notably well received, but no one has subsequently sought to produce the complete work. Musgrave has what so many younger composers lack: a real sense of what works theatrically. It seems to me ludicrous that her output is so little known. Nevertheless, she remains positive, always cheerful and a joy to be with, although she has every reason to feel bitter and unregarded, but it is not in her nature.

It is unimaginable that Musgrave could behave as badly as did Luciano Berio, who tried to pass off as new a work which we had paid for but which turned out to have been performed a few weeks earlier in Germany. It was only by chance that we stumbled on the would-be deception. The *Financial Times* carried a review of the German concert, and since the work it described seemed so similar to our Prom commission I set about getting details of it and obtaining a tape. It was immediately apparent that, apart from forty seconds of the introduction, our piece had already been performed elsewhere. Berio's agent refused to accept this. Berio himself came to London, but I refused to see him. My poor former assistant Jacky Guter, who now worked for Berio's manager, was dragged into this row, which rumbled on for several days and came close to ruining for me the last week of my last season. Berio eventually tried to prevent us from performing the piece. I insisted we went ahead, but removed the words 'BBC Commission' from the programme, simply saying it was a UK première. The whole episode left a very sour taste in the mouth. I had, over the years, done a great deal to support Berio and his music. The BBC's 1990 Berio Festival had been the most extensive and expensive of all the Barbican festivals. I believe in his music, but every time we worked together there were disputes. I have never received a word of explanation from Berio or his manager, Andrew Rosner, about the episode in the 1995 Proms. Some months later, after I had left, Nicholas Kenyon received in the post a cheque returning the commission fee. It would have been nice to have had an apology too.

But, if there were occasional problems, there was nevertheless a very happy atmosphere around the 1995 season. The BBC Symphony Orchestra had a particularly distinguished roster of conductors: as well as Andrew Davis, Lazarev, Knussen and Eötvös there were Salonen and Kreizberg, and it looked as if, after several years of cancellations, Günter Wand would be coming back. Sadly, the Wand concert was to become one of the problems. I had persuaded him to conduct Mozart's Fortieth Symphony and Tchaikovsky's Fifth for a change. It was one of the first concerts to sell out – hardly surprising in view of the programme and Wand's reputation. A couple of weeks before it, he told me that he would come only if he could conduct Bruckner's Eighth. His interpretation of the Bruckner is absolutely superb, but it would have been the third time in less than ten years that he had conducted it at the Proms. But those were his terms, so we advertised the change of programme and a regrettably large number of people asked for refunds. But at least he turned up. He was very frail, short-tempered and endlessly critical of the orchestra – too many women players, too many young players, too many people he didn't know. His great friend Bela Dekany, who had been leader, had retired and Wand felt distanced from the orchestra, in which no one spoke good German. As usual we made every effort to look after him, and the concert itself went off well.

After Wand's concerts there was always a dinner at the Hyde Park Hotel, in the very expensive restaurant where he ate every meal. He ordered the food in advance, and there was no discussion. He had invited an assortment of people, none of whom was ever introduced and some of whom spoke no English. We waited while Wand changed, and on this occasion it was well over an hour before he appeared. He was already snapping at his wife. When the wine waiter brought wine of the wrong year, he exploded. His wife tried to calm him down, but that only made things worse. Everyone sat in embarrassed silence while he shouted at the waiters, muttering to himself in German. Eventually I said, as emolliently as I could, 'We've had a great concert and now we're hoping to have a happy dinner. Could you not cheer up a bit?' He screamed at me, 'How dare you speak like that! Who do you think you are?' and so on. Something snapped. I got up, thanked him for the concert, and left. I had sent my driver away for his supper, so I spent the next forty-five minutes pacing the pavement outside the Hyde Park Hotel.

It was a highly regrettable incident and I suppose I should have sat it out, but we had just had the sixty-second concert of the season and, up to my neck in the Berio business, I was on the edge of exhaustion. I had never accustomed myself to Wand's Janus-like behaviour: all sweetness and light and 'Du, mein lieber Freund' one moment and foul language and boorish behaviour the next. I would go to endless lengths to ensure his presence on the platform, but I felt less responsibility over the dinner table. He is certainly a great conductor, but much less impressive as a human being. He no longer comes back to the BBC Symphony Orchestra, but still finds it possible to go to Edinburgh every year with his old colleagues of the North German Radio Orchestra.

Another great conductor who happily returned to the BBC Symphony Orchestra in the centenary year was Pierre Boulez. Over the years, I had devoted considerable energy and time to trying to make sure that Boulez was still part of our lives, only to see plans abandoned or cancelled. We worked on a possible twentieth-century-music festival in Tokyo, but once he insisted on the Chicago Symphony Orchestra also taking part the Japanese promoters lost interest in the BBC SO. We made a complicated series of deals with youth orchestras. He was to conduct the National Youth Orchestra one year, the European Union Youth Orchestra the next. Both engagements were cancelled, since he said he needed time for a summer rest – but somehow this did not stop him appearing in Salzburg. During the 1990s, while he constantly claimed he was giving up conducting to return to composition, in Britain alone he conducted the LSO, the CBSO and the Welsh National Opera Orchestra, while elsewhere he was working with the orchestras of Cleveland, Vienna, Chicago, Los Angeles and Amsterdam. But, ironically, the less we saw him with the BBC Symphony Orchestra, the warmer our personal relations became. However, I was absolutely determined he should take part in my last Proms season – and with the BBC SO.

I went to Paris to see him, and we had a superb lunch in a very good restaurant – enjoying food was another aspect of the new, humanized, Boulez. We made a programme – a very good one, it seemed to me – and after lunch we went back to his office to see his long-time assistant, the splendid Astrid Schirmer. I enthusiastically told her what we had decided. She did not seem to share our enthusiasm, and hardly spoke. I returned to London, and the following day Astrid rang and asked if I realized that the programme we had discussed was identical to one he was giving earlier in the year at the Barbican with the LSO? I rang Boulez, and we both fell about with laughter. 'The years are beginning to tell!' he exclaimed, and went on, 'Well, in the circumstances, you had better tell me what you want.' In that way, I got not only exactly what I wanted but as near ideal a Boulez programme as it is possible to imagine: Bartók's *Music for Strings, Percussion and Celeste*, Debussy's *Jeux* and the *Three Villon Ballads*, his own *Le Soleil des eaux* and Messiaen's *Et Exspecto Resurrectionem Mortuorum*. We had begun our relationship thirty years earlier with *Jeux* in the television Debussy programme, and here it was again – a still undervalued masterpiece.

The concert was one of the happiest I can recall, and afterwards at dinner Boulez and Peter Diamand held the company enthralled for two hours telling stories about near-disasters or perilous situations from their shared experiences. Whatever disappointment I had from Boulez's so frequent cancelling and so rarely completing compositions was always compensated for by the joy of being with him, and of relishing the growing warmth and maturity of his interpretations. I count myself immensely lucky to have known him and to have had a chance to experience his many accomplishments. His *Pelléas et Mélisande* at the Royal Opera House in the 1960s and his conducting of the Peter Stein production in Wales in the 1990s are two of the high points of my opera-going life. The concerts with the BBC Symphony Orchestra in Russia in 1967 and the Barbican Boulez Festival are unforgettable. For all that he dislikes much more music than he likes, he brings to the things he admires not only deep commitment but the keenest sense of realization. How can people find the music of the twentieth century impenetrable with advocates like him? Once in the 1980s he gave a pre-concert talk before a programme that included the Schoenberg *Variations*. I admitted that I had always had difficulty with the work. He talked simply and convincingly about it, and after the concert I wondered why I had ever had a problem. He is a very great musician, and in the best possible way quintessentially French.

I had spent May 1995 in France, working on my book about Diaghilev. Having launched the Proms at a press conference, there was not much reason to hang about in London until nearer the start. It was at this time that I received a letter from 10 Downing Street, announcing the Prime Minister's intention to recommend me for a knighthood in the Birthday Honours. I was astonished. I had received the CBE five years earlier at the behest of the then Arts Minister, Richard Luce, whom I had come to know and very much like. We had seen each other quite often, and discussed policy and ideas. He had come to the Proms several times, and wrote me a generous letter saying how much he liked the combination of musical seriousness and social informality. My predecessor at the Edinburgh Festival and several earlier Controllers of Radio 3 had been awarded the CBE, but honours for the BBC were not in fashion in the Thatcher years and the time when most BBC Directors of Radio, Television and Engineering had knighthoods and Controllers CBEs was long gone. Checkland was given a 'K' as a sop for the shabby way in which he was eased out, but one had to go back to William Glock, David Attenborough or Huw Wheldon to find a 'K' for people actually concerned with programmes.

I was wondering how and why the idea of awarding me a knighthood had come about – and was quite sure that it had not come from the BBC, where my presence was hardly recognized – when I recalled a conversation with the Prime Minister some months earlier. I had been at a dinner given by Sotheby's to mark the sale of Joan Sutherland's opera costumes. Since Norma Major had written a biography of La Stupenda, it was not surprising that she and the Prime Minister were there. As we were collecting our coats to leave, the Prime Minister asked me what I was going to do after I left the Proms. I was astonished that he knew it was my last year. I explained that I really had no plans, but I thought it time to go. I had been incredibly lucky, I said, to have had some of the very best jobs in British life: the Edinburgh Festival, Radio 3 and the Proms. I record his reply not out of vanity or arrogance, but because it surprised me so much. He said, 'Luck has nothing to do with it, John. You are an outstanding public servant, and have contributed enormously to the life of this country.' I drove home reflectively, thinking that, even if Major was not the greatest Prime Minister we had ever had, it was quite a nice thing at the age of sixty to have the Prime Minister say something like that – and, as always with Major, in a way that I knew was sincere. When the offer of the 'K' came, I thought there might be a connection, and wondered if it was also a recognition of what I had tried to do with the European Arts Festival – something he had personally encouraged. In any event, I had no trouble in accepting – as much on behalf of the Proms and the other institutions I had worked for as for myself.

On the weekend of the Birthday Honours announcement, I arranged to be out of the country – in Bologna with Elizabeth Cavendish and Bob Lockyer, listening to *Rosenkavalier*, looking at Morandi and eating rather well. I had told no one of the impending announcement except my press officer, since I felt he had to know to have CVs or photographs ready if they were required. The Honours List is relayed to the press and the broadcasters on a Friday afternoon, to be announced at midnight on the radio and in Saturday's papers. My press officer said he would keep in touch with the BBC's corporate press office on the Friday and ring me to confirm that the award had gone ahead, since one is never told this in advance. You are asked if you will accept, and then there is silence until the day. I had written my acceptance letter from France, and was worried that it might not have arrived safely since there had been frequent postal strikes that summer. It was nearly seven o'clock in the evening before my colleague rang, after I had spent a rather restless afternoon in my hotel room. But we had a good dinner.

The following day close friends like John and Ann Tusa, Sheila

Colvin and Gillian Reynolds all found out where I was and phoned or faxed, but there was silence from the BBC. I returned to London a week later to a barrage of letters and cards – over seven hundred in all. There was a very nice letter from Hussey and a perfectly adequate one from Birt, but no personal contact. No one telephoned or offered me a drink. My press officer then showed me the BBC's corporate press release for the Honours List. It led with a piece about the Director of Planning, Patricia Hodgson, who had been awarded a CBE, but it contained no mention of me. He had rung to ask why and had been told that, as the citation said 'for services to music', the award was nothing to do with the BBC. In a way I was not really surprised, but I was deeply offended. I wrote to Hussey to thank him for his letter and to ask for an explanation of the absence of my name from the BBC's press release. I never received even an acknowledgement let alone an explanation, and at no time during the Proms that year did the BBC make any gesture towards me except for a suggestion that at some time later in the year there might be an occasion to mark my retirement. I replied that I intended to be in Australia all autumn.

Unknown to me, my real friends had clubbed together to give me a spectacular party, which, ironically, was held in the Council Chamber of Broadcasting House under the gaze of the portraits of previous Director-Generals. I knew nothing of it until I was inveigled there and, on opening the door, saw a hundred and twenty of the people I cared about most – headed by Alistair Cooke and David Attenborough. Friends had come from Scotland, Wales, France and all over England. It was a wonderful compensation, and I recounted for the first time the story of my parents' having their fortunes told in different parts of the world long before they met. In each case they were correctly told the nationality of the person they would marry and that they would have one son called John. This part I had known from my childhood, but it was only on my twenty-first birthday that my father told me that the fortune-tellers had also said that the son would eventually be knighted. I recalled that evening that 'eventually' was the key word, since I had had a wait of nearly forty years.

But I had been, as I had said to John Major, incredibly lucky. Others might have done better, but I had tried my best. I had sought to live up to the traditions I inherited and to maintain and revitalize them as best I could. I had been hugely helped by my colleagues, had had considerable success in making teams, and, despite a normal level of irritation,

455

had a great deal of fun and a largely happy life. I had also made a remarkable number of true friends who have featured far too little in this account, which has concentrated on my professional life. I had had much recognition from professional bodies, such as receiving the annual award of the Association of British Orchestras and of the National Federation of Music Societies, and I am the only person in the world of music who has received the annual award of the Critics' Circle.

But there was one last slap in the face. The French Ambassador, the brilliant and mercurial Jean Guéginou, told me he had recommended me for a French decoration – not the Ordre des Arts et des Lettres, which would have been more usual, but the Légion d'Honneur, much rarer for a foreigner. It was refused on my behalf by the Foreign Office, who wrote to him saying, 'For the purposes of foreign honours, BBC employees count as Crown servants and are not allowed to accept.' So much for the much vaunted independence of the BBC! Happily the Ambassador was generous enough to wait until the following year and resubmitted my name, when, after I had left the BBC, the Foreign Office could no longer block it. After a lifetime of affectionate involvement with France, I am as proud of the red ribbon as of anything I have achieved.

The final weeks of the Centenary Proms season brought back old friends like Riccardo Chailly and the Concertgebouw and new ones like Marc Minkowski and Les Musiciens du Louvre, as well as works I had long wanted to programme, such as Ravel's *L'Enfant et les sortilèges*, with a brilliant young French cast. The Mahler cycle sold well, and the concert opera performances – Purcell's *Dido and Aeneas* and *King Arthur*, Janáček's *The Makropoulos Case* and Hindemith's *Sancta Susanna*, one of his best works – were all in different ways highly effective. The visiting orchestras were exciting, and the level of playing from all the BBC's orchestras was outstanding. We had a big family party in the gallery of the hall on the penultimate night, and I was able to thank the many people who had contributed over the years, inviting all my former Proms helpers and as many colleagues as we could find. I made an interminable speech, but got a few laughs.

When I began at the Proms I had had a long wish list ranging right across the classical field to gamelan music and the best of young jazz performers. Over the years, much of the list had found its place. I would go into semi-obscurity with very happy memories and a sense of fulfilment, even if I was not quite certain how I would survive financially. When in 1994 I had been interviewed by Sue Lawley on *Desert Island Discs*, she had claimed that I needed an official post from which to voice my opinions. In a sense she was right: speaking out is easier when you are identified with a job. But I had had so many years of that, and was now ready to be quieter – perhaps even more fulfilled, with time to do things that interested me but which had hardly been possible on the treadmills I had occupied. I had done the three jobs I wanted, fighting hard for the things I believed in, and each time had moved on before I was required to and before I had lost my enthusiasm. Now, at sixty, I might have a chance to explore whether I was a person in my own right, not just a bulwark of an institution.

# Postscript – Keeping Faith

Five years have passed since Birtwistle's *Panic* frightened viewers of BBC1. There is a different government, a new Director-General of the BBC, a new Chairman of the Arts Council and a new team at the Royal Opera House. So rapidly did the cast change that, within a couple of years, I found myself with as little direct involvement with the people running the arts as the general public – and, what's more, happy to be out of it after so many years. I found a positive pleasure in not having to go to endless meetings or read impenetrable pages of management-speak. Within a year the newspapers had stopped asking me to react to every trumped-up 'scandal' involving the arts. And, just as had happened when I left Television, I no longer felt I had to listen to the increasingly trivial chit-chat that now characterized so much of Radio 3. I was better out of it. My temper improved, I felt years younger, and I could find time to read again. But this did not mean that I had lost faith in what I believed, or that I stopped looking for signs that things might be returning to a state of greater sanity.

There certainly were improvements, like Jenny Abramsky running BBC Radio and John Tusa at the Barbican in place of their totally unsuitable predecessors. But there is still a long way to go before our world is free from the legacy of Birt and his management consultants, or the influence of Tim Bell and the PR monsters, ready to give anything or anyone a new image at a price.

Several close friends advised me not to write this book. They said I would risk appearing as an embittered old person who had lost his battles and did not have the decency to shut up – 'an old soldier rattling his sabre', in Birt's offensive phrase about Mark Tully, the doyen of BBC foreign correspondents. Ian McKellen was sure it would make me terminally depressed by bringing home what profound damage had been done to the achievements of the post-war years, which had so marked my life and formed my taste. Some said that, like my old boss Stephen Hearst, I would come to feel that my life had been wasted, since so little of what I had worked for seems valued today. Tainted by Experience indeed.

But it has not been quite as straightforward as that. The world may still be full of hapless victims of political correctness, focus groups and marketing departments. It is still run by 'managers' who seem unable to recognize what is meant by dumbing down and who are haunted by the insecurity that comes from having authority without knowing how to use it. But everywhere I look the arts are full of emerging talent – new people who may not share all my values, but who certainly reject the whole-hearted materialism of the past two decades.

In the past five years I have spent a fair amount of time working with these young people – musicians mostly, but also students of all kinds. Despite being visibly enslaved to the dictates of fashion (rather more extremely so than my generation was in our day), they show every sign of having real ideas and aspirations for their future, tailored to their age and their interests. To my considerable surprise, I have often found them willing to listen to other voices, even if they do not agree with them. Only the devotees of information technology seem totally brain-washed, confusing a delivery system with a culture. The many who can still think recognize that something has gone wrong.

It might have been expected that I would devote much of this book to arguing the case for subsidy or to explaining why public-service broadcasting at its best is preferable to the alternatives. I have taken it for granted that anyone who has got this far shares my belief that, far from culture needing to make its case, it is the people who want to get rid of it who should be justifying themselves. At one of our last meetings, Isaiah Berlin asked me why I remained so concerned about everything. He suggested that, since I had my eyesight, my hearing, my friends and my library, I might enjoy life more not by caring less but by not letting my dissatisfaction with the world show quite as much. 'Not yet,' I replied. 'Too soon!'

I believe it still matters to demonstrate that some of us have not lost faith. After the onslaught of recent years, it might have been much easier to give up. But for someone like me, born in the 1930s, the word 'appeasement' will always hang in the air like smoke. The lowest-common-denominator, accessibility-at-any-price, anti-intellectual laziness of so many of today's leaders – not only in politics, but also in education and the arts – is for me a form of appeasement. Failing or refusing to differentiate between the good and the indifferent, while sheltering under a cloak of spurious democracy, is simply not good enough. It is a betrayal of all our civilization has stood for.

The new century will bring new problems, new opportunities and perhaps new solutions. But it will be worth much less if it cannot incorporate some of the old values. The most satisfactory sight I know is of a pendulum returning. If I still have the strength to help it on its way, then much of my earlier efforts may not have been wasted.

# Index

461